MORTON A[LLAN]

DIRECTORY

of

EUROPEAN PASSENGER
STEAMSHIP ARRIVALS

FOR THE YEARS
1 8 9 0 *to* 1 9 3 0
AT THE PORT OF
N E W Y O R K

and

FOR THE YEARS
1 9 0 4 *to* 1 9 2 6
AT THE PORTS OF
NEW YORK, PHILA-
DELPHIA, BOSTON
and BALTIMORE

Originally published: New York, 1931
Reprinted: Genealogical Publishing Co., Inc.
1001 N. Calvert St., Baltimore, Md. 21202
1979, 1980, 1987, 1993, 1998, 2001
Reprinted from a volume in the Enoch Pratt Free Library
Baltimore, Maryland
Library of Congress Catalogue Card Number 78-65163
International Standard Book Number 0-8063-0830-3
Made in the United States of America

FOREWORD

The Morton Allan Directory of European Passenger Steamship Arrivals contains the arrivals of passenger steamships, carefully compiled by the calendar year and indexed alphabetically by Steamship Line. The port of arrival and port of departure are shown at the top of each column.

PUBLISHERS' NOTES

The Lines mentioned below are no longer in operation as passenger carriers to U. S. Ports.

Allan Line	Polish American Line
Allan State Line	Prince Line
American Near East and Black Sea Line	Russian-American Line
Austro American Line	Russian East Asiatic S. S. Co.
Booras Line	Russian Volunteer Fleet
Hellenic Trans. Line	Sicula American Line
Insular Navigation Co.	Transoceanica Line
Linha de Vapores Portuguezes	United American Line
Lloyd Italiana	U. S. Mail S. S. Co.
N. Y. and Continental Line	Uranium Line
North West Transp. Line	Warren Line
Ottoman-American Line	Wilson Line

The Compagnie Generale Transatlantique is identical with the French Line.

The Compania Transatlantica is also known as the Spanish Line.

Many of the Steamship Lines now operating are in possession of record books containing the names of passengers arriving as far back as 1912, some further. Others have records available for post-war years only.

In making application for verification of landing for naturalization, permits to re-enter the United States or other reasons, care should be taken to furnish all possible information regarding particulars of the arrival, such as:

1. Name, as spelled at the time of arrival.
2. Approximate date of arrival.
3. Port of departure in Europe.
4. Name of steamship line.
5. Country of birth.
6. Age at time of arrival.
7. Class of accommodation traveled by.
8. Names of any persons traveling with same sailing.
9. Port of arrival in the United States.

To insure practical accuracy and completeness this volume has been compiled with all reasonable care and industry and therefore forms a comprehensive and valuable directory.

The Publisher.

November, 1931.

INDEX

Year 1890

ALLAN STATE LINE
Glasgow—New York
N. Y.

Arrival	Steamer
Jan. 2	State of Nebraska
Jan. 27	State of Indiana
Feb. 1	State of Georgia
Feb. 13	State of Nebraska
Feb. 27	State of Indiana
Apr. 7	State of Georgia
Apr. 10	State of Nebraska
Apr. 18	State of Indiana
May 8	State of Georgia
May 14	State of Nebraska
May 23	State of Indiana
June 11	State of Georgia
June 19	State of Nebraska
June 27	State of Indiana
July 16	State of Georgia
July 23	State of Nebraska
July 31	State of Indiana
Aug. 20	State of Georgia
Aug. 26	State of Nebraska
Sept. 4	State of Indiana
Sept. 24	State of Georgia
Oct. 2	State of Nebraska
Oct. 9	State of Indiana
Nov. 5	State of Nebraska
Nov. 17	State of Georgia
Nov. 22	State of Indiana
Dec. 22	State of Georgia

ANCHOR LINE
Glasgow—New York
N. Y.

Arrival	Steamer
Jan. 2	Furnessia
Jan. 9	Circassia
Jan. 25	Anchoria
Jan. 30	Ethiopia
Feb. 6	Devonia
Feb. 20	Circassia
Feb. 26	Anchoria
Mar. 3	Ethiopia
Mar. 21	Devonia
Mar. 27	Circassia
Apr. 3	Anchoria
Apr. 10	Ethiopia
Apr. 15	Furnessia
Apr. 23	Devonia
Apr. 29	Circassia
May 7	Anchoria
May 13	Ethiopia
May 21	Furnessia
May 27	Devonia
June 3	Circassia
June 9	Anchoria
June 17	Ethiopia
June 26	Furnessia
July 5	Devonia
July 8	Circassia
July 14	Anchoria
July 22	Ethiopia
Aug. 6	Devonia
Aug. 12	Circassia
Aug. 18	Anchoria
Aug. 25	Ethiopia

ANCHOR LINE
Glasgow—New York
(Continued)
N. Y.

Arrival	Steamer
Sept. 2	Furnessia
Sept. 9	Devonia
Sept. 15	Circassia
Sept. 23	Anchoria
Sept. 30	Ethiopia
Oct. 7	Furnessia
Oct. 21	Circassia
Oct. 28	Anchoria
Nov. 13	Ethiopia
Nov. 26	Circassia
Dec. 2	Anchoria

ANCHOR LINE
Mediterranean—New York
N. Y.

Arrival	Steamer
Jan. 2	Columbia
Jan. 14	Elysia
Feb. 24	Bolivia
Mar. 5	California
Mar. 8	Caledonia
Mar. 12	Alsatia
Mar. 31	Belgravia
Apr. 10	Victoria
May 8	Olympia
May 22	Bolivia
May 26	Caledonia
June 27	Italia
July 16	Belgravia
July 21	Columbia
July 31	Elysia
Aug. 25	Victoria
Sept. 4	Assyria
Sept. 8	Trinacria
Sept. 16	Caledonia
Sept. 18	Scotia
Sept. 24	California
Oct. 25	Alsatia
Nov. 3	Belgravia
Nov. 21	Victoria
Nov. 26	Assyria
Nov. 26	Devonia
Dec. 8	Caledonia
Dec. 22	California

CANADA SHIPPING COMPANY
Liverpool—New York
N. Y.

Arrival	Steamer
Mar. 1	Lake Nepigon
Apr. 13	Lake Superior
Dec. 12	Lake Ontario

COMPANIA TRANSATLANTICA LINE
(Spanish Line)
Spanish Ports—New York
N. Y.

Arrival	Steamer
Jan. 4	Ciudad Condal
Jan. 15	Mendez Nunez

COMPANIA TRANSATLANTICA LINE
(Spanish Line)
Spanish Ports—New York
(Continued)
N. Y.

Arrival	Steamer
Jan. 25	Vizcaya
Feb. 4	Ciudad Condal
Feb. 15	Habana
Feb. 26	Mendez Nunez
Mar. 5	Ciudad Condal
Mar. 15	Vizcaya
Mar. 25	Habana
Apr. 4	Ciudad Condal
Apr. 15	Mendez Nunez
Apr. 25	Vizcaya
May 5	Ciudad Condal
May 15	Habana
May 26	Mendez Nunez
June 4	Ciudad Condal
June 16	Vizcaya
June 26	Habana
July 5	Ciudad Condal
July 16	Mendez Nunez
July 25	Vizcaya
Aug. 4	Ciudad Condal
Aug. 15	Habana
Aug. 25	Mendez Nunez
Sept. 4	Ciudad Condal
Sept. 15	Vizcaya
Sept. 26	Baldomero Iglesias
Sept. 30	Habana
Oct. 7	Ciudad Condal
Oct. 15	Mendez Nunez
Oct. 27	Vizcaya
Nov. 5	Habana
Nov. 8	Baldomero Iglesias
Nov. 15	Ciudad Condal
Nov. 25	Baldomero Iglesias
Dec. 5	Habana
Dec. 8	San Augustin
Dec. 15	Ciudad Condal
Dec. 26	San Augustin

CUNARD LINE
Liverpool—New York
N. Y.

Arrival	Steamer
Jan. 9	Gallia
Jan. 14	Umbria
Jan. 22	Servia
Jan. 30	Bothnia
Feb. 3	Aurania
Feb. 10	Umbria
Feb. 19	Gallia
Feb. 26	Bothnia
Mar. 3	Aurania
Mar. 10	Servia
Mar. 20	Gallia
Mar. 24	Etruria
Apr. 5	Bothnia
Apr. 7	Umbria
Apr. 14	Servia
Apr. 21	Etruria
Apr. 28	Aurania
May 5	Umbria

Year 1890

CUNARD LINE
Liverpool—New York
(Continued)

N. Y. Arrival	Steamer
May 5	Bothnia
May 12	Servia
May 16	Gallia
May 19	Etruria
May 26	Aurania
May 31	Bothnia
June 2	Umbria
June 9	Servia
June 13	Gallia
June 16	Etruria
June 23	Aurania
June 29	Bothnia
June 30	Umbria
July 7	Servia
July 11	Gallia
July 14	Etruria
July 21	Aurania
July 28	Umbria
Aug. 4	Servia
Aug. 11	Etruria
Aug. 18	Aurania
Aug. 23	Bothnia
Aug. 25	Umbria
Sept. 1	Servia
Sept. 5	Gallia
Sept. 8	Etruria
Sept. 15	Aurania
Sept. 20	Bothnia
Sept. 22	Umbria
Sept. 29	Servia
Oct. 4	Etruria
Oct. 4	Gallia
Oct. 13	Aurania
Oct. 18	Bothnia
Oct. 20	Umbria
Oct. 27	Servia
Nov. 3	Etruria
Nov. 10	Aurania
Nov. 17	Umbria
Nov. 25	Servia
Dec. 1	Etruria
Dec. 8	Aurania
Dec. 16	Gallia
Dec. 23	Servia
Dec. 30	Umbria

FABRE LINE
Mediterranean—New York

N. Y. Arrival	Steamer
Jan. 8	Alesia
Jan. 31	Nuestria
Feb. 24	Britannia
Mar. 6	Alesia
Mar. 31	Nuestria
Apr. 12	Burgundia
Apr. 21	Pictavia
May 1	Britannia
May 7	Alesia
May 27	Nuestria
June 10	Burgundia
June 30	Britannia
July 9	Alesia
July 22	Nuestria
Aug. 6	Burgundia

FABRE LINE
Mediterranean—New York
(Continued)

N. Y. Arrival	Steamer
Aug. 26	Britannia
Sept. 17	Nuestria
Oct. 1	Burgundia
Oct. 14	Alesia
Oct. 25	Britannia
Nov. 17	Nuestria
Nov. 29	Burgundia
Dec. 17	Alesia
Dec. 27	Britannia

FRENCH LINE
(Compagnie Generale Transatlantique)
Havre—New York

N. Y. Arrival	Steamer
Jan. 8	La Normandie
Jan. 14	La Bourgoyne
Jan. 22	La Gascogne
Jan. 28	La Champagne
Feb. 5	La Normandie
Feb. 10	La Bretagne
Feb. 17	La Gascogne
Feb. 26	La Champagne
Mar. 3	La Normandie
Mar. 10	La Bretagne
Mar. 17	La Gascogne
Mar. 26	La Champagne
Apr. 1	La Normandie
Apr. 7	La Bretagne
Apr. 14	La Gascogne
Apr. 22	La Champagne
Apr. 29	La Normandie
May 5	La Bretagne
May 12	La Gascogne
May 20	La Champagne
May 26	La Normandie
June 3	La Bourgoyne
June 9	La Bretagne
June 16	La Gascogne
June 23	La Normandie
June 30	La Bourgoyne
July 7	La Bretagne
July 21	La Normandie
July 28	La Bourgoyne
Aug. 4	La Bretagne
Aug. 11	La Champagne
Aug. 18	La Normandie
Aug. 25	La Bourgoyne
Sept. 1	La Bretagne
Sept. 8	La Champagne
Sept. 15	La Normandie
Sept. 22	La Bourgoyne
Sept. 29	La Bretagne
Oct. 1	Ville de Marseilles
Oct. 6	La Champagne
Oct. 13	La Gascogne
Oct. 20	La Bourgoyne
Oct. 27	La Bretagne
Nov. 3	La Champagne
Nov. 10	La Gascogne
Nov. 19	La Normandie
Nov. 24	La Bourgoyne
Dec. 1	La Champagne
Dec. 8	La Gascogne
Dec. 16	La Normandie

FRENCH LINE
(Compagnie Generale Transatlantique)
Havre—New York
(Continued)

N. Y. Arrival	Steamer
Dec. 22	La Bourgoyne
Dec. 29	La Bretagne

GUION STEAMSHIP LINE
Liverpool—New York

N. Y. Arrival	Steamer
Feb. 26	Arizona
Apr. 21	Alaska
May 26	Alaska
June 9	Arizona
June 30	Alaska
July 14	Arizona
Aug. 4	Alaska
Aug. 18	Arizona
Sept. 8	Alaska
Sept. 22	Arizona
Oct. 13	Alaska
Oct. 27	Arizona
Nov. 17	Alaska
Dec. 1	Arizona

HAMBURG-AMERICAN LINE
Hamburg—New York

N. Y. Arrival	Steamer
Jan. 2	Marsala
Jan. 7	Bohemia
Jan. 14	Scandia
Jan. 15	Rugia
Jan. 23	Italia
Jan. 25	California
Jan. 25	Rhaetia
Jan. 27	Moravia
Jan. 27	Sorrento
Jan. 28	Russia
Feb. 4	Gellert
Feb. 10	Dania
Feb. 13	Amalfi
Feb. 20	Bohemia
Feb. 20	Taormina
Feb. 26	Rugia
Feb. 27	Suevia
Mar. 3	Marsala
Mar. 3	Rhaetia
Mar. 10	Moravia
Mar. 21	Sorrento
Mar. 25	Italia
Mar. 25	Russia
Mar. 31	Dania
Apr. 1	California
Apr. 7	Rugia
Apr. 14	Amalfi
Apr. 14	Gellert
Apr. 15	Taormina
Apr. 18	Bohemia
Apr. 19	Columbia
Apr. 21	Rhaetia
Apr. 26	Augusta Victoria
Apr. 26	Scandia
Apr. 28	Marsala
May 5	Moravia

Year 1890

HAMBURG-AMERICAN LINE
Hamburg—New York
(Continued)

N. Y. Arrival	Steamer
May 5	Wieland
May 9	Russia
May 12	Sorrento
May 16	California
May 17	Gellert
May 17	Columbia
May 19	Italia
May 22	Dania
May 24	Augusta Victoria
May 26	Suevia
May 31	Normannia
June 2	Amalfi
June 2	Bohemia
June 2	Rhaetia
June 6	Wieland
June 9	Taormina
June 10	Scandia
June 13	Columbia
June 16	Rugia
June 21	Augusta Victoria
June 23	Gellert
June 23	Marsala
June 23	Moravia
June 27	Russia
June 28	Normannia
June 30	Suevia
July 7	Rhaetia
July 7	Sorrento
July 8	Dania
July 11	Columbia
July 12	Wieland
July 14	California
July 19	Augusta Victoria
July 19	Scandia
July 21	Slavonia
July 24	Bohemia
July 26	Normannia
July 26	Rugia
July 28	Moravia
Aug. 2	Gellert
Aug. 4	Amalfi
Aug. 5	Russia
Aug. 8	Columbia
Aug. 11	Suevia
Aug. 16	Augusta Victoria
Aug. 18	Rhaetia
Aug. 18	Taormina
Aug. 22	Normannia
Aug. 23	Dania
Aug. 23	Wieland
Aug. 30	Rugia
Sept. 1	Marsala
Sept. 5	Columbia
Sept. 6	Gellert
Sept. 6	Slavonia
Sept. 9	Italia
Sept. 13	Augusta Victoria
Sept. 13	Suevia
Sept. 15	Sorrento
Sept. 17	Moravia
Sept. 19	Russia
Sept. 20	Normannia
Sept. 22	Rhaetia
Sept. 25	California

HAMBURG-AMERICAN LINE
Hamburg—New York
(Continued)

N. Y. Arrival	Steamer
Sept. 26	Wieland
Sept. 29	Amalfi
Oct. 2	Bohemia
Oct. 3	Columbia
Oct. 6	Rugia
Oct. 11	Augusta Victoria
Oct. 11	Gellert
Oct. 11	Scandia
Oct. 13	Taormina
Oct. 17	Normannia
Oct. 20	Suevia
Oct. 27	Marsala
Oct. 27	Rhaetia
Oct. 27	Slavonia
Oct. 29	Moravia
Oct. 31	Columbia
Nov. 1	Wieland
Nov. 8	Augusta Victoria
Nov. 11	Russia
Nov. 12	Sorrento
Nov. 17	Bohemia
Nov. 17	Normannia
Nov. 22	California
Nov. 22	Rugia
Nov. 24	Gellert
Nov. 28	Amalfi
Nov. 28	Scandia
Dec. 8	Rhaetia
Dec. 16	Dania
Dec. 16	Taormina
Dec. 23	Russia
Dec. 26	Slavonia

HAMBURG-AMERICAN LINE
Scandinavian Ports—New York

N. Y. Arrival	Steamer
Jan. 2	Polynesia
Jan. 13	Slavonia
Feb. 11	Polaria
Feb. 26	Polynesia
Mar. 13	Slavonia
Apr. 10	Polaria
Apr. 22	Polynesia
May 7	Slavonia
June 2	Polaria
June 16	Polynesia
July 31	Polaria
Aug. 11	Polynesia
Sept. 26	Polaria
Oct. 10	Polynesia
Nov. 28	Polaria

HOLLAND-AMERICA LINE
Rotterdam, Amsterdam, Flushing—New York

N. Y. Arrival	Steamer
Jan. 13	Rotterdam
Jan. 14	P. Caland
Jan. 30	Edam

HOLLAND-AMERICA LINE
Rotterdam, Amsterdam, Flushing—New York
(Continued)

N. Y. Arrival	Steamer
Feb. 4	Obdam
Feb. 10	Amsterdam
Feb. 24	Rotterdam
Mar. 3	P. Caland
Mar. 8	Werkendam
Mar. 27	Amsterdam
Mar. 31	Maasdam
Apr. 7	Rotterdam
Apr. 12	Spaarndam
Apr. 21	P. Caland
Apr. 25	Werkendam
May 5	Amsterdam
May 9	Maasdam
May 16	Rotterdam
May 23	Spaarndam
May 31	Werkendam
June 9	P. Caland
June 14	Amsterdam
June 21	Obdam
June 23	Maasdam
June 30	Rotterdam
July 3	Spaarndam
July 14	Werkendam
July 21	Veendam
July 25	Amsterdam
July 31	Obdam
Aug. 4	Maasdam
Aug. 11	Rotterdam
Aug. 14	Spaarndam
Aug. 23	Werkendam
Aug. 27	Venndam
Sept. 8	Amsterdam
Sept. 12	Obdam
Sept. 15	Maasdam
Sept. 20	Rotterdam
Sept. 25	P. Caland
Sept. 29	Spaarndam
Oct. 4	Werkendam
Oct. 6	Zaandam
Oct. 9	Veendam
Oct. 16	Edam
Oct. 18	Amsterdam
Oct. 27	Maasdam
Oct. 27	Obdam
Nov. 3	Rotterdam
Nov. 8	Spaarndam
Nov. 17	Werkendam
Nov. 20	Veendam
Nov. 25	Zaandam
Dec. 1	Amsterdam
Dec. 8	Obdam
Dec. 9	Maasdam
Dec. 15	Rotterdam
Dec. 29	Spaarndam
Dec. 29	Werkendam

INMAN & INTERNATIONAL STEAMSHIP COMPANY
Liverpool—New York

N. Y. Arrival	Steamer
Jan. 13	City of Berlin

Year 1890

INMAN & INTERNATIONAL STEAMSHIP COMPANY
Liverpool—New York
(Continued)

N. Y.

Arrival	Steamer
Jan. 21	City of Chester
Jan. 28	City of Chicago
Feb. 8	City of Berlin
Feb. 13	City of Paris
Feb. 24	City of Chester
Mar. 8	City of Chicago
Mar. 13	City of Paris
Mar. 25	City of Berlin
Apr. 1	City of Richmond
Apr. 7	City of Chester
Apr. 14	City of Chicago
Apr. 21	City of Berlin
Apr. 28	City of Richmond
May 5	City of Chester
May 12	City of Chicago
May 15	City of New York
May 23	City of Berlin
June 2	City of Chester
June 9	City of Chicago
June 12	City of New York
June 21	City of Berlin
June 30	City of Chester
July 7	City of Chicago
July 10	City of New York
July 21	City of Richmond
July 25	City of Berlin
Aug. 2	City of Chester
Aug. 9	City of Chicago
Aug. 13	City of New York
Aug. 22	City of Berlin
Aug. 30	City of Chester
Sept. 6	City of Chicago
Sept. 10	City of New York
Sept. 27	City of Chester
Oct. 4	City of Chicago
Oct. 8	City of New York
Oct. 18	City of Berlin
Oct. 25	City of Chester
Nov. 1	City of Chicago
Nov. 6	City of New York
Nov. 17	City of Berlin
Nov. 22	City of Chester
Dec. 1	City of Chicago
Dec. 4	City of New York
Dec. 13	City of Berlin
Dec. 29	City of Chester

INSULAR NAVIGATION COMPANY
Azores—Lisbon—New Bedford, Massachusetts—New York

N. Y.

Arrival	Steamer
Feb. 6	Benguella
Mar. 24	Benguella
May 2	Benguella
June 16	Benguella
Nov. 29	Vega

LINHA DE VAPORES PORTUGUEZES
Azores—Lisbon—New Bedford, Massachusetts—New York

N. Y.

Arrival	Steamer
May 3	Olinda
June 21	Olinda
Aug. 4	Olinda

LIVERPOOL & GREAT WESTERN STEAMSHIP COMPANY
Liverpool—New York

N. Y.

Arrival	Steamer
Jan. 2	Nevada
Jan. 18	Wyoming
Feb. 1	Wisconsin
Feb. 6	Nevada
Feb. 21	Wyoming
Mar. 5	Wisconsin
Mar. 12	Nevada
Apr. 11	Wyoming
Apr. 16	Nevada
May 1	Wisconsin
May 14	Wyoming
May 22	Nevada
June 4	Wisconsin
June 12	Vandyck
June 19	Wyoming
June 26	Nevada
July 10	Wisconsin
July 23	Wyoming
July 30	Nevada
Aug. 13	Wisconsin
Aug. 27	Wyoming
Sept. 3	Nevada
Sept. 17	Wisconsin
Oct. 1	Wyoming
Oct. 8	Nevada
Oct. 23	Wisconsin
Nov. 5	Wyoming
Nov. 15	Nevada
Nov. 28	Wisconsin
Dec. 11	Wyoming
Dec. 18	Nevada

NATIONAL NAVIGATION COMPANY
Mediterranean—New York

N. Y.

Arrival	Steamer
Apr. 17	Cachemire
Nov. 1	Canton
Nov. 17	Chandernagor
Dec. 24	Hindoustan

NATIONAL STEAMSHIP COMPANY
London, Liverpool—New York

N. Y.

Arrival	Steamer
Jan. 3	Canada
Jan. 8	Italy
Jan. 20	Denmark
Jan. 27	Egypt
Jan. 29	England
Feb. 3	France

NATIONAL STEAMSHIP COMPANY
London, Liverpool—New York
(Continued)

N. Y.

Arrival	Steamer
Feb. 4	Greece
Feb. 24	The Queen
Mar. 1	Spain
Mar. 1	Italy
Mar. 6	Helvetia
Mar. 17	Denmark
Mar. 24	Egypt
Mar. 29	Canada
Apr. 3	France
Apr. 6	Canada
Apr. 12	The Queen
Apr. 15	Greece
Apr. 21	Spain
Apr. 25	Italy
May 5	Helvetia
May 8	Denmark
May 12	Egypt
May 20	France
May 22	The Queen
May 30	England
June 4	Greece
June 6	Italy
June 10	Spain
June 21	Canada
June 27	Denmark
July 3	Egypt
July 5	The Queen
July 10	France
July 11	Helvetia
July 17	England
July 28	Greece
July 30	Italy
Aug. 2	Spain
Aug. 11	Canada
Aug. 11	Italy
Aug. 16	The Queen
Aug. 19	Denmark
Aug. 28	England
Aug. 29	France
Sept. 20	Greece
Sept. 27	The Queen
Sept. 28	Canada
Oct. 8	Denmark
Oct. 11	England
Oct. 22	France
Oct. 27	Italy
Nov. 10	Greece
Nov. 11	The Queen
Nov. 26	England
Dec. 1	Denmark
Dec. 12	France
Dec. 27	Italy
Dec. 29	Greece

NAVIGAZIONE GENERALE ITALIANA LINE
Mediterranean—New York

N. Y.

Arrival	Steamer
Feb. 4	Iniziativa
Feb. 17	Entella
Mar. 3	Letimbro
Mar. 28	Giava
Apr. 10	Stura

Year 1890

NAVIGAZIONE GENER-ALE ITALIANA LINE
Mediterranean—New York
(Continued)

N. Y.

Arrival	Steamer
Apr. 16	Iniziativa
May 7	Entella
May 12	Letimbro
May 24	Birmania
June 9	Giava
July 12	Stura
July 18	Washington
July 19	Entella
July 30	Iniziativa
Aug. 18	Birmania
Aug. 30	Letimbro
Sept. 29	Stura
Oct. 6	Iniziativa
Oct. 23	Giava
Nov. 4	Birmania
Nov. 11	Letimbro
Dec. 19	Stura

NORTH GERMAN LLOYD
Bremen—New York

N. Y.

Arrival	Steamer
Jan. 2	Neckar
Jan. 4	Fulda
Jan. 8	Weser
Jan. 14	Eider
Jan. 20	Werra
Jan. 27	America
Jan. 27	Saale
Feb. 1	Trave
Feb. 5	Fulda
Feb. 7	Lahn
Feb. 11	Eider
Feb. 15	Aller
Feb. 19	Werra
Feb. 24	Saale
Feb. 26	Ems
Feb. 27	Karlsruhe
Mar. 1	Trave
Mar. 4	Fulda
Mar. 7	Lahn
Mar. 11	Eider
Mar. 15	Aller
Mar. 19	Werra
Mar. 21	Main
Mar. 24	Saale
Mar. 29	Trave
Apr. 2	Elbe
Apr. 4	Lahn
Apr. 5	Fulda
Apr. 7	Leipzig
Apr. 8	Eider
Apr. 12	Aller
Apr. 15	Werra
Apr. 19	Saale
Apr. 22	Ems
Apr. 23	Graf Bismarck
Apr. 25	Trave
Apr. 29	Elbe
May 1	Hermann
May 3	Lahn
May 3	Fulda
May 7	Eider
May 10	Aller

NORTH GERMAN LLOYD
Bremen—New York
(Continued)

N. Y.

Arrival	Steamer
May 13	Werra
May 19	Saale
May 20	Ems
May 24	Trave
May 24	Weser
May 27	Elbe
May 30	Fulda
May 30	Lahn
June 3	Eider
June 7	Aller
June 10	Werra
June 14	Saale
June 18	Ems
June 20	Hermann
June 21	Trave
June 25	Elbe
June 25	Karlsruhe
June 27	Lahn
July 1	Eider
July 5	Aller
July 8	Fulda
July 11	Weser
July 12	Saale
July 15	Werra
July 19	Trave
July 22	Ems
July 25	Lahn
July 29	Kaiser Wilhelm II
July 30	Hermann
Aug. 5	Eider
Aug. 9	Fulda
Aug. 12	Werra
Aug. 15	Saale
Aug. 19	Ems
Aug. 22	Weser
Aug. 23	Trave
Aug. 26	Elbe
Aug. 29	Lahn
Sept. 2	Eider
Sept. 6	Aller
Sept. 6	Kaiser Wilhelm II
Sept. 9	Fulda
Sept. 12	Saale
Sept. 12	Werra
Sept. 16	Ems
Sept. 20	Trave
Sept. 24	Elbe
Sept. 26	Lahn
Sept. 30	Eider
Oct. 4	Aller
Oct. 7	Fulda
Oct. 8	Munchen
Oct. 10	Werra
Oct. 11	Saale
Oct. 14	Ems
Oct. 18	Trave
Oct. 21	Spree
Oct. 25	Lahn
Oct. 28	Eider
Nov. 1	Aller
Nov. 5	Werra
Nov. 8	Saale
Nov. 12	Ems
Nov. 17	Trave
Nov. 21	Fulda

NORTH GERMAN LLOYD
Bremen—New York
(Continued)

N. Y.

Arrival	Steamer
Nov. 21	Lahn
Nov. 25	Eider
Nov. 29	Aller
Dec. 2	Werra
Dec. 8	Saale
Dec. 9	Ems
Dec. 15	Trave
Dec. 20	Lahn
Dec. 22	Spree
Dec. 29	Aller

RED STAR LINE
Antwerp—New York

N. Y.

Arrival	Steamer
Jan. 3	Noordland
Jan. 10	Westernland
Jan. 24	Rhynland
Jan. 25	Friesland
Feb. 3	Waesland
Feb. 7	Noordland
Feb. 15	Belgenland
Feb. 24	Pennland
Feb. 27	Westernland
Mar. 7	Waesland
Mar. 12	Friesland
Mar. 24	Noordland
Mar. 31	Rhynland
Apr. 4	Westernland
Apr. 11	Waesland
Apr. 16	Friesland
Apr. 24	Noordland
Apr. 24	Nederland
May 2	Rhynland
May 8	Westernland
May 15	Waesland
May 21	Friesland
May 29	Noordland
June 5	Nederland
June 6	Rhynland
June 11	Westernland
June 20	Waesland
June 25	Friesland
June 26	Pennland
July 3	Noordland
July 11	Rhynland
July 15	Nederland
July 16	Westernland
July 24	Waesland
July 30	Friesland
Aug. 7	Noordland
Aug. 14	Rhynland
Aug. 20	Westernland
Aug. 23	Nederland
Aug. 27	Waesland
Sept. 3	Friesland
Sept. 11	Noordland
Sept. 17	Rhynland
Sept. 24	Westernland
Oct. 2	Waesland
Oct. 8	Friesland
Oct. 9	Nederland
Oct. 15	Noordland
Oct. 23	Rhynland
Oct. 29	Westernland

Year 1890

RED STAR LINE
Antwerp—New York
(Continued)

N.Y. Arrival	Steamer
Nov. 8	Pennland
Nov. 15	Friesland
Nov. 21	Noordland
Nov. 22	Nederland
Nov. 28	Rhynland
Dec. 4	Westernland
Dec. 11	Waesland
Dec. 19	Belgenland
Dec. 27	Noordland

SCANDINAVIAN-AMERICAN LINE
Scandinavian Ports—New York

N.Y. Arrival	Steamer
Jan. 7	Hekla
Feb. 4	Thingvalla
Feb. 26	Norge
Mar. 3	Hekla
Mar. 20	Island
Apr. 21	Norge
Apr. 26	Hekla
May 8	Island
May 26	Thingvalla
June 5	Island
June 23	Hekla
Aug. 11	Thingvalla
Aug. 22	Hekla
Sept. 6	Island
Sept. 22	Norge
Oct. 6	Thingvalla
Oct. 20	Hekla
Nov. 5	Island
Dec. 2	Thingvalla
Dec. 16	Hekla

STATE STEAMSHIP COMPANY
Glasgow—New York

N.Y. Arrival	Steamer
Feb. 10	State of Nevada
Feb. 20	State of Alabama
Mar. 24	State of Nevada
Apr. 24	State of Nevada
May 27	State of Alabama
May 29	State of Nevada
June 4	State of Pennsylvania
July 3	State of Nevada
July 21	State of Alabama
Aug. 6	State of Nevada
Sept. 10	State of Nevada
Oct. 10	State of Alabama
Oct. 23	State of Nevada
Nov. 28	State of Nevada
Dec. 12	State of Pennsylvania
Dec. 12	State of Alabama

WHITE STAR LINE
Liverpool—New York

N.Y. Arrival	Steamer
Jan. 3	Cufic
Jan. 6	Celtic

WHITE STAR LINE
Liverpool—New York
(Continued)

N.Y. Arrival	Steamer
Jan. 13	Germanic
Jan. 20	Britannic
Jan. 27	Adriatic
Feb. 3	Celtic
Feb. 6	Runic
Feb. 8	Germanic
Feb. 13	Cufic
Feb. 15	Britannic
Feb. 24	Adriatic
Feb. 27	Teutonic
Mar. 8	Celtic
Mar. 15	Britannic
Mar. 22	Germanic
Apr. 7	Adriatic
Apr. 10	Majestic
Apr. 15	Cufic
Apr. 19	Germanic
Apr. 24	Teutonic
May 2	Runic
May 3	Britannic
May 8	Majestic
May 17	Germanic
May 22	Teutonic
May 27	Cufic
May 30	Britannic
June 5	Majestic
June 10	Runic
June 13	Germanic
June 19	Teutonic
June 27	Britannic
July 3	Majestic
July 8	Cufic
July 11	Germanic
July 16	Teutonic
July 23	Runic
July 25	Britannic
July 30	Majestic
Aug. 8	Germanic
Aug. 13	Teutonic
Aug. 18	Cufic
Aug. 22	Britannic
Aug. 27	Majestic
Sept. 2	Runic
Sept. 5	Germanic
Sept. 10	Teutonic
Sept. 19	Britannic
Sept. 24	Majestic
Sept. 24	Cufic
Oct. 3	Germanic
Oct. 8	Teutonic
Oct. 14	Runic
Oct. 17	Britannic
Oct. 23	Majestic
Oct. 31	Germanic
Nov. 3	Cufic
Nov. 6	Teutonic
Nov. 17	Britannic
Nov. 20	Majestic
Nov. 28	Germanic
Nov. 28	Runic
Dec. 5	Teutonic
Dec. 10	Cufic
Dec. 13	Britannic
Dec. 18	Majestic
Dec. 27	Germanic

WILSON LINE
Hull, London—New York

N.Y. Arrival	Steamer
Jan. 24	Egyptian Monarch
Jan. 27	Colorado
Jan. 28	Lydian Monarch
Mar. 8	Othello
Mar. 12	Colorado
Mar. 24	Egyptian Monarch
Mar. 25	Lydian Monarch
Apr. 17	Marengo
Apr. 23	Chicago
Apr. 24	Colorado
Apr. 30	Othello
May 12	Egyptian Monarch
May 12	Lydian Monarch
June 3	Marengo
June 9	Chicago
June 11	Colorado
June 27	Lydian Monarch
July 3	Egyptian Monarch
July 24	Colorado
July 28	Chicago
Aug. 18	Lydian Monarch
Sept. 8	Colorado
Oct. 13	Lydian Monarch
Oct. 25	Colorado
Dec. 8	Lydian Monarch
Dec. 16	Colorado

ADDITIONAL ARRIVALS
Antwerp—New York

N.Y. Arrival	Steamer
July 28	Volturno

Bordeaux—New York

N.Y. Arrival	Steamer
Jan. 17	Chateau Lafite
Mar. 4	Chateau Lafite
Apr. 26	Chateau Lafite
June 23	Chateau Lafite
Oct. 20	Chateau Lafite
Dec. 10	Chateau Lafite

British Ports—New York

N.Y. Arrival	Steamer
Jan. 3	Croma
Jan. 4	Lux
Jan. 31	Critic
Feb. 3	Jersey City
Feb. 10	Exeter City
Feb. 24	Sorrento
Feb. 28	Croma
Mar. 26	Critic
Apr. 8	Exeter City
Apr. 21	Jersey City
Apr. 24	Croma
Apr. 26	Lux
May 16	Llandaff City
May 17	Critic
June 2	Exeter City
June 9	Jersey City
June 20	Croma
July 14	Llandaff City
July 24	Lux
July 29	Jersey City

Year 1890

ADDITIONAL ARRIVALS
British Ports—New York
(Continued)

N.Y.

Arrival	Steamer
Aug. 9	Croma
Sept. 4	Llandaff City
Sept. 12	Exeter City
Sept. 29	Critic
Oct. 11	Jersey City
Oct. 25	Llandaff City
Nov. 3	Exeter City
Nov. 25	Critic
Dec. 1	Jersey City
Dec. 2	Croma
Dec. 20	Llandaff City
Dec. 29	Exeter City

Hamburg—New York

N.Y.

Arrival	Steamer
Jan. 17	India
Mar. 31	India
May 12	Britannic
Aug. 2	Aller
Nov. 28	Liscard

Liverpool—New York

N.Y.

Arrival	Steamer
Feb. 28	Crown of Arragon
Apr. 28	City of Rome
May 26	City of Rome
June 2	Britannia
July 21	City of Rome
Aug. 18	City of Rome
Sept. 15	City of Rome
Oct. 13	City of Rome

ADDITIONAL ARRIVALS
London—New York

N.Y.

Arrival	Steamer
Jan. 25	Ludgate Hill
Feb. 10	Tower Hill
Mar. 5	Furnessia
Mar. 25	Ludgate Hill
Apr. 2	Tower Hill
May 6	Bayonne
May 12	Ludgate Hill
June 2	Connemara
June 2	Tower Hill
June 27	Ludgate Hill
July 21	Tower Hill
July 28	Bencroy
Aug. 13	Connemara
Aug. 18	Ludgate Hill
Aug. 28	St. Dunstan
Sept. 2	Bayonne
Sept. 8	Tower Hill
Oct. 13	Ludgate Hill
Oct. 28	Connemara
Oct. 31	Tower Hill
Dec. 1	Bear Creek
Dec. 8	Ludgate Hill
Dec. 20	Tower Hill

Mediterranean—New York

N.Y.

Arrival	Steamer
Jan. 2	Sacrobosco
Jan. 9	Alexandria
Feb. 10	Rhosina
Mar. 5	Wingates
May 12	Urbino
May 20	Netley Abbey
June 12	Yoxford

ADDITIONAL ARRIVALS
Mediterranean—New York
(Continued)

N.Y.

Arrival	Steamer
June 21	Wydale
July 8	Stelvio
Aug. 5	Florida
Oct. 27	Yoxford
Dec. 9	Wetherby

Rotterdam, Amsterdam,
Flushing—New York

N.Y.

Arrival	Steamer
Jan. 30	Oranje Nassau
Mar. 6	Prins Willem III
Mar. 25	Prins Fred'k Hendrik
Apr. 12	Prins Maurits
May 5	Prins Willem II
May 26	Oranje Nassau
June 13	Borneo
July 3	Prins Willem III
July 25	Prins Fred'k Hendrik
Aug. 15	Prins Maurits

Scandinavian Ports—New
York

N.Y.

Arrival	Steamer
Nov. 24	Christina

Spanish Ports—New York

N.Y.

Arrival	Steamer
July 22	Palentino
Aug. 29	Miguel M. Pinillos
Sept. 11	Palentino

Year 1891

ALLAN STATE LINE
Glasgow—New York
N.Y.

Arrival	Steamer
Jan. 8	State of Nevada
Jan. 22	State of Pennsylvania
Feb. 7	State of Indiana
Feb. 20	State of Nevada
Mar. 6	State of Pennsylvania
Mar. 20	State of Georgia
Apr. 2	State of Nevada
Apr. 9	State of Pennsylvania
Apr. 24	Pomeranian
May 1	State of Indiana
May 8	State of Nevada
May 15	Assyrian
May 20	State of Nebraska
May 27	Siberian
June 4	State of Georgia
June 10	Pomeranian
June 18	State of Nevada
June 26	Assyrian
June 30	State of Nebraska
July 7	Siberian
July 16	State of Georgia
July 22	Pomeranian
July 29	State of Nevada
Aug. 5	Assyrian
Aug. 12	State of Nebraska
Aug. 19	Siberian
Aug. 26	State of California
Sept. 3	Pomeranian
Sept. 10	State of Nevada
Sept. 16	Assyrian
Sept. 23	State of Nebraska
Sept. 30	Siberian
Oct. 9	State of California
Oct. 17	Pomeranian
Oct. 23	State of Nevada
Oct. 30	Assyrian
Nov. 4	State of Nebraska
Nov. 12	Siberian
Nov. 18	State of California
Nov. 25	Pomeranian
Dec. 3	Norwegian
Dec. 10	State of Nebraska
Dec. 21	Assyrian
Dec. 24	Siberian

ANCHOR LINE
Glasgow—New York
N.Y.

Arrival	Steamer
Jan. 2	Circassia
Jan. 14	Anchoria
Jan. 30	Ethiopia
Feb. 13	Circassia
Feb. 26	Anchoria
Mar. 11	Ethiopia
Mar. 24	Circassia
Mar. 31	Devonia
Apr. 14	Anchoria
Apr. 21	Ethiopia
Apr. 28	Circassia
May 5	Devonia

ANCHOR LINE
Glasgow—New York
(Continued)
N.Y.

Arrival	Steamer
May 13	Anchoria
May 18	City of Rome
May 25	Ethiopia
June 2	Furnessia
June 9	Circassia
June 16	Anchoria
June 22	City of Rome
June 29	Ethiopia
July 7	Furnessia
July 14	Circassia
July 20	Anchoria
July 27	Devonia
Aug. 3	Ethiopia
Aug. 10	Furnessia
Aug. 18	Circassia
Aug. 24	Anchoria
Aug. 29	City of Rome
Sept. 8	Ethiopia
Sept. 14	Furnessia
Sept. 22	Circassia
Sept. 28	Anchoria
Oct. 14	Ethiopia
Oct. 20	Furnessia
Oct. 28	Devonia
Nov. 2	Anchoria
Nov. 9	Circassia
Nov. 17	Ethiopia
Nov. 23	Furnessia
Dec. 1	Devonia
Dec. 8	Anchoria
Dec. 15	Circassia
Dec. 23	Ethiopia
Dec. 29	Furnessia

ANCHOR LINE
Mediterranean—New York
N.Y.

Arrival	Steamer
Feb. 6	Alexandria
Feb. 10	Scotia
Feb. 24	Belgravia
Mar. 7	Alsatia
Mar. 12	Victoria
Mar. 25	Caledonia
Mar. 28	Trinacria
Apr. 13	Columbia
Apr. 28	Assyria
May 4	Elysia
May 18	Scotia
May 26	Victoria
June 3	Alsatia
June 22	Italia
July 6	Alexandria
July 17	Trinacria
July 22	Anglia
Aug. 6	Assyria
Aug. 13	Elysia
Sept. 7	Hesperia
Sept. 17	Alexandria
Sept. 19	Victoria

ANCHOR LINE
Mediterranean—New York
(Continued)
N.Y.

Arrival	Steamer
Oct. 12	Anglia
Oct. 20	Alsatia
Oct. 24	Assyria
Oct. 27	California
Nov. 10	Olympia
Nov. 30	Trinacria
Dec. 15	Bolivia

COMPANIA TRANSATLANTICA LINE
(Spanish Line)
Spanish Ports—New York
N.Y.

Arrival	Steamer
Jan. 5	Habana
Jan. 8	Baldomero Iglesias
Jan. 15	Ciudad Condal
Jan. 26	Baldomero Iglesias
Feb. 4	Habana
Feb. 9	San Agustin
Feb. 16	Ciudad Condal
Feb. 25	San Agustin
Mar. 5	Habana
Mar. 9	Baldomero Iglesias
Mar. 16	Ciudad Condal
Mar. 26	Panama
Apr. 4	Habana
Apr. 8	Baldomero Iglesias
Apr. 15	Ciudad Condal
Apr. 25	Baldomero Iglesias
May 5	Habana
May 8	Panama
May 15	Ciudad Condal
May 25	Panama
June 4	Habana
June 8	Mexico
June 15	Ciudad Condal
June 25	Mexico
July 6	Habana
July 8	Panama
July 15	Ciudad Condal
July 27	Baldomero Iglesias
Aug. 3	Habana
Aug. 8	Mexico
Aug. 14	Ciudad Condal
Aug. 25	Mexico
Aug. 31	Panama
Sept. 3	Habana
Sept. 15	Ciudad Condal
Sept. 25	Baldomero Iglesias
Oct. 6	Panama
Oct. 8	Mexico
Oct. 15	Ciudad Condal
Oct. 26	Mexico
Nov. 5	Panama
Nov. 16	Ciudad Condal
Nov. 25	Panama
Dec. 5	Habana
Dec. 8	Mexico
Dec. 22	Baldomero Iglesias
Dec. 26	Mexico

Year 1891

CUNARD LINE
Liverpool—New York
N.Y.

Arrival	Steamer
Jan. 7	Bothnia
Jan. 12	Etruria
Jan. 20	Gallia
Jan. 26	Aurania
Feb. 2	Umbria
Feb. 10	Servia
Feb. 16	Etruria
Feb. 23	Aurania
Mar. 2	Umbria
Mar. 9	Servia
Mar. 16	Etruria
Mar. 23	Aurania
Mar. 30	Umbria
Apr. 6	Servia
Apr. 13	Etruria
Apr. 20	Aurania
Apr. 24	Gallia
Apr. 27	Umbria
May 4	Servia
May 9	Bothnia
May 11	Etruria
May 18	Aurania
May 22	Gallia
May 25	Umbria
June 2	Servia
June 5	Bothnia
June 8	Etruria
June 15	Aurania
June 19	Gallia
June 22	Umbria
June 29	Servia
July 6	Etruria
July 13	Aurania
July 20	Umbria
July 27	Gallia
Aug. 3	Etruria
Aug. 10	Aurania
Aug. 17	Umbria
Aug. 24	Servia
Aug. 29	Bothnia
Aug. 31	Etruria
Sept. 7	Aurania
Sept. 11	Gallia
Sept. 14	Umbria
Sept. 21	Servia
Sept. 28	Etruria
Sept. 28	Bothnia
Oct. 5	Aurania
Oct. 10	Gallia
Oct. 12	Umbria
Oct. 19	Servia
Oct. 26	Etruria
Oct. 27	Bothnia
Nov. 2	Aurania
Nov. 9	Umbria
Nov. 16	Servia
Nov. 23	Etruria
Nov. 30	Aurania
Dec. 7	Umbria
Dec. 15	Servia
Dec. 21	Etruria
Dec. 28	Aurania

FABRE LINE
Mediterranean—New York
N.Y.

Arrival	Steamer
Jan. 30	Burgundia
Feb. 28	Britannia
Mar. 12	Nuestria
Apr. 2	Burgundia
Apr. 7	Gergovia
May 1	Britannia
May 13	Nuestria
May 25	Massilia
June 3	Burgundia
June 9	Gergovia
June 22	Alesia
July 1	Britannia
July 13	Nuestria
July 27	Massilia
Aug. 10	Burgundia
Aug. 28	Alesia
Sept. 11	Nuestria
Sept. 23	Massilia
Oct. 6	Burgundia
Oct. 30	Alesia
Nov. 9	Nuestria
Nov. 18	Massilia
Dec. 7	Burgundia

FRENCH LINE
(Compagnie Generale Transatlantique)
Havre—New York
N.Y.

Arrival	Steamer
Jan. 5	La Gascogne
Jan. 12	La Normandie
Jan. 19	La Burgoyne
Jan. 26	La Bretogne
Feb. 3	La Champagne
Feb. 16	La Normandie
Feb. 23	La Bretogne
Mar. 2	La Champagne
Mar. 9	La Gascogne
Mar. 16	La Burgoyne
Mar. 23	La Bretogne
Mar. 30	La Champagne
Apr. 6	La Gascogne
Apr. 13	La Normandie
Apr. 22	La Burgoyne
Apr. 27	La Bretogne
May 4	La Gascogne
May 11	La Champagne
May 18	La Burgoyne
May 25	La Bretogne
June 1	La Gascogne
June 8	La Champagne
June 15	La Burgoyne
June 22	La Bretogne
June 27	La Touraine
July 6	La Gascogne
July 13	La Champagne
July 20	La Burgoyne
July 27	La Normandie
Aug. 3	La Gascogne
Aug. 10	La Touraine
Aug. 17	La Burgoyne
Aug. 24	La Champagne
Aug. 31	La Normandie
Sept. 7	La Touraine
Sept. 14	La Bretogne
Sept. 21	La Champagne

FRENCH LINE
(Compagnie Generale Transatlantique)
Havre—New York
(Continued)
N.Y.

Arrival	Steamer
Sept. 28	La Burgoyne
Oct. 5	La Touraine
Oct. 12	La Bretogne
Oct. 19	La Champagne
Oct. 26	La Gascogne
Nov. 2	La Touraine
Nov. 9	La Bretogne
Nov. 16	La Burgoyne
Nov. 23	La Gascogne
Nov. 30	La Champagne
Dec. 7	La Bretogne
Dec. 14	La Burgoyne
Dec. 21	La Gascogne
Dec. 28	La Champagne

GUION STEAMSHIP LINE
Liverpool—New York
N.Y.

Arrival	Steamer
Apr. 13	Arizona
Apr. 27	Alaska
May 11	Arizona
May 25	Alaska
June 8	Arizona
June 22	Alaska
July 6	Arizona
July 20	Alaska
Aug. 3	Arizona
Aug. 17	Alaska
Aug. 31	Arizona
Sept. 14	Alaska
Sept. 28	Arizona
Oct. 13	Alaska
Oct. 27	Arizona
Nov. 9	Alaska
Nov. 23	Arizona

HAMBURG-AMERICAN LINE
Hamburg—New York
N.Y.

Arrival	Steamer
Jan. 2	Bohemia
Jan. 3	Marsala
Jan. 5	Scandia
Jan. 6	Sorrento
Jan. 15	Suevia
Jan. 20	Rhaetia
Feb. 2	Rugia
Feb. 9	Moravia
Feb. 11	Russia
Feb. 16	Amalfi
Feb. 16	Scandia
Feb. 24	Suevia
Feb. 24	Bohemia
Mar. 2	Rhaetia
Mar. 2	Taormina
Mar. 4	Marsala
Mar. 6	Slavonia
Mar. 9	Wieland
Mar. 14	Sorrento
Mar. 14	Gothia
Mar. 16	Rugia

Year 1891

HAMBURG-AMERICAN LINE
Hamburg—New York
(Continued)

N. Y. Arrival	Steamer
Mar. 20	Moravia
Mar. 23	Russia
Mar. 26	Scandia
Mar. 28	Gellert
Apr. 3	Amalfi
Apr. 6	Dania
Apr. 13	Bohemia
Apr. 13	Rhaetia
Apr. 22	Suevia
Apr. 22	Taormina
Apr. 22	Wieland
Apr. 27	Marsala
Apr. 27	Augusta Victoria
Apr. 29	Russia
May 4	Normannia
May 4	Rugia
May 8	Gellert
May 9	Sorrento
May 11	Scandia
May 15	Dania
May 16	Furst Bismarck
May 16	California
May 22	Amalfi
May 25	Rhaetia
May 28	Bohemia
June 1	Suevia
June 1	Normannia
June 5	Wieland
June 6	Columbia
June 6	Taormina
June 9	Moravia
June 13	Rugia
June 15	Furst Bismarck
June 20	Gellert
June 20	Marsala
June 22	Augusta Victoria
June 23	Slavonia
June 24	Russia
June 26	Dania
June 27	Normannia
July 3	California
July 6	Rhaetia
July 6	Columbia
July 10	Scandia
July 11	Sorrento
July 11	Furst Bismarck
July 15	Suevia
July 17	Gothia
July 18	Wieland
July 20	Augusta Victoria
July 23	Bohemia
July 25	Normannia
July 27	Gellert
July 31	Amalfi
Aug. 1	Columbia
Aug. 3	Russia
Aug. 4	Moravia
Aug. 8	Furst Bismarck
Aug. 8	Dania
Aug. 14	Taormina
Aug. 15	Rugia
Aug. 17	Slavonia
Aug. 17	Augusta Victoria
Aug. 21	Marsala

HAMBURG-AMERICAN LINE
Hamburg—New York
(Continued)

N. Y. Arrival	Steamer
Aug. 24	Normannia
Aug. 27	Suevia
Aug. 27	Scandia
Aug. 28	California
Aug. 29	Columbia
Aug. 31	Wieland
Sept. 5	Sorrento
Sept. 7	Furst Bismarck
Sept. 8	Rhaetia
Sept. 12	Bohemia
Sept. 14	Gothia
Sept. 14	Gellert
Sept. 14	Augusta Victoria
Sept. 15	Moravia
Sept. 18	Dania
Sept. 21	Normannia
Sept. 26	Columbia
Sept. 26	Amalfi
Sept. 28	Rugia
Sept. 28	Russia
Oct. 5	Furst Bismarck
Oct. 6	Suevia
Oct. 12	Augusta Victoria
Oct. 12	Wieland
Oct. 12	Taormina
Oct. 13	Slavonia
Oct. 16	California
Oct. 19	Normannia
Oct. 20	Rhaetia
Oct. 23	Scandia
Oct. 26	Columbia
Oct. 26	Marsala
Oct. 31	Dania
Oct. 31	Furst Bismarck
Nov. 2	Bohemia
Nov. 9	Gothia
Nov. 9	Rugia
Nov. 9	Sorrento
Nov. 9	Augusta Victoria
Nov. 12	Moravia
Nov. 12	Normannia
Nov. 18	Russia
Nov. 23	Suevia
Nov. 28	Scandia
Nov. 28	Furst Bismarck
Nov. 28	California
Dec. 8	Rhaetia
Dec. 8	Taormina
Dec. 15	Dania
Dec. 21	Bohemia
Dec. 22	Rugia
Dec. 24	Marsala
Dec. 28	Moravia
Dec. 31	Russia

HAMBURG-AMERICAN LINE
Scandinavian Ports
Stettin, Copenhagen—New York

N. Y. Arrival	Steamer
Feb. 9	Polaria
Mar. 3	Italia

HAMBURG-AMERICAN LINE
Scandinavian Ports
Stettin, Copenhagen—New York
(Continued)

N. Y. Arrival	Steamer
Apr. 27	Polynesia
May 11	Polaria
May 21	Italia
June 20	Polaria
July 16	Italia
July 31	Polaria
Aug. 14	Polynesia
Sept. 3	Italia
Sept. 26	Polaria
Oct. 13	Polynesia
Nov. 2	Italia
Nov. 23	Polaria
Dec. 9	Polynesia

HOLLAND-AMERICA LINE
Rotterdam, Amsterdam & Boulogne—New York

N. Y. Arrival	Steamer
Feb. 5	Rotterdam
Feb. 7	Spaarndam
Feb. 14	Werkendam
Feb. 20	Veendam
Mar. 2	Amsterdam
Mar. 9	Obdam
Mar. 12	Maasdam
Mar. 23	Rotterdam
Mar. 26	Spaarndam
Apr. 4	Werkendam
Apr. 9	Veendam
Apr. 20	Obdam
Apr. 22	Maasdam
Apr. 27	Zaandam
May 4	Amsterdam
May 7	Spaarndam
May 11	Schiedam
May 15	Werkendam
May 19	Rotterdam
May 26	Veendam
May 29	Obdam
June 3	Didam
June 4	Maasdam
June 11	Zaandam
June 12	Amsterdam
June 19	Spaarndam
June 25	Edam
June 26	Werkendam
July 2	Rotterdam
July 10	Obdam
July 14	Didam
July 14	Schiedam
July 16	Maasdam
July 28	P. Caland
July 29	Spaarndam
Aug. 6	Werkendam
Aug. 12	Veendam
Aug. 14	Rotterdam
Aug. 21	Obdam
Sept. 5	Amsterdam
Sept. 11	Spaarndam
Sept. 18	Werkendam

Year 1891

HOLLAND-AMERICA LINE
Rotterdam, Amsterdam & Boulogne—New York
(Continued)

N.Y.

Arrival	Steamer
Sept. 22	Dubbledam
Sept. 23	Rotterdam
Sept. 24	Veendam
Oct. 2	Zaandam
Oct. 3	Obdam
Oct. 7	Maasdam
Oct. 20	Didam
Oct. 28	Amsterdam
Nov. 2	Werkendam
Nov. 4	Veendam
Nov. 6	Rotterdam
Nov. 9	Dubbledam
Nov. 13	Obdam
Nov. 23	Spaarndam
Nov. 25	Maasdam
Dec. 2	Edam
Dec. 8	Amsterdam
Dec. 10	Didam
Dec. 14	Werkendam
Dec. 19	Veendam
Dec. 19	Rotterdam
Dec. 28	Obdam

INMAN & INTERNATIONAL STEAMSHIP LINE
Liverpool—New York

N.Y.

Arrival	Steamer
Jan. 10	City of Chicago
Jan. 23	City of Berlin
Feb. 9	City of Chicago
Feb. 12	City of New York
Feb. 21	City of Berlin
Mar. 9	City of Chicago
Mar. 14	City of New York
Mar. 21	City of Berlin
Mar. 28	City of Chester
Apr. 6	City of Chicago
Apr. 9	City of New York
Apr. 18	City of Berlin
Apr. 27	City of Chester
May 4	City of Chicago
May 7	City of New York
May 16	City of Berlin
May 21	City of Paris
June 1	City of Richmond
June 4	City of New York
June 10	City of Chester
June 13	City of Berlin
June 18	City of Paris
June 27	City of Chicago
July 2	City of New York
July 11	City of Paris
July 16	City of Paris
July 25	City of Chicago
July 30	City of New York
Aug. 8	City of Berlin
Aug. 13	City of Paris
Aug. 22	City of Chicago
Aug. 26	City of New York
Sept. 5	City of Berlin
Sept. 9	City of Paris

INMAN & INTERNATIONAL STEAMSHIP LINE
Liverpool—New York
(Continued)

N.Y.

Arrival	Steamer
Sept. 19	City of Chicago
Sept. 24	City of New York
Oct. 8	City of Paris
Oct. 19	City of Chicago
Oct. 22	City of New York
Oct. 30	City of Berlin
Nov. 4	City of Paris
Nov. 14	City of Chicago
Nov. 19	City of New York
Nov. 27	City of Berlin
Dec. 3	City of Paris
Dec. 14	City of Chicago
Dec. 21	City of Chester

INSULAR NAVIGATION COMPANY
Azores, Lisbon—New Bedford, Mass., New York

N.Y.

Arrival	Steamer
Jan. 27	Vega
Mar. 24	Vega
May 21	Vega
July 11	Vega
Aug. 31	Vega
Dec. 14	Vega

LINHA DE VAPORES PORTUGUEZES
Azores, Lisbon—New Bedford, Mass., New York

N.Y.

Arrival	Steamer
Jan. 17	Olinda
Mar. 14	Olinda
Mar. 17	Oevenum
May 18	Oevenum
June 2	Olinda
July 15	Oevenum
Sept. 7	Oevenum
Sept. 14	Olinda
Nov. 23	Oevenum
Dec. 21	Oevenum

LIVERPOOL & GREAT WESTERN STEAMSHIP COMPANY
Liverpool—New York

N.Y.

Arrival	Steamer
Jan. 3	Wisconsin
Jan. 14	Wyoming
Jan. 30	Nevada
Feb. 7	Wisconsin
Feb. 20	Wyoming
Feb. 26	Nevada
Mar. 12	Wisconsin
Mar. 25	Wyoming
Apr. 2	Nevada
Apr. 23	Wisconsin
May 6	Nevada
May 21	Wyoming
June 3	Wisconsin

LIVERPOOL & GREAT WESTERN STEAMSHIP COMPANY
Liverpool—New York
(Continued)

N.Y.

Arrival	Steamer
June 18	Nevada
June 29	Wyoming
July 15	Wisconsin
July 29	Nevada
Aug. 12	Wyoming
Aug. 26	Wisconsin
Sept. 10	Nevada
Sept. 23	Wyoming
Oct. 9	Wisconsin
Oct. 22	Nevada
Nov. 4	Wyoming
Nov. 19	Wisconsin
Dec. 2	Nevada
Dec. 18	Wyoming
Dec. 26	Wisconsin

NATIONAL NAVIGATION COMPANY
Mediterranean—New York

N.Y.

Arrival	Steamer
Feb. 16	Chandernagor
Mar. 18	Cachar
Apr. 9	Cachemire
May 5	Chandernagor
June 2	Cachemire
June 15	Cachar
July 8	Chandernagor
Aug. 8	Cachemire
Oct. 9	Cachemire
Nov. 14	Hindoustan
Dec. 10	Chandernagor

NATIONAL STEAMSHIP COMPANY
London and Liverpool—New York

N.Y.

Arrival	Steamer
Jan. 7	The Queen
Jan. 16	England
Feb. 6	Denmark
Feb. 10	Spain
Feb. 18	Italy
Feb. 26	France
Mar. 2	America
Mar. 9	Greece
Mar. 17	England
Mar. 23	Canada
Apr. 7	Italy
Apr. 10	Spain
Apr. 13	Helvetia
Apr. 21	France
Apr. 27	America
Apr. 29	The Queen
May 5	Greece
May 12	Denmark
May 13	England
May 21	Canada
May 23	Holland
May 28	Europe
June 8	Italy
June 15	France

Year 1891

NATIONAL STEAMSHIP COMPANY
London and Liverpool—New York
(Continued)

N. Y.

Arrival	Steamer
June 22	America
June 26	The Queen
June 29	Spain
July 6	Greece
July 11	Denmark
July 13	England
July 21	Canada
July 23	Italy
July 24	Europe
Aug. 3	France
Aug. 6	Holland
Aug. 10	America
Aug. 17	Spain
Aug. 24	Greece
Aug. 25	Helvetia
Sept. 4	Denmark
Sept. 4	England
Sept. 12	The Queen
Sept. 17	Canada
Sept. 18	Italy
Sept. 21	Europe
Sept. 28	Holland
Oct. 1	France
Oct. 6	America
Oct. 12	Greece
Oct. 19	Spain
Oct. 26	Denmark
Oct. 26	England
Nov. 6	Italy
Nov. 11	Canada
Nov. 12	Holland
Nov. 27	Greece
Nov. 28	America
Dec. 7	Spain
Dec. 10	Denmark
Dec. 16	England
Dec. 19	The Queen
Dec. 28	Europe
Dec. 31	Helvetia

NAVIGAZIONE GENERALE ITALIANA LINE
Mediterranean—New York

N. Y.

Arrival	Steamer
Jan. 7	Giava
Jan. 21	Birmania
Feb. 12	Letimbro
Feb. 23	Entella
Mar. 17	Stura
Apr. 2	Iniziativa
Apr. 9	Birmania
Apr. 16	Giava
Apr. 28	Letimbro
May 9	Entella
June 11	Palcevera
June 24	Washington
June 29	Birmania
July 13	Iniziativa
July 28	Plata
Aug. 27	Entella
Sept. 29	Birmania
Oct. 3	Iniziativa

NAVIGAZIONE GENERALE ITALIANA LINE
Mediterranean—New York
(Continued)

N. Y.

Arrival	Steamer
Oct. 16	Plata
Nov. 12	Palcevera
Nov. 27	Entella
Dec. 14	San Antonio
Dec. 21	Iniziativa

NORTH GERMAN LLOYD
Bremen—New York

N. Y.

Arrival	Steamer
Jan. 5	Saale
Jan. 14	Eider
Jan. 17	Lahn
Jan. 21	Fulda
Jan. 23	Spree
Jan. 24	Stuttgart
Jan. 30	Werra
Feb. 3	Trave
Feb. 9	Salier
Feb. 9	Ems
Feb. 11	Eider
Feb. 14	Havel
Feb. 19	Fulda
Feb. 23	Saale
Feb. 25	Werra
Feb. 27	Spree
Mar. 3	Aller
Mar. 6	Lahn
Mar. 11	Ems
Mar. 13	Havel
Mar. 17	Eider
Mar. 21	Fulda
Mar. 23	Trave
Mar. 24	Saale
Mar. 25	Spree
Mar. 28	Werra
Mar. 31	Aller
Apr. 3	Lahn
Apr. 7	Ems
Apr. 9	Havel
Apr. 13	Elbe
Apr. 14	Eider
Apr. 18	Fulda
Apr. 21	Trave
Apr. 23	Saale
Apr. 23	Spree
Apr. 25	Werra
Apr. 28	Aller
Apr. 30	Lahn
May 5	Ems
May 6	Havel
May 11	Elbe
May 12	Eider
May 15	Trave
May 16	Fulda
May 19	Saale
May 20	Spree
May 23	Werra
May 26	Aller
May 28	Lahn
June 1	Kaiser Willem II
June 2	Ems
June 4	Havel
June 6	Elbe

NORTH GERMAN LLOYD
Bremen—New York
(Continued)

N. Y.

Arrival	Steamer
June 9	Eider
June 12	Trave
June 13	Fulda
June 17	Saale
June 18	Spree
June 20	Werra
June 24	Aller
June 25	Lahn
June 27	Kaiser Willem II
June 30	Ems
July 2	Havel
July 6	Elbe
July 7	Eider
July 10	Trave
July 14	Saale
July 15	Spree
July 21	Fulda
July 23	Werra
July 27	Aller
July 29	Lahn
Aug. 3	Ems
Aug. 6	Havel
Aug. 11	Eider
Aug. 13	Trave
Aug. 15	Elbe
Aug. 18	Saale
Aug. 19	Spree
Aug. 21	Fulda
Aug. 25	Aller
Aug. 27	Lahn
Aug. 29	Werra
Sept. 1	Ems
Sept. 3	Havel
Sept. 5	Kaiser Willem II
Sept. 8	Eider
Sept. 11	Trave
Sept. 12	Elbe
Sept. 15	Saale
Sept. 16	Spree
Sept. 19	Fulda
Sept. 22	Aller
Sept. 24	Lahn
Sept. 26	Werra
Sept. 29	Ems
Oct. 1	Havel
Oct. 5	Kaiser Willem II
Oct. 6	Eider
Oct. 10	Elbe
Oct. 14	Saale
Oct. 15	Spree
Oct. 19	Fulda
Oct. 20	Aller
Oct. 22	Lahn
Oct. 26	Werra
Oct. 28	Ems
Oct. 29	Havel
Nov. 3	Eider
Nov. 7	Elbe
Nov. 12	Spree
Nov. 20	Lahn
Nov. 20	Werra
Nov. 24	Ems
Nov. 27	Havel
Dec. 4	Trave
Dec. 10	Elbe

Year 1891

NORTH GERMAN LLOYD
Bremen—New York
(Continued)

N.Y. Arrival	Steamer
Dec. 12	Spree
Dec. 22	Ems
Dec. 24	Havel
Dec. 31	Weimar

NORTH GERMAN LLOYD
Mediterranean—New York

N.Y. Arrival	Steamer
Nov. 28	Fulda
Dec. 30	Fulda

RED STAR LINE
Antwerp—New York

N.Y. Arrival	Steamer
Jan. 5	Rhynland
Jan. 7	Westernland
Feb. 7	Waesland
Feb. 9	Friesland
Feb. 20	Noordland
Mar. 5	Rhynland
Mar. 11	Friesland
Mar. 18	Waesland
Mar. 25	Noordland
Apr. 1	Westernland
Apr. 10	Nederland
Apr. 15	Friesland
Apr. 23	Waesland
May 1	Rhynland
May 6	Westernland
May 14	Nederland
May 18	Pennland
May 20	Friesland
May 26	Waesland
June 3	Nederland
June 4	Rhynland
June 9	Westernland
June 18	Noordland
June 23	Pennland
June 24	Friesland
July 1	Waesland
July 22	Noordland
July 28	Friesland
Aug. 5	Waesland
Aug. 14	Rhynland
Aug. 19	Westernland
Aug. 27	Noordland
Sept. 2	Friesland
Sept. 9	Waesland
Sept. 17	Rhynland
Sept. 23	Westernland
Sept. 24	Nederland
Oct. 1	Noordland
Oct. 7	Friesland
Oct. 15	Waesland
Oct. 23	Rhynland
Oct. 29	Westernland
Nov. 4	Noordland
Nov. 5	Nederland
Nov. 9	Friesland
Nov. 18	Waesland
Nov. 27	Rhynland
Dec. 1	Westernland
Dec. 11	Noordland

RED STAR LINE
Antwerp—New York
(Continued)

N.Y. Arrival	Steamer
Dec. 18	Friesland
Dec. 24	Waesland
Dec. 26	Nederland

SCANDINAVIAN-AMERICAN LINE
Scandinavian Ports—New York

N.Y. Arrival	Steamer
Jan. 10	Norge
Jan. 28	Thingvalla
Feb. 11	Hekla
Feb. 24	Island
Mar. 11	Norge
Mar. 23	Thingvalla
Apr. 6	Hekla
Apr. 10	Christine
Apr. 18	Island
May 4	Norge
May 18	Thingvalla
June 11	Island
June 27	Norge
July 9	Thingvalla
July 24	Hekla
Aug. 7	Island
Aug. 22	Norge
Sept. 4	Thingvalla
Sept. 18	Hekla
Oct. 5	Island
Oct. 19	Norge
Nov. 2	Thingvalla
Nov. 14	Hekla
Nov. 28	Island
Dec. 14	Norge
Dec. 28	Thingvalla

WHITE STAR LINE
Liverpool—New York

N.Y. Arrival	Steamer
Jan. 5	Adriatic
Jan. 9	Britannic
Jan. 17	Celtic
Jan. 23	Germanic
Jan. 30	Cufic
Feb. 2	Adriatic
Feb. 5	Teutonic
Feb. 16	Celtic
Feb. 20	Majestic
Mar. 2	Adriatic
Mar. 4	Teutonic
Mar. 10	Cufic
Mar. 13	Britannic
Mar. 27	Germanic
Apr. 2	Teutonic
Apr. 7	Runic
Apr. 11	Britannic
Apr. 15	Majestic
Apr. 21	Cufic
Apr. 24	Germanic
Apr. 30	Teutonic
May 8	Britannic
May 13	Majestic
May 19	Runic

WHITE STAR LINE
Liverpool—New York
(Continued)

N.Y. Arrival	Steamer
May 22	Germanic
May 27	Teutonic
June 2	Tauric
June 5	Britannic
June 10	Majestic
June 19	Germanic
June 24	Cufic
June 25	Teutonic
June 29	Runic
July 3	Britannic
July 8	Majestic
July 13	Tauric
July 17	Germanic
July 22	Teutonic
July 31	Britannic
Aug. 5	Majestic
Aug. 10	Runic
Aug. 14	Germanic
Aug. 17	Cufic
Aug. 19	Teutonic
Aug. 24	Tauric
Aug. 28	Britannic
Sept. 2	Majestic
Sept. 11	Germanic
Sept. 14	Runic
Sept. 16	Teutonic
Sept. 23	Cufic
Sept. 26	Britannic
Oct. 1	Majestic
Oct. 6	Tauric
Oct. 9	Germanic
Oct. 15	Teutonic
Oct. 15	Nomadic
Oct. 21	Runic
Oct. 23	Britannic
Oct. 28	Majestic
Oct. 29	Cufic
Nov. 6	Germanic
Nov. 9	Tauric
Nov. 11	Teutonic
Nov. 21	Britannic
Nov. 23	Runic
Nov. 25	Majestic
Dec. 3	Cufic
Dec. 5	Germanic
Dec. 10	Teutonic
Dec. 15	Tauric
Dec. 21	Britannic
Dec. 24	Majestic
Dec. 29	Runic

WILSON LINE
Hull, London—New York

N.Y. Arrival	Steamer
Jan. 5	Egyptian Monarch
Jan. 19	Lydian Monarch
Jan. 21	Persian Monarch
Feb. 2	Colorado
Mar. 2	Egyptian Monarch
Mar. 14	Persian Monarch
Mar. 23	Lydian Monarch
Mar. 26	Colorado
Apr. 27	Egyptian Monarch
May 8	Lydian Monarch

Year 1891

WILSON LINE
Hull, London—New York
(Continued)
N.Y.

Arrival	Steamer
May 11	Colorado
May 16	Persian Monarch
May 20	Galileo
June 20	Egyptian Monarch
June 22	Colorado
June 29	Galileo
July 1	Lydian Monarch
July 9	Persian Monarch
Aug. 1	Hindoo
Aug. 8	Egyptian Monarch
Aug. 10	Colorado
Aug. 21	Lydian Monarch
Aug. 28	Persian Monarch
Sept. 21	Egyptian Monarch
Sept. 21	Colorado
Oct. 5	Lydian Monarch
Oct. 9	Francisco
Oct. 14	Persian Monarch
Nov. 2	Colorado
Nov. 6	Egyptian Monarch
Nov. 19	Francisco
Nov. 20	Lydian Monarch
Nov. 30	Persian Monarch
Dec. 17	Hindoo
Dec. 28	Colorado
Dec. 30	Egyptian Monarch

ADDITIONAL ARRIVALS
Antwerp—New York
N.Y.

Arrival	Steamer
Dec. 7	Volturno

Bordeaux—New York
N.Y.

Arrival	Steamer
Mar. 14	Chateau Yquem
Apr. 6	Chateau Lafite
Dec. 23	Chateau Lafite

British Ports—New York
N.Y.

Arrival	Steamer
Jan. 19	Wells City
Feb. 2	Croma
Feb. 6	Jersey City
Feb. 20	Llandaff
Feb. 23	Otranto
Feb. 28	Critic

ADDITIONAL ARRIVALS
British Ports—New York
(Continued)
N.Y.

Arrival	Steamer
Mar. 2	Exeter City
Mar. 19	Wells City
Mar. 27	Jersey City
Apr. 11	Mineola
Apr. 21	Llandaff
Apr. 30	Exeter City
May 16	Wells City
May 18	Critic
May 28	Mineola
June 6	Jersey City
June 10	Llandaff
June 19	Exeter City
June 29	Wells City
July 7	Critic
July 13	Mineola
July 18	Jersey City
July 20	Croft
July 24	Llandaff
July 31	Exeter City
Aug. 10	Wells City
Aug. 25	Croma
Aug. 29	Jersey City
Sept. 5	Llandaff
Sept. 7	Croft
Sept. 14	Exeter City
Sept. 16	Critic
Sept. 19	Wells City
Oct. 17	Jersey City
Oct. 31	Exeter City
Oct. 31	Croft
Nov. 7	Wells City
Nov. 11	Critic
Dec. 4	Jersey City
Dec. 11	Llandaff
Dec. 16	Exeter City
Dec. 22	Croft
Dec. 29	Wells City

Hamburg—New York
N.Y.

Arrival	Steamer
Jan. 10	India
May 7	Drot
June 2	India
Aug. 7	Volturno
Oct. 1	Virginia
Oct. 29	Venetia
Nov. 24	Virginia
Dec. 24	Venetia

ADDITIONAL ARRIVALS
Liverpool—New York
N.Y.

Arrival	Steamer
Jan. 21	Lake Ontario
Feb. 9	Lake Huron
Mar. 6	Lake Ontario
Dec. 11	Abyssinia

London—New York
N.Y.

Arrival	Steamer
Feb. 16	Ludgate Hill
Feb. 26	Tower Hill
Apr. 7	Ludgate Hill
Apr. 17	Tower Hill
May 23	Ludgate Hill
May 25	Bayonne
June 23	Tower Hill
July 18	Ludgate Hill
Aug. 12	Tower Hill
Sept. 7	Ludgate Hill
Sept. 28	Tower Hill
Oct. 24	Ludgate Hill
Nov. 11	Tower Hill
Dec. 9	Ludgate Hill
Dec. 30	Tower Hill

Mediterranean—New York
N.Y.

Arrival	Steamer
Feb. 17	Simpatia
Mar. 9	Peeress
Apr. 11	Wetherby
Aug. 6	Fitzroy

Rotterdam, Amsterdam—
New York
N.Y.

Arrival	Steamer
July 3	Prins Willem III
Aug. 28	Prins Willem I

Spanish Ports—New York
N.Y.

Arrival	Steamer
Aug. 3	Palentino
Aug. 13	Ponce De Leon

Year 1892

ALLAN STATE LINE
Glasgow—New York

N.Y.

Arrival	Steamer
Jan. 2	State of California
Jan. 9	Pomeranian
Jan. 12	Norwegian
Jan. 19	State of Nebraska
Jan. 30	Assyrian
Feb. 5	Siberian
Feb. 11	State of California
Feb. 19	Pomeranian
Feb. 24	Norwegian
Mar. 1	State of Nebraska
Mar. 10	Siberian
Mar. 18	Corean
Mar. 26	State of California
Mar. 31	Pomeranian
Apr. 6	Norwegian
Apr. 14	State of Nebraska
Apr. 20	Siberian
Apr. 26	State of California
May 4	Corean
May 11	State of Nevada
May 18	Norwegian
May 25	State of Nebraska
June 1	Siberian
June 6	State of California
June 15	Corean
June 21	State of Nevada
June 28	Norwegian
July 6	State of Nebraska
July 13	Siberian
July 18	State of California
July 26	Corean
Aug. 2	State of Nevada
Aug. 8	Norwegian
Aug. 16	State of Nebraska
Aug. 24	Siberian
Aug. 30	State of California
Sept. 9	Corean
Sept. 17	State of Nevada
Sept. 21	Norwegian
Sept. 29	State of Nebraska
Oct. 7	Siberian
Oct. 12	State of California
Oct. 19	Corean
Oct. 26	Norwegian
Nov. 1	State of Nebraska
Nov. 11	Siberian
Nov. 16	State of California
Nov. 22	Corean
Nov. 28	Norwegian
Dec. 7	State of Nebraska
Dec. 15	Siberian
Dec. 20	State of California
Dec. 30	Pomeranian

ANCHOR LINE
Glasgow—New York

N.Y.

Arrival	Steamer
Jan. 6	Devonia
Jan. 16	Algeria
Jan. 26	Circassia
Feb. 3	Anchoria
Feb. 11	Ethiopia

ANCHOR LINE
Glasgow—New York
(Continued)

N.Y.

Arrival	Steamer
Feb. 17	Devonia
Mar. 2	Anchoria
Mar. 7	Circassia
Mar. 16	Ethiopia
Mar. 23	Devonia
Mar. 28	Furnessia
Apr. 4	Anchoria
Apr. 12	Circassia
Apr. 19	Ethiopia
Apr. 27	Devonia
May 2	Furnessia
May 9	Anchoria
May 17	Circassia
May 23	City of Rome
May 31	Ethiopia
June 6	Furnessia
June 14	Anchoria
June 21	Circassia
June 25	City of Rome
July 5	Ethiopia
July 11	Furnessia
July 19	Anchoria
July 25	Circassia
Aug. 2	Bolivia
Aug. 8	Ethiopia
Aug. 15	Furnessia
Aug. 22	Anchoria
Sept. 1	Circassia
Sept. 5	City of Rome
Sept. 20	Furnessia
Sept. 23	Ethiopia
Sept. 27	Anchoria
Oct. 10	City of Rome
Oct. 18	Circassia
Oct. 24	Furnessia
Oct. 31	Anchoria
Nov. 10	Devonia
Nov. 17	Ethiopia
Nov. 28	Furnessia
Dec. 7	Anchoria
Dec. 23	Ethiopia

ANCHOR LINE
Mediterranean—New York

N.Y.

Arrival	Steamer
Jan. 2	Victoria
Jan. 12	Anglia
Jan. 14	Assyria
Jan. 18	Hesperia
Feb. 19	Alsatia
Mar. 1	Bolivia
Mar. 14	California
Mar. 28	India
Apr. 4	Olympia
Apr. 8	Victoria
Apr. 20	Trinacria
Apr. 26	Hesperia
May 2	Anglia
May 9	Assyria
May 13	Alsatia
June 6	India

ANCHOR LINE
Mediterranean—New York
(Continued)

N.Y.

Arrival	Steamer
June 15	California
June 24	Belgravia
July 21	Olympia
July 30	Trinacria
Aug. 13	Victoria
Aug. 31	Italia
Sept. 10	Alsatia
Sept. 21	California
Oct. 12	Britannia
Oct. 17	India
Oct. 18	Assyria
Nov. 5	Belgravia
Dec. 2	Victoria
Dec. 5	Alsatia
Dec. 20	Italia

ATLANTIC TRANSPORT LINE
London—New York

N.Y.

Arrival	Steamer
Apr. 27	Manitoba
May 5	Massachusetts
June 6	Manitoba
June 17	Massachusetts
July 18	Manitoba
July 28	Massachusetts
Aug. 18	Mississippi
Sept. 7	Massachusetts
Sept. 29	Mississippi
Oct. 5	Manitoba
Oct. 18	Massachusetts
Nov. 11	Mississippi
Nov. 17	Manitoba
Dec. 1	Massachusetts
Dec. 22	Mississippi
Dec. 29	Manitoba

COMPANIA TRANSATLANTICA LINE
(Spanish Line)
Spanish Ports—New York

N.Y.

Arrival	Steamer
Jan. 4	Habana
Jan. 8	Panama
Jan. 16	Ciudad Condal
Jan. 25	Panama
Feb. 4	Habana
Feb. 8	Mexico
Feb. 15	Baldomero Iglisias
Feb. 27	Mexico
Mar. 5	Habana
Mar. 8	Panama
Mar. 15	Ciudad Condal
Mar. 25	Panama
Apr. 5	Mexico
Apr. 15	Habana
Apr. 25	Mexico
May 5	Panama
May 16	Ciudad Condal
May 25	Panama

Year 1892

COMPANIA TRANSATLANTICA LINE
(Spanish Line)
Spanish Ports—New York
(Continued)

N. Y.

Arrival	Steamer
June 4	Mexico
June 15	Ciudad Condal
June 25	Mexico
July 5	Panama
July 15	Ciudad Condal
July 25	Panama
Aug. 4	Mexico
Aug. 16	Habana
Aug. 25	Mexico
Sept. 5	Panama
Sept. 15	Ciudad Condal
Sept. 26	Panama
Oct. 6	Habana
Oct. 19	Panama
Oct. 25	Habana
Nov. 4	Mexico
Nov. 15	Ciudad Condal
Nov. 25	Mexico
Dec. 5	Panama
Dec. 15	Ciudad Condal
Dec. 26	Panama

CUNARD LINE
Liverpool—New York

N. Y.

Arrival	Steamer
Jan. 6	Bothnia
Jan. 11	Umbria
Jan. 18	Gallia
Jan. 25	Etruria
Feb. 1	Aurania
Feb. 8	Umbria
Feb. 8	Bothnia
Feb. 16	Servia
Feb. 22	Etruria
Feb. 29	Aurania
Mar. 7	Umbria
Mar. 15	Servia
Mar. 21	Etruria
Mar. 28	Aurania
Apr. 2	Bothnia
Apr. 4	Umbria
Apr. 11	Servia
Apr. 18	Etruria
Apr. 25	Aurania
Apr. 30	Bothnia
May 2	Umbria
May 9	Servia
May 13	Gallia
May 16	Etruria
May 23	Aurania
May 30	Umbria
May 30	Bothnia
June 6	Servia
June 10	Gallia
June 13	Etruria
June 20	Aurania
June 27	Umbria
July 5	Servia
July 11	Etruria
July 18	Aurania
July 25	Gallia
Aug. 1	Servia

CUNARD LINE
Liverpool—New York
(Continued)

N. Y.

Arrival	Steamer
Aug. 6	Umbria
Aug. 15	Aurania
Aug. 20	Etruria
Aug. 29	Servia
Sept. 3	Gallia
Sept. 5	Umbria
Sept. 12	Aurania
Sept. 19	Bothnia
Sept. 19	Etruria
Sept. 26	Servia
Sept. 30	Gallia
Oct. 3	Umbria
Oct. 10	Aurania
Oct. 17	Etruria
Oct. 24	Servia
Oct. 31	Umbria
Nov. 8	Aurania
Nov. 14	Etruria
Nov. 21	Servia
Nov. 28	Umbria
Dec. 5	Aurania
Dec. 12	Etruria
Dec. 20	Gallia
Dec. 31	Umbria

FABRE LINE
Mediterranean—New York

N. Y.

Arrival	Steamer
Jan. 2	Nuestria
Jan. 30	Massilia
Feb. 19	Burgundia
Mar. 10	Nuestria
Apr. 4	Massilia
Apr. 25	Burgundia
May 2	Britannia
May 12	Nuestria
May 13	Alesia
June 6	Massilia
June 27	Britannia
July 14	Nuestria
Aug. 3	Massilia
Aug. 25	Britannia
Sept. 13	Nuestria
Oct. 11	Massilia
Nov. 2	Britannia
Nov. 15	Burgundia
Nov. 23	Nuestria
Dec. 6	Massilia

FRENCH LINE
(Compagnie Generale Transatlantique)
Havre—New York

N. Y.

Arrival	Steamer
Jan. 5	La Normandie
Jan. 11	La Bourgoyne
Jan. 18	La Gascogne
Jan. 25	La Bretogne
Feb. 4	La Bourgoyne
Feb. 9	La Normandie
Feb. 15	La Gascogne
Feb. 22	La Bretogne

FRENCH LINE
(Compagnie Generale Transatlantique)
Havre—New York
(Continued)

N. Y.

Arrival	Steamer
Feb. 29	La Champagne
Mar. 7	La Bourgoyne
Mar. 15	La Normandie
Mar. 21	La Bretogne
Mar. 26	La Touraine
Apr. 4	La Champagne
Apr. 11	La Gascogne
Apr. 18	La Bretogne
Apr. 25	La Touraine
May 2	La Champagne
May 9	La Bourgoyne
May 16	La Gascogne
May 23	La Touraine
May 30	La Champagne
June 6	La Bourgoyne
June 13	La Bretogne
June 18	La Touraine
June 27	La Gascogne
July 5	La Bourgoyne
July 11	La Bretogne
July 18	La Champagne
July 25	La Gascogne
July 30	La Touraine
Aug. 8	La Bourgoyne
Aug. 15	La Champagne
Aug. 27	La Touraine
Sept. 8	La Bourgoyne
Sept. 14	La Champagne
Oct. 3	La Gascogne
Oct. 10	La Champagne
Oct. 17	La Bourgoyne
Oct. 24	La Touraine
Oct. 31	La Gascogne
Nov. 8	La Bretogne
Nov. 14	La Bourgoyne
Nov. 21	La Champagne
Nov. 28	La Gascogne
Dec. 7	La Bretogne
Dec. 11	La Bourgoyne
Dec. 19	La Champagne
Dec. 27	La Normandie

GUION STEAMSHIP LINE
Liverpool—New York

N. Y.

Arrival	Steamer
Feb. 5	Arizona
Apr. 11	Arizona
Apr. 25	Alaska
May 9	Arizona
May 23	Alaska
June 6	Arizona
June 20	Alaska
July 5	Arizona
July 18	Alaska
Aug. 1	Arizona
Aug. 15	Alaska
Aug. 29	Arizona
Sept. 14	Alaska
Sept. 27	Arizona
Oct. 10	Alaska
Oct. 25	Arizona
Nov. 22	Arizona

Year 1892

HAMBURG-AMERICAN LINE
Hamburg—New York

N. Y.

Arrival	Steamer
Jan. 4	Suevia
Jan. 5	Sorrento
Jan. 7	Gothia
Jan. 9	California
Jan. 12	Scandia
Jan. 16	Amalfi
Jan. 20	Virginia
Jan. 21	Rhaetia
Jan. 23	Dania
Feb. 2	Rugia
Feb. 3	Taormina
Feb. 9	Bohemia
Feb. 12	Slavonia
Feb. 15	Russia
Feb. 16	Suevia
Feb. 17	Venetia
Feb. 19	Marsala
Feb. 20	Moravia
Feb. 22	Scandia
Feb. 26	Sorrento
Feb. 29	Gothia
Feb. 29	Rhaetia
Mar. 5	California
Mar. 7	Dania
Mar. 14	Amalfi
Mar. 14	Gellert
Mar. 16	Virginia
Mar. 17	Rugia
Mar. 21	Wieland
Mar. 24	Russia
Mar. 28	Suevia
Mar. 28	Taormina
Mar. 30	Moravia
Mar. 31	Bohemia
Apr. 2	Scandia
Apr. 9	Marsala
Apr. 11	Rhaetia
Apr. 11	Venetia
Apr. 16	Dania
Apr. 18	California
Apr. 16	Slavonia
Apr. 18	Normannia
Apr. 22	Gothia
Apr. 25	Columbia
Apr. 29	Sorrento
Apr. 30	Furst Bismarck
May 2	Rugia
May 7	Amalfi
May 7	Wieland
May 9	Augusta Victoria
May 11	Russia
May 14	Normannia
May 16	Suevia
May 20	Scandia
May 23	Columbia
May 23	Rhaetia
May 23	Taormina
May 26	Moravia
May 28	Furst Bismarck
May 30	Dania
June 3	Gellert
June 4	Augusta Victoria
June 4	Marsala
June 6	Venetia
June 10	Bohemia

HAMBURG-AMERICAN LINE
Hamburg—New York
(Continued)

N. Y.

Arrival	Steamer
June 13	Normannia
June 13	Rugia
June 18	Columbia
June 18	Wieland
June 20	Gothia
June 20	Sorrento
June 22	California
June 24	Virginia
June 25	Furst Bismarck
June 25	Suevia
July 2	Amalfi
July 2	Russia
July 5	Augusta Victoria
July 5	Rhaetia
July 7	Moravia
July 9	Dania
July 9	Normannia
July 16	Columbia
July 18	Gellert
July 18	Scandia
July 19	Taormina
July 22	Bohemia
July 23	Furst Bismarck
July 25	Rugia
July 29	Albingia
July 30	Augusta Victoria
July 30	Polynesia
July 30	Venetia
July 30	Wieland
Aug. 3	Virginia
Aug. 6	Normannia
Aug. 6	Suevia
Aug. 12	Marsala
Aug. 13	Columbia
Aug. 13	Rhaetia
Aug. 15	California
Aug. 19	Slavonia
Aug. 20	Dania
Aug. 20	Furst Bismarck
Aug. 27	Gellert
Aug. 29	Augusta Victoria
Aug. 29	Russia
Aug. 29	Sorrento
Sept. 15	Amalfi
Sept. 19	Wieland
Sept. 22	Moravia
Sept. 22	Normannia
Sept. 22	Rugia
Sept. 23	Suevia
Sept. 27	Taormina
Sept. 29	Rhaetia
Sept. 29	Scandia
Oct. 4	Dania
Oct. 7	Slavonia
Oct. 8	Bohemia
Oct. 11	Marsala
Oct. 15	California
Oct. 31	Russia
Nov. 7	Suevia
Nov. 15	Amalfi
Nov. 18	Dania
Nov. 28	Rhaetia
Nov. 30	Sorrento
Dec. 5	Scandia

HAMBURG-AMERICAN LINE
Hamburg—New York
(Continued)

N. Y.

Arrival	Steamer
Dec. 6	Marsala
Dec. 11	Taormina
Dec. 12	Russia
Dec. 13	Bohemia
Dec. 20	Suevia
Dec. 20	Columbia
Dec. 29	Moravia

HAMBURG-AMERICAN LINE
Scandinavian Ports—New York

N. Y.

Arrival	Steamer
Jan. 11	Italia
Jan. 29	Polaria
Feb. 12	Polynesia
Mar. 2	Italia
Mar. 25	Polaria
Apr. 29	Italia
May 30	Polaria
June 15	Polynesia
June 28	Italia
July 22	Polaria
Aug. 8	Gothia
Aug. 26	Italia
Oct. 4	Gothia
Oct. 10	Polaria
Nov. 28	Gothia
Dec. 12	Polaria

HAMBURG-AMERICAN LINE
Southampton—New York

N. Y.

Arrival	Steamer
Sept. 12	Columbia
Sept. 19	Furst Bismarck
Sept. 26	Augusta Victoria
Oct. 1	Columbia
Oct. 10	Furst Bismarck
Oct. 17	Augusta Victoria
Oct. 29	Columbia
Nov. 14	Furst Bismarck

HOLLAND-AMERICA LINE
Rotterdam, Amsterdam—New York

N. Y.

Arrival	Steamer
Jan. 4	Spaarndam
Jan. 6	Maasdam
Jan. 18	Edam
Jan. 23	Zaandam
Jan. 26	Amsterdam
Feb. 3	Werkendam
Feb. 4	Rotterdam
Feb. 15	Obdam
Feb. 19	Spaarndam
Feb. 22	Schiedam
Feb. 23	P. Caland
Feb. 24	Maasdam
Mar. 5	Amsterdam
Mar. 9	Edam

Year 1892

HOLLAND-AMERICA LINE
Rotterdam, Amsterdam—New York
(Continued)

N.Y. Arrival	Steamer
Mar. 11	Werkendam
Mar. 17	Veendam
Mar. 26	Obdam
Mar. 26	Zaandam
Apr. 1	Rotterdam
Apr. 6	Maasdam
Apr. 7	Spaarndam
Apr. 13	Didam
Apr. 18	Amsterdam
Apr. 20	P. Caland
Apr. 22	Werkendam
Apr. 28	Veendam
Apr. 30	Edam
May 5	Dubbledam
May 6	Obdam
May 10	Maasdam
May 16	Zaandam
May 19	Spaarndam
May 28	Didam
June 4	Werkendam
June 8	Schiedam
June 8	Veendam
June 13	P. Caland
June 17	Dubbledam
June 17	Obdam
June 22	Maasdam
June 24	Edam
June 30	Spaarndam
July 6	Rotterdam
July 9	Amsterdam
July 15	Werkendam
July 18	Zaandam
July 22	Dubbledam
July 26	Veendam
July 28	Schiedam
Aug. 2	Maasdam
Aug. 5	Didam
Aug. 11	P. Caland
Aug. 16	Rotterdam
Aug. 22	Amsterdam
Aug. 26	Werkendam
Aug. 27	Edam
Sept. 3	Veendam
Sept. 12	Obdam
Sept. 12	Zaandam
Sept. 14	Didam
Sept. 14	Maasdam
Sept. 22	Spaarndam
Sept. 28	Rotterdam
Sept. 28	Schiedam
Oct. 3	Amsterdam
Oct. 8	Werkendam
Oct. 10	P. Caland
Oct. 13	Veendam
Oct. 17	Dubbledam
Oct. 21	Obdam
Oct. 24	Edam
Oct. 25	Didam
Oct. 26	Maasdam
Nov. 5	Spaarndam
Nov. 14	Rotterdam
Nov. 14	Zaandam
Nov. 16	Amsterdam

HOLLAND-AMERICA LINE
Rotterdam, Amsterdam—New York
(Continued)

N.Y. Arrival	Steamer
Nov. 19	Werkendam
Nov. 25	Veendam
Nov. 26	Dubbledam
Nov. 28	P. Caland
Dec. 2	Obdam
Dec. 6	Didam
Dec. 6	Schiedam
Dec. 9	Maasdam
Dec. 15	Spaarndam
Dec. 16	Edam
Dec. 27	Rotterdam

INMAN & INTERNATIONAL STEAMSHIP COMPANY
Liverpool—New York

N.Y. Arrival	Steamer
Jan. 2	City of Paris
Jan. 16	City of Berlin
Feb. 1	City of Chicago
Feb. 15	City of Berlin
Feb. 27	City of Chicago
Mar. 14	City of Berlin
Mar. 17	City of New York
Mar. 26	City of Chicago
Mar. 30	City of Paris
Apr. 9	City of Berlin
Apr. 14	City of New York
Apr. 23	City of Chicago
Apr. 27	City of Paris
May 7	City of Berlin
May 11	City of New York
May 23	City of Chicago
May 26	City of Paris
June 4	City of Berlin
June 9	City of New York
June 15	City of Chester
June 18	City of Chicago
June 22	City of Paris
July 2	City of Berlin
July 7	City of New York
July 23	City of Chester
July 27	City of Paris
Aug. 5	City of Berlin
Aug. 13	City of New York
Aug. 20	City of Chester
Aug. 24	City of Paris
Sept. 3	City of Berlin
Sept. 9	City of New York
Sept. 17	City of Chester
Sept. 22	City of Paris
Oct. 1	City of Berlin
Oct. 6	City of New York
Oct. 15	City of Chester
Oct. 19	City of Paris
Oct. 29	City of Berlin
Nov. 4	City of New York
Nov. 14	City of Chester
Nov. 16	City of Paris
Nov. 26	City of Berlin
Nov. 30	City of New York
Dec. 10	City of Chester

INMAN & INTERNATIONAL STEAMSHIP COMPANY
Liverpool—New York
(Continued)

N.Y. Arrival	Steamer
Dec. 14	City of Paris
Dec. 27	City of Berlin

INSULAR NAVIGATION COMPANY
Azores, Lisbon—New Bedford, Mass., New York

N.Y. Arrival	Steamer
Mar. 16	Vega
May 4	Vega
June 27	Vega
Aug. 13	Vega
Dec. 29	Vega

LA VELOCE LINE
Mediterranean—New York

Apr. 21	Matteo Bruzzo

LINHA DE VAPORES PORTUGUEZES
Azores, Lisbon—New Bedford, Mass., New York

N.Y. Arrival	Steamer
Feb. 1	Olinda
Mar. 19	Oevenum
May 2	Olinda
May 23	Oevenum
July 2	Olinda
July 9	Oevenum
Sept. 1	Olinda
Sept. 8	Oevenum
Nov. 12	Olinda
Nov. 15	Oevenum
Dec. 8	Dona Maria

LIVERPOOL & GREAT WESTERN STEAMSHIP COMPANY
Liverpool—New York

N.Y. Arrival	Steamer
Jan. 2	Nevada
Jan. 20	Wyoming
Jan. 30	Wisconsin
Feb. 13	Nevada
Feb. 24	Wyoming
Mar. 3	Wisconsin
Mar. 18	Nevada
Mar. 30	Wyoming
Apr. 7	Wisconsin
Apr. 21	Nevada
May 5	Wyoming
May 19	Wisconsin
June 2	Nevada
June 16	Wyoming
June 30	Wisconsin
July 14	Nevada
July 27	Wyoming
Aug. 10	Wisconsin
Aug. 25	Nevada
Sept. 22	Wisconsin

Year 1892

LIVERPOOL & GREAT WESTERN STEAMSHIP COMPANY
Liverpool—New York
(Continued)

N. Y.

Arrival	Steamer
Sept. 26	Wyoming
Oct. 3	Nevada
Nov. 3	Wisconsin
Nov. 17	Nevada
Nov. 30	Wyoming

NATIONAL STEAMSHIP COMPANY
London, Liverpool—New York

N. Y.

Arrival	Steamer
Jan. 2	Holland
Jan. 7	Canada
Jan. 12	America
Jan. 25	France
Feb. 2	Spain
Feb. 8	The Queen
Feb. 9	England
Feb. 12	Europe
Feb. 18	Italy
Feb. 22	Holland
Feb. 25	America
Mar. 7	Canada
Mar. 16	France
Mar. 24	Spain
Mar. 28	Europe
Mar. 28	The Queen
Apr. 5	Buffalo
Apr. 6	England
Apr. 11	America
Apr. 25	Italy
Apr. 30	Canada
May 3	France
May 14	Spain
May 16	Europe
May 20	Buffalo
May 30	England
June 1	America
June 6	The Queen
June 20	Canada
June 25	France
July 1	Buffalo
July 6	Spain
July 11	America
July 25	England
July 25	Europe
Aug. 4	Canada
Aug. 8	France
Aug. 15	Greece
Aug. 17	Buffalo
Aug. 23	Spain
Aug. 27	America
Sept. 3	Europe
Sept. 14	England
Sept. 20	Canada
Sept. 29	France
Oct. 4	Greece
Oct. 10	Spain
Oct. 17	America
Oct. 22	Europe
Nov. 1	Italy
Nov. 12	Canada

NATIONAL STEAMSHIP COMPANY
London, Liverpool—New York
(Continued)

N. Y.

Arrival	Steamer
Nov. 14	England
Nov. 18	France
Nov. 18	The Queen
Nov. 26	Greece
Nov. 28	Holland
Nov. 30	Spain
Dec. 5	America
Dec. 14	Europe
Dec. 19	Italy

NAVIGAZIONE GENERALE ITALIANA LINE
Mediterranean—New York

N. Y.

Arrival	Steamer
Jan. 2	Plata
Jan. 25	Letimbro
Feb. 26	Stura
Mar. 7	Entella
Mar. 19	Po
Mar. 22	Iniziativa
Mar. 31	Plata
Apr. 20	Letimbro
Apr. 27	Birmania
May 9	Stura
May 28	Entella
June 8	Arno
June 25	Plata
July 18	Stura
July 27	Letimbro
Aug. 16	Birmania
Sept. 14	Plata
Sept. 27	Iniziativa
Oct. 10	Entella
Oct. 27	Letimbro
Dec. 7	Giava
Dec. 9	Stura

NORTH GERMAN LLOYD
Bremen—New York

N. Y.

Arrival	Steamer
Jan. 2	Trave
Jan. 9	Elbe
Jan. 16	Saale
Jan. 19	Eider
Jan. 21	Havel
Jan. 27	Aller
Jan. 30	Trave
Feb. 4	Ems
Feb. 8	Lahn
Feb. 12	Elbe
Feb. 13	Saale
Feb. 18	Spree
Feb. 18	Weimar
Feb. 23	Aller
Feb. 26	Trave
Mar. 1	Oldenburg
Mar. 2	Ems
Mar. 3	Lahn
Mar. 10	Elbe
Mar. 11	Saale
Mar. 17	Spree
Mar. 22	Aller

NORTH GERMAN LLOYD
Bremen—New York
(Continued)

N. Y.

Arrival	Steamer
Mar. 22	Darmstadt
Mar. 25	Trave
Mar. 29	Ems
Mar. 31	Havel
Apr. 5	America
Apr. 6	Saale
Apr. 7	Lahn
Apr. 9	Hermann
Apr. 12	Braunschweig
Apr. 13	Elbe
Apr. 16	Spree
Apr. 19	Aller
Apr. 21	Weser
Apr. 22	Trave
Apr. 26	Darmstadt
Apr. 26	Ems
Apr. 28	Havel
May 3	Saale
May 5	Lahn
May 9	America
May 10	Elbe
May 12	Spree
May 17	Aller
May 17	Munchen
May 20	Trave
May 24	Ems
May 24	Hermann
May 26	Havel
May 31	Dresden
June 1	Saale
June 2	Lahn
June 6	Darmstadt
June 8	Elbe
June 9	Spree
June 14	Aller
June 15	America
June 17	Trave
June 21	Ems
June 22	Havel
June 28	Saale
June 29	Hermann
June 30	Lahn
July 6	Elbe
July 6	Munchen
July 7	Spree
July 13	Dresden
July 13	Kaiser Wilhelm II
July 15	Aller
July 20	Havel
July 21	Darmstadt
July 25	Ems
July 26	Stuttgart
July 28	Saale
Aug. 1	Weimar
Aug. 2	Elbe
Aug. 4	Lahn
Aug. 9	Gera
Aug. 9	Kaiser Wilhelm II
Aug. 10	Spree
Aug. 15	Aller
Aug. 16	Munchen
Aug. 19	Trave
Aug. 23	Dresden
Aug. 23	Ems
Aug. 25	Havel

Year 1892

NORTH GERMAN LLOYD
Bremen—New York
(Continued)

N. Y.

Arrival	Steamer
Aug. 29	America
Aug. 30	Saale
Sept. 3	Lahn
Sept. 7	Darmstadt
Sept. 8	Elbe
Sept. 10	Spree
Sept. 12	Kaiser Wilhelm II
Sept. 13	Aller
Sept. 16	Trave
Sept. 20	Ems
Sept. 22	Havel
Sept. 27	Hermann
Sept. 27	Saale
Sept. 29	Lahn
Oct. 6	Elbe
Oct. 6	Spree
Oct. 11	Aller
Oct. 12	Dresden
Oct. 14	Trave
Oct. 18	Ems
Oct. 20	Havel
Oct. 25	Saale
Oct. 26	Stuttgart
Oct. 27	Lahn
Nov. 2	Kaiser Wilhelm II
Nov. 4	Spree
Nov. 8	Aller
Nov. 11	Salier
Nov. 11	Trave
Nov. 16	Elbe
Nov. 17	Havel
Nov. 22	Saale
Nov. 26	Hermann
Nov. 26	Lahn
Nov. 30	Dresden
Dec. 6	America
Dec. 9	Trave
Dec. 15	Havel
Dec. 16	Stuttgart
Dec. 17	Elbe
Dec. 26	Saale
Dec. 30	Lahn

NORTH GERMAN LLOYD
Mediterranean—New York

N. Y.

Arrival	Steamer
Jan. 18	Werra
Feb. 1	Fulda
Feb. 22	Werra
Mar. 7	Fulda
Mar. 28	Werra
Apr. 11	Fulda
May 2	Werra
June 6	Werra
June 27	Fulda
July 18	Werra
Aug. 1	Fulda
Aug. 22	Werra
Sept. 7	Fulda
Sept. 26	Werra
Oct. 10	Fulda
Nov. 1	Werra
Nov. 17	Fulda
Nov. 23	Ems

NORTH GERMAN LLOYD
Mediterranean—New York
(Continued)

N. Y.

Arrival	Steamer
Dec. 5	Werra
Dec. 12	Kaiser Wilhelm II
Dec. 28	Fulda
Dec. 29	Ems

RED STAR LINE
Antwerp—New York

N. Y.

Arrival	Steamer
Jan. 2	Rhynland
Jan. 6	Westernland
Jan. 19	Friesland
Feb. 1	Pennland
Feb. 8	Rhynland
Feb. 15	Belgenland
Feb. 17	Waesland
Feb. 23	Westernland
Mar. 2	Noordland
Mar. 8	Friesland
Mar. 18	Rhynland
Mar. 25	Pennland
Mar. 29	Westernland
Apr. 7	Noordland
Apr. 12	Friesland
Apr. 20	Waesland
Apr. 28	Rhynland
May 4	Westernland
May 9	Belgenland
May 11	Noordland
May 17	Friesland
May 24	Pennland
May 26	Waesland
June 2	Rhynland
June 8	Westernland
June 16	Noordland
June 20	Belgenland
June 21	Friesland
June 29	Waesland
July 5	Pennland
July 7	Rhynland
July 13	Westernland
July 21	Noordland
July 26	Friesland
Aug. 1	Belgenland
Aug. 3	Waesland
Aug. 10	Rhynland
Aug. 15	Pennland
Aug. 17	Westernland
Aug. 25	Noordland
Aug. 31	Friesland
Sept. 9	Waesland
Sept. 14	Belgenland
Sept. 15	Rhynland
Sept. 22	Westernland
Sept. 28	Pennland
Sept. 29	Noordland
Oct. 5	Friesland
Oct. 13	Waesland
Oct. 20	Rhynland
Oct. 26	Westernland
Nov. 4	Noordland
Nov. 10	Friesland
Nov. 11	Pennland
Nov. 19	Belgenland
Nov. 25	Rhynland
Nov. 30	Westernland

RED STAR LINE
Antwerp—New York
(Continued)

N. Y.

Arrival	Steamer
Dec. 8	Noordland
Dec. 13	Friesland
Dec. 20	Pennland
Dec. 21	Waesland
Dec. 30	Rhynland

SCANDINAVIAN-AMERICAN LINE
Scandinavian Ports—New York

N. Y.

Arrival	Steamer
Jan. 11	Hekla
Feb. 11	Norge
Feb. 20	Thingvalla
Mar. 5	Hekla
Mar. 23	Island
Apr. 16	Thingvalla
Apr. 30	Hekla
May 12	Island
May 30	Norge
June 10	Thingvalla
June 25	Hekla
July 9	Island
July 22	Norge
Aug. 5	Thingvalla
Aug. 18	Hekla
Sept. 3	Island
Sept. 20	Norge
Oct. 10	Thingvalla
Oct. 31	Island
Nov. 21	Norge
Nov. 26	Thingvalla
Dec. 19	Hekla

WHITE STAR LINE
Liverpool—New York

N. Y.

Arrival	Steamer
Jan. 7	Cufic
Jan. 9	Adriatic
Jan. 14	Teutonic
Jan. 18	Tauric
Jan. 22	Britannic
Jan. 28	Majestic
Jan. 28	Nomadic
Feb. 3	Runic
Feb. 8	Adriatic
Feb. 11	Teutonic
Feb. 12	Cufic
Feb. 19	Britannic
Feb. 23	Tauric
Feb. 24	Majestic
Feb. 29	Nomadic
Mar. 4	Germanic
Mar. 8	Runic
Mar. 9	Teutonic
Mar. 16	Cufic
Mar. 19	Britannic
Mar. 24	Majestic
Mar. 28	Tauric
Apr. 1	Germanic
Apr. 5	Nomadic
Apr. 6	Teutonic
Apr. 12	Runic

Year 1892

WHITE STAR LINE
Liverpool—New York
(Continued)

N. Y.

Arrival	Steamer
Apr. 15	Britannic
Apr. 19	Cufic
Apr. 20	Majestic
Apr. 29	Germanic
May 2	Tauric
May 4	Teutonic
May 10	Nomadic
May 13	Britannic
May 17	Runic
May 19	Majestic
May 24	Cufic
May 28	Germanic
June 1	Teutonic
June 6	Taurid
June 11	Britannic
June 15	Majestic
June 15	Nomadic
June 22	Runic
June 24	Germanic
June 28	Cufic
June 29	Teutonic
July 9	Britannic
July 12	Tauric
July 16	Adriatic
July 20	Nomadic
July 20	Majestic
July 29	Germanic
Aug. 1	Runic
Aug. 3	Teutonic
Aug. 8	Cufic
Aug. 12	Britannic
Aug. 16	Tauric
Aug. 17	Majestic
Aug. 23	Nomadic
Aug. 26	Germanic
Aug. 30	Naronic
Sept. 1	Teutonic
Sept. 6	Bovic
Sept. 10	Britannic
Sept. 13	Cufic
Sept. 15	Majestic
Sept. 20	Tauric
Sept. 24	Germanic
Sept. 26	Adriatic
Sept. 27	Nomadic
Sept. 28	Teutonic
Oct. 3	Naronic
Oct. 7	Britannic
Oct. 12	Bovic
Oct. 13	Majestic
Oct. 17	Cufic
Oct. 22	Germanic
Oct. 26	Tauric
Oct. 27	Teutonic
Nov. 1	Nomadic
Nov. 5	Britannic
Nov. 9	Naronic
Nov. 10	Majestic
Nov. 16	Bovic
Nov. 18	Germanic
Nov. 23	Teutonic
Nov. 23	Runic
Nov. 28	Tauric
Dec. 2	Britannic
Dec. 6	Nomadic

WHITE STAR LINE
Liverpool—New York
(Continued)

N. Y.

Arrival	Steamer
Dec. 7	Majestic
Dec. 13	Naronic
Dec. 16	Germanic
Dec. 20	Bovic
Dec. 22	Teutonic
Dec. 29	Runic
Dec. 31	Britannic

WILSON LINE
Hull—New York

N. Y.

Arrival	Steamer
Jan. 26	Marengo
Feb. 3	Hindoo
Feb. 11	Colorado
Mar. 8	Marengo
Mar. 24	Hindoo
Apr. 2	Colorado
Apr. 26	Egyptian Monarch
May 2	Marengo
May 11	Galileo
May 18	Hindoo
May 26	Colorado
June 14	Egyptian Monarch
June 24	Marengo
June 27	Galileo
July 5	Hindoo
July 16	Colorado
Aug. 1	Francisco
Aug. 10	Galileo
Aug. 15	Hindoo
Aug. 22	Marengo
Aug. 31	Colorado
Sept. 12	Martello
Sept. 24	Galileo
Sept. 26	Francisco
Oct. 1	Egyptian Monarch
Oct. 13	Hindoo
Oct. 18	Marengo
Oct. 24	Colorado
Nov. 3	Martello
Nov. 15	Galileo
Nov. 17	Francisco
Nov. 28	Hindoo
Dec. 7	Colorado
Dec. 12	Marengo
Dec. 22	Martello
Dec. 29	Galileo

WILSON LINE
London—New York

N. Y.

Arrival	Steamer
Jan. 16	Lydian Monarch
Mar. 1	Persian Monarch
Mar. 5	Lydian Monarch
Apr. 14	Persian Monarch
Apr. 20	Lydian Monarch
May 31	Persian Monarch
June 6	Lydian Monarch
July 27	Persian Monarch
Aug. 29	Lydian Monarch
Sept. 8	Persian Monarch
Oct. 24	Persian Monarch
Nov. 14	Lydian Monarch
Dec. 10	Persian Monarch

ADDITIONAL ARRIVALS
Antwerp—New York

N. Y.

Arrival	Steamer
Jan. 7	Chicago
Feb. 26	Chicago
Apr. 23	Chicago
June 20	Chicago
Aug. 12	Chicago
Oct. 14	Chicago
Dec. 2	Chicago

Bordeaux—New York

N. Y.

Arrival	Steamer
May 30	Chateau Lafite
July 29	Chateau Lafite
Sept. 26	Chateau Lafite
Nov. 12	Chateau Lafite

British Ports—New York

N. Y.

Arrival	Steamer
Jan. 6	Croma
Jan. 14	Critic
Feb. 6	Exeter City
Mar. 1	Croma
Mar. 22	Critic
Mar. 25	Exeter City
Apr. 29	Glenavon
May 4	Critic
May 12	Croma
May 12	Exeter City
May 31	Mareca
June 20	Critic
June 23	Exeter City
July 1	Croma
July 18	Mareca
Aug. 5	Critic
Aug. 9	Exeter City
Aug. 15	Wells City
Aug. 23	Principia
Aug. 24	Merrimac
Aug. 29	Llandaff City
Sept. 3	Mohican
Sept. 10	Mannheim
Sept. 15	Croft
Sept. 16	Monomoy
Sept. 19	Oranje Prince
Sept. 23	Critic
Oct. 1	Exeter City
Oct. 11	Principia
Oct. 17	Croma
Oct. 18	Mohican
Nov. 1	Croft
Nov. 1	Monomoy
Nov. 7	Oranje Prince
Nov. 11	Critic
Nov. 25	Exeter City
Nov. 28	Principia
Dec. 1	Mohican
Dec. 7	Wells City
Dec. 12	Croma
Dec. 13	Monomoy
Dec. 27	Croft

Glasgow—New York

N. Y.

Arrival	Steamer
Feb. 23	Belgenland

Year 1892

ADDITIONAL ARRIVALS
Hamburg—New York

N.Y. Arrival	Steamer
May 2	Pickhuben
July 16	Steinhoft
Aug. 20	Pickhuben

Hull—New York

N.Y. Arrival	Steamer
Feb. 1	Guildford

Liverpool—New York

N.Y. Arrival	Steamer
Jan. 14	Lake Winnipeg
Feb. 18	Lake Winnipeg
Mar. 28	Lake Winnipeg
Oct. 3	Indiana

London—New York

N.Y. Arrival	Steamer
Jan. 27	Ludgate Hill
Feb. 11	Richmond Hill

ADDITIONAL ARRIVALS
London—New York
(Continued)

N.Y. Arrival	Steamer
Mar. 16	Ludgate Hill
Mar. 28	Richmond Hill
Apr. 28	Tower Hill
May 12	Richmond Hill
June 13	Tower Hill
June 20	Ludgate Hill
June 25	Mohawk
June 27	Richmond Hill
Aug. 5	Mohawk
Aug. 8	Richmond Hill
Sept. 19	Mohawk
Sept. 21	Richmond Hill
Oct. 14	Ludgate Hill
Oct. 27	Mohawk
Nov. 4	Montezuma
Nov. 9	Richmond Hill
Nov. 28	Mariposa
Nov. 28	Tower Hill
Dec. 3	Ludgate Hill
Dec. 7	Mohawk
Dec. 14	Montezuma
Dec. 30	Richmond Hill

ADDITIONAL ARRIVALS
Mediterranean—New York

N.Y. Arrival	Steamer
Sept. 10	Tiverton

Rotterdam, Amsterdam—
New York

N.Y. Arrival	Steamer
Jan. 4	Prins Willem I
Mar. 5	Prins Willem III
Mar. 6	Prins Willem I
May 27	Prins Willem II
June 18	Oranje Nassau
July 8	Prins Willem III
July 29	Prins Frederik Hendrik
Aug. 19	Prins Maurits
Sept. 30	Prins Willem II
Nov. 12	Prins Willem III
Dec. 3	Prins Frederik Hendrik
Dec. 27	Prins Maurits

Year 1893

ALLAN STATE LINE
Glasgow—New York
N. Y.

Arrival	Steamer
Jan. 6	Corean
Jan. 12	State of Nebraska
Jan. 19	Norwegian
Jan. 26	Siberian
Feb. 2	State of California
Feb. 20	Corean
Feb. 25	State of Nebraska
Mar. 4	Norwegian
Mar. 13	Siberian
Mar. 14	State of California
Mar. 23	Grecian
Mar. 30	Corean
Apr. 10	State of Nebraska
Apr. 14	Norwegian
Apr. 20	Siberian
Apr. 25	State of California
May 3	Grecian
May 10	State of Nebraska
May 20	Peruvian
May 24	Norwegian
May 30	State of California
June 7	Grecian
June 13	State of Nebraska
June 21	Peruvian
June 27	Norwegian
July 3	State of California
July 11	Grecian
July 18	State of Nebraska
July 26	Peruvian
Aug. 2	Norwegian
Aug. 8	State of California
Aug. 15	Peruvian
Aug. 22	State of Nebraska
Aug. 31	Peruvian
Sept. 5	Norwegian
Sept. 11	State of California
Sept. 21	Grecian
Sept. 26	State of Nebraska
Oct. 9	Peruvian
Oct. 12	Norwegian
Oct. 23	State of California
Nov. 2	Grecian
Nov. 7	State of Nebraska
Nov. 15	Peruvian
Nov. 21	Norwegian
Nov. 29	State of California
Dec. 8	Siberian
Dec. 23	State of Nebraska

AMERICAN LINE
Southampton—New York
N. Y.

Arrival	Steamer
Mar. 18	New York
Apr. 1	Paris
Apr. 15	New York
Apr. 29	Paris
May 13	New York
May 27	Paris
June 10	New York
June 24	Paris
July 8	New York
July 22	Paris

AMERICAN LINE
Southampton—New York
(Continued)
N. Y.

Arrival	Steamer
Aug. 5	New York
Aug. 12	Paris
Aug. 26	New York
Sept. 2	Paris
Sept. 16	New York
Sept. 23	Paris
Oct. 7	New York
Oct. 14	Paris
Oct. 28	New York
Nov. 4	Paris
Nov. 18	New York
Nov. 25	Paris
Dec. 9	New York
Dec. 18	Paris

ANCHOR LINE
Glasgow—New York
N. Y.

Arrival	Steamer
Jan. 9	Bolivia
Feb. 3	Devonia
Feb. 24	Bolivia
Mar. 3	Anchoria
Mar. 15	Devonia
Mar. 20	Circassia
Mar. 27	Furnessia
Apr. 5	Ethiopia
Apr. 12	Anchoria
Apr. 18	Devonia
Apr. 24	Circassia
May 1	Furnessia
May 9	Ethiopia
May 17	Anchoria
May 22	City of Rome
May 29	Circassia
June 5	Furnessia
June 13	Ethiopia
June 19	Anchoria
June 24	City of Rome
July 3	Circassia
July 10	Furnessia
July 17	Ethiopia
July 24	Anchoria
Aug. 7	Circassia
Aug. 14	Furnessia
Aug. 22	Ethiopia
Aug. 28	Anchoria
Sept. 2	City of Rome
Sept. 11	Circassia
Sept. 18	Furnessia
Sept. 26	Devonia
Oct. 3	Ethiopia
Oct. 9	City of Rome
Oct. 16	Circassia
Oct. 23	Furnessia
Oct. 31	Devonia
Nov. 14	Anchoria
Nov. 22	Bolivia
Nov. 30	Furnessia
Dec. 16	Ethiopia
Dec. 27	Anchoria

ANCHOR LINE
Mediterranean—New York
N. Y.

Arrival	Steamer
Jan. 5	California
Jan. 14	Olympia
Feb. 3	India
Feb. 16	Victoria
Feb. 21	Britannia
Mar. 15	Italia
Apr. 1	Elysia
Apr. 1	Assyria
Apr. 10	Olympia
Apr. 22	California
May 5	Hesperia
May 15	Bolivia
May 15	India
May 29	Victoria
June 8	Britannia
June 16	Alsatia
June 19	Victoria
June 20	Italia
June 28	Assyria
July 5	Elysia
Aug. 14	Karamania
Sept. 7	California
Oct. 23	Alsatia
Oct. 23	Hesperia
Oct. 30	Victoria
Nov. 29	California
Dec. 21	Elysia
Dec. 30	Italia

ATLANTIC TRANSPORT LINE
London—New York
N. Y.

Arrival	Steamer
Jan. 13	Massachusetts
Feb. 11	Manitoba
Feb. 25	Massachusetts
Mar. 15	Mississippi
Mar. 22	Manitoba
Apr. 6	Massachusetts
Apr. 21	Michigan
May 1	Manitoba
May 22	Massachusetts
June 15	Manitoba
June 28	Massachusetts
July 25	Manitoba
Aug. 9	Massachusetts
Sept. 2	Manitoba
Sept. 23	Massachusetts
Oct. 16	Manitoba
Nov. 4	Massachusetts
Nov. 21	Manitoba
Dec. 8	Massachusetts
Dec. 15	Mississippi
Dec. 29	Manitoba

COMPANIA TRANSATLANTICA LINE
(Spanish Line)
Spanish Ports—New York
N. Y.

Arrival	Steamer
Jan. 6	Mexico

Year 1893

COMPANIA TRANSATLANTICA LINE
(Spanish Line)
Spanish Ports—New York
(Continued)

N. Y.

Arrival	Steamer
Jan. 16	Ciudad Condal
Jan. 25	Mexico
Feb. 6	Panama
Feb. 15	Ciudad Condal
Feb. 25	Panama
Mar. 7	Mexico
Mar. 15	Ciudad Condal
Mar. 25	Mexico
Mar. 28	Habana
Apr. 4	Panama
Apr. 25	Panama
May 5	Habana
May 15	Ciudad Condal
May 25	Habana
June 5	Panama
June 15	Ciudad Condal
June 26	Panama
July 6	Habana
July 14	Ciudad Condal
July 25	Habana
Aug. 4	Panama
Aug. 14	Ciudad Condal
Aug. 25	Habana
Sept. 6	Mexico
Sept. 15	Ciudad Condal
Sept. 25	Mexico
Oct. 6	Panama
Oct. 25	Panama
Oct. 30	Ciudad Condal
Nov. 6	Mexico
Nov. 16	Habana
Nov. 25	Mexico
Dec. 5	Panama
Dec. 15	Habana
Dec. 26	Panama

CUNARD LINE
Liverpool—New York

N. Y.

Arrival	Steamer
Jan. 4	Bothnia
Jan. 10	Servia
Jan. 17	Gallia
Jan. 23	Aurania
Jan. 30	Etruria
Feb. 7	Servia
Feb. 15	Gallia
Feb. 21	Aurania
Feb. 27	Etruria
Mar. 6	Servia
Mar. 14	Gallia
Mar. 20	Aurania
Mar. 27	Etruria
Apr. 4	Servia
Apr. 10	Umbria
Apr. 17	Aurania
Apr. 21	Gallia
Apr. 24	Etruria
May 1	Compania
May 5	Servia
May 8	Umbria
May 15	Aurania
May 20	Gallia

CUNARD LINE
Liverpool—New York
(Continued)

N. Y.

Arrival	Steamer
May 22	Etruria
May 27	Compania
June 1	Servia
June 5	Umbria
June 12	Aurania
June 19	Etruria
June 24	Compania
June 29	Gallia
July 3	Umbria
July 10	Aurania
July 17	Servia
July 22	Etruria
July 29	Compania
Aug. 7	Umbria
Aug. 14	Aurania
Aug. 19	Etruria
Aug. 28	Compania
Aug. 31	Gallia
Sept. 2	Umbria
Sept. 9	Lucania
Sept. 18	Etruria
Sept. 23	Compania
Sept. 30	Umbria
Oct. 7	Lucania
Oct. 14	Etruria
Oct. 21	Compania
Oct. 30	Umbria
Nov. 4	Lucania
Nov. 13	Etruria
Nov. 18	Compania
Nov. 27	Umbria
Dec. 2	Lucania
Dec. 11	Etruria
Dec. 19	Aurania
Dec. 26	Umbria

FABRE LINE
Mediterranean—New York

N. Y.

Arrival	Steamer
Jan. 4	Britannia
Jan. 19	Burgundia
Jan. 31	Nuestria
Feb. 11	Massilia
Mar. 13	Britannia
Mar. 22	Alesia
Apr. 8	Nuestria
Apr. 12	Gergovia
Apr. 15	Massilia
May 19	Alesia
May 22	Burgundia
June 3	Nuestria
June 13	Massilia
July 3	Britannia
July 17	Burgundia
July 26	Nuestria
Aug. 11	Massilia
Sept. 13	Burgundia
Sept. 25	Britannia
Oct. 6	Massilia
Nov. 1	Alesia
Nov. 10	Burgundia
Nov. 27	Massilia
Dec. 27	Nuestria

FRENCH LINE
(Compagnie Generale Transatlantique)
Havre—New York

N. Y.

Arrival	Steamer
Jan. 3	La Gascogne
Jan. 9	La Bourgoyne
Jan. 16	La Champagne
Jan. 23	La Normandie
Jan. 30	La Gascogne
Feb. 6	La Bretagne
Feb. 13	La Bourgoyne
Feb. 23	La Normandie
Feb. 27	La Gascogne
Mar. 6	La Bretagne
Mar. 13	La Bourgoyne
Mar. 20	La Champagne
Mar. 27	La Touraine
Mar. 31	La Normandie
Apr. 3	La Bretagne
Apr. 10	La Gascogne
Apr. 17	La Champagne
Apr. 24	La Touraine
May 1	La Bretagne
May 8	La Gascogne
May 15	La Champagne
May 20	La Touraine
May 29	La Bretagne
June 5	La Bourgoyne
June 12	La Champagne
June 17	La Touraine
June 26	La Bretagne
July 10	La Champagne
July 17	La Touraine
July 24	La Bretagne
July 31	La Bourgoyne
Aug. 7	La Champagne
Aug. 14	La Normandie
Aug. 19	La Touraine
Aug. 28	La Bourgoyne
Sept. 4	La Champagne
Sept. 11	La Gascogne
Sept. 16	La Touraine
Sept. 25	La Bourgoyne
Oct. 2	La Bretagne
Oct. 9	La Gascogne
Oct. 14	La Touraine
Oct. 23	La Champagne
Oct. 30	La Bretagne
Nov. 6	La Gascogne
Nov. 11	La Touraine
Nov. 20	La Champagne
Nov. 27	La Bretagne
Dec. 4	La Bourgoyne
Dec. 11	La Gascogne
Dec. 18	La Champagne
Dec. 26	La Bretagne

GUION STEAMSHIP LINE
Liverpool—New York

N. Y.

Arrival	Steamer
Apr. 17	Arizona
May 1	Alaska
May 15	Arizona
May 29	Alaska
June 13	Arizona
June 26	Alaska
July 10	Arizona

Year 1893

GUION STEAMSHIP LINE
Liverpool—New York (Continued)

N. Y. Arrival	Steamer
July 24	Alaska
Aug. 14	Arizona
Aug. 29	Alaska
Sept. 11	Arizona
Sept. 25	Alaska
Oct. 9	Arizona
Oct. 24	Alaska

HAMBURG-AMERICAN LINE
Hamburg—New York

N. Y. Arrival	Steamer
Jan. 3	Dania
Jan. 5	Amalfi
Jan. 10	Cheraskia
Jan. 25	Russia
Jan. 30	Furst Bismarck
Feb. 8	Bohemia
Feb. 13	Dania
Feb. 18	Slavonia
Feb. 27	Augusta Victoria
Feb. 27	Moravia
Feb. 28	Scandia
Mar. 3	Suevia
Mar. 7	Rugia
Mar. 13	Marsala
Mar. 20	Amalfi
Mar. 20	Rhaetia
Mar. 25	Dania
Mar. 25	Normannia
Apr. 1	Gellert
Apr. 10	Columbia
Apr. 10	Moravia
Apr. 10	Scandia
Apr. 15	Augusta Victoria
Apr. 15	Markomannia
Apr. 17	Rugia
Apr. 24	Taormina
Apr. 24	Wieland
Apr. 28	Furst Bismarck
Apr. 29	California
May 1	Suevia
May 5	Columbia
May 5	Marsala
May 6	Gellert
May 12	Augusta Victoria
May 12	Dania
May 19	Normannia
May 20	Rhaetia
May 22	Amalfi
May 26	Furst Bismarck
May 29	Rugia
May 30	Moravia
June 2	Columbia
June 3	Wieland
June 10	Augusta Victoria
June 10	Suevia
June 16	Normannia
June 17	Gellert
June 17	Taormina
June 19	Russia
June 23	Furst Bismarck
June 24	Dania

HAMBURG-AMERICAN LINE
Hamburg—New York (Continued)

N. Y. Arrival	Steamer
June 29	Marsala
June 30	Columbia
July 1	Rhaetia
July 7	Augusta Victoria
July 8	Rugia
July 14	Normannia
July 14	Wieland
July 15	Amalfi
July 18	Moravia
July 21	Furst Bismarck
July 22	Suevia
July 28	Columbia
July 29	Gellert
July 29	Sorrento
Aug. 3	Dania
Aug. 4	Augusta Victoria
Aug. 11	Normannia
Aug. 12	Taormina
Aug. 14	Rhaetia
Aug. 17	Gothia
Aug. 18	Furst Bismarck
Aug. 19	Rugia
Aug. 25	Columbia
Aug. 26	Marsala
Aug. 26	Wieland
Aug. 29	Moravia
Sept. 1	Augusta Victoria
Sept. 2	Suevia
Sept. 8	Gellert
Sept. 8	Normannia
Sept. 9	Amalfi
Sept. 14	Dania
Sept. 15	Furst Bismarck
Sept. 22	Columbia
Sept. 23	Rhaetia
Sept. 29	Gothia
Oct. 2	Augusta Victoria
Oct. 2	Rugia
Oct. 10	Taormina
Oct. 12	Moravia
Oct. 13	Russia
Oct. 14	Suevia
Oct. 20	Dania
Oct. 21	Marsala
Oct. 27	Gellert
Oct. 30	Amalfi
Nov. 6	Rhaetia
Nov. 10	Furst Bismarck
Nov. 11	Gothia
Nov. 11	Rugia
Nov. 19	Sorrento
Nov. 20	Russia
Nov. 25	Columbia
Nov. 25	Moravia
Nov. 28	Dania
Dec. 4	Suevia
Dec. 4	Taormina
Dec. 8	Normannia
Dec. 9	Scandia
Dec. 20	Rhaetia
Dec. 21	Marsala
Dec. 29	Gothia
Dec. 30	Rugia

HAMBURG-AMERICAN LINE
Scandinavian Ports—New York

N. Y. Arrival	Steamer
Jan. 3	Italia
Mar. 25	Gothia
Mar. 27	Venetia
Apr. 24	Italia
Apr. 28	Virginia
May 5	Russia
May 19	Venetia
June 20	Italia
June 30	Virginia
July 14	Venetia
July 30	Bohemia
Aug. 12	Italia
Aug. 24	Virginia
Sept. 8	Venetia
Oct. 9	Italia
Oct. 19	Virginia
Oct. 27	Columbia
Nov. 6	Venetia
Dec. 8	Italia
Dec. 20	Virginia

HOLLAND-AMERICA LINE
Rotterdam, Amsterdam—New York

N. Y. Arrival	Steamer
Jan. 2	Werkendam
Jan. 6	Veendam
Jan. 13	Obdam
Jan. 21	Didam
Jan. 25	Maasdam
Feb. 4	Spaarndam
Feb. 14	Rotterdam
Feb. 20	Werkendam
Feb. 25	Veendam
Mar. 6	Obdam
Mar. 9	Maasdam
Mar. 13	Edam
Mar. 15	P. Caland
Mar. 16	Spaarndam
Mar. 24	Rotterdam
Mar. 25	Zaandam
Mar. 29	Didam
Apr. 1	Werkendam
Apr. 7	Veendam
Apr. 12	Dubbledam
Apr. 15	Obdam
Apr. 19	Maasdam
Apr. 29	Amsterdam
May 2	Rotterdam
May 2	Edam
May 4	Spaarndam
May 11	P. Caland
May 12	Werkendam
May 16	Didam
May 17	Veendam
May 20	Dubbledam
May 25	Obdam
May 27	Zaandam
May 31	Maasdam
June 10	Rotterdam
June 12	Schiedam
June 14	Spaarndam

Year 1893

HOLLAND-AMERICA LINE
Rotterdam, Amsterdam—New York
(Continued)

N. Y.

Arrival	Steamer
June 16	Edam
June 26	Veendam
June 30	P. Caland
July 5	Obdam
July 8	Maasdam
July 13	Zaandam
July 14	Rotterdam
July 18	Amsterdam
July 24	Spaarndam
July 26	Didam
July 31	Edam
July 31	Veendam
Aug. 4	Werkendam
Aug. 7	Schiedam
Aug. 8	Obdam
Aug. 12	Maasdam
Aug. 16	Dubbledam
Aug. 21	Amsterdam
Aug. 24	Zaandam
Aug. 26	Rotterdam
Aug. 28	Spaarndam
Sept. 1	Didam
Sept. 2	Veendam
Sept. 8	Edam
Sept. 12	Obdam
Sept. 25	Amsterdam
Sept. 28	Schiedam
Sept. 29	Veendam
Oct. 2	Spaarndam
Oct. 5	Veendam
Oct. 11	Rotterdam
Oct. 13	Zaandam
Oct. 13	Didam
Oct. 18	Obdam
Oct. 25	Edam
Oct. 26	Werkendam
Oct. 30	Amsterdam
Nov. 7	Spaarndam
Nov. 9	Dubbledam
Nov. 13	Schiedam
Nov. 13	Veendam
Nov. 14	P. Caland
Nov. 17	Rotterdam
Nov. 22	Obdam
Nov. 27	Zaandam
Nov. 27	Maasdam
Nov. 29	Didam
Dec. 4	Didam
Dec. 8	Werkendam
Dec. 12	Amsterdam
Dec. 18	Dubbledam
Dec. 20	Spaarndam
Dec. 28	Rotterdam

INMAN & INTERNATIONAL STEAMSHIP COMPANY
Liverpool—New York

N. Y.

Arrival	Steamer
Feb. 16	City of New York
Feb. 27	City of Chester
Mar. 2	City of Paris
Mar. 13	Berlin

INMAN & INTERNATIONAL STEAMSHIP COMPANY
Southampton—New York

N. Y.

Arrival	Steamer
Mar. 30	Chester
Apr. 11	Berlin
Apr. 25	Chester
May 8	Berlin
May 22	Chester
June 5	Berlin
June 20	Chester
July 3	Berlin
July 19	Chester
July 31	Berlin
Aug. 21	Chester
Sept. 11	Berlin
Oct. 2	Berlin
Oct. 23	Berlin
Nov. 13	Berlin
Dec. 5	Berlin
Dec. 28	Berlin

INSULAR NAVIGATION COMPANY
Azores, Lisbon—New Bedford, Mass., New York

N. Y.

Arrival	Steamer
Feb. 24	Vega
Mar. 20	Peninsular
Apr. 19	Vega
May 9	Peninsular
June 13	Vega
Aug. 1	Vega
Sept. 28	Vega
Dec. 1	Vega
Dec. 13	Peninsular

LINHA DE VAPORES PORTUGUEZES
Azores, Lisbon—New Bedford, Mass., New York

N. Y.

Arrival	Steamer
Jan. 19	Olinda
Feb. 4	Dona Maria
Mar. 18	Olinda
Apr. 5	Oevenum
Apr. 6	Dona Maria
May 15	Olinda
June 1	Oevenum
June 10	Dona Maria
July 5	Olinda
July 24	Dona Maria
Aug. 25	Olinda
Sept. 8	Dona Maria
Oct. 6	Oevenum
Oct. 24	Olinda
Oct. 26	Dona Maria
Dec. 18	Dona Maria
Dec. 23	Olinda

LIVERPOOL & GREAT WESTERN STEAMSHIP COMPANY
Liverpool—New York

N. Y.

Arrival	Steamer
Apr. 26	Nevada
May 24	Nevada

NATIONAL NAVIGATION COMPANY
Mediterranean—New York

N. Y.

Arrival	Steamer
Feb. 3	Hindoustan
Feb. 27	Cheribon
Mar. 14	Cachemire
Apr. 1	Colombo
Apr. 17	Chandernagor
May 8	Hindoustan
May 13	Cheribon
May 29	Cachemire
June 21	Chandernagor
July 21	Hindoustan
Aug. 21	Cachemire
Dec. 14	Chandernagor

NATIONAL STEAMSHIP COMPANY
London—New York

N. Y.

Arrival	Steamer
Mar. 20	America
Apr. 10	America
Apr. 24	France
May 23	America
July 15	America
Sept. 6	America
Oct. 27	America
Dec. 20	America

NAVIGAZIONE GENERALE ITALIANA LINE
Mediterranean—New York

N. Y.

Arrival	Steamer
Jan. 3	San Giorgio
Jan. 16	Letimbro
Mar. 20	Giava
Apr. 7	Entella
Apr. 20	San Giorgio
Apr. 24	Iniziativa
May 23	Letimbro
June 10	Montebello
June 16	Giava
July 5	Entella
July 10	Iniziativa
Aug. 2	Letimbro
Sept. 25	Entella

NORTH GERMAN LLOYD
Bremen—New York

N. Y.

Arrival	Steamer
Jan. 5	Weimar
Jan. 6	Hermann
Jan. 9	H. H. Meier
Jan. 13	Dresden
Jan. 14	Elbe
Jan. 20	Aller
Feb. 2	Salier
Feb. 4	Stuttgart
Feb. 4	Trave
Feb. 13	Elbe
Feb. 20	H. H. Meier
Feb. 27	Braunschweig
Feb. 27	Werra
Mar. 3	Aller
Mar. 10	Havel

Year 1893

NORTH GERMAN LLOYD	
Bremen—New York	
(Continued)	
N. Y.	
Arrival	**Steamer**
Mar. 10............	Weimar
Mar. 14.............	Saale
Mar. 17............	Dresden
Mar. 21............	America
Mar. 24............	Trave
Mar. 30.........	Strassburg
Mar. 31.........H.	H. Meier
Apr. 1............	Aller
Apr. 5.........	Darmstadt
Apr. 6.............	Havel
Apr. 10.......	Braunschweig
Apr. 11............	Saale
Apr. 19.............	Elbe
Apr. 21.............	Trave
Apr. 25............	Dresden
Apr. 25.............	Fulda
Apr. 28.............	Aller
May 2............	Stuttgart
May 4............	America
May 4.............	Havel
May 11.............	Gera
May 12.........H.	H. Meier
May 16.........	Darmstadt
May 16.............	Saale
May 19.............	Spree
May 23............	Munchen
May 23.............	Trave
May 25.........	Strassburg
May 26............	Aller
May 31.............	Ems
June 1.............	Havel
June 3.............	Weimar
June 6.............	Elbe
June 8............	Dresden
June 13............	Saale
June 14............	Stuttgart
June 15............	Spree
June 20............	Trave
June 21.........H.	H. Meier
June 23............	Aller
June 26............	Ems
June 28.............	Havel
July 5.............	Elbe
July 5............	Munchen
July 6............	Strassburg
July 11.............	Saale
July 11............	Weimar
July 13............	Spree
July 18....Kaiser	Wilhelm II
July 19............	Dresden
July 20............	Trave
July 24.............	Ems
July 25..........	Stuttgart
July 26............	Havel
Aug. 1.............	Elbe
Aug. 1.........H.	H. Meier
Aug. 3.............	Aller
Aug. 7............	Stuttgart
Aug. 8.........	Darmstadt
Aug. 8.............	Saale
Aug. 10............	Spree
Aug. 17...........	Munchen
Aug. 17............	Strassburg
Aug. 22............	Ems
Aug. 22............	Weimar

NORTH GERMAN LLOYD	
Bremen—New York	
(Continued)	
N. Y.	
Arrival	**Steamer**
Aug. 23.............	Havel
Aug. 25.............	Trave
Aug. 30............	Dresden
Aug. 30.............	Elbe
Aug. 31............	Aller
Sept. 5............	Saale
Sept. 7.............	Spree
Sept. 11.........H.	H. Meier
Sept. 12....Kaiser	Wilhelm II
Sept. 19.........	Darmstadt
Sept. 20............	Havel
Sept. 22............	Trave
Sept. 26............	Elbe
Sept. 28............	Aller
Oct. 3.............	Saale
Oct. 5.............	Spree
Oct. 11....Kaiser	Wilhelm II
Oct. 11............	Dresden
Oct. 17.............	Ems
Oct. 18.............	Havel
Oct. 24............	America
Oct. 24.............	Elbe
Oct. 26.............	Aller
Oct. 30.............	Saale
Nov. 2.............	Spree
Nov. 6.............	Trave
Nov. 14.............	Ems
Nov. 14............	Weimar
Nov. 15.............	Havel
Nov. 21.............	Dresden
Nov. 21.............	Elbe
Nov. 24.............	Aller
Nov. 28.............	Saale
Nov. 30.............	Spree
Dec. 5.............	Trave
Dec. 14.............	Havel
Dec. 19.........H.	H. Meier
Dec. 23............	Aller
Dec. 26............	Karlsruhe
Dec. 30.............	Ems

NORTH GERMAN LLOYD	
Mediterranean—New York	
N. Y.	
Arrival	**Steamer**
Jan. 23...Kaiser	Wilhelm II
Jan. 30.............	Fulda
Feb. 11.............	Ems
Feb. 18.............	Lahn
Feb. 28...Kaiser	Wilhelm II
Mar. 16............	Lahn
Mar. 22............	Ems
Apr. 4...Kaiser	Wilhelm II
Apr. 13.K. Frederich	Wilhelm
Apr. 14.............	Lahn
Apr. 17.............	Werra
May 9...Kaiser	Wilhelm II
May 12.............	Lahn
May 15.............	Weser
May 22.............	Werra
May 26.K. Frederich	Wilhelm
June 8.............	Lahn
June 26.............	Werra
July 6.............	Lahn
July 7.K. Frederich	Wilhelm

NORTH GERMAN LLOYD	
Mediterranean—New York	
(Continued)	
N. Y.	
Arrival	**Steamer**
July 31.............	Werra
Aug. 17.............	Lahn
Aug. 21.............	Weser
Sept. 4.............	Werra
Sept. 12.K. Frederich	Wilhelm
Sept. 14.............	Lahn
Oct. 9.............	Werra
Oct. 12.............	Lahn
Oct. 27.K. Frederich	Wilhelm
Nov. 9.............	Lahn
Nov. 13.............	Werra
Nov. 20...Kaiser	Wilhelm II
Dec. 7.............	Lahn
Dec. 11.K. Frederich	Wilhelm
Dec. 21.............	Werra
Dec. 26...Kaiser	Wilhelm II

PRINCE LINE	
Mediterranean—New York	
N. Y.	
Arrival	**Steamer**
Apr. 3........Stuart	Prince
June 17......Grecian	Prince
Oct. 21......Grecian	Prince

RED STAR LINE	
Antwerp—New York	
N. Y.	
Arrival	**Steamer**
Jan. 17............	Friesland
Jan. 25..........	Waesland
Feb. 2.........	Belgenland
Feb. 4..........	Rhynland
Feb. 13.........	Westernland
Feb. 27..........	Noordland
Mar. 3............	Waesland
Mar. 8............	Friesland
Mar. 16............	Rhynland
Mar. 23............	Belgenland
Mar. 29............	Nederland
Mar. 30............	Noordland
Apr. 7............	Waesland
Apr. 11............	Friesland
Apr. 12............	Pennland
Apr. 28............	Belgenland
May 3............	Noordland
May 11............	Nederland
May 11............	Waesland
May 16............	Friesland
May 22............	Pennland
May 31.........	Westernland
June 7............	Noordland
June 19.........	Belgenland
June 20.........	Friesland
June 28............	Rhynland
July 5.........	Westernland
July 12............	Noordland
July 19............	Waesland
July 25............	Friesland
Aug. 2.........	Belgenland
Aug. 9.........	Rhynland
Aug. 15.........	Westernland
Aug. 23............	Noordland
Sept. 5............	Friesland
Sept. 11.........	Belgenland

Year 1893

RED STAR LINE
Antwerp—New York
(Continued)

N.Y. Arrival	Steamer
Sept. 14	Rhynland
Sept. 20	Westernland
Sept. 26	Noordland
Oct. 4	Waesland
Oct. 10	Friesland
Oct. 18	Rhynland
Oct. 25	Westernland
Nov. 9	Waesland
Nov. 13	Friesland
Nov. 23	Rhynland
Nov. 29	Westernland
Dec. 16	Waesland
Dec. 20	Friesland

SCANDINAVIAN-AMERICAN LINE
Scandinavian Ports, Stettin, Copenhagen, Christiania—New York

N.Y. Arrival	Steamer
Jan. 4	Island
Jan. 5	Christine
Jan. 14	Norge
Jan. 31	Thingvalla
Mar. 13	Island
Mar. 21	Christine
Apr. 3	Norge
Apr. 10	Hekla
Apr. 15	Thingvalla
Apr. 29	Island
May 23	Norge
June 2	Christine
June 8	Thingvalla
June 23	Island
July 6	Hekla
July 13	Christine
July 31	Amerika
Aug. 5	Thingvalla
Aug. 18	Island
Aug. 22	Christine
Aug. 31	Hekla
Sept. 9	Amerika
Sept. 15	Norge
Sept. 29	Thingvalla
Oct. 9	Christine
Oct. 14	Island
Oct. 26	Hekla
Dec. 11	Island
Dec. 20	Norge
Dec. 27	Hekla

WHITE STAR LINE
Liverpool—New York

N.Y. Arrival	Steamer
Jan. 4	Tauric
Jan. 7	Adriatic
Jan. 15	Germanic
Jan. 18	Majestic
Jan. 28	Britannic
Feb. 2	Teutonic
Feb. 11	Tauric
Feb. 13	Germanic
Feb. 16	Majestic

WHITE STAR LINE
Liverpool—New York
(Continued)

N.Y. Arrival	Steamer
Feb. 27	Britannic
Mar. 2	Teutonic
Mar. 8	Runic
Mar. 11	Germanic
Mar. 14	Tauric
Mar. 15	Majestic
Mar. 21	Nomadic
Mar. 25	Britannic
Mar. 29	Teutonic
Apr. 5	Bovic
Apr. 10	Germanic
Apr. 12	Runic
Apr. 12	Majestic
Apr. 18	Tauric
Apr. 22	Britannic
Apr. 25	Nomadic
Apr. 27	Teutonic
May 1	Cufic
May 6	Germanic
May 10	Majestic
May 16	Runic
May 19	Britannic
May 23	Tauric
May 25	Teutonic
May 30	Nomadic
June 3	Germanic
June 8	Majestic
June 12	Bovic
June 17	Adriatic
June 20	Runic
June 21	Teutonic
June 26	Tauric
June 30	Germanic
July 5	Majestic
July 5	Nomadic
July 10	Cufic
July 15	Adriatic
July 17	Bovic
July 21	Britannic
July 26	Teutonic
Aug. 1	Tauric
Aug. 4	Germanic
Aug. 7	Nomadic
Aug. 9	Majestic
Aug. 14	Cufic
Aug. 18	Britannic
Aug. 21	Bovic
Aug. 23	Teutonic
Sept. 1	Germanic
Sept. 4	Tauric
Sept. 6	Majestic
Sept. 12	Nomadic
Sept. 15	Britannic
Sept. 20	Teutonic
Sept. 25	Bovic
Sept. 29	Germanic
Oct. 2	Runic
Oct. 5	Majestic
Oct. 10	Tauric
Oct. 13	Britannic
Oct. 16	Nomadic
Oct. 18	Teutonic
Oct. 27	Germanic
Oct. 30	Bovic
Nov. 1	Majestic

WHITE STAR LINE
Liverpool—New York
(Continued)

N.Y. Arrival	Steamer
Nov. 7	Runic
Nov. 10	Britannic
Nov. 14	Tauric
Nov. 15	Teutonic
Nov. 20	Nomadic
Nov. 24	Germanic
Nov. 28	Cufic
Nov. 29	Majestic
Dec. 5	Bovic
Dec. 9	Britannic
Dec. 15	Teutonic
Dec. 20	Tauric
Dec. 25	Adriatic
Dec. 28	Nomadic
Dec. 30	Germanic

WILSON LINE
Hull, London—New York

N.Y. Arrival	Steamer
Jan. 9	Egyptian Monarch
Jan. 17	Buffalo
Jan. 30	Colorado
Feb. 21	Persian Monarch
Mar. 14	Egyptian Monarch
Mar. 22	Colorado
Apr. 11	Persian Monarch
Apr. 13	Buffalo
May 8	Egyptian Monarch
May 9	Galileo
May 31	Persian Monarch
June 10	Colorado
June 17	Lydian Monarch
June 26	Buffalo
June 26	Egyptian Monarch
July 22	Persian Monarch
July 24	Colorado
July 31	Lydian Monarch
Aug. 8	Buffalo
Aug. 14	Egyptian Monarch
Aug. 23	Francisco
Aug. 28	Martello
Sept. 2	Persian Monarch
Sept. 4	Colorado
Sept. 18	Buffalo
Oct. 18	Colorado
Oct. 20	Galileo
Oct. 21	Persian Monarch
Oct. 30	Buffalo
Nov. 6	Hindoo
Nov. 13	Francisco
Dec. 11	Colorado
Dec. 12	Persian Monarch
Dec. 14	Buffalo

ADDITIONAL ARRIVALS
Antwerp—New York

N.Y. Arrival	Steamer
Feb. 24	Lepanto
Apr. 17	Lepanto
June 5	Lepanto
Sept. 15	Lepanto
Nov. 10	Lepanto

Year 1893

ADDITIONAL ARRIVALS
Bordeaux—New York
N. Y.

Arrival	Steamer
Jan. 25	Chateau Lafite
Mar. 20	Chateau Yquem
Apr. 7	Ville du Havre
Apr. 10	Chateau Lafite
Sept. 4	Chateau Lafite
Oct. 23	Chateau Lafite
Dec. 20	Chateau Lafite

Bremen—New York
N. Y.

Arrival	Steamer
May 1	Gulf of Mexico
May 16	Laughton
June 16	Gulf of Mexico
July 14	Red Sea
Aug. 9	Laughton
Oct. 19	Laughton

British Ports—New York
N. Y.

Arrival	Steamer
Jan. 6	Broadmayne
Mar. 11	Exeter City
Apr. 3	Llandaff City
Apr. 7	Croma
Apr. 19	Croft
May 3	Manhanset
May 8	Principia
May 22	Croma
June 6	Croft
June 16	Chicago City
June 21	Manhanset
June 26	Principia
July 1	Brooklyn City
July 3	Llandaff City
July 3	Sarah Radcliffe
July 7	Abana
July 10	Carib Prince
July 13	Boston City
July 13	Croma
July 24	Croft
July 28	Chicago City
Aug. 21	Abana
Aug. 25	Boston City
Sept. 1	Croma
Sept. 11	Croft

ADDITIONAL ARRIVALS
British Ports—New York
(Continued)
N. Y.

Arrival	Steamer
Oct. 10	Abana
Oct. 12	Boston City
Oct. 17	Monomoy
Oct. 19	Croma
Oct. 30	Croft
Dec. 2	Abana
Dec. 26	Brooklyn City
Dec. 26	Manhanset
Dec. 27	Croft

Hamburg—New York
N. Y.

Arrival	Steamer
Mar. 25	Essen
May 12	Essen
June 16	Solingen
July 8	Chemnitz
Aug. 4	Solingen
Aug. 28	Essen

Liverpool—New York
N. Y.

Arrival	Steamer
Mar. 31	Lake Superior
Apr. 14	Lake Ontario

London—New York
N. Y.

Arrival	Steamer
Jan. 6	Mariposa
Jan. 23	Ludgate Hill
Jan. 26	Montezuma
Feb. 18	Mariposa
Mar. 3	Mohawk
Mar. 13	Montezuma
Mar. 20	Ludgate Hill
Mar. 30	Mariposa
Apr. 24	Richmond Hill
May 11	Montezuma
May 19	Ludgate Hill
May 31	Mohawk
June 8	Richmond Hill
July 7	Ludgate Hill
July 12	Mohawk
Aug. 2	Richmond Hill
Aug. 22	Mohawk

ADDITIONAL ARRIVALS
London—New York
(Continued)
N. Y.

Arrival	Steamer
Aug. 25	Ludgate Hill
Sept. 13	Mobile
Sept. 15	Richmond Hill
Oct. 3	Mohawk
Oct. 10	Ludgate Hill
Oct. 24	Mobile
Nov. 1	Richmond Hill
Nov. 13	Mohawk
Nov. 23	Ludgate Hill
Nov. 30	Mobile
Dec. 21	Mohawk
Dec. 22	Richmond Hill

Mediterranean—New York
N. Y.

Arrival	Steamer
Apr. 5	Guildhall
June 2	Peconic
June 5	Charles Martel
Aug. 16	Madonna Della Costa
Oct. 4	Peconic

Rotterdam, Amsterdam— New York
N. Y.

Arrival	Steamer
Feb. 6	Prins Willem II
Mar. 20	Prins Willem III
Apr. 10	Pr. Frederik Hendrik
May 19	Prins Willem I
June 12	Prins Willem II
June 23	Winchester
July 22	Prins Willem III
July 27	Winchester
Aug. 11	Pr. Frederik Hendrik
Sept. 5	Prins Maurits
Sept. 23	Prins Willem I
Sept. 25	Winchester
Nov. 7	Winchester
Nov. 27	Prins Willem III

Spanish Ports—New York
N. Y.

Arrival	Steamer
July 20	Madrileno
July 24	J. Jover Serra
Oct. 18	Madrileno

Year 1894

ALLAN STATE LINE
Glasgow—New York
N.Y.

Arrival	Steamer
Jan. 2	Peruvian
Jan. 6	Grecian
Jan. 12	Norwegian
Jan. 19	Siberian
Jan. 25	State of Nebraska
Feb. 17	Grecian
Feb. 23	Norwegian
Feb. 24	Corean
Mar. 1	State of California
Mar. 12	Siberian
Mar. 15	State of Nebraska
Mar. 28	Grecian
Apr. 3	Peruvian
Apr. 5	State of California
Apr. 14	Norwegian
Apr. 18	State of Nebraska
Apr. 27	Grecian
May 7	Peruvian
May 8	State of California
May 15	Norwegian
May 22	State of Nebraska
May 29	Grecian
June 4	State of California
June 13	Peruvian
June 20	State of Nebraska
June 27	Norwegian
July 2	State of California
July 13	Grecian
July 17	State of Nebraska
July 31	State of California
Aug. 14	State of Nebraska
Aug. 28	State of California
Sept. 7	Norwegian
Sept. 11	State of Nebraska
Sept. 24	Grecian
Sept. 24	State of California
Oct. 8	Peruvian
Oct. 10	State of Nebraska
Oct. 16	Norwegian
Oct. 22	State of California
Oct. 30	Grecian
Nov. 7	State of Nebraska
Nov. 19	Peruvian
Nov. 23	State of California
Dec. 3	Norwegian
Dec. 5	State of Nebraska
Dec. 15	Grecian
Dec. 21	Peruvian

AMERICAN LINE
Southampton—New York
N.Y.

Arrival	Steamer
Jan. 1	New York
Jan. 6	Paris
Jan. 22	New York
Jan. 27	Paris
Feb. 11	New York
Mar. 26	New York
Apr. 14	New York
Apr. 20	Paris
May 7	New York

AMERICAN LINE
Southampton—New York
(Continued)
N.Y.

Arrival	Steamer
May 12	Paris
May 26	New York
June 2	Paris
June 16	New York
June 23	Paris
July 7	New York
July 14	Paris
Aug. 11	Paris
Aug. 25	New York
Sept. 1	Paris
Sept. 15	New York
Sept. 22	Paris
Oct. 6	New York
Oct. 13	Paris
Oct. 27	New York
Nov. 3	Paris
Nov. 19	New York
Nov. 26	Paris
Dec. 8	New York
Dec. 31	New York

ANCHOR LINE
Glasgow—New York
N.Y.

Arrival	Steamer
Jan. 15	Bolivia
Jan. 26	Ethiopia
Feb. 12	Anchoria
Feb. 23	Furnessia
Mar. 12	Ethiopia
Mar. 21	Anchoria
Mar. 31	Furnessia
Apr. 12	Circassia
Apr. 17	Ethiopia
Apr. 23	Anchoria
Apr. 30	Furnessia
May 16	Circassia
May 21	City of Rome
May 28	Ethiopia
June 4	Furnessia
June 11	Anchoria
June 19	Circassia
June 25	City of Rome
July 9	Furnessia
July 16	Anchoria
July 25	Circassia
Aug. 6	Ethiopia
Aug. 13	Furnessia
Aug. 20	Anchoria
Sept. 1	City of Rome
Sept. 10	Ethiopia
Sept. 17	Furnessia
Sept. 24	Anchoria
Oct. 6	City of Rome
Oct. 16	Ethiopia
Oct. 22	Furnessia
Oct. 29	Anchoria
Nov. 14	Circassia
Nov. 30	Furnessia
Dec. 11	Anchoria
Dec. 26	Circassia

ANCHOR LINE
Mediterranean—New York
N.Y.

Arrival	Steamer
Jan. 4	Belgravia
Jan. 15	Victoria
Mar. 12	California
Mar. 19	Victoria
Apr. 7	Italia
Apr. 10	Elysia
Apr. 28	Belgravia
May 7	Olympia
May 11	Bolivia
May 21	Victoria
June 2	Britannia
June 15	Scotia
June 25	Italia
July 3	California
July 5	Victoria
July 27	Elysia
Aug. 20	Olympia
Sept. 5	Britannia
Sept. 17	Italia
Sept. 19	Victoria
Oct. 19	Victoria
Oct. 31	Bolivia
Nov. 9	Alsatia
Nov. 17	Elysia
Dec. 4	Italia
Dec. 20	Olympia

ATLANTIC TRANSPORT LINE
London—New York
N.Y.

Arrival	Steamer
Jan. 10	Massachusetts
Feb. 1	Manitoba
Feb. 14	Massachusetts
Feb. 24	Mississippi
Mar. 7	Manitoba
Mar. 21	Massachusetts
Apr. 12	Manitoba
Apr. 25	Massachusetts
May 14	Manitoba
May 28	Massachusetts
June 5	Mississippi
June 18	Manitoba
July 2	Massachusetts
July 10	Mississippi
July 23	Manitoba
Aug. 6	Massachusetts
Aug. 13	Mississippi
Aug. 27	Manitoba
Sept. 10	Massachusetts
Sept. 17	Mississippi
Oct. 1	Manitoba
Oct. 16	Massachusetts
Nov. 2	Manitoba
Nov. 22	Massachusetts
Nov. 30	Mississippi
Dec. 4	Manitoba
Dec. 26	Massachusetts

Year 1894

COMPANIA TRANSATLANTICA LINE
(Spanish Line)
Spanish Ports—New York

N.Y.

Arrival	Steamer
Jan. 4	Mexico
Jan. 15	Ciudad Condal
Jan. 25	Mexico
Feb. 5	Panama
Feb. 15	Ciudad Condal
Feb. 26	Panama
Mar. 5	Mexico
Mar. 15	Ciudad Condal
Mar. 26	Mexico
Apr. 4	Panama
Apr. 16	Ciudad Condal
Apr. 25	Panama
May 7	Habana
May 14	Ciudad Condal
May 25	Habana
June 4	Panama
June 14	Ciudad Condal
June 25	Panama
July 5	Habana
July 16	Ciudad Condal
July 25	Mexico
Aug. 4	Panama
Aug. 14	Ciudad Condal
Aug. 25	Panama
Sept. 4	Habana
Sept. 15	Ciudad Condal
Sept. 25	Habana
Oct. 5	Panama
Oct. 15	Ciudad Condal
Oct. 25	Panama
Nov. 5	Habana
Nov. 14	Ciudad Condal
Nov. 26	Habana
Dec. 5	Panama
Dec. 17	Habana
Dec. 26	Panama

CUNARD LINE
Liverpool—New York

N.Y.

Arrival	Steamer
Jan. 3	Gallia
Jan. 8	Servia
Jan. 16	Aurania
Jan. 22	Etruria
Feb. 3	Gallia
Feb. 5	Umbria
Feb. 14	Servia
Feb. 19	Etruria
Feb. 27	Aurania
Mar. 5	Lucania
Mar. 12	Umbria
Mar. 19	Campania
Mar. 26	Etruria
Mar. 31	Lucania
Apr. 9	Umbria
Apr. 16	Campania
Apr. 23	Etruria
Apr. 28	Lucania
May 7	Umbria
May 14	Campania
May 21	Etruria
May 26	Lucania
June 4	Umbria
June 9	Campania

CUNARD LINE
Liverpool—New York
(Continued)

N.Y.

Arrival	Steamer
June 18	Etruria
June 23	Lucania
June 28	Aurania
July 2	Umbria
July 7	Campania
July 21	Lucania
July 30	Umbria
Aug. 6	Aurania
Aug. 13	Etruria
Aug. 18	Campania
Aug. 27	Umbria
Sept. 1	Lucania
Sept. 5	Aurania
Sept. 10	Etruria
Sept. 15	Campania
Sept. 20	Servia
Sept. 22	Umbria
Sept. 29	Lucania
Oct. 8	Etruria
Oct. 13	Campania
Oct. 20	Umbria
Oct. 27	Lucania
Nov. 5	Etruria
Nov. 10	Campania
Nov. 20	Aurania
Nov. 26	Lucania
Dec. 3	Etruria
Dec. 8	Campania
Dec. 17	Umbria
Dec. 22	Lucania
Dec. 31	Etruria

FABRE LINE
Mediterranean—New York

N.Y.

Arrival	Steamer
Jan. 25	Burgundia
Feb. 7	Massilia
Feb. 27	Nuestria
Apr. 4	Massilia
Apr. 30	Britannia
May 3	Nuestria
May 11	Gergovia
June 5	Alesia
June 13	Massilia
June 25	Britannia
July 11	Gergovia
July 25	Nuestria
Aug. 9	Alesia
Aug. 27	Britannia
Sept. 6	Massilia
Sept. 24	Nuestria
Oct. 12	Alesia
Nov. 1	Burgundia
Nov. 13	Massilia
Dec. 10	Alesia
Dec. 31	Burgundia

FRENCH LINE
(Compagnie Generale Transatlantique)
Havre—New York

N.Y.

Arrival	Steamer
Jan. 1	La Bourgoyne
Jan. 8	La Gascogne
Jan. 16	La Champagne

FRENCH LINE
(Compagnie Generale Transatlantique)
Havre—New York
(Continued)

N.Y.

Arrival	Steamer
Jan. 22	La Bretagne
Feb. 6	La Gascogne
Feb. 12	La Champagne
Feb. 19	La Bretagne
Feb. 26	La Bourgoyne
Mar. 5	La Gascogne
Mar. 12	La Champagne
Mar. 19	La Bretagne
Mar. 26	La Touraine
Apr. 2	La Bourgoyne
Apr. 9	La Gascogne
Apr. 16	La Bretagne
Apr. 23	La Touraine
Apr. 30	La Bourgoyne
May 7	La Champagne
May 14	La Bretagne
May 21	La Touraine
May 28	La Bourgoyne
June 4	La Champagne
June 11	La Bretagne
June 16	La Touraine
June 25	La Bourgoyne
July 2	La Normandie
July 9	La Champagne
July 14	La Touraine
July 23	La Bourgoyne
July 30	La Normandie
Aug. 6	La Navarre
Aug. 13	La Champagne
Aug. 18	La Touraine
Sept. 3	La Bretagne
Sept. 10	La Bourgoyne
Sept. 17	La Champagne
Sept. 22	La Touraine
Oct. 1	La Bretagne
Oct. 8	La Bourgoyne
Oct. 15	La Champagne
Oct. 20	La Touraine
Oct. 29	La Bretagne
Nov. 3	La Bourgoyne
Nov. 12	La Champagne
Nov. 19	La Touraine
Nov. 30	La Bretagne
Dec. 3	La Bourgoyne
Dec. 10	La Champagne
Dec. 17	La Normandie
Dec. 24	La Bretagne

GUION STEAMSHIP LINE
Liverpool—New York

N.Y.

Arrival	Steamer
Apr. 23	Arizona
May 7	Alaska
May 21	Arizona

HAMBURG-AMERICAN LINE
Hamburg—New York

N.Y.

Arrival	Steamer
Jan. 3	Russia
Jan. 4	Amalfi

Year 1894

Column 1

HAMBURG-AMERICAN LINE
Hamburg—New York

N.Y. Arrival	Steamer
Jan. 9	Moravia
Jan. 15	Wieland
Jan. 18	Sorrento
Jan. 20	Dania
Jan. 27	Furst Bismarck
Jan. 29	Scandia
Feb. 5	Taormina
Feb. 8	Rhaetia
Feb. 14	Rugia
Feb. 16	Marsala
Feb. 20	Augusta Victoria
Feb. 21	Russia
Feb. 28	Moravia
Mar. 5	Dania
Mar. 6	Amalfi
Mar. 10	Suevia
Mar. 20	Rhaetia
Mar. 20	Sorrento
Mar. 21	Scandia
Mar. 26	Gellert
Mar. 29	Bohemia
Apr. 3	Russia
Apr. 6	Taormina
Apr. 10	Moravia
Apr. 14	Dania
Apr. 16	Marsala
Apr. 19	Stubbenhuk
Apr. 23	Rhaetia
Apr. 28	Augusta Victoria
Apr. 30	Scandia
May 4	Normannia
May 7	Amalfi
May 8	Bohemia
May 11	Furst Bismarck
May 15	Russia
May 19	Columbia
May 21	Moravia
May 21	Sorrento
May 25	Dania
May 26	Augusta Victoria
May 28	Grimm
June 1	Normannia
June 4	Rhaetia
June 4	Taormina
June 8	Furst Bismarck
June 9	Scandia
June 15	Columbia
June 16	Marsala
June 18	Rugia
June 23	Augusta Victoria
June 26	Russia
June 27	Bohemia
June 29	Normannia
June 30	Amalfi
July 2	Moravia
July 6	Furst Bismarck
July 9	Prussia
July 13	Columbia
July 16	Rhaetia
July 16	Sorrento
July 20	California
July 21	Scandia
July 27	Normannia
July 27	Persia

Column 2

HAMBURG-AMERICAN LINE
Hamburg—New York
(Continued)

N.Y. Arrival	Steamer
July 28	Taormina
Aug. 3	Furst Bismarck
Aug. 4	Polaria
Aug. 6	Russia
Aug. 10	Columbia
Aug. 10	Marsala
Aug. 13	Rugia
Aug. 16	Bohemia
Aug. 17	Augusta Victoria
Aug. 18	Prussia
Aug. 24	Normannia
Aug. 25	Amalfi
Aug. 27	Rhaetia
Aug. 29	Moravia
Aug. 31	Furst Bismarck
Sept. 1	Scandia
Sept. 7	Columbia
Sept. 7	Sorrento
Sept. 8	Persia
Sept. 10	Wieland
Sept. 15	Augusta Victoria
Sept. 17	Russia
Sept. 21	Dania
Sept. 21	Normannia
Sept. 22	Taormina
Sept. 28	Furst Bismarck
Sept. 29	Prussia
Oct. 5	Marsala
Oct. 6	Columbia
Oct. 8	Rhaetia
Oct. 12	Scandia
Oct. 13	Augusta Victoria
Oct. 19	Amalfi
Oct. 22	Persia
Oct. 26	Furst Bismarck
Oct. 29	Moravia
Nov. 3	Columbia
Nov. 3	Sorrento
Nov. 5	Dania
Nov. 12	Prussia
Nov. 13	Suevia
Nov. 22	Rhaetia
Nov. 26	Scandia
Dec. 1	Taormina
Dec. 3	Persia
Dec. 3	Polaria
Dec. 10	Amalfi
Dec. 11	Moravia
Dec. 17	Marsala
Dec. 22	Normannia
Dec. 24	Dania
Dec. 31	Prussia

HAMBURG-AMERICAN LINE
Mediterranean—New York

N.Y. Arrival	Steamer
Jan. 2	Columbia
Feb. 8	Gellert
Mar. 9	Wieland
Mar. 26	Rugia
Apr. 7	Furst Bismarck
Apr. 27	Suevia

Column 3

HAMBURG-AMERICAN LINE
Mediterranean—New York
(Continued)

N.Y. Arrival	Steamer
May 7	Wieland
May 19	Gellert
June 15	Suevia
June 26	Wieland
July 16	Gellert
Aug. 10	Suevia
Sept. 24	Rugia
Oct. 22	Wieland
Nov. 12	Augusta Victoria
Nov. 13	Rugia
Dec. 4	Furst Bismarck

HAMBURG-AMERICAN LINE
Scandinavian Ports—New York

N.Y. Arrival	Steamer
Jan. 2	Venetia
Mar. 5	Virginia
Mar. 26	Venetia
Apr. 11	Slavonia
Apr. 23	Gothia
May 4	Virginia
May 10	Venetia
June 2	Slavonia
June 18	Gothia
June 30	Virginia
July 14	Venetia
July 28	Slavonia
Aug. 13	Gothia
Aug. 24	Virginia
Sept. 22	Slavonia
Oct. 5	Venetia
Oct. 19	Virginia
Nov. 7	Polynesia
Nov. 24	Slavonia
Dec. 3	Venetia
Dec. 17	Virginia

HOLLAND-AMERICA LINE
Rotterdam, Amsterdam Boulogne—New York

N.Y. Arrival	Steamer
Jan. 5	Obdam
Jan. 5	Schiedam
Jan. 17	Amsterdam
Jan. 17	Zaandam
Jan. 25	Edam
Jan. 27	Dubbledam
Jan. 31	Spaarndam
Feb. 10	Rotterdam
Feb. 19	Obdam
Feb. 20	Schiedam
Feb. 26	Amsterdam
Mar. 5	Zaandam
Mar. 5	Maasdam
Mar. 7	Edam
Mar. 9	Schiedam
Mar. 10	Dubbledam
Mar. 12	Spaarndam
Mar. 20	Didam
Mar. 21	Werkendam

Year 1894

HOLLAND-AMERICA LINE
Rotterdam, Amsterdam
Boulogne—New York
(Continued)

N. Y.

Arrival	Steamer
Mar. 30	Rotterdam
Mar. 30	P. Caland
Apr. 3	Amsterdam
Apr. 9	Veendam
Apr. 16	Maasdam
Apr. 16	Edam
Apr. 19	Dubbledam
Apr. 23	Spaarndam
May 1	Werkendam
May 7	Amsterdam
May 11	Rotterdam
May 16	Maasdam
May 21	Veendam
May 26	Zaandam
May 28	Spaarndam
May 31	Dubbledam
June 4	Werkendam
June 11	Amsterdam
June 18	Maasdam
June 23	Rotterdam
June 25	Veendam
July 2	Spaarndam
July 10	Werkendam
July 16	Amsterdam
July 16	Zaandam
July 23	Maasdam
July 23	Edam
July 28	Veendam
July 31	Schiedam
Aug. 3	Rotterdam
Aug. 6	Spaarndam
Aug. 14	Obdam
Aug. 14	P. Caland
Aug. 17	Werkendam
Aug. 20	Amsterdam
Aug. 27	Maasdam
Sept. 3	Zaandam
Sept. 7	Edam
Sept. 10	Spaarndam
Sept. 15	Rotterdam
Sept. 17	Obdam
Sept. 24	Amsterdam
Sept. 24	Schiedam
Sept. 27	Werkendam
Sept. 29	Maasdam
Oct. 8	P. Caland
Oct. 8	Veendam
Oct. 15	Spaarndam
Oct. 20	Edam
Oct. 23	Obdam
Oct. 29	Rotterdam
Oct. 29	Zaandam
Nov. 7	Amsterdam
Nov. 12	Veendam
Nov. 17	Schiedam
Nov. 22	Spaarndam
Nov. 30	Obdam
Dec. 3	Maasdam
Dec. 3	Edam
Dec. 11	Amsterdam
Dec. 17	Veendam
Dec. 19	Zaandam
Dec. 26	Werkendam

INMAN & INTERNATIONAL STEAMSHIP COMPANY
Southampton—New York

N. Y.

Arrival	Steamer
Jan. 20	Berlin
Feb. 9	Chester
Feb. 27	Berlin
Mar. 8	Chester
Mar. 20	Berlin
Apr. 5	Chester
Apr. 10	Berlin
May 1	Berlin
May 22	Chester
June 13	Chester
July 5	Chester
July 31	Chester
Aug. 20	Berlin
Sept. 11	Berlin
Oct. 1	Berlin
Oct. 22	Berlin
Nov. 15	Chester
Dec. 3	Berlin
Dec. 26	Berlin

INSULAR NAVIGATION COMPANY
Azores, Lisbon—New Bedford, Mass., New York

N. Y.

Arrival	Steamer
Jan. 25	Vega
Feb. 5	Peninsular
Mar. 17	Vega
Apr. 9	Peninsular
May 7	Vega
June 6	Peninsular
June 25	Vega
Aug. 9	Vega
Sept. 15	Peninsular
Nov. 13	Vega

LINHA DE VAPORES PORTUGUEZES
Azores, Lisbon—New Bedford Mass., New York

N. Y.

Arrival	Steamer
Feb. 2	Dona Maria
Feb. 19	Olinda
Mar. 29	Dona Maria
Apr. 19	Olinda
May 19	Dona Maria
May 28	Oevenum
June 12	Olinda
July 2	Dona Maria
Aug. 8	Oevenum
Aug. 10	Dona Maria
Nov. 16	Oevenum

NATIONAL NAVIGATION COMPANY
Mediterranean—New York

N. Y.

Arrival	Steamer
Apr. 21	Cachemire
May 15	Hindoustan

NAVIGAZIONE GENERALE ITALIANA LINE
Mediterranean—New York

N. Y.

Arrival	Steamer
Jan. 23	Letimbro
Feb. 21	Plata
Mar. 15	San Giorgio
Mar. 23	Entella
Apr. 28	Letimbro
May 19	Plata
June 4	Entella
June 15	Iniziativa
July 16	Plata
July 17	Letimbro
Aug. 9	Iniziativa
Nov. 15	Letimbro

NORTH GERMAN LLOYD
Bremen—New York

N. Y.

Arrival	Steamer
Jan. 1	America
Jan. 1	Darmstadt
Jan. 4	Trave
Jan. 4	Weimar
Jan. 11	Spree
Jan. 15	Dresden
Jan. 20	Stuttgart
Jan. 22	Saale
Jan. 27	Ems
Jan. 31	Braunschweig
Feb. 5	Elbe
Feb. 5	H. H. Meier
Feb. 10	Trave
Feb. 13	America
Feb. 16	Lahn
Feb. 24	Aller
Feb. 24	Weimar
Mar. 2	Munchen
Mar. 3	Saale
Mar. 9	Trave
Mar. 12	Dresden
Mar. 15	Lahn
Mar. 19	Braunschweig
Mar. 21	Werra
Mar. 23	Stuttgart
Mar. 24	Aller
Mar. 29	Havel
Apr. 3	Saale
Apr. 4	Darmstadt
Apr. 6	Trave
Apr. 12	Elbe
Apr. 12	Spree
Apr. 17	Gera
Apr. 18	Aller
Apr. 19	Lahn
Apr. 26	Havel
Apr. 28	Wittekind
May 1	Saale
May 4	Trave
May 9	Elbe
May 10	Spree
May 15	Aller
May 17	Lahn
May 23	Havel
May 26	Braunschweig
May 29	Saale
May 31	Trave
June 5	Elbe

Year 1894

NORTH GERMAN LLOYD
Bremen—New York
(Continued)

N. Y.

Arrival	Steamer
June 7	Willehad
June 7	Spree
June 12	Aller
June 14	Lahn
June 21	Havel
June 23	Wittekind
June 28	Stuttgart
June 28	Trave
July 3	Saale
July 5	Spree
July 10	Elbe
July 11	Darmstadt
July 12	Lahn
July 17	Ems
July 18	Willehad
July 19	Havel
July 23	Aller
July 25	H. H. Meier
July 26	Trave
July 30	Saale
Aug. 2	Spree
Aug. 4	Weser
Aug. 7	Elbe
Aug. 7	Weimar
Aug. 9	Lahn
Aug. 14	Kaiser Wilhelm II
Aug. 15	Wittekind
Aug. 16	Havel
Aug. 20	Ems
Aug. 23	Aller
Aug. 27	Saale
Aug. 29	Willehad
Aug. 30	Spree
Sept. 4	Elbe
Sept. 5	Lahn
Sept. 11	Trave
Sept. 12	Habsburg
Sept. 13	Havel
Sept. 17	Ems
Sept. 17	Kaiser Wilhelm II
Sept. 20	Aller
Sept. 24	Saale
Sept. 25	Wittekind
Sept. 27	Spree
Oct. 2	Dresden
Oct. 2	Elbe
Oct. 4	Lahn
Oct. 9	Trave
Oct. 11	Willehad
Oct. 11	Havel
Oct. 15	Ems
Oct. 16	Stuttgart
Oct. 19	Aller
Oct. 23	H. H. Meier
Oct. 23	Saale
Oct. 25	Spree
Oct. 29	Weimar
Oct. 30	Elbe
Nov. 1	Lahn
Nov. 6	Trave
Nov. 8	Havel
Nov. 10	Wittekind
Nov. 16	Aller
Nov. 17	Dresden
Nov. 24	Saale

NORTH GERMAN LLOYD
Bremen—New York
(Continued)

N. Y.

Arrival	Steamer
Nov. 28	Stuttgart
Nov. 30	Lahn
Dec. 3	Weser
Dec. 6	Trave
Dec. 8	Braunschweig
Dec. 15	Salier
Dec. 17	Elbe
Dec. 21	Ems
Dec. 21	Weimar
Dec. 31	Wittekind

NORTH GERMAN LLOYD
Mediterranean—New York

N. Y.

Arrival	Steamer
Jan. 4	Fulda
Jan. 29	Werra
Feb. 7	Kaiser Wilhelm II
Feb. 12	Spree
Feb. 19	Weser
Feb. 27	Fulda
Mar. 3	Neckar
Mar. 12	Kaiser Wilhelm II
Mar. 16	Kron. Fred. Wilhelm
Mar. 19	Spree
Apr. 5	Fulda
Apr. 19	Kaiser Wilhelm II
Apr. 20	Weser
Apr. 23	Neckar
May 7	Fulda
May 14	Kron. Fred. Wilhelm
May 22	Kaiser Wilhelm II
May 28	Werra
June 4	Neckar
June 11	Fulda
June 11	Weser
June 26	Kaiser Wilhelm II
July 2	Werra
July 5	Kron. Fred. Wilhelm
July 16	Fulda
July 23	Neckar
Aug. 6	Werra
Aug. 20	Kron. Fred. Wilhelm
Aug. 20	Fulda
Sept. 10	Neckar
Sept. 10	Werra
Sept. 24	Fulda
Oct. 17	Kron. Fred. Wilhelm
Oct. 17	Werra
Oct. 23	Kaiser Wilhelm II
Nov. 3	Neckar
Nov. 7	Fulda
Nov. 20	Werra
Nov. 27	Kaiser Wilhelm II
Dec. 4	Kron. Fred. Wilhelm
Dec. 24	Neckar
Dec. 26	Werra

PRINCE LINE
Mediterranean—New York

N. Y.

Arrival	Steamer
Jan. 8	Carib Prince
Feb. 12	Carib Prince
Mar. 16	Carib Prince

PRINCE LINE
Mediterranean—New York
(Continued)

N. Y.

Arrival	Steamer
Mar. 19	Danish Prince
Apr. 23	Carib Prince
May 25	Carib Prince
July 5	Carib Prince
Aug. 13	Carib Prince
Sept. 26	Carib Prince
Nov. 5	Carib Prince
Dec. 18	Carib Prince

RED STAR LINE
Antwerp—New York

N. Y.

Arrival	Steamer
Jan. 1	Rhynland
Jan. 3	Westernland
Jan. 10	Noordland
Jan. 17	Waesland
Jan. 26	Belgenland
Feb. 6	Pennland
Feb. 12	Rhynland
Feb. 15	Westernland
Feb. 23	Noordland
Mar. 1	Waesland
Mar. 9	Belgenland
Mar. 16	Rhynland
Mar. 22	Westernland
Mar. 30	Noordland
Apr. 6	Waesland
Apr. 10	Friesland
Apr. 19	Rhynland
Apr. 25	Westernland
May 3	Noordland
May 8	Waesland
May 23	Rhynland
May 30	Westernland
June 5	Noordland
June 13	Waesland
June 19	Friesland
June 28	Rhynland
July 5	Westernland
July 11	Noordland
July 19	Belgenland
July 25	Waesland
July 31	Friesland
Aug. 8	Rhynland
Aug. 14	Westernland
Aug. 22	Noordland
Aug. 29	Waesland
Sept. 3	Belgenland
Sept. 4	Friesland
Sept. 12	Rhynland
Sept. 17	Pennland
Sept. 18	Westernland
Sept. 25	Noordland
Oct. 2	Waesland
Oct. 9	Friesland
Oct. 17	Rhynland
Oct. 23	Westernland
Oct. 30	Noordland
Nov. 8	Waesland
Nov. 14	Friesland
Nov. 26	Rhynland
Nov. 30	Westernland
Dec. 5	Noordland
Dec. 13	Waesland

Year 1894

RED STAR LINE
Antwerp—New York
(Continued)

N.Y. Arrival	Steamer
Dec. 18	Friesland
Dec. 29	Pennland

SCANDINAVIAN-AMERICAN LINE
Scandinavian Ports—New York

N.Y. Arrival	Steamer
Jan. 20	Thingvalla
Feb. 23	Norge
Mar. 5	Hekla
Mar. 28	Island
Apr. 14	Norge
Apr. 27	Hekla
May 12	Island
May 23	Hekla
June 8	Norge
June 25	Hekla
July 5	Island
July 23	Thingvalla
Aug. 6	Norge
Aug. 31	Island
Sept. 22	Thingvalla
Oct. 5	Hekla
Nov. 1	Island
Nov. 21	Thingvalla
Nov. 30	Hekla

WHITE STAR LINE
Liverpool—New York

N.Y. Arrival	Steamer
Jan. 5	Britannic
Jan. 11	Teutonic
Jan. 17	Majestic
Jan. 24	Cevic
Jan. 27	Germanic
Feb. 6	Adriatic
Feb. 10	Britannic
Feb. 14	Bovic
Feb. 16	Majestic
Feb. 24	Germanic
Mar. 1	Teutonic
Mar. 10	Britannic
Mar. 13	Nomadic
Mar. 15	Majestic
Mar. 24	Germanic
Mar. 29	Teutonic
Apr. 7	Britannic
Apr. 12	Majestic
Apr. 20	Germanic
Apr. 25	Teutonic
May 4	Britannic
May 7	Cevic
May 9	Majestic
May 19	Germanic
May 23	Teutonic
June 1	Britannic
June 6	Majestic
June 11	Cevic
June 15	Germanic
June 19	Tauric
June 20	Teutonic
June 29	Britannic

WHITE STAR LINE
Liverpool—New York
(Continued)

N.Y. Arrival	Steamer
July 2	Bovic
July 5	Majestic
July 13	Germanic
July 17	Cevic
July 18	Teutonic
July 27	Britannic
July 30	Nomadic
Aug. 1	Majestic
Aug. 6	Bovic
Aug. 10	Germanic
Aug. 15	Teutonic
Aug. 21	Cevic
Aug. 24	Britannic
Aug. 27	Tauric
Aug. 29	Majestic
Sept. 4	Nomadic
Sept. 7	Germanic
Sept. 10	Bovic
Sept. 12	Teutonic
Sept. 21	Britannic
Sept. 24	Cevic
Sept. 26	Majestic
Oct. 1	Tauric
Oct. 5	Germanic
Oct. 10	Teutonic
Oct. 16	Bovic
Oct. 19	Britannic
Oct. 24	Majestic
Oct. 29	Cevic
Nov. 3	Germanic
Nov. 5	Tauric
Nov. 12	Adriatic
Nov. 14	Nomadic
Nov. 15	Teutonic
Nov. 23	Bovic
Nov. 26	Britannic
Nov. 30	Majestic
Dec. 4	Cevic
Dec. 8	Adriatic
Dec. 11	Tauric
Dec. 13	Teutonic
Dec. 19	Nomadic
Dec. 22	Britannic
Dec. 26	Bovic
Dec. 27	Majestic

WILSON LINE
Hull, London—New York

N.Y. Arrival	Steamer
Jan. 3	Egyptian Monarch
Jan. 6	Lydian Monarch
Jan. 27	Alecto
Feb. 7	Persian Monarch
Feb. 27	Lydian Monarch
Mar. 14	Alecto
Mar. 20	Persian Monarch
Apr. 9	Francisco
Apr. 13	Lydian Monarch
Apr. 27	Alecto
May 7	Persian Monarch
May 23	Francisco
May 28	Lydian Monarch
June 15	Buffalo
June 18	Alecto

WILSON LINE
Hull, London—New York
(Continued)

N.Y. Arrival	Steamer
June 25	Hindoo
July 16	Lydian Monarch
July 28	Buffalo
July 30	Alecto
Aug. 3	Hindoo
Aug. 13	Francisco
Aug. 27	Lydian Monarch
Aug. 30	Colorado
Sept. 10	Buffalo
Sept. 13	Alecto
Sept. 17	Hindoo
Sept. 24	Francisco
Oct. 10	Lydian Monarch
Oct. 17	Colorado
Oct. 24	Buffalo
Oct. 29	Hindoo
Oct. 29	Alecto
Nov. 9	Francisco
Dec. 1	Lydian Monarch
Dec. 3	Colorado
Dec. 10	Buffalo
Dec. 12	Alecto
Dec. 17	Hindoo
Dec. 26	Francisco

ADDITIONAL ARRIVALS
Antwerp—New York

N.Y. Arrival	Steamer
July 13	Sorrento
Dec. 21	Sorrento

Bordeaux—New York

N.Y. Arrival	Steamer
Feb. 28	Chateau Lafite
Apr. 16	Chateau Lafite
June 8	Chateau Lafite
July 24	Chateau Lafite
Sept. 7	Chateau Lafite
Oct. 23	Chateau Lafite
Dec. 8	Chateau Lafite

British Ports—New York

N.Y. Arrival	Steamer
Jan. 4	Trinidad
Apr. 16	Croma
Apr. 29	Wells City
May 11	Exeter City
May 24	Brooklyn City
July 16	Brooklyn City
Aug. 1	Llandaff City
Aug. 22	Exeter City
Sept. 5	Brooklyn City
Oct. 20	Llandaff City
Oct. 25	Boston City

Hamburg—New York

N.Y. Arrival	Steamer
Apr. 5	Essen
Dec. 17	Patria
Dec. 28	Hispania

Year 1894

ADDITIONAL ARRIVALS
London—New York
N. Y.

Arrival	Steamer
Jan. 3	Mobile
Jan. 11	Ludgate Hill
Jan. 24	Mohawk
Feb. 9	Mobile
Feb. 15	Richmond Hill
Feb. 28	Mohawk
Mar. 3	Ludgate Hill
Mar. 14	Mobile
Mar. 29	Tower Hill
Apr. 3	Mohawk
Apr. 3	Richmond Hill
Apr. 17	Mobile
Apr. 18	Ludgate Hill
May 7	Mohawk
May 14	Richmond Hill
May 21	Mobile
June 7	Ludgate Hill
June 11	Mohawk
June 25	Mobile
July 3	Richmond Hill
July 16	Mohawk
July 30	Mobile

ADDITIONAL ARRIVALS
London—New York
(Continued)
N. Y.

Arrival	Steamer
Aug. 16	Richmond Hill
Aug. 20	Mohawk
Sept. 3	Mobile
Sept. 24	Mohawk
Sept. 27	Richmond Hill
Oct. 11	Mobile
Nov. 7	Mohawk
Nov. 13	Mobile
Nov. 15	Richmond Hill
Dec. 11	Mohawk
Dec. 19	Mobile
Dec. 24	Ludgate Hill
Dec. 31	Richmond Hill

Mediterranean—New York
N. Y.

Arrival	Steamer
Apr. 24	Charles Martel
Nov. 7	Sicilia
Dec. 20	Nyassa

ADDITIONAL ARRIVALS
Rotterdam, Amsterdam—New York
N. Y.

Arrival	Steamer
Jan. 6	Prins Maurits
Jan. 29	Prins Willem I
Feb. 20	Prins Willem II
Mar. 12	Oranje Nassau
Mar. 31	Prins Willem III
Apr. 24	Pr. Frederik Hendrik
May 14	Prins Maurits
June 2	Prins Willem I
July 16	Oranje Nassau
Aug. 25	Pr. Frederik Hendrik
Sept. 17	Prins Maurits

Southampton—New York
N. Y.

Arrival	Steamer
Aug. 8	Pennland

Year 1895

ALLAN STATE LINE
Glasgow—New York
N. Y.

Arrival	Steamer
Jan. 2	State of California
Jan. 12	Norwegian
Jan. 22	Grecian
Jan. 30	State of Nebraska
Feb. 12	State of California
Feb. 28	Norwegian
Mar. 15	State of Nebraska
Mar. 27	State of California
Apr. 12	Siberian
Apr. 24	State of Nebraska
May 9	State of California
May 21	State of Nebraska
June 3	State of California
June 18	State of Nebraska
July 1	State of California
July 16	State of Nebraska
July 30	State of California
Aug. 13	State of Nebraska
Aug. 27	State of California
Sept. 11	State of Nebraska
Sept. 24	State of California
Oct. 11	State of Nebraska
Oct. 23	State of California
Nov. 12	State of Nebraska
Nov. 30	Corean
Dec. 18	Pomeranian
Dec. 26	State of Nebraska

AMERICAN LINE
Southampton—New York
N. Y.

Arrival	Steamer
Jan. 12	Paris
Jan. 19	New York
Jan. 29	Berlin
Feb. 2	Paris
Feb. 20	Berlin
Feb. 23	Paris
Mar. 2	New York
Mar. 12	Berlin
Mar. 23	Paris
Apr. 2	Berlin
Apr. 6	New York
Apr. 13	Paris
Apr. 22	Berlin
May 4	Paris
May 14	Berlin
May 18	New York
May 25	Paris
June 4	Berlin
June 8	New York
June 15	Paris
June 24	Saint Louis
June 25	Berlin
June 29	New York
July 6	Paris
July 13	Saint Louis
July 20	New York
July 27	Paris
Aug. 3	Saint Louis
Aug. 13	Berlin
Aug. 17	New York

AMERICAN LINE
Southampton—New York
(Continued)
N. Y.

Arrival	Steamer
Aug. 24	Paris
Aug. 31	Saint Louis
Sept. 7	New York
Sept. 16	Paris
Sept. 21	Saint Louis
Sept. 28	New York
Oct. 7	Paris
Oct. 12	Saint Louis
Oct. 19	New York
Oct. 26	Saint Paul
Nov. 4	Berlin
Nov. 11	New York
Nov. 18	Saint Louis
Nov. 23	Saint Paul
Nov. 30	New York
Dec. 7	Saint Louis
Dec. 14	Saint Paul
Dec. 21	Paris
Dec. 28	Saint Louis

ANCHOR LINE
Glasgow—New York
N. Y.

Arrival	Steamer
Jan. 9	Furnessia
Jan. 21	Anchoria
Feb. 8	Circassia
Feb. 19	Furnessia
Mar. 4	Anchoria
Mar. 21	Ethiopia
Apr. 2	Furnessia
Apr. 15	Anchoria
Apr. 22	Ethiopia
May 1	Furnessia
May 15	Circassia
May 18	City of Rome
May 28	Ethiopia
June 4	Furnessia
June 11	Anchoria
June 19	Circassia
June 22	City of Rome
July 1	Ethiopia
July 8	Furnessia
July 22	Anchoria
Aug. 5	Ethiopia
Aug. 12	Furnessia
Aug. 20	Circassia
Aug. 26	Anchoria
Aug. 31	City of Rome
Sept. 10	Ethiopia
Sept. 16	Furnessia
Sept. 24	Circassia
Sept. 30	Anchoria
Oct. 5	City of Rome
Oct. 15	Ethiopia
Oct. 22	Furnessia
Oct. 30	Circassia
Nov. 6	Anchoria
Nov. 25	Ethiopia
Dec. 3	Furnessia
Dec. 19	Anchoria

ANCHOR LINE
Mediterranean—New York
N. Y.

Arrival	Steamer
Feb. 12	Bolivia
Feb. 28	California
Mar. 30	Italia
Apr. 22	Olympia
May 25	Bohemia
June 5	Italia
July 2	Olympia
Aug. 9	Elysia
Aug. 14	Italia
Aug. 24	Bolivia
Sept. 6	Olympia
Sept. 19	California
Oct. 18	Olympia
Oct. 21	Italia
Oct. 23	Belgravia
Nov. 1	Scotia
Dec. 3	California
Dec. 5	Britannia
Dec. 10	Bolivia

ATLANTIC TRANSPORT LINE
London—New York
N. Y.

Arrival	Steamer
Jan. 3	Manitoba
Jan. 9	Mississippi
Jan. 29	Massachusetts
Feb. 11	Manitoba
Feb. 14	Mississippi
Mar. 4	Massachusetts
Mar. 13	Manitoba
Mar. 22	Mississippi
Apr. 10	Massachusetts
Apr. 16	Manitoba
Apr. 23	Mississippi
May 14	Massachusetts
May 20	Manitoba
May 29	Mississippi
June 17	Massachusetts
June 24	Manitoba
July 3	Mississippi
July 22	Massachusetts
July 29	Manitoba
Aug. 6	Mississippi
Aug. 27	Massachusetts
Sept. 3	Manitoba
Sept. 11	Mississippi
Sept. 30	Massachusetts
Oct. 8	Manitoba
Oct. 17	Mississippi
Nov. 4	Massachusetts
Nov. 12	Manitoba
Nov. 25	Mississippi
Dec. 11	Massachusetts
Dec. 19	Manitoba
Dec. 28	Mississippi

Year 1895

COMPANIA TRANSATLANTICA LINE
(Spanish Line)
Spanish Ports—New York
N.Y.

Arrival	Steamer
Jan. 4	Habana
Jan. 15	Ciudad Condal
Jan. 24	Habana
Feb. 7	Panama
Feb. 15	Ciudad Condal
Feb. 25	Panama
Mar. 5	Habana
Mar. 15	Ciudad Condal
Apr. 4	Panama
Apr. 15	Ciudad Condal
Apr. 25	Panama
May 6	Habana
May 15	Ciudad Condal
May 25	Habana
June 4	Panama
June 14	Ciudad Condal
June 25	Panama
July 5	Habana
July 15	Ciudad Condal
July 25	Habana
Aug. 5	Panama
Aug. 14	Ciudad Condal
Aug. 26	Panama
Sept. 12	Habana
Sept. 16	Ciudad Condal
Oct. 7	Panama
Oct. 15	Ciudad Condal
Oct. 28	Panama
Nov. 8	Mexico
Nov. 16	Ciudad Condal
Nov. 25	Mexico
Dec. 5	Panama
Dec. 16	Ciudad Condal
Dec. 26	Panama

CUNARD LINE
Liverpool—New York
N.Y.

Arrival	Steamer
Jan. 7	Aurania
Jan. 12	Umbria
Jan. 19	Lucania
Jan. 28	Etruria
Feb. 4	Aurania
Feb. 11	Umbria
Feb. 19	Servia
Feb. 25	Etruria
Mar. 4	Aurania
Mar. 11	Umbria
Mar. 16	Lucania
Mar. 25	Etruria
Apr. 2	Aurania
Apr. 8	Umbria
Apr. 13	Lucania
Apr. 20	Etruria
Apr. 27	Campania
May 6	Umbria
May 11	Lucania
May 18	Etruria
May 25	Campania
June 3	Umbria
June 8	Lucania
June 15	Etruria
June 22	Campania

CUNARD LINE
Liverpool—New York
(Continued)
N.Y.

Arrival	Steamer
June 27	Aurania
July 1	Umbria
July 6	Lucania
July 15	Etruria
July 20	Campania
July 30	Aurania
Aug. 3	Umbria
Aug. 10	Lucania
Aug. 17	Etruria
Aug. 23	Campania
Sept. 2	Umbria
Sept. 5	Aurania
Sept. 7	Lucania
Sept. 14	Etruria
Sept. 19	Servia
Sept. 21	Campania
Sept. 28	Umbria
Oct. 3	Aurania
Oct. 5	Lucania
Oct. 14	Etruria
Oct. 19	Campania
Oct. 26	Umbria
Nov. 2	Lucania
Nov. 11	Etruria
Nov. 18	Campania
Nov. 25	Umbria
Nov. 30	Lucania
Dec. 9	Etruria
Dec. 14	Campania
Dec. 23	Umbria
Dec. 30	Lucania

FABRE LINE
Mediterranean—New York
N.Y.

Arrival	Steamer
Jan. 30	Massilia
Mar. 2	Alesia
Mar. 23	Nuestria
Apr. 15	Pictavia
Apr. 16	Britannia
May 2	Alesia
May 13	Burgundia
May 23	Nuestria
June 12	Britannia
June 28	Alesia
July 12	Burgundia
July 24	Nuestria
Aug. 9	Britannia
Aug. 28	Alesia
Sept. 23	Nuestria
Oct. 7	Britannia
Oct. 31	Alesia
Nov. 7	Burgundia

FRENCH LINE
(Compagnie Generale Transatlantique)
Havre—New York
N.Y.

Arrival	Steamer
Jan. 2	La Gascogne
Jan. 7	La Champagne
Jan. 14	La Normandie
Jan. 21	La Bourgoyne
Jan. 28	La Bretagne

FRENCH LINE
(Compagnie Generale Transatlantique)
Havre—New York
(Continued)
N.Y.

Arrival	Steamer
Jan. 31	La Touraine
Feb. 11	La Normandie
Feb. 12	La Gascogne
Feb. 19	La Bourgoyne
Feb. 25	La Champagne
Mar. 4	La Bretagne
Mar. 12	La Normandie
Mar. 18	La Gascogne
Mar. 25	La Champagne
Apr. 1	La Bourgoyne
Apr. 8	La Normandie
Apr. 15	La Gascogne
Apr. 22	La Champagne
Apr. 29	La Bourgoyne
May 6	La Normandie
May 11	La Touraine
May 23	La Gascogne
May 27	La Champagne
June 3	La Bourgoyne
June 10	La Touraine
June 17	La Normandie
June 24	La Champagne
July 1	La Bourgoyne
July 8	La Touraine
July 15	La Normandie
July 22	La Champagne
July 29	La Bourgoyne
Aug. 5	La Touraine
Aug. 12	La Normandie
Aug. 19	La Gascogne
Aug. 26	La Champagne
Sept. 2	La Bourgoyne
Sept. 7	La Touraine
Sept. 16	La Gascogne
Sept. 23	La Champagne
Sept. 30	La Bourgoyne
Oct. 7	La Touraine
Oct. 14	La Gascogne
Oct. 21	La Champagne
Oct. 28	La Bourgoyne
Nov. 4	La Touraine
Nov. 11	La Gascogne
Nov. 18	La Champagne
Nov. 25	La Bourgoyne
Dec. 2	La Normandie
Dec. 9	La Gascogne
Dec. 17	La Champagne
Dec. 23	La Bourgoyne

HAMBURG-AMERICAN LINE
Hamburg—New York
N.Y.

Arrival	Steamer
Jan. 17	Slavonia
Jan. 17	Augusta Victoria
Jan. 24	Persia
Jan. 28	Amalfi
Jan. 29	Phoenicia
Feb. 4	Patria
Feb. 12	Dania
Feb. 13	Taormina
Feb. 18	Scandia
Feb. 25	Prussia

Year 1895

HAMBURG-AMERICAN LINE
Hamburg—New York
(Continued)

N.Y. Arrival	Steamer
Mar. 4	Russia
Mar. 12	Persia
Mar. 18	Phoenicia
Mar. 25	Amalfi
Apr. 1	Dania
Apr. 8	Scandia
Apr. 11	Taormina
Apr. 15	Russia
Apr. 19	Normannia
Apr. 20	Marsala
Apr. 20	Prussia
Apr. 27	Phoenicia
Apr. 27	Polaria
May 3	Albano
May 3	Persia
May 4	Columbia
May 11	Augusta Victoria
May 11	Palatia
May 13	Markomannia
May 17	Dania
May 17	Normannia
May 20	Amalfi
May 24	Furst Bismarck
May 24	Patria
June 1	Columbia
June 1	Prussia
June 3	Taormina
June 6	Augusta Victoria
June 8	California
June 10	Phoenicia
June 14	Normannia
June 14	Persia
June 15	Marsala
June 21	Furst Bismarck
June 22	Palatia
June 25	Polaria
June 27	Taormina
June 28	Albano
July 5	Columbia
July 5	Patria
July 12	Prussia
July 15	Amalfi
July 19	Furst Bismarck
July 19	Phoenicia
July 20	Italia
July 26	Persia
Aug. 1	Palatia
Aug. 6	Bohemia
Aug. 12	Marsala
Aug. 15	Patria
Aug. 16	Furst Bismarck
Aug. 22	Prussia
Aug. 24	Columbia
Aug. 30	Phoenicia
Aug. 30	Moravia
Aug. 31	Augusta Victoria
Sept. 7	Persia
Sept. 7	Normannia
Sept. 9	Amalfi
Sept. 12	Palatia
Sept. 14	Furst Bismarck
Sept. 20	Columbia
Sept. 20	Dania
Sept. 23	Taormina

HAMBURG-AMERICAN LINE
Hamburg—New York
(Continued)

N.Y. Arrival	Steamer
Sept. 27	Patria
Sept. 28	Augusta Victoria
Oct. 4	Normannia
Oct. 4	Prussia
Oct. 7	Marsala
Oct. 12	Bohemia
Oct. 12	Furst Bismarck
Oct. 12	Phoenicia
Oct. 18	Persia
Oct. 19	Albano
Oct. 24	Palatia
Oct. 28	Moravia
Oct. 31	Dania
Nov. 2	Amalfi
Nov. 9	Patria
Nov. 18	Prussia
Nov. 21	Taormina
Nov. 25	Phoenicia
Nov. 29	Markomannia
Nov. 30	Persia
Dec. 2	Marsala
Dec. 11	Palatia
Dec. 16	Albano
Dec. 16	Scotia
Dec. 20	Moravia
Dec. 21	Normannia
Dec. 26	Patria
Dec. 28	Christiania
Dec. 30	Prussia
Dec. 31	Amalfi

HAMBURG-AMERICAN LINE
Mediterranean—New York

N.Y. Arrival	Steamer
Jan. 2	Suevia
Jan. 25	Furst Bismarck
Feb. 14	Normannia
Mar. 4	Suevia
Mar. 20	Normannia
Apr. 5	Furst Bismarck
Apr. 30	Suevia
Nov. 18	Furst Bismarck

HAMBURG-AMERICAN LINE
Scandinavian Ports—New York

N.Y. Arrival	Steamer
May 15	Georgia
May 25	Sicilia
June 21	Virginia
July 5	Georgia
Aug. 1	Venetia
Aug. 15	Virginia
Aug. 31	Georgia
Sept. 13	Sicilia
Oct. 12	Virginia
Oct. 26	Georgia
Nov. 21	Venetia
Dec. 4	Virginia

HOLLAND-AMERICA LINE
Rotterdam, Amsterdam—New York

N.Y. Arrival	Steamer
Jan. 4	Obdam
Jan. 4	Schiedam
Jan. 9	Maasdam
Jan. 22	Edam
Jan. 25	Amsterdam
Feb. 5	Werkendam
Feb. 11	Maasdam
Feb. 20	Obdam
Mar. 4	Zaandam
Mar. 13	Amsterdam
Mar. 21	Werkendam
Mar. 25	Maasdam
Apr. 4	Obdam
Apr. 8	Spaarndam
Apr. 15	Veendam
Apr. 22	Amsterdam
Apr. 29	Maasdam
May 6	Zaandam
May 8	Obdam
May 13	Spaarndam
May 20	Veendam
May 23	Werkendam
June 3	Maasdam
June 10	Edam
June 11	Obdam
June 17	Spaarndam
June 24	Veendam
June 29	Werkendam
July 1	Amsterdam
July 8	Maasdam
July 16	Obdam
July 20	Edam
July 22	Spaarndam
July 27	Veendam
Aug. 3	Zaandam
Aug. 12	Maasdam
Aug. 17	Werkendam
Aug. 20	Obdam
Aug. 26	Spaarndam
Sept. 2	Edam
Sept. 3	Veendam
Sept. 9	Amsterdam
Sept. 16	Maasdam
Sept. 17	Rotterdam
Sept. 21	Werkendam
Sept. 24	Edam
Sept. 30	Spaarndam
Oct. 7	Veendam
Oct. 16	Zaandam
Oct. 17	Amsterdam
Oct. 21	Maasdam
Oct. 29	Werkendam
Oct. 31	Rotterdam
Nov. 4	Spaarndam
Nov. 11	Veendam
Nov. 12	Obdam
Nov. 13	Schiedam
Nov. 20	Amsterdam
Nov. 25	Maasdam
Nov. 29	Spaarndam
Dec. 3	Rotterdam
Dec. 3	Werkendam
Dec. 9	P. Caland
Dec. 14	Edam

Year 1895

HOLLAND-AMERICA LINE
Rotterdam, Amsterdam—
New York
(Continued)

N. Y.

Arrival	Steamer
Dec. 17	Veendam
Dec. 24	Amsterdam
Dec. 30	Obdam
Dec. 30	Maasdam

INSULAR NAVIGATION COMPANY
Azores, Lisbon—New Bedford, Mass., New York

N. Y.

Arrival	Steamer
Feb. 15	Peninsular
Mar. 26	Vega
May 31	Peninsular
July 18	Peninsular
Sept. 7	Peninsular
Oct. 31	Peninsular
Dec. 23	Peninsular

LA VELOCE LINE
Mediterranean—New York

N. Y.

Arrival	Steamer
June 6	Citta di Messina

LINHA DE VAPORES PORTUGUEZES
Azores—New Bedford, Mass., New York

N. Y.

Arrival	Steamer
Jan. 10	Olinda
Jan. 18	Oevenum
Apr. 2	Dona Maria
Apr. 5	Olinda
Apr. 11	Oevenum
June 10	Oevenum
Oct. 3	Oevenum
Oct. 26	Dona Maria
Nov. 26	Oevenum

NAVIGAZIONE GENER- ALE ITALIANA LINE
Mediterranean—New York

N. Y.

Arrival	Steamer
Feb. 22	Letimbro
Apr. 8	San Giorgio
Dec. 23	Sicilia

NORTH GERMAN LLOYD
Bremen—New York

N. Y.

Arrival	Steamer
Jan. 2	Hohenzollern
Jan. 4	Dresden
Jan. 12	Elbe
Jan. 12	Weser
Jan. 22	Stuttgart
Jan. 25	Lahn
Jan. 25	Salier
Feb. 1	Ems
Feb. 1	Weimar

NORTH GERMAN LLOYD
Bremen—New York
(Continued)

N. Y.

Arrival	Steamer
Feb. 11	Wittikind
Feb. 15	Karlsruhe
Feb. 15	Saale
Feb. 21	Lahn
Feb. 25	Braunschweig
Mar. 1	Ems
Mar. 1	Stuttgart
Mar. 8	Havel
Mar. 8	Salier
Mar. 16	Saale
Mar. 18	Weimar
Mar. 20	Fulda
Mar. 21	Lahn
Mar. 21	Willehad
Mar. 29	Trave
Mar. 30	Munchen
Apr. 4	Havel
Apr. 8	Wittikind
Apr. 10	Stuttgart
Apr. 12	Saale
Apr. 15	Braunschweig
Apr. 18	Lahn
Apr. 19	Oldenburg
Apr. 23	Weimar
Apr. 25	Salier
Apr. 26	Trave
Apr. 30	Ems
May 10	Munchen
May 10	Saale
May 13	Habsburg
May 16	Lahn
May 17	Wittikind
May 21	Fulda
May 22	Stuttgart
May 23	Trave
May 28	Ems
May 29	Oldenburg
May 30	Havel
June 4	Weimar
June 7	Saale
June 10	Braunschweig
June 12	Willehad
June 13	Lahn
June 14	Salier
June 18	Fulda
June 19	Munchen
June 20	Spree
June 27	Weser
June 27	Havel
June 28	Neckar
July 3	Stuttgart
July 5	Trave
July 11	Lahn
July 12	Wittikind
July 16	Weimar
July 17	Fulda
July 17	Kaiser Wilhelm II
July 18	Spree
July 23	Ems
July 24	Havel
July 24	Willehad
July 30	Munchen
July 30	Saale
Aug. 1	Aller
Aug. 5	Trave

NORTH GERMAN LLOYD
Bremen—New York
(Continued)

N. Y.

Arrival	Steamer
Aug. 7	Dresden
Aug. 8	Lahn
Aug. 13	Fulda
Aug. 14	Stuttgart
Aug. 15	Spree
Aug. 19	Ems
Aug. 20	Wittikind
Aug. 22	Havel
Aug. 26	Saale
Aug. 30	Braunschweig
Sept. 3	Salier
Sept. 3	Trave
Sept. 4	Willehad
Sept. 5	Lahn
Sept. 10	Fulda
Sept. 11	Neckar
Sept. 12	Spree
Sept. 17	Ems
Sept. 18	Dresden
Sept. 19	Havel
Sept. 23	Saale
Sept. 25	Crefeld
Sept. 26	Aller
Sept. 30	Trave
Oct. 1	Weimar
Oct. 3	Lahn
Oct. 8	Fulda
Oct. 9	Habsburg
Oct. 10	Spree
Oct. 15	Ems
Oct. 17	Havel
Oct. 18	Braunschweig
Oct. 24	Aller
Oct. 24	Munchen
Oct. 29	Dresden
Oct. 29	Trave
Nov. 5	Fulda
Nov. 6	Crefeld
Nov. 7	Spree
Nov. 14	Havel
Nov. 15	H. H. Meier
Nov. 23	Ems
Nov. 25	Weimar
Nov. 29	Munchen
Nov. 30	Kaiser Wilhelm II
Dec. 5	Stuttgart
Dec. 5	Spree
Dec. 13	Aller
Dec. 14	Dresden
Dec. 19	Havel
Dec. 24	Braunschweig
Dec. 28	Saale
Dec. 30	H. H. Meier

NORTH GERMAN LLOYD
Mediterranean—New York

N. Y.

Arrival	Steamer
Jan. 24	K. Frederick Wilhelm
Feb. 21	Kaiser Wilhelm II
Feb. 25	Neckar
Mar. 7	Werra
Mar. 27	Kaiser Wilhelm II
Apr. 1	K. Frederick Wilhelm
Apr. 10	Neckar

Year 1895

NORTH GERMAN LLOYD
Mediterranean—New York
(Continued)

N.Y. Arrival	Steamer
Apr. 24	Fulda
May 16	Werra
May 24	K. Frederick Wilhelm
June 1	Kaiser Wilhelm II
June 18	Werra
June 26	Ems
July 22	Werra
Aug. 20	Kaiser Wilhelm II
Sept. 24	Kaiser Wilhelm II
Oct. 7	Werra
Nov. 14	Werra
Nov. 30	Saale
Dec. 19	Fulda

RED STAR LINE
Antwerp—New York

N.Y. Arrival	Steamer
Jan. 2	Westernland
Jan. 9	Noordland
Jan. 17	Waesland
Jan. 24	Belgenland
Feb. 11	Rhynland
Feb. 12	Westernland
Feb. 20	Noordland
Feb. 27	Waesland
Mar. 6	Belgenland
Mar. 15	Rhynland
Mar. 21	Westernland
Apr. 5	Waesland
Apr. 11	Friesland
Apr. 18	Rhynland
Apr. 23	Westernland
May 9	Waesland
May 14	Friesland
May 23	Rhynland
May 29	Westernland
June 6	Noordland
June 12	Waesland
June 18	Friesland
June 26	Rhynland
July 2	Westernland
July 12	Noordland
July 24	Waesland
July 30	Friesland
Aug. 8	Rhynland
Aug. 21	Noordland
Aug. 29	Waesland
Sept. 3	Friesland
Sept. 18	Westernland
Sept. 24	Noordland
Oct. 8	Friesland
Oct. 23	Westernland
Oct. 30	Noordland
Nov. 12	Friesland
Nov. 27	Westernland
Dec. 3	Noordland
Dec. 18	Friesland

SCANDINAVIAN-AMERICAN LINE
Scandinavian Ports—New York

N.Y. Arrival	Steamer
Jan. 2	Island

SCANDINAVIAN-AMERICAN LINE
Scandinavian Ports—New York
(Continued)

N.Y. Arrival	Steamer
Feb. 23	Island
Apr. 6	Hekla
Apr. 20	Island
May 6	Norge
May 17	Thingvalla
May 31	Hekla
June 14	Island
June 27	Norge
July 15	Thingvalla
Aug. 10	Island
Aug. 21	Hekla
Sept. 7	Thingvalla
Oct. 5	Island
Oct. 17	Hekla
Nov. 1	Thingvalla
Nov. 15	Norge
Nov. 26	Island
Dec. 16	Hekla
Dec. 28	Thingvalla

SCANDINAVIAN-AMERICAN LINE
Mediterranean—New York

N.Y. Arrival	Steamer
Oct. 29	Norge

WHITE STAR LINE
Liverpool—New York

N.Y. Arrival	Steamer
Jan. 2	Runic
Jan. 5	Adriatic
Jan. 9	Teutonic
Jan. 9	Cevic
Jan. 19	Britannic
Jan. 23	Majestic
Jan. 29	Bovic
Feb. 4	Adriatic
Feb. 5	Runic
Feb. 11	Teutonic
Feb. 13	Cevic
Feb. 16	Britannic
Feb. 21	Majestic
Mar. 2	Adriatic
Mar. 4	Bovic
Mar. 7	Teutonic
Mar. 14	Runic
Mar. 16	Britannic
Mar. 21	Majestic
Mar. 21	Cevic
Apr. 1	Adriatic
Apr. 4	Teutonic
Apr. 4	Nomadic
Apr. 9	Bovic
Apr. 13	Britannic
Apr. 17	Majestic
Apr. 17	Runic
Apr. 22	Cevic
Apr. 27	Adriatic
May 1	Teutonic
May 7	Nomadic
May 11	Britannic

WHITE STAR LINE
Liverpool—New York
(Continued)

N.Y. Arrival	Steamer
May 13	Bovic
May 15	Majestic
May 20	Runic
May 24	Germanic
May 28	Cevic
May 30	Teutonic
June 8	Britannic
June 11	Nomadic
June 12	Majestic
June 17	Bovic
June 21	Germanic
June 25	Runic
June 29	Adriatic
July 1	Cevic
July 3	Teutonic
July 12	Britannic
July 16	Nomadic
July 17	Majestic
July 22	Bovic
July 25	Germanic
July 30	Runic
July 31	Teutonic
Aug. 5	Cevic
Aug. 9	Britannic
Aug. 14	Majestic
Aug. 20	Nomadic
Aug. 22	Germanic
Aug. 27	Georgic
Aug. 29	Teutonic
Sept. 3	Bovic
Sept. 6	Britannic
Sept. 11	Majestic
Sept. 11	Cevic
Sept. 19	Germanic
Sept. 24	Nomadic
Sept. 25	Teutonic
Sept. 30	Georgic
Oct. 4	Britannic
Oct. 7	Bovic
Oct. 10	Majestic
Oct. 16	Cevic
Oct. 18	Germanic
Oct. 23	Teutonic
Oct. 28	Nomadic
Nov. 1	Britannic
Nov. 4	Georgic
Nov. 7	Majestic
Nov. 11	Bovic
Nov. 18	Adriatic
Nov. 21	Cevic
Nov. 23	Germanic
Nov. 27	Teutonic
Dec. 2	Nomadic
Dec. 6	Britannic
Dec. 12	Majestic
Dec. 12	Georgic
Dec. 19	Bovic
Dec. 26	Teutonic
Dec. 26	Cevic

WILSON LINE
Hull, London—New York

N.Y. Arrival	Steamer
Jan. 14	Colorado

Year 1895

WILSON LINE
Hull, London—New York
(Continued)

N.Y.

Arrival	Steamer
Jan. 17	Lydian Monarch
Feb. 2	Alecto
Feb. 12	Francisco
Mar. 2	Colorado
Mar. 12	Ontario
Mar. 26	Alecto
Apr. 1	Francisco
Apr. 8	Galileo
Apr. 19	Colorado
Apr. 24	Ontario
May 20	Francisco
May 24	Galileo
June 3	Colorado
June 12	Martello
June 17	Buffalo
June 17	Ontario
June 25	Francisco
June 29	Hindoo
July 8	Galileo
July 18	Colorado
July 23	Martello
July 30	Ontario
Aug. 8	Francisco
Aug. 16	Hindoo
Aug. 19	Galileo
Aug. 31	Colorado
Sept. 9	Buffalo
Sept. 16	Ontario
Sept. 17	Martello
Sept. 27	Galileo
Oct. 3	Francisco
Oct. 5	Hindoo
Oct. 15	Colorado
Oct. 29	Ontario
Oct. 31	Martello
Nov. 11	Galileo
Nov. 16	Francisco
Nov. 29	Colorado
Nov. 29	Buffalo
Nov. 30	Hindoo
Dec. 12	Martello
Dec. 23	Ontario
Dec. 30	Galileo

ADDITIONAL ARRIVALS
Antwerp—New York

N.Y.

Arrival	Steamer
Jan. 17	Lepanto
May 13	Lepanto
June 25	Lepanto

ADDITIONAL ARRIVALS
Antwerp—New York
(Continued)

N.Y.

Arrival	Steamer
Aug. 21	Lepanto
Sept. 10	Berlin
Sept. 11	Southwark
Oct. 16	Southwark
Nov. 7	Kensington
Nov. 22	Southwark
Dec. 13	Kensington
Dec. 27	Southwark

Bordeaux—New York

N.Y.

Arrival	Steamer
Jan. 30	Chateau Lafite
May 22	Chateau Lafite
Aug. 14	Chateau Lafite
Sept. 23	Chateau Lafite
Dec. 30	Chateau Lafite

British Ports—New York

N.Y.

Arrival	Steamer
Jan. 7	Manhanset
Jan. 15	Chicago City
Jan. 29	Exeter City
Mar. 5	Manhanset
Mar. 8	Chicago City
Mar. 25	Exeter City
Apr. 15	Wells City
Apr. 19	Chicago City
Apr. 22	Manhanset
May 13	Exeter City
June 3	Wells City
June 4	Menantic
June 8	Chicago City
June 20	Manhanset
July 5	Exeter City
July 27	Wells City
Aug. 5	Chicago City
Aug. 16	Menantic
Aug. 29	Exeter City
Sept. 21	Chicago City
Oct. 4	Menantic
Oct. 14	Exeter City
Oct. 28	Wells City
Nov. 9	Chicago City
Nov. 29	Exeter City
Dec. 24	Chicago City

Hamburg—New York

N.Y.

Arrival	Steamer
Jan. 2	Westernland

ADDITIONAL ARRIVALS
London—New York

N.Y.

Arrival	Steamer
Jan. 15	Mohawk
Jan. 23	Mobile
Feb. 20	Mohawk
Feb. 26	Mobile
Mar. 26	Mohawk
Apr. 4	Mobile
Apr. 10	Richmond Hill
Apr. 30	Mohawk
May 7	Mobile
May 15	Muriel
May 29	Richmond Hill
June 4	Mohawk
June 11	Mobile
July 9	Mohawk
July 16	Mobile
Aug. 13	Mohawk
Aug. 19	Mobile
Sept. 17	Mohawk
Sept. 24	Mobile
Sept. 27	Richmond Hill
Oct. 22	Mohawk
Oct. 23	Ludgate Hill
Oct. 29	Mobile
Nov. 13	Richmond Hill
Nov. 27	Mohawk
Dec. 2	Mobile
Dec. 9	Ludgate Hill
Dec. 31	Mohawk
Dec. 31	Richmond Hill

Mediterranean—New York

N.Y.

Arrival	Steamer
Feb. 20	Bannwall
Apr. 9	La Touraine

Rotterdam, Amsterdam—
New York

N.Y.

Arrival	Steamer
Jan. 22	Prins Maurits
Feb. 13	Prins Willem I
Mar. 27	Prins Willem IV
June 15	Prins Willem I
Sept. 9	P. Frederick Hendrick

Spanish Ports—New York

N.Y.

Arrival	Steamer
Aug. 19	M. L. Villaverdo

Year 1896

ALLAN STATE LINE
Glasgow—New York

N. Y.

Arrival	Steamer
Jan. 11	Norwegian
Jan. 25	Carthaginian
Feb. 10	Pomeranian
Feb. 27	Norwegian
Mar. 6	Carthaginian
Mar. 23	Pomeranian
Apr. 2	Norwegian
Apr. 30	Hibernian
May 12	State of California
May 19	Norwegian
May 26	State of Nebraska
June 9	State of California
June 16	Norwegian
June 24	State of Nebraska
July 7	State of California
July 22	State of Nebraska
Aug. 4	State of California
Aug. 19	State of Nebraska
Aug. 31	State of California
Sept. 15	State of Nebraska
Sept. 29	State of California
Oct. 14	State of Nebraska
Oct. 29	Siberian
Nov. 2	State of California
Nov. 4	Norwegian
Nov. 19	State of Nebraska
Nov. 30	Pomeranian
Dec. 3	Siberian
Dec. 10	Norwegian
Dec. 10	State of California
Dec. 26	State of Nebraska

AMERICAN LINE
Southampton—New York

N. Y.

Arrival	Steamer
Jan. 11	Paris
Jan. 18	Saint Louis
Feb. 3	Paris
Feb. 4	Saint Paul
Feb. 10	New York
Feb. 17	Saint Louis
Feb. 24	Paris
Mar. 2	New York
Mar. 7	Saint Louis
Mar. 16	Saint Paul
Mar. 21	New York
Mar. 30	Saint Louis
Apr. 6	Saint Paul
Apr. 11	New York
Apr. 18	Paris
Apr. 25	Saint Paul
May 2	New York
May 9	Paris
May 16	Saint Paul
May 23	New York
May 28	Berlin
May 30	Paris
June 6	Saint Paul
June 13	New York
June 20	Saint Louis
June 27	Saint Paul

AMERICAN LINE
Southampton—New York
(Continued)

N. Y.

Arrival	Steamer
July 1	Paris
July 6	New York
July 11	Saint Louis
July 18	Saint Paul
July 25	New York
Aug. 1	Paris
Aug. 7	Saint Louis
Aug. 14	Saint Paul
Aug. 22	Paris
Aug. 25	New York
Aug. 28	Saint Louis
Aug. 29	Ohio
Sept. 4	Saint Paul
Sept. 12	Paris
Sept. 15	New York
Sept. 19	Saint Louis
Sept. 26	Saint Paul
Oct. 3	Paris
Oct. 6	New York
Oct. 10	Saint Louis
Oct. 17	Saint Paul
Oct. 27	Berlin
Oct. 31	Saint Louis
Nov. 7	Saint Paul
Nov. 17	New York
Nov. 21	Saint Louis
Nov. 28	Saint Paul
Dec. 7	New York
Dec. 14	Saint Louis
Dec. 21	Paris
Dec. 26	New York

ANCHOR LINE
Glasgow—New York

N. Y.

Arrival	Steamer
Jan. 2	Ethiopia
Jan. 15	Furnessia
Jan. 29	Anchoria
Feb. 14	Ethiopia
Feb. 27	Furnessia
Mar. 13	Anchoria
Mar. 26	Ethiopia
Apr. 7	Furnessia
Apr. 23	Anchoria
Apr. 29	Ethiopia
May 6	Circassia
May 11	Furnessia
May 21	Anchoria
May 28	Ethiopia
June 1	City of Rome
June 15	Furnessia
June 23	Anchoria
June 29	City of Rome
July 7	Ethiopia
July 15	Furnessia
July 22	Circassia
Aug. 3	Anchoria
Aug. 10	Ethiopia
Aug. 17	Furnessia

ANCHOR LINE
Glasgow—New York
(Continued)

N. Y.

Arrival	Steamer
Aug. 25	Circassia
Aug. 31	City of Rome
Sept. 8	Anchoria
Sept. 14	Ethiopia
Sept. 21	Furnessia
Sept. 29	Circassia
Oct. 5	City of Rome
Oct. 13	Anchoria
Oct. 20	Ethiopia
Oct. 26	Furnessia
Nov. 9	Circassia
Nov. 19	Anchoria
Nov. 27	Ethiopia
Nov. 30	Furnessia
Dec. 17	Circassia
Dec. 23	Anchoria
Dec. 30	Ethiopia

ANCHOR LINE
Mediterranean—New York

N. Y.

Arrival	Steamer
Jan. 6	Italia
Jan. 13	Victoria
Jan. 24	Olympia
Feb. 7	Elysia
Feb. 22	Scotia
Mar. 9	Alsatia
Mar. 19	Italia
Mar. 28	California
Apr. 6	Caledonia
Apr. 13	Bolivia
Apr. 22	Elysia
Apr. 24	Victoria
Apr. 30	Belgravia
May 4	Hesperia
May 11	Alsatia
May 18	Olympia
May 20	Scindia
May 28	Dalmatia
June 3	Italia
June 8	Algeria
June 20	Caledonia
July 2	Elysia
July 8	Victoria
July 11	California
July 25	Olympia
Aug. 1	Karamania
Aug. 15	Algeria
Aug. 24	Bolivia
Sept. 14	Italia
Oct. 1	Alsatia
Oct. 5	Elysia
Oct. 22	Karamania
Oct. 26	Olympia
Nov. 5	Victoria
Nov. 11	Elysia
Nov. 23	Italia
Dec. 7	Britannia
Dec. 7	California
Dec. 26	Alsatia

Year 1896

ATLANTIC TRANSPORT LINE
London—New York
N. Y.

Arrival	Steamer
Jan. 9	Mobile
Jan. 14	Massachusetts
Jan. 21	Manitoba
Jan. 29	Mississippi
Feb. 6	Mohawk
Feb. 14	Mobile
Feb. 19	Massachusetts
Feb. 27	Manitoba
Mar. 5	Mississippi
Mar. 13	Mohawk
Mar. 18	Mobile
Mar. 25	Massachusetts
Apr. 1	Manitoba
Apr. 6	Michigan
Apr. 8	Mississippi
Apr. 15	Mohawk
Apr. 21	Mobile
Apr. 28	Massachusetts
May 4	Manitoba
May 11	Mississippi
May 15	Michigan
May 19	Mohawk
May 26	Mobile
June 2	Massachusetts
June 9	Manitoba
June 17	Mississippi
June 23	Mohawk
June 25	Michigan
June 30	Mobile
July 7	Massachusetts
July 14	Manitoba
July 22	Mississippi
July 28	Mohawk
Aug. 5	Mobile
Aug. 10	Michigan
Aug. 17	Manitoba
Aug. 25	Mississippi
Sept. 1	Mohawk
Sept. 7	Mobile
Sept. 16	Massachusetts
Sept. 21	Michigan
Sept. 25	Manitoba
Sept. 30	Mississippi
Oct. 6	Mohawk
Oct. 14	Mobile
Oct. 20	Massachusetts
Oct. 28	Manitoba
Oct. 30	Michigan
Nov. 4	Mississippi
Nov. 9	Mohawk
Nov. 17	Mobile
Nov. 27	Massachusetts
Dec. 1	Manitoba
Dec. 3	Michigan
Dec. 10	Mississippi
Dec. 17	Mohawk
Dec. 23	Mobile
Dec. 29	Massachusetts

COMPANIA TRANSATLANTICA LINE
(Spanish Line)
Spanish Ports—New York
N. Y.

Arrival	Steamer
Jan. 7	Habana

COMPANIA TRANSATLANTICA LINE
(Spanish Line)
Spanish Ports—New York
(Continued)
N. Y.

Arrival	Steamer
Jan. 15	Ciudad Condal
Jan. 25	Habana
Feb. 4	Panama
Feb. 15	Ciudad Condal
Feb. 25	Panama
Mar. 7	Habana
Mar. 16	Ciudad Condal
Mar. 27	Habana
Apr. 3	Panama
Apr. 15	Ciudad Condal
Apr. 17	Mexico
Apr. 25	Panama
May 5	Habana
May 14	Mexico
May 25	Habana
June 4	Panama
June 15	Ciudad Condal
June 25	Panama
July 6	Habana
July 14	Ciudad Condal
July 25	Habana
Aug. 3	Panama
Aug. 14	Ciudad Condal
Aug. 24	Panama
Sept. 4	Habana
Sept. 15	Ciudad Condal
Sept. 25	Habana
Oct. 5	San Augustin
Oct. 16	Ciudad Condal
Oct. 26	Mexico
Nov. 4	Habana
Nov. 16	Ciudad Condal
Nov. 25	Habana
Dec. 5	Mexico
Dec. 15	Ciudad Condal
Dec. 26	Panama

CUNARD LINE
Liverpool—New York
N. Y.

Arrival	Steamer
Jan. 20	Servia
Jan. 27	Campania
Feb. 3	Umbria
Feb. 8	Aurania
Feb. 17	Etruria
Feb. 24	Campania
Mar. 2	Umbria
Mar. 16	Etruria
Mar. 21	Campania
Mar. 30	Umbria
Apr. 4	Lucania
Apr. 13	Etruria
Apr. 18	Campania
Apr. 27	Umbria
May 2	Lucania
May 11	Etruria
May 16	Campania
May 25	Umbria
May 30	Lucania
June 4	Aurania
June 8	Etruria
June 13	Campania

CUNARD LINE
Liverpool—New York
(Continued)
N. Y.

Arrival	Steamer
June 22	Umbria
June 27	Lucania
July 2	Aurania
July 6	Etruria
July 11	Campania
July 20	Umbria
July 25	Lucania
Aug. 1	Etruria
Aug. 8	Campania
Aug. 15	Umbria
Aug. 22	Lucania
Aug. 26	Aurania
Aug. 29	Etruria
Sept. 5	Campania
Sept. 9	Servia
Sept. 12	Umbria
Sept. 19	Lucania
Sept. 28	Etruria
Oct. 3	Campania
Oct. 12	Umbria
Oct. 17	Lucania
Oct. 26	Etruria
Oct. 31	Campania
Nov. 7	Umbria
Nov. 14	Lucania
Nov. 23	Etruria
Nov. 28	Campania
Dec. 7	Umbria
Dec. 14	Lucania
Dec. 21	Etruria
Dec. 26	Campania

FABRE LINE
Mediterranean—New York
N. Y.

Arrival	Steamer
Jan. 11	Burgundia
Feb. 7	Massilia
Feb. 20	Britannia
Feb. 27	Nuestria
Mar. 9	Patria
Mar. 30	Massilia
Apr. 13	Alesia
Apr. 18	Britannia
May 25	Massilia
June 8	Alesia
June 22	Nuestria
July 21	Massilia
Aug. 3	Alesia
Aug. 17	Nuestria
Sept. 1	Patria
Oct. 10	Nuestria
Oct. 27	Patria
Nov. 13	Burgundia
Nov. 24	Massilia
Dec. 23	Patria

FRENCH LINE
(Compagnie Generale Transatlantique)
Havre—New York
N. Y.

Arrival	Steamer
Jan. 6	La Gascogne
Jan. 20	La Bretagne
Jan. 27	La Bourgoyne

Year 1896

FRENCH LINE
(Compagnie Generale Transatlantique)
Havre—New York

N.Y. Arrival	Steamer
Feb. 3	La Touraine
Feb. 10	La Gascogne
Feb. 17	La Normandie
Feb. 24	La Bourgoyne
Mar. 2	La Bretagne
Mar. 9	La Gascogne
Mar. 16	La Touraine
Mar. 23	La Normandie
Mar. 30	La Bretagne
Apr. 6	La Bourgoyne
Apr. 13	La Touraine
Apr. 20	La Gascogne
Apr. 27	La Bretagne
May 4	La Bourgoyne
May 11	La Touraine
May 18	La Normandie
May 25	La Bretagne
June 1	La Bourgoyne
June 8	La Touraine
June 15	La Gascogne
June 22	La Bretagne
June 29	La Bourgoyne
July 6	La Touraine
July 13	La Normandie
July 20	La Gascogne
July 27	La Bretagne
Aug. 3	La Bourgoyne
Aug. 10	La Normandie
Aug. 17	La Gascogne
Aug. 24	La Bretagne
Aug. 31	La Bourgoyne
Sept. 7	La Normandie
Sept. 12	La Touraine
Sept. 21	La Gascogne
Sept. 28	La Bretagne
Oct. 5	La Bourgoyne
Oct. 10	Ville De Brest
Oct. 10	La Touraine
Oct. 19	La Gascogne
Oct. 26	La Bretagne
Nov. 2	La Bourgoyne
Nov. 9	La Champagne
Nov. 14	La Touraine
Nov. 23	La Gascogne
Nov. 30	La Bretagne
Dec. 7	La Champagne
Dec. 14	La Bourgoyne
Dec. 21	La Gascogne
Dec. 28	La Bretagne

HAMBURG-AMERICAN LINE
Hamburg—New York

N.Y. Arrival	Steamer
Jan. 6	Phoenicia
Jan. 6	Sicilia
Jan. 13	Persia
Jan. 23	Furst Bismarck
Jan. 27	Marsala
Jan. 27	Palatia
Feb. 3	Scotia
Feb. 4	Moravia
Feb. 10	Patria

HAMBURG-AMERICAN LINE
Hamburg—New York
(Continued)

N.Y. Arrival	Steamer
Feb. 14	Albano
Mar. 3	Amalfi
Mar. 9	California
Mar. 9	Italia
Mar. 18	Taormina
Mar. 24	Moravia
Apr. 2	Scotia
Apr. 8	Prussia
Apr. 11	Phoenicia
Apr. 13	Albano
Apr. 17	Persia
Apr. 18	Augusta Victoria
Apr. 18	Georgia
Apr. 27	Palatia
May 1	Columbia
May 1	Scandia
May 2	Amalfi
May 8	Patria
May 9	Normannia
May 11	Sorrento
May 15	California
May 16	Augusta Victoria
May 18	Prussia
May 18	Taormina
May 22	Furst Bismarck
May 25	Marsala
May 25	Phoenicia
May 29	Columbia
May 29	Persia
June 5	Bohemia
June 5	Normannia
June 5	Scandia
June 10	Albano
June 13	Palatia
June 15	Augusta Victoria
June 19	Furst Bismarck
June 19	Patria
June 20	Hispania
June 26	Columbia
June 27	Prussia
June 29	Sorrento
July 6	California
July 6	Normannia
July 6	Phoenicia
July 11	Augusta Victoria
July 11	Persia
July 11	Taormina
July 17	Furst Bismarck
July 20	Scotia
July 20	Scandia
July 25	Palatia
July 25	Marsala
July 30	Patria
July 31	Normannia
Aug. 7	Albano
Aug. 7	Augusta Victoria
Aug. 8	Prussia
Aug. 14	Hispania
Aug. 14	Phoenicia
Aug. 14	Furst Bismarck
Aug. 21	Columbia
Aug. 21	Persia
Aug. 22	Sorrento
Aug. 27	Moravia

HAMBURG-AMERICAN LINE
Hamburg—New York
(Continued)

N.Y. Arrival	Steamer
Aug. 28	Normannia
Aug. 28	Scandia
Sept. 4	Augusta Victoria
Sept. 7	Palatia
Sept. 7	Russia
Sept. 11	Furst Bismarck
Sept. 11	Patria
Sept. 18	Columbia
Sept. 19	Prussia
Sept. 21	Italia
Sept. 21	Marsala
Sept. 26	Bohemia
Sept. 28	Phoenicia
Oct. 2	Persia
Oct. 3	Augusta Victoria
Oct. 9	Furst Bismarck
Oct. 9	Scandia
Oct. 16	Columbia
Oct. 16	Palatia
Oct. 17	Armenia
Oct. 19	Sorrento
Oct. 23	California
Oct. 23	Patria
Oct. 24	Normannia
Oct. 30	Prussia
Oct. 31	Augusta Victoria
Nov. 7	Furst Bismarck
Nov. 7	Phoenicia
Nov. 14	Marsala
Nov. 14	Persia
Nov. 21	Normannia
Nov. 21	Patria
Nov. 25	Bohemia
Nov. 30	Albano
Nov. 30	Armenia
Dec. 1	Palatia
Dec. 11	California
Dec. 26	Asturia
Dec. 28	Prussia

HAMBURG-AMERICAN LINE
Mediterranean—New York

N.Y. Arrival	Steamer
Jan. 24	Columbia
Jan. 24	Italia
Feb. 14	Normannia
Mar. 24	Normannia
Apr. 6	Furst Bismarck
May 7	Italia
Nov. 24	Columbia
Dec. 23	Columbia

HAMBURG-AMERICAN LINE
Scandinavian Ports—New York

N.Y. Arrival	Steamer
Jan. 7	Venetia
Mar. 2	Venetia
Mar. 31	Venetia
Apr. 30	Virginian

Year 1896

HAMBURG-AMERICAN LINE
Scandinavian Ports—New York
(Continued)

N.Y. Arrival	Steamer
May 16	Venetia
June 6	Georgia
June 17	Virginia
July 2	Venetia
July 28	Georgia
Aug. 7	Virginia
Sept. 15	Georgia
Sept. 29	Virginia
Oct. 13	Venetia
Nov. 5	Georgia
Nov. 16	Virginia
Dec. 3	Venetia

HOLLAND-AMERICA LINE
Rotterdam, Amsterdam, Boulogne—New York

N.Y. Arrival	Steamer
Jan. 2	Schiedam
Jan. 13	Zaandam
Jan. 18	Rotterdam
Jan. 21	Werkendam
Jan. 23	Veendam
Jan. 27	Spaarndam
Feb. 5	Amsterdam
Feb. 10	Maasdam
Feb. 21	Edam
Feb. 24	Schiedam
Feb. 27	Rotterdam
Feb. 27	Werkendam
Mar. 10	Amsterdam
Mar. 16	Veendam
Mar. 19	Zaandam
Mar. 23	Maasdam
Apr. 2	Rotterdam
Apr. 2	Edam
Apr. 7	Spaarndam
Apr. 9	Schiedam
Apr. 14	Amsterdam
Apr. 20	Veendam
Apr. 27	Zaandam
Apr. 27	Maasdam
May 4	Werkendam
May 11	Spaarndam
May 11	Rotterdam
May 18	Amsterdam
May 25	Veendam
May 27	Schiedam
June 5	Zaandam
June 8	Maasdam
June 12	Werkendam
June 15	Spaarndam
June 23	Amsterdam
June 29	Edam
June 29	Veendam
July 6	Obdam
July 13	Maasdam
July 22	Rotterdam
July 24	Werkendam
July 27	Amsterdam
Aug. 3	Veendam
Aug. 5	Edam

HOLLAND-AMERICA LINE
Rotterdam, Amsterdam, Boulogne—New York
(Continued)

N.Y. Arrival	Steamer
Aug. 10	Obdam
Aug. 15	Maasdam
Aug. 17	Zaandam
Aug. 24	Spaarndam
Aug. 31	Amsterdam
Aug. 31	Schiedam
Sept. 3	Werkendam
Sept. 7	Veendam
Sept. 8	Rotterdam
Sept. 11	Edam
Sept. 14	Obdam
Sept. 21	Maasdam
Sept. 28	Spaarndam
Oct. 3	Zaandam
Oct. 7	Amsterdam
Oct. 10	Veendam
Oct. 13	Schiedam
Oct. 13	Rotterdam
Oct. 16	Werkendam
Oct. 19	Obdam
Oct. 24	Maasdam
Oct. 26	Edam
Nov. 2	Spaarndam
Nov. 9	Veendam
Nov. 16	Zaandam
Nov. 18	Rotterdam
Nov. 20	Werkendam
Nov. 24	Obdam
Dec. 3	Schiedam
Dec. 7	Maasdam
Dec. 9	Edam
Dec. 15	Spaarndam
Dec. 26	Werkendam
Dec. 28	Veendam
Dec. 28	Rotterdam
Dec. 30	Zaandam

INSULAR NAVIGATION COMPANY
Azores, Lisbon—New Bedford, Mass., New York

N.Y. Arrival	Steamer
Mar. 16	Peninsular
May 5	Peninsular
June 22	Peninsular
Aug. 10	Peninsular
Sept. 28	Peninsular
Nov. 20	Peninsular
Nov. 28	Vega

LINHA DE VAPORES PORTUGUEZES
Azores, Lisbon—New Bedford, Mass., New York

N.Y. Arrival	Steamer
Jan. 30	Oevenum
Mar. 30	Dona Maria
Mar. 30	Oevenum
May 25	Oevenum
July 14	Oevenum
Aug. 21	Dona Maria

LINHA DE VAPORES PORTUGUEZES
Azores, Lisbon—New Bedford, Mass., New York
(Continued)

N.Y. Arrival	Steamer
Oct. 14	Oevenum
Oct. 19	Dona Amelia
Nov. 25	Dona Maria

NATIONAL NAVIGATION COMPANY
Mediterranean—New York

N.Y. Arrival	Steamer
Mar. 23	Hindoustan
May 9	Chamdernager

NORTH GERMAN LLOYD
Bremen—New York

N.Y. Arrival	Steamer
Jan. 6	Bonn
Jan. 10	Weimar
Jan. 16	Aller
Jan. 18	Stuttgart
Jan. 28	Aachen
Feb. 3	Willehad
Feb. 6	Spree
Feb. 12	Braunschweig
Feb. 15	Aller
Feb. 20	Munchen
Feb. 21	Havel
Feb. 24	Weimar
Mar. 2	Halle
Mar. 3	Dresden
Mar. 6	Spree
Mar. 7	Stuttgart
Mar. 13	Saale
Mar. 17	Aachen
Mar. 19	Havel
Mar. 21	H. H. Meier
Mar. 27	Aller
Mar. 31	Bonn
Apr. 2	Spree
Apr. 9	Lahn
Apr. 10	Halle
Apr. 14	Saale
Apr. 16	Havel
Apr. 16	Stuttgart
Apr. 27	Aller
Apr. 27	Aachen
Apr. 29	H. H. Meier
May 1	Spree
May 7	Lahn
May 11	Bonn
May 12	Saale
May 13	Dresden
May 14	Havel
May 21	Trave
May 22	Halle
May 25	Aller
May 27	Stuttgart
May 28	Spree
June 4	Aachen
June 4	Lahn
June 8	Saale
June 10	H. H. Meier
June 11	Havel

Year 1896

NORTH GERMAN LLOYD
Bremen—New York
(Continued)

N. Y.

Arrival	Steamer
June 19	Bonn
June 23	Aller
June 25	Dresden
July 2	Lahn
July 3	Munchen
July 6	Saale
July 9	Havel
July 9	Halle
July 17	Weimar
July 20	Aller
July 22	H. H. Meier
July 23	Spree
July 30	Karlsruhe
July 30	Lahn
Aug. 4	Saale
Aug. 6	Bonn
Aug. 6	Havel
Aug. 12	Munchen
Aug. 17	Aller
Aug. 18	Weimar
Aug. 20	Spree
Aug. 26	Lahn
Aug. 27	H. H. Meier
Sept. 3	Aachen
Sept. 3	Havel
Sept. 9	Karlsruhe
Sept. 16	Munchen
Sept. 17	Spree
Sept. 24	Lahn
Sept. 25	Weimar
Sept. 29	Saale
Oct. 1	Havel
Oct. 2	Bonn
Oct. 8	H. H. Meier
Oct. 8	Trave
Oct. 13	Aller
Oct. 15	Spree
Oct. 22	Karlsruhe
Oct. 22	Lahn
Oct. 29	Havel
Oct. 29	Willehad
Nov. 5	Munchen
Nov. 5	Trave
Nov. 11	Weimar
Nov. 12	Aller
Nov. 19	Lahn
Nov. 20	H. H. Meier
Nov. 27	Havel
Nov. 28	Stuttgart
Dec. 4	Dresden
Dec. 11	Spree
Dec. 14	Karlsruhe
Dec. 17	Lahn
Dec. 21	Willehad
Dec. 22	Havel
Dec. 26	H. H. Meier

NORTH GERMAN LLOYD
Mediterranean—New York
N. Y.

Arrival	Steamer
Jan. 16	Kaiser Wilhelm II
Feb. 2	Ems
Feb. 5	Fulda
Feb. 20	Werra

NORTH GERMAN LLOYD
Mediterranean—New York
(Continued)

N. Y.

Arrival	Steamer
Mar. 5	Kaiser Wilhelm II
Mar. 14	Fulda
Apr. 7	Kaiser Wilhelm II
Apr. 15	Werra
Apr. 22	Fulda
May 11	Kaiser Wilhelm II
May 20	Werra
June 3	Ems
June 16	Kaiser Wilhelm II
June 17	Braunschweig
June 24	Werra
June 29	Fulda
July 8	Ems
Aug. 5	Werra
Aug. 18	Fulda
Aug. 26	Ems
Sept. 8	Kaiser Wilhelm II
Sept. 16	Werra
Sept. 22	Fulda
Sept. 30	Ems
Oct. 13	Kaiser Wilhelm II
Oct. 29	Werra
Nov. 3	Fulda
Nov. 18	Kaiser Wilhelm II
Dec. 10	Fulda
Dec. 19	Ems
Dec. 29	Kaiser Wilhelm II

PRINCE LINE
Mediterranean—New York
N. Y.

Arrival	Steamer
Mar. 16	Asiatic Prince
Oct. 14	Eastern Prince

RED STAR LINE
Antwerp—New York
N. Y.

Arrival	Steamer
Jan. 8	Westernland
Jan. 16	Kensington
Jan. 23	Noordland
Jan. 28	Friesland
Feb. 14	Westernland
Feb. 21	Southwark
Feb. 27	Noordland
Mar. 3	Friesland
Mar. 12	Kensington
Mar. 18	Westernland
Mar. 27	Southwark
Apr. 2	Noordland
Apr. 8	Friesland
Apr. 22	Westernland
Apr. 29	Southwark
May 6	Noordland
May 12	Friesland
May 19	Kensington
May 27	Westernland
June 2	Southwark
June 10	Noordland
June 16	Friesland
June 23	Kensington
June 30	Westernland
July 8	Southwark
July 14	Berlin

RED STAR LINE
Antwerp—New York
(Continued)

N. Y.

Arrival	Steamer
July 22	Noordland
July 28	Friesland
Aug. 4	Kensington
Aug. 12	Westernland
Aug. 19	Southwark
Aug. 26	Noordland
Sept. 1	Friesland
Sept. 8	Kensington
Sept. 15	Westernland
Sept. 23	Southwark
Sept. 30	Noordland
Oct. 6	Friesland
Oct. 13	Kensington
Oct. 20	Westernland
Oct. 28	Southwark
Nov. 4	Noordland
Nov. 9	Friesland
Nov. 18	Kensington
Nov. 25	Westernland
Dec. 10	Noordland
Dec. 17	Friesland
Dec. 23	Kensington
Dec. 31	Westernland

SCANDINAVIAN-AMERICAN LINE
Scandinavian Ports—New York
N. Y.

Arrival	Steamer
Jan. 13	Norge
Jan. 27	Island
Feb. 10	Hekla
Feb. 26	Thingvalla
Mar. 9	Norge
Mar. 23	Island
Apr. 4	Hekla
Apr. 20	Thingvalla
May 4	Norge
May 15	Island
May 30	Hekla
June 13	Thingvalla
June 27	Norge
July 13	Island
July 30	Hekla
Aug. 7	Thingvalla
Aug. 20	Norge
Sept. 5	Island
Sept. 16	Hekla
Oct. 3	Thingvalla
Oct. 16	Norge
Oct. 31	Island
Nov. 11	Hekla
Dec. 7	Thingvalla
Dec. 31	Island

WHITE STAR LINE
Liverpool—New York
N. Y.

Arrival	Steamer
Jan. 3	Britannic
Jan. 9	Majestic
Jan. 16	Germanic
Jan. 23	Teutonic
Feb. 5	Tauric

Year 1896

WHITE STAR LINE Liverpool—New York		WHITE STAR LINE Liverpool—New York (Continued)		WILSON LINE Hull, London—New York (Continued)	
N. Y. Arrival	**Steamer**	**N. Y. Arrival**	**Steamer**	**N. Y. Arrival**	**Steamer**
Feb. 6	Majestic	Oct. 13	Cevic	Oct. 19	Francisco
Feb. 13	Nomadic	Oct. 14	Majestic	Oct. 26	Ontario
Feb. 15	Germanic	Oct. 19	Nomadic	Nov. 2	Martello
Feb. 20	Teutonic	Oct. 22	Germanic	Nov. 4	Colorado
Feb. 28	Britannic	Oct. 27	Georgic	Nov. 6	Buffalo
Mar. 5	Majestic	Oct. 28	Teutonic	Nov. 11	Idaho
Mar. 11	Tauric	Nov. 2	Bovic	Nov. 30	Francisco
Mar. 13	Germanic	Nov. 6	Britannic	Dec. 9	Ontario
Mar. 17	Nomadic	Nov. 9	Tauric	Dec. 17	Martello
Mar. 19	Teutonic	Nov. 12	Majestic	Dec. 21	Colorado
Mar. 27	Georgic	Nov. 16	Cevic	Dec. 28	Hindoo
Mar. 28	Britannic	Nov. 20	Germanic		
Mar. 31	Bovic	Nov. 25	Nomadic	**ADDITIONAL ARRIVALS** Bourdeaux—New York	
Apr. 2	Majestic	Nov. 27	Teutonic	**N. Y.**	
Apr. 8	Cufic	Dec. 1	Georgic	**Arrival**	**Steamer**
Apr. 10	Germanic	Dec. 4	Britannic	May 18	Chateau Lafite
Apr. 13	Tauric	Dec. 8	Bovic	July 3	Chateau Lafite
Apr. 16	Teutonic	Dec. 10	Majestic	Oct. 8	Chateau Lafite
Apr. 24	Britannic	Dec. 17	Tauric	Nov. 24	Chateau Lafite
Apr. 28	Nomadic	Dec. 18	Germanic		
Apr. 29	Majestic	Dec. 24	Teutonic	British Ports—New York	
May 5	Georgic	Dec. 29	Nomadic	**N. Y.**	
May 8	Germanic			**Arrival**	**Steamer**
May 11	Bovic	**WILSON LINE** Hull, London—New York		Jan. 8	Kansas City
May 13	Teutonic	**N. Y.**		Jan. 14	Llandaff City
May 19	Cufic	**Arrival**	**Steamer**	Jan. 17	Exeter City
May 22	Britannic	Jan. 2	Francisco	Feb. 18	Brooklyn City
May 27	Majestic	Jan. 15	Colorado	Feb. 18	Jersey City
June 1	Nomadic	Jan. 17	Buffalo	Feb. 24	Kansas City
June 4	Germanic	Jan. 25	Martello	Feb. 27	Critic
June 8	Georgic	Feb. 5	Ontario	Mar. 3	Llandaff City
June 10	Teutonic	Feb. 17	Francisco	Apr. 1	Wells City
June 15	Bovic	Feb. 27	Colorado	Apr. 10	Brooklyn City
June 19	Britannic	Mar. 5	Buffalo	Apr. 16	Jersey City
June 22	Tauric	Mar. 12	Martello	Apr. 20	Critic
June 22	Cufic	Mar. 25	Ontario	Apr. 25	Llandaff City
June 25	Majestic	Mar. 31	Francisco	May 15	Wells City
July 3	Germanic	Apr. 7	Galileo	May 24	Croft
July 6	Nomadic	Apr. 18	Buffalo	June 1	Jersey City
July 8	Teutonic	May 7	Martello	June 5	Critic
July 14	Georgic	May 8	Ontario	June 13	Exeter City
July 17	Britannic	May 8	Francisco	July 1	Exeter City
July 20	Bovic	May 18	Galileo	July 3	Brooklyn City
July 27	Tauric	May 26	Colorado	July 15	Croft
July 30	Germanic	June 4	Buffalo	July 16	Jersey City
Aug. 3	Cevic	June 10	Idaho	July 20	Howick Hall
Aug. 5	Teutonic	June 22	Martello	July 27	Critic
Aug. 10	Nomadic	June 22	Ontario	July 27	Llandaff City
Aug. 14	Britannic	June 26	Francisco	Aug. 3	Delaware
Aug. 17	Georgic	July 6	Colorado	Aug. 7	Wells City
Aug. 19	Majestic	July 14	Buffalo	Aug. 21	Brooklyn City
Aug. 24	Bovic	July 20	Idaho	Aug. 31	Croft
Aug. 27	Germanic	Aug. 3	Francisco	Sept. 3	Llandaff City
Aug. 31	Tauric	Aug. 3	Ontario	Sept. 12	Exeter City
Sept. 2	Teutonic	Aug. 12	Martello	Sept. 16	Critic
Sept. 8	Cevic	Aug. 17	Colorado	Oct. 5	Brooklyn City
Sept. 11	Britannic	Aug. 24	Buffalo	Oct. 9	Jersey City
Sept. 14	Nomadic	Aug. 31	Idaho	Oct. 9	Delaware
Sept. 16	Majestic	Sept. 8	Francisco	Oct. 13	Croft
Sept. 22	Georgic	Sept. 14	Ontario	Oct. 30	Kansas City
Sept. 25	Germanic	Sept. 23	Martello	Oct. 31	Critic
Sept. 28	Bovic	Sept. 25	Colorado	Nov. 4	Wells City
Oct. 1	Teutonic	Sept. 29	Buffalo	Nov. 6	Chicago City
Oct. 6	Tauric	Oct. 6	Idaho	Nov. 13	Brooklyn City
Oct. 9	Britannic				

Year 1896

ADDITIONAL ARRIVALS
British Ports—New York
(Continued)
N. Y.

Arrival	Steamer
Nov. 17	Jersey City
Nov. 20	Llandaff City
Dec. 2	Exeter City
Dec. 3	Croft
Dec. 8	Kansas City
Dec. 18	Chicago City
Dec. 18	Critic
Dec. 18	Wells City
Dec. 26	Jersey City

German Ports—New York
N. Y.

Arrival	Steamer
May 13	Harald

Hamburg—New York
N. Y.

Arrival	Steamer
Feb. 14	Mobile

ADDITIONAL ARRIVALS
Havre—New York
N. Y.

Arrival	Steamer
Oct. 23	Chateau Yquem

London—New York
N. Y.

Arrival	Steamer
Feb. 15	Ludgate Hill
Apr. 2	Ludgate Hill
Sept. 7	America
Oct. 5	Georgian
Oct. 5	Europe
Oct. 20	America
Oct. 21	Ludgate Hill
Nov. 2	Tower Hill
Nov. 12	Georgian
Nov. 30	America

ADDITIONAL ARRIVALS
Mediterranean—New York
N. Y.

Arrival	Steamer
Mar. 26	Chateau Yquem
May 12	Acacia
May 26	Chateau Yquem
June 1	Capac
June 27	Ardanmhor
Nov. 4	Clive
Nov. 6	Boyne
Dec. 2	Oregon
Dec. 14	Sarnia

Rotterdam—New York
N. Y.

Arrival	Steamer
Oct. 8	Massapequa

Year 1897

ALLAN STATE LINE
Glasgow—New York
N.Y.

Arrival	Steamer
Jan. 14	Siberian
Feb. 1	Corean
Feb. 23	Siberian
Mar. 18	Carthaginian
Apr. 29	Buenos Ayrean
May 26	Mongolian
May 31	City of Rome
June 23	Mongolian
July 20	Mongolian
Aug. 18	Mongolian
Sept. 5	City of Rome
Sept. 7	Roumanian
Sept. 15	Mongolian
Oct. 14	Mongolian
Nov. 15	Mongolian
Nov. 27	Corean
Dec. 27	Buenos Ayrean

AMERICAN LINE
Southampton—New York
N.Y.

Arrival	Steamer
Jan. 2	Saint Louis
Jan. 11	Paris
Jan. 16	New York
Jan. 23	Saint Louis
Feb. 1	Saint Paul
Feb. 8	New York
Mar. 1	New York
Mar. 8	Saint Louis
Mar. 15	Paris
Mar. 22	Saint Paul
Apr. 5	Paris
Apr. 12	Saint Paul
Apr. 19	New York
May 1	Saint Paul
May 8	Saint Louis
May 15	Paris
May 22	Saint Paul
May 29	Saint Louis
June 5	Paris
June 12	Saint Paul
June 19	Saint Louis
July 3	Saint Paul
July 10	Saint Louis
July 17	New York
July 24	Paris
July 31	Saint Paul
Aug. 7	Saint Louis
Aug. 14	Paris
Aug. 21	Saint Paul
Aug. 28	Saint Louis
Sept. 4	Paris
Sept. 7	New York
Sept. 11	Saint Paul
Sept. 18	Saint Louis
Sept. 25	Paris
Oct. 2	Saint Paul
Oct. 9	Saint Louis
Oct. 16	Paris
Oct. 23	Saint Paul
Oct. 30	Saint Louis
Nov. 6	Paris

AMERICAN LINE
Southampton—New York
(Continued)
N.Y.

Arrival	Steamer
Nov. 15	Saint Paul
Nov. 20	Saint Louis
Nov. 27	Paris
Dec. 4	Saint Paul
Dec. 13	Saint Louis
Dec. 19	Paris
Dec. 27	Saint Paul

ANCHOR LINE
Glasgow—New York
N.Y.

Arrival	Steamer
Jan. 5	Furnessia
Jan. 13	State of California
Jan. 29	Anchoria
Feb. 8	Furnessia
Feb. 15	State of California
Mar. 6	Ethiopia
Mar. 20	Circassia
Mar. 26	State of California
Mar. 30	Anchoria
Apr. 6	Furnessia
Apr. 15	Ethiopia
Apr. 28	Circassia
Apr. 29	Anchoria
May 11	Furnessia
May 19	Ethiopia
June 8	Anchoria
June 14	Furnessia
June 22	Ethiopia
July 5	State of Nebraska
July 7	Anchoria
July 20	Circassia
July 26	Ethiopia
Aug. 9	Anchoria
Aug. 16	Furnessia
Aug. 24	Circassia
Aug. 31	Ethiopia
Sept. 13	Anchoria
Sept. 20	Furnessia
Oct. 12	Ethiopia
Oct. 18	Anchoria
Oct. 19	Alexandria
Oct. 25	Furnessia
Nov. 13	Ethiopia
Nov. 23	Anchoria
Dec. 1	Furnessia
Dec. 16	Ethiopia
Dec. 31	Anchoria

ANCHOR LINE
Mediterranean—New York
N.Y.

Arrival	Steamer
Jan. 4	Olympia
Feb. 6	Italia
Feb. 26	Victoria
Mar. 1	Bolivia
Mar. 9	California
Mar. 22	Olympia
Apr. 5	Alsatia
Apr. 14	Scindia

ANCHOR LINE
Mediterranean—New York
(Continued)
N.Y.

Arrival	Steamer
Apr. 21	Karamania
Apr. 27	Hesperia
Apr. 28	Victoria
May 6	Italia
May 13	Bolivia
May 20	California
May 29	Scotia
June 4	Britannia
June 14	Alsatic
July 20	Hesperia
Aug. 10	Victoria
Aug. 26	Scotia
Sept. 13	Scindia
Sept. 28	Karamania
Oct. 15	Hesperia
Oct. 30	Victoria
Nov. 24	Bolivia
Dec. 17	Karamania

ATLANTIC TRANSPORT LINE
London—New York
N.Y.

Arrival	Steamer
Jan. 7	Manitoba
Jan. 8	Michigan
Jan. 14	Mississippi
Jan. 20	Mohawk
Jan. 29	Mobile
Feb. 2	Massachusetts
Feb. 10	Manitoba
Feb. 20	Mississippi
Feb. 26	Mohawk
Mar. 5	Mobile
Mar. 12	Massachusetts
Mar. 19	Manitoba
Mar. 26	Mississippi
Apr. 8	Mobile
Apr. 14	Massachusetts
Apr. 21	Manitoba
Apr. 28	Mississippi
May 4	Mohawk
May 12	Mobile
May 17	Massachusetts
May 24	Manitoba
June 2	Mississippi
June 8	Mohawk
June 15	Mobile
June 21	Massachusetts
June 29	Manitoba
July 10	Mississippi
July 13	Mohawk
July 15	Michigan
July 19	Mobile
July 27	Massachusetts
Aug. 3	Manitoba
Aug. 10	Mississippi
Aug. 17	Mohawk
Aug. 24	Mobile
Aug. 31	Massachusetts
Sept. 7	Manitoba
Sept. 15	Mississippi

Year 1897

ATLANTIC TRANSPORT LINE
London—New York
(Continued)
N.Y.

Arrival	Steamer
Sept. 23	Mohawk
Sept. 27	Mobile
Oct. 1	Michigan
Oct. 4	Massachusetts
Oct. 11	Manitoba
Oct. 19	Mississippi
Oct. 26	Mohawk
Nov. 1	Mobile
Nov. 8	Massachusetts
Nov. 8	Michigan
Nov. 17	Manitoba
Nov. 26	Mississippi
Nov. 30	Mohawk
Dec. 7	Mobile
Dec. 14	Michigan
Dec. 15	Massachusetts
Dec. 24	Manitoba
Dec. 30	Mississippi

COMPANIA TRANSATLANTICA LINE
(Spanish Line)
Spanish Ports, Havana, Cienfuegos—New York
N.Y.

Arrival	Steamer
Jan. 3	Habana
Jan. 14	Santo Domingo
Jan. 25	Habana
Feb. 4	Ciudad Condal
Feb. 15	Santo Domingo
Feb. 24	Ciudad Condal
Mar. 5	Panama
Mar. 15	Santo Domingo
Mar. 25	Habana
Apr. 5	Panama
Apr. 14	Santo Domingo
Apr. 28	Mexico
May 5	Habana
May 14	Santo Domingo
May 25	Habana
June 14	Santo Domingo
July 5	Habana
July 14	Santo Domingo
July 24	Habana
Aug. 14	Santo Domingo
Sept. 3	San Augustin
Sept. 14	Santo Domingo
Sept. 25	San Augustin
Nov. 3	San Augustin
Nov. 26	San Augustin
Dec. 14	Santo Domingo

CUNARD LINE
Liverpool—New York
N.Y.

Arrival	Steamer
Jan. 4	Aurania
Jan. 11	Lucania
Jan. 18	Servia
Jan. 23	Campania
Feb. 1	Umbria
Feb. 8	Aurania
Feb. 15	Servia

CUNARD LINE
Liverpool—New York
(Continued)
N.Y.

Arrival	Steamer
Feb. 22	Lucania
Mar. 1	Umbria
Mar. 11	Aurania
Mar. 15	Etruria
Mar. 22	Campania
Mar. 27	Umbria
Apr. 3	Lucania
Apr. 12	Etruria
Apr. 26	Umbria
Apr. 29	Servia
May 1	Lucania
May 10	Etruria
May 15	Campania
May 20	Aurania
May 24	Umbria
May 29	Lucania
June 7	Etruria
June 12	Campania
June 17	Aurania
June 21	Umbria
June 26	Lucania
June 30	Servia
July 3	Etruria
July 10	Campania
July 19	Aurania
July 24	Umbria
July 31	Lucania
Aug. 7	Etruria
Aug. 14	Campania
Aug. 19	Servia
Aug. 21	Umbria
Aug. 28	Lucania
Sept. 2	Aurania
Sept. 4	Etruria
Sept. 11	Campania
Sept. 16	Servia
Sept. 18	Umbria
Sept. 25	Lucania
Sept. 30	Aurania
Oct. 2	Etruria
Oct. 9	Campania
Oct. 16	Umbria
Oct. 25	Lucania
Oct. 30	Etruria
Nov. 6	Campania
Nov. 15	Umbria
Nov. 20	Lucania
Nov. 29	Etruria
Dec. 4	Campania
Dec. 13	Umbria
Dec. 20	Lucania
Dec. 27	Etruria

FABRE LINE
Mediterranean—New York
N.Y.

Arrival	Steamer
Jan. 7	Alesia
Jan. 23	Massilia
Feb. 24	Patria
Mar. 10	Alesia
Mar. 17	Massilia
Apr. 2	Burgundia
Apr. 15	Britannia
Apr. 17	Patria

FABRE LINE
Mediterranean—New York
(Continued)
N.Y.

Arrival	Steamer
May 10	Alesia
May 14	Massilia
May 27	Burgundia
June 7	Patria
July 19	Burgundia
July 30	Patria
Aug. 20	Nuestria
Aug. 30	Massilia
Sept. 20	Britannia
Sept. 30	Burgundia
Oct. 7	Patria
Oct. 18	Nuestria
Oct. 29	Massilia
Nov. 18	Britannia
Nov. 29	Patria
Dec. 16	Alesia
Dec. 30	Nuestria

FRENCH LINE
(Compagnie Generale Transatlantique)
Havre—New York
N.Y.

Arrival	Steamer
Jan. 2	Ville De St. Nazaire
Jan. 4	La Normandie
Jan. 11	La Champagne
Jan. 11	Ville De Brest
Jan. 18	La Bourgoyne
Jan. 25	La Gascogne
Feb. 1	La Bretagne
Feb. 8	La Normandie
Feb. 9	Ville De Broudeaux
Feb. 15	La Bourgoyne
Feb. 22	La Champagne
Mar. 1	La Gascogne
Mar. 9	La Bretagne
Mar. 15	La Normandie
Mar. 15	Ville De Brest
Mar. 22	La Champagne
Mar. 28	Ville De St. Nazaire
Mar. 29	La Touraine
Apr. 5	La Bretagne
Apr. 12	La Normandie
Apr. 19	La Champagne
Apr. 26	La Gascogne
May 3	La Touraine
May 5	Ville De Brest
May 10	La Bourgoyne
May 17	La Champagne
May 24	La Gascogne
May 31	La Touraine
June 7	La Bretagne
June 14	La Champagne
June 21	La Gascogne
June 26	Ville De Marseille
June 28	La Touraine
July 5	La Bretagne
July 12	La Normandie
July 19	La Gascogne
Aug. 2	La Champagne
Aug. 9	La Normandie
Aug. 16	La Bretagne
Aug. 23	La Gascogne
Aug. 30	La Champagne
Sept. 4	La Touraine

Year 1897

FRENCH LINE
(Compagnie Generale Transatlantique)
Havre—New York
(Continued)

N. Y.

Arrival	Steamer
Sept. 13	La Bretagne
Sept. 20	La Gascogne
Sept. 27	La Champagne
Oct. 2	La Touraine
Oct. 11	La Bretagne
Oct. 18	La Gascogne
Oct. 25	La Champagne
Oct. 30	La Touraine
Nov. 8	La Bretagne
Nov. 15	La Gascogne
Nov. 22	La Champagne
Nov. 29	La Touraine
Dec. 6	La Bretagne
Dec. 13	La Gascogne
Dec. 20	La Normandie
Dec. 27	La Champagne

HAMBURG-AMERICAN LINE
Hamburg—New York

N. Y.

Arrival	Steamer
Jan. 6	Phoenicia
Jan. 6	Sicilia
Jan. 12	Persia
Jan. 16	Taormina
Jan. 23	Andalusia
Feb. 1	Marsala
Feb. 2	Armenia
Feb. 9	Albano
Feb. 11	Palatia
Feb. 19	Patria
Feb. 23	Prussia
Mar. 1	Phoenicia
Mar. 1	Italia
Mar. 6	Sorrento
Mar. 9	Persia
Mar. 21	Andalusia
Mar. 25	Palatia
Mar. 27	Taormina
Apr. 5	Pennsylvania
Apr. 14	Patria
Apr. 16	Marsala
Apr. 19	Phoenicia
Apr. 20	Albano
Apr. 21	Bohemia
Apr. 23	Normannia
Apr. 24	Persia
May 4	Andalusia
May 7	Palatia
May 8	Columbia
May 10	Sorrento
May 20	Pennsylvania
May 22	Taormina
May 22	Furst Bismarck
May 29	Phoenicia
May 29	Normannia
June 1	Pisa
June 4	Patria
June 5	Columbia
June 11	Persia
June 12	Adria
June 18	Furst Bismarck

HAMBURG-AMERICAN LINE
Hamburg—New York
(Continued)

N. Y.

Arrival	Steamer
June 18	Marsala
June 21	Andalusia
June 25	Palatia
June 26	Normannia
July 1	Albano
July 3	Prussia
July 5	Columbia
July 9	Asturia
July 9	Pennsylvania
July 16	Patria
July 16	Furst Bismarck
July 17	Taormina
July 22	Phoenicia
July 23	Normannia
July 29	Persia
July 30	Columbia
July 30	Sorrento
Aug. 6	Andalusia
Aug. 7	Christiania
Aug. 9	Pisa
Aug. 11	Palatia
Aug. 13	Furst Bismarck
Aug. 19	Prussia
Aug. 23	California
Aug. 25	Normannia
Aug. 25	Pennsylvania
Aug. 28	Columbia
Aug. 30	Marsala
Sept. 1	Albano
Sept. 1	Patria
Sept. 4	Augusta Victoria
Sept. 9	Phoenicia
Sept. 11	Furst Bismarck
Sept. 16	Persia
Sept. 18	Normannia
Sept. 24	Andalusia
Sept. 24	Columbia
Oct. 1	Palatia
Oct. 4	California
Oct. 6	Pisa
Oct. 7	Prussia
Oct. 9	Furst Bismarck
Oct. 14	Pennsylvania
Oct. 15	Normannia
Oct. 15	Patria
Oct. 22	Phoenicia
Oct. 23	Columbia
Oct. 25	Marsala
Oct. 28	Persia
Oct. 29	Albano
Nov. 6	Andalusia
Nov. 6	Furst Bismarck
Nov. 12	Palatia
Nov. 12	Prussia
Nov. 15	California
Nov. 16	Normannia
Nov. 20	Taormina
Nov. 26	Patria
Nov. 29	Pennsylvania
Nov. 29	Scotia
Dec. 1	Pisa
Dec. 6	Phoenicia
Dec. 13	Persia
Dec. 24	Andalusia

HAMBURG-AMERICAN LINE
Hamburg—New York
(Continued)

N. Y.

Arrival	Steamer
Dec. 27	Palatia
Dec. 30	Albano

HAMBURG-AMERICAN LINE
Mediterranean—New York

N. Y.

Arrival	Steamer
Mar. 23	Columbia
Apr. 5	Furst Bismarck
Dec. 7	Augusta Victoria

HAMBURG-AMERICAN LINE
Scandinavian Ports—New York

Jan. 22	Virginia
Mar. 22	Sicilia
Apr. 10	Georgia
Apr. 28	Adria
May 1	Aragonia
May 17	Asturia
May 19	Sicilia
June 2	Georgia
July 1	Aragonia
July 12	Sicilia
July 23	Ambria
July 29	Georgia
Aug. 23	Aragonia
Sept. 6	Sicilia
Sept. 18	Ambria
Oct. 4	Georgia
Oct. 18	Aragonia
Nov. 29	Georgia
Dec. 17	Aragonia
Dec. 29	Sicilia

HOLLAND-AMERICA LINE
Rotterdam, Amsterdam, Boulogne—New York

N. Y.

Arrival	Steamer
Jan. 6	Obdam
Jan. 12	Amsterdam
Jan. 18	Edam
Jan. 19	Spaarndam
Feb. 1	Veendam
Feb. 1	Werkendam
Feb. 5	Schiedam
Feb. 13	Zaandam
Feb. 16	Maasdam
Feb. 24	Spaarndam
Mar. 2	Edam
Mar. 3	Amsterdam
Mar. 15	Werkendam
Mar. 19	Obdam
Mar. 23	Veendam
Mar. 25	Schiedam
Mar. 29	Spaarndam
Apr. 7	Amsterdam
Apr. 9	Zaandam
Apr. 13	Maasdam
Apr. 16	Edam
Apr. 20	Werkendam

Year 1897

HOLLAND-AMERICA LINE
Rotterdam, Amsterdam, Boulogne—New York
(Continued)

N. Y.

Arrival	Steamer
Apr. 21	Obdam
Apr. 26	Veendam
Apr. 28	P. Caland
Apr. 30	Spaarndam
May 10	Amsterdam
May 10	Schiedam
May 17	Maasdam
May 24	Zaandam
May 26	Werkendam
May 31	'Obdam
June 7	Veendam
June 14	Spaarndam
June 19	Edam
June 21	Amsterdam
June 29	Schiedam
June 29	Maasdam
July 6	Obdam
July 12	Veendam
July 19	Spaarndam
July 26	Amsterdam
Aug. 2	Maasdam
Aug. 9	Obdam
Aug. 14	Veendam
Aug. 23	Spaarndam
Aug. 28	Rotterdam
Sept. 1	Amsterdam
Sept. 6	Maasdam
Sept. 13	Obdam
Sept. 24	Edam
Oct. 4	Rotterdam
Oct. 11	Maasdam
Oct. 1C	Obdam
Oct. 23	Werkendam
Nov. 1	Spaarndam
Nov. 5	Edam
Nov. 6	Rotterdam
Nov. 19	Amsterdam
Nov. 23	Obdam
Nov. 29	Veendam
Dec. 9	Spaarndam
Dec. 20	Edam
Dec. 23	Amsterdam
Dec. 23	Rotterdam
Dec. 28	Obdam

INSULAR NAVIGATION COMPANY
Azores, Lisbon—New Bedford, Mass., New York

N. Y.

Arrival	Steamer
Jan. 8	Peninsular
Jan. 23	Vega
Mar. 4	Peninsular
Mar. 25	Vega
Apr. 22	Peninsular
May 21	Vega
June 21	Peninsular
July 12	Vega
Sept. 29	Peninsular
Oct. 16	Vega
Nov. 19	Peninsular
Dec. 29	Vega

LINHA DE VAPORES PORTUGUEZES
Azores, Lisbon—New Bedford, Mass., New York

N. Y.

Arrival	Steamer
Feb. 1	Dona Amelia
Feb. 3	Dona Maria
Feb. 17	Oevenum
Apr. 9	Dona Maria
Apr. 17	Oevenum
May 26	Dona Maria
July 9	Dona Maria
Sept. 16	Oevenum
Dec. 27	Dona Maria
Dec. 29	Oevenum

NATIONAL STEAMSHIP COMPANY
London—New York

N. Y.

Arrival	Steamer
Feb. 11	America
Sept. 7	Europe
Sept. 22	America
Oct. 11	Europe
Oct. 29	America
Nov. 16	Europe
Dec. 4	America
Dec. 27	Europe

NORTH GERMAN LLOYD
Bremen—New York

N. Y.

Arrival	Steamer
Jan. 2	Aller
Jan. 6	Stuttgart
Jan. 7	Spree
Jan. 14	Dresden
Jan. 14	Lahn
Jan. 18	Karlsruhe
Jan. 27	Oldenburg
Jan. 29	Munchen
Jan. 29	Trave
Feb. 3	H. H. Meir
Feb. 6	Aller
Feb. 8	Weimar
Feb. 11	Havel
Feb. 13	Stuttgart
Feb. 20	Spree
Feb. 25	Dresden
Feb. 26	Trave
Mar. 1	Karlsruhe
Mar. 2	Roland
Mar. 6	Aller
Mar. 8	Oldenburg
Mar. 12	Havel
Mar. 19	Spree
Mar. 22	Weimar
Mar. 25	H. H. Meir
Mar. 26	Trave
Mar. 29	Stuttgart
Apr. 1	Lahn
Apr. 9	Havel
Apr. 12	Willehad
Apr. 16	Spree
Apr. 17	Fredrich der Grosse
Apr. 22	Trave
Apr. 23	Bonn
Apr. 26	Weimar

NORTH GERMAN LLOYD
Bremen—New York
(Continued)

N. Y.

Arrival	Steamer
Apr. 29	Lahn
Apr. 29	Munchen
Apr. 30	H. H. Meir
May 6	Havel
May 7	Halle
May 11	Aller
May 14	Prinz Regent Luitpold
May 14	Saale
May 20	Trave
May 21	Crefeld
May 24	Spree
May 27	Fredrich der Grosse
May 27	Lahn
June 3	Havel
June 7	Aller
June 7	Barbarossa
June 10	Konigen Luise
June 10	Saale
June 17	Bremen
June 17	Trave
June 21	Spree
June 24	Lahn
June 29	H. H. Meir
June 30	Havel
July 8	Fredrich der Grosse
July 15	Trave
July 16	Barbarossa
July 22	Konigen Luise
July 22	Lahn
July 29	Havel
July 29	Prinz Regent Luitpold
Aug. 5	Bremen
Aug. 12	Trave
Aug. 19	Fredrich der Grosse
Aug. 19	Lahn
Aug. 21	Havel
Aug. 27	Bremen
Aug. 30	Aller
Sept. 2	Saale
Sept. 3	Karlsruhe
Sept. 8	Konigen Luise
Sept. 9	Trave
Sept. 13	Spree
Sept. 16	Lahn
Sept. 20	Havel
Sept. 23	Bremen
Sept. 27	K. William der Grosse
Sept. 28	Aller
Oct. 1	Saale
Oct. 2	Stuttgart
Oct. 7	Trave
Oct. 14	Lahn
Oct. 18	Havel
Oct. 19	K. William der Grosse
Oct. 22	Konigan Luise
Oct. 29	Saale
Nov. 4	Trave
Nov. 4	Weimar
Nov. 11	Lahn
Nov. 12	Stuttgart
Nov. 17	K. William der Grosse
Nov. 22	Munchen
Nov. 26	Karlsruhe
Dec. 6	Gera
Dec. 10	Trave

Year 1897

NORTH GERMAN LLOYD
Bremen—New York
(Continued)
N. Y.

Arrival	Steamer
Dec. 11	Havel
Dec. 17	Saale
Dec. 18	Weimar
Dec. 23	K. William der Grosse
Dec. 27	Stuttgart

NORTH GERMAN LLOYD
Mediterranean—New York
N. Y.

Arrival	Steamer
Jan. 12	Werra
Feb. 5	Fulda
Feb. 16	Kaiser Wilhelm II
Feb. 24	Ems
Mar. 2	Werra
Mar. 11	Fulda
Mar. 22	Kaiser Wilhelm II
Mar. 31	Ems
Apr. 15	Werra
Apr. 21	Fulda
May 6	Kaiser Wilhelm II
May 12	Ems
May 19	Werra
May 26	Fulda
June 10	Kaiser Wilhelm II
June 16	Ems
July 1	Werra
July 7	Fulda
July 22	Kaiser Wilhelm II
Aug. 6	Ems
Aug. 11	Werra
Sept. 8	Ems
Sept. 15	Werra
Sept. 23	Fulda
Oct. 5	Kaiser Wilhelm II
Oct. 13	Ems
Oct. 21	Werra
Oct. 28	Fulda
Nov. 1	Aller
Nov. 9	Kaiser Wilhelm II
Nov. 18	Ems
Nov. 24	Werra
Dec. 1	Fulda
Dec. 16	Kaiser Wilhelm II
Dec. 30	Werra

PRINCE LINE
Mediterranean—New York
N. Y.

Arrival	Steamer
Dec. 6	Trojan Prince
Dec. 23	Trojan Prince

RED STAR LINE
Antwerp—New York
N. Y.

Arrival	Steamer
Jan. 7	Southwark
Jan. 20	Noordland
Jan. 27	Friesland
Feb. 3	Kensington
Feb. 10	Westernland
Feb. 26	Noordland
Mar. 4	Friesland
Mar. 12	Kensington

RED STAR LINE
Antwerp—New York
(Continued)
N. Y.

Arrival	Steamer
Mar. 19	Westernland
Apr. 1	Noordland
Apr. 7	Friesland
Apr. 14	Kensington
Apr. 28	Southwark
May 5	Noordland
May 11	Friesland
May 18	Kensington
May 26	Westernland
June 2	Southwark
June 10	Noordland
June 16	Friesland
June 22	Kensington
June 30	Westernland
July 21	Noordland
July 27	Friesland
Aug. 3	Kensington
Aug. 10	Westernland
Aug. 17	Southwark
Aug. 25	Noordland
Aug. 31	Friesland
Sept. 7	Kensington
Sept. 15	Westernland
Sept. 21	Southwark
Sept. 29	Noordland
Oct. 5	Friesland
Oct. 12	Kensington
Oct. 20	Westernland
Nov. 3	Noordland
Nov. 9	Friesland
Nov. 16	Kensington
Nov. 24	Westernland
Dec. 1	Southwark
Dec. 9	Noordland
Dec. 15	Friesland
Dec. 23	Kensington
Dec. 29	Westernland

SCANDINAVIAN-AMERICAN LINE
Scandinavian Ports—New York
N. Y.

Arrival	Steamer
Jan. 15	Hekla
Feb. 8	Thingvalla
Feb. 24	Norge
Mar. 1	Island
Mar. 22	Hekla
Apr. 19	Norge
May 7	Island
May 17	Hekla
May 26	Amerika
June 11	Norge
June 28	Island
July 17	Thingvalla
Aug. 5	Hekla
Aug. 19	Island
Sept. 9	Thingvalla
Sept. 24	Amerika
Oct. 8	Hekla
Oct. 23	Island
Nov. 18	Norge
Nov. 24	Hekla
Dec. 20	Island

WHITE STAR LINE
Liverpool—New York
N. Y.

Arrival	Steamer
Jan. 7	Majestic
Jan. 15	Germanic
Jan. 21	Teutonic
Jan. 30	Britannic
Feb. 4	Majestic
Feb. 12	Germanic
Feb. 22	Adriatic
Mar. 1	Britannic
Mar. 4	Majestic
Mar. 5	Cevic
Mar. 13	Germanic
Mar. 18	Teutonic
Mar. 27	Britannic
Apr. 1	Majestic
Apr. 9	Germanic
Apr. 15	Teutonic
Apr. 24	Britannic
Apr. 29	Majestic
May 7	Germanic
May 11	Tauric
May 13	Teutonic
May 17	Cevic
May 21	Britannic
May 27	Majestic
June 4	Germanic
June 9	Teutonic
June 18	Britannic
June 24	Majestic
June 30	Nomadic
July 2	Germanic
July 7	Teutonic
July 17	Adriatic
July 19	Tauric
July 23	Britannic
July 26	Cevic
July 28	Majestic
Aug. 2	Nomadic
Aug. 5	Germanic
Aug. 11	Teutonic
Aug. 20	Britannic
Aug. 23	Tauric
Aug. 25	Majestic
Aug. 30	Cevic
Sept. 2	Bovic
Sept. 3	Germanic
Sept. 8	Teutonic
Sept. 17	Britannic
Sept. 22	Majestic
Sept. 27	Tauric
Oct. 1	Germanic
Oct. 4	Cevic
Oct. 6	Teutonic
Oct. 11	Nomadic
Oct. 15	Britannic
Oct. 21	Majestic
Oct. 26	Bovic
Oct. 28	Germanic
Nov. 1	Tauric
Nov. 3	Teutonic
Nov. 8	Cevic
Nov. 13	Britannic
Nov. 16	Nomadic
Nov. 17	Majestic
Nov. 27	Adriatic
Nov. 29	Bovic
Dec. 1	Germanic

Year 1897

WHITE STAR LINE
Liverpool—New York
(Continued)

N.Y. Arrival	Steamer
Dec. 7	Tauric
Dec. 9	Teutonic
Dec. 15	Cevic
Dec. 18	Britannic
Dec. 23	Majestic
Dec. 23	Nomadic

WILSON, FURNESS, LEYLAND LINE
London—New York

N.Y. Arrival	Steamer
Jan. 30	Idaho
Mar. 8	Megantic
Mar. 15	Georgian
Apr. 30	Idaho
May 29	Megantic
June 1	Georgian
June 19	Cambrian
July 26	Cambrian
Aug. 3	Megantic
Aug. 16	Idaho
Sept. 2	Cambrian
Sept. 14	Georgian
Sept. 20	Idaho
Oct. 5	Cambrian
Oct. 11	Megantic
Oct. 26	Idaho
Nov. 11	Cambrian
Nov. 19	Megantic
Nov. 30	Idaho
Dec. 15	Cambrian
Dec. 2⁴	Megantic

WILSON LINE
Hull, London—New York

N.Y. Arrival	Steamer
Jan. 4	Buffalo
Jan. 22	Ontario
Feb. 1	Martello
May 1	Martello
May 13	Ontario
May 29	Hindoo
June 10	Colorado
June 14	Martello
June 28	Galileo
July 13	Hindoo
July 17	Colorado
July 29	Buffalo
Aug. 6	Francisco
Aug. 25	Ontario
Aug. 27	Colorado
Sept. 4	Martello
Sept. 9	Buffalo
Sept. 18	Francisco
Sept. 28	Galileo
Oct. 2	Hindoo
Oct. 11	Colorado
Oct. 16	Martello

WILSON LINE
Hull, London—New York
(Continued)

N.Y. Arrival	Steamer
Oct. 25	Buffalo
Oct. 29	Francisco
Nov. 15	Hindoo
Nov. 20	Colorado
Nov. 27	Martello
Dec. 3	Buffalo
Dec. 13	Francisco
Dec. 24	Galileo
Dec. 28	Hindoo

ADDITIONAL ARRIVALS
Antwerp—New York

N.Y. Arrival	Steamer
Jan. 14	Berlin
Apr. 27	Berlin
July 14	Berlin

Bordeaux—New York

N.Y. Arrival	Steamer
Jan. 11	Chateau Lafite
Apr. 9	Chateau Lafite
May 11	Jeanne Conseil
Sept. 14	Chateau Lafite
Nov. 18	Chateau Lafite

British Ports—New York

N.Y. Arrival	Steamer
Jan. 8	Boston City
Jan. 9	Jersey City
Feb. 1	Chicago City
Mar. 24	Wells City
Apr. 26	Kansas City
May 10	Wells City
May 23	Brooklyn City
May 26	Critic
May 27	Exeter City
July 5	Brooklyn City
July 14	Exeter City
July 16	Astrakhan
Sept. 17	Wells City
Sept. 18	Croft
Sept. 20	Boston City
Sept. 24	Kansas City
Oct. 2	Jersey City
Oct. 6	Critic
Oct. 7	Chicago City
Oct. 11	Brooklyn City
Oct. 15	Menantic
Oct. 16	Exeter City
Oct. 27	Wells City
Nov. 3	Kansas City
Nov. 5	Croft
Nov. 15	Jersey City
Nov. 22	Brooklyn City
Nov. 26	Critic
Nov. 30	Exeter City
Dec. 9	Wells City

ADDITIONAL ARRIVALS
British Ports—New York
(Continued)

N.Y. Arrival	Steamer
Dec. 13	Boston City
Dec. 22	Kansas City
Dec. 29	Croft
Dec. 29	Jersey City

Hamburg—New York

N.Y. Arrival	Steamer
Apr. 24	Normannia

Mediterranean—New York

N.Y. Arrival	Steamer
Jan. 21	Clive
Jan. 27	Elysia
Feb. 10	Oregon
Mar. 2	Sarnia
Apr. 14	Elysia
Apr. 19	Oregon
Apr. 26	Chateau Yquem
Apr. 28	Heaton
May 8	Sarnia
May 26	Clive
June 1	Chateau Lafite
June 21	Tampico
June 24	Oregon
June 26	Chateau Yquem
July 6	Elysia
July 16	Sarnia

Rotterdam, Amsterdam, Boulogne—New York

N.Y. Arrival	Steamer
Jan. 27	Hendric
Feb. 15	Prinz Maurits
Mar. 29	Prins Willem 11
Apr. 19	Prins Willem IV
May 11	Prins Willem III
May 29	P. Frederic Hendric
June 18	Prinz Maurits
July 12	Prins Willem I
July 31	Prins Willem II
Sept. 11	Prins Willem III
Oct. 4	P. Frederic Hendric
Nov. 16	Prins Willem I
Nov. 29	Prins Willem V
Nov. 30	Prins Willem II
Dec. 29	Prins Willem IV

Spanish Ports—New York

N.Y. Arrival	Steamer
May 14	Amethyst
June 16	Santiago De Cuba
Aug. 7	Cienfuegos
Sept. 6	Cienfuegos
Sept. 20	Santiago De Cuba
Nov. 20	Santiago De Cuba
Dec. 28	Cienfuegos

Year 1898

ALLAN STATE LINE
Glasgow—New York
N. Y.

Arrival	Steamer
Jan. 11	Peruvian
Feb. 4	Buenos Ayrean
Feb. 14	State of Nebraska
Feb. 23	Peruvian
Mar. 12	Corean
Mar. 14	Turanian
Mar. 17	Buenos Ayrean
Mar. 26	State of Nebraska
Apr. 8	Siberian
Apr. 23	Corean
May 2	State of Nebraska
May 16	Mongolian
May 31	State of Nebraska
June 14	Mongolian
June 30	State of Nebraska
July 12	Mongolian
July 28	State of Nebraska
Aug. 9	Mongolian
Aug. 27	State of Nebraska
Sept. 8	Mongolian
Sept. 28	State of Nebraska
Oct. 12	Mongolian
Oct. 28	State of Nebraska
Nov. 11	Mongolian
Dec. 8	State of Nebraska

AMERICAN LINE
Southampton—New York
N. Y.

Arrival	Steamer
Jan. 3	Saint Louis
Jan. 10	New York
Jan. 15	Saint Paul
Jan. 22	Saint Louis
Jan. 29	New York
Feb. 7	Paris
Feb. 12	Saint Louis
Feb. 26	Paris
Mar. 5	Saint Paul
Mar. 12	New York
Mar. 26	Saint Paul
Apr. 2	Saint Louis
Apr. 11	Paris
Apr. 16	Saint Paul
Apr. 24	Saint Louis
Apr. 24	New York
Apr. 30	Paris
May 25	Chester
June 6	Berlin
June 21	Chester
July 5	Berlin
July 19	Chester
Nov. 12	Saint Louis
Nov. 21	Paris
Nov. 26	Saint Paul
Dec. 5	Saint Louis
Dec. 12	Paris
Dec. 17	Saint Paul
Dec. 24	Saint Louis

ANCHOR LINE
Glasgow—New York
N. Y.

Arrival	Steamer
Jan. 11	Furnessia
Jan. 26	Ethiopia
Feb. 10	Anchoria
Feb. 23	Furnessia
Mar. 8	Ethiopia
Mar. 22	Anchoria
Apr. 5	Furnessia
Apr. 13	Ethiopia
Apr. 27	Anchoria
May 9	Furnessia
May 17	Ethiopia
May 25	Anchoria
May 31	City of Rome
June 13	Furnessia
June 21	Ethiopia
June 29	Anchoria
July 13	Furnessia
July 19	Ethiopia
Aug. 2	Anchoria
Aug. 15	Furnessia
Aug. 29	Ethiopia
Sept. 6	City of Rome
Sept. 12	Anchoria
Sept. 19	Furnessia
Oct. 4	Ethiopia
Oct. 18	Anchoria
Oct. 24	Furnessia
Nov. 7	Ethiopia
Nov. 16	Anchoria
Nov. 28	Furnessia
Dec. 15	Ethiopia
Dec. 27	Anchoria

ANCHOR LINE
Mediterranean—New York
N. Y.

Arrival	Steamer
Jan. 3	Alsatia
Jan. 13	California
Jan. 24	Victoria
Feb. 7	Bolivia
Feb. 21	Scindia
Mar. 7	Karamania
Mar. 19	Alsatia
Apr. 2	California
Apr. 13	Victoria
Apr. 23	Bolivia
May 2	Hesperia
May 6	Scindia
May 16	Karamania
May 27	Alsatia
June 8	California
June 22	Victoria
July 1	Bolivia
July 15	Hesperia
July 26	Karamania
Aug. 18	California
Sept. 10	Alsatia
Sept. 28	Hesperia
Oct. 10	Karamania

ANCHOR LINE
Mediterranean—New York
(Continued)
N. Y.

Arrival	Steamer
Oct. 22	Victoria
Nov. 18	Alsatia
Dec. 6	Hesperia
Dec. 23	Karamania

ATLANTIC TRANSPORT LINE
London—New York
N. Y.

Arrival	Steamer
Jan. 7	Mohawk
Jan. 13	Mobile
Jan. 18	Massachusetts
Jan. 26	Manitoba
Feb. 8	Mohawk
Feb. 18	Mobile
Feb. 19	Michigan
Feb. 21	Massachusetts
Feb. 23	Victoria
Feb. 28	Manitoba
Mar. 1	Boadicea
Mar. 8	Minnewaska
Mar. 14	Mohawk
Mar. 22	Mobile
Mar. 29	Massachusetts
Apr. 5	Manitoba
Apr. 6	Boadicea
Apr. 12	Minnewaska
Apr. 21	Mohawk
Apr. 27	Mobile
May 3	Massachusetts
May 9	Boadicea
May 10	Manitoba
May 16	Minnewaska
May 31	Mobile
June 6	Victoria
June 6	Massachusetts
June 13	Boadicea
June 13	Manitoba
June 28	Mohawk
July 5	Mobile
July 11	Victoria
July 11	Massachusetts
July 18	Boadicea
Aug. 14	Victoria
Aug. 22	Boadicea
Sept. 19	Victoria
Sept. 27	Marquette
Oct. 4	Menominee
Oct. 9	Mesaba
Oct. 20	Manitou
Nov. 8	Menominee
Nov. 14	Mesaba
Nov. 22	Manitou
Dec. 6	Marquette
Dec. 14	Menominee
Dec. 10	Mesaba
Dec. 27	Manitou

Year 1898

COMPANIA TRANSATLANTICA LINE
(Spanish Line)
Spanish Ports—New York

N. Y.

Arrival	Steamer
Jan. 4	Mexico
Feb. 4	Mexico
Mar. 7	Mexico
Apr. 4	Mexico
Apr. 18	Panama

CUNARD LINE
Liverpool—New York

N. Y.

Arrival	Steamer
Jan. 3	Aurania
Jan. 10	Umbria
Jan. 17	Servia
Jan. 22	Campania
Jan. 31	Aurania
Feb. 7	Lucania
Feb. 14	Etruria
Feb. 21	Campania
Feb. 28	Umbria
Mar. 5	Lucania
Mar. 12	Etruria
Mar. 19	Campania
Mar. 28	Umbria
Apr. 11	Etruria
Apr. 18	Campania
Apr. 25	Umbria
Apr. 30	Lucania
May 5	Servia
May 7	Etruria
May 14	Campania
May 19	Aurania
May 23	Umbria
May 28	Lucania
June 2	Servia
June 4	Etruria
June 11	Campania
June 20	Umbria
June 25	Lucania
June 30	Servia
July 2	Etruria
July 9	Campania
July 18	Umbria
July 30	Lucania
Aug. 6	Etruria
Aug. 13	Campania
Aug. 18	Servia
Aug. 20	Umbria
Aug. 27	Lucania
Sept. 1	Aurania
Sept. 3	Etruria
Sept. 10	Campania
Sept. 15	Servia
Sept. 19	Umbria
Sept. 24	Lucania
Oct. 3	Etruria
Oct. 4	Scythia
Oct. 8	Campania
Oct. 17	Umbria
Oct. 22	Lucania
Oct. 31	Etruria
Nov. 5	Campania
Nov. 14	Umbria
Nov. 19	Lucania
Nov. 28	Etruria

CUNARD LINE
Liverpool—New York
(Continued)

N. Y.

Arrival	Steamer
Dec. 3	Campania
Dec. 12	Umbria
Dec. 17	Lucania
Dec. 26	Etruria

FABRE LINE
Mediterranean—New York

N. Y.

Arrival	Steamer
Jan. 5	Massilia
Jan. 26	Patria
Feb. 8	Burgundia
Feb. 23	Nuestria
Mar. 10	Massilia
Mar. 22	Patria
Apr. 15	Burgundia
Apr. 22	Nuestria
May 3	Alesia
May 14	Patria
June 6	Britannia
June 13	Burgundia
June 20	Nuestria
June 27	Alesia
July 7	Patria
July 27	Britannia
Aug. 12	Burgundia
Aug. 22	Nuestria
Sept. 6	Patria
Sept. 24	Alesia
Oct. 13	Burgundia
Oct. 24	Nuestria
Nov. 1	Patria
Dec. 5	Alesia
Dec. 19	Burgundia
Dec. 27	Patria

FRENCH LINE
(Compagnie Generale Transatlantique)
Havre—New York

N. Y.

Arrival	Steamer
Jan. 3	La Bretagne
Jan. 10	La Gascogne
Jan. 17	La Normandie
Jan. 27	La Champagne
Jan. 31	La Bretagne
Feb. 7	La Gascogne
Feb. 14	La Normandie
Feb. 27	La Bretagne
Mar. 7	La Gascogne
Mar. 14	La Normandie
Mar. 21	La Navarre
Mar. 28	La Bourgoyne
Apr. 4	La Bretagne
Apr. 11	La Champagne
Apr. 11	La Gascogne
Apr. 18	La Navarre
Apr. 26	La Normandie
May 2	La Bourgoyne
May 9	La Touraine
May 16	La Gascogne
May 23	La Navarre
May 30	La Bourgoyne
June 6	La Touraine
June 13	La Bretagne

FRENCH LINE
(Compagnie Generale Transatlantique)
Havre—New York
(Continued)

N. Y.

Arrival	Steamer
June 20	La Navarre
June 27	La Bourgoyne
July 5	La Touraine
July 11	La Bretagne
July 18	La Navarre
July 25	La Gascogne
Aug. 1	La Touraine
Aug. 8	La Bretagne
Aug. 15	La Normandie
Aug. 22	La Gascogne
Aug. 29	La Touraine
Sept. 5	La Champagne
Sept. 12	La Navarre
Sept. 19	La Normandie
Sept. 26	La Gascogne
Oct. 3	La Touraine
Oct. 10	La Champagne
Oct. 17	La Navarre
Oct. 24	La Normandie
Oct. 31	La Touraine
Nov. 7	La Gascogne
Nov. 14	La Champagne
Nov. 22	La Normandie
Nov. 28	La Touraine
Dec. 5	La Gascogne
Dec. 12	La Champagne
Dec. 19	La Bretagne
Dec. 27	La Normandie

HAMBURG-AMERICAN LINE
Hamburg—New York

N. Y.

Arrival	Steamer
Jan. 3	Prussia
Jan. 8	Patria
Jan. 14	Pennsylvania
Jan. 20	Furst Bismarck
Jan. 21	Phoenicia
Jan. 24	Scotia
Feb. 4	Palatia
Feb. 4	Alesia
Feb. 18	Prussia
Feb. 23	Furst Bismarck
Feb. 25	Pretoria
Mar. 3	Albano
Mar. 3	Patria
Mar. 10	Phoenicia
Mar. 12	Scotia
Mar. 16	Pennsylvania
Mar. 21	Hercynia
Mar. 22	Pisa
Mar. 31	Palatia
Apr. 1	Taormina
Apr. 9	Pretoria
Apr. 18	Patria
Apr. 23	Furst Bismarck
Apr. 26	Moravia
Apr. 28	Bulgaria
Apr. 29	Albano
Apr. 30	Phoenicia
May 2	Pennsylvania
May 6	Scotia
May 16	Augusta Victoria

Year 1898

HAMBURG-AMERICAN LINE
Hamburg—New York
(Continued)

N. Y.

Arrival	Steamer
May 16	Palatia
May 16	Sorrento
May 21	Pretoria
May 24	Cheruskia
May 27	Furst Bismarck
May 27	Patria
May 30	Pisa
June 6	Bulgaria
June 10	Phoenicia
June 11	Augusta Victoria
June 17	Pennsylvania
June 23	Albano
June 24	Furst Bismarck
June 24	Palatia
July 5	Pretoria
July 6	Cheruskia
July 7	Patria
July 15	Bulgaria
July 22	Furst Bismarck
July 22	Phoenicia
July 22	Syria
July 25	Pisa
July 28	Pennsylvania
Aug. 5	Augusta Victoria
Aug. 5	Palatia
Aug. 12	Pretoria
Aug. 19	Cheruskia
Aug. 19	Furst Bismarck
Aug. 26	Bulgaria
Sept. 2	Phoenicia
Sept. 3	Augusta Victoria
Sept. 7	Albano
Sept. 9	Pennsylvania
Sept. 16	Furst Bismarck
Sept. 16	Palatia
Sept. 21	Pisa
Sept. 24	Pretoria
Oct. 1	Augusta Victoria
Oct. 4	Patria
Oct. 8	Bulgaria
Oct. 15	Furst Bismarck
Oct. 17	Phoenicia
Oct. 21	Pennsylvania
Oct. 29	Augusta Victoria
Nov. 1	Brasilia
Nov. 1	Polaria
Nov. 4	Albano
Nov. 7	Palatia
Nov. 11	Furst Bismarck
Nov. 14	Pretoria
Nov. 16	Pisa
Nov. 18	Patria
Nov. 26	Bulgaria
Dec. 5	Phoenicia
Dec. 13	Pennsylvania
Dec. 15	Moravia
Dec. 19	Palatia
Dec. 26	Pretoria

HAMBURG-AMERICAN LINE
Mediterranean—New York

N. Y.

Arrival	Steamer
Jan. 17	Augusta Victoria

HAMBURG-AMERICAN LINE
Mediterranean—New York
(Continued)

N. Y.

Arrival	Steamer
Feb. 8	Normannia
Mar. 17	Normannia
Apr. 4	Augusta Victoria
Dec. 5	Augusta Victoria

HOLLAND-AMERICA LINE
Rotterdam, Amsterdam—New York

N. Y.

Arrival	Steamer
Jan. 4	Veendam
Jan. 22	Amsterdam
Jan. 24	Rotterdam
Jan. 31	Obdam
Feb. 10	Spaarndam
Feb. 23	Amsterdam
Feb. 28	Rotterdam
Mar. 7	Obdam
Mar. 15	Spaarndam
Mar. 29	Werkendam
Apr. 4	Rotterdam
Apr. 12	Obdam
Apr. 20	Amsterdam
Apr. 27	Spaarndam
May 4	Werkendam
May 7	Edam
May 9	Rotterdam
May 16	Obdam
May 24	Amsterdam
May 31	Spaarndam
June 6	Maasdam
June 9	Werkendam
June 13	Rotterdam
June 20	Obdam
June 28	Amsterdam
July 5	Spaarndam
July 11	Maasdam
July 18	Rotterdam
Aug. 1	Amsterdam
Aug. 5	Edam
Aug. 9	Spaarndam
Aug. 15	Maasdam
Aug. 22	Rotterdam
Aug. 30	Werkendam
Sept. 8	Amsterdam
Sept. 14	Spaarndam
Sept. 19	Maasdam
Sept. 26	Rotterdam
Oct. 10	Statendam
Oct. 19	Spaarndam
Oct. 24	Maasdam
Oct. 31	Rotterdam
Nov. 10	Werkendam
Nov. 14	Statendam
Nov. 25	Spaarndam
Nov. 29	Maasdam
Dec. 5	Rotterdam
Dec. 17	Werkendam
Dec. 19	Statendam
Dec. 28	Spaarndam

INSULAR NAVIGATION COMPANY
Azores, Lisbon—New Bedford, Mass.—New York

N. Y.

Arrival	Steamer
Jan. 13	Peninsular
Mar. 7	Peninsular
Apr. 4	Vega
May 30	Vega
June 18	Peninsular
July 11	Vega
July 22	Peninsular
Aug. 29	Vega
Sept. 15	Peninsular
Oct. 22	Vega
Nov. 2	Peninsular
Dec. 16	Peninsular

LINHA DE VAPORES PORTUGUEZES
Azores, Lisbon—New Bedford, Mass.—New York

	Steamer
Feb. 10	Oevenum
Feb. 11	Dona Maria
Mar. 31	Dona Maria
May 19	Dona Maria
June 3	Oevenum
June 30	Dona Maria
Aug. 9	Dona Maria
Sept. 17	Oevenum
Nov. 15	Dona Maria
Dec. 16	Oevenum

NORTH GERMAN LLOYD
Bremen—New York

N. Y.

Arrival	Steamer
Jan. 3	Munchen
Jan. 7	Trave
Jan. 10	Karlsruhe
Jan. 14	Gera
Jan. 14	Lahn
Jan. 21	H. H. Meier
Jan. 27	Weimar
Jan. 28	Aller
Feb. 4	Havel
Feb. 4	Stuttgart
Feb. 10	Saale
Feb. 18	Lahn
Feb. 19	Karlsruhe
Feb. 24	Trave
Feb. 25	Friedrich der Grosse
Mar. 3	Havel
Mar. 3	H. H. Meier
Mar. 9	K. William der Grosse
Mar. 10	Weimar
Mar. 16	Oldenburg
Mar. 17	Lahn
Mar. 25	Trave
Mar. 31	Friedrich der Grosse
Apr. 6	K. William der Grosse
Apr. 8	Karlsruhe
Apr. 15	Lahn
Apr. 16	H. H. Meier
Apr. 21	Koenigin Luise
Apr. 21	Trave
Apr. 28	Havel
May 4	K. William der Grosse
May 5	Oldenburg

Year 1898

NORTH GERMAN LLOYD
Bremen—New York
(Continued)

N. Y.

Arrival	Steamer
May 12	Lahn
May 20	Barbarossa
May 24	Koenigin Luise
May 24	Trave
May 31	K. William der Grosse
June 8	Prinz Regent Luitpold
June 9	Lahn
June 16	Friedrich der Grosse
June 16	Kaiser Friedrich
June 23	Barbarossa
June 23	Trave
June 29	Koenigin Luise
July 1	K. William der Grosse
July 7	Lahn
July 16	Prinz Regent Luitpold
July 20	Friedrich der Grosse
July 21	Trave
July 28	Barbarossa
Aug. 2	Koenigin Luise
Aug. 4	Lahn
Aug. 10	K. William der Grosse
Aug. 18	Havel
Aug. 18	Trave
Aug. 23	Friedrich der Grosse
Sept. 7	K. William der Grosse
Sept. 7	Koenigin Luise
Sept. 15	Trave
Sept. 15	Weimar
Sept. 21	Kaiser Friedrich
Sept. 29	Lahn
Sept. 30	Havel
Oct. 5	K. William der Grosse
Oct. 6	Barbarossa
Oct. 13	Trave
Oct. 14	Karlsruhe
Oct. 19	Koenigin Luise
Oct. 20	Kaiser Friedrich
Oct. 28	Weimar
Nov. 3	Lahn
Nov. 4	Oldenberg
Nov. 9	K. William der Grosse
Nov. 11	Havel
Nov. 17	Barbarossa
Nov. 17	Trave
Nov. 25	Kaiser Friedrich
Nov. 25	Karlsruhe
Dec. 2	Lahn
Dec. 10	Weimar
Dec. 17	Oldenburg
Dec. 21	K. William der Grosse
Dec. 23	Havel
Dec. 27	Roland

NORTH GERMAN LLOYD
Mediterranean—New York

N. Y.

Arrival	Steamer
Jan. 27	Ems
Feb. 2	Kaiser Wilhelm II
Feb. 17	Fulda
Mar. 2	Werra
Mar. 10	Kaiser Wilhelm II
Mar. 24	Fulda
Mar. 30	Ems
Apr. 13	Saale

NORTH GERMAN LLOYD
Mediterranean—New York
(Continued)

N. Y.

Arrival	Steamer
Apr. 22	Werra
Apr. 28	Kaiser Wilhelm II
May 5	Fulda
May 11	Ems
May 17	Aller
May 26	Werra
June 1	Kaiser Wilhelm II
June 9	Fulda
June 15	Ems
June 21	Aller
July 7	Kaiser Wilhelm II
July 21	Fulda
Aug. 13	Kaiser Wilhelm II
Aug. 24	Werra
Sept. 7	Aller
Sept. 22	Ems
Sept. 28	Kaiser Wilhelm II
Oct. 6	Fulda
Oct. 12	Aller
Oct. 20	Werra
Nov. 3	Kaiser Wilhelm II
Nov. 10	Fulda
Nov. 16	Aller
Nov. 25	Werra
Nov. 27	Ems
Dec. 3	Ems
Dec. 16	Kaiser Wilhelm II
Dec. 29	Aller

PRINCE LINE
Mediterranean—New York

N. Y.

Arrival	Steamer
Jan. 8	Spartan Prince
Jan. 27	Tartar Prince
Feb. 8	Asiatic Prince
Feb. 24	Trojan Prince
Feb. 24	Castillian Prince
Mar. 16	Spartan Prince
Mar. 31	Roman Prince
Apr. 4	Tartar Prince
Apr. 23	Trojan Prince
Apr. 25	Asiatic Prince
May 16	Spartan Prince
June 4	Tartar Prince
July 5	Trojan Prince
July 23	Spartan Prince
Aug. 15	Tartar Prince
Aug. 19	Roman Prince
Sept. 5	Trojan Prince
Sept. 24	Spartan Prince
Oct. 17	Tartar Prince
Nov. 7	Trojan Prince
Nov. 26	Spartan Prince
Dec. 19	Tartar Prince

RED STAR LINE
Antwerp—New York

N. Y.

Arrival	Steamer
Jan. 7	Southwark
Jan. 17	Noordland
Jan. 25	Friesland
Feb. 2	Kensington
Feb. 10	Westernland

RED STAR LINE
Antwerp—New York
(Continued)

N. Y.

Arrival	Steamer
Feb. 23	Noordland
Mar. 3	Friesland
Mar. 8	Kensington
Mar. 15	Westernland
Mar. 23	Southwark
Mar. 30	Noordland
Apr. 5	Friesland
Apr. 12	Kensington
Apr. 21	Westernland
May 4	Noordland
May 10	Friesland
May 24	Westernland
May 31	Kensington
June 8	Noordland
June 14	Friesland
June 21	Southwark
June 29	Westernland
July 5	Kensington
July 13	Noordland
July 23	Friesland
July 26	Southwark
Aug. 2	Westernland
Aug. 9	Kensington
Aug. 17	Noordland
Aug. 31	Southwark
Sept. 7	Westernland
Sept. 13	Kensington
Sept. 21	Noordland
Sept. 28	Friesland
Oct. 4	Southwark
Oct. 12	Westernland
Oct. 19	Kensington
Oct. 26	Noordland
Nov. 1	Friesland
Nov. 9	Southwark
Nov. 15	Westernland
Nov. 22	Kensington
Nov. 30	Noordland
Dec. 14	Friesland
Dec. 20	Southwark
Dec. 28	Westernland

SCANDINAVIAN-AMERICAN LINE
Scandinavian Ports—New York

N. Y.

Arrival	Steamer
Jan. 3	Thingvalla
Jan. 21	Norge
Feb. 15	Island
Feb. 28	Thingvalla
Mar. 14	Norge
Mar. 28	Hekla
Apr. 4	Venus
Apr. 7	Island
Apr. 27	Thingvalla
May 6	Norge
May 21	Hekla
June 3	Island
June 18	Thingvalla
July 2	Norge
July 14	Hekla
July 30	Island
Aug. 12	Thingvalla

Year 1898

SCANDINAVIAN-AMERICAN LINE
Scandinavian Ports—New York
(Continued)

N. Y.

Arrival	Steamer
Aug. 25	Norge
Sept. 7	Venus
Sept. 9	Hekla
Sept. 27	Island
Oct. 8	Thingvalla
Oct. 20	Norge
Oct. 31	Venus
Nov. 7	Hekla
Nov. 28	Thingvalla
Dec. 20	Norge

WHITE STAR LINE
Liverpool—New York

N. Y.

Arrival	Steamer
Jan. 6	Teutonic
Jan. 15	Britannic
Jan. 16	Cufic
Jan. 19	Majestic
Jan. 28	Germanic
Feb. 3	Teutonic
Feb. 11	Britannic
Feb. 17	Majestic
Feb. 24	Germanic
Mar. 2	Teutonic
Mar. 12	Nomadic
Mar. 12	Britannic
Mar. 16	Majestic
Mar. 23	Bovic
Mar. 25	Germanic
Mar. 30	Teutonic
Apr. 9	Britannic
Apr. 14	Majestic
Apr. 22	Germanic
Apr. 26	Bovic
Apr. 28	Teutonic
May 2	Tauric
May 6	Britannic
May 9	Cymric
May 12	Majestic
May 26	Teutonic
May 31	Bovic
June 3	Britannic
June 9	Majestic
June 13	Cymric
June 17	Germanic
June 23	Teutonic
July 1	Britannic
July 5	Bovic
July 7	Majestic
July 15	Germanic
July 22	Cymric
July 25	Cevic
July 28	Teutonic
Aug. 5	Britannic
Aug. 9	Georgic
Aug. 11	Majestic
Aug. 19	Germanic
Aug. 22	Cymric
Aug. 24	Teutonic
Sept. 2	Britannic
Sept. 5	Cevic

WHITE STAR LINE
Liverpool—New York
(Continued)

N. Y.

Arrival	Steamer
Sept. 8	Majestic
Sept. 15	Germanic
Sept. 15	Georgic
Sept. 22	Teutonic
Sept. 26	Cymric
Sept. 30	Britannic
Oct. 5	Tauric
Oct. 5	Majestic
Oct. 13	Cevic
Oct. 14	Germanic
Oct. 19	Teutonic
Oct. 19	Georgic
Oct. 29	Britannic
Nov. 7	Cymric
Nov. 9	Majestic
Nov. 18	Germanic
Nov. 22	Georgic
Nov. 23	Teutonic
Dec. 5	Cymric
Dec. 5	Britannic
Dec. 8	Majestic
Dec. 16	Germanic
Dec. 19	Cevic
Dec. 23	Teutonic
Dec. 27	Georgic

WILSON, FURNESS, LEYLAND LINE
London—New York

N. Y.

Arrival	Steamer
Jan. 31	Alexandra
Feb. 18	Londonian
Mar. 7	Alexandra
Apr. 27	Georgian
May 16	Alexandra
May 31	Georgian
June 20	Alexandra
July 5	Georgian
July 25	Alexandra
Aug. 12	Cleopatra
Aug. 29	Alexandra
Sept. 13	Georgian

WILSON LINE
Hull—New York

N. Y.

Arrival	Steamer
Jan. 14	Martello
Feb. 26	Buffalo
May 27	Buffalo
June 2	Francisco
June 20	Colorado
July 23	Ohio
Aug. 15	Buffalo
Aug. 19	Idaho
Aug. 26	Francisco
Sept. 17	Ontario
Sept. 26	Buffalo
Oct. 3	Idaho
Nov. 7	Buffalo
Nov. 29	Francisco
Dec. 17	Buffalo

ADDITIONAL ARRIVALS
Amsterdam, Rotterdam—New York

N. Y.

Arrival	Steamer
Jan. 31	P. Frederick Hendrik
June 27	Prins Willem V
Aug. 15	Oranje Nassau

Antwerp—New York

N. Y.

Arrival	Steamer
Jan. 13	Berlin
Jan. 22	British King
Feb. 15	Berlin
Mar. 15	British King
Aug. 26	British King
Sept. 20	Equatoria
Nov. 21	British King
Nov. 25	Scotia
Dec. 13	Italia

Bordeaux—New York

N. Y.

Arrival	Steamer
Jan. 7	Chateau Lafite
Feb. 14	Chateau Lafite
Apr. 11	Chateau Lafite
Apr. 25	Panama
Oct. 31	Panama

British Ports—New York

N. Y.

Arrival	Steamer
Feb. 26	Croft
May 30	Croft
July 13	Croft
Aug. 27	Croft
Aug. 30	Mohican
Nov. 6	Kansas City

French Ports—New York

N. Y.

Arrival	Steamer
June 23	Port Chalmers

German Ports—New York

N. Y.

Arrival	Steamer
Mar. 12	Aragonia
Apr. 16	Hispania
May 10	Aragonia
May 16	Ellen Rickmers
June 6	Hispania
July 5	Aragonia

Glasgow—New York

N. Y.

Arrival	Steamer
Jan. 28	Boadicea

Hamburg—New York

N. Y.

Arrival	Steamer
Jan. 17	Christiana
Feb. 14	Arabia
Feb. 23	Hispania
Mar. 10	Geestemunde
Mar. 29	Arabia
July 21	Knight Errant

Year 1898

ADDITIONAL ARRIVALS
Hamburg—New York
(Continued)
N. Y.

Arrival	Steamer
Aug. 8	Hispania
Aug. 19	Washington
Sept. 20	Hispania
Oct. 4	Christiana

London—New York
N. Y.

Arrival	Steamer
Mar. 14	Winifreda
Apr. 19	Winifreda
May 23	Winifreda
June 27	Winifreda
July 25	Europa
Aug. 1	Winifreda
Aug. 23	Menantic
Aug. 30	Europa
Sept. 6	Winifreda
Sept. 19	Port Melbourne
Oct. 10	Europa
Dec. 6	Port Melbourne

ADDITIONAL ARRIVALS
Mediterranean—New York
N. Y.

Arrival	Steamer
Feb. 2	Altai
Mar. 1	Altai
Apr. 12	Notre Dame De Salut
May 24	Altai
May 30	Sahara
June 21	Altai
July 19	Altai
Aug. 7	Laughton
Aug. 29	Altai
Sept. 26	Altai
Oct. 24	Altai
Oct. 31	Vienna
Nov. 22	Altai
Dec. 19	Altai

Scandinavian Ports—New York
N. Y.

Arrival	Steamer
Feb. 27	Manitoban

ADDITIONAL ARRIVALS
Scandinavian Ports—New York
(Continued)
N. Y.

Arrival	Steamer
Aug. 22	Wieneland
Oct. 8	Polarstjernen

Southampton—New York
N. Y.

Arrival	Steamer
Aug. 30	Pennland
Sept. 14	Rhynland
Sept. 29	Pennland

Spanish Ports—New York
N. Y.

Arrival	Steamer
Jan. 14	Santo Domingo
Jan. 24	San Augustin
Feb. 14	Santo Domingo
Mar. 13	Santo Domingo
Mar. 25	San Augustin
Sept. 17	Gran Antilla

Year 1899

ALLAN STATE LINE
Glasgow—New York
N. Y.

Arrival	Steamer
Jan. 10	Pomeranian
Jan. 18	State of Nebraska
Jan. 24	Assyrian
Jan. 30	Norwegian
Feb. 23	Pomeranian
Mar. 6	Assyrian
Mar. 17	State of Nebraska
Apr. 1	Siberian
Apr. 17	Pomeranian
Apr. 27	State of Nebraska
May 15	Buenos Ayrean
May 23	Mongolian
June 21	Mongolian
July 5	State of Nebraska
July 19	Mongolian
Aug. 2	State of Nebraska
Aug. 17	Mongolian
Aug. 22	Orcadian
Aug. 28	Numidian
Sept. 5	State of Nebraska
Sept. 11	Laurentian
Sept. 19	Mongolian
Sept. 29	Orcadian
Oct. 3	Numidian
Oct. 11	State of Nebraska
Oct. 16	Laurentian
Nov. 3	Orcadian
Nov. 11	State of Nebraska
Nov. 18	Pomeranian
Dec. 16	State of Nebraska
Dec. 30	Pomeranian

AMERICAN LINE
Southampton—New York
N. Y.

Arrival	Steamer
Jan. 2	Paris
Jan. 6	Saint Louis
Jan. 11	Saint Paul
Jan. 23	Paris
Feb. 14	Paris
Feb. 20	Saint Paul
Feb. 25	Saint Louis
Mar. 11	Saint Paul
Mar. 18	Saint Louis
Apr. 3	New York
Apr. 24	New York
Apr. 29	Saint Louis
May 8	Paris
May 15	Saint Paul
May 17	New York
May 20	Saint Louis
June 3	Saint Paul
June 10	Saint Louis
June 19	New York
June 26	Saint Paul
July 1	Saint Louis
July 10	New York
July 15	Saint Paul
July 31	New York
Aug. 5	Saint Louis
Aug. 12	Saint Paul
Aug. 21	New York

AMERICAN LINE
Southampton—New York
(Continued)
N. Y.

Arrival	Steamer
Aug. 26	Saint Louis
Sept. 2	Saint Paul
Sept. 11	New York
Sept. 16	Saint Louis
Oct. 2	New York
Oct. 7	Saint Louis
Oct. 14	Saint Paul
Oct. 28	Saint Louis
Nov. 6	Saint Paul
Nov. 13	New York
Nov. 20	Saint Louis
Dec. 11	Saint Louis
Dec. 23	Saint Paul

ANCHOR LINE
Glasgow—New York
N. Y.

Arrival	Steamer
Jan. 13	Furnessia
Jan. 28	Ethiopia
Feb. 14	Anchoria
Feb. 23	Furnessia
Mar. 8	Ethiopia
Mar. 22	Anchoria
Apr. 6	Furnessia
Apr. 21	Ethiopia
May 2	Anchoria
May 10	Furnessia
May 23	Ethiopia
May 29	City of Rome
June 6	Anchoria
June 14	Furnessia
June 22	Ethiopia
July 5	Anchoria
July 13	Furnessia
July 25	Ethiopia
Aug. 14	Furnessia
Aug. 28	Ethiopia
Sept. 19	Furnessia
Sept. 29	Ethiopia
Oct. 9	City of Rome
Oct. 16	Anchoria
Oct. 23	Furnessia
Nov. 10	Ethiopia
Nov. 22	Anchoria
Dec. 22	Ethiopia
Dec. 27	Anchoria

ANCHOR LINE
Mediterranean—New York
N. Y.

Arrival	Steamer
Jan. 5	Victoria
Jan. 11	California
Jan. 30	Bolivia
Mar. 4	Alsatia
Mar. 4	Karamania
Mar. 17	Victoria
Mar. 28	California
Apr. 17	Hesperia
May 1	Bolivia
May 17	Karamania

ANCHOR LINE
Mediterranean—New York
(Continued)
N. Y.

Arrival	Steamer
May 29	Victoria
June 10	California
July 10	Bolivia
July 24	Karamania
Aug. 12	Victoria
Sept. 2	Hesperia
Sept. 20	Bolivia
Oct. 2	Karamania
Oct. 12	Alsatia
Oct. 18	Victoria
Oct. 30	California
Nov. 8	Hesperia
Dec. 1	Bolivia
Dec. 18	Karamania
Dec. 26	Alsatia

ATLANTIC TRANSPORT LINE
London—New York
N. Y.

Arrival	Steamer
Jan. 17	Marquette
Jan. 19	Menominee
Jan. 24	Mesaba
Feb. 1	Manitou
Feb. 23	Menominee
Mar. 1	Marquette
Mar. 6	Mesaba
Mar. 14	Manitou
Mar. 23	Menominee
Apr. 4	Marquette
Apr. 11	Mesaba
Apr. 17	Manitou
May 1	Menominee
May 11	Marquette
May 15	Mesaba
May 22	Manitou
May 31	Menominee
June 12	Marquette
June 19	Mesaba
June 26	Manitou
July 3	Menominee
July 17	Marquette
July 24	Mesaba
July 31	Manitou
Aug. 7	Menominee
Aug. 21	Marquette
Aug. 28	Mesaba
Sept. 5	Manitou
Sept. 11	Menominee
Sept. 19	Mohawk
Sept. 25	Marquette
Oct. 2	Mesaba
Oct. 9	Manitou
Oct. 16	Menominee
Oct. 26	Marquette
Nov. 9	Mesaba
Nov. 16	Manitou
Nov. 22	Menominee
Dec. 11	Mesaba
Dec. 20	Manitou
Dec. 27	Menominee

Year 1899

AUSTRO-AMERICANA LINE
Mediterranean—New York

N. Y.

Arrival	Steamer
Sept. 25	Gottfried Schenker

COMPANIA TRANSATLANTICA LINE
(Spanish Line)
Spanish Ports—New York

N. Y.

Arrival	Steamer
Jan. 25	Manuel S. Villaverde
Feb. 6	Mexico
Feb. 23	Mexico
Feb. 27	Manuel S. Villaverde
Mar. 6	San Agustin
Mar. 16	Mexico
Mar. 27	Manuel S. Villaverde
Apr. 10	Manuel S. Villaverde
Apr. 15	San Agustin
Apr. 25	Manuel S. Villaverde
May 9	Rabat
May 15	San Agustin
May 25	Rabat
June 5	Manuel S. Villaverde
June 15	San Agustin
June 26	Manuel S. Villaverde
July 6	Rabat
July 15	San Agustin
July 25	Rabat
Aug. 4	Manuel S. Villaverde
Aug. 21	San Agustin
Aug. 25	Manuel S. Villaverde
Sept. 5	Rabat
Sept. 14	San Agustin
Sept. 25	Rabat
Oct. 4	Manuel S. Villaverde
Oct. 16	San Agustin
Oct. 27	Manuel S. Villaverde
Nov. 6	Rabat
Nov. 17	San Agustin

CUNARD LINE
Liverpool, Queenstown—New York

N. Y.

Arrival	Steamer
Jan. 4	Aurania
Jan. 9	Umbria
Jan. 17	Servia
Jan. 21	Campania
Jan. 30	Aurania
Feb. 14	Etruria
Feb. 27	Umbria
Mar. 4	Lucania
Mar. 13	Etruria
Mar. 18	Campania
Mar. 27	Umbria
Apr. 3	Lucania
Apr. 10	Etruria
Apr. 15	Campania
Apr. 24	Umbria
Apr. 29	Lucania
May 4	Aurania
May 8	Etruria

CUNARD LINE
Liverpool, Queenstown—New York
(Continued)

N. Y.

Arrival	Steamer
May 13	Campania
May 18	Servia
May 22	Umbria
May 27	Lucania
June 5	Etruria
June 10	Campania
June 15	Servia
June 19	Umbria
June 24	Lucania
June 29	Aurania
July 3	Etruria
July 17	Umbria
July 22	Lucania
July 31	Etruria
Aug. 5	Campania
Aug. 19	Lucania
Aug. 24	Aurania
Aug. 26	Etruria
Sept. 2	Campania
Sept. 7	Servia
Sept. 18	Lucania
Sept. 21	Aurania
Sept. 25	Etruria
Oct. 2	Campania
Oct. 6	Servia
Oct. 9	Umbria
Oct. 14	Lucania
Oct. 23	Etruria
Oct. 30	Campania
Nov. 6	Umbria
Nov. 13	Lucania
Nov. 20	Etruria
Nov. 25	Campania
Dec. 4	Umbria
Dec. 9	Lucania
Dec. 18	Etruria
Dec. 23	Campania

FABRE LINE
Mediterranean—New York

N. Y.

Arrival	Steamer
Jan. 9	Britannia
Feb. 9	Alesia
Feb. 24	Patria
Feb. 25	Burgundia
Apr. 3	Nuestria
April 11	Alesia
Apr. 29	Patria
May 1	Burgundia
May 9	Massilia
May 27	Nuestria
June 17	Patria
June 29	Britannia
July 26	Massilia
Aug. 8	Patria
Aug. 23	Nuestria
Oct. 2	Patria
Oct. 2	Massilia
Oct. 23	Nuestria
Nov. 24	Massilia
Dec. 1	Patria
Dec. 21	Nuestria

FRENCH LINE
(Compagnie Generale Transatlantique)
Havre—New York

N. Y.

Arrival	Steamer
Jan. 3	La Gascogne
Jan. 9	La Champagne
Jan. 15	La Bretagne
Jan. 24	La Normandie
Feb. 6	La Champagne
Feb. 15	La Bretagne
Feb. 20	La Touraine
Feb. 28	La Normandie
Mar. 6	La Champagne
Mar. 13	La Bretagne
Mar. 20	La Touraine
Mar. 27	La Normandie
Apr. 3	La Champagne
Apr. 10	La Bretagne
Apr. 17	La Touraine
Apr. 24	La Gascogne
May 1	La Normandie
May 8	La Champagne
May 15	La Bretagne
May 22	La Touraine
May 29	La Gascogne
June 5	La Champagne
June 12	La Touraine
June 19	La Bretagne
June 26	La Gascogne
July 3	La Champagne
July 10	La Normandie
July 17	La Bretagne
July 24	La Gascogne
July 29	La Touraine
Aug. 7	La Champagne
Aug. 14	La Bretagne
Aug. 21	La Normandie
Aug. 26	La Touraine
Sept. 4	La Champagne
Sept. 11	La Gascogne
Sept. 18	La Bretagne
Sept. 25	La Touraine
Oct. 2	La Normandie
Oct. 9	La Champagne
Oct. 16	La Gascogne
Oct. 23	La Bretagne
Oct. 30	La Touraine
Nov. 7	La Champagne
Nov. 13	La Gascogne
Nov. 20	La Bretagne
Nov. 27	La Normandie
Dec. 4	La Champagne
Dec. 11	La Gascogne
Dec. 18	L'Aquitaine
Dec. 26	La Bretagne

HAMBURG-AMERICAN LINE
Hamburg—New York

N. Y.

Arrival	Steamer
Jan. 2	Patria
Jan. 3	Albano
Jan. 19	Phoenicia
Jan. 21	Bulgaria
Jan. 21	Pisa
Jan. 23	Pennsylvania
Jan. 31	Brasilia
Feb. 6	Palatia

Year 1899

HAMBURG-AMERICAN LINE
Hamburg—New York
(Continued)

N. Y.

Arrival	Steamer
Feb. 21	Patria
Feb. 27	Phoenicia
Mar. 1	Brasilia
Mar. 2	Albano
Mar. 3	Pennsylvania
Mar. 13	Arcadia
Mar. 16	Bohemia
Mar. 18	Palatia
Mar. 23	Pisa
Mar. 27	Pretoria
Apr. 1	Patria
Apr. 15	Graf Waldersee
Apr. 17	Sorrento
Apr. 22	Pennsylvania
Apr. 25	Albano
Apr. 29	Furst Bismarck
Apr. 29	Palatia
May 8	Pretoria
May 12	Brasilia
May 13	Patria
May 13	Pompeji
May 19	Patricia
May 24	Phoenicia
May 26	Arabia
May 27	Graf Waldersee
May 27	Furst Bismarck
May 31	Pisa
June 2	Pennsylvania
June 8	Bulgaria
June 10	Augusta Victoria
June 10	Palatia
June 10	Sorrento
June 17	Pretoria
June 21	Albano
June 21	Brasilia
June 23	Patria
June 27	Furst Bismarck
June 30	Patricia
July 5	Phoenicia
July 7	Pompeji
July 14	Pennsylvania
July 19	Bulgaria
July 21	Furst Bismarck
July 22	Palatia
July 28	Pretoria
Aug. 2	Brasilia
Aug. 4	Patria
Aug. 4	Sorrento
Aug. 5	Augusta Victoria
Aug. 11	Patricia
Aug. 14	Phoenicia
Aug. 15	Albano
Aug. 18	Furst Bismarck
Aug. 18	Graf Waldersee
Aug. 24	Pennsylvania
Aug. 29	Bulgaria
Aug. 31	Pompeji
Sept. 2	Augusta Victoria
Sept. 2	Palatia
Sept. 8	Columbia
Sept. 9	Pretoria
Sept. 13	Brasilia
Sept. 15	Furst Bismarck
Sept. 15	Patria

HAMBURG-AMERICAN LINE
Hamburg—New York
(Continued)

N. Y.

Arrival	Steamer
Sept. 22	Patricia
Sept. 25	Phoenicia
Sept. 30	Graf Waldersee
Sept. 30	Sorrento
Oct. 2	Augusta Victoria
Oct. 6	Columbia
Oct. 7	Pennsylvania
Oct. 12	Albano
Oct. 13	Furst Bismarck
Oct. 20	Pretoria
Oct. 24	Brasilia
Oct. 26	Italia
Oct. 28	Patria
Oct. 30	Augusta Victoria
Nov. 4	Patricia
Nov. 13	Graf Waldersee
Nov. 13	Furst Bismarck
Nov. 18	Pennsylvania
Nov. 28	Belgravia
Nov. 28	Bulgaria
Dec. 9	Albano
Dec. 11	Pennsylvania
Dec. 18	Patricia
Dec. 22	Columbia
Dec. 26	Graf Waldersee
Dec. 26	Phoenicia
Dec. 28	Italia

HAMBURG-AMERICAN LINE
Mediterranean—New York

N. Y.

Arrival	Steamer
Jan. 16	Augusta Victoria
Feb. 11	Furst Bismarck
Apr. 4	Augusta Victoria
Dec. 5	Augusta Victoria
Dec. 19	Furst Bismarck

HOLLAND-AMERICA LINE
Rotterdam, Amsterdam, Boulogne—New York

N. Y.

Arrival	Steamer
Jan. 4	Maasdam
Jan. 11	Rotterdam
Jan. 19	Amsterdam
Jan. 23	Werkendam
Feb. 6	Edam
Feb. 15	Spaarndam
Feb. 18	Maasdam
Feb. 23	Amsterdam
Mar. 4	Werkendam
Mar. 11	Edam
Mar. 23	Spaarndam
Mar. 27	Rotterdam
Apr. 5	Amsterdam
Apr. 7	Werkendam
Apr. 10	Statendam
Apr. 19	Maasdam
Apr. 25	Spaarndam
May 1	Rotterdam

HOLLAND-AMERICA LINE
Rotterdam, Amsterdam, Bou-
logne—New York
(Continued)

N. Y.

Arrival	Steamer
May 10	Amsterdam
May 15	Statendam
May 22	Maasdam
May 31	Spaarndam
June 5	Rotterdam
June 5	Spaarndam
June 9	Edam
June 12	Amsterdam
June 19	Statendam
June 26	Maasdam
July 10	Rotterdam
July 18	Amsterdam
July 24	Statendam
July 31	Maasdam
Aug. 7	Spaarndam
Aug. 14	Rotterdam
Aug. 22	Amsterdam
Sept. 4	Statendam
Sept. 11	Maasdam
Sept. 19	Spaarndam
Sept. 25	Rotterdam
Oct. 3	Amsterdam
Oct. 9	Statendam
Oct. 12	Werkendam
Oct. 16	Maasdam
Oct. 24	Spaarndam
Oct. 30	Rotterdam
Nov. 9	Amsterdam
Nov. 15	Statendam
Nov. 20	Maasdam
Nov. 28	Spaarndam
Dec. 4	Rotterdam
Dec. 19	Statendam
Dec. 26	Maasdam

INSULAR NAVIGATION COMPANY
Azores, Lisbon—New Bedford,
Mass.—New York

N. Y.

Arrival	Steamer
Jan. 9	Vega
Feb. 6	Peninsular
Mar. 9	Vega
Apr. 22	Vega
June 6	Peninsular
July 24	Peninsular
Sept. 9	Peninsular
Oct. 30	Peninsular
Dec. 19	Peninsular

LA VELOCE LINE
Mediterranean—New York

N. Y.

Arrival	Steamer
Sept. 8	Citta di Palermo

LINHA DE VAPORES PORTUGUEZES
Azores, Lisbon—New Bedford,
Mass.—New York

N. Y.

Arrival	Steamer
Mar. 6	Dona Maria

Year 1899

LINHA DE VAPORES PORTUGUEZES
Azores, Lisbon—New Bedford, Mass.—New York
(Continued)
N. Y.

Arrival	Steamer
Mar. 16	Oevenum
Apr. 28	Dona Maria
May 18	Oevenum
June 14	Dona Maria
July 10	Oevenum
July 24	Dona Maria
Sept. 4	Oevenum
Oct. 2	Dona Maria
Nov. 24	Dona Maria

NAVIGAZIONE GENERALE ITALIANA LINE
Mediterranean—New York
N. Y.

Arrival	Steamer
Feb. 24	Sempione
Mar. 27	Archimede
Apr. 25	Sempione
May 25	Archimede
June 27	Sempione
Aug. 5	Archimede
Sept. 1	Sempione
Oct. 10	Archimede
Nov. 4	Sempione
Nov. 29	Archimede

NORTH GERMAN LLOYD
Bremen—New York
N. Y.

Arrival	Steamer
Jan. 2	Karlsruhe
Jan. 6	Trave
Jan. 10	Gera
Jan. 17	Weimar
Jan. 19	Lahn
Jan. 21	Oldenburg
Jan. 28	Saale
Feb. 2	H. H. Meier
Feb. 7	Stuttgart
Feb. 16	Gera
Feb. 18	Lahn
Feb. 20	Fr'drich der Grosse
Feb. 24	Saale
Feb. 25	Weimar
Mar. 2	Trave
Mar. 4	Oldenburg
Mar. 8	K. William der Grosse
Mar. 9	H. H. Meier
Mar. 16	Lahn
Mar. 23	Kaiser Friedrich
Mar. 27	Bonn
Mar. 31	Trave
Apr. 5	K. William der Grosse
Apr. 7	Weimar
Apr. 13	Koenigin Luise
Apr. 14	Lahn
Apr. 20	Fr'drich der Grosse
Apr. 20	Kaiser Friedrich
Apr. 24	Willehad
Apr. 27	Trave
May 3	K. William der Grosse
May 4	H. H. Meier

NORTH GERMAN LLOYD
Bremen—New York
(Continued)
N. Y.

Arrival	Steamer
May 11	Lahn
May 15	Barbarossa
May 17	Koenigin Luise
May 23	Fr'drich der Grosse
May 25	Trave
May 31	Bremen
May 31	K. William der Grosse
June 8	Lahn
June 15	Kaiser Friedrich
June 16	H. H. Meier
June 20	Barbarossa
June 20	Koenigin Luise
June 22	Trave
June 28	Fr'drich der Grosse
June 28	K. William der Grosse
July 6	Bremen
July 6	Lahn
July 15	P. Regent Luitpold
July 20	Trave
July 22	Barbarossa
July 31	Koenigin Luise
Aug. 1	Fr'drich der Grosse
Aug. 5	Lahn
Aug. 9	K. William der Grosse
Aug. 16	P. Regent Luitpold
Aug. 17	Trave
Aug. 23	Barbarossa
Aug. 24	Saale
Aug. 29	Koenigin Luise
Sept. 2	Lahn
Sept. 5	Fr'drich der Grosse
Sept. 5	K. William der Grosse
Sept. 14	Bremen
Sept. 14	Trave
Sept. 21	Saale
Sept. 22	Oldenburg
Sept. 23	Kaiser Wilhelm II
Sept. 27	Barbarossa
Oct. 4	K. William der Grosse
Oct. 4	Koenigin Luise
Oct. 5	Werra
Oct. 12	Fr'drich der Grosse
Oct. 12	Trave
Oct. 18	H. H. Meier
Oct. 20	Saale
Oct. 26	Darmstadt
Oct. 26	Lahn
Oct. 30	K. William der Grosse
Nov. 6	Barbarossa
Nov. 10	Trave
Nov. 17	Saale
Nov. 18	Oldenburg
Nov. 22	K. William der Grosse
Nov. 23	H. H. Meier
Dec. 1	Darmstadt
Dec. 7	Trave
Dec. 16	Stuttgart
Dec. 23	Rhein
Dec. 28	H. H. Meier

NORTH GERMAN LLOYD
Mediterranean—New York
N. Y.

Arrival	Steamer
Jan. 12	Ems

NORTH GERMAN LLOYD
Mediterranean—New York
(Continued)
N. Y.

Arrival	Steamer
Jan. 30	Kaiser Wilhelm II
Feb. 1	Aller
Feb. 23	Ems
Mar. 18	Aller
Mar. 27	Kaiser Wilhelm II
Mar. 31	Ems
Apr. 12	Saale
Apr. 20	Aller
May 1	Kaiser Wilhelm II
May 4	Ems
May 18	Saale
May 24	Aller
June 3	Kaiser Wilhelm II
June 7	Ems
June 22	Saale
June 28	Aller
July 12	Ems
Aug. 9	Aller
Sept. 6	Ems
Sept. 20	Aller
Oct. 12	Ems
Oct. 26	Aller
Nov 2	Kaiser Wilhelm II
Nov. 16	Werra
Nov. 23	Ems
Nov. 29	Aller
Dec. 14	Kaiser Wilhelm II
Dec. 29	Werra

PRINCE LINE
Mediterranean—New York
N. Y.

Arrival	Steamer
Jan. 6	Roman Prince
Jan. 6	Trojan Prince
Jan. 21	Kaffir Prince
Feb. 2	Spartan Prince
Feb. 23	Tartar Prince
Mar. 11	Trojan Prince
Mar. 21	Roman Prince
Apr. 5	Kaffir Prince
Apr. 6	Spartan Prince
May 8	Tartar Prince
May 18	Trojan Prince
May 23	Cyprian Prince
June 6	Roman Prince
June 14	Spartan Prince
June 26	Grecian Prince
July 10	Tartar Prince
July 22	Kaffir Prince
July 27	Trojan Prince
Aug. 5	Cyprian Prince
Aug. 17	Spartan Prince
Sept. 5	Roman Prince
Sept. 13	Tartar Prince
Sept. 27	Trojan Prince
Oct. 14	Cyprian Prince
Oct. 19	Spartan Prince
Oct. 25	Grecian Prince
Nov. 16	Tartar Prince
Nov. 24	Trojan Prince
Dec. 5	Roman Prince
Dec. 19	Spartan Prince

Year 1899

RED STAR LINE
Antwerp—New York
N. Y.

Arrival	Steamer
Jan. 9	Noordland
Jan. 18	Friesland
Jan. 26	Southwark
Feb. 1	Westernland
Feb. 11	Kensington
Feb. 20	Noordland
Feb. 28	Friesland
Mar. 1	Southwark
Mar. 8	Westernland
Mar. 15	Kensington
Mar. 23	Noordland
Mar. 28	Friesland
Apr. 5	Southwark
Apr. 13	Westernland
Apr. 19	Kensington
Apr. 26	Noordland
May 2	Friesland
May 11	Southwark
May 17	Westernland
May 24	Kensington
May 31	Noordland
June 6	Friesland
June 14	Southwark
June 21	Westernland
June 28	Kensington
July 6	Noordland
July 11	Friesland
July 25	Southwark
Aug. 2	Westernland
Aug. 9	Kensington
Aug. 16	Noordland
Aug. 22	Friesland
Aug. 26	Westernland
Aug. 29	Southwark
Sept. 11	Kensington
Sept. 16	Westernland
Sept. 20	Noordland
Sept. 26	Friesland
Oct. 4	Southwark
Oct. 17	Kensington
Oct. 25	Noordland
Nov. 2	Friesland
Nov. 9	Southwark
Nov. 22	Kensington
Nov. 29	Noordland
Dec. 5	Friesland
Dec. 13	Southwark
Dec. 27	Kensington

SCANDINAVIAN-AMERICAN LINE
Scandinavian Ports—New York
N. Y.

Arrival	Steamer
Jan. 5	Hekla
Jan. 6	Venus
Jan. 18	Island
Jan. 30	Thingvalla
Feb. 16	Norge
Feb. 25	Hekla
Mar. 11	Island
Mar. 28	Thingvalla
Apr. 10	Norge
Apr. 22	Hekla
May 5	Island

SCANDINAVIAN-AMERICAN LINE
Scandinavian Ports—New York
(Continued)
N. Y.

Arrival	Steamer
June 2	Norge
June 17	Hekla
June 30	Island
July 15	Thingvalla
Aug. 11	Hekla
Aug. 25	Island
Sept. 9	Thingvalla
Sept. 23	Norge
Oct. 6	Hekla
Oct. 20	Wineland
Oct. 23	Island
Nov. 8	Thingvalla
Nov. 20	Norge
Nov. 27	Hekla
Dec. 6	Venus
Dec. 18	Island

WHITE STAR LINE
Liverpool—New York
N. Y.

Arrival	Steamer
Jan. 2	Britannic
Jan. 5	Majestic
Jan. 9	Nomadic
Jan. 11	Cymric
Jan. 16	Germanic
Jan. 19	Teutonic
Jan. 19	Tauric
Feb. 1	Cevic
Feb. 2	Majestic
Feb. 11	Germanic
Feb. 15	Nomadic
Feb. 16	Cymric
Feb. 17	Teutonic
Feb. 23	Tauric
Mar. 1	Bovic
Mar. 2	Majestic
Mar. 6	Cevic
Mar. 16	Teutonic
Mar. 22	Nomadic
Mar. 25	Cymric
Mar. 28	Tauric
Mar. 30	Majestic
Apr. 5	Cevic
Apr. 8	Britannic
Apr. 13	Cevic
Apr. 13	Teutonic
Apr. 22	Cymric
Apr. 24	Nomadic
May 2	Tauric
May 6	Britannic
May 9	Bovic
May 11	Teutonic
May 16	Cevic
May 19	Cymric
May 24	Majestic
May 30	Nomadic
June 2	Britannic
June 6	Tauric
June 8	Teutonic
June 13	Bovic
June 16	Germanic
June 19	Cevic

WHITE STAR LINE
Liverpool—New York
(Continued)
N. Y.

Arrival	Steamer
June 22	Majestic
July 3	Cymric
July 3	Nomadic
July 6	Teutonic
July 11	Tauric
July 14	Germanic
July 17	Bovic
July 20	Majestic
July 24	Cevic
July 28	Britannic
July 31	Georgic
Aug. 2	Teutonic
Aug. 4	Nomadic
Aug. 11	Germanic
Aug. 14	Tauric
Aug. 16	Majestic
Aug. 21	Bovic
Aug. 25	Britannic
Aug. 28	Cevic
Aug. 30	Teutonic
Sept. 5	Georgic
Sept. 8	Germanic
Sept. 9	Nomadic
Sept. 11	Cymric
Sept. 13	Oceanic
Sept. 19	Tauric
Sept. 21	Majestic
Sept. 26	Bovic
Sept. 28	Teutonic
Oct. 5	Cevic
Oct. 6	Germanic
Oct. 12	Oceanic
Oct. 12	Georgic
Oct. 16	Cymric
Oct. 19	Majestic
Oct. 24	Tauric
Oct. 25	Teutonic
Oct. 30	Bovic
Nov. 9	Oceanic
Nov. 10	Cevic
Nov. 16	Majestic
Nov. 17	Georgic
Nov. 22	Cymric
Nov. 23	Teutonic
Nov. 27	Tauric
Dec. 1	Germanic
Dec. 5	Bovic
Dec. 6	Oceanic
Dec. 15	Cevic
Dec. 21	Teutonic
Dec. 22	Georgic
Dec. 29	Germanic

WILSON LINE
Hull—New York
N. Y.

Arrival	Steamer
Jan. 13	Francisco
Jan. 20	Martello
Jan. 21	Colorado
Feb. 1	Buffalo
Feb. 15	Idaho
Feb. 27	Francisco
Mar. 6	Martello
Mar. 16	Colorado

Year 1899

WILSON LINE
Hull—New York
(Continued)

N.Y. Arrival	Steamer
Mar. 27	Buffalo
Apr. 3	Idaho
Apr. 12	Francisco
Apr. 22	Martello
Apr. 27	Colorado
May 15	Idaho
May 22	Francisco
May 27	Hindoo
June 12	Colorado
June 26	Idaho
July 1	Buffalo
July 10	Francisco
July 18	Martello
July 24	Colorado
Aug. 12	Buffalo
Aug. 18	Francisco
Aug. 28	Hindoo
Sept. 2	Colorado
Sept. 15	Idaho
Sept. 22	Buffalo
Oct. 2	Francisco
Oct. 13	Colorado
Oct. 30	Galileo
Nov. 6	Buffalo
Nov. 21	Hindoo
Nov. 27	Colorado
Dec. 11	Galileo

ADDITIONAL ARRIVALS
Antwerp—New York

N.Y. Arrival	Steamer
June 22	Kentucky
Sept. 23	Saxon Prince
Oct. 12	Saint Andrew

British Ports—New York

N.Y. Arrival	Steamer
Jan. 23	Wells City
Feb. 2	Croma
Feb. 15	Kansas City
Feb. 23	Llandaff City
Mar. 2	Boston City
Mar. 15	Wells City
Apr. 11	Exeter City
Apr. 17	Llandaff City
Apr. 22	Boston City
May 16	Wells City
May 27	Exeter City
June 5	Llandaff City
June 15	Kansas City

ADDITIONAL ARRIVALS
British Ports—New York
(Continued)

N.Y. Arrival	Steamer
June 23	Jersey City
July 3	Wells City
July 17	Croma
July 18	Exeter City
July 24	Llandaff City
Aug. 1	Kansas City
Aug. 5	Jersey City
Aug. 12	Critic
Aug. 14	Wells City
Aug. 25	Exeter City
Aug. 28	Boston City
Sept. 2	Llandaff City
Sept. 11	Kansas City
Sept. 18	Masconomo
Sept. 22	Jersey City
Sept. 23	Saxon Prince
Sept. 27	Wells City
Sept. 28	British Princess
Oct. 2	Critic
Oct. 2	Dona Maria
Oct. 6	Boston City
Oct. 9	Exeter City
Oct. 16	Llandaff City
Oct. 19	Kansas City
Nov. 8	Jersey City
Nov. 20	Wells City
Nov. 22	Boston City
Nov. 25	Critic
Nov. 27	Exeter City
Nov. 28	Llandaff City
Dec. 2	Kansas City
Dec. 28	Jersey City

Glasgow—New York

N.Y. Arrival	Steamer
Dec. 9	Tainui

Hamburg—New York

N.Y. Arrival	Steamer
Sept. 10	Kaiser Friedrich
Sept. 14	Barcelona
Nov. 8	Barcelona
Nov. 8	Kaiser Friedrich

London—New York

N.Y. Arrival	Steamer
Feb. 25	Montcalm
Apr. 3	Montcalm
May 5	Montcalm

ADDITIONAL ARRIVALS
London—New York
(Continued)

N.Y. Arrival	Steamer
June 16	Montcalm
July 24	Montcalm
Aug. 24	Montcalm
Sept. 23	Europa
Oct. 2	Montcalm
Nov. 8	Europa
Nov. 15	Montcalm
Dec. 26	Montcalm

Mediterranean—New York

N.Y. Arrival	Steamer
Feb. 24	Chateau Yquem
Mar. 13	Massalia
Apr. 15	Alesia
May 16	Chateau Yquem
June 15	Chateau Lafite
July 10	Chateau Yquem
July 29	Chateau Lafite
Aug. 9	Mark Lane
Aug. 28	Gardenia
Sept. 5	Chateau Yquem
Sept. 18	Chateau Lafite
Nov. 2	Chateau Lafite
Nov. 3	Chateau Yquem
Dec. 26	Chateau Lafite

Rotterdam, Amsterdam— New York

N.Y. Arrival	Steamer
Dec. 20	Deutschland

Scandinavian Ports—New York

N.Y. Arrival	Steamer
May 18	Orion
May 22	Arkansas
Oct. 2	Polarstjirnan
Nov. 28	S. P. Holmblad
Dec. 11	Alexandra

Southampton—New York

N.Y. Arrival	Steamer
May 18	Kaiser Friedrich

Spanish Ports—New York

N.Y. Arrival	Steamer
Feb. 6	Santiago de Cuba
Apr. 21	Santiago de Cuba

Year 1900

ALLAN STATE LINE
Glasgow—New York
N. Y.

Arrival	Steamer
Jan. 8	Sarmatian
Mar. 3	Corean
Mar. 10	State of Nebraska
Mar. 28	Sarmatian
Apr. 17	State of Nebraska
Apr. 27	Laurentian
May 14	Norwegian
May 22	State of Nebraska
May 28	City of Rome
June 5	Laurentian
June 13	Sardinian
June 25	City of Rome
June 27	State of Nebraska
July 9	Laurentian
July 17	Sardinian
Aug. 2	State of Nebraska
Aug. 13	Laurentian
Aug. 21	Sardinian
Sept. 4	City of Rome
Sept. 5	State of Nebraska
Sept. 11	Californian
Sept. 19	Laurentian
Sept. 27	Sardinian
Oct. 9	City of Rome
Oct. 11	State of Nebraska
Oct 23	Laurentian
Oct. 31	Sardinian
Nov. 15	State of Nebraska
Nov. 28	Californian
Dec. 6	Sardinian
Dec. 27	Laurentian

AMERICAN LINE
Southampton—New York
N. Y.

Arrival	Steamer
Jan. 2	Saint Louis
Jan. 15	Saint Paul
Jan. 22	New York
Jan. 29	Saint Louis
Feb. 5	Saint Paul
Feb. 12	New York
Feb. 19	Saint Louis
Mar. 10	Saint Paul
Mar. 26	New York
Mar. 31	Saint Paul
Apr. 9	Saint Louis
Apr. 16	New York
Apr. 21	Saint Paul
May 7	New York
May 14	Saint Paul
May 21	Saint Louis
May 28	New York
June 2	Saint Paul
June 11	Saint Louis
June 25	Saint Paul
July 2	Saint Louis
July 14	Saint Paul
July 21	Saint Louis
Aug. 6	New York
Aug. 18	Saint Louis
Aug. 25	New York
Sept. 1	Saint Paul

AMERICAN LINE
Southampton—New York
(Continued)
N. Y.

Arrival	Steamer
Sept. 8	Saint Louis
Sept. 17	New York
Sept. 24	Saint Paul
Sept. 29	Saint Louis
Oct. 8	New York
Oct. 13	Saint Paul
Oct. 20	Saint Louis
Nov. 12	Saint Louis
Nov. 19	New York
Dec. 3	Saint Louis
Dec. 10	New York
Dec. 22	Saint Louis

ANCHOR LINE
Glasgow—New York
N. Y.

Arrival	Steamer
Jan. 16	Astoria
Feb. 1	Ethiopia
Feb. 5	Anchoria
Feb. 19	Astoria
Mar. 10	Anchoria
Apr. 18	Anchoria
May 9	Ethiopia
May 21	Anchoria
June 9	Astoria
June 12	Ethiopia
June 18	Furnessia
July 2	Anchoria
July 9	Astoria
July 17	Ethiopia
July 23	Furnessia
Aug. 10	Anchoria
Aug. 13	Astoria
Aug. 21	Ethiopia
Aug. 27	Furnessia
Sept. 12	Anchoria
Sept. 18	Astoria
Sept. 26	Furnessia
Oct. 3	Ethiopia
Oct. 24	Astoria
Oct. 29	Furnessia
Nov. 6	Ethiopia
Nov. 23	Anchoria
Nov. 28	Astoria
Dec. 4	Furnessia
Dec. 12	Ethiopia
Dec. 27	Anchoria

ANCHOR LINE
Mediterranean—New York
N. Y.

Arrival	Steamer
Jan. 5	Victoria
Jan. 22	Hesperia
Mar. 13	Victoria
Mar. 23	California
Apr. 5	Hesperia
Apr. 23	Bolivia
May 16	Victoria
May 25	California
June 5	Hesperia

ANCHOR LINE
Mediterranean—New York
(Continued)
N. Y.

Arrival	Steamer
July 2	Bolivia
July 19	Victoria
July 30	California
Aug. 10	Alsatia
Aug. 10	Hesperia
Oct. 1	Victoria
Nov. 8	Karamania
Nov. 23	Bolivia
Dec. 17	Victoria
Dec. 28	Alsatia

ATLANTIC TRANSPORT LINE
London—New York
N. Y.

Arrival	Steamer
Jan. 15	Marquette
Jan. 16	Mesaba
Jan. 27	Manitou
Feb. 3	Menominee
Feb. 5	Tuscarora
Feb. 15	Marquette
Feb. 20	Mesaba
Mar. 2	Manitou
Mar. 8	Menominee
Mar. 16	Tuscarora
Mar. 21	Marquette
Mar. 28	Mesaba
Apr. 3	Manitou
Apr. 12	Menominee
Apr. 21	Tuscarora
Apr. 24	Marquette
Apr. 30	Mesaba
May 11	Manitou
May 17	Menominee
May 21	Minneapolis
May 28	Tuscarora
May 29	Marquette
June 4	Mesaba
June 8	Manitou
June 19	Menominee
June 25	Minneapolis
July 2	Tuscarora
July 3	Marquette
July 9	Mesaba
July 16	Manitou
July 23	Menominee
July 30	Minneapolis
Aug. 6	Marquette
Aug. 6	Tuscarora
Aug. 13	Mesaba
Aug. 22	Minnehaha
Aug. 27	Manitou
Sept. 1	Minneapolis
Sept. 10	Marquette
Sept. 17	Mesaba
Sept. 17	Tuscarora
Sept. 18	Minnehaha
Sept. 25	Menominee
Oct. 1	Manitou
Oct. 16	Minnehaha
Oct. 17	Marquette

Year 1900

ATLANTIC TRANSPORT LINE
London—New York
(Continued)
N. Y.

Arrival	Steamer
Oct. 20	Tuscarora
Oct. 22	Minneapolis
Oct. 24	Mesaba
Oct. 29	Menominee
Nov. 5	Manitou
Nov. 14	Minnehaha
Nov. 22	Marquette
Nov. 26	Minneapolis
Nov. 27	Mesaba
Nov. 27	Tuscarora
Dec. 5	Menominee
Dec. 12	Manitou
Dec. 18	Minnehaha
Dec. 31	Minneapolis

AUSTRO-AMERICANA LINE
Mediterranean—New York
N. Y.

Arrival	Steamer
Aug. 2	Abbazia

COMPANIA TRANSATLANTICA LINE
(Spanish Line)
Spanish Ports—New York
N. Y.

Arrival	Steamer
June 11	Leon XIII
June 11	Gran Antilla
July 5	Leon XIII
July 11	Montserrat
Aug. 3	Montserrat
Aug. 31	Leon XIII
Sept. 10	Montserrat
Oct. 1	Montserrat
Oct. 12	Leon XIII
Nov. 5	Leon XIII
Nov. 10	Montserrat
Dec. 1	Montserrat
Dec. 14	Leon XIII

CUNARD LINE
Liverpool—New York
N. Y.

Arrival	Steamer
Jan. 6	Lucania
Jan. 15	Etruria
Jan. 22	Campania
Feb. 3	Lucania
Feb. 17	Campania
Mar. 5	Lucania
Mar. 12	Etruria
Mar. 17	Campania
Mar. 31	Lucania
Apr. 9	Etruria
Apr. 14	Campania
Apr. 24	Ivernia
Apr. 28	Lucania
May 7	Etruria

CUNARD LINE
Liverpool—New York
(Continued)
N. Y.

Arrival	Steamer
May 14	Campania
May 22	Ivernia
May 26	Lucania
June 4	Etruria
June 9	Campania
June 18	Servia
June 23	Lucania
July 2	Etruria
July 7	Campania
July 16	Servia
July 21	Lucania
July 30	Umbria
Aug. 4	Campania
Aug. 13	Etruria
Aug. 16	Servia
Aug. 18	Lucania
Aug. 27	Umbria
Sept. 1	Campania
Sept. 8	Etruria
Sept. 15	Lucania
Sept. 24	Umbria
Oct. 1	Campania
Oct. 8	Etruria
Oct. 12	Servia
Oct. 13	Lucania
Oct. 22	Umbria
Oct. 27	Campania
Nov. 5	Etruria
Nov. 10	Lucania
Nov. 19	Umbria
Nov. 26	Campania
Dec. 3	Etruria
Dec. 8	Lucania
Dec. 17	Umbria
Dec. 22	Campania
Dec. 31	Etruria

FABRE LINE
Mediterranean—New York
N. Y.

Arrival	Steamer
Jan. 3	Chateau Yquem
Jan. 5	Burgundia
Jan. 25	Massilia
Feb. 5	Patria
Feb. 17	Nuestria
Mar. 5	Chateau Yquem
Mar. 23	Massilia
Apr. 4	Patria
Apr. 19	Nuestria
Apr. 28	Chateau Yquem
May 16	Massilia
May 29	Patria
June 11	Nuestria
June 23	Chateau Yquem
July 14	Massilia
July 23	Patria
Aug. 6	Burgundia
Sept. 10	Nuestria
Oct. 2	Burgundia
Nov. 5	Patria
Nov. 12	Nuestria
Nov. 26	Burgundia
Dec. 29	Patria

FRENCH LINE
(Compagnie Generale Transatlantique)
Havre—New York
N. Y.

Arrival	Steamer
Jan. 2	La Normandie
Jan. 8	La Champagne
Jan. 15	La Gascogne
Jan. 22	La Bretagne
Jan. 30	La Champagne
Feb. 5	La Champagne
Feb. 12	La Gascogne
Feb. 19	La Touraine
Feb. 27	La Normandie
Mar. 5	La Champagne
Mar. 12	L'Aquitaine
Mar. 19	La Gascogne
Mar. 26	La Touraine
Apr. 2	La Bretagne
Apr. 9	L'Aquitaine
Apr. 16	Saint Germain
Apr. 16	La Gascogne
Apr. 23	La Touraine
Apr. 30	La Bretagne
May 7	La Champagne
May 14	La Gascogne
May 21	L'Aquitaine
May 28	La Touraine
June 4	La Bretagne
June 11	La Gascogne
June 18	La Champagne
June 25	L'Aquitaine
July 2	La Touraine
July 9	La Gascogne
July 16	La Bretagne
July 23	La Champagne
July 30	L'Aquitaine
Aug. 16	La Bretagne
Aug. 20	La Lorraine
Aug. 27	L'Aquitaine
Sept. 3	La Touraine
Sept. 10	La Bretagne
Sept. 15	La Lorraine
Sept. 21	Saint Germain
Sept. 24	La Gascogne
Oct. 1	L'Aquitaine
Oct. 8	La Touraine
Oct. 15	La Lorraine
Oct. 22	La Bretagne
Oct. 27	L'Aquitaine
Oct. 31	Saint Germain
Nov. 5	La Touraine
Nov. 12	La Champagne
Nov. 20	L'Aquitaine
Nov. 26	La Lorraine
Dec. 3	La Gascogne
Dec. 10	La Bretagne
Dec. 26	La Normandie
Dec. 31	La Gascogne

HAMBURG-AMERICAN LINE
Hamburg—New York
N. Y.

Arrival	Steamer
Jan. 4	Barcelona
Jan. 8	Belgravia
Jan. 13	Pennsylvania
Jan. 22	Pretoria
Jan. 22	Pisa

Year 1900

HAMBURG-AMERICAN LINE
Hamburg—New York

N. Y.

Arrival	Steamer
Jan. 29	Palatia
Feb. 5	Albano
Feb. 5	Patricia
Feb. 12	Graf Waldersee
Feb. 26	Pennsylvania
Mar. 5	Barcelona
Mar. 5	Pretoria
Mar. 10	Palatia
Mar. 14	Pisa
Mar. 16	Patricia
Mar. 23	Graf Waldersee
Mar. 29	Albano
Mar. 31	Phoenicia
Apr. 7	Kaiser Friedrich
Apr. 7	Pennsylvania
Apr. 14	Columbia
Apr. 16	Milano
Apr. 16	Pretoria
Apr. 17	Belgravia
Apr. 21	Palatia
Apr. 27	Barcelona
Apr. 27	Furst Bismarck
Apr. 30	Batavia
May 4	Kaiser Friedrich
May 4	Patricia
May 12	Columbia
May 12	Pisa
May 14	Graf Waldersee
May 19	Augusta Victoria
May 19	Phoenicia
May 25	Pennsylvania
May 25	Albano
May 26	Furst Bismarck
June 1	Kaiser Friedrich
June 4	Pretoria
June 8	Milano
June 8	Palatia
June 9	Columbia
June 13	Batavia
June 16	Albano
June 16	Patricia
June 20	Barcelona
June 22	Graf Waldersee
June 23	Furst Bismarck
June 30	Phoenicia
June 30	Kaiser Friedrich
July 5	Pisa
July 6	Pennsylvania
July 7	Columbia
July 10	Belgravia
July 13	Deutschland
July 19	Albano
July 20	Palatia
July 21	Furst Bismarck
July 27	Patricia
July 28	Kaiser Friedrich
Aug. 3	Milano
Aug. 4	Columbia
Aug. 4	Graf Waldersee
Aug. 6	Deutschland
Aug. 13	Bulgaria
Aug. 16	Barcelona
Aug. 17	Pennsylvania
Aug. 18	Furst Bismarck

HAMBURG-AMERICAN LINE
Hamburg—New York
(Continued)

N. Y.

Arrival	Steamer
Aug. 21	Belgravia
Aug. 25	Kaiser Friedrich
Sept. 1	Deutschland
Sept. 1	Columbia
Sept. 7	Patricia
Sept. 8	Augusta Victoria
Sept. 12	Albano
Sept. 14	Furst Bismarck
Sept. 14	Graf Waldersee
Sept. 24	Deutschland
Sept. 24	Bulgaria
Sept. 27	Pennsylvania
Sept. 28	Milano
Sept. 29	Columbia
Oct. 6	Augusta Victoria
Oct. 12	Barcelona
Oct. 13	Furst Bismarck
Oct. 15	Deutschland
Oct. 19	Kaiser Friedrich
Oct. 19	Patricia
Oct. 26	Columbia
Oct. 27	Graf Waldersee
Nov. 3	Augusta Victoria
Nov. 5	Deutschland
Nov. 5	Bulgaria
Nov. 8	Albano
Nov. 10	Pennsylvania
Nov. 14	Belgravia
Nov. 16	Furst Bismarck
Nov. 19	Pretoria
Nov. 30	Milano
Dec. 3	Patricia
Dec. 7	Deutschland
Dec. 8	Barcelona
Dec. 10	Graf Waldersee
Dec. 21	Bulgaria
Dec. 21	Furst Bismarck
Dec. 24	Pennsylvania

HAMBURG-AMERICAN LINE
Mediterranean—New York

N. Y.

Arrival	Steamer
Jan. 16	Augusta Victoria
Feb. 7	Lauenberg
Feb. 9	Furst Bismarck
Feb. 12	Columbia
Mar. 12	Lauenberg
Mar. 12	Furst Bismarck
Apr. 3	Augusta Victoria
Apr. 9	Lauenberg
Apr. 23	Georgia
May 7	Lauenberg
May 21	Christiania
May 30	Lauenberg
June 20	Lauenberg
July 6	Christiania
Aug. 2	Lauenberg
Sept. 17	Lauenberg
Dec. 6	Columbia
Dec. 11	Lauenberg
Dec. 21	Furst Bismarck

HOLLAND-AMERICA LINE
Rotterdam, Amsterdam—New York

N. Y.

Arrival	Steamer
Jan. 17	Amsterdam
Jan. 25	Rotterdam
Jan. 31	Maasdam
Feb. 5	Statendam
Feb. 13	Werkendam
Feb. 21	Spaarndam
Mar. 6	Maasdam
Mar. 12	Statendam
Mar. 20	Werkendam
Mar. 28	Spaarndam
Apr. 2	Rotterdam
Apr. 18	Amsterdam
Apr. 23	Statendam
May 1	Spaarndam
May 7	Rotterdam
May 16	Maasdam
May 22	Amsterdam
May 29	Potsdam
June 4	Statendam
June 13	Spaarndam
June 18	Rotterdam
June 25	Maasdam
July 2	Potsdam
July 9	Statendam
July 17	Spaarndam
July 23	Rotterdam
July 30	Maasdam
Aug. 7	Amsterdam
Aug. 13	Statendam
Aug. 21	Spaarndam
Aug. 27	Rotterdam
Sept. 4	Maasdam
Sept. 10	Amsterdam
Sept. 17	Statendam
Sept. 26	Spaarndam
Oct. 1	Rotterdam
Oct. 8	Maasdam
Oct. 16	Amsterdam
Oct. 22	Statendam
Oct. 30	Spaarndam
Nov. 5	Rotterdam
Nov. 12	Maasdam
Nov. 22	Amsterdam
Nov. 26	Statendam
Dec. 13	Spaarndam
Dec. 19	Rotterdam
Dec. 26	Amsterdam
Dec. 31	Statendam

INSULAR NAVIGATION COMPANY
Azores, Lisbon—New Bedford, Mass., New York

N. Y.

Arrival	Steamer
Feb. 7	Peninsular
May 26	Peninsular
July 19	Peninsular
Sept. 4	Peninsular
Nov. 2	Peninsular

Year 1900

LA VELOCE LINE
Mediterranean—New York

N. Y.

Arrival	Steamer
May 28	Citta di Messina
Sept. 4	Citta di Messina
Nov. 9	Citta di Messina

LINHA DE VAPORES PORTUGUEZES
Azores, Lisbon—New Bedford, Mass., New York

N. Y.

Arrival	Steamer
Jan. 23	Dona Maria
Mar. 23	Oevenum
Mar. 27	Dona Maria
May 14	Dona Maria
May 14	Oevenum
Oct. 26	Dona Maria
Nov. 7	Dona Amelia
Dec. 7	Dona Maria

NAVIGAZIONE GENERALE ITALIANA LINE
Mediterranean—New York

N. Y.

Arrival	Steamer
Jan. 9	Sempione
Feb. 17	Archimede
Mar. 17	Marco Minghetti
Apr. 6	Manilla
Apr. 24	Archimede
May 11	Sempione
May 16	Marco Minghetti
May 31	Manilla
June 26	Archimede
July 9	Sempione
Aug. 7	Archimede
Aug. 28	Vincenzo Florio
Sept. 18	Archimede
Oct. 30	Vincenzo Florio
Nov. 20	Archimede
Dec. 18	Vincenzo Florio

NORTH GERMAN LLOYD
Bremen—New York

N. Y.

Arrival	Steamer
Jan. 5	Darmstadt
Jan. 12	Trave
Jan. 18	Lahn
Jan. 22	Gera
Jan. 29	Aller
Jan. 29	Rhein
Feb. 2	Saale
Feb. 3	Dresden
Feb. 10	H. H. Meier
Feb. 10	Trave
Feb. 15	Darmstadt
Feb. 24	Aller
Mar. 2	Saale
Mar. 8	K. William der Grosse
Mar. 8	Bremen
Mar. 8	Bremen
Mar. 8	Rhein
Mar. 15	Lahn
Mar. 16	H. H. Meier
Mar. 22	Darmstadt
Mar. 22	Ka'in Maria Theresia

NORTH GERMAN LLOYD
Bremen—New York
(Continued)

N. Y.

Arrival	Steamer
Mar. 28	Fr'drich der Grosse
Mar. 30	Saale
Apr. 6	Munchen
Apr. 12	Lahn
Apr. 13	Rhein
Apr. 18	Bremen
Apr. 18	Bremen
Apr. 21	Ka'in Maria Theresia
Apr. 25	Koenigin Luise
Apr. 27	Saale
May 1	Fr'drich der Grosse
May 2	K. William der Grosse
May 11	Lahn
May 14	Main
May 17	Ka'in Maria Theresia
May 23	Bremen
May 25	Saale
May 31	Barbarossa
May 31	K. William der Grosse
June 6	Koenigin Luise
June 7	Lahn
June 13	Fr'drich der Grosse
June 14	Ka'in Maria Theresia
June 27	Bremen
June 20	Grosser Kurfuerst
June 22	Saale
June 26	Main
June 27	Bremen
June 27	K. William der Grosse
July 5	Barbarossa
July 5	Lahn
July 11	Koenigin Luise
July 12	Ka'in Maria Theresia
July 18	Fr'drich der Grosse
July 28	Grosser Kurfuerst
Aug. 1	K. William der Grosse
Aug. 4	Roland
Aug. 9	Barbarossa
Aug. 9	Lahn
Aug. 16	Ka'in Maria Theresia
Aug. 16	Koenigin Luise
Aug. 20	Trave
Aug. 24	Fr'drich der Grosse
Aug. 28	Grosser Kurfuerst
Aug. 29	K. William der Grosse
Sept. 6	Lahn
Sept. 7	Trave
Sept. 13	Barbarossa
Sept. 13	Ka'in Maria Theresia
Sept. 20	Prinzess Irene
Sept. 25	Aller
Sept. 26	Fr'drich der Grosse
Sept. 26	K. William der Grosse
Oct. 3	Grosser Kurfuerst
Oct. 4	Lahn
Oct. 9	Trave
Oct. 11	Ka'in Maria Theresia
Oct. 15	Bonn
Oct. 19	Aller
Oct. 24	K. William der Grosse
Oct. 26	Trier
Oct. 29	Weimar
Nov. 1	Fr'drich der Grosse
Nov. 1	Lahn
Nov. 8	Ka'in Maria Theresia

NORTH GERMAN LLOYD
Bremen—New York
(Continued)

N. Y.

Arrival	Steamer
Nov. 16	Trave
Nov. 19	Bonn
Nov. 23	K. William der Grosse
Nov. 30	Mainz
Dec. 6	Lahn
Dec. 20	K. William der Grosse
Dec. 22	H. H. Meier
Dec. 28	Trave
Dec. 29	Oldenburg

NORTH GERMAN LLOYD
Mediterranean—New York

N. Y.

Arrival	Steamer
Jan. 5	Ems
Jan. 25	Kaiser Wilhelm II
Feb. 1	Werra
Feb. 23	Ems
Mar. 8	Werra
Mar. 21	Trave
Mar. 28	Aller
Apr. 5	Ems
Apr. 13	Werra
Apr. 20	Kaiser Wilhelm II
Apr. 25	Trave
May 2	Aller
May 10	Ems
May 17	Werra
May 24	Kaiser Wilhelm II
May 31	Trave
June 14	Ems
June 21	Werra
July 5	Kaiser Wilhelm II
July 19	Ems
Aug. 2	Werra
Aug. 6	Aller
Aug. 16	Kaiser Wilhelm II
Aug. 30	Ems
Sept. 13	Werra
Sept. 21	Kaiser Wilhelm II
Oct. 3	Ems
Oct. 20	Werra
Nov. 3	Kaiser Wilhelm II
Nov. 8	Ems
Nov. 21	Aller
Nov. 30	Werra
Dec. 2	Kaiser Wilhelm II

PRINCE LINE
Mediterranean—New York

N. Y.

Arrival	Steamer
Jan. 25	Tartar Prince
Feb. 7	Trojan Prince
Mar. 5	Spartan Prince
Mar. 26	Tartar Prince
Apr. 13	Trojan Prince
May 28	Tartar Prince
June 18	Trojan Prince
July 6	Spartan Prince
Aug. 17	Trojan Prince
Aug. 27	Tartar Prince
Sept. 10	Spartan Prince
Oct. 3	Tartar Prince
Oct. 19	Trojan Prince

Year 1900

PRINCE LINE
Mediterranean—New York
(Continued)
N. Y.

Arrival	Steamer
Nov. 13	Spartan Prince
Nov. 27	Tartar Prince
Dec. 20	Trojan Prince

RED STAR LINE
Antwerp—New York
N. Y.

Arrival	Steamer
Jan. 5	Noordland
Jan. 18	Friesland
Feb. 2	Westernland
Feb. 14	Noordland
Feb. 21	Friesland
Mar. 1	Southwark
Mar. 7	Westernland
Mar. 14	Kensington
Mar. 21	Noordland
Mar. 27	Friesland
Apr. 5	Southwark
Apr. 12	Westernland
Apr. 18	Kensington
Apr. 25	Noordland
May 1	Friesland
May 16	Westernland
May 23	Kensington
May 31	Noordland
June 5	Friesland
June 13	Southwark
June 20	Westernland
June 27	Kensington
July 5	Noordland
July 11	Friesland
Aug. 1	Kensington
Aug. 16	Noordland
Aug. 21	Friesland
Aug. 28	Southwark
Sept. 5	Westernland
Sept. 12	Kensington
Sept. 19	Noordland
Sept. 25	Friesland
Oct. 17	Kensington
Oct. 25	Noordland
Oct. 30	Friesland
Nov. 8	Southwark
Nov. 14	Westernland
Nov. 30	Noordland
Dec. 13	Southwark
Dec. 20	Vaderland

SCANDINAVIAN-AMERICAN LINE
Scandinavian Ports—New York
N. Y.

Arrival	Steamer
Jan. 2	Thingvalla
Jan. 2	Wineland
Jan. 15	Norge
Feb. 7	Hekla
Feb. 10	Island
Feb. 27	Thingvalla
Mar. 12	Norge
Mar. 24	Hekla

SCANDINAVIAN-AMERICAN LINE
Scandinavian Ports—New York
(Continued)
N. Y.

Arrival	Steamer
Apr. 9	Island
Apr. 24	Thingvalla
May 4	Norge
May 19	Hekla
June 4	Island
June 18	Thingvalla
July 2	Norge
July 16	Hekla
Aug. 25	Norge
Sept. 7	Hekla
Sept. 21	Thingvalla
Sept. 24	Island
Oct. 8	Norge
Oct. 29	Hekla
Nov. 12	Island
Nov. 24	Norge
Dec. 1	Hekla

WHITE STAR LINE
Liverpool—New York
N. Y.

Arrival	Steamer
Jan. 17	Oceanic
Jan. 22	Cevic
Jan. 25	Teutonic
Feb. 3	Germanic
Feb. 14	Oceanic
Feb. 14	Bovic
Feb. 23	Teutonic
Mar. 2	Cevic
Mar. 3	Germanic
Mar. 14	Oceanic
Mar. 22	Teutonic
Mar. 28	Bovic
Mar. 30	Germanic
Apr. 6	Cevic
Apr. 11	Oceanic
Apr. 12	Georgic
Apr. 19	Teutonic
Apr. 27	Germanic
Apr. 30	Bovic
May 9	Cevic
May 10	Oceanic
May 16	Teutonic
May 16	Georgic
May 25	Germanic
May 31	Majestic
June 2	Bovic
June 4	Cymric
June 6	Oceanic
June 14	Teutonic
June 19	Georgic
June 22	Germanic
July 2	Bovic
July 5	Oceanic
July 9	Cymric
July 17	Cevic
July 20	Germanic
July 24	Georgic
July 26	Majestic
July 31	Bovic
Aug. 1	Oceanic

WHITE STAR LINE
Liverpool—New York
(Continued)
N. Y.

Arrival	Steamer
Aug. 7	Tauric
Aug. 9	Teutonic
Aug. 13	Cymric
Aug. 17	Germanic
Aug. 20	Cevic
Aug. 22	Majestic
Aug. 28	Georgic
Sept. 4	Bovic
Sept. 5	Teutonic
Sept. 10	Tauric
Sept. 14	Germanic
Sept. 17	Cymric
Sept. 20	Majestic
Sept. 26	Oceanic
Sept. 26	Cevic
Oct. 4	Georgic
Oct. 4	Teutonic
Oct. 9	Bovic
Oct. 12	Germanic
Oct. 16	Tauric
Oct. 18	Majestic
Oct. 22	Cymric
Oct. 24	Oceanic
Oct. 31	Teutonic
Oct. 31	Cevic
Nov. 7	Georgic
Nov. 9	Germanic
Nov. 13	Bovic
Nov. 15	Majestic
Nov. 21	Tauric
Nov. 22	Oceanic
Nov. 26	Cymric
Nov. 30	Teutonic
Dec. 7	Germanic
Dec. 8	Cevic
Dec. 14	Majestic
Dec. 14	Georgic
Dec. 21	Bovic
Dec. 26	Tauric
Dec. 27	Teutonic

WILSON, FURNESS, LEYLAND LINE
Liverpool—New York
N. Y.

Arrival	Steamer
July 23	Caledonian
July 28	Columbian
Aug. 7	Georgian
Sept. 3	Iberian
Sept. 10	Georgian
Sept. 24	Philadelphian
Oct. 1	Caledonian
Oct. 8	Iberian
Oct. 15	Georgian
Oct. 27	Philadelphian
Nov. 5	Caledonian
Nov. 12	Iberian
Nov. 20	Georgian
Nov. 30	Philadelphian
Dec. 11	Caledonian
Dec. 20	Iberian
Dec. 24	Gregian

Year 1900

WILSON LINE
Hull—New York
N. Y.

Arrival	Steamer
June 14	Buffalo
June 19	Ontario
July 20	Buffalo
Aug. 4	Ontario
Aug. 14	Colorado
Aug. 20	Consuelo
Sept. 1	Buffalo
Sept. 10	Toronto
Sept. 22	Colorado
Sept. 29	Consuelo
Oct. 15	Buffalo
Oct. 27	Toronto
Nov. 3	Colorado
Nov. 12	Consuelo
Nov. 26	Buffalo
Dec. 10	Toronto
Dec. 20	Colorado
Dec. 24	Consuelo

ADDITIONAL ARRIVALS
Antwerp—New York
N. Y.

Arrival	Steamer
June 19	British Trader
July 28	British Trader
Aug. 11	Aragonia
Sept. 8	British Trader

ADDITIONAL ARRIVALS
Antwerp—New York
(Continued)
N. Y.

Arrival	Steamer
Oct. 22	British Trader
Dec. 7	British Trader

Bordeaux—New York
N. Y.

Arrival	Steamer
Apr. 4	Chateau Lafite
May 17	Chateau Lafite
July 6	Chateau Lafite

British Ports—New York
N. Y.

Arrival	Steamer
July 21	Boston City
Aug. 30	Boston City
Sept. 8	Critic
Sept. 10	Llandaff City
Sept. 29	Bristol City
Oct. 15	Boston City
Oct. 19	Jersey City
Oct. 27	Llandaff City
Nov. 14	Bristol City
Nov. 28	Boston City
Dec. 5	Jersey City
Dec. 12	Critic
Dec. 17	Llandaff City

ADDITIONAL ARRIVALS
French Ports—New York
N. Y.

Arrival	Steamer
Feb. 3	Melbourne
Apr. 19	Thornhill

Hamburg—New York
N. Y.

Arrival	Steamer
Feb. 16	Italia
Aug. 31	Cap Frio
Oct. 15	Cap Frio
Oct. 19	Laura
Nov. 28	Cap Frio

Mediterranean—New York
N. Y.

Arrival	Steamer
Dec. 31	Balilla

Rotterdam, Amsterdam— New York
N. Y.

Arrival	Steamer
Oct. 15	Deutschland
Oct. 22	Californian
Nov. 14	Deutschland

Southampton—New York
N. Y.

Arrival	Steamer
Jan. 26	Saint Jerome

Year 1901

ALLAN STATE LINE
Glasgow—New York
N. Y.

Arrival	Steamer
Jan. 3	Californian
Jan. 14	Sardinian
Jan. 31	Laurentian
Feb. 16	Sardinian
Mar. 11	Siberian
Mar. 22	Sardinian
Apr. 5	State of Nebraska
Apr. 27	Laurentian
Apr. 30	Sicilian
May 17	State of Nebraska
May 27	City of Rome
May 31	Laurentian
June 15	Sardinian
June 24	City of Rome
June 26	State of Nebraska
July 5	Laurentian
July 19	Sardinian
July 25	Mongolian
Aug. 2	State of Nebraska
Aug. 10	Laurentian
Aug. 22	Sardinian
Aug. 29	Mongolian
Sept. 2	City of Rome
Sept. 5	State of Nebraska
Sept. 14	Laurentian
Sept. 28	Sardinian
Oct. 5	Mongolian
Oct. 7	City of Rome
Oct. 12	State of Nebraska
Oct. 26	Laurentian
Nov. 9	Mongolian
Nov. 25	Buenos Ayrean
Dec. 20	Laurentian

AMERICAN LINE
Southampton—New York
N. Y.

Arrival	Steamer
Jan. 28	Saint Louis
Feb. 4	New York
Feb. 25	New York
Mar. 11	Saint Louis
Mar. 18	New York
Apr. 1	Saint Louis
Apr. 22	Saint Louis
Apr. 30	New York
May 13	Saint Louis
May 25	Saint Paul
June 1	Saint Louis
June 15	Saint Paul
June 24	Saint Louis
July 8	Saint Paul
July 15	Saint Louis
Aug. 3	Saint Paul
Aug. 12	Saint Louis
Aug. 24	Saint Paul
Aug. 31	Saint Louis
Sept. 7	Philadelphia
Sept. 14	Saint Paul
Sept. 23	Saint Louis
Sept. 30	Philadelphia
Oct. 5	Saint Paul
Oct. 14	Saint Louis

AMERICAN LINE
Southampton—New York
(Continued)
N. Y.

Arrival	Steamer
Oct. 19	Philadelphia
Oct. 26	Saint Paul
Nov. 2	Saint Louis
Nov. 9	Philadelphia
Nov. 16	Saint Paul
Dec. 9	Saint Paul
Dec. 21	Philadelphia
Dec. 30	Saint Paul

ANCHOR LINE
Glasgow—New York
N. Y.

Arrival	Steamer
Jan. 2	Astoria
Jan. 8	Furnessia
Jan. 31	Anchoria
Feb. 7	Astoria
Feb. 18	Furnessia
Feb. 26	Ethiopia
Mar. 13	Astoria
Mar. 26	Furnessia
Apr. 2	Ethiopia
Apr. 15	Astoria
Apr. 24	Anchoria
May 6	Furnessia
May 14	Ethiopia
May 20	Astoria
June 10	Furnessia
June 18	Ethiopia
July 1	Astoria
July 9	Anchoria
July 15	Furnessia
July 15	Hesperia
July 23	Ethiopia
Aug. 5	Astoria
Aug. 13	Anchoria
Aug. 19	Furnessia
Aug. 27	Ethiopia
Sept. 9	Astoria
Sept. 18	Anchoria
Sept. 24	Furnessia
Oct. 2	Ethiopia
Oct. 15	Astoria
Oct. 23	Anchoria
Oct. 28	Furnessia
Nov. 12	Ethiopia
Nov. 26	Astoria
Dec. 26	Furnessia

ANCHOR LINE
Mediterranean—New York
N. Y.

Arrival	Steamer
Jan. 4	Hesperia
Jan. 12	California
Jan. 26	Victoria
Jan. 29	Karamania
Feb. 28	Victoria
Mar. 13	Hesperia
Mar. 18	California
Mar. 26	Britannia
Apr. 5	Karamania

ANCHOR LINE
Mediterranean—New York
(Continued)
N. Y.

Arrival	Steamer
May 1	Victoria
May 11	Hesperia
May 20	Bolivia
May 23	California
June 3	Britannia
June 12	Calabria
June 13	Karamania
June 24	Armenia
July 8	Victoria
July 15	Hesperia
July 29	California
July 29	Karamania
Aug. 10	Calabria
Aug. 30	Karamania
Sept. 11	Perugia
Sept. 20	Victoria
Oct. 10	Hesperia
Oct. 17	Calabria
Oct. 19	Bolivia
Nov. 4	Perugia
Nov. 25	Karamania
Dec. 3	Calabria
Dec. 18	Victoria
Dec. 26	Bolivia

ATLANTIC TRANSPORT LINE
London—New York
N. Y.

Arrival	Steamer
Jan. 10	Menominee
Jan. 15	Marquette
Jan. 18	Manitou
Jan. 28	Minnehaha
Jan. 30	Mesaba
Feb. 4	Minneapolis
Feb. 15	Menominee
Feb. 23	Marquette
Feb. 23	Manitou
Feb. 25	Minnehaha
Mar. 7	Mesaba
Mar. 12	Minneapolis
Mar. 28	Marquette
Apr. 1	Minnehaha
Apr. 9	Manitou
Apr. 16	Minneapolis
Apr. 19	Mesaba
Apr. 29	Menominee
Apr. 30	Minnehaha
May 9	Manitou
May 14	Minneapolis
May 27	Marquette
May 28	Minnehaha
June 3	Menominee
June 10	Manitou
June 10	Minneapolis
June 20	Mesaba
June 24	Minnehaha
July 2	Marquette
July 8	Menominee
July 16	Manitou
July 22	Minnehaha

Year 1901

ATLANTIC TRANSPORT LINE
London—New York
(Continued)

N.Y.

Arrival	Steamer
July 23	Mesaba
Aug. 3	Marquette
Aug. 6	Minneapolis
Aug. 12	Menominee
Aug. 20	Manitou
Aug. 21	Minnehaha
Aug. 26	Mesaba
Sept. 3	Minneapolis
Sept. 7	Menominee
Sept. 9	Marquette
Sept. 18	Minnehaha
Sept. 24	Manitou
Oct. 1	Mesaba
Oct. 1	Minneapolis
Oct. 10	Marquette
Oct. 15	Minnehaha
Oct. 22	Menominee
Oct. 29	Manitou
Nov. 4	Mesaba
Nov. 12	Marquette
Nov. 18	Minnehaha
Nov. 27	Menominee
Dec. 2	Minneapolis
Dec. 11	Manitou
Dec. 17	Mesaba
Dec. 18	Marquette
Dec. 23	Minnehaha

COMPANIA TRANSATLANTICA LINE
(Spanish Line)
Spanish Ports—New York

N.Y.

Arrival	Steamer
Jan. 7	Leon XIII
Jan. 11	Cuidad di Cadiz
Jan. 31	Cuidad di Cadiz
Feb. 23	Leon XIII
Mar. 9	Leon XIII
Mar. 13	Cuidad di Cadiz
Apr. 12	Buenos Aires
May 4	Buenos Aires
May 11	Mexico
May 13	Cuidad di Cadiz
June 1	Cuidad di Cadiz
June 11	Montserrat
July 1	Montserrat
July 11	Buenos Aires
July 31	Buenos Aires
Aug. 9	Montserrat
Aug. 31	Montserrat
Sept. 10	Buenos Aires
Oct. 1	Buenos Aires
Oct. 11	Montserrat
Nov. 4	Montserrat
Nov. 14	Buenos Aires
Dec. 3	Buenos Aires
Dec. 14	P. de Satrustegue

CUNARD LINE
Liverpool—New York

N.Y.

Arrival	Steamer
Jan. 8	Servia

CUNARD LINE
Liverpool—New York
(Continued)

N.Y.

Arrival	Steamer
Jan. 14	Umbria
Jan. 21	Campania
Jan. 28	Etruria
Feb. 4	Lucania
Feb. 11	Umbria
Feb. 19	Servia
Feb. 25	Etruria
Mar. 4	Lucania
Mar. 11	Umbria
Mar. 18	Campania
Mar. 25	Etruria
Apr. 8	Servia
Apr. 13	Campania
Apr. 22	Umbria
Apr. 27	Lucania
May 6	Etruria
May 9	Servia
May 11	Campania
May 20	Umbria
May 25	Lucania
June 3	Etruria
June 6	Servia
June 8	Campania
June 17	Umbria
June 22	Lucania
July 1	Etruria
July 5	Servia
July 8	Campania
July 15	Umbria
July 20	Lucania
July 29	Etruria
Aug. 3	Campania
Aug. 12	Umbria
Aug. 17	Lucania
Aug. 26	Etruria
Aug. 28	Servia
Aug. 31	Campania
Sept. 9	Umbria
Sept. 14	Lucania
Sept. 23	Etruria
Sept. 28	Campania
Oct. 7	Umbria
Oct. 12	Lucania
Oct. 21	Etruria
Oct. 26	Campania
Nov. 4	Umbria
Nov. 9	Lucania
Nov. 18	Etruria
Nov. 25	Campania
Dec. 2	Umbria
Dec. 7	Lucania
Dec. 16	Etruria
Dec. 21	Campania

FABRE LINE
Mediterranean—New York

N.Y.

Arrival	Steamer
Jan. 9	Nuestria
Jan. 26	Burgundia
Feb. 20	Massilia
Feb. 26	Britannia
Feb. 27	Gallia
Mar. 2	Patria
Mar. 14	Nuestria

FABRE LINE
Mediterranean—New York
(Continued)

N.Y.

Arrival	Steamer
Apr. 24	Britannia
Apr. 29	Patria
May 6	Massilia
May 16	Nuestria
May 29	Gallia
June 18	Britannia
June 25	Patria
July 19	Olbia
Aug. 5	Nuestria
Aug. 17	Patria
Aug. 29	Britannia
Sept. 16	Burgundia
Sept. 30	Nuestria
Oct. 19	Patria
Oct. 24	Britannia
Nov. 6	Gallia
Nov. 20	Burgundia
Nov. 25	Gergovia
Dec. 7	Nuestria
Dec. 21	Patria
Dec. 31	Gallia

FRENCH LINE
(Compagnie Generale Transatlantique)
Havre—New York

N.Y.

Arrival	Steamer
Jan. 7	La Bretagne
Jan. 14	La Champagne
Jan. 21	L'Aquitaine
Jan. 28	La Gascogne
Feb. 4	La Bretagne
Feb. 11	La Champagne
Feb. 18	L'Aquitaine
Feb. 25	La Gascogne
Mar. 4	La Bretagne
Mar. 12	La Champagne
Mar. 18	L'Aquitaine
Mar. 26	La Gascogne
Apr. 1	La Bretagne
Apr. 8	La Champagne
Apr. 15	La Lorraine
Apr. 22	L'Aquitaine
Apr. 23	La Gascogne
Apr. 29	La Bretagne
May 6	La Champagne
May 13	La Lorraine
May 20	La Gascogne
May 20	L'Aquitaine
May 27	La Bretagne
June 3	La Champagne
June 10	La Lorraine
June 17	L'Aquitaine
June 24	La Bretagne
July 1	La Champagne
July 8	La Normandie
July 15	L'Aquitaine
July 22	La Gascogne
July 29	La Champagne
Aug. 5	La Normandie
Aug. 12	La Bretagne
Aug. 19	La Gascogne
Aug. 26	L'Aquitaine
Sept. 2	La Champagne
Sept. 7	La Savoie

Year 1901

FRENCH LINE
(Compagnie Generale Transatlantique)
Havre—New York
(Continued)

N. Y.

Arrival	Steamer
Sept. 16	La Bretagne
Sept. 23	L'Aquitaine
Sept. 30	La Champagne
Oct. 5	La Savoie
Oct. 14	La Bretagne
Oct. 21	L'Aquitaine
Oct. 28	La Champagne
Nov. 4	La Gascogne
Nov. 9	La Savoie
Nov. 18	La Bretagne
Nov. 25	La Champagne
Dec. 2	La Gascogne
Dec. 9	L'Aquitaine
Dec. 16	La Bretagne
Dec. 21	La Savoie
Dec. 31	La Champagne

HAMBURG-AMERICAN LINE
Hamburg—New York

N. Y.

Arrival	Steamer
Jan. 2	Pretoria
Jan. 14	Phoenicia
Jan. 19	Patricia
Jan. 25	Augusta Victoria
Jan. 28	Graf Waldersee
Feb. 2	Deutschland
Feb. 9	Bulgaria
Feb. 11	Pennsylvania
Feb. 16	Milano
Feb. 18	Pretoria
Feb. 25	Phoenicia
Mar. 2	Patricia
Mar. 11	Pisa
Mar. 12	Graf Waldersee
Mar. 20	Batavia
Mar. 22	Pennsylvania
Apr. 1	Bulgaria
Apr. 4	Milano
Apr. 6	Pretoria
Apr. 9	Augusta Victoria
Apr. 12	Deutschland
Apr. 15	Phoenicia
Apr. 20	Patricia
Apr. 22	Albano
Apr. 27	Graf Waldersee
May 3	Pisa
May 4	Furst Bismarck
May 6	Batavia
May 10	Deutschland
May 10	Pennsylvania
May 18	Augusta Victoria
May 20	Pretoria
May 25	Phoenicia
May 31	Milano
June 1	Furst Bismarck
June 1	Patricia
June 6	Deutschland
June 8	Graf Waldersee
June 15	Augusta Victoria
June 17	Armenia
June 21	Pennsylvania
June 29	Pretoria

HAMBURG-AMERICAN LINE
Hamburg—New York
(Continued)

N. Y.

Arrival	Steamer
July 5	Deutschland
July 6	Phoenicia
July 13	Patricia
July 19	Albano
July 19	Graf Waldersee
July 27	Bulgaria
July 27	Furst Bismarck
July 27	Milano
Aug. 1	Deutschland
Aug. 2	Pennsylvania
Aug. 9	Pretoria
Aug. 10	Augusta Victoria
Aug. 17	Phoenicia
Aug. 23	Patricia
Aug. 24	Furst Bismarck
Aug. 29	Deutschland
Aug. 29	Graf Waldersee
Sept. 7	Albano
Sept. 7	Augusta Victoria
Sept. 7	Bulgaria
Sept. 13	Pennsylvania
Sept. 20	Belgravia
Sept. 20	Furst Bismarck
Sept. 21	Pretoria
Sept. 26	Deutschland
Sept. 30	Phoenicia
Oct. 5	Augusta Victoria
Oct. 5	Patricia
Oct. 11	Graf Waldersee
Oct. 19	Furst Bismarck
Oct. 21	Palatia
Oct. 24	Deutschland
Oct. 25	Pennsylvania
Nov. 1	Pisa
Nov. 2	Augusta Victoria
Nov. 2	Pretoria
Nov. 7	Albano
Nov. 11	Phoenicia
Nov. 16	Milano
Nov. 18	Patricia
Nov. 25	Graf Waldersee
Dec. 2	Palatia
Dec. 6	Deutschland
Dec. 7	Pennsylvania
Dec. 16	Pretoria
Dec. 23	Phoenicia
Dec. 28	Patricia

HAMBURG-AMERICAN LINE
Mediterranean—New York

N. Y.

Arrival	Steamer
Jan. 16	Columbia
Feb. 9	Furst Bismarck
Apr. 3	Sicilia
May 13	Georgia
May 28	Sicilia
July 1	Georgia
July 15	Sicilia
Aug. 29	Georgia
Sept. 9	Sicilia
Nov. 2	Sicilia
Nov. 19	Furst Bismarck

HAMBURG-AMERICAN LINE
Mediterranean—New York
(Continued)

N. Y.

Arrival	Steamer
Dec. 23	Sicilia
Dec. 23	Furst Bismarck

HAMBURG-AMERICAN LINE
Scandinavian Ports—New York

N. Y.

Arrival	Steamer
Feb. 23	Xenia
Aug. 22	Xenia
Nov. 6	Xenia
Dec. 24	Xenia

HOLLAND-AMERICA LINE
Rotterdam—New York

N. Y.

Arrival	Steamer
Jan. 8	Potsdam
Jan. 16	Spaarndam
Jan. 21	Rotterdam
Jan. 30	Amsterdam
Feb. 6	Statendam
Feb. 11	Potsdam
Feb. 19	Maasdam
Feb. 25	Rotterdam
Mar. 8	Amsterdam
Mar. 12	Statendam
Mar. 18	Potsdam
Mar. 26	Maasdam
Apr. 1	Rotterdam
Apr. 16	Amsterdam
Apr. 22	Statendam
Apr. 29	Potsdam
May 6	Maasdam
May 13	Rotterdam
May 21	Amsterdam
May 27	Statendam
June 3	Potsdam
June 10	Maasdam
June 15	Rotterdam
June 25	Amsterdam
July 1	Statendam
July 8	Potsdam
July 15	Maasdam
July 22	Rotterdam
July 30	Amsterdam
Aug. 5	Statendam
Aug. 12	Potsdam
Aug. 26	Rotterdam
Sept. 2	Amsterdam
Sept. 9	Statendam
Sept. 16	Potsdam
Sept. 30	Rotterdam
Oct. 8	Amsterdam
Oct. 14	Statendam
Oct. 21	Ryndam
Oct. 28	Potsdam
Nov. 4	Rotterdam
Nov. 12	Amsterdam
Nov. 18	Statendam
Nov. 25	Ryndam
Dec. 2	Potsdam

Year 1901

HOLLAND-AMERICA LINE
Rotterdam—New York
(Continued)

N.Y. Arrival	Steamer
Dec. 10	Maasdam
Dec. 18	Amsterdam
Dec. 23	Statendam
Dec. 31	Ryndam

INSULAR NAVIGATION COMPANY
Azores, Lisbon—New Bedford, Mass., New York

N.Y. Arrival	Steamer
Apr. 2	Peninsular
May 17	Peninsular
July 8	Peninsular
Sept. 21	Peninsular
Nov. 18	Peninsular

LA VELOCE LINE
Mediterranean—New York

N.Y. Arrival	Steamer
Apr. 13	Citta di Torino
May 23	Citta di Messina
May 28	Citta di Torino
July 22	Citta di Messina
July 29	Nord America
Sept. 5	Nord America
Sept. 28	Citta di Messina
Oct. 1	Citta di Torino
Oct. 28	Nord America
Nov. 19	Citta di Torino
Dec. 7	Citta di Palermo
Dec. 14	Nord America
Dec. 31	Citta di Torino

LINHA DE VAPORES PORTUGUEZES
Azores, Lisbon—New Bedford, Mass., New York

N.Y. Arrival	Steamer
Jan. 14	Dona Maria
Feb. 25	Dona Maria
Apr. 12	Dona Maria
May 4	Dona Amelia
July 13	Dona Maria
Sept. 13	Patria
Sept. 25	Dona Maria
Nov. 4	Patria

NAVIGAZIONE GENERALE ITALIANA LINE
Mediterranean—New York

N.Y. Arrival	Steamer
Mar. 5	Liguria
Apr. 8	Manilla
Apr. 13	Marco Minghetti
Apr. 26	Liguria
May 7	Vincenzo Florio
May 14	Semphione
May 17	Washington
May 27	Marco Minghetti
June 3	Sicilia

NAVIGAZIONE GENERALE ITALIANA LINE
Mediterranean—New York
(Continued)

N.Y. Arrival	Steamer
June 8	Manilla
June 13	Liguria
June 21	Vincenzo Florio
June 28	Lombardia
July 12	Marco Minghetti
Aug. 3	Liguria
Aug. 19	Lombardia
Aug. 27	Sicilia
Sept. 20	Liguria
Oct. 4	Lombardia
Oct. 18	Sicilia
Nov. 8	Liguria
Nov. 22	Lombardia
Dec. 4	Sicilia
Dec. 27	Liguria

NORTH GERMAN LLOYD
Bremen—New York

N.Y. Arrival	Steamer
Jan. 7	K. Maria Theresia
Jan. 17	Karlsruhe
Jan. 25	Lahn
Jan. 26	Weimar
Feb. 4	Dresden
Feb. 8	Koenigin Luise
Feb. 8	Trave
Feb. 16	Oldenburg
Feb. 21	Lahn
Feb. 23	Rhein
Feb. 27	K. William der Grosse
Feb. 28	Frankfurt
Mar. 4	Karlsruhe
Mar. 11	Hannover
Mar. 16	Barbarossa
Mar. 20	Koenigin Luise
Mar. 21	Lahn
Mar. 27	K. William der Grosse
Mar. 28	Grosse Kurfuerst
Apr. 5	Rhein
Apr. 11	Frankfurt
Apr. 18	Barbarossa
Apr. 22	Lahn
Apr. 24	K. William der Grosse
Apr. 24	Koenigin Luise
May 1	Grosse Kurfuerst
May 9	H. H. Meier
May 14	K. Maria Theresia
May 16	Lahn
May 16	Neckar
May 22	Barbarossa
May 22	K. William der Grosse
May 29	Koenigin Luise
June 5	Fr'drich der Grosse
June 6	K. Maria Theresia
June 11	Grosse Kurfuerst
June 13	Lahn
June 19	K. William der Grosse
June 24	Koln
June 26	Barbarossa
July 6	Koenigin Luise
July 13	Fr'drich der Grosse
July 16	Grosse Kurfuerst
July 24	K. William der Grosse

NORTH GERMAN LLOYD
Bremen—New York
(Continued)

N.Y. Arrival	Steamer
July 26	H. H. Meier
July 31	Barbarossa
Aug. 6	Koenigin Luise
Aug. 8	K. Maria Theresia
Aug. 13	Fr'drich der Grosse
Aug. 15	Lahn
Aug. 21	Grosse Kurfuerst
Aug. 29	Gera
Sept. 4	Barbarossa
Sept. 4	K. Maria Theresia
Sept. 10	Koenigin Luise
Sept. 12	Lahn
Sept. 17	K. William der Grosse
Sept. 18	Fr'drich der Grosse
Sept. 25	Grosse Kurfuerst
Sept. 25	Kronprinz Wilhelm
Oct. 3	K. Maria Theresia
Oct. 4	H. H. Meier
Oct. 9	Barbarossa
Oct. 11	Lahn
Oct. 15	K. William der Grosse
Oct. 16	Koenigin Luise
Oct. 23	Bremen
Oct. 23	Bremen
Oct. 23	Kronprinz Wilhelm
Oct. 31	K. Maria Theresia
Nov. 1	Koln
Nov. 8	Cassel
Nov. 13	K. William der Grosse
Nov. 14	H. H. Meier
Nov. 19	Koenigin Luise
Nov. 27	Bremen
Nov. 27	Bremen
Nov. 27	Kronprinz Wilhelm
Dec. 6	Breslau
Dec. 11	K. William der Grosse
Dec. 14	Cassel
Dec. 20	Barbarossa
Dec. 23	Kronprinz Wilhelm
Dec. 28	Darmstadt

NORTH GERMAN LLOYD
Mediterranean—New York

N.Y. Arrival	Steamer
Jan. 3	Werra
Jan. 24	Hohenzollern
Jan. 30	Aller
Feb. 13	K. Maria Theresia
Feb. 21	Werra
Mar. 7	Hohenzollern
Apr. 1	Werra
Apr. 11	Hohenzollern
Apr. 15	K. Maria Theresia
May 6	Werra
May 16	Hohenzollern
May 29	Aller
June 12	Trave
June 19	Werra
June 21	Hohenzollern
July 3	Aller
July 16	Trave
July 31	Werra
Sept. 4	Hohenzollern
Sept. 11	Werra

Year 1901

NORTH GERMAN LLOYD
Mediterranean—New York
(Continued)

N.Y. Arrival	Steamer
Sept. 18	Aller
Oct. 9	Hohenzollern
Oct. 23	Aller
Nov. 4	Trave
Nov. 13	Hohenzollern
Nov. 25	Lahn
Dec. 2	Aller
Dec. 18	Hohenzollern

PRINCE LINE
Mediterranean—New York

N.Y. Arrival	Steamer
Jan. 24	Spartan Prince
Feb. 11	Tartar Prince
Feb. 23	Trojan Prince
Apr. 11	Tartar Prince
Apr. 29	Trojan Prince
June 11	Tartar Prince
June 25	Trojan Prince
July 18	Spartan Prince
Aug. 7	Tartar Prince
Aug. 26	Trojan Prince
Sept. 13	Spartan Prince
Oct. 11	Tartar Prince
Oct. 24	Trojan Prince
Nov. 18	Spartan Prince
Dec. 16	Trojan Prince
Dec. 31	Tartar Prince

RED STAR LINE
Antwerp, Southampton—New York

N.Y. Arrival	Steamer
Jan. 5	Kensington
Jan. 17	Southwark
Jan. 22	Vaderland
Feb. 7	Westernland
Feb. 9	Kensington
Feb. 15	Noordland
Feb. 19	Friesland
Feb. 21	Vaderland
Feb. 27	Southwark
Mar. 13	Westernland
Mar. 15	Kensington
Mar. 27	Vaderland
Apr. 2	Southwark
Apr. 11	Westernland
Apr. 18	Vaderland
Apr. 18	Kensington
Apr. 23	Zeeland
Apr. 30	Friesland
May 8	Southwark
May 17	Pennland
May 23	Kensington
June 4	Friesland
June 11	Southwark
June 18	Vaderland
June 27	Kensington
July 2	Zeeland
July 9	Friesland
July 23	Southwark
July 30	Vaderland
Aug. 7	Kensington

RED STAR LINE
Antwerp, Southampton—New York
(Continued)

N.Y. Arrival	Steamer
Aug. 12	Zeeland
Aug. 20	Friesland
Aug. 27	Southwark
Sept. 2	Vaderland
Sept. 10	Kensington
Sept. 16	Zeeland
Sept. 24	Friesland
Oct. 3	Southwark
Oct. 7	Vaderland
Oct. 16	Kensington
Oct. 22	Zeeland
Oct. 29	Friesland
Nov. 6	Southwark
Nov. 12	Vaderland
Nov. 26	Zeeland
Dec. 3	Friesland
Dec. 11	Southwark
Dec. 17	Vaderland

SCANDINAVIAN-AMERICAN LINE
Scandinavian Ports—New York

N.Y. Arrival	Steamer
Jan. 15	Norge
Feb. 8	Hekla
Feb. 16	Island
Feb. 20	Oscar II
Mar. 4	Norge
Mar. 29	Oscar II
Mar. 30	Hekla
Apr. 4	Island
Apr. 19	Norge
May 11	Hekla
May 23	Oscar II
May 25	Island
June 7	Norge
June 28	Hekla
July 12	Island
July 23	Oscar II
July 29	Norge
Aug. 17	Hekla
Aug. 30	Island
Sept. 13	Norge
Oct. 7	Hekla
Oct. 21	Island
Nov. 22	Hekla
Dec. 9	Island

WHITE STAR LINE
Liverpool—New York

N.Y. Arrival	Steamer
Jan. 7	Cymric
Jan. 11	Germanic
Jan. 17	Majestic
Jan. 24	Bovic
Jan. 24	Oceanic
Jan. 30	Tauric
Jan. 31	Teutonic
Feb. 6	Cymric
Feb. 8	Germanic
Feb. 14	Majestic

WHITE STAR LINE
Liverpool—New York
(Continued)

N.Y. Arrival	Steamer
Feb. 15	Cevic
Feb. 20	Oceanic
Feb. 28	Teutonic
Mar. 1	Bovic
Mar. 8	Tauric
Mar. 11	Germanic
Mar. 14	Majestic
Mar. 19	Cymric
Mar. 20	Oceanic
Mar. 28	Teutonic
Mar. 28	Cevic
Apr. 4	Germanic
Apr. 8	Bovic
Apr. 11	Majestic
Apr. 15	Tauric
Apr. 17	Oceanic
Apr. 22	Cymric
Apr. 25	Teutonic
May 3	Germanic
May 9	Majestic
May 15	Oceanic
May 20	Tauric
May 23	Teutonic
May 27	Cymric
May 31	Germanic
June 4	Cevic
June 6	Majestic
June 14	Oceanic
June 17	Bovic
June 20	Teutonic
June 28	Germanic
July 6	Cymric
July 8	Cevic
July 11	Majestic
July 17	Oceanic
July 23	Bovic
July 25	Teutonic
July 29	Tauric
Aug. 2	Germanic
Aug. 5	Celtic
Aug. 13	Cevic
Aug. 15	Oceanic
Aug. 19	Cymric
Aug. 22	Teutonic
Aug. 29	Germanic
Sept. 4	Bovic
Sept. 5	Majestic
Sept. 9	Celtic
Sept. 11	Oceanic
Sept. 17	Cevic
Sept. 20	Teutonic
Sept. 23	Cymric
Sept. 27	Germanic
Oct. 3	Majestic
Oct. 8	Bovic
Oct. 9	Oceanic
Oct. 14	Celtic
Oct. 17	Teutonic
Oct. 23	Cevic
Oct. 25	Germanic
Oct. 28	Cymric
Oct. 31	Majestic
Nov. 6	Oceanic
Nov. 12	Bovic
Nov. 14	Teutonic

Year 1901

WHITE STAR LINE
Liverpool—New York
(Continued)

N. Y.

Arrival	Steamer
Nov. 18	Celtic
Nov. 22	Germanic
Nov. 29	Majestic
Nov. 29	Cevic
Dec. 2	Cymric
Dec. 4	Oceanic
Dec. 12	Teutonic
Dec. 18	Bovic
Dec. 20	Germanic
Dec. 23	Celtic
Dec. 26	Majestic

WILSON LINE
Hull—New York

N. Y.

Arrival	Steamer
Jan. 21	Toronto
Jan. 28	Colorado
Feb. 5	Consuelo
Mar. 11	Colorado
Mar. 18	Consuelo
Mar. 25	Hindoo
Apr. 26	Consuelo
Apr. 30	Colorado
May 13	Hindoo
May 20	Toronto
June 7	Consuelo
June 15	Colorado
June 26	Hindoo
June 29	Buffalo
July 8	Toronto
July 20	Consuelo
July 27	Colorado
Aug. 17	Toronto
Aug. 30	Consuelo
Sept. 11	Colorado
Sept. 14	Hindoo
Sept. 30	Toronto
Oct. 12	Consuelo
Oct. 28	Hindoo
Nov. 8	Toronto
Nov. 25	Consuelo

WILSON LINE
Hull—New York
(Continued)

N. Y.

Arrival	Steamer
Dec. 7	Colorado
Dec. 20	Hindoo
Dec. 21	Toronto

ADDITIONAL ARRIVALS
Amsterdam—New York

N. Y.

Arrival	Steamer
June 8	Campania

Antwerp—New York

N. Y.

Arrival	Steamer
Sept. 13	British Prince
Oct. 5	British Princess
Oct. 26	British Prince
Nov. 20	Haverford
Dec. 3	British King

Bordeaux—New York

N. Y.

Arrival	Steamer
Apr. 10	Chateau Lafite
May 27	Chateau Lafite
July 15	Chateau Lafite
Oct. 16	Chateau Lafite
Dec. 2	Chateau Lafite

Bremen—New York

N. Y.

Arrival	Steamer
Jan. 4	Prins Regent Leitpold
Jan. 7	Trier

British Ports—New York

N. Y.

Arrival	Steamer
Feb. 20	Bristol City
Apr. 27	Chicago City
June 10	Southern Cross
July 5	Wells City
July 20	Llandaff City

ADDITIONAL ARRIVALS
British Ports—New York
(Continued)

N. Y.

Arrival	Steamer
Aug. 28	Kansas City
Sept. 6	Boston City
Sept. 9	Critic
Nov. 4	Chicago City
Dec. 21	Chicago City

Glasgow—New York

N. Y.

Arrival	Steamer
Dec. 5	Pretorian

Liverpool—New York

N. Y.

Arrival	Steamer
Aug. 22	Suevia

Mediterranean—New York

N. Y.

Arrival	Steamer
Jan. 14	Isola di Favignano
Jan. 22	Antilia
Feb. 18	Antilia
Feb. 20	Urania
Mar. 18	Antilia
Apr. 8	Dutchessa di Genova
Apr. 17	Antilia
May 8	Balilla
May 14	Antilia
May 14	Dutchessa di Genova
June 10	Campania
June 12	Isola di Seranzo
July 1	Dinnamare
July 8	Antilia
Aug. 5	Antilia
Aug. 12	Dutchessa di Genova
Sept. 3	Antilia
Sept. 21	Isola di Seranzo
Sept. 30	Antilia
Oct. 7	Dinnamare
Oct. 29	Antilia
Nov. 25	Antilia
Dec. 24	Antilia

Year 1902

ALLAN STATE LINE
Glasgow—New York
N. Y.

Arrival	Steamer
Jan. 8	Mongolian
Feb. 14	Mongolian
Mar. 15	Laurientian
Mar. 29	Mongolian
Apr. 11	Carthaginian
Apr. 24	Laurientian
May 15	Carthaginian
May 23	Mongolian
June 6	Laurientian
June 19	Carthaginian
July 10	Laurientian
July 24	Carthaginian
Aug. 13	Laurientian
Aug. 27	Carthaginian
Sept. 17	Laurientian
Sept. 25	Mongolian
Oct. 9	Carthaginian
Oct. 24	Laurientian
Nov. 7	Mongolian
Dec. 6	Laurientian
Dec. 22	Mongolian

AMERICAN LINE
Southampton—New York
N. Y.

Arrival	Steamer
Jan. 13	Saint Louis
Jan. 17	Germanic
Jan. 18	Philadelphia
Jan. 25	Saint Paul
Feb. 3	Saint Louis
Feb. 10	Philadelphia
Feb. 14	Germanic
Feb. 17	Saint Paul
Feb. 24	Saint Louis
Mar. 1	Philadelphia
Mar. 10	Saint Louis
Mar. 14	Germanic
Mar. 22	Philadelphia
Mar. 31	Saint Paul
Apr. 7	Saint Louis
Apr. 11	Germanic
Apr. 12	Philadelphia
Apr. 19	Saint Paul
May 3	Philadelphia
May 9	Germanic
May 12	Saint Louis
May 19	Saint Louis
May 26	Philadelphia
May 31	Saint Paul
June 6	Germanic
June 9	Saint Louis
June 14	Philadelphia
June 23	Saint Paul
June 30	Saint Louis
July 5	Philadelphia
July 14	Saint Paul
July 21	Saint Louis
Aug. 2	Philadelphia
Aug. 8	Germanic
Aug. 23	Philadelphia
Aug. 30	Saint Paul
Sept. 4	Germanic

AMERICAN LINE
Southampton—New York
(Continued)
N. Y.

Arrival	Steamer
Sept. 8	Saint Louis
Sept. 13	Philadelphia
Sept. 29	Saint Louis
Oct. 4	Philadelphia
Oct. 11	Saint Paul
Oct. 20	Saint Louis
Oct. 25	Philadelphia
Oct. 31	Germanic
Nov. 3	Saint Paul
Nov. 10	Saint Louis
Nov. 17	Philadelphia
Nov. 22	Saint Paul
Dec. 1	Saint Louis
Dec. 8	Philadelphia
Dec. 15	Saint Paul
Dec. 27	Philadelphia

ANCHOR LINE
Glasgow—New York
N. Y.

Arrival	Steamer
Jan. 8	Astoria
Jan. 21	Anchoria
Feb. 20	Astoria
Mar. 6	Anchoria
Mar. 20	Furnessia
Apr. 3	Astoria
Apr. 15	Anchoria
Apr. 26	Furnessia
May 5	Ethiopia
May 12	Astoria
May 20	Anchoria
May 26	Columbia
June 2	Furnessia
June 10	Ethiopia
June 16	Astoria
June 23	Columbia
July 1	Furnessia
July 7	Anchoria
July 15	Ethiopia
July 21	Columbia
July 28	Astoria
Aug. 4	Furnessia
Aug. 12	Anchoria
Aug. 18	Columbia
Aug. 25	Ethiopia
Sept. 1	Astoria
Sept. 8	Furnessia
Sept. 15	Columbia
Sept. 23	Anchoria
Oct. 1	Ethiopia
Oct. 6	Astoria
Oct. 13	Columbia
Oct. 21	Furnessia
Oct. 30	Anchoria
Nov. 5	Ethiopia
Nov. 10	Columbia
Nov. 25	Astoria
Dec. 3	Furnessia
Dec. 15	Ethiopia
Dec. 29	Anchoria

ANCHOR LINE
Mediterranean—New York
N. Y.

Arrival	Steamer
Jan. 6	Perguia
Jan. 28	Calabria
Feb. 24	California
Mar. 4	Perguia
Mar. 27	Calabria
Apr. 10	Victoria
Apr. 29	California
May 3	Perguia
May 24	Calabria
June 16	Victoria
June 30	Perguia
July 25	Calabria
Aug. 11	Algeria
Aug. 22	Perguia
Dec. 17	Perguia

ATLANTIC TRANSPORT LINE
London—New York
N. Y.

Arrival	Steamer
Jan. 4	Menominee
Jan. 7	Minneapolis
Jan. 15	Manitou
Jan. 20	Mesaba
Jan. 28	Minnehaha
Feb. 11	Minneapolis
Feb. 12	Menominee
Feb. 20	Manitou
Feb. 26	Mesaba
Mar. 4	Minnehaha
Mar. 18	Minneapolis
Mar. 28	Manitou
Apr. 1	Mesaba
Apr. 7	Minnehaha
Apr. 15	Menominee
Apr. 19	Minneapolis
Apr. 30	Manitou
May 5	Minnehaha
May 13	Mesaba
May 20	Minneapolis
May 26	Menominee
May 26	Minnetonka
June 2	Minnehaha
June 7	Manitou
June 11	Mesaba
June 16	Minneapolis
June 26	Menominee
July 2	Minnehaha
July 12	Manitou
July 16	Minneapolis
July 23	Minnetonka
July 30	Minnehaha
Aug. 6	Mesaba
Aug. 13	Minneapolis
Aug. 20	Minnetonka
Aug. 27	Minnehaha
Sept. 3	Mesaba
Sept. 6	Menominee
Sept. 10	Minneapolis
Sept. 17	Minnetonka
Sept. 19	Manitou
Sept. 24	Minnehaha

Year 1902

ATLANTIC TRANSPORT LINE
London—New York
(Continued)

N. Y.

Arrival	Steamer
Oct. 1	Mesaba
Oct. 8	Minneapolis
Oct. 9	Menominee
Oct. 15	Minnetonka
Oct. 22	Minnehaha
Nov. 10	Minneapolis
Nov. 12	Minnetonka
Nov. 25	Minnehaha
Dec. 3	Mesaba
Dec. 11	Manitou
Dec. 15	Minnetonka
Dec. 22	Minneapolis
Dec. 29	Minnehaha

COMPANIA TRANSATLANTICA LINE
(Spanish Line)
Spanish Ports—New York

N. Y.

Arrival	Steamer
Jan. 7	P. de Satrustegui
Jan. 10	Buenos Aires
Jan. 30	Buenos Aires
Feb. 15	P. de Satrustegui
Mar. 8	P. de Satrustegui
Mar. 17	Buenos Aires
Mar. 31	Buenos Aires
Apr. 11	Manuel Calva
May 1	Manuel Calva
May 12	Leon XIII
May 31	Leon XIII
June 11	Buenos Aires
July 1	Buenos Aires
July 31	Manuel Calva
Aug. 11	Montevideo
Sept. 10	Montserrat
Oct. 1	Montserrat
Oct. 13	Leon XIII
Nov. 3	Leon XIII
Nov. 11	Buenos Aires
Dec. 1	Buenos Aires
Dec. 15	Manuel Calva

CUNARD LINE
Liverpool—New York

N. Y.

Arrival	Steamer
Jan. 7	Saxonia
Jan. 13	Etruria
Jan. 20	Ivernia
Jan. 27	Umbria
Feb. 5	Saxonia
Feb. 10	Lucania
Feb. 17	Etruria
Feb. 24	Campania
Mar. 3	Umbria
Mar. 8	Lucania
Mar. 22	Campania
Apr. 5	Lucania
Apr. 14	Saxonia
Apr. 19	Campania
Apr. 28	Umbria
May 3	Lucania
May 12	Saxonia

CUNARD LINE
Liverpool—New York
(Continued)

N. Y.

Arrival	Steamer
May 17	Campania
May 26	Umbria
May 31	Lucania
June 14	Campania
June 23	Umbria
June 28	Lucania
July 12	Campania
July 21	Umbria
July 26	Lucania
Aug. 4	Etruria
Aug. 9	Campania
Aug. 18	Umbria
Aug. 23	Lucania
Aug. 30	Etruria
Sept. 6	Campania
Sept. 13	Umbria
Sept. 20	Lucania
Sept. 29	Etruria
Oct. 4	Campania
Oct. 13	Umbria
Oct. 18	Lucania
Oct. 28	Saxonia
Nov. 1	Campania
Nov. 10	Umbria
Nov. 17	Lucania
Nov. 24	Etruria
Dec. 1	Campania
Dec. 8	Umbria
Dec. 15	Lucania
Dec. 22	Etruria
Dec. 30	Saxonia

CUNARD LINE
Mediterranean—New York

N. Y.

Arrival	Steamer
June 4	Umbria

FABRE LINE
Mediterranean—New York

N. Y.

Arrival	Steamer
Feb. 6	Nuestria
Feb. 28	Patria
Mar. 18	Massilia
Mar. 28	Gallia
Apr. 7	Nuestria
Apr. 21	Patria
May 12	Massilia
May 17	Gallia
May 19	Roma
May 27	Nuestria
July 7	Roma
July 22	Gallia
Aug. 7	Nuestria
Aug. 18	Roma
Sept. 6	Massilia
Sept. 16	Gallia
Oct. 3	Roma
Oct. 17	Patria
Nov. 3	Massilia
Nov. 10	Roma
Nov. 26	Gallia
Dec. 17	Roma

FRENCH LINE
(Compagnie Generale Transatlantique)
Havre—New York

N. Y.

Arrival	Steamer
Jan. 6	L'Aquitaine
Jan. 13	La Gascogne
Jan. 18	La Savoie
Jan. 27	La Champagne
Feb. 3	L'Aquitaine
Feb. 11	La Gascogne
Feb. 17	La Touraine
Feb. 25	La Champagne
Mar. 3	La Bretagne
Mar. 10	L'Aquitaine
Mar. 17	La Gascogne
Mar. 24	La Touraine
Mar. 29	La Savoie
Apr. 1	La Bretagne
Apr. 7	L'Aquitaine
Apr. 14	La Champagne
Apr. 19	La Touraine
Apr. 22	La Gascogne
Apr. 26	La Savoie
May 5	La Bretagne
May 10	La Lorraine
May 13	La Champagne
May 17	La Touraine
May 24	La Savoie
May 27	La Gascogne
June 2	L'Aquitaine
June 9	La Lorraine
June 14	La Touraine
June 21	La Savoie
June 30	La Bretagne
July 5	La Lorraine
July 12	La Touraine
July 19	La Savoie
July 28	La Gascogne
Aug. 4	La Bretagne
Aug. 11	La Touraine
Aug. 16	La Lorraine
Aug. 25	La Gascogne
Aug. 30	La Savoie
Sept. 8	La Bretagne
Sept. 13	La Lorraine
Sept. 20	La Touraine
Sept. 27	La Savoie
Sept. 30	La Gascogne
Oct. 6	La Champagne
Oct. 11	La Lorraine
Oct. 20	La Touraine
Oct. 25	La Savoie
Oct. 29	La Gascogne
Nov. 3	La Champagne
Nov. 8	La Lorraine
Nov. 17	La Touraine
Nov. 24	La Gascogne
Dec. 2	La Champagne
Dec. 8	La Lorraine
Dec. 15	La Touraine
Dec. 20	La Savoie
Dec. 20	La Champagne

HAMBURG-AMERICAN LINE
Hamburg—New York

N. Y.

Arrival	Steamer
Jan. 4	Pisa

Year 1902

HAMBURG-AMERICAN LINE
Hamburg—New York
(Continued)

N. Y.

Arrival	Steamer
Jan. 6	Graf Waldersee
Jan. 13	Augusta Victoria
Jan. 17	Pennsylvania
Jan. 25	Pretoria
Feb. 14	Graf Waldersee
Feb. 28	Pennsylvania
Feb. 25	Palatia
Mar. 3	Pisa
Mar. 10	Pretoria
Mar. 17	Phoenicia
Mar. 20	Moltke
Mar. 22	Assyria
Mar. 29	Patricia
Apr. 5	Graf Waldersee
Apr. 7	Arcadia
Apr. 14	Palatia
Apr. 23	Pisa
Apr. 30	Moltke
May 3	Columbia
May 3	Bulgaria
May 8	Patricia
May 15	Graf Waldersee
May 17	Augusta Victoria
May 22	Pennsylvania
May 31	Pretoria
May 31	Columbia
June 3	Moltke
June 12	Patricia
June 14	Augusta Victoria
June 18	Bluecher
June 26	Graf Waldersee
June 28	Columbia
June 30	Albano
July 2	Pennsylvania
July 14	Palatia
July 17	Patricia
July 22	Bluecher
July 26	Columbia
July 30	Graf Waldersee
Aug. 6	Pennsylvania
Aug. 9	Augusta Victoria
Aug. 12	Moltke
Aug. 21	Albano
Aug. 21	Patricia
Aug. 22	Columbia
Aug. 26	Bluecher
Sept. 3	Graf Waldersee
Sept. 6	Augusta Victoria
Sept. 11	Pennsylvania
Sept. 16	Moltke
Sept. 19	Columbia
Sept. 25	Patricia
Oct. 1	Pretoria
Oct. 2	Bluecher
Oct. 4	Augusta Victoria
Oct. 6	Albano
Oct. 9	Graf Waldersee
Oct. 18	Columbia
Oct. 22	Moltke
Nov. 1	Augusta Victoria
Nov. 5	Bluecher
Nov. 7	Pisa
Nov. 15	Pretoria
Nov. 18	Palatia

HAMBURG-AMERICAN LINE
Hamburg—New York
(Continued)

N. Y.

Arrival	Steamer
Nov. 21	Graf Waldersee
Nov. 28	Pennsylvania
Dec. 4	Moltke
Dec. 15	Patricia
Dec. 16	Albano
Dec. 17	Bluecher
Dec. 30	Belgravia

HAMBURG-AMERICAN LINE
Mediterranean—New York

N. Y.

Arrival	Steamer
Jan. 20	Georgia
Feb. 27	Sicilia
Mar. 21	Georgia
Apr. 7	Augusta Victoria
May 19	Seriphos
June 2	Sicilia
June 20	Phoenicia
June 23	Sicilia
Sept. 17	Sicilia
Nov. 29	Phoenicia
Dec. 30	Sicilia

HOLLAND-AMERICA LINE
Rotterdam—New York

N. Y.

Arrival	Steamer
Jan. 20	Rotterdam
Jan. 28	Amsterdam
Feb. 4	Statendam
Feb. 25	Rotterdam
Mar. 4	Amsterdam
Mar. 10	Statendam
Mar. 24	Ryndam
Mar. 31	Rotterdam
Apr. 8	Amsterdam
Apr. 14	Statendam
Apr. 21	Potsdam
Apr. 28	Ryndam
May 5	Rotterdam
May 12	Noordam
May 19	Statendam
May 26	Potsdam
June 2	Ryndam
June 9	Rotterdam
June 16	Noordam
June 23	Statendam
June 30	Potsdam
July 7	Ryndam
July 14	Rotterdam
July 21	Noordam
July 28	Statendam
Aug. 4	Potsdam
Aug. 11	Ryndam
Aug. 18	Rotterdam
Aug. 25	Noordam
Sept. 1	Statendam
Sept. 8	Potsdam
Sept. 13	Ryndam

HOLLAND-AMERICA LINE
Rotterdam—New York
(Continued)

N. Y.

Arrival	Steamer
Sept. 22	Rotterdam
Sept. 29	Noordam
Oct. 6	Statendam
Oct. 13	Potsdam
Oct. 20	Ryndam
Oct. 27	Rotterdam
Nov. 3	Noordam
Nov. 10	Statendam
Nov. 24	Potsdam
Dec. 1	Ryndam
Dec. 8	Rotterdam
Dec. 15	Noordam
Dec. 24	Amsterdam
Dec. 31	Potsdam

INSULAR NAVIGATION COMPANY
Azores, Lisbon—New Bedford, Mass., New York

N. Y.

Arrival	Steamer
Jan. 11	Peninsular
May 17	Peninsular
July 7	Peninsular
Aug. 25	Peninsular
Oct. 18	Peninsular
Dec. 13	Peninsular

LA VELOCE LINE
Mediterranean—New York

N. Y.

Arrival	Steamer
Jan. 30	Nord America
Feb. 26	Citta di Milano
Mar. 15	Citta di Torino
Mar. 25	Nord America
Apr. 8	Citta di Genova
Apr. 12	Citta di Milano
May 8	Nord America
May 31	Citta di Milano
June 7	Citta di Genova
June 23	Citta di Torino
June 26	Nord America
July 18	Citta di Milano
Aug. 13	Nord America
Sept. 2	Citta di Milano
Oct. 2	Nord America
Nov. 1	Citta di Milano
Nov. 17	Citta di Torino
Nov. 28	Nord America
Dec. 15	Citta di Napoli
Dec. 26	Citta di Milano

LINHA DE VAPORES PORTUGUEZES
Azores, Lisbon—New Bedford, Mass., New York

N. Y.

Arrival	Steamer
Apr. 7	Patria
June 6	Patria
Sept. 16	Patria

Year 1902

NAVIGAZIONE GENER-ALE ITALIANA LINE
Mediterranean—New York
N. Y.

Arrival	Steamer
Jan. 14	Lombardia
Jan. 22	Sardegna
Feb. 6	Sicilia
Feb. 13	Liguria
Feb. 27	Lombardia
Mar. 13	Sardegna
Mar. 25	Sicilia
Apr. 2	Liguria
Apr. 16	Marco Minghetti
Apr. 17	Lombardia
May 12	Liguria
May 14	Sicilia
May 22	Lombardia
June 2	Marco Minghetti
June 4	Umbria
July 2	Sicilia
July 9	Liguria
July 23	Lombardia
Aug. 28	Liguria
Sept. 10	Lombardia
Sept. 23	Sicilia
Oct. 8	Sardegna
Oct. 23	Lombardia
Nov. 6	Liguria
Nov. 20	Sicilia
Dec. 4	Sardegna
Dec. 19	Lombardia
Dec. 31	Liguria

NORTH GERMAN LLOYD
Bremen—New York
N. Y.

Arrival	Steamer
Jan. 6	Gera
Jan. 14	K. William der Grosse
Jan. 24	Kronprinz Wilhelm
Feb. 3	Rhein
Feb. 10	Breslau
Feb. 12	K. William der Grosse
Feb. 14	Cassel
Mar. 18	Rhein
Mar. 19	K. William der Grosse
Mar. 21	Hanover
Mar. 27	Crefeld
Mar. 27	Gera
Apr. 2	Kronprinz Wilhelm
Apr. 7	Brandenburg
Apr. 9	Friederich der Grosse
Apr. 15	K. William der Grosse
Apr. 19	Cassel
Apr. 21	Neckar
Apr. 23	Grosser Kurfuerst
Apr. 29	Kronprinz Wilhelm
May 3	Rhein
May 6	Bremen
May 13	K. William der Grosse
May 14	Friederich der Grosse
May 22	Cassel
May 26	Brandenburg
May 28	Kronprinz Wilhelm
June 9	Barbarossa
June 10	K. William der Grosse
June 11	Bremen
June 18	Friederich der Grosse
June 24	Kronprinz Wilhelm

NORTH GERMAN LLOYD
Bremen—New York
(Continued)
N. Y.

Arrival	Steamer
June 25	Koenigin Luise
July 2	Grosser Kurfuerst
July 9	K. William der Grosse
July 11	Barbarossa
July 18	Bremen
July 22	Kronprinz Wilhelm
July 23	Friederich der Grosse
July 30	Koenigin Luise
Aug. 5	Grosser Kurfuerst
Aug. 5	K. William der Grosse
Aug. 15	Barbarossa
Aug. 19	Bremen
Aug. 26	Friederich der Grosse
Sept. 2	Koenigin Luise
Sept. 2	Main
Sept. 2	K. William der Grosse
Sept. 10	Grosser Kurfuerst
Sept. 16	Kronprinz Wilhelm
Sept. 22	Neckar
Sept. 24	Bremen
Oct. 1	Friederich der Grosse
Oct. 1	K. William der Grosse
Oct. 13	Main
Oct. 15	Grosser Kurfuerst
Oct. 15	Kronprinz Wilhelm
Oct. 24	Cassel
Oct. 29	K. William der Grosse
Nov. 1	Breslau
Nov. 5	Bremen
Nov. 11	Kronprinz Wilhelm
Nov. 12	Neckar
Nov. 26	K. William der Grosse
Dec. 1	Main
Dec. 12	Kronprinz Wilhelm
Dec. 15	Chemnitz
Nov. 20	Friederich der Grosse
Dec. 22	K. William der Grosse
Dec. 22	Brandenburg
Dec. 29	Frankfurt

NORTH GERMAN LLOYD
Mediterranean—New York
N. Y.

Arrival	Steamer
Jan. 21	Lahn
Jan. 29	Hohenzollern
Feb. 27	Lahn
Mar. 19	Hohenzollern
Apr. 1	Lahn
Apr. 23	Hohenzollern
May 6	Lahn
May 26	Neckar
May 28	Hohenzollern
June 9	Lahn
July 2	Hohenzollern
July 14	Lahn
Aug. 12	Hohenzollern
Aug. 18	Lahn
Sept. 16	Hohenzollern
Sept. 22	Lahn
Oct. 27	Lahn
Dec. 2	Lahn

PRINCE LINE
Mediterranean—New York
N. Y.

Arrival	Steamer
Oct. 20	Sicilian Prince
Dec. 9	Sicilian Prince
Dec. 23	Napolitan Prince

RED STAR LINE
Antwerp—New York
N. Y.

Arrival	Steamer
Jan. 2	Zeeland
Jan. 21	Vaderland
Feb. 5	Zeeland
Mar. 4	Vaderland
Mar. 12	Kensington
Apr. 8	Vaderland
Apr. 16	Kensington
Apr. 22	Zeeland
Apr. 30	Friesland
May 12	Vaderland
May 21	Kensington
May 27	Zeeland
June 3	Friesland
June 16	Vaderland
June 25	Kensington
June 30	Zeeland
July 9	Friesland
July 15	Vaderland
July 22	Kroonland
July 28	Zeeland
Aug. 5	Friesland
Aug. 11	Vaderland
Aug. 18	Kroonland
Aug. 25	Zeeland
Sept. 2	Friesland
Sept. 8	Vaderland
Sept. 15	Kroonland
Sept. 22	Zeeland
Oct. 6	Vaderland
Oct. 14	Kroonland
Oct. 20	Zeeland
Oct. 28	Finland
Nov. 5	Kensington
Nov. 11	Friesland
Nov. 18	Vaderland
Nov. 24	Kroonland
Dec. 4	Zeeland
Dec. 10	Finland
Dec. 17	Vaderland
Dec. 23	Kroonland
Dec. 30	Zeeland

SCANDINAVIAN-AMERICAN LINE
Scandinavian Ports—New York
N. Y.

Arrival	Steamer
Jan. 18	Hekla
Feb. 7	Norge
Feb. 14	Island
Mar. 1	Hekla
Mar. 24	Norge
Apr. 14	Island
Apr. 25	Hekla
May 6	Oscar II
May 17	Norge
June 2	Island

Year 1902

SCANDINAVIAN-AMERICAN LINE
Scandinavian Ports—New York
(Continued)

N.Y.

Arrival	Steamer
June 13	.Hekla
June 17	Oscar II
July 7	Norge
July 19	Island
July 28	Oscar II
Aug. 21	Norge
Sept. 5	Island
Sept. 8	Oscar II
Sept. 25	Hekla
Oct. 10	Norge
Oct. 21	Oscar II
Nov. 4	Island
Nov. 17	Hekla
Nov. 29	Norge
Dec. 2	Oscar II
Dec. 22	Island

WHITE STAR LINE
Liverpool—New York

N.Y.

Arrival	Steamer
Jan. 6	Cymric
Jan. 9	Teutonic
Jan. 24	Celtic
Jan. 28	Cevic
Jan. 30	Oceanic
Feb. 10	Cymric
Feb. 21	Teutonic
Feb. 26	Oceanic
Mar. 6	Majestic
Mar. 20	Teutonic
Mar. 27	Oceanic
Apr. 3	Majestic
Apr. 15	Tauric
Apr. 22	Cymric
Apr. 23	Oceanic
May 1	Majestic
May 5	Celtic
May 15	Teutonic
May 21	Oceanic
May 29	Majestic
June 2	Celtic
June 12	Teutonic
June 16	Cymric
June 18	Oceanic
June 26	Majestic
June 30	Celtic

WHITE STAR LINE
Liverpool—New York
(Continued)

N.Y.

Arrival	Steamer
July 8	Tauric
July 14	Cymric
July 16	Oceanic
July 24	Majestic
July 28	Cevic
Aug. 1	Celtic
Aug. 14	Teutonic
Aug. 18	Cymric
Aug. 20	Oceanic
Aug. 28	Majestic
Sept. 1	Celtic
Sept. 9	Cevic
Sept. 11	Teutonic
Sept. 15	Cymric
Sept. 17	Oceanic
Sept. 25	Majestic
Sept. 29	Celtic
Oct. 9	Teutonic
Oct. 13	Cymric
Oct. 15	Oceanic
Oct. 16	Cevic
Oct. 23	Majestic
Nov. 5	Teutonic
Nov. 10	Cymric
Nov. 12	Oceanic
Nov. 19	Cevic
Nov. 20	Majestic
Nov. 28	Celtic
Dec. 5	Teutonic
Dec. 11	Oceanic
Dec. 22	Cymric
Dec. 26	Celtic

WILSON LINE
Hull—New York

N.Y.

Arrival	Steamer
Jan. 7	Consuelo
Jan. 22	Colorado
Feb. 5	Toronto
Feb. 24	Consuelo
Mar. 7	Colorado
Mar. 20	Toronto
Apr. 8	Consuelo
Apr. 30	Toronto
May 21	Consuelo
June 9	Toronto
June 19	Colorado
July 10	Consuelo

WILSON LINE
Hull—New York
(Continued)

N.Y.

Arrival	Steamer
Aug. 1	Toronto
Aug. 2	Colorado
Aug. 20	Consuelo
Sept. 18	Toronto
Sept. 22	Colorado
Oct. 8	Consuelo
Nov. 3	Toronto
Nov. 7	Colorado
Nov. 25	Consuelo
Dec. 26	Toronto

ADDITIONAL ARRIVALS
Bremen—New York

N.Y.

Arrival	Steamer
Apr. 1	Batavia

British Ports—New York

N.Y.

Arrival	Steamer
Jan. 13	Wells City
Aug. 13	Exeter City
Sept. 2	Brooklyn City
Oct. 14	Boston City

Liverpool—New York

N.Y.

Arrival	Steamer
May 3	Canadian
June 9	Canadian
July 14	Canadian
Aug. 16	Canadian
Sept. 20	Canadian
Oct. 27	Canadian
Dec. 1	Canadian

Mediterranean—New York

N.Y.

Arrival	Steamer
Apr. 5	Balilla
Apr. 9	Regina Elena
May 6	Attivita
May 15	Regina Elena
May 23	Balilla
June 3	Equita
July 14	Regina Elena
Aug. 5	Regina Elena
Oct. 24	Balilla
Dec. 11	Regina Elena

Year 1903

ALLAN STATE LINE
Glasgow—New York
N. Y.

Arrival	Steamer
Jan. 16	Laurentian
Feb. 5	Pomerinian
Feb. 16	Carthaginian
Mar. 3	Laurentian
Mar. 16	Pomerinian
Mar. 30	Mongolian
Apr. 13	Laurentian
Apr. 25	Pomerinian
May 9	Mongolian
May 21	Laurentian
June 4	Numidian
June 17	Mongolian
July 1	Laurentian
July 8	Numidian
July 23	Mongolian
Aug. 5	Laurentian
Aug. 13	Numidian
Aug. 27	Mongolian
Sept. 9	Laurentian
Sept. 24	Numidian
Oct. 1	Mongolian
Oct. 14	Laurentian
Oct. 31	Numidian
Nov. 6	Mongolian
Nov. 21	Laurentian
Dec. 5	Siberian
Dec. 18	Corinthian

AMERICAN LINE
Southampton, Cherbourg—
New York
N. Y.

Arrival	Steamer
Jan. 5	St. Paul
Jan. 10	Germanic
Jan. 17	St. Louis
Jan. 19	Philadelphia
Feb. 2	St. Paul
Feb. 14	Germanic
Feb. 16	Philadelphia
Feb. 24	St. Paul
Mar. 9	Philadelphia
Mar. 13	Germanic
Mar. 16	St. Paul
Mar. 30	Philadelphia
Apr. 17	Germanic
Apr. 18	Philadelphia
Apr. 27	St. Paul
May 4	New York
May 9	Philadelphia
May 15	Germanic
May 18	St. Paul
May 25	New York
May 30	Philadelphia
June 8	St. Paul
June 12	Germanic
June 15	New York
June 20	Philadelphia
June 29	St. Paul
July 6	New York
July 10	Germanic
July 11	Philadelphia
July 20	St. Paul

AMERICAN LINE
Southampton—Cherbourg—
New York
(Continued)
N. Y.

Arrival	Steamer
Aug. 3	New York
Aug. 7	Germanic
Aug. 8	Philadelphia
Aug. 17	St. Paul
Aug. 22	New York
Aug. 29	Philadelphia
Sept. 4	Germanic
Sept. 5	St. Louis
Sept. 12	New York
Sept. 19	Philadelphia
Sept. 26	St. Louis
Oct. 2	Germanic
Oct. 3	New York
Oct. 10	Philadelphia
Oct. 17	St. Louis
Oct. 26	New York
Oct. 31	Philadelphia
Nov. 7	St. Louis
Nov. 14	New York
Nov. 28	Philadelphia
Dec. 5	St. Louis
Dec. 14	New York
Dec. 21	St. Paul
Dec. 28	Philadelphia

ANCHOR LINE
Glasgow—New York
N. Y.

Arrival	Steamer
Jan. 9	Furnessia
Jan. 26	Ethiopia
Feb. 9	Anchoria
Feb. 19	Furnessia
Mar. 11	Ethiopia
Mar. 18	Astoria
Mar. 30	Columbia
Apr. 10	Anchoria
Apr. 14	Furnessia
Apr. 20	Astoria
Apr. 27	Columbia
May 6	Ethiopia
May 11	Anchoria
May 18	Furnessia
May 25	Columbia
June 1	Astoria
June 10	Ethiopia
June 15	Anchoria
June 22	Columbia
June 29	Furnessia
July 6	Astoria
July 14	Ethiopia
July 20	Columbia
July 27	Anchoria
Aug. 3	Furnessia
Aug. 10	Astoria
Aug. 17	Columbia
Aug. 25	Ethiopia
Sept. 1	Anchoria
Sept. 7	Furnessia
Sept. 14	Columbia
Sept. 22	Astoria

ANCHOR LINE
Glasgow—New York
(Continued)
N. Y.

Arrival	Steamer
Sept. 29	Ethiopia
Oct. 6	Anchoria
Oct. 12	Columbia
Oct. 19	Furnessia
Oct. 26	Astoria
Nov. 4	Ethiopia
Nov. 10	Columbia
Nov. 23	Furnessia
Nov. 30	Astoria
Dec. 11	Ethiopia
Dec. 26	Anchoria

ANCHOR LINE
Mediterranean—New York
N. Y.

Arrival	Steamer
Jan. 20	Calabria
Feb. 4	Algeria
Feb. 16	Perugia
Mar. 2	Victoria
Mar. 16	Calabria
Apr. 6	Perugia
Apr. 25	California
May 7	Victoria
May 11	Calabria
June 5	Perugia
June 19	Algeria
June 30	California
July 9	Calabria
July 21	Victoria
Aug. 1	Perugia
Aug. 25	California
Sept. 3	Calabria
Sept. 30	Perugia
Oct. 12	Victoria
Oct. 26	California
Nov. 4	Calabria
Nov. 21	Perugia

ATLANTIC TRANSPORT LINE
London—New York
N. Y.

Arrival	Steamer
Jan. 5	Mesaba
Jan. 16	Manitou
Jan. 28	Minneapolis
Feb. 3	Minnehaha
Feb. 13	Mesaba
Feb. 19	Menominee
Feb. 24	Minnetonka
Mar. 5	Minneapolis
Mar. 11	Minnehaha
Mar. 18	Mesaba
Mar. 27	Menominee
Mar. 31	Minnetonka
Apr. 7	Minneapolis
Apr. 13	Minnehaha
Apr. 21	Manitou
Apr. 29	Minnetonka
May 4	Menominee
May 6	Minneapolis

Year 1903

ATLANTIC TRANSPORT LINE
London—New York
(Continued)
N. Y.

Arrival	Steamer
May 12	Minnehaha
May 18	Marquette
May 27	Minnetonka
June 1	Manitou
June 2	Minneapolis
June 10	Minnehaha
June 15	Menominee
June 17	Mesaba
June 23	Minnetonka
July 2	Manitou
July 8	Minnehaha
July 15	Mesaba
July 22	Minnetonka
July 29	Minneapolis
July 29	Menominee
Aug. 6	Marquette
Aug. 13	Mesaba
Aug. 18	Minnetonka
Aug. 26	Minneapolis
Sept. 1	Minnehaha
Sept. 9	Mesaba
Sept. 16	Minnetonka
Sept. 23	Minneapolis
Sept. 30	Minnehaha
Oct. 7	Mesaba
Oct. 14	Minnetonka
Oct. 21	Minneapolis
Oct. 28	Minnehaha
Nov. 5	Menominee
Nov. 11	Minnetonka
Nov. 18	Minneapolis
Nov. 30	Mesaba
Dec. 8	Minnetonka
Dec. 21	Minneapolis
Dec. 28	Minnehaha

COMPANIA TRANSATLANTICA LINE
(Spanish Line)
Spanish Ports—New York
N. Y.

Arrival	Steamer
Jan. 2	Manuel Calva
Jan. 15	Montevideo
Feb. 5	Montevideo
Feb. 13	Montserrat
Mar. 6	Montserrat
Mar. 12	Leon XIII
Apr. 3	Leon XIII
Apr. 18	Buenos Aires
May 9	Buenos Aires
May 12	Manuel Calva
June 3	Manuel Calva
June 11	Montevideo
July 6	Montevideo
July 11	Montserrat
Aug. 3	Montserrat
Aug. 10	Leon XIII
Sept. 3	Leon XIII
Sept. 11	Buenos Aires
Oct. 5	Buenos Aires
Oct. 14	Manuel Calva
Nov. 4	Manuel Calva
Dec. 12	Montserrat

CUNARD LINE
Liverpool—New York
N. Y.

Arrival	Steamer
Jan. 5	Umbria
Jan. 13	Ivernia
Jan. 19	Lucania
Feb. 4	Saxonia
Feb. 11	Ivernia
Feb. 16	Lucania
Feb. 23	Etruria
Mar. 2	Campania
Mar. 9	Umbria
Mar. 16	Ivernia
Mar. 23	Etruria
Mar. 30	Campania
Apr. 6	Umbria
Apr. 13	Ivernia
Apr. 20	Etruria
Apr. 23	Aurania
Apr. 25	Campania
May 4	Umbria
May 11	Ivernia
May 18	Etruria
May 21	Aurania
May 23	Campania
June 1	Umbria
June 8	Carpathia
June 8	Lucania
June 15	Etruria
June 18	Aurania
June 20	Campania
July 3	Carpathia
July 6	Lucania
July 13	Etruria
July 16	Aurania
July 18	Campania
July 27	Umbria
July 31	Carpathia
Aug. 1	Lucania
Aug. 10	Etruria
Aug. 13	Aurania
Aug. 15	Campania
Aug. 24	Umbria
Aug. 28	Carpathia
Aug. 29	Lucania
Sept. 5	Etruria
Sept. 10	Aurania
Sept. 12	Campania
Sept. 21	Umbria
Sept. 24	Carpathia
Sept. 26	Lucania
Oct. 3	Etruria
Oct. 8	Aurania
Oct. 10	Campania
Oct. 19	Umbria
Oct. 24	Lucania
Nov. 2	Etruria
Nov. 7	Campania
Nov. 16	Umbria
Nov. 20	Carpathia
Nov. 21	Lucania
Dec. 5	Campania
Dec. 15	Umbria
Dec. 19	Lucania
Dec. 28	Etruria

CUNARD LINE
Mediterranean—New York
N. Y.

Arrival	Steamer
Dec. 1	Aurania

FABRE LINE
Mediterranean—New York
N. Y.

Arrival	Steamer
Jan. 28	Massilia
Feb. 16	Gallia
Feb. 26	Roma
Mar. 16	Patria
Mar. 27	Massilia
Apr. 1	Roma
Apr. 9	Germania
Apr. 18	Gallia
Apr. 20	Germania
May 6	Patria
May 6	Roma
May 16	Massilia
May 25	Germania
June 2	Gallia
June 8	Nuestria
June 11	Roma
June 29	Patria
July 1	Germania
July 23	Massilia
July 28	Roma
Aug. 19	Germania
Aug. 31	Patria
Sept. 11	Roma
Oct. 6	Gallia
Oct. 21	Roma
Nov. 4	Gallia
Nov. 24	Germania
Dec. 4	Roma

FRENCH LINE
(Compagnie Generale Transatlantique)
Havre—New York
N. Y.

Arrival	Steamer
Jan. 3	La Lorraine
Jan. 12	La Bretagne
Jan. 19	La Savoie
Jan. 27	La Champagne
Feb. 2	La Lorraine
Feb. 10	La Bretagne
Feb. 17	L'Aquitaine
Feb. 24	La Champagne
Mar. 2	La Savoie
Mar. 10	La Bretagne
Mar. 16	La Lorraine
Mar. 24	La Champagne
Mar. 30	La Savoie
Apr. 3	L'Aquitaine
Apr. 6	La Bretagne
Apr. 13	La Lorraine
Apr. 20	La Champagne
Apr. 28	La Gascogne
May 2	La Savoie
May 5	L'Aquitaine
May 11	La Bretagne
May 16	La Lorraine
May 18	La Champagne
May 25	La Gascogne
May 30	La Savoie
June 8	La Bretagne

Year 1903

FRENCH LINE
(Compagnie Generale Transatlantique)
Havre—New York
(Continued)

N.Y.

Arrival	Steamer
June 13	La Lorraine
June 22	La Gascogne
July 6	La Touraine
July 11	La Lorraine
July 20	La Gascogne
July 27	La Bretagne
Aug. 1	La Touraine
Aug. 10	La Champagne
Aug. 15	La Savoie
Aug. 24	La Bretagne
Aug. 29	La Lorraine
Sept. 5	La Touraine
Sept. 12	La Savoie
Sept. 14	La Gascogne
Sept. 21	La Bretagne
Sept. 26	La Lorraine
Sept. 28	La Champagne
Oct. 5	La Touraine
Oct. 10	La Savoie
Oct. 12	La Gascogne
Oct. 19	La Bretagne
Oct. 24	La Lorraine
Nov. 2	La Touraine
Nov. 2	La Champagne
Nov. 9	La Gascogne
Nov. 14	La Savoie
Nov. 23	La Bretagne
Nov. 28	La Touraine
Dec. 7	La Champagne
Dec. 14	La Savoie
Dec. 21	La Bretagne
Dec. 28	La Touraine

HAMBURG-AMERICAN LINE
Hamburg—New York

N.Y.

Arrival	Steamer
Jan. 5	Palatia
Jan. 7	Moltke
Jan. 17	Pennsylvania
Jan. 23	Patricia
Jan. 27	Phoenicia
Jan. 29	Bluecher
Jan. 31	Augusta Victoria
Feb. 2	Moltke
Feb. 14	Bulgaria
Feb. 16	Graf Waldersee
Feb. 24	Belgravia
Feb. 27	Palatia
Mar. 10	Patricia
Mar. 11	Bluecher
Mar. 16	Phoenicia
Mar. 23	Pretoria
Mar. 30	Graf Waldersee
Apr. 8	Belgravia
Apr. 10	Pennsylvania
Apr. 10	Bulgaria
Apr. 13	Moltke
Apr. 17	Patricia
Apr. 27	Bluecher
May 2	Deutschland
May 2	Phoenicia
May 2	Pretoria

HAMBURG-AMERICAN LINE
Hamburg—New York

N.Y.

Arrival	Steamer
May 8	Graf Waldersee
May 16	Augusta Victoria
May 18	Arcadia
May 21	Pennsylvania
May 25	Bluecher
May 29	Patricia
May 29	Deutschland
June 2	Moltke
June 12	Pretoria
June 13	Augusta Victoria
June 18	Graf Waldersee
June 20	Phoenicia
June 22	Bluecher
June 26	Deutschland
June 27	Bulgaria
June 27	Belgravia
July 1	Pennsylvania
July 6	Moltke
July 9	Patricia
July 20	Bluecher
July 20	Bulgaria
July 24	Pretoria
July 30	Graf Waldersee
Aug. 3	Moltke
Aug. 12	Pennsylvania
Aug. 17	Bluecher
Aug. 20	Patricia
Aug. 22	Augusta Victoria
Aug. 28	Phoenicia
Sept. 4	Pretoria
Sept. 8	Deutschland
Sept. 10	Graf Waldersee
Sept. 14	Bluecher
Sept. 19	Augusta Victoria
Sept. 23	Pennsylvania
Sept. 28	Moltke
Oct. 1	Patricia
Oct. 6	Deutschland
Oct. 9	Phoenicia
Oct. 12	Bluecher
Oct. 17	Augusta Victoria
Oct. 23	Graf Waldersee
Nov. 2	Belgravia
Nov. 4	Moltke
Nov. 9	Deutschland
Nov. 12	Pennsylvania
Nov. 20	Patricia
Nov. 27	Pretoria
Dec. 5	Moltke
Dec. 10	Graf Waldersee
Dec. 22	Belgravia
Dec. 23	Bluecher
Dec. 26	Prinz Osker

HAMBURG-AMERICAN LINE
Mediterranean—New York

N.Y.

Arrival	Steamer
Jan. 2	Pisa
Feb. 19	Georgia
Mar. 3	Pisa
Apr. 10	Sicilia
May 5	Seriphos
May 26	Georgia

HAMBURG-AMERICAN LINE
Mediterranean—New York
(Continued)

N.Y.

Arrival	Steamer
July 17	Pisa
Aug. 1	Sicilia
Aug. 29	Seriphos
Sept. 14	Pisa
Sept. 22	Georgia
Oct. 30	Tenedos
Nov. 12	Sicilia
Nov. 20	Pisa
Dec. 29	Seriphos

HAMBURG-AMERICAN LINE
Scandinavian Ports—New York

N.Y.

Arrival	Steamer
Mar. 6	Adria

HOLLAND-AMERICA LINE
Rotterdam—New York

N.Y.

Arrival	Steamer
Jan. 21	Rotterdam
Jan. 31	Amsterdam
Feb. 12	Ryndam
Feb. 26	Rotterdam
Mar. 9	Amsterdam
Mar. 12	Statendam
Mar. 18	Ryndam
Mar. 25	Noordam
Apr. 1	Rotterdam
Apr. 9	Potsdam
Apr. 14	Statendam
Apr. 21	Ryndam
Apr. 28	Noordam
May 6	Rotterdam
May 12	Potsdam
May 19	Statendam
May 26	Ryndam
June 2	Noordam
June 9	Rotterdam
June 23	Statendam
June 30	Ryndam
July 7	Noordam
July 16	Amsterdam
July 21	Rotterdam
Aug. 4	Statendam
Aug. 11	Ryndam
Aug. 18	Noordam
Aug. 25	Rotterdam
Sept. 1	Potsdam
Sept. 8	Statendam
Sept. 14	Ryndam
Sept. 22	Noordam
Sept. 29	Rotterdam
Oct. 6	Potsdam
Oct. 13	Statendam
Oct. 20	Ryndam
Oct. 28	Noordam
Nov. 4	Rotterdam
Nov. 13	Amsterdam
Nov. 17	Statendam
Dec. 1	Noordam

Year 1903

HOLLAND-AMERICA LINE
Rotterdam—New York
(Continued)
N. Y.

Arrival	Steamer
Dec. 19.........	Amsterdam
Dec. 22.........	Rotterdam

INSULAR NAVIGATION COMPANY
Azores, Lisbon—New Bedford, Mass., New York
N. Y.

Arrival	Steamer
Apr. 20.........	Peninsular
June 5.........	Peninsular
July 24.........	Peninsular
Sept. 11.........	Peninsular
Nov. 5.........	Peninsular

LA VELOCE LINE
Mediterranean—New York
N. Y.

Arrival	Steamer
Jan. 30......	Nord America
Feb. 14......	Citta di Napoli
Mar. 2......	Citta di Milano
Mar. 17......	Citta di Torino
Mar. 18......	Nord America
Apr. 2......	Citta di Napoli
Apr. 17......	Citta di Milano
May 5......	Citta di Genova
May 7......	Nord America
May 13......	Citta di Torino
May 20......	Citta di Napoli
June 5......	Citta di Milano
June 25......	Nord America
July 9......	Citta di Napoli
July 24......	Citta di Milano
Aug. 13......	Nord America
Aug. 26......	Citta di Napoli
Oct. 1......	Nord America
Oct. 15......	Citta di Napoli
Oct. 31......	Citta di Milano
Nov. 19......	Nord America
Dec. 3......	Citta di Napoli
Dec. 21......	Citta di Milano

LINHA DE VAPORES PORTUGUEZES
Azores, Lisbon—New Bedford, Mass., New York
N. Y.

Arrival	Steamer
Jan. 2.........	Patria
Feb. 27.........	Patria
May 11.........	Patria
Aug. 28.........	Patria
Nov. 2.........	Patria

NAVIGAZIONE GENERALE ITALIANA LINE
Mediterranean—New York
N. Y.

Arrival	Steamer
Jan. 22.........	Sicilia
Feb. 5.........	Lombardia
Feb. 19.........	Sardegna
Feb. 28.........	Sicilia

NAVIGAZIONE GENERALE ITALIANA LINE
Mediterranean—New York
(Continued)
N. Y.

Arrival	Steamer
Mar. 6.........	Liguria
Mar. 11.........	Sicilia
Mar. 30.........	Sardegna
Apr. 9.........	Liguria
Apr. 17......	Marco Minghetti
Apr. 25.........	Sicilia
Apr. 29.........	Lombardia
May 13.........	Sardegna
May 27.........	Liguria
June 10.........	Umbria
June 10......	Marco Minghetti
June 17.........	Lombardia
July 13.........	Liguria
July 24.........	Sicilia
July 29.........	Umbria
Aug. 20.........	Lombardia
Sept. 2.........	Liguria
Sept. 23.........	Sardegna
Oct. 8.........	Lombardia
Oct. 22.........	Liguria
Nov. 5.........	Sicilia
Nov. 11.........	Sardegna
Nov. 25.........	Lombardia
Dec. 21......	Vincenzo Florio

NORTH GERMAN LLOYD
Bremen—New York
N. Y.

Arrival	Steamer
Jan. 2.........	Neckar
Jan. 15.........	Main
Jan. 16.........	Hanover
Jan. 19.........	Cassel
Feb. 13.........	Neckar
Feb. 19...	Kronprinz Wilhelm
Feb. 24.........	Main
Mar. 5...K. Wm. der Grosse
Mar. 12.........	Hanover
Mar. 13.........	Barbarossa
Mar. 18...Kronprinz Wilhelm
Mar. 21....	Grosser Kurfuerst
Mar. 26......	Koenig Albert
Apr. 1...K. Wm. der Grosse
Apr. 10.........	Gera
Apr. 14...Kronprinz Wilhelm
Apr. 15.........	Barbarossa
Apr. 22...Grosser Kurfuerst
Apr. 22...Kaiser Wilhelm II
Apr. 30.........	Neckar
May 6...Kronprinz Wilhelm
May 13...Fr'drich der Grosse
May 13...K. Wm. der Grosse
May 18.........	Chemnitz
May 20.........	Barbarossa
May 20.. Kaiser Wilhelm II
May 21.........	Gera
May 27...Grosser Kurfuerst
June 2.........	Bremen
June 2...Kronprinz Wilhelm
June 10...K. Wm. der Grosse
June 16...Fr'drich der Grosse
June 17...Kaiser Wilhelm II
June 25.........	Barbarossa
June 30....Grosser Kurfuerst

NORTH GERMAN LLOYD
Bremen—New York
(Continued)
N. Y.

Arrival	Steamer
July 1...Kronprinz Wilhelm
July 8...K. Wm. der Grosse
July 15...Kaiser Wilhelm II
July 22...Fr'drich der Grosse
July 29...K. Wm. der Grosse
July 30.........	Barbarossa
Aug. 6....Grosser Kurfuerst
Aug. 4...Kronprinz Wilhelm
Aug. 12.........	Bremen
Aug. 18...Kaiser Wilhelm II
Aug. 25...K. Wm. der Grosse
Aug. 26...Fr'drich der Grosse
Sept. 1...Kronprinz Wilhelm
Sept. 4.........	Barbarossa
Sept. 9....Grosser Kurfuerst
Sept. 15.......Koenig Albert
Sept. 16...Kaiser Wilhelm II
Sept. 22.........	Bremen
Sept. 22...K. Wm. der Grosse
Sept. 30...Fr'drich der Grosse
Sept. 30.........	Main
Oct. 10.........	Chemnitz
Oct. 13...Kaiser Wilhelm II
Oct. 14....Grosser Kurfuerst
Oct. 21...K. Wm. der Grosse
Oct. 23.........	Neckar
Oct. 28...Kronprinz Wilhelm
Oct. 31.........	Rhein
Nov. 4...Fr'drich der Grosse
Nov. 10...Kaiser Wilhelm II
Nov. 12.........	Main
Nov. 18....Grosser Kurfuerst
Nov. 18...K. Wm. der Grosse
Nov. 24...Kronprinz Wilhelm
Nov. 25.........	Neckar
Dec. 4.........	Rhein
Dec. 8...Kaiser Wilhelm II
Dec. 12.........	Chemnitz
Dec. 22.........	Main
Dec. 24...Kronprinz Wilhelm
Dec. 26.........	Bradenburg

NORTH GERMAN LLOYD
Mediterranean—New York
N. Y.

Arrival	Steamer
Jan. 31.........	Lahn
Feb. 27......	Koenigin Luise
Mar. 4.........	Lahn
Mar. 27.........	Neckar
Apr. 4......	Koenigin Luise
Apr. 9......	Prinzess Irene
Apr. 15.........	Lahn
Apr. 29......	Koenig Albert
May 6......	Koenigin Luise
May 13......	Prinzess Irene
May 27......	Hohenzollern
June 10......	Koenig Albert
June 10......	Koenigin Luise
June 25.........	Lahn
June 25......	Prinzess Irene
July 8......	Hohenzollern
July 14......	Koenigin Luise
Aug. 5.........	Lahn

Year 1903

NORTH GERMAN LLOYD
Mediterranean—New York
(Continued)

N.Y. Arrival	Steamer
Aug. 5	Koenigin Luise
Aug. 26	Hohenzollern
Sept. 10	Prinzess Irene
Sept. 16	Lahn
Sept. 16	Koenigin Luise
Oct. 1	Hohenzollern
Oct. 14	Prinzess Irene
Oct. 28	Lahn
Nov. 12	Hohenzollern
Nov. 27	Prinzess Irene
Dec. 7	Lahn
Dec. 23	Hohenzollern

PRINCE LINE
Mediterranean—New York

N.Y. Arrival	Steamer
Jan. 30	Sicilian Prince
Feb. 24	Napolitan Prince
Mar. 30	Sicilian Prince
Apr. 9	II Piemonte
Apr. 16	Napolitan Prince
May 16	Sicilian Prince
May 26	Napolitan Prince
May 27	II Piemonte
June 29	Sicilian Prince
July 9	Napolitan Prince
Aug. 7	II Piemonte
Aug. 12	Sicilian Prince
Sept. 8	Napolitan Prince
Sept. 14	II Piemonte
Sept. 25	Sicilian Prince
Oct. 21	Napolitan Prince
Oct. 21	II Piemonte
Nov. 9	Sicilian Prince
Nov. 30	Napolitan Prince
Nov. 30	II Piemonte
Dec. 24	Sicilian Prince

RED STAR LINE
Antwerp—New York

N.Y. Arrival	Steamer
Jan. 8	Finland
Jan. 14	Vaderland
Jan. 24	Kroonland
Feb. 3	Zeeland
Feb. 11	Finland
Feb. 18	Vaderland
Feb. 25	Kroonland
Mar. 4	Zeeland
Mar. 11	Finland
Mar. 17	Vaderland
Mar. 27	Kensington
Apr. 7	Kroonland
Apr. 14	Zeeland
Apr. 21	Finland
Apr. 28	Vaderland
May 5	Kroonland
May 12	Zeeland
May 18	Finland
May 26	Vaderland
June 9	Zeeland
June 15	Finland

RED STAR LINE
Antwerp—New York
(Continued)

N.Y. Arrival	Steamer
June 23	Vaderland
June 29	Kroonland
July 7	Zeeland
July 13	Finland
July 21	Vaderland
July 28	Kroonland
Aug. 10	Finland
Aug. 18	Vaderland
Aug. 25	Kroonland
Aug. 31	Zeeland
Sept. 8	Finland
Sept. 14	Vaderland
Sept. 21	Kroonland
Sept. 29	Zeeland
Oct. 6	Finland
Oct. 13	Vaderland
Oct. 20	Kroonland
Oct. 27	Zeeland
Nov. 4	Finland
Nov. 10	Vaderland
Nov. 17	Kroonland
Nov. 23	Zeeland
Dec. 1	Finland
Dec. 7	Vaderland
Dec. 22	Zeeland

SCANDINAVIAN-AMERICAN LINE
Scandinavian Ports—New York

N.Y. Arrival	Steamer
Jan. 7	Hekla
Jan. 29	Norge
Feb. 16	Island
Feb. 23	Hekla
Mar. 17	Norge
Apr. 1	Island
Apr. 9	Hellig Olav
Apr. 20	Hekla
May 6	Norge
May 16	Island
May 18	Hellig Olav
June 6	Hekla
June 16	United States
June 27	Norge
June 30	Hellig Olav
July 11	Island
July 14	Oscar II
July 24	Hekla
July 27	United States
Aug. 10	Hellig Olav
Aug. 21	Norge
Aug. 24	Oscar II
Sept. 4	Island
Sept. 8	United States
Sept. 18	Hekla
Sept. 21	Hellig Olav
Oct. 6	Oscar II
Oct. 15	Norge
Oct. 19	United States
Oct. 31	Island
Nov. 2	Hellig Olav
Nov. 14	Hekla

SCANDINAVIAN-AMERICAN LINE
Scandinavian Ports—New York
(Continued)

N.Y. Arrival	Steamer
Nov. 17	Oscar II
Dec. 1	United States
Dec. 14	Norge
Dec. 15	Hellig Olav
Dec. 28	Island

WHITE STAR LINE
Liverpool—New York

N.Y. Arrival	Steamer
Jan. 2	Teutonic
Jan. 24	Celtic
Feb. 5	Oceanic
Feb. 21	Cedric
Mar. 5	Oceanic
Mar. 21	Cedric
Apr. 9	Teutonic
Apr. 20	Cedric
Apr. 24	Celtic
Apr. 30	Oceanic
May 7	Teutonic
May 18	Cedric
May 21	Majestic
May 25	Celtic
May 28	Oceanic
June 4	Teutonic
June 15	Cedric
June 18	Majestic
June 22	Celtic
June 24	Oceanic
July 2	Teutonic
July 6	Arabic
July 16	Majestic
July 18	Celtic
July 22	Oceanic
July 30	Teutonic
Aug. 3	Arabic
Aug. 10	Cedric
Aug. 13	Majestic
Aug. 17	Celtic
Aug. 19	Oceanic
Aug. 27	Teutonic
Sept. 5	Cedric
Sept. 9	Majestic
Sept. 12	Celtic
Sept. 17	Oceanic
Sept. 24	Teutonic
Oct. 3	Cedric
Oct. 8	Majestic
Oct. 12	Celtic
Oct. 14	Oceanic
Oct. 22	Teutonic
Oct. 26	Arabic
Oct. 30	Cedric
Nov. 5	Majestic
Nov. 9	Celtic
Nov. 11	Oceanic
Nov. 19	Teutonic
Nov. 27	Cedric
Dec. 10	Oceanic
Dec. 17	Teutonic
Dec. 26	Cedric

Year 1903

WILSON LINE		WILSON LINE		ADDITIONAL ARRIVALS	
Hull—New York		Hull—New York		Mediterranean—New York	
N.Y.			(Continued)	N.Y.	
Arrival	Steamer	N.Y.		Arrival	Steamer
Jan. 12	Colorado	Arrival	Steamer	Feb. 25	Equita
Jan. 26	Consuelo	July 31	Colorado	Mar. 24	Regina Elena
Feb. 19	Toronto	Aug. 4	Consuelo	Apr. 8	Balilla
Mar. 3	Colorado	Aug. 28	Toronto	Apr. 22	Regina Elena
Mar. 26	Consuelo	Sept. 14	Colorado	May 11	Regina Elena
Apr. 9	Toronto	Sept. 19	Consuelo	May 21	Attivita
Apr. 24	Colorado	Oct. 16	Toronto	Nov. 18	Regina Elena
May 8	Consuelo	Oct. 31	Colorado		
May 29	Toronto	Nov. 28	Toronto		
June 15	Colorado	Dec. 11	Idaho		
June 17	Consuelo	Dec. 15	Colorado		
July 17	Toronto	Dec. 26	Consuelo		

Year 1904

ALLAN LINE
Glasgow—Boston
Boston

Arrival	Steamer
Mar. 18	Sardinian
Apr. 2	Sarmatian
Apr. 18	Siberian
Apr. 24	Pomeranian
May 11	Sarmatian
June 12	Sarmatian
July 24	Sarmatian
Aug. 8	Corean
Aug. 29	Sarmatian
Oct. 3	Sarmatian

ALLAN STATE LINE
Glasgow—New York
N. Y.

Arrival	Steamer
Jan. 2	Mongolian
Jan. 16	Siberian
Jan. 29	Corinthian
Feb. 16	Corean
Feb. 29	Numidian
Mar. 11	Corinthian
Mar. 26	Laurientian
Apr. 11	Numidian
Apr. 23	Mongolian
May 6	Laurientian
May 20	Numidian
June 4	Mongolian
June 15	Laurentian
June 30	Numidian
July 7	Mongolian
July 19	Laurentian
Aug. 4	Numidian
Aug. 17	Mongolian
Aug. 25	Laurentian
Sept. 8	Numidian
Sept. 23	Mongolian
Sept. 28	Laurentian
Oct. 14	Numidian
Nov. 7	Laurentian
Nov. 18	Numidian
Dec. 1	Pomeranian
Dec. 16	Mongolian
Dec. 28	Numidian

AMERICAN LINE
Southampton—New York
N. Y.

Arrival	Steamer
Jan. 3	St. Louis
Jan. 10	New York
Jan. 17	St. Paul
Jan. 23	Philadelphia
Jan. 31	St. Louis
Feb. 7	New York
Feb. 14	St. Paul
Feb. 21	Philadelphia
Feb. 28	St. Louis
Mar. 5	New York
Mar. 13	St. Paul
Mar. 27	St. Louis
Apr. 10	St. Paul
Apr. 16	Philadelphia
Apr. 23	St. Louis
May 2	Germanic

AMERICAN LINE
Southampton—New York
(Continued)
N. Y.

Arrival	Steamer
May 8	St. Paul
May 15	Philadelphia
May 21	St. Louis
May 30	Germanic
June 4	St. Paul
June 11	Philadelphia
June 18	St. Louis
June 27	Germanic
July 3	St. Paul
July 9	Philadelphia
July 17	St. Louis
July 24	New York
Aug. 3	St. Paul
Aug. 6	Philadelphia
Aug. 14	Germanic
Aug. 20	New York
Aug. 27	St. Paul
Sept. 3	Philadelphia
Sept. 12	Germanic
Sept. 17	New York
Sept. 24	St. Paul
Oct. 1	Philadelphia
Oct. 11	Germanic
Oct. 15	New York
Oct. 22	St. Paul
Oct. 29	Philadelphia
Nov. 12	New York
Nov. 20	St. Paul
Nov. 26	Philadelphia
Dec. 12	New York
Dec. 18	St. Paul
Dec. 25	St. Louis

AMERICAN LINE
Liverpool—Philadelphia
Phila.

Arrival	Steamer
Jan. 5	Haverford
Jan. 15	Noordland
Jan. 18	Friesland
Jan. 25	Merion
Feb. 10	Haverford
Feb. 20	Noordland
Mar. 3	Merion
Mar. 7	Westernland
Mar. 14	Haverford
Mar. 20	Friesland
Apr. 4	Noordland
Apr. 14	Merion
Apr. 17	Westernland
Apr. 25	Haverford
May 1	Friesland
May 10	Noordland
May 16	Merion
May 22	Westernland
May 30	Haverford
June 13	Noordland
June 19	Merion
June 27	Westernland
July 3	Haverford
July 10	Friesland
July 18	Noordland

AMERICAN LINE
Liverpool—Philadelphia
(Continued)
Phila.

Arrival	Steamer
July 24	Merion
July 31	Westernland
Aug. 1	Haverford
Aug. 14	Friesland
Aug. 22	Noordland
Aug. 28	Merion
Sept. 4	Westernland
Sert. 10	Haverford
Sept. 18	Friesland
Sept. 26	Noordland
Oct. 2	Merion
Oct. 9	Westernland
Oct. 17	Haverland
Oct. 31	Friesland
Nov. 13	Merion
Nov. 27	Haverford
Dec. 13	Friesland
Dec. 28	Merion

ANCHOR LINE
Glasgow—New York
N. Y.

Arrival	Steamer
Jan. 9	Furnessia
Jan. 23	Ethiopia
Feb. 8	Anchoria
Feb. 18	Furnessia
Mar. 5	Ethiopia
Mar. 16	Astoria
Mar. 28	Columbia
Apr. 12	Furnessia
Apr. 25	Columbia
May 2	Astoria
May 11	Anchoria
May 15	Furnessia
May 22	Columbia
June 1	Ethiopia
June 6	Astoria
June 13	Anchoria
June 19	Columbia
June 27	Furnessia
July 4	Ethiopia
July 10	Astoria
July 17	Columbia
July 26	Anchoria
July 31	Furnessia
Aug. 8	Ethiopia
Aug. 14	Columbia
Aug. 21	Astoria
Aug. 29	Anchoria
Sept. 5	Furnessia
Sept. 12	Columbia
Sept. 20	Ethiopia
Sept. 26	Anchoria
Oct. 5	Anchoria
Oct. 9	Columbia
Oct. 18	Furnessia
Oct. 31	Astoria
Nov. 6	Columbia
Nov. 23	Furnessia
Dec. 9	Astoria
Dec. 24	Ethiopia

Year 1904

ANCHOR LINE
Mediterranean—New York

N. Y.

Arrival	Steamer
Jan. 2	Calabria
Jan. 11	California
Jan. 24	Perugia
Feb. 12	Victoria
Feb. 27	Calabria
Mar. 6	Italia
Mar. 18	Perugia
Mar. 25	California
Apr. 13	Victoria
Apr. 16	Calabria
Apr. 19	Algeria
Apr. 23	Italia
May 4	Perugia
June 2	Calabria
June 10	Italia
June 26	Perugia
July 14	Algeria
July 25	Calabria
Aug. 2	Italia
Aug. 24	Perugia
Sept. 9	Algeria
Sept. 23	Calabria
Oct. 8	Italia
Oct. 24	Perugia
Nov. 12	Algeria
Nov. 23	Calabria
Nov. 29	Italia
Dec. 21	Perugia

ATLANTIC TRANSPORT LINE
London—New York

N. Y.

Arrival	Steamer
Jan. 5	Minnehaha
Jan. 18	Minnetonka
Jan. 27	Marquette
Feb. 1	Minnehaha
Feb. 14	Manitou
Feb. 16	Mesaba
Feb. 23	Minnetonka
Mar. 2	Marquette
Mar. 9	Menominee
Mar. 12	Minneapolis
Mar. 21	Mesaba
Mar. 27	Minnetonka
Apr. 6	Marquette
Apr. 11	Minnehaha
Apr. 19	Minneapolis
Apr. 26	Mesaba
May 2	Minnetonka
May 9	Minnehaha
May 16	Minneapolis
May 24	Mesaba
May 31	Minnetonka
June 6	Minnehaha
June 13	Minneapolis
June 21	Mesaba
June 27	Minnetonka
July 4	Minnehaha
July 11	Minneapolis
July 19	Mesaba
July 25	Minnetonka
Aug. 2	Minnehaha
Aug. 8	Minneapolis
Aug. 16	Mesaba

ATLANTIC TRANSPORT LINE
London—New York
(Continued)

N. Y.

Arrival	Steamer
Aug. 22	Minnetonka
Aug. 29	Minnehaha
Sept. 5	Minneapolis
Sept. 13	Mesaba
Sept. 19	Minnetonka
Sept. 26	Minnehaha
Oct. 3	Minneapolis
Oct. 10	Menominee
Oct. 17	Minnetonka
Oct. 24	Mesaba
Oct. 31	Minnehaha
Nov. 7	Minneapolis
Nov. 14	Menominee
Nov. 20	Minnetonka
Nov. 29	Mesaba
Dec. 6	Minnehaha
Dec. 16	Manitou
Dec. 21	Menominee
Dec. 24	Minnetonka

AUSTRO-AMERICANA LINE
Mediterranean—New York

N. Y.

Arrival	Steamer
July 5	Gerty
Aug. 8	Giulia
Aug. 23	Frieda
Sept. 6	Gerty
Oct. 4	Giulia
Nov. 7	Gerty
Nov. 25	Giulia
Dec. 20	Georgia

COMPANIA TRANSATLANTICA LINE
(Spanish Line)
Spanish Ports—New York

N. Y.

Arrival	Steamer
Jan. 12	Leon XIII
Feb. 14	Buenos Aires
Mar. 13	Manuel Calva
Apr. 10	Montevideo
May 11	Montserrat
June 11	Leon XIII
July 11	P. de Satrustegui
Aug. 10	Manuel Calvo
Sept. 10	Montevideo
Oct. 12	Buenos Aires
Nov. 12	Antonio Lopez
Dec. 12	Montserrat

CUNARD LINE
Liverpool—New York

N. Y.

Arrival	Steamer
Jan. 5	Ivernia
Jan. 10	Umbria
Jan. 16	Lucania
Jan. 25	Saxonia
Jan. 31	Etruria
Feb. 7	Umbria
Feb. 16	Ivernia
Feb. 20	Campania

CUNARD LINE
Liverpool—New York
(Continued)

N. Y.

Arrival	Steamer
Feb. 28	Etruria
Mar. 5	Lucania
Mar. 13	Umbria
Mar. 19	Campania
Mar. 27	Etruria
Apr. 2	Lucania
Apr. 10	Umbria
Apr. 16	Campania
Apr. 23	Etruria
Apr. 30	Lucania
May 8	Umbria
May 13	Campania
May 21	Etruria
May 26	Aurania
May 28	Lucania
June 5	Umbria
June 10	Carpathia
June 11	Campania
June 18	Etruria
June 23	Aurania
June 25	Lucania
July 2	Umbria
July 7	Carpathia
July 9	Campania
July 16	Etruria
July 20	Aurania
July 22	Lucania
July 30	Umbria
Aug. 4	Carpathia
Aug. 6	Campania
Aug. 13	Etruria
Aug. 18	Aurania
Aug. 20	Lucania
Aug. 27	Umbria
Sept. 1	Carpathia
Sept. 2	Campania
Sept. 10	Etruria
Sept. 14	Aurania
Sept. 17	Lucania
Sept. 24	Umbria
Sept. 29	Carpathia
Sept. 30	Campania
Oct. 8	Etruria
Oct. 14	Lucania
Oct. 22	Umbria
Oct. 27	Carpathia
Oct. 28	Campania
Nov. 5	Etruria
Nov. 11	Lucania
Nov. 19	Umbria
Nov. 25	Campania
Dec. 4	Etruria
Dec. 10	Lucania
Dec. 17	Umbria
Dec. 24	Campania

CUNARD LINE
Mediterranean—New York

N. Y.

Arrival	Steamer
Jan. 7	Carpathia
Jan. 19	Aurania
Feb. 25	Carpathia
Mar. 7	Aurania
Apr. 19	Slavonia

Year 1904

CUNARD LINE
Mediterranean—New York
(Continued)
N. Y.

Arrival	Steamer
May 4	Carpathia
May 21	Ultonia
June 4	Slavonia
June 18	Pannonia
July 4	Ultonia
July 15	Slavonia
July 28	Pannonia
Aug. 23	Ultonia
Aug. 29	Slavonia
Sept. 17	Pannonia
Oct. 13	Ultonia
Oct. 23	Slavonia
Nov. 7	Pannonia
Dec. 5	Ultonia
Dec. 14	Slavonia
Dec. 28	Pannonia

CUNARD LINE
Liverpool—Boston
Boston

Arrival	Steamer
Jan. 25	Ultonia
Feb. 21	Ultonia
Feb. 26	Saxonia
Mar. 11	Ivernia
Mar. 25	Saxonia
Apr. 7	Ivernia
Apr. 22	Saxonia
May 5	Ivernia
May 19	Saxonia
June 2	Ivernia
June 16	Saxonia
June 30	Ivernia
July 14	Saxonia
July 28	Ivernia
Aug. 11	Saxonia
Aug. 24	Ivernia
Sept. 8	Saxonia
Sept. 22	Ivernia
Oct. 6	Saxonia
Oct. 19	Ivernia
Nov. 2	Saxonia
Nov. 23	Ivernia
Dec. 9	Saxonia

FABRE LINE
Mediterranean—New York
N. Y.

Arrival	Steamer
Jan. 1	Patria
Jan. 18	Germania
Jan. 29	Massila
Feb. 25	Roma
Mar. 13	Neustria
Mar. 16	Germania
Mar. 26	Patria
Apr. 3	Gallia
Apr. 7	Roma
Apr. 16	Massilia
Apr. 27	Germania
May 9	Neustria
May 10	Roma
May 21	Patria
June 7	Germania
June 19	Gallia

FABRE LINE
Mediterranean—New York
(Continued)
N. Y.

Arrival	Steamer
July 1	Roma
July 18	Patria
July 28	Germania
Aug. 15	Roma
Sept. 5	Gallia
Sept. 23	Roma
Oct. 19	Patria
Oct. 26	Germania
Nov. 1	Roma
Nov. 18	Gallia
Dec. 7	Germania
Dec. 18	Roma

FRENCH LINE
(Compagnie Generale Transatlantique)
Havre—New York
N. Y.

Arrival	Steamer
Jan. 5	La Champagne
Jan. 10	La Savoie
Jan. 18	La Bretagne
Jan. 23	La Touraine
Feb. 1	La Champagne
Feb. 7	La Lorraine
Feb. 15	La Bretagne
Feb. 21	La Touraine
Feb. 29	La Champagne
Mar. 5	La Lorraine
Mar. 13	La Bretagne
Mar. 19	La Savoie
Mar. 28	La Gascogne
Apr. 2	La Touraine
Apr. 5	L'Aquitaine
Apr. 9	La Lorraine
Apr. 17	La Bretagne
Apr. 23	La Savoie
Apr. 30	La Touraine
May 2	La Gascogne
May 9	La Lorraine
May 15	La Bretagne
May 21	La Savoie
May 28	La Touraine
June 4	La Lorraine
June 12	La Gascogne
June 17	La Bretagne
June 26	La Champagne
July 1	La Lorraine
July 9	La Touraine
July 15	La Savoie
July 24	La Bretagne
July 31	La Champagne
Aug. 7	La Gascogne
Aug. 13	La Touraine
Aug. 20	La Lorraine
Aug. 28	La Bretagne
Sept. 2	La Savoie
Sept. 10	La Touraine
Sept. 18	La Lorraine
Sept. 24	La Bretagne
Sept. 30	La Savoie
Oct. 8	La Touraine
Oct. 14	La Lorraine
Oct. 23	La Gascogne
Oct. 28	La Savoie
Nov. 5	La Touraine

FRENCH LINE
(Compagnie Generale Transatlantique)
Havre—New York
(Continued)
N. Y.

Arrival	Steamer
Nov. 11	La Lorraine
Nov. 19	La Gascogne
Nov. 26	La Savoie
Dec. 3	La Touraine
Dec. 10	La Lorraine
Dec. 20	La Gascogne
Dec. 24	La Savoie

HAMBURG-AMERICAN LINE
Hamburg—New York
N. Y.

Arrival	Steamer
Jan. 10	Patricia
Jan. 12	Deutschland
Jan. 16	Pretoria
Jan. 22	Graf Waldersee
Jan. 25	Auguste Victoria
Jan. 29	Prinz Adalbert
Jan. 30	Belgravia
Feb. 5	Bluecher
Feb. 9	Palatia
Feb. 13	Pennsylvania
Feb. 20	Patricia
Feb. 22	Prinz Oskar
Feb. 24	Moltke
Mar. 5	Pretoria
Mar. 10	Graf Waldersee
Mar. 15	Bluecher
Mar. 17	Prinz Adalbert
Mar. 26	Pennsylvania
Mar. 28	Moltke
Mar. 29	Palatia
Mar. 31	Deutschland
Apr. 2	Patricia
Apr. 10	Belgravia
Apr. 10	Prinz Oskar
Apr. 16	Pretoria
Apr. 16	Columbia
Apr. 22	Graf Waldersee
Apr. 24	Bluecher
Apr. 30	Bulgaria
May 1	Moltke
May 3	Prinz Adalbert
May 5	Pennsylvania
May 5	Deutschland
May 13	Patricia
May 17	Palatia
May 19	Belgravia
May 21	Bluecher
May 25	Prinz Oskar
May 26	Pretoria
May 29	Moltke
June 2	Graf Waldersee
June 2	Deutschland
June 12	Hamburg
June 12	Arcadia
June 16	Pennsylvania
June 19	Bluecher
June 21	Prinz Adalbert
June 23	Patricia
June 26	Moltke
June 29	Deutschland
July 1	Belgravia

Year 1904

HAMBURG-AMERICAN LINE
Hamburg—New York
(Continued)

N. Y.

Arrival	Steamer
July 8	Pretoria
July 12	Prinz Oskar
July 17	Hamburg
July 17	Graf Waldersee
July 23	Moltke
July 22	Bulgaria
July 27	Pennsylvania
July 28	Deutschland
Aug. 4	Patricia
Aug. 10	Prinz Adalbert
Aug. 12	Phoenicia
Aug. 14	Hamburg
Aug. 19	Pretoria
Aug. 21	Bluecher
Aug. 24	Graf Waldersee
Aug. 25	Deutschland
Aug. 30	Prinz Oskar
Sept. 1	Moltke
Sept. 1	Belgravia
Sept 7	Pennsylvania
Sept. 11	Hamburg
Sept. 15	Patricia
Sept. 18	Bluecher
Sept. 22	Deutschland
Sept. 23	Phoenicia
Sept. 27	Prinz Adalbert
Sept. 29	Pretoria
Sept. 30	Moltke
Oct. 6	Graf Waldersee
Oct. 9	Hamburg
Oct. 13	Belgravia
Oct. 15	Bluecher
Oct. 20	Pennsylvania
Oct. 20	Deutschland
Oct. 20	Prinz Oskar
Oct. 27	Patricia
Oct. 31	Moltke
Nov. 10	Phoenicia
Nov. 14	Hamburg
Nov. 18	Prinz Adalbert
Nov. 19	Pretoria
Nov. 24	Graf Waldersee
Nov. 29	Bluecher
Dec. 4	Prinz Oskar
Dec. 11	Belgravia
Dec. 14	Moltke
Dec. 22	Deutschland
Dec. 25	Patricia
Dec. 31	Pretoria

HAMBURG-AMERICAN LINE
Levant—New York

N. Y.

Arrival	Steamer
Jan. 7	Georgia
Mar. 5	Pisa
Apr. 3	Tenedos
Apr. 18	Seriphos
May 11	Georgia
June 3	Sicilia
July 23	Tenedos
Aug. 4	Seriphos

HAMBURG-AMERICAN LINE
Levant—New York
(Continued)

N. Y.

Arrival	Steamer
Sept. 15	Sicilia

HAMBURG-AMERICAN LINE
(Scandia Line)
Scandinavian Ports—New York

N. Y.

Arrival	Steamer
Apr. 25	Adria
May 19	Willehad
June 18	Adria
July 15	Willehad
Aug. 12	Adria
Sept. 8	Willehad
Oct. 7	Adria

HOLLAND-AMERICAN LINE
Rotterdam—New York

N. Y.

Arrival	Steamer
Jan. 14	Statendam
Jan. 21	Amsterdam
Jan. 26	Rotterdam
Feb. 17	Statendam
Feb. 27	Amsterdam
Mar. 1	Rotterdam
Mar. 15	Noordam
Mar. 31	Potsdam
Apr. 5	Rotterdam
Apr. 13	Ryndam
Apr. 19	Noordam
Apr. 29	Amsterdam
May 3	Potsdam
May 11	Rotterdam
May 17	Ryndam
May 24	Noordam
May 31	Statendam
June 8	Potsdam
June 14	Rotterdam
June 21	Ryndam
June 28	Noordam
July 5	Statendam
July 11	Potsdam
July 25	Rotterdam
Aug. 2	Ryndam
Aug. 8	Noordam
Aug. 16	Statendam
Aug. 23	Potsdam
Aug. 29	Rotterdam
Sept. 5	Ryndam
Sept. 12	Noordam
Sept. 20	Statendam
Sept. 27	Potsdam
Oct. 4	Rottendam
Oct. 10	Ryndam
Oct. 18	Noordam
Oct. 25	Statendam
Nov. 2	Amsterdam
Nov. 7	Rotterdam
Nov. 15	Ryndam
Nov. 29	Statendam
Dec. 9	Amsterdam
Dec. 14	Rotterdam

INSULAR NAVIGATION COMPANY
Azores, Lisbon—New York—New Bedford, Mass.

N. Y.
New Bedford

Arrival	Steamer
Jan. 10	Peninsular
Mar. 1	Peninsular
Apr. 16	Peninsular
June 11	Peninsular
June 30	Peninsular
Sept. 21	Peninsular
Nov. 11	Peninsular

LA VELOCE
Mediterranean—New York

N. Y.

Arrival	Steamer
Jan. 28	Nord America
Feb. 6	Citta di Napoli
Feb. 28	Citta di Torino
Mar. 16	Nord America
Mar. 27	Citta di Milano
Mar. 31	Citta di Napoli
Apr. 15	Citta di Torino
Apr. 30	Citta di Genova
May 3	Nord America
May 9	Citta di Milano
May 18	Citta di Napoli
June 4	Citta di Torino
June 23	Nord America
July 6	Citta di Napoli
July 23	Citta di Torina
Aug. 11	Nord America
Aug. 24	Citta di Napoli
Sept. 10	Citta di Torino
Sept. 29	Nord America
Oct. 14	Citta di Napoli
Nov. 20	Nord America
Dec. 1	Citta di Napoli
Dec. 28	Citta di Torino

LEYLAND LINE
Liverpool—Boston

Boston

Arrival	Steamer
Jan. 7	Devonian
Jan. 13	Winifredian
Jan. 22	Bohemian
Jan. 27	Canadian
Feb. 5	Cestrian
Feb. 11	Devonian
Feb. 17	Winifredian
Feb. 25	Bohemian
Mar. 5	Canadian
Mar. 8	Cestrian
Mar. 18	Devonian
Mar. 30	Bohemian
Apr. 6	Canadian
Apr. 13	Cestrian
Apr. 19	Winifredian
May 3	Bohemian
May 16	Cestrian
May 23	Winifredian
May 31	Devonian
June 8	Bohemian
June 15	Canadian
June 21	Cestrian
June 28	Winifredian

Year 1904

LEYLAND LINE
Liverpool—Boston
(Continued)

Boston

Arrival	Steamer
July 11	Devonian
July 25	Cestrian
Aug. 8	Winifredian
Aug. 16	Bohemian
Aug. 24	Canadian
Sept. 5	Devonian
Sept. 13	Winifredian
Sept. 21	Bohemian
Sept. 27	Canadian
Oct. 4	Cestrian
Oct. 11	Devonian
Oct. 17	Winifredian
Oct. 25	Bohemian
Nov. 1	Canadian
Nov. 15	Devonian
Nov. 22	Winifredian
Nov. 29	Bohemian
Dec. 8	Canadian
Dec. 21	Devonian
Dec. 27	Winifredian

LINHA DE VAPORES PORTUGUEZES
Azores, Lisbon—N. Y., New Bedford

N. Y.
N. Bedford

Arrival	Steamer
Jan. 2	Patria
Mar. 6	Patria
May 3	Patria
July 7	Patria

NAVIGAZIONE GENE-RALE ITALIANA
Mediterranean—New York

N. Y.

Arrival	Steamer
Jan. 5	Sardegna
Jan. 20	Lombardia
Feb. 5	Liguria
Feb. 18	Sicilia
Mar. 7	Vincenzo Florio
Mar. 10	Lombardia
Mar. 23	Liguria
Apr. 6	Sicilia
Apr. 10	Marco Minghetti
Apr. 13	Umbria
Apr. 20	Sardegna
Apr. 26	Lombardia
May 1	Vincenzo Florio
May 11	Liguria
May 25	Sicilia
June 16	Sardegna
June 28	Lombardia
July 13	Liguria
Aug. 3	Sardegna
Aug. 18	Lombardia
Aug. 31	Liguria
Sept. 22	Sardegna
Oct. 7	Lombardia
Nov. 13	Vincenzo Florio
Nov. 24	Lombardia
Dec. 5	Liguria

NORTH GERMAN LLOYD
Mediterranean—New York

N. Y.

Arrival	Steamer
Jan. 20	Prinzess Irene
Feb. 4	Hohenzollern
Feb. 18	Lahn
Feb. 25	Prinzess Irene
Mar. 10	Koenigin Luise
Mar. 16	Hohenzollern
Mar. 23	Neckar
Mar. 31	Prinzess Irene
Apr. 10	Koenig Albert
Apr. 14	Koenigin Luise
Apr. 27	Neckar
May 4	Prinzess Irene
May 18	Koenig Albert
May 25	Koenigin Luise
June 9	Prinzess Irene
June 22	Koenig Albert
June 29	Koenigin Luise
July 13	Prinzess Irene
Aug. 3	Koenigin Luise
Aug. 24	Prinzess Irene
Sept. 6	Hohenzollern
Sept. 21	Koenigin Luise
Oct. 5	Prinzess Irene
Oct. 12	Hohenzollern
Oct. 27	Koenigin Luise
Nov. 13	Prinzess Irene
Nov. 17	Hohenzollern
Nov. 23	Koenig Albert
Dec. 4	Koenigin Luise
Dec. 6	Neckar
Dec. 27	Prinzess Irene

NORTH GERMAN LLOYD
Bremen—New York

N. Y.

Arrival	Steamer
Jan. 20	Kaiser Wilhelm II
Feb. 4	K. Wm. der Grosse
Mar. 1	K. Wm. der Grosse
Mar. 8	Kaiser Wilhelm II
Mar. 15	Kronprinz Wilhelm
Mar. 23	K. Wm. der Grosse
Apr. 6	Kaiser Wilhelm II
Apr. 20	K. Wm. der Grosse
Apr. 26	Kronprinz Wilhelm
May 11	Kaiser Wilhelm II
May 17	K. Wm. der Grosse
May 24	Kronprinz Wilhelm
June 7	Kaiser Wilhelm II
June 14	K. Wm. der Grosse
June 21	Kronprinz Wilhelm
July 5	Kaiser Wilhelm II
July 12	K. Wm. der Grosse
July 19	Kronprinz Wilhelm
Aug. 2	Kaiser Wilhelm II
Aug. 9	K. Wm. der Grosse
Aug. 16	Kronprinz Wilhelm
Aug. 30	Kaiser Wilhelm II
Sept. 6	K. Wm. der Grosse
Sept. 13	Kronprinz Wilhelm
Sept. 27	Kaiser Wilhelm II
Oct. 5	K. Wm. der Grosse
Oct. 11	Kronprinz Wilhelm
Nov. 1	Kaiser Wilhelm II
Nov. 16	K. Wm. der Grosse
Nov. 29	Kaiser Wilhelm II

NORTH GERMAN LLOYD
Bremen—New York
(Continued)

N. Y.

Arrival	Steamer
Dec. 14	K. Wm. der Grosse

NORTH GERMAN LLOYD
Bremen—New York
Express Service

N. Y.

Arrival	Steamer
Jan. 1	Breslau
Jan. 12	Rhein
Jan. 15	Cassel
Jan. 22	Neckar
Jan. 30	Frankfurt
Feb. 8	Brandenburg
Feb. 14	Main
Feb. 21	Chemnitz
Feb. 27	Rhein
Mar. 2	Grosser Kurfuerst
Mar. 8	Bremen
Mar. 17	Main
Mar. 24	Barbarossa
Apr. 2	Prinzess Alice
Apr. 11	Brandenburg
Apr. 13	Bremen
Apr. 22	Rhein
Apr. 26	Barbarossa
May 3	Prinzess Alice
May 11	Fr'drich der Grosse
May 17	Bremen
May 26	Chemnitz
June 3	Prinzess Alice
June 9	Barbarossa
June 15	Fr'drich der Grosse
June 22	Bremen
June 28	Grosser Kurfuerst
July 5	Prinzess Alice
July 13	Barbarossa
July 19	Fr'drich der Grosse
July 27	Bremen
Aug. 2	Grosser Kurfuerst
Aug. 9	Prinzess Alice
Aug. 17	Barbarossa
Aug. 23	Fr'drich der Grosse
Aug. 29	Bremen
Sept. 6	Koenig Albert
Sept. 8	Main
Sept. 13	Grosser Kurfuerst
Sept. 21	Neckar
Sept. 27	Fr'drich der Grosse
Oct. 4	Bremen
Oct. 4	Rhein
Oct. 11	Koenig Albert
Oct. 20	Main
Oct. 26	Neckar
Nov. 1	Fr'drich der Grosse
Nov. 8	Breslau
Nov. 8	Bremen
Nov. 16	Frankfurt
Nov. 18	Cassel
Nov. 25	Main
Dec. 2	Chemnitz
Dec. 11	Hannover
Dec. 14	Gera
Dec. 18	Brandenburg
Dec. 24	Frankfurt
Dec. 30	Main

Year 1904

NORTH GERMAN LLOYD
Bremen—Baltimore
Baltimore

Arrival	Steamer
Jan. 24	Hannover
Jan. 27	Oldenburg
Feb. 8	Willehad
Feb. 24	Chemnitz
Mar. 2	Rhein
Mar. 4	Koein
Mar. 9	Breslau
Mar. 17	Cassel
Mar. 26	Hannover
Apr. 3	Chemnitz
Apr. 13	Brandenburg
Apr. 16	Frankfurt
Apr. 25	Rhein
May 4	Breslau
May 14	Koein
May 19	Brandenburg
May 26	Hannover
June 2	Cassel
June 9	Breslau
June 14	Neckar
June 23	Frankfurt
June 30	Brandenburg
July 6	Chemnitz
July 21	Cassel
Aug. 4	Hannover
Aug. 10	Brandenburg
Aug. 24	Chemnitz
Aug. 31	Cassel
Sept. 8	Main
Sept. 17	Frankfurt
Sept. 21	Brandenburg
Sept. 28	Breslau
Oct. 6	Rhein
Oct. 13	Hannover
Oct. 20	Chemnitz
Nov. 2	Brandenburg
Nov. 11	Breslau
Nov. 20	Cassel
Dec. 5	Chemnitz
Dec. 8	Darmstadt
Dec. 21	Brandenburg
Dec. 24	Weimar

PRINCE LINE
Mediterranean—New York
N. Y.

Arrival	Steamer
Feb. 25	Sicilian Prince
Mar. 4	Napolitan Prince
Apr. 13	Sicilian Prince
Apr. 25	Napolitan Prince
May 20	II Piemonte
May 28	Napolitan Prince
June 14	Napolitan Prince
July 11	Sicilian Prince
July 27	Napolitan Prince
Aug. 23	Sicilian Prince
Sept. 10	Napolitan Prince
Oct. 22	Napolitan Prince
Nov. 20	Sicilian Prince
Dec. 2	Napolitan Prince

RED STAR LINE
Antwerp—New York
N. Y.

Arrival	Steamer
Jan. 8	Vaderland

RED STAR LINE
Antwerp—New York
(Continued)
N. Y.

Arrival	Steamer
Jan. 20	Kroonland
Jan. 26	Zeeland
Feb. 5	Finland
Feb. 11	Vaderland
Feb. 16	Kroonland
Feb. 23	Zeeland
Mar. 1	Finland
Mar. 8	Vaderland
Mar. 15	Kroonland
Mar. 22	Zeeland
Mar. 30	Finland
Apr. 5	Vaderland
Apr. 12	Kroonland
Apr. 19	Zeeland
Apr. 26	Finland
May 3	Vaderland
May 11	Kroonland
May 17	Zeeland
May 24	Finland
June 1	Vaderland
June 14	Zeeland
June 21	Finland
June 28	Vaderland
July 4	Kroonland
July 12	Zeeland
July 18	Finland
July 26	Vaderland
Aug. 1	Kroonland
Aug. 8	Zeeland
Aug. 15	Finland
Aug. 23	Vaderland
Aug. 29	Kroonland
Sept. 5	Zeeland
Sept. 13	Finland
Sept. 30	Vaderland
Sept. 26	Kroonland
Oct. 3	Zeeland
Oct. 11	Finland
Oct. 17	Vaderland
Oct. 24	Kroonland
Oct. 31	Zeeland
Nov. 7	Finland
Nov. 15	Vaderland
Nov. 22	Kroonland
Dec. 7	Finland
Dec. 13	Zeeland
Dec. 21	Kroonland
Dec. 27	Vaderland

RED STAR LINE
Antwerp—Philadelphia
Phila.

Arrival	Steamer
Jan. 1	Switzerland
Jan. 16	Rhynland
Jan. 30	Belgenland
Feb. 24	Switzerland
Feb. 26	Rhynland
Mar. 9	Belgenland
Mar. 30	Switzerland
Apr. 6	Rhynland
Apr. 21	Belgenland
May 5	Switzerland
May 19	Rhynland
June 15	Switzerland

RED STAR LINE
Antwerp—Philadelphia
(Continued)
Phila.

Arrival	Steamer
July 6	Rhynland
July 27	Switzerland
Aug. 17	Rhynland
Sept. 7	Switzerland
Sept. 28	Rhynland
Oct. 19	Switzerland
Nov. 8	Rhynland
Nov. 30	Belgenland
Dec. 24	Rhynland

SCANDINAVIAN-AMER. LINE
Scandinavian Ports—New York
N. Y.

Arrival	Steamer
Jan. 10	Kehla
Feb. 3	Norge
Feb. 11	Oscar II
Feb. 20	Island
Feb. 22	United States
Mar. 6	Hekla
Mar. 7	Hellig Olav
Mar. 20	Norge
Apr. 2	United States
Apr. 21	Island
Apr. 19	Hellig Olav
May 1	Hekla
May 16	Norge
May 16	United States
June 4	Island
June 14	Hellig Olav
June 25	Hekla
June 27	United States
July 10	Oscar II
July 23	Island
July 25	Hellig Olav
Aug. 7	United States
Aug. 17	Hekla
Aug. 21	Oscar II
Sept. 4	Hellig Olav
Sept. 20	Island
Sept. 19	United States
Oct. 3	Oscar II
Oct. 16	Hekla
Oct. 19	Hellig Olav
Oct. 31	United States
Nov. 15	Oscar II
Nov. 30	Hellig Olav
Dec. 12	United States
Dec. 14	Hekla
Dec. 26	Oscar II

WHITE STAR LINE
Liverpool—New York
N. Y.

Arrival	Steamer
Jan. 9	Celtic
Jan. 14	Teutonic
Jan. 23	Cedric
Jan. 28	Majestic
Feb. 4	Oceanic
Feb. 13	Celtic
Feb. 20	Cedric
Feb. 25	Majestic

Year 1904

WHITE STAR LINE Liverpool—New York	
N. Y. Arrival	Steamer
Mar. 2	Oceanic
Mar. 10	Celtic
Mar. 18	Cedric
Mar. 24	Majestic
Mar. 30	Oceanic
Apr. 7	Teutonic
Apr. 11	Celtic
Apr. 15	Cedric
Apr. 21	Majestic
Apr. 24	Arabic
Apr. 27	Oceanic
May 5	Teutonic
May 8	Celtic
May 13	Cedric
May 19	Majestic
May 22	Arabic
May 25	Oceanic
June 2	Teutonic
June 6	Celtic
June 10	Cedric
June 16	Majestic
June 18	Arabic
June 22	Oceanic
June 30	Teutonic
July 3	Celtic
July 8	Baltic
July 14	Majestic
July 16	Cedric
July 20	Oceanic
July 24	Arabic
July 28	Teutonic
July 30	Celtic
Aug. 4	Baltic
Aug. 10	Majestic
Aug. 14	Cedric
Aug. 17	Oceanic
Aug. 17	Arabic
Aug. 24	Teutonic
Aug. 27	Celtic
Sept. 1	Baltic
Sept. 7	Majestic
Sept. 11	Cedric
Sept. 14	Oceanic
Sept. 18	Arabic
Sept. 21	Teutonic
Sept. 24	Celtic
Sept. 30	Baltic
Oct. 5	Majestic
Oct. 8	Cedric
Oct. 12	Oceanic

WHITE STAR LINE Liverpool—New York (Continued)	
N. Y. Arrival	Steamer
Oct. 16	Arabic
Oct. 21	Teutonic
Oct. 23	Celtic
Oct. 28	Baltic
Nov. 3	Cedric
Nov. 9	Oceanic
Nov. 17	Majestic
Nov. 25	Baltic
Dec. 2	Cedric
Dec. 8	Oceanic
Dec. 15	Majestic
Dec. 23	Baltic

WHITE STAR LINE Mediterranean—New York	
N. Y. Arrival	Steamer
Nov. 24	Republic
Dec. 7	Cretic

WHITE STAR LINE Liverpool—Boston	
Boston Arrival	Steamer
Jan. 17	Cymric
Jan. 23	Canopic
Jan. 31	Cretic
Feb. 14	Cymric
Feb. 28	Cretic
Mar. 12	Cymric
Mar. 27	Cretic
Apr. 17	Cymric
Apr. 30	Cretic
May 14	Cymric
May 28	Cretic
June 3	Republic
June 11	Cymric
June 25	Cretic
July 1	Republic
July 9	Cymric
July 23	Cretic
Aug. 5	Republic
Aug. 20	Cretic
Sept. 2	Republic
Sept. 10	Cymric
Sept. 17	Cretic
Sept. 30	Republic
Oct. 8	Cymric
Oct. 22	Cretic
Nov. 12	Cymric

WHITE STAR LINE Liverpool—Boston (Continued)	
Boston Arrival	Steamer
Dec. 14	Cymric

WHITE STAR LINE Mediterranean—Boston	
Boston Arrival	Steamer
Jan. 10	Romanic
Feb. 9	Republic
Feb. 23	Romanic
Mar. 7	Canopic
Mar. 22	Republic
Apr. 5	Romanic
Apr. 21	Canopic
Apr. 27	Republic
May 10	Romanic
May 24	Canopic
June 15	Romanic
June 27	Canopic
Sept. 11	Romanic
Oct. 1	Canopic
Oct. 24	Romanic
Nov. 12	Canopic
Dec. 1	Romanic

WILSON LINE Hull—New York	
N. Y. Arrival	Steamer
Feb. 20	Consuelo
Apr. 18	Consuelo
May 6	Toronto
May 30	Colorado
June 13	Consuelo
July 21	Colorado
Aug. 20	Idaho
Sept. 6	Colorado
Oct. 7	Idaho
Oct. 20	Toronto
Nov. 2	Consuelo

ADDITIONAL ARRIVALS Mediterranean—New York	
N. Y. Arrival	Steamer
Mar. 27	Regina Elena
Mar. 28	Attivita
Apr. 11	Balilla
Apr. 25	Equita
May 8	Regina Elena
May 14	San Gottardo

Year 1905

ALLAN LINE
Glasgow—Boston
Boston

Arrival	Steamer
Mar. 23	Sarmatian
Mar. 30	Laurentian
Apr. 13	Sicilian
Apr. 20	Sardinian
May 5	Corean
May 18	Numidian
June 10	Corean
June 25	Buenos Ayrean
July 17	Corean
Aug. 7	Monte Videan
Aug. 20	Corean
Oct. 9	Corean
Nov. 7	Siberian
Nov. 20	Buenos Ayrean
Dec. 9	Mongolian
Dec. 24	Carthaginian

ALLAN-STATE LINE
Glasgow—New York
N. Y.

Arrival	Steamer
Jan. 12	Pomeranian
Jan. 27	Mongolian
Feb. 14	Corean
Feb. 22	Laurentian
Mar. 12	Mongolian
Mar. 23	Corinthian
Apr. 6	Pomeranian
Apr. 27	Mongolian
June 5	Parisian
June 19	Numidian
July 1	Parisian
July 15	Numidian
July 30	Parisian
Aug. 14	Numidian
Aug. 28	Parisian
Sept. 12	Numidian
Oct. 1	Carthaginian
Oct. 8	Numidian

AMERICAN LINE
Southampton—New York
N. Y.

Arrival	Steamer
Jan. 1	Philadelphia
Jan. 15	New York
Jan. 22	St. Louis
Jan. 28	Philadelphia
Feb. 5	St. Paul
Feb. 12	New York
Feb. 18	St. Louis
Feb. 25	Philadelphia
Mar. 5	St. Paul
Mar. 13	New York
Mar. 20	St. Louis
Mar. 25	Philadelphia
Apr. 2	St. Paul
Apr. 9	New York
Apr. 16	St. Louis
Apr. 22	Philadelphia
Apr. 30	St. Paul
May 7	New York
May 14	St. Louis

AMERICAN LINE
Southampton—New York
(Continued)
N. Y.

Arrival	Steamer
May 20	Philadelphia
May 28	St. Paul
June 3	New York
June 10	St. Louis
June 17	Philadelphia
June 25	St. Paul
July 1	New York
July 8	St. Louis
July 15	Philadelphia
July 29	St. Paul
Aug. 5	New York
Aug. 12	St. Louis
Aug. 19	Philadelphia
Aug. 26	St. Paul
Sept. 2	New York
Sept. 9	St. Louis
Sept. 16	Philadelphia
Sept. 23	St. Paul
Sept. 30	New York
Oct. 7	St. Louis
Oct. 14	Philadelphia
Oct. 21	St. Paul
Oct. 28	New York
Nov. 5	St. Louis
Nov. 11	Philadelphia
Nov. 19	St. Paul
Nov. 25	New York
Dec. 3	St. Louis
Dec. 10	Philadelphia
Dec. 16	St. Paul
Dec. 23	New York

AMERICAN LINE
Liverpool—Philadelphia
Phila.

Arrival	Steamer
Jan. 10	Haversford
Jan. 24	Friesland
Feb. 7	Merion
Feb. 22	Harverford
Mar. 7	Friesland
Mar. 23	Merion
Apr. 3	Haverford
Apr. 11	Friesland
Apr. 18	Westernland
Apr. 24	Merion
May 1	Noordland
May 9	Haverford
May 16	Friesland
May 22	Westernland
May 28	Merion
June 6	Noordland
June 12	Haverland
June 18	Friesland
June 26	Westernland
July 3	Merion
July 10	Noordland
July 17	Haverford
July 31	Westernland
Aug. 6	Merion
Aug. 14	Noordland
Aug. 20	Haverford

AMERICAN LINE
Liverpool—Philadelphia
(Continued)
Phila.

Arrival	Steamer
Aug. 27	Friesland
Sept. 3	Westernland
Sept. 10	Merion
Sept. 19	Noordland
Sept. 26	Haverford
Sept. 30	Friesland
Oct. 8	Westernland
Oct. 16	Merion
Oct. 23	Noordland
Oct. 29	Haverford
Nov. 5	Friesland
Nov. 20	Merion
Dec. 6	Haverford
Dec. 13	Noordland
Dec. 29	Merion

ANCHOR LINE
Glasgow—New York
N. Y.

Arrival	Steamer
Jan. 5	Furnessia
Jan. 20	Astoria
Feb. 5	Ethiopia
Feb. 16	Furnessia
Mar. 2	Astoria
Mar. 19	Ethiopia
Mar. 20	Columbia
Apr. 2	Caledonia
Apr. 10	Astoria
Apr. 16	Columbia
Apr. 25	Furnessia
Apr. 30	Caledonia
May 9	Astoria
May 14	Columbia
May 23	Furnessia
May 28	Caledonia
June 7	Astoria
June 11	Columbia
June 19	Furnessia
June 25	Caledonia
July 3	Astoria
July 9	Columbia
July 17	Furnessia
July 23	Caledonia
July 31	Astoria
Aug. 6	Columbia
Aug. 14	Furnessia
Aug. 20	Caledonia
Aug. 28	Astoria
Sept. 3	Columbia
Sept. 11	Furnessia
Sept. 17	Caledonia
Sept. 26	Astoria
Oct. 1	Columbia
Oct. 10	Furnessia
Oct. 15	Caledonia
Oct. 24	Astoria
Oct. 29	Columbia
Nov. 7	Furnessia
Nov. 12	Caledonia
Nov. 22	Astoria
Nov. 28	Columbia

Year 1905

ANCHOR LINE
Glasgow—New York
(Continued)

N. Y. Arrival	Steamer
Dec. 8	Furnessia
Dec. 15	Caledonia
Dec. 19	Astoria
Dec. 25	Columbia

ANCHOR LINE
Mediterranean—New York

N. Y. Arrival	Steamer
Jan. 10	Algeria
Jan. 27	Calabria
Feb. 5	Italia
Feb. 21	Perugia
Mar. 12	Algeria
Mar. 21	Calabria
Mar. 30	Italia
Apr. 14	Perugia
May 7	Algeria
May 12	Calabria
May 19	Italia
June 4	Perugia
June 26	Algeria
July 5	Calabria
July 19	Italia
Aug. 4	Perugia
Aug. 19	Algeria
Sept. 1	Calabria
Sept. 13	Italia
Sept. 25	Perugia
Oct. 16	Algeria
Oct. 23	Calabria
Nov. 7	Italia
Nov. 20	Perugia
Dec. 18	Algeria

ATLANTIC TRANSPORT LINE
London—New York

N. Y. Arrival	Steamer
Jan. 10	Minnehaha
Jan. 19	Manitou
Jan. 25	Menominee
Jan. 29	Minneapolis
Feb. 6	Mesaba
Feb. 12	Minnetonka
Feb. 22	Manitou
Feb. 27	Menominee
Mar. 5	Minneapolis
Mar. 13	Minnehaha
Mar. 21	Minnetonka
Apr. 3	Mesaba
Apr. 10	Minneapolis
Apr. 17	Minnehaha
Apr. 24	Minnetonka
May 2	Mesaba
May 9	Minneapolis
May 16	Minnehaha
May 22	Minnetonka
May 30	Mesaba
June 6	Minneapolis
June 12	Minnehaha
June 19	Minnetonka
June 27	Mesaba
July 7	Minneapolis

ATLANTIC TRANSPORT LINE
London—New York
(Continued)

N. Y. Arrival	Steamer
July 10	Minnehaha
July 17	Minnetonka
July 25	Mesaba
Aug. 2	Minneapolis
Aug. 8	Minnehaha
Aug. 14	Minnetonka
Aug. 22	Mesaba
Aug. 28	Minneapolis
Sept. 4	Minnehaha
Sept. 11	Minnetonka
Sept. 19	Mesaba
Sept. 25	Minneapolis
Oct. 2	Minnehaha
Oct. 9	Minnetonka
Oct. 17	Mesaba
Oct. 23	Minneapolis
Oct. 30	Minnehaha
Nov. 12	Minnetonka
Nov. 21	Mesaba
Nov. 26	Minneapolis
Dec. 3	Minnehaha
Dec. 16	Minnetonka

AUSTRO-AMERICANA LINE
Adriatic Ports—New York

N. Y. Arrival	Steamer
Jan. 9	Gerty
Jan. 23	Giulia
Feb. 16	Georgia
Mar. 10	Gerty
Mar. 21	Giulia
Apr. 15	Georgia
May 7	Gerty
May 21	Giulia
June 8	Georgia
June 18	Erny
July 4	Gerty
July 18	Giulia
Aug. 3	Georgia
Aug. 19	Erny
Sept. 5	Giulia
Sept. 18	Francesca
Sept. 26	Gerty
Oct. 6	Georgia
Oct. 18	Erny
Oct. 31	Giulia
Nov. 4	Francesca
Dec. 4	Gerty
Dec. 8	Georgia
Dec. 20	Erny

AUSTRO-AMERICANA LINE
Italian Ports—New York

N. Y. Arrival	Steamer
Feb. 16	Georgia
Mar. 21	Giulia
May 21	Giulia
June 8	Georgia
July 4	Gerty
July 18	Giulia

AUSTRO-AMERICANA LINE
Italian Ports—New York
(Continued)

N. Y. Arrival	Steamer
Sept. 18	Francesca
Oct. 31	Giulia
Nov. 4	Francesca
Dec. 4	Gerty
Dec. 8	Georgia
Dec. 20	Erny

COMPANIA TRANSATLANTICA LINE
(Spanish Line)
Italian Ports—New York

N. Y. Arrival	Steamer
Jan. 11	Manuel Calvo
Feb. 11	Montevideo
Mar. 13	Buenos Aires
Apr. 11	Manuel Calvo
May 12	Antonio Lopez
June 10	Buenos Aires
July 10	Montserrat
Aug. 10	Montevideo
Sept. 10	Manuel Calvo
Oct. 11	Antonio Lopez
Nov. 10	Buenos Aires
Dec. 11	Montserrat

COMPANIA TRANSATLANTICA LINE
(Spanish Line)
Spanish Ports—New York

N. Y. Arrival	Steamer
Jan. 11	Manuel Calvo
Feb. 11	Montevido
Mar. 13	Buenos Aires
Apr. 11	Manuel Calvo
May 12	Antonio Lopez
June 10	Buenos Aires
July 10	Montserrat
Aug. 10	Montevideo
Sept. 10	Manuel Calvo
Oct. 11	Antonio Lopez
Nov. 10	Buenos Aires
Dec. 11	Montserrat

CUNARD LINE
Liverpool—New York

N. Y. Arrival	Steamer
Jan. 3	Ivernia
Jan. 7	Lucania
Jan. 15	Umbria
Jan. 21	Campania
Jan. 29	Etruria
Feb. 4	Lucania
Feb. 12	Umbria
Feb. 18	Campania
Feb. 25	Etruria
Mar. 5	Caronia
Mar. 13	Umbria
Mar. 20	Lucania
Mar. 25	Etruria
Apr. 1	Campania
Apr. 9	Caronia
Apr. 15	Lucania

Year 1905

CUNARD LINE
Liverpool—New York

N. Y. Arrival	Steamer
Apr. 22	Etruria
Apr. 29	Campania
May 7	Umbria
May 10	Caronia
May 13	Lucania
May 20	Etruria
May 27	Campania
June 4	Umbria
June 7	Caronia
June 10	Lucania
June 17	Etruria
June 23	Carpathia
June 24	Campania
July 2	Umbria
July 5	Caronia
July 8	Lucania
July 15	Etruria
July 21	Carpathia
July 22	Campania
July 30	Umbria
Aug. 2	Caronia
Aug. 5	Lucania
Aug. 12	Etruria
Aug. 19	Campania
Aug. 26	Umbria
Aug. 29	Caronia
Sept. 1	Lucania
Sept. 9	Etruria
Sept. 14	Carpathia
Sept. 15	Campania
Sept. 23	Umbria
Sept. 27	Caronia
Sept. 29	Lucania
Oct. 7	Etruria
Oct. 13	Campania
Oct. 22	Umbria
Oct. 24	Caronia
Oct. 27	Lucania
Nov. 4	Etruria
Nov. 11	Campania
Nov. 19	Caronia
Nov. 24	Lucania
Dec. 4	Umbria
Dec. 10	Carmania
Dec. 16	Etruria
Dec. 24	Caronia
Dec. 31	Campania

CUNARD LINE
Mediterranean—New York

N. Y. Arrival	Steamer
Jan. 7	Carpathia
Jan. 31	Ultonia
Jan. 31	Slavonia
Feb. 13	Pannonia
Feb. 25	Carpathia
Mar. 20	Ultonia
Mar. 21	Slavonia
Apr. 2	Pannonia
Apr. 15	Carpathia
May 8	Ultonia
May 14	Slavonia
May 25	Carpathia
June 4	Pannonia

CUNARD LINE
Mediterranean—New York
(Continued)

N. Y. Arrival	Steamer
June 30	Ultonia
July 1	Slavonia
July 23	Pannonia
Aug. 20	Slavonia
Sept. 10	Pannonia
Sept. 24	Ultonia
Oct. 9	Slavonia
Oct. 27	Pannonia
Nov. 13	Carpathia
Nov. 30	Slavonia
Dec. 11	Pannonia

CUNARD LINE
Liverpool—Boston

Boston Arrival	Steamer
Jan. 12	Saxonia
Jan. 27	Ivernia
Feb. 10	Saxonia
Feb. 24	Ivernia
Mar. 10	Saxonia
Apr. 6	Ivernia
Apr. 20	Saxonia
May 4	Ivernia
May 18	Saxonia
June 1	Ivernia
June 15	Saxonia
June 29	Ivernia
July 13	Saxonia
July 27	Ivernia
Aug. 10	Saxonia
Aug. 24	Ivernia
Sept. 7	Saxonia
Sept. 20	Ivernia
Oct. 4	Saxonia
Oct. 18	Ivernia
Nov. 15	Ivernia
Nov. 30	Saxonia
Dec. 14	Ivernia
Dec. 28	Saxonia

FABRE LINE
Mediterranean—New York

N. Y. Arrival	Steamer
Jan. 10	Patria
Jan. 25	Germania
Feb. 14	Gallia
Feb. 20	Roma
Mar. 14	Neustria
Mar. 15	Germania
Mar. 27	Patria
Apr. 3	Massilia
Apr. 4	Roma
Apr. 20	Gallia
Apr. 23	Germania
May 2	Neustria
May 10	Roma
May 11	Madonna
May 22	Massilia
May 28	Patria
June 1	Germania
June 11	Gallia
June 14	Roma
June 24	Neustria

FABRE LINE
Mediterranean—New York
(Continued)

N. Y. Arrival	Steamer
June 29	Madonna
July 17	Germania
July 27	Roma
Aug. 14	Madonna
Sept. 2	Germania
Sept. 13	Roma
Sept. 29	Madonna
Oct. 14	Gallia
Oct. 20	Roma
Nov. 11	Massilia
Nov. 14	Madonna
Dec. 2	Roma
Dec. 19	Gallia

FRENCH LINE
(Compagnie Generale Transatlantique)
Havre—New York

N. Y. Arrival	Steamer
Jan. 1	La Champagne
Jan. 7	La Touraine
Jan. 15	La Gascogne
Jan. 21	La Savoie
Jan. 29	La Champagne
Feb. 4	La Lorraine
Feb. 11	La Touraine
Feb. 20	La Gascogne
Feb. 26	La Bretagne
Mar. 4	La Lorraine
Mar. 12	La Touraine
Mar. 18	La Savoie
Mar. 21	La Gascogne
Mar. 26	La Bretagne
Mar. 30	Quebec
Apr. 2	La Lorraine
Apr. 4	L'Aquitaine
Apr. 5	Lafayette
Apr. 5	Montreal
Apr. 8	La Touraine
Apr. 14	La Savoie
Apr. 17	La Gascogne
Apr. 23	La Bretagne
Apr. 28	La Lorraine
May 6	La Touraine
May 7	Hudson
May 8	L'Aquitaine
May 12	La Savoie
May 16	La Gascogne
May 21	La Bretagne
May 26	La Lorraine
June 2	Montreal
June 3	La Touraine
June 9	La Savoie
June 15	Hudson
June 18	La Bretagne
June 23	La Lorraine
July 2	La Gascogne
July 7	La Savoie
July 13	Louisiane
July 16	La Bretagne
July 21	La Lorraine
July 27	Hudson
July 29	La Touraine
Aug. 6	La Touraine
Aug. 13	La Bretagne

Year 1905

FRENCH LINE
(Compagnie Generale Transatlantique)
Havre—New York
(Continued)

N. Y. Arrival	Steamer
Aug. 18	La Savoie
Aug. 22	Louisiane
Aug. 26	La Touraine
Sept. 2	La Lorraine
Sept. 8	Hudson
Sept. 10	La Bretagne
Sept. 16	La Touraine
Sept. 17	L'Aquitaine
Sept. 24	La Gascogne
Sept. 30	La Lorraine
Oct. 6	Montreal
Oct. 8	La Bretagne
Oct. 14	La Savoie
Oct. 21	La Touraine
Oct. 21	Hudson
Oct. 27	La Lorraine
Oct. 30	La Gascogne
Nov. 5	La Bretagne
Nov. 11	La Savoie
Nov. 18	La Touraine
Nov. 18	Californie
Nov. 25	La Lorraine
Dec. 4	La Gascogne
Dec. 9	La Savoie
Dec. 17	La Bretagne
Dec. 23	La Lorraine

HAMBURG-AMERICAN LINE
Hamburg—New York

N. Y. Arrival	Steamer
Jan. 5	Graf Waldersee
Jan. 10	Bluecher
Jan. 21	Pennsylvania
Jan. 26	Moltke
Feb. 2	Patricia
Feb. 11	Pretoria
Feb. 17	Graf Waldersee
Feb. 21	Bluecher
Mar. 2	Pennsylvania
Mar. 21	Patricia
Mar. 24	Roland
Mar. 26	Armenia
Mar. 26	Pretoria
Mar. 30	Graf Waldersee
Apr. 4	Bluecher
Apr. 7	Silvia
Apr. 11	Dania
Apr. 14	Allemania
Apr. 20	Christiania
Apr. 20	Deutschland
Apr. 21	Pennsylvania
Apr. 24	Albingia
Apr. 28	Patricia
May 7	Bluecher
May 7	Pretoria
May 18	Deutschland
May 19	Graf Waldersee
May 25	Sardinia
May 28	Hamburg
May 28	Armenia
June 2	Pennsylvania
June 4	Bluecher

HAMBURG-AMERICAN LINE
Hamburg—New York
(Continued)

N. Y. Arrival	Steamer
June 10	Rhaetia
June 11	Moltke
June 15	Deutschland
June 15	Patricia
June 23	Pretoria
June 25	Hamburg
June 29	Graf Waldersee
July 2	Bluecher
July 7	Batavia
July 13	Pennsylvania
July 13	Deutschland
July 20	Armenia
July 21	Rhaetia
July 27	Patricia
July 30	Bluecher
Aug. 5	Bulgaria
Aug. 11	Graf Waldersee
Aug. 13	Moltke
Aug. 17	Batavia
Aug. 17	Deutschland
Aug. 24	Pennsylvania
Aug. 27	Hamburg
Aug. 29	Fuerst Bismarck
Sept. 3	Bluecher
Sept. 7	Patricia
Sept. 10	Moltke
Sept. 14	Deutschland
Sept. 15	Pretoria
Sept. 21	Graf Waldersee
Sept. 24	Hamburg
Sept. 30	Batavia
Oct. 2	Bluecher
Oct. 5	Pennsylvania
Oct. 7	Molke
Oct. 10	Fuerst Bismarck
Oct. 12	Deutschland
Oct. 19	Patricia
Oct. 20	Amerika
Oct. 27	Scotia
Oct. 27	Pretoria
Oct. 29	Bluecher
Nov. 2	Graf Waldersee
Nov. 7	Moltke
Nov. 11	Venetia
Nov. 18	Batavia
Nov. 24	Pennsylvania
Nov. 27	Amerika
Dec. 10	Patricia
Dec. 15	Pretoria
Dec. 19	Bluecher
Dec. 29	Graf Waldersee

HAMBURG-AMERICAN LINE
Mediterranean—New York

N. Y. Arrival	Steamer
Jan. 6	Prinz Adalbert
Jan. 26	Prinz Oskar
Feb. 1	Deutschland
Feb. 22	Prinz Adalbert
Mar. 15	Prinz Oskar
Apr. 6	Prinz Adalbert
Apr. 18	Moltke

HAMBURG-AMERICAN LINE
Mediterranean—New York
(Continued)

N. Y. Arrival	Steamer
Apr. 27	Hamburg
May 4	Prinz Oskar
May 24	Prinz Adalbert
June 21	Prinz Oskar
July 12	Prinz Adalbert
Aug. 9	Prinz Oskar
Sept. 5	Prinz Adalbert
Oct. 4	Prinz Oskar
Oct. 25	Prinz Adalbert
Nov. 4	Hamburg
Nov. 22	Prinz Oskar
Nov. 29	Fuerst Bismarck
Dec. 14	Prinz Adalbert
Dec. 21	Hamburg

HAMBURG-AMERICAN LINE
(Union Line)
Hamburg—New York

N. Y. Arrival	Steamer
Feb. 2	Pallanza
June 23	Pallanza
Oct. 11	Albano
Oct. 20	Barcelona
Nov. 25	Pallanza
Dec. 10	Albano

HOLLAND-AMERICA LINE
Rotterdam—New York

N. Y. Arrival	Steamer
Jan. 3	Statendam
Jan. 11	Amsterdam
Jan. 18	Ryndam
Jan. 26	Rotterdam
Feb. 7	Statendam
Feb. 17	Amsterdam
Feb. 21	Ryndam
Mar. 1	Rotterdam
Mar. 16	Noordam
Mar. 23	Statendam
Mar. 28	Ryndam
Apr. 4	Rotterdam
Apr. 11	Potsdam
Apr. 18	Noordam
Apr. 25	Statendam
May 2	Ryndam
May 10	Rotterdam
May 17	Potsdam
May 23	Noordam
May 29	Statendam
June 6	Ryndam
June 13	Rotterdam
June 20	Potsdam
June 27	Noordam
July 3	Statendam
July 11	Ryndam
July 25	Rotterdam
Aug. 1	Potsdam
Aug. 8	Noordam
Aug. 14	Statendam
Aug. 22	Ryndam
Aug. 29	Rotterdam

Year 1905

HOLLAND-AMERICA LINE
Rotterdam—New York
(Continued)

N. Y.

Arrival	Steamer
Sept. 5	Potsdam
Sept. 11	Noordam
Sept. 19	Statendam
Sept. 25	Ryndam
Oct. 2	Rotterdam
Oct. 9	Potsdam
Oct. 17	Noordam
Oct. 24	Statendam
Oct. 30	Ryndam
Nov. 8	Rotterdam
Nov. 14	Potsdam
Nov. 22	Noordam
Nov. 29	Statendam
Dec. 14	Rotterdam
Dec. 26	Noordam

INSULAR NAVIGATION COMPANY
Azores, Lisbon—New York,
New Bedford, Mass.

N. Y.
N. Bedford

Arrival	Steamer
Mar. 19	Peninsular
May 8	Peninsular
July 1	Peninsular
Aug. 31	Peninsular
Oct. 28	Peninsular
Dec. 16	Peninsular

LA VELOCE LINE
Mediterranean—New York

N. Y.

Arrival	Steamer
Jan. 19	Nord America
Feb. 12	Citta di Torino
Feb. 28	Citta di Torino
Mar. 10	Nord America
Mar. 16	Citta di Milano
Mar. 27	Citta di Napoli
Mar. 30	Citta di Reggio
Apr. 11	Citta di Torino
Apr. 15	Citta di Genova
Apr. 16	Washington
Apr. 23	Nord America
Apr. 30	Citta di Milano
May 7	Citta di Napoli
May 18	Citta di Reggio
May 29	Citta di Torino
June 5	Nord America
June 6	Citta di Genova
June 18	Citti di Milano
June 29	Citta di Napoli
July 13	Citta di Torino
July 29	Nord America
Aug. 18	Citta di Napoli
Sept. 7	Nord America
Sept. 24	Citta di Torino
Oct. 6	Citta di Napoli
Oct. 27	Nord America
Nov. 12	Citta di Torino
Nov. 24	Citta di Napoli
Dec. 7	Nord America

LEYLAND LINE
Liverpool—Boston

Boston

Arrival	Steamer
Jan. 3	Bohemian
Jan. 11	Canadian
Jan. 26	Devonian
Jan. 31	Winifredian
Feb. 8	Bohemian
Feb. 17	Canadian
Mar. 3	Devonian
Mar. 8	Winifredian
Mar. 19	Bohemian
Mar. 24	Canadian
Apr. 4	Devonian
Apr. 17	Bohemian
Apr. 25	Cestrian
May 2	Winifredian
May 9	Devonian
May 18	Canadian
May 26	Bohemian
May 30	Cestrian
June 6	Winifredian
June 12	Devonian
June 20	Canadian
July 2	Bohemian
July 11	Cestrian
July 17	Devonian
July 25	Canadian
Aug. 12	Cestrian
Aug. 15	Winifredian
Aug. 22	Devonian
Aug. 29	Canadian
Sept. 5	Bohemian
Sept. 12	Cestrian
Sept. 18	Winifredian
Sept. 25	Devonian
Oct. 3	Canadian
Oct. 9	Bohemian
Oct. 17	Cestrian
Oct. 24	Winifredian
Oct. 30	Devonian
Nov. 9	Canadian
Nov. 14	Bohemian
Nov. 26	Winifredian
Dec. 6	Devonian
Dec. 15	Canadian
Dec. 23	Bohemian
Dec. 26	Winifredian

LLOYD ITALIANA
Mediterranean—New York

N. Y.

Arrival	Steamer
Dec. 4	Florida

NAVIGAZIONE GENE-RALE ITALIANA
Mediterranean—New York

N. Y.

Arrival	Steamer
Jan. 2	Vincenzo Florio
Jan. 12	Lombardia
Jan. 28	Liguria
Feb. 10	Sicilia
Mar. 3	Lombardia
Mar. 15	Vincenzo Florio
Mar. 16	Liguria

NAVIGAZIONE GENE-RALE ITALIANA
Mediterranean—New York
(Continued)

N. Y.

Arrival	Steamer
Mar. 27	Il Piemonte
Mar. 28	Sardegna
Mar. 30	Sicilia
Apr. 20	Lombardia
Apr. 24	Marco Minghetti
Apr. 29	Liguria
May 4	Sardegna
May 8	Italia
May 15	Il Piemonte
May 17	Sicilia
June 1	Lombardia
June 6	Marco Minghetti
June 8	Liguria
June 22	Sardegna
June 23	Italia
July 3	Il Piemonte
July 5	Sicilia
July 26	Lombardia
Aug. 9	Liguria
Aug. 24	Sicilia
Sept. 3	Italia
Sept. 14	Lombardia
Sept. 29	Liguria
Oct. 11	Sicilia
Nov. 2	Lombardia
Nov. 13	Italia
Nov. 30	Sicilia

NORTH GERMAN LLOYD
Bremen—New York

N. Y.

Arrival	Steamer
Jan. 10	Kronprinz Wilhelm
Feb. 1	K. Wm. der Grosse
Feb. 15	Kronprinz Wilhelm
Mar. 1	K. Wm. der Grosse
Mar. 16	Kronprinz Wilhelm
Mar. 29	K. Wm. der Grosse
Apr. 11	Kaiser Wilhelm II
Apr. 25	Kronprinz Wilhelm
May 2	K. Wm. der Grosse
May 9	Kaiser Wilhelm II
May 23	Kronprinz Wilhelm
May 30	K. Wm. der Grosse
June 6	Kaiser Wilhelm II
June 20	Kronprinz Wilhelm
June 28	K. Wm. der Grosse
July 4	Kaiser Wilhelm II
July 25	Kronprinz Wilhelm
Aug. 3	K. Wm. der Grosse
Aug. 8	Kaiser Wilhelm II
Aug. 22	Kronprinz Wilhelm
Aug. 29	K. Wm. der Grosse
Sept. 5	Kaiser Wilhelm II
Sept. 19	Kronprinz Wilhelm
Sept. 26	K. Wm. der Grosse
Oct. 3	Kaiser Wilhelm II
Oct. 13	Kronprinz Wilhelm
Oct. 24	K. Wm. der Grosse
Nov. 2	Kaiser Wilhelm II
Nov. 14	Kronprinz Wilhelm
Nov. 21	K. Wm. der Grosse
Dec. 6	Kaiser Wilhelm II
Dec. 20	K. Wm. der Grosse

Year 1905

NORTH GERMAN LLOYD
Bremen—New York
Express Service

N. Y.

Arrival	Steamer
Jan. 5	Cassel
Jan. 13	Breslau
Jan. 22	Chemnitz
Jan. 29	Brandenburg
Feb. 4	Hannover
Feb. 10	Main
Feb. 16	Barbarossa
Feb. 24	Breslau
Mar. 1	Grosser Kurfuerst
Mar. 11	Gera
Mar. 12	Brandenburg
Mar. 20	Main
Mar. 23	Oldenburg
Mar. 24	Barbarossa
Mar. 29	Gneisenau
Apr. 4	Grosser Kurfuerst
Apr. 10	Chemnitz
Apr. 13	Rhein
Apr. 21	Main
Apr. 26	Barbarossa
May 4	Gneisenau
May 9	Grosser Kurfuerst
May 20	Prinzess Alice
May 23	Bremen
June 1	Barbarossa
June 7	Fried. der Grosse
June 13	Grosser Kurfuerst
June 20	Prinzess Alice
June 27	Bremen
July 5	Barbarossa
July 11	Fried. der Grosse
July 18	Grosser Kurfuerst
July 27	Main
Aug. 1	Bremen
Aug. 10	Barbarossa
Aug. 15	Fried. der Grosse
Aug. 21	Grosser Kurfuerst
Aug. 31	Main
Sept. 5	Bremen
Sept. 11	Oldenburg
Sept. 14	Rhein
Sept. 19	Fried. der Grosse
Sept. 26	Grosser Kurfuerst
Oct. 5	Main
Oct. 11	Oldenburg
Oct. 12	Brandenburg
Oct. 18	Rhein
Oct. 25	Fried. der Grosse
Nov. 1	Neckar
Nov. 11	Main
Nov. 14	Bremen
Nov. 23	Rhein
Nov. 30	Fried. der Grosse
Dec. 10	Chemnitz
Dec. 16	Main
Dec. 19	Bremen
Dec. 29	Rhein

NORTH GERMAN LLOYD
Mediterranean—New York

N. Y.

Arrival	Steamer
Jan. 19	Koenig Albert
Jan. 28	Koenigin Luise
Feb. 5	Neckar

NORTH GERMAN LLOYD
Mediterranean—New York
(Continued)

N. Y.

Arrival	Steamer
Feb. 16	Prinzess Irene
Mar. 1	Koenig Albert
Mar. 9	Koenigin Luise
Mar. 15	Neckar
Mar. 23	Prinzess Irene
Mar. 31	Weimar
Apr. 5	Koenig Albert
Apr. 13	Koenigin Luise
Apr. 21	Neckar
Apr. 28	Prinzess Irene
May 7	Weimar
May 10	Koenig Albert
May 18	Koenigin Luise
May 25	Neckar
June 1	Prinzess Irene
June 11	Weimar
June 15	Koenig Albert
June 23	Koenigin Luise
July 5	Prinzess Irene
July 19	Koenig Albert
Aug. 1	Koenigin Luise
Aug. 14	Prinzess Irene
Aug. 28	Koenig Albert
Sept. 8	Koenigin Luise
Sept. 20	Prinzess Irene
Oct. 4	Koenig Albert
Oct. 12	Koenigin Luise
Oct. 26	Prinzess Irene
Nov. 8	Koenig Albert
Nov. 17	Koenigin Luise
Dec. 2	Prinzess Irene
Dec. 5	Neckar
Dec. 21	Koenig Albert

NORTH GERMAN LLOYD
Bremen—Baltimore

Baltimore

Arrival	Steamer
Jan. 5	Koeln
Jan. 20	Darmstadt
Jan. 27	Gera
Feb. 1	Oldenburg
Feb. 9	Weimar
Feb. 17	Cassel
Feb. 24	Karlsruhe
Feb. 26	Stuttgart
Mar. 2	Chemnitz
Mar. 6	Darmstadt
Mar. 11	Koeln
Mar. 14	Borkum
Mar. 22	Wittekind
Mar. 26	Cassel
Mar. 29	Hannover
Apr. 2	Breslau
Apr. 6	Stuttgart
Apr. 7	Darmstadt
Apr. 12	Chemnitz
Apr. 15	Gera
Apr. 19	Brandenburg
Apr. 24	Main
Apr. 25	Koeln
May 5	Hannover
May 18	Breslau
May 25	Frankfurt
May 25	Cassel

NORTH GERMAN LLOYD
Bremen—Baltimore
(Continued)

Baltimore

Arrival	Steamer
June 1	Brandenburg
June 7	Main
June 15	Chemnitz
June 21	Hannover
June 28	Breslau
July 5	Cassel
July 12	Brandenburg
July 19	Frankfurt
July 26	Chemnitz
Aug. 9	Breslau
Aug. 17	Koeln
Aug. 23	Cassel
Aug. 30	Brandenburg
Sept. 6	Chemnitz
Sept. 13	Neckar
Sept. 20	Breslau
Sept. 27	Darmstadt
Oct. 2	Cassel
Oct. 14	Brandenburg
Oct. 19	Koeln
Oct. 25	Chemnitz
Oct. 31	Breslau
Nov. 15	Cassel
Nov. 23	Brandenburg
Dec. 13	Chemnitz
Dec. 21	Breslau
Dec. 27	Cassel

PRINCE LINE
Mediterranean—New York

N. Y.

Arrival	Steamer
Jan. 26	Napolitan Prince
Feb. 19	Sicilian Prince
Mar. 11	Napolitan Prince
Apr. 2	Sicilian Prince
Apr. 22	Napolitan Prince
May 13	Sicilian Prince
June 8	Napolitan Prince
June 27	Sicilian Prince
July 23	Napolitan Prince
Aug. 12	Sicilian Prince
Sept. 2	Napolitan Prince
Sept. 22	Sicilian Prince
Oct. 15	Napolitan Prince
Nov. 7	Sicilian Prince
Nov. 27	Napolitan Prince
Dec. 21	Sicilian Prince

RED STAR LINE
Antwerp—New York

N. Y.

Arrival	Steamer
Jan. 9	Zeeland
Jan. 18	Finland
Jan. 25	Vaderland
Jan. 31	Kroonland
Feb. 6	Zeeland
Feb. 15	Finland
Feb. 24	Vaderland
Feb. 28	Kroonland
Mar. 7	Zeeland
Mar. 15	Finland
Mar. 22	Vaderland
Mar. 28	Kroonland

Year 1905

RED STAR LINE
Antwerp—New York
(Continued)

N. Y.

Arrival	Steamer
Apr. 4	Zeeland
Apr. 11	Rynland
Apr. 11	Finland
Apr. 18	Vaderland
Apr. 24	Kroonland
Apr. 26	Nederland
May 2	Zeeland
May 9	Finland
May 16	Vaderland
May 22	Kroonland
May 30	Zeeland
June 6	Finland
June 13	Vaderland
June 20	Kroonland
June 27	Zeeland
July 3	Finland
July 10	Vaderland
July 18	Kroonland
July 25	Zeeland
Aug. 1	Finland
Aug. 8	Vaderland
Aug. 14	Kroonland
Aug. 21	Zeeland
Aug. 28	Finland
Sept. 5	Vaderland
Sept. 12	Kroonland
Sept. 18	Zeeland
Sept. 25	Finland
Oct. 2	Vaderland
Oct. 10	Kroonland
Oct. 16	Zeeland
Oct. 24	Finland
Oct. 30	Vaderland
Nov. 7	Kroonland
Nov. 13	Zeeland
Nov. 22	Finland
Nov. 29	Southwark
Dec. 8	Kroonland
Dec. 13	Vaderland
Dec. 18	Finland
Dec. 26	Zeeland

RED STAR LINE
Antwerp—Phila.—Boston

Boston

Arrival	Steamer
Sept. 8	Manitou
Sept. 19	Menominee
Oct. 3	Marquette
Oct. 17	Manitou
Nov. 7	Menominee
Nov. 14	Marquette
Dec. 15	Menominee
Dec. 27	Marquette

SCANDINAVIAN AMERICAN LINE
Scandinavian Ports—N. Y.

N. Y.

Arrival	Steamer
Jan. 30	Hekla
Feb. 7	Hellig Olav
Feb. 22	United States
Mar. 6	Oscar II
Mar. 21	Hellig Olav

SCANDINAVIAN AMERICAN LINE
Scandinavian Ports—N. Y.
(Continued)

N. Y.

Arrival	Steamer
Apr. 6	United States
Apr. 17	Oscar II
May 1	Hellig Olav
May 16	United States
May 29	Oscar II
June 12	Hellig Olav
June 25	United States
July 9	Oscar II
July 24	Hellig Olav
Aug. 6	United States
Aug. 20	Oscar II
Sept. 4	Hellig Olav
Sept. 18	United States
Oct. 1	Oscar II
Oct. 15	Hellig Olav
Oct. 29	United States
Nov. 13	Oscar II
Dec. 5	Hellig Olav
Dec. 13	United States
Dec. 26	Oscar II

WHITE STAR LINE
Liverpool—New York

N. Y.

Arrival	Steamer
Jan. 1	Cedric
Jan. 5	Teutonic
Jan. 12	Majestic
Jan. 20	Arabic
Jan. 27	Baltic
Feb. 2	Teutonic
Feb. 8	Oceanic
Feb. 16	Majestic
Feb. 24	Baltic
Mar. 2	Teutonic
Mar. 9	Oceanic
Mar. 20	Cedric
Mar. 24	Baltic
Mar. 24	Celtic
Mar. 30	Teutonic
Apr. 5	Oceanic
Apr. 13	Majestic
Apr. 16	Cedric
Apr. 21	Baltic
Apr. 27	Teutonic
May 1	Celtic
May 3	Oceanic
May 11	Majestic
May 14	Cedric
May 19	Baltic
May 25	Teutonic
May 28	Celtic
May 31	Oceanic
June 8	Majestic
June 10	Cedric
June 16	Baltic
June 22	Teutonic
June 25	Celtic
June 28	Oceanic
July 6	Majestic
July 13	Cedric
July 20	Baltic
July 27	Teutonic
July 29	Celtic

WHITE STAR LINE
Liverpool—New York
(Continued)

N. Y.

Arrival	Steamer
Aug. 3	Oceanic
Aug. 12	Cedric
Aug. 18	Baltic
Aug. 23	Teutonic
Aug. 27	Celtic
Aug. 30	Oceanic
Sept. 6	Majestic
Sept. 9	Cedric
Sept. 14	Baltic
Sept. 23	Teutonic
Sept. 23	Celtic
Sept. 27	Oceanic
Oct. 4	Majestic
Oct. 7	Cedric
Oct. 12	Baltic
Oct. 19	Teutonic
Oct. 22	Celtic
Oct. 25	Oceanic
Nov. 3	Cedric
Nov. 10	Baltic
Nov. 15	Majestic
Nov. 22	Oceanic
Dec. 1	Cedric
Dec. 8	Baltic
Dec. 14	Majestic
Dec. 20	Oceanic
Dec. 30	Celtic

WHITE STAR LINE
Mediterranean—New York

N. Y.

Arrival	Steamer
Jan. 9	Republic
Jan. 28	Cretic
Feb. 20	Republic
Mar. 14	Cretic
Apr. 4	Republic
Apr. 24	Cretic
May 23	Republic
June 6	Cretic
July 3	Romanic
July 21	Cretic
Sept. 18	Cretic
Oct. 31	Cretic
Nov. 23	Republic
Dec. 4	Cretic

WHITE STAR LINE
Liverpool—Boston

Boston

Arrival	Steamer
Jan. 19	Cymric
Feb. 21	Cymric
Mar. 20	Cymric
Apr. 23	Arabic
May 7	Cymric
May 13	Arabic
June 4	Cymric
June 17	Arabic
July 2	Republic
July 9	Cymric
July 15	Arabic
Aug. 5	Republic
Aug. 13	Cymric
Aug. 19	Arabic

Year 1905

WHITE STAR LINE
Liverpool—Boston
(Continued)

Boston Arrival	Steamer
Sept. 2	Republic
Sept. 10	Cymric
Sept. 16	Arabic
Sept. 30	Republic
Oct. 7	Cymric
Oct. 14	Arabic
Nov. 6	Cymric
Nov. 11	Arabic
Nov. 30	Cymric

WHITE STAR LINE
Mediterranean—Boston

Boston Arrival	Steamer
Jan. 2	Canopic
Jan. 20	Romanic
Feb. 14	Canopic
Mar. 7	Romanic
Mar. 27	Canopic
Apr. 18	Romanic
May 8	Canopic
May 29	Romanic

WHITE STAR LINE
Mediterranean—Boston
(Continued)

Boston Arrival	Steamer
June 19	Canopic
July 31	Canopic
Sept. 7	Romanic
Oct. 2	Canopic
Oct. 24	Romanic
Nov. 13	Canopic
Nov. 30	Romanic

WILSON LINE
Hull—New York

N. Y. Arrival	Steamer
May 14	Consuelo
June 8	Toronto
June 14	Idaho
July 2	Colorado
July 26	Toronto
Aug. 20	Consuelo
Sept. 8	Toronto
Sept. 13	Colorado
Sept. 24	Idaho
Oct. 18	Consuelo

WILSON LINE
Hull—New York
(Continued)

N. Y. Arrival	Steamer
Nov. 22	Consuelo
Dec. 11	Toronto

ADDITIONAL ARRIVALS
Mediterranean—New York

N. Y. Arrival	Steamer
Apr. 8	Citta di New York
Apr. 12	Regina Elena
Apr. 30	Equita
May 11	America (Fabre, Marseilles)
May 25	Citta di New York
June 11	Equita
July 24	Citta di New York
Oct. 16	Germania (Fabre, Marseilles)
Oct. 28	Neustria (Fabre, Marseilles)
Nov. 29	Germania (Fabre, Marseilles)
Dec. 4	Brooklyn (Zotti)

Year 1906

ALLAN LINE
Glasgow—Boston

Boston

Arrival	Steamer
Jan. 6	Sardinian
Jan. 21	Mongolian
Feb. 2	Siberian
Feb. 15	Sardinian
Mar. 2	Mongolian
Mar. 19	Siberian
Mar. 26	Sardinian
Mar. 29	Numidian
Apr. 6	Mongolian
Apr. 14	Corinthian
Apr. 20	Sicilian
May 11	Corean
May 21	Laurentian
June 6	Parisian
June 18	Laurentian
July 2	Parisian
July 17	Laurentian
July 30	Parisian
Aug. 13	Laurentian
Aug. 26	Parisian
Sept. 10	Laurentian
Sept. 23	Parisian
Oct. 8	Laurentian
Oct. 22	Parisian
Nov. 7	Laurentian
Nov. 21	Pretorian
Dec. 7	Numidian
Dec. 23	Corinthian

AMERICAN LINE
Southampton—New York

N. Y.

Arrival	Steamer
Jan. 1	St. Louis
Jan. 6	Philadelphia
Jan. 14	St. Paul
Jan. 27	New York
Feb. 3	St. Louis
Feb. 10	Philadelphia
Feb. 18	St. Paul
Feb. 25	New York
Mar. 4	St. Louis
Mar. 11	Philadelphia
Mar. 18	St. Paul
Mar. 25	New York
Mar. 31	St. Louis
Apr. 7	Philadelphia
Apr. 15	St. Paul
Apr. 21	New York
Apr. 28	St. Louis
May 5	Philadelphia
May 13	St. Paul
May 19	New York
May 26	St. Louis
June 2	Philadelphia
June 9	St. Paul
June 17	New York
June 23	St. Louis
July 1	Philadelphia
July 8	St. Paul
July 22	New York
July 28	St. Louis

AMERICAN LINE
Southampton—New York
(Continued)

N. Y.

Arrival	Steamer
Aug. 4	Philadelphia
Aug. 11	St. Paul
Aug. 18	New York
Aug. 25	St. Louis
Sept. 1	Philadelphia
Sept. 8	St. Paul
Sept. 16	New York
Sept. 22	St. Louis
Sept. 29	Philadelphia
Oct. 6	St. Paul
Oct. 13	New York
Oct. 20	St. Louis
Oct. 27	Philadelphia
Nov. 4	St. Paul
Nov. 10	New York
Nov. 17	St. Louis
Nov. 25	Philadelphia
Dec. 2	St. Paul
Dec. 9	New York
Dec. 16	St. Louis
Dec. 22	Philadelphia
Dec. 29	St. Paul

AMERICAN LINE
Liverpool—Philadelphia

Phila.

Arrival	Steamer
Jan. 9	Haverford
Jan. 20	Noordland
Jan. 29	Merion
Feb. 12	Haverford
Feb. 26	Noordland
Mar. 6	Merion
Mar. 22	Haverford
Mar. 26	Friesland
Apr. 9	Merion
Apr. 25	Haverford
Apr. 30	Friesland
May 14	Merion
May 27	Haverford
June 3	Friesland
June 11	Westernland
June 18	Merion
June 25	Noordland
July 9	Friesland
July 15	Westernland
July 22	Merion
July 29	Noordland
Aug. 13	Friesland
Aug. 19	Westernland
Aug. 25	Merion
Sept. 2	Noordland
Sept. 9	Haverford
Sept. 16	Friesland
Sept. 22	Westernland
Sept. 30	Merion
Oct. 7	Noordland
Oct. 15	Haverford
Oct. 21	Friesland
Oct. 29	Westernland

AMERICAN LINE
Liverpool—Philadelphia
(Continued)

Phila.

Arrival	Steamer
Nov. 7	Merion
Nov. 22	Haverford
Nov. 27	Noordland
Dec. 11	Merion
Dec. 26	Haverford

ANCHOR LINE
Glasgow—New York

N. Y.

Arrival	Steamer
Jan. 4	Ethiopia
Jan. 9	Furnessia
Jan. 22	Caledonia
Jan. 30	Astoria
Feb. 5	Columbia
Feb. 14	Ethiopia
Feb. 22	Furnessia
Feb. 28	Astoria
Mar. 5	Caledonia
Mar. 19	Columbia
Mar. 26	Furnessia
Mar. 31	Caledonia
Apr. 13	Astoria
Apr. 15	Columbia
Apr. 24	Furnessia
Apr. 29	Caledonia
May 10	Ethiopia
May 13	Columbia
May 21	Furnessia
May 26	Caledonia
June 5	Astoria
June 10	Columbia
June 18	Furnessia
June 23	Caledonia
July 4	Astoria
July 8	Columbia
July 17	Furnessia
July 22	Caledonia
July 31	Astoria
Aug. 5	Columbia
Aug. 14	Furnessia
Aug. 19	Caledonia
Aug. 28	Astoria
Sept. 2	Columbia
Sept. 11	Furnessia
Sept. 16	Caledonia
Sept. 25	Astoria
Sept. 30	Columbia
Oct. 9	Furnessia
Oct. 14	Caledonia
Oct. 24	Astoria
Oct. 29	Columbia
Nov. 7	Furnessia
Nov. 10	Caledonia
Nov. 22	Astoria
Nov. 25	Columbia
Dec. 8	Ethiopia
Dec. 11	Caledonia
Dec. 19	Furnessia
Dec. 24	Columbia

Year 1906

ANCHOR LINE
Mediterranean—New York
N. Y.

Arrival	Steamer
Jan. 1	Calabria
Jan. 14	Italia
Feb. 3	Perugia
Feb. 23	Algeria
Mar. 4	Calabria
Mar. 15	Italia
Apr. 2	Perugia
Apr. 16	Algeria
Apr. 27	Calabria
May 10	Italia
May 26	Perugia
June 11	Algeria
June 22	Calabria
June 29	Italia
July 19	Perugia
Aug. 4	Algeria
Aug. 16	Calabria
Aug. 16	Calabria
Aug. 30	Italia
Sept. 14	Perugia
Oct. 1	Algeria
Oct. 7	Calabria
Oct. 19	Italia
Nov. 5	Perugia
Dec. 2	Algeria
Dec. 10	Calabria
Dec. 22	Italia

ATLANTIC TRANSPORT LINE
London—New York
N. Y.

Arrival	Steamer
Jan. 2	Minneapolis
Jan. 7	Minnehaha
Jan. 22	Minnetonka
Feb. 4	Minneapolis
Feb. 25	Minnehaha
Mar. 6	Minneapolis
Mar. 12	Minnetonka
Mar. 22	Mesaba
Mar. 31	Minnehaha
Apr. 9	Minnetonka
Apr. 18	Mesaba
Apr. 21	Minneapolis
Apr. 30	Minnehaha
May 7	Minnetonka
May 16	Mesaba
May 21	Minneapolis
May 29	Minnehaha
June 4	Minnetonka
June 13	Mesaba
June 18	Minneapolis
June 26	Minnehaha
July 2	Minnetonka
July 11	Mesaba
July 16	Minneapolis
July 24	Minnehaha
July 30	Minnehaha
Aug. 7	Mesaba
Aug. 13	Minneapolis
Aug. 20	Minnehaha
Aug. 27	Minnetonka
Sept. 4	Mesaba
Sept. 10	Minneapolis
Sept. 17	Minnehaha

ATLANTIC TRANSPORT LINE
London—New York
(Continued)
N. Y.

Arrival	Steamer
Sept. 24	Minnetonka
Oct. 2	Mesaba
Oct. 9	Minneapolis
Oct. 16	Minnehaha
Oct. 22	Minnetonka
Nov. 1	Mesaba
Nov. 12	Minneapolis
Nov. 18	Minnehaha
Nov. 29	Mesaba
Dec. 3	Minnetonka
Dec. 15	Minneapolis
Dec. 23	Minnehaha
Dec. 30	Mesaba

AUSTRO-AMERICANA LINE
Adriatic Ports—New York
N. Y.

Arrival	Steamer
Jan. 2	Giulia
Jan. 4	Francesca
Jan. 8	Sofia Hohenberg
Jan. 31	Georgia
Feb. 14	Erny
Feb. 28	Francesca
Mar 1	Gerty
Mar. 11	Sofia Hohenberg
Mar. 20	Giulia
Mar. 30	Georgia
Apr. 9	Dora
Apr. 17	Francesca
Apr. 18	Erny
May 2	Gerty
May 4	Sofia Hohenberg
May 15	Giulia
May 23	Georgia
June 6	Francesca
June 21	Sofia Hohenberg
June 27	Gerty
July 5	Giulia
July 19	Georgia
July 24	Francesca
Aug. 11	Sofia Hohenberg
Aug. 20	Gerty
Aug. 28	Giulia
Sept. 8	Francesca
Sept. 23	Erny
Sept. 28	Sofia Hohenberg
Oct. 18	Gerty
Oct. 27	Giulia
Nov. 1	Francesca
Nov. 20	Sofia Hohenberg
Nov. 21	Erny
Dec. 11	Gerty
Dec. 30	Giulia

AUSTRO-AMERICANA LINE
Italian Ports—New York
(Including Greek Ports)
N. Y.

Arrival	Steamer
Jan. 2	Giulia
Jan. 4	Francesca

AUSTRO-AMERICANA LINE
Italian Ports—New York
(Including Greek Ports)
(Continued)
N. Y.

Arrival	Steamer
Jan. 31	Georgia
Feb. 28	Francesca
Mar. 11	Sofia Hohenberg
Mar. 20	Giulia
Apr. 9	Dora
Apr. 17	Francesca
Apr. 18	Erny
May 2	Gerty
May 4	Sofia Hohenberg
May 15	Giulia
May 23	Georgia
June 6	Francesca
June 21	Sofia Hohenberg
June 27	Erny
June 27	Gerty
June 29	Virginia
July 5	Giulia
July 7	Dora
July 19	Georgia
July 24	Francesca
Aug. 11	Sofia Hohenberg
Aug. 28	Giulia
Sept. 8	Francesca
Sept. 23	Erny
Sept. 28	Sofia Hohenberg
Oct. 18	Gerty
Oct. 18	Carolina
Oct. 27	Giulia
Nov. 1	Francesca
Nov. 20	Sofia Hohenberg
Dec. 11	Gerty
Dec. 18	Dora
Dec. 30	Giulia

COMPANIA TRANSATLANTICA LINE
(Spanish Line)
Italian Ports—New York
N. Y.

Arrival	Steamer
Jan. 11	Montevideo
Feb. 10	Manuel Calvo
Mar. 14	Antonio Lopez
Apr. 13	Manuel Calvo
May 11	Buenos Aires
June 10	Montevideo
July 11	Montserrat
Aug. 10	Antonio Lopez
Sept. 11	Manuel Calvo
Oct. 11	Buenos Aires
Nov. 10	Montevideo
Dec. 11	Montserrat

CUNARD LINE
Liverpool—New York
N. Y.

Arrival	Steamer
Jan. 8	Carmania
Jan. 14	Lucania
Jan. 21	Umbria
Jan. 27	Campania

Year 1906

CUNARD LINE
Liverpool—New York

N. Y.

Arrival	Steamer
Feb. 3	Carmania
Feb. 9	Lucania
Feb. 18	Umbria
Feb. 24	Campania
Mar. 4	Carmania
Mar. 10	Lucania
Mar. 18	Umbria
Mar. 23	Campania
Mar. 31	Etruria
Apr. 4	Carmania
Apr. 6	Lucania
Apr. 14	Umbria
Apr. 18	Caronia
Apr. 21	Campania
Apr. 28	Etruria
May 2	Carmania
May 4	Lucania
May 12	Umbria
May 16	Caronia
May 19	Campania
May 26	Etruria
May 30	Carmania
June 2	Lucania
June 10	Umbria
June 12	Caronia
June 16	Campania
June 23	Etruria
June 27	Carmania
June 30	Lucania
July 8	Umbria
July 11	Caronia
July 13	Campania
July 21	Etruria
July 24	Carmania
July 27	Lucania
Aug. 4	Umbria
Aug. 7	Caronia
Aug. 10	Campania
Aug. 18	Etruria
Aug. 21	Carmania
Aug. 24	Lucania
Sept. 1	Umbria
Sept. 4	Caronia
Sept. 8	Campania
Sept. 15	Etruria
Sept. 19	Carmania
Sept. 21	Lucania
Sept. 29	Umbria
Oct. 2	Caronia
Oct. 5	Campania
Oct. 13	Etruria
Oct. 16	Carmania
Oct. 19	Lucania
Oct. 28	Umbria
Oct. 31	Caronia
Nov. 3	Campania
Nov. 10	Carmania
Nov. 16	Lucania
Nov. 25	Caronia
Dec. 1	Campania
Dec. 9	Etruria
Dec. 15	Lucania
Dec. 23	Umbria
Dec. 30	Caronia

CUNARD LINE
Mediterranean—Adriatic—
New York
(Continued)

N. Y.

Arrival	Steamer
Jan. 2	Carpathia
Jan. 24	Slavonia
Jan. 29	Pannonia
Feb. 10	Caronia
Feb. 26	Carpathia
Mar. 15	Ultonia
Mar. 26	Slavonia
Apr. 1	Pannonia
Apr. 16	Carpathia
May 1	Ultonia
May 13	Slavonia
May 20	Pannonia
June 5	Carpathia
June 24	Ultonia
July 3	Slavonia
July 9	Pannonia
July 23	Carpathia
Aug. 21	Slavonia
Aug. 29	Pannonia
Sept. 9	Carpathia
Sept. 22	Ultonia
Oct. 9	Slavonia
Oct. 22	Pannonia
Nov. 6	Carpathia
Nov. 14	Ultonia
Nov. 29	Slavonia
Dec. 13	Pannonia

CUNARD LINE
Liverpool—Boston

Boston

Arrival	Steamer
Jan. 19	Ivernia
Feb. 1	Saxonia
Feb. 15	Ivernia
Mar. 2	Saxonia
Mar. 16	Ivernia
Mar. 29	Saxonia
Apr. 12	Ivernia
Apr. 26	Saxonia
May 11	Ivernia
May 24	Saxonia
June 7	Ivernia
June 21	Saxonia
July 5	Ivernia
July 19	Saxonia
Aug. 2	Ivernia
Aug. 16	Saxonia
Aug. 30	Ivernia
Sept. 13	Saxonia
Sept. 26	Ivernia
Oct. 11	Saxonia
Oct. 24	Ivernia
Nov. 8	Saxonia
Nov. 22	Ivernia
Dec. 6	Saxonia
Dec. 20	Ivernia

FABRE LINE
Mediterranean—New York

N. Y.

Arrival	Steamer
Jan. 1	Madonna
Jan. 19	Massilia
Jan. 29	Roma

FABRE LINE
Mediterranean—New York
(Continued)

N. Y.

Arrival	Steamer
Feb. 16	Madonna
Feb. 27	Germania
Mar. 17	Massilia
Mar. 22	Roma
Mar. 24	Neustria
Apr. 4	Madonna
Apr. 10	Germania
Apr. 25	Roma
May 8	Massilia
May 15	Madonna
May 21	Neustria
May 23	Germania
May 28	Gallia
June 9	Gallia
June 29	Germania
July 3	Madonna
July 13	Massilia
July 19	Roma
Aug. 4	Gallia
Aug. 13	Germania
Aug. 22	Madonna
Sept. 5	Roma
Sept. 17	Massilia
Sept. 25	Germania
Oct. 6	Gallia
Oct. 10	Madonna
Oct. 23	Roma
Nov. 6	Massilia
Nov. 15	Germania
Nov. 27	Madonna
Dec. 5	Roma

FRENCH LINE
(Compagnie Generale Transatlantique)
Havre—New York

N. Y.

Arrival	Steamer
Jan. 1	La Touraine
Jan. 7	La Gascogne
Jan. 14	La Savoie
Jan. 21	La Bretagne
Jan. 27	La Touraine
Feb. 4	La Gascogne
Feb. 10	La Savoie
Feb. 18	La Bretagne
Feb. 24	La Touraine
Feb. 26	St. Laurent
Mar. 4	La Gascogne
Mar. 10	La Lorraine
Mar. 13	Hudson
Mar. 20	La Champagne
Mar. 31	La Touraine
Apr. 5	St. Laurent
Apr. 7	La Lorraine
Apr. 9	La Gascogne
Apr. 15	La Champagne
Apr. 16	La Bretagne
Apr. 21	La Savoie
Apr. 26	Hudson
Apr. 27	La Provence
May 5	La Lorraine
May 7	La Gascogne
May 12	La Touraine
May 16	La Bretagne
May 18	La Savoie

Year 1906

FRENCH LINE (Compagnie Generale Transatlantique) Havre—New York		HAMBURG-AMERICAN LINE Hamburg—New York (Continued)		HAMBURG-AMERICAN LINE Hamburg—New York (Continued)	
N. Y. Arrival	**Steamer**	**N. Y. Arrival**	**Steamer**	**N. Y. Arrival**	**Steamer**
May 23	St. Laurent	Feb. 12	Armenia	Oct. 20	Amerika
May 25	La Provence	Feb. 15	Graf Waldersee	Oct. 25	Graf Waldersee
June 2	La Lorraine	Feb. 20	Amerika	Oct. 28	Bluecher
June 8	Hudson	Mar. 2	Pennsylvania	Nov. 3	K. Aug'e Victoria
June 9	La Touraine	Mar. 10	Patricia	Nov. 9	Armenia
June 16	La Savoie	Mar. 14	Bluecher	Nov. 9	Pennsylvania
June 22	La Provence	Mar. 24	Pretoria	Nov. 15	Batavia
June 25	La Gascogne	Mar. 31	Amerika	Nov. 17	Amerika
June 30	La Lorraine	Mar. 28	Graf Waldersee	Nov. 23	Patricia
July 6	St. Laurent	Apr. 4	Armenia	Dec. 1	Pretoria
July 7	La Touraine	Apr. 7	Rugia	Dec. 7	Graf Waldersee
July 15	La Bretagne	Apr. 12	Pennsylvania	Dec. 8	K. Aug'e Victoria
July 20	La Provence	Apr. 15	Bluecher	Dec. 11	Bluecher
July 20	Hudson	Apr. 21	Batavia	Dec. 22	Pennsylvania
July 27	La Lorraine	Apr. 26	Deutschland	Dec. 22	Amerika
Aug. 5	La Gascogne	Apr. 26	Pr. Eitel Friedrich	Dec. 31	Batavia
Aug. 12	La Bretagne	Apr. 27	Patricia		
Aug. 16	St. Laurent	Apr. 28	Christiania	**HAMBURG-AMERICAN LINE**	
Aug. 18	La Touraine	May 5	Pretoria	Mediterranean—New York	
Aug. 25	La Savoie	May 6	Amerika	**N. Y.**	
Aug. 31	Hudson	May 12	Graf Waldersee	**Arrival**	**Steamer**
Aug. 31	La Provence	May 14	Bluecher	Jan. 11	Prinz Oskar
Sept. 7	La Lorraine	May 19	K. Aug'e Victoria	Jan. 29	Prinz Adalbert
Sept. 10	La Bretagne	May 24	Deutschland	Feb. 14	Hamburg
Sept. 15	La Touraine	May 25	Pennsylvania	Mar. 5	Prinz Oskar
Sept. 24	La Savoie	June 2	Batavia	Mar. 6	Deutschland
Sept. 23	La Gascogne	June 3	Amerika	Mar. 17	Prinz Adalbert
Sept. 28	La Provence	June 9	Patricia	Mar. 31	Bulgaria
Oct. 4	St. Laurent	June 10	Bluecher	Apr. 16	Prinz Oskar
Oct. 5	La Lorraine	June 16	Pretoria	Apr. 17	Moltke
Oct. 7	La Bretagne	June 17	K. Aug'e Victoria	May 2	Prinz Adalbert
Oct. 13	La Touraine	June 21	Deutschland	May 15	Bulgaria
Oct. 19	Hudson	June 22	Graf Waldersee	June 1	Moltke
Oct. 20	La Savoie	June 30	Amerika	June 2	Prinz Oskar
Oct. 22	La Gascogne	July 2	Bulgaria	June 17	Prinz Adalbert
Oct. 26	La Provence	July 6	Pennsylvania	July 14	Prinz Oskar
Nov. 3	La Lorraine	July 14	K. Aug'e Victoria	July 16	Moltke
Nov. 5	La Bretagne	July 14	Batavia	Aug. 5	Prinz Adalbert
Nov. 10	La Touraine	July 20	Patricia	Sept. 4	Moltke
Nov. 15	St. Laurent	July 27	Pretoria	Sept. 24	Prinz Adalbert
Nov. 16	La Savoie	July 28	Amerika	Oct. 15	Moltke
Nov. 19	La Gascogne	Aug. 3	Graf Waldersee	Nov. 8	Hamburg
Nov. 23	La Provence	Aug. 5	Bluecher	Nov. 30	Moltke
Dec. 1	La Lorraine	Aug. 11	K. Aug'e Victoria	Dec. 21	Hamburg
Dec. 3	Hudson	Aug. 11	Bulgaria		
Dec. 9	La Bretagne	Aug. 16	Pennsylvania	**HOLLAND-AMERICAN LINE**	
Dec. 15	La Touraine	Aug. 24	Batavia	Rotterdam—New York	
Dec. 21	La Provence	Aug. 25	Amerika	**N. Y.**	
Dec. 28	St. Laurent	Aug. 30	Patricia	**Arrival**	**Steamer**
Dec. 29	La Lorraine	Sept. 2	Bluecher	Jan. 3	Statendam
		Sept. 6	Pretoria	Jan. 24	Rotterdam
HAMBURG-AMERICAN LINE		Sept. 8	K. Aug'e Victoria	Jan. 29	Noordam
Hamburg—New York		Sept. 13	Graf Waldersee	Feb. 13	Statendam
N. Y.		Sept. 13	Deutschland	Feb. 21	Ryndam
Arrival	**Steamer**	Sept. 14	Oceana	Feb. 27	Potsdam
Jan. 5	Pennsylvania	Sept. 19	Hamburg	Mar. 7	Noordam
Jan. 13	Amerika	Sept. 22	Amerika	Mar. 21	Statendam
Jan. 15	Batavia	Sept. 26	Pennsylvania	Mar. 27	Ryndam
Jan. 24	Moltke	Sept. 30	Bluecher	Apr. 3	Potsdam
Jan. 24	Bulgaria	Oct. 4	Batavia	Apr. 10	Noordam
Jan. 29	Patricia	Oct. 6	K. Aug'e Victoria	Apr. 16	New Amsterdam
Feb. 2	Pretoria	Oct. 10	Deutschland	Apr. 24	Statendam
Feb. 6	Bluecher	Oct. 12	Patricia	May 1	Ryndam
		Oct. 18	Pretoria		

Year 1906

HOLLAND-AMERICAN LINE
Rotterdam—New York
(Continued)

N. Y.

Arrival	Steamer
May 9	Potsdam
May 15	Noordam
May 21	New Amsterdam
May 29	Statendam
June 5	Ryndam
June 12	Potsdam
June 19	Noordam
June 25	New Amsterdam
July 3	Statendam
July 9	Ryndam
July 23	Potsdam
July 31	Noordam
Aug. 6	New Amsterdam
Aug. 13	Statendam
Aug. 20	Ryndam
Aug. 28	Potsdam
Sept. 3	Noordam
Sept. 10	New Amsterdam
Sept. 17	Statendam
Sept. 24	Ryndam
Oct. 1	Potsdam
Oct. 8	Noordam
Oct. 15	New Amsterdam
Oct. 23	Statendam
Oct. 30	Ryndam
Nov. 7	Potsdam
Nov. 12	Noordam
Nov. 19	New Amsterdam
Nov. 27	Statendam
Dec. 11	Ryndam
Dec. 26	Potsdam

INSULAR NAVIGATION COMPANY
Azores, Lisbon—New York,
New Bedford, Mass.

N. Y.
N. Bedford

Arrival	Steamer
Mar. 19	Peninsular
May 7	Peninsular
June 28	Peninsular
Aug. 14	Peninsular
Oct. 12	Peninsular
Dec. 6	Peninsular

LA VELOCE LINE
Mediterranean—New York

N. Y.

Arrival	Steamer
Jan. 13	Brasile
Feb. 1	Nord America
Feb. 24	Brasile
Mar. 7	Citta di Napoli
Mar. 15	Nord America
Mar. 28	Citta di Milano
Apr. 3	Citta di Torino
Apr. 5	Italia
Apr. 16	Citta di Genova
Apr. 19	Citta di Napoli
May 3	Nord America
May 14	Citta di Milano
May 28	Citta di Torino
June 7	Citta di Genova
June 9	Citta di Napoli

LA VELOCE LINE
Mediterranean—New York
(Continued)

N. Y.

Arrival	Steamer
June 11	Nord America
June 28	Citta di Milano
July 15	Citta di Torino
Aug. 9	Nord America
Sept. 4	Citta di Milano
Sept. 26	Nord America
Oct. 17	Citta di Napoli
Nov. 10	Nord America
Dec. 4	Citta di Napoli

LEYLAND LINE
Liverpool—Boston

Boston

Arrival	Steamer
Jan. 10	Devonian
Jan. 23	Canadian
Jan. 24	Bohemian
Jan. 29	Winifredian
Feb. 7	Cestrian
Feb. 16	Devonian
Feb. 26	Bohemian
Mar. 6	Winifredian
Mar. 16	Cestrian
Mar. 27	Bohemian
Apr. 10	Winifredian
Apr. 18	Cestrian
Apr. 23	Devonian
May 1	Bohemian
May 9	Canadian
May 21	Winifredian
May 28	Devonian
June 5	Bohemian
June 12	Canadian
June 24	Winifredian
June 29	Cestrian
July 10	Bohemian
July 17	Canadian
July 31	Cestrian
Aug. 13	Winifredian
Aug. 21	Canadian
Sept. 1	Bohemian
Sept. 4	Cestrian
Sept. 10	Devonian
Sept. 18	Winifredian
Sept. 25	Canadian
Oct. 2	Bohemian
Oct. 9	Cestrian
Oct. 16	Devonian
Oct. 22	Winifredian
Oct. 31	Canadian
Nov. 7	Bohemian
Nov. 13	Cestrian
Nov. 20	Devonian
Nov. 27	Winifredian
Dec. 6	Canadian
Dec. 12	Bohemian
Dec. 23	Devonian

LLOYD ITALIANO
Mediterranean—New York

N. Y.

Arrival	Steamer
Feb. 21	Indiana
Mar. 22	Florida
Apr. 12	Indiana

LLOYD ITALIANO
Mediterranean—New York
(Continued)

N. Y.

Arrival	Steamer
Apr. 21	Luisiana
May 5	Florida
May 22	Indiana
June 5	Luisiana
June 13	Florida
July 6	Indiana
Aug. 1	Luisiana
Sept. 1	Indiana
Sept. 22	Luisiana
Oct. 23	Virginia
Nov. 26	Florida

NAVIGAZIONE GENERALE ITALIANA
Mediterranean—New York

N. Y.

Arrival	Steamer
Jan. 10	Liguria
Jan. 23	Sicilia
Feb. 7	Lombardia
Feb. 28	Liguria
Mar. 1	Italia
Mar. 7	Sicilia
Mar. 17	Il Piemonte
Mar. 23	Vincenzo Florio
Mar. 26	Lombardia
Apr. 8	Lazio
Apr. 13	Liguria
Apr. 18	Ravenna
Apr. 23	Sicilia
Apr. 26	Marco Minghetti
May 6	Il Piemonte
May 10	Lombardia
May 18	Italia
May 28	Liguria
May 29	Lazio
June 12	Sicilia
June 18	Il Piemonte
June 27	Italia
June 28	Lombardia
July 12	Sannio
July 28	Lazio
Aug. 9	Italia
Aug. 14	Sicilia
Aug. 24	Sannio
Sept. 6	Lombardia
Oct. 5	Sicilia
Oct. 6	Italia
Oct. 20	Liguria
Dec. 1	Liguria
Dec. 1	Italia

NORTH GERMAN LLOYD
Bremen—New York

N. Y.

Arrival	Steamer
Jan. 17	Kaiser Wilhelm II
Jan. 31	K. Wm. der Grosse
Feb. 13	Kaiser Wilhelm II
Feb. 28	K. Wm. der Grosse
Mar. 21	Kaiser Wilhelm II
Apr. 4	Kronprinz Wilhelm
Apr. 11	K. Wm. der Grosse
Apr. 20	Kaiser Wilhelm II
May 2	Kronprinz Wilhelm

Year 1906

NORTH GERMAN LLOYD
Bremen—New York
(Continued)

N. Y.

Arrival	Steamer
May 9	K. Wm. der Grosse
May 16	Kaiser Wilhelm II
May 30	Kronprinz Wilhelm
June 7	K. Wm. der Grosse
June 13	Kaiser Wilhelm II
June 27	Kronprinz Wilhelm
July 3	K. Wm. der Grosse
July 10	Kaiser Wilhelm II
July 24	Kronprinz Wilhelm
Aug. 1	K. Wm. der Grosse
Aug. 14	Kaiser Wilhelm II
Aug. 28	Kronprinz Wilhelm
Sept. 5	K. Wm. der Grosse
Sept. 11	Kaiser Wilhelm II
Sept. 25	Kronprinz Wilhelm
Oct. 2	K. Wm. der Grosse
Oct. 10	Kaiser Wilhelm II
Oct. 24	Kronprinz Wilhelm
Oct. 31	K. Wm. der Grosse
Nov. 13	Kaiser Wilhelm II
Dec. 11	Kronprinz Wilhelm
Dec. 22	Kaiser Wilhelm II

NORTH GERMAN LLOYD
Bremen—New York
Express Service

N. Y.

Arrival	Steamer
Jan. 5	Brandenburg
Jan. 15	Hannover
Jan. 19	Neckar
Jan. 26	Main
Feb. 1	Koenigin Luise
Feb. 5	Rhein
Feb. 8	Cassel
Feb. 15	Barbarossa
Feb. 24	Breslau
Feb. 28	Wuerzburg
Mar. 3	Chemnitz
Mar. 10	Main
Mar. 16	Gneisenau
Mar. 22	Grosser Kurfuerst
Mar. 23	Trave
Mar. 30	Rhein
Apr. 5	Wuerzburg
Apr. 6	Chemnitz
Apr. 12	Seydlitz
Apr. 17	Gneisenau
Apr. 26	Main
Apr. 26	Grosser Kurfuerst
May 5	Cassel
May 12	Rhein
May 17	Prinzess Alice
May 23	Fried. der Grosse
May 29	Main
May 31	Grosser Kurfuerst
June 3	Trave
June 7	Barbarossa
June 13	Bremen
June 20	Prinzess Alice
June 27	Fried. der Grosse
July 5	Grosser Kurfuerst
July 12	Barbarossa
July 18	Bremen
July 24	Prinzess Alice

NORTH GERMAN LLOYD
Bremen—New York
Express Service
(Continued)

N. Y.

Arrival	Steamer
Aug. 2	Fried. der Grosse
Aug. 7	Grosser Kurfuerst
Aug. 15	Barbarossa
Aug. 21	Bremen
Aug. 30	Main
Sept. 5	Fried. der Grosse
Sept. 11	Grosser Kurfuerst
Sept. 20	Barbarossa
Sept. 26	Neckar
Oct. 2	Bremen
Oct. 9	Main
Oct. 10	Fried. der Grosse
Oct. 19	Chemnitz
Oct. 25	Rhein
Nov. 3	Brandenburg
Nov. 8	Bremen
Nov. 12	Neckar
Nov. 14	Fried. der Grosse
Nov. 20	Oldenburg
Nov. 23	Main
Nov. 30	Chemnitz
Dec. 2	Trave
Dec. 9	Rhein
Dec. 7	Yorek
Dec. 15	Hannover
Dec. 20	Fried. der Grosse
Dec. 28	Cassel

NORTH GERMAN LLOYD
Mediterranean—New York

N. Y.

Arrival	Steamer
Jan. 25	Prinzess Irene
Feb. 14	Koenig Albert
Feb. 28	Prinzess Irene
Mar. 8	Koenigin Luise
Mar. 17	Weimar
Mar. 22	Koenig Albert
Mar. 31	Barbarossa
Apr. 6	Prinzess Irene
Apr. 23	Weimar
Apr. 26	Koenig Albert
May 2	Hohenzollern
May 4	Barbarossa
May 10	Prinzess Irene
May 17	Koenigin Luise
May 27	Weimar
May 31	Gera
June 1	Koenig Albert
June 8	Hohenzollern
June 14	Prinzess Irene
June 21	Koenigin Luise
July 5	Koenig Albert
July 18	Prinzess Irene
Aug 2	Koenigin Luise
Aug. 16	Koenig Albert
Aug. 30	Prinzess Irene
Sept. 13	Koenigin Luise
Sept. 27	Koenig Albert
Oct. 4	Prinzess Irene
Oct. 18	Koenigin Luise
Nov. 1	Koenig Albert
Nov. 19	Prinzess Irene
Nov. 30	Koenigin Luise
Dec. 20	Koenig Albert

NORTH GERMAN LLOYD
Bremen—Baltimore

Baltimore

Arrival	Steamer
Jan. 23	Chemnitz
Jan. 29	Main
Feb. 1	Frankfurt
Feb. 7	Darmstadt
Feb. 15	Brandenburg
Feb. 26	Oldenburg
Mar. 3	Roland
Mar. 12	Main
Mar. 15	Wittekind
Mar. 17	Hannover
Mar. 18	Cassel
Mar. 31	Breslau
Apr. 1	Rhein
Apr. 1	Oldenburg
Apr. 8	Brandenburg
Apr. 11	Koeln
Apr. 13	Erlangen
Apr. 17	Karlsruhe
Apr. 18	Gneisenau
Apr. 21	Frankfurt
May 4	Wittekind
May 10	Breslau
May 17	Chemnitz
May 21	Hannover
May 21	Gneisenau
May 31	Main
June 8	Brandenburg
June 15	Cassel
June 22	Rhein
June 26	Neckar
July 6	Hannover
July 11	Main
July 20	Brandenburg
July 26	Koeln
Aug. 1	Rhein
Aug. 7	Neckar
Aug. 15	Chemnitz
Aug. 22	Breslau
Aug. 30	Brandenburg
Sept. 7	Wittekind
Sept. 11	Rhein
Sept. 20	Cassel
Sept. 26	Frankfurt
Oct. 4	Breslau
Oct. 11	Main
Oct. 19	Koeln
Oct. 22	Trave
Nov. 4	Halle
Nov. 10	Breslau
Nov. 19	Neckar
Nov. 22	Cassel
Nov. 30	Frankfurt
Dec. 11	Brandenburg
Dec. 15	Halle
Dec. 23	Karlsruhe

PRINCE LINE
Mediterranean—New York

N. Y.

Arrival	Steamer
Jan. 26	Napolitan Prince
Feb. 11	Sicilian Prince
Mar. 9	Napolitan Prince
Mar. 26	Sicilian Prince
Apr. 19	Napolitan Prince
May 11	Sicilian Prince

Year 1906

PRINCE LINE
Mediterranean—New York
(Continued)

N. Y.

Arrival	Steamer
June 2	Napolitan Prince
June 25	Sicilian Prince
July 15	Napolitan Prince
Aug. 6	Sicilian Prince
Aug. 29	Napolitan Prince
Sept. 20	Sicilian Prince
Oct. 10	Napolitan Prince
Nov. 7	Sicilian Prince
Nov. 28	Napolitan Prince
Dec. 21	Sicilian Prince

RED STAR LINE
Antwerp—New York

N. Y.

Arrival	Steamer
Jan. 4	Southwark
Jan. 9	Vaderland
Jan. 17	Kroonland
Jan. 24	Zeeland
Jan. 29	Finland
Feb. 6	Vaderland
Feb. 12	Kroonland
Feb. 21	Zeeland
Feb. 27	Finland
Mar. 6	Vaderland
Mar. 13	Kroonland
Mar. 17	Rhynland
Mar. 21	Zeeland
Mar. 26	Westernland
Mar. 26	Finland
Apr. 3	Vaderland
Apr. 10	Noordland
Apr. 12	Kroonland
Apr. 16	Zeeland
Apr. 23	Finland
Apr. 30	Vaderland
May 8	Kroonland
May 10	Westernland
May 14	Zeeland
May 21	Noordland
May 21	Finland
May 29	Vaderland
June 5	Rhynland
July 5	Kroonland
June 11	Zeeland
June 19	Finland
June 25	Vaderland
July 3	Kroonland
July 9	Zeeland
July 20	Mississippi
July 23	Vaderland
July 31	Finland
Aug. 7	Zeeland
Aug. 14	Kroonland
Aug. 21	Vaderland
Aug. 27	Finland
Sept. 4	Zeeland
Sept. 11	Kroonland
Sept. 18	Vaderland
Sept. 24	Finland
Oct. 1	Zeeland
Oct. 8	Kroonland
Oct. 16	Vaderland
Oct. 22	Finland
Oct. 31	Zeeland

RED STAR LINE
Antwerp—New York
(Continued)

N. Y.

Arrival	Steamer
Nov. 8	Samland
Nov. 12	Kroonland
Nov. 27	Vaderland
Dec. 5	Finland
Dec. 13	Samland
Dec. 19	Zeeland
Dec. 25	Kroonland
Dec. 31	Vaderland

RED STAR LINE
Antwerp—Phila.—Boston

Boston

Arrival	Steamer.
Mar. 8	Menominee
Mar. 22	Marquette
Apr. 3	Manitou
Apr. 17	Menominee
Apr. 30	Marquette
May 14	Manitou
May 27	Menominee
June 11	Marquette
June 25	Manitou
July 9	Menominee
July 23	Marquette
Aug. 20	Manitou
Sept. 3	Menominee
Sept. 17	Marquette
Oct. 1	Manitou
Oct. 15	Menominee
Oct. 29	Marquette
Nov. 28	Menominee
Dec. 14	Marquette
Dec. 25	Manitou

RUSSIAN EAST ASIATIC STEAMSHIP COMPANY
Libau—New York

N. Y.

Arrival	Steamer
Aug. 18	Kowno
Sept. 9	Grodno
Oct. 2	Korea
Nov. 5	Kowno
Nov. 19	Grodno

RUSSIAN VOLUNTEER FLEET
Libau—New York

N. Y.

Arrival	Steamer
July 24	Smolensk
Sept. 13	Smolensk
Nov. 8	Petersburg
Nov. 23	Smolensk
Dec. 27	Petersburg

SCANDINAVIAN-AMERICAN LINE
Scandinavian Ports—N. Y.

N. Y.

Arrival	Steamer
Jan. 8	Hellig Olav
Jan. 29	United States
Feb. 10	Oscar II
Feb. 22	Hellig Olav

SCANDINAVIAN-AMERICAN LINE
Scandinavian Ports—N. Y.
(Continued)

N. Y.

Arrival	Steamer
Mar. 6	United States
Mar. 21	Oscar II
Apr. 3	Hellig Olav
Apr. 17	United States
May 2	Oscar II
May 10	C. F. Tietgen
May 15	Hellig Olav
May 29	United States
June 12	Oscar II
June 20	C. F. Tietgen
June 26	Hellig Olav
July 9	United States
July 24	Oscar II
Aug. 1	C. F. Tietgen
Aug. 7	Hellig Olav
Aug. 20	United States
Sept. 3	Oscar II
Sept. 11	C. F. Tietgen
Sept. 18	Hellig Olav
Oct. 2	United States
Oct. 16	Oscar II
Oct. 24	C. F. Tietgen
Oct. 30	Hellig Olav
Nov. 12	Manitou
Nov. 12	United States
Nov. 27	Oscar II
Dec. 8	C. F. Tietgen
Dec. 13	Hellig Olav
Dec. 26	United States

UNION LINE
Hamburg—New York

N. Y.

Arrival	Steamer
Mar. 16	Pallanza
Mar. 25	Barcelona
Mar. 28	Albano
Mar. 29	Pisa
May 4	Pallanza
May 21	Barcelona
May 30	Albano
June 28	Pallanza
July 12	Barcelona
Sept. 2	Barcelona
Sept. 5	Albano
Sept. 18	Pisa
Dec. 6	Pallanza
Dec. 20	Barcelona
Dec. 21	Albano

WHITE STAR LINE
Liverpool—New York

N. Y.

Arrival	Steamer
Jan. 4	Cedric
Jan. 13	Baltic
Jan. 19	Majestic
Jan. 26	Arabic
Feb. 1	Teutonic
Feb. 8	Baltic
Feb. 15	Majestic
Feb. 23	Cedric
Mar. 1	Teutonic

Year 1906

WHITE STAR LINE Liverpool—New York N. Y. **Arrival**	**Steamer**
Mar. 9	Baltic
Mar. 15	Majestic
Mar. 24	Cedric
Mar. 29	Teutonic
Apr. 6	Baltic
Apr. 12	Majestic
Apr. 16	Celtic
Apr. 18	Oceanic
Apr. 26	Teutonic
Apr. 28	Cedric
May 4	Baltic
May 10	Majestic
May 13	Celtic
May 17	Oceanic
May 24	Teutonic
May 26	Cedric
June 1	Baltic
June 7	Majestic
June 10	Celtic
June 13	Oceanic
June 21	Teutonic
June 24	Cedric
June 29	Baltic
July 5	Majestic
July 8	Celtic
July 11	Oceanic
July 19	Teutonic
July 22	Cedric
July 26	Baltic

WHITE STAR LINE Liverpool—New York (Continued) N. Y. **Arrival**	**Steamer**
Aug. 2	Majestic
Aug. 5	Celtic
Aug. 8	Oceanic
Aug. 15	Teutonic
Aug. 18	Cedric
Aug. 23	Baltic
Aug. 29	Majestic
Sept. 1	Celtic
Sept. 5	Oceanic
Sept. 12	Teutonic
Sept. 15	Cedric
Sept. 20	Baltic
Sept. 26	Majestic
Sept. 29	Celtic
Oct. 3	Oceanic
Oct. 11	Teutonic
Oct. 14	Cedric
Oct. 19	Baltic
Oct. 24	Majestic
Oct. 27	Celtic
Oct. 31	Oceanic
Nov. 8	Teutonic
Nov. 15	Baltic
Nov. 23	Cedric
Nov. 28	Oceanic
Dec. 7	Celtic
Dec. 15	Baltic
Dec. 20	Majestic
Dec. 26	Oceanic

ADDITIONAL ARRIVALS Mediterranean—New York N. Y. **Arrival**	**Steamer**
Jan. 23	Brooklyn (Zotti, Naples)
Mar. 20	Brooklyn (Zotti, Naples)
Apr. 16	Equita (Naples)
Apr. 29	America (Fabre, Marseilles)
May 28	Brooklyn (Zotti, Marseilles)
July 9	Brooklyn (Zotti, Marseilles)
July 19	America (Fabre, Marseilles)
Aug. 22	Madonna (Fabre, Marseilles)
Oct. 31	Neustria (Fabre, Marseilles)
Nov. 24	Gregory Morch (R's'n-Od'sa Line)
Nov. 29	Gallia (Fabre, Marseilles)
Dec. 26	Neustria (Fabre, Marseilles)

Year 1907

ALLAN LINE
Glasgow—Boston
Boston

Arrival	Steamer
Jan. 4	Sicilian
Jan. 25	Numidian
Feb. 9	Laurentian
Feb. 25	Corinthian
Mar. 11	Sicilian
Mar. 24	Laurentian
Apr. 5	Pretorian
Apr. 20	Numidian
Apr. 27	Laurentian
May 7	Sarmatian
May 21	Corean
May 27	Laurentian
June 10	Sarmatian
June 25	Laurentian
July 5	Corean
July 13	Sarmatian
July 22	Laurentian
Aug. 5	Numidian
Aug. 19	Laurentian
Sept. 2	Numidian
Sept. 16	Laurentian
Oct. 1	Numidian
Oct. 14	Laurentian
Oct. 31	Numidian
Nov. 18	Laurentian
Dec. 5	Numidian
Dec. 18	Grampian

AMERICAN LINE
Southampton—New York
N. Y.

Arrival	Steamer
Jan. 6	New York
Jan. 13	St. Louis
Jan. 20	Philadelphia
Jan. 27	St. Paul
Feb. 3	New York
Feb. 17	St. Louis
Feb. 24	Philadelphia
Mar. 9	New York
Mar. 17	St. Louis
Mar. 24	Philadelphia
Apr. 7	New York
Apr. 14	St. Louis
Apr. 21	Philadelphia
Apr. 29	Celtic
May 5	New York
May 12	St. Louis
May 19	Philadelphia
May 27	Celtic
June 1	New York
June 10	St. Louis
June 15	Philadelphia
June 23	New York
June 30	New York
July 6	St. Louis
July 13	Philadelphia
July 27	St. Paul
Aug. 3	New York
Aug. 10	St. Louis
Aug. 17	Philadelphia
Aug. 24	St. Paul

AMERICAN LINE
Southampton—New York
(Continued)
N. Y.

Arrival	Steamer
Aug. 31	New York
Sept. 7	St. Louis
Sept. 14	Philadelphia
Sept. 21	St. Paul
Sept. 28	New York
Oct. 5	St. Louis
Oct. 12	Philadelphia
Oct. 19	St. Paul
Oct. 26	New York
Nov. 2	St. Louis
Nov. 9	Philadelphia
Nov. 16	St. Paul
Nov. 24	New York
Dec. 1	St. Louis
Dec. 8	Philadelphia
Dec. 15	St. Paul
Dec. 22	New York
Dec. 29	St. Louis

AMERICAN LINE
Liverpool—Philadelphia
Phila.

Arrival	Steamer
Jan. 2	Noordland
Jan. 15	Merion
Jan. 28	Haverford
Feb. 5	Noordland
Feb. 20	Merion
Mar. 6	Haverford
Mar. 14	Noordland
Mar. 18	Friesland
Mar. 30	Westernland
Apr. 9	Haverford
Apr. 18	Noordland
Apr. 22	Friesland
Apr. 30	Merion
May 5	Westmoreland
May 13	Haverford
May 22	Noordland
May 26	Friesland
June 3	Merion
June 10	Westernland
June 17	Haverford
June 25	Noordland
June 30	Friesland
July 7	Merion
July 14	Westmoreland
July 22	Haverford
July 29	Noordland
Aug. 4	Friesland
Aug. 11	Merion
Aug. 19	Westernland
Aug. 25	Haverford
Sept. 2	Noordland
Sept. 7	Friesland
Sept. 15	Merion
Sept. 23	Westernland
Sept. 30	Haverford
Oct. 7	Noordland
Oct. 13	Friesland
Oct. 20	Merion
Oct. 29	Westernland

AMERICAN LINE
Liverpool—Philadelphia
(Continued)
Phila.

Arrival	Steamer
Nov. 4	Haverford
Nov. 11	Noordland
Nov. 26	Friesland
Dec. 6	Haverford
Dec. 25	Noordland

ANCHOR LINE
Glasgow—New York
N. Y.

Arrival	Steamer
Jan. 8	Caledonia
Jan. 25	Ethiopia
Jan. 29	Furnessia
Feb. 2	Columbia
Feb. 15	Astoria
Feb. 18	Caledonia
Mar. 3	Ethiopia
Mar. 4	Columbia
Mar. 15	Furnessia
Mar. 18	Caledonia
Mar. 29	Astoria
Apr. 1	Columbia
Apr. 12	Furnessia
Apr. 15	Caledonia
Apr. 26	Ethiopia
Apr. 28	Columbia
May 10	Furnessia
May 12	Caledonia
May 21	Astoria
May 26	Columbia
June 3	Ethiopia
June 9	Caledonia
June 18	Astoria
June 22	Columbia
July 2	Furnessia
July 7	Caledonia
July 16	Astoria
July 21	Columbia
July 29	Furnessia
Aug. 4	Caledonia
Aug. 13	Astoria
Aug. 18	Columbia
Aug. 27	Furnessia
Sept. 1	Caledonia
Sept. 11	Astoria
Sept. 15	Columbia
Sept. 24	Furnessia
Sept. 29	Caledonia
Oct. 10	Astoria
Oct. 13	Columbia
Oct. 21	California
Oct. 28	Caledonia
Nov. 5	Furnessia
Nov. 10	Columbia
Nov. 19	California
Nov. 25	Caledonia
Dec. 3	Furnessia
Dec. 15	Astoria
Dec. 17	California
Dec. 22	Caledonia
Dec. 30	Columbia

Year 1907

ANCHOR LINE
Mediterranean—New York
N. Y.

Arrival	Steamer
Jan. 4	Perugia
Feb. 4	Algeria
Feb. 19	Calabria
Mar. 3	Italia
Mar. 18	Perugia
Apr. 6	Algeria
Apr. 13	Calabria
Apr. 25	Italia
May 9	Perugia
June 3	Algeria
June 8	Calabria
June 14	Italia
June 30	Perugia
July 22	Algeria
Aug. 1	Calabria
Aug. 14	Italia
Aug. 30	Perugia
Sept. 14	Algeria
Sept. 28	Calabria
Oct. 5	Italia
Oct. 19	Perugia
Nov. 6	Algeria
Nov. 20	Calabria
Nov. 27	Italia
Dec. 14	Perugia

ATLANTIC TRANSPORT LINE
London—New York
N. Y.

Arrival	Steamer
Jan. 7	Minnetonka
Jan. 21	Minneapolis
Jan. 26	Minnehaha
Feb. 14	Mesaba
Feb. 18	Minnetonka
Mar. 5	Minneapolis
Mar. 18	Minnehaha
Mar. 25	Mesaba
Apr. 1	Minnetonka
Apr. 7	Minneapolis
Apr. 16	Minnehaha
Apr. 25	Mesaba
Apr. 30	Minnetonka
May 6	Minneapolis
May 14	Minnehaha
May 22	Mesaba
May 27	Minnetonka
June 3	Minneapolis
June 11	Minnehaha
June 19	Mesaba
June 25	Minnetonka
July 2	Minneapolis
July 8	Minnehaha
July 17	Mesaba
July 22	Minnetonka
July 30	Minneapolis
Aug. 5	Minnehaha
Aug. 14	Mesaba
Aug. 19	Minnetonka
Aug. 26	Minneapolis
Sept. 2	Minnehaha
Sept. 11	Mesaba

ATLANTIC TRANSPORT LINE
London—New York
(Continued)
N. Y.

Arrival	Steamer
Sept. 26	Minnetonka
Sept. 23	Minneapolis
Sept. 30	Minnehaha
Oct. 8	Mesaba
Oct. 14	Minnetonka
Oct. 22	Minneapolis
Oct. 29	Minnehaha
Nov. 11	Minnetonka
Nov. 18	Mesaba
Nov. 24	Minneapolis
Dec. 1	Minnehaha
Dec. 15	Minnetonka
Dec. 30	Minneapolis

AUSTRO-AMERICANA LINE
Mediterranean—New York
N. Y.

Arrival	Steamer
Jan. 1	Francesca
Jan. 14	Sofia Hohenberg
Jan. 28	Erny
Feb. 16	Gerty
Feb. 22	Francesca
Mar. 4	Carolina
Mar. 9	Giulia
Mar. 10	Eugenia
Mar. 18	Teresa
Mar. 23	Sofia Hohenberg
Apr. 1	Erny
Apr. 6	Ida
Apr. 17	Gerty
Apr. 17	Francesca
Apr. 21	Irene
Apr. 30	Giulia
May 8	Eugenia
May 10	Sofia Hohenberg
May 29	Lura
June 7	Francesca
June 23	Gerty
June 29	Giulia
July 2	Sofia Hohenberg
July 7	Carolina
July 17	Laura
July 19	Eugenia
Aug. 2	Francesca
Aug. 20	Gerty
Sept. 2	Laura
Sept. 17	Alice
Sept. 27	Francesca
Oct. 10	Giulia
Oct. 18	Laura
Nov. 2	Alice
Nov. 8	Erny
Nov. 16	Francesca
Nov. 17	Carolina
Dec. 1	Giulia
Dec. 5	Laura
Dec. 9	Ida
Dec. 20	Alice
Dec. 20	Hermine

COMPANIA TRANSATLANTICA LINE
(Spanish Line)
Italian Ports—New York
N. Y.

Arrival	Steamer
Jan. 13	Manuel Calvo
Feb. 11	Antonio Lopez
Mar. 12	Buenos Aires
Apr. 10	Montevideo
Apr. 26	Leon XIII
May 11	Antonio Lopez
June 11	Manuel Calvo
July 10	Montevideo
Aug. 10	Buenos Aires
Sept. 10	Montserrat
Oct. 11	Antonio Lopez
Nov. 11	Manuel Calvo
Dec. 12	Montevideo

CUNARD LINE
Liverpool—New York
N. Y.

Arrival	Steamer
Jan. 6	Etruria
Jan. 13	Carmania
Jan. 19	Campania
Jan. 26	Umbria
Feb. 2	Lucania
Feb. 10	Carmania
Feb. 16	Campania
Feb. 24	Etruria
Mar. 2	Lucania
Mar. 10	Carmania
Mar. 16	Campania
Mar. 24	Etruria
Mar. 30	Lucania
Apr. 3	Caronia
Apr. 7	Umbria
Apr. 13	Campania
Apr. 17	Carmania
Apr. 21	Etruria
Apr. 27	Lucania
May 1	Caronia
May 5	Umbria
May 11	Campania
May 15	Carmania
May 19	Etruria
May 24	Lucania
May 29	Caronia
June 1	Umbria
June 8	Campania
June 12	Carmania
June 15	Etruria
June 22	Lucania
June 26	Caronia
June 29	Umbria
July 6	Campania
July 10	Carmania
July 13	Etruria
July 20	Lucania
July 24	Caronia
July 27	Umbria
Aug. 3	Campania
Aug. 7	Carmania
Aug. 10	Etruria
Aug. 17	Lucania
Aug. 21	Caronia
Aug. 24	Umbria

Year 1907

CUNARD LINE
Liverpool—New York
(Continued)

N. Y.

Arrival	Steamer
Aug. 30	Campania
Sept. 3	Carmania
Sept. 7	Etruria
Sept. 13	Lucania
Sept. 13	Lusitania
Sept. 17	Caronia
Sept. 21	Umbria
Sept. 27	Campania
Oct. 1	Carmania
Oct. 5	Etruria
Oct. 8	Lucania
Oct. 11	Lusitania
Oct. 15	Caronia
Oct. 20	Umbria
Oct. 26	Campania
Oct. 30	Carmania
Nov. 2	Lucania
Nov. 8	Lusitania
Nov. 16	Caronia
Nov. 22	Mauretania
Dec. 1	Carmania
Dec. 8	Lusitania
Dec. 15	Lucania
Dec. 20	Mauretania
Dec. 28	Campania

CUNARD LINE
Med. Adriatic—New York

N. Y.

Arrival	Steamer
Jan. 4	Ultonia
Jan. 9	Carpathia
Jan. 31	Slavonia
Feb. 9	Caronia
Mar. 4	Ultonia
Mar. 7	Pannonia
Mar. 16	Carpathia
Apr. 2	Slavonia
Apr. 24	Pannonia
May 6	Carpathia
May 22	Slavonia
May 28	Ultonia
June 13	Pannonia
June 25	Carpathia
July 11	Slavonia
July 17	Ultonia
Aug. 1	Pannonia
Aug. 13	Carpathia
Aug. 28	Slavonia
Sept. 3	Ultonia
Sept. 18	Pannonia
Oct. 2	Carpathia
Oct. 18	Slavonia
Oct. 27	Ultonia
Nov. 8	Pannonia
Nov. 20	Carpathia
Dec. 7	Slavonia
Dec. 19	Ultonia
Dec. 28	Caronia
Dec. 29	Pannonia

CUNARD LINE
Liverpool—Boston

Boston

Arrival	Steamer
Jan. 18	Saxonia
Jan. 31	Ivernia
Feb. 15	Saxonia
Feb. 28	Ivernia
Mar. 15	Saxonia
Mar. 29	Ivernia
Apr. 12	Saxonia
Apr. 25	Ivernia
May 10	Saxonia
May 23	Ivernia
June 6	Saxonia
June 20	Ivernia
July 4	Saxonia
July 18	Ivernia
Aug. 1	Saxonia
Aug. 15	Ivernia
Aug. 29	Saxonia
Sept. 12	Ivernia
Sept. 26	Saxonia
Oct. 10	Ivernia
Oct. 22	Saxonia
Nov. 7	Ivernia
Nov. 22	Saxonia
Dec. 5	Ivernia
Dec. 19	Saxonia

FABRE LINE
Mediterranean—New York

N. Y.

Arrival	Steamer
Jan. 28	Madonna
Feb. 4	Roma
Feb. 13	Germania
Mar. 5	Madonna
Mar. 19	Germania
Mar. 25	Roma
Apr. 8	Madonna
Apr. 16	Gallia
Apr. 25	Germania
May 3	Roma
May 14	Madonna
June 7	Germania
June 16	Roma
June 17	Gallia
June 22	Massilia
June 26	Madonna
July 24	Germania
July 30	Roma
Aug. 9	Madonna
Sept. 10	Germania
Sept. 17	Roma
Sept. 24	Madonna
Oct. 1	Venezia
Oct. 1	Massilia
Oct. 20	Germania
Oct. 21	Neustria
Oct. 27	Roma
Nov. 11	Madonna
Nov. 19	Venezia
Nov. 28	Germania
Dec. 9	Massilia
Dec. 13	Roma
Dec. 31	Madonna

FRENCH LINE
(Compagnie Generale Transatlantique)
Havre—New York

N. Y.

Arrival	Steamer
Jan. 6	La Bretagne
Jan. 12	La Savoie
Jan. 20	La Gascogne
Jan. 26	La Lorraine
Feb. 3	La Bretagne
Feb. 9	La Savoie
Feb. 11	St. Laurent
Feb. 19	La Gascogne
Feb. 22	La Provence
Feb. 27	Hudson
Mar. 3	La Bretagne
Mar. 9	La Savoie
Mar. 17	La Touraine
Mar. 21	Californie
Mar. 21	La Gascogne
Mar. 22	La Provence
Mar. 30	St. Laurent
Apr. 2	La Bretagne
Apr. 7	La Touraine
Apr. 13	La Savoie
Apr. 14	Hudson
Apr. 17	La Gascogne
Apr. 19	La Provence
Apr. 27	La Lorraine
Apr. 29	Californie
Apr. 30	La Bretagne
May 4	La Savoie
May 10	Sa Laurent
May 11	La Touraine
May 15	La Gascogne
May 17	La Provence
May 24	Hudson
May 25	La Lorraine
May 27	La Bretagne
June 1	La Savoie
June 7	Californie
June 12	La Provence
June 15	La Lorraine
June 22	La Savoie
June 23	St. Laurent
June 29	La Touraine
July 5	La Provence
July 5	Hudson
July 14	La Bretagne
July 20	La Savoie
July 20	Californie
July 28	La Touraine
Aug. 1	St. Laurent
Aug. 3	La Lorraine
Aug. 11	La Bretagne
Aug. 16	La Provence
Aug. 16	Hudson
Aug. 25	La Touraine
Aug. 31	La Lorraine
Sept. 5	Mexico
Sept. 8	La Savoie
Sept. 9	La Gascogne
Sept. 13	La Provence
Sept. 18	St. Laurent
Sept. 21	La Lorraine
Sept. 23	La Bretagne
Sept. 28	La Savoie
Oct. 3	Californie
Oct. 4	La Provence
Oct. 7	La Gascogne

Year 1907

FRENCH LINE
(Compagnie Generale Transatlantique)
Havre—New York
(Continued)

N. Y.

Arrival	Steamer
Oct. 12	La Touraine
Oct. 17	Hudson
Oct. 19	La Lorraine
Oct. 21	La Bretagne
Oct. 26	La Savoie
Nov. 2	La Provence
Nov. 2	St. Laurent
Nov. 4	La Gascogne
Nov. 9	La Touraine
Nov. 15	Californie
Nov. 16	La Lorraine
Nov. 23	La Savoie
Nov. 30	La Provence
Nov. 30	Hudson
Dec. 2	La Gascogne
Dec. 8	La Touraine
Dec. 15	La Lorraine
Dec. 20	Floride
Dec. 24	La Bretagne
Dec. 28	La Provence

HAMBURG-AMERICAN LINE
Hamburg—New York

N. Y.

Arrival	Steamer
Jan. 5	Patricia
Jan. 16	Pretoria
Jan. 19	K. Auguste Victoria
Jan. 23	Bluecher
Jan. 24	Deutschland
Feb. 1	Pennsylvania
Feb. 10	Badenia
Feb. 10	Amerika
Feb. 16	Graf Waldersee
Feb. 23	Prinz Sigismund
Feb. 26	Batavia
Feb. 26	K. Auguste Victoria
Mar. 2	Pisa
Mar. 10	Pretoria
Mar. 11	Acilia
Mar. 12	Arcadia
Mar. 17	Bosnia
Mar. 17	Amerika
Mar. 17	Patricia
Mar. 22	Pennsylvania
Mar. 30	Graf Waldersee
Mar. 30	Pallanza
Apr. 7	Badenia
Apr. 9	K. Auguste Victoria
Apr. 13	Batavia
Apr. 21	Amerika
Apr. 21	Barcelonia
Apr. 24	Pretoria
Apr. 25	Deutschland
Apr. 27	Patricia
May 2	Andalusia
May 2	Pisa
May 4	Silvia
May 5	Bluecher
May 10	Arcadia
May 10	Graf Waldersee
May 11	K. Auguste Victoria
May 17	Pennsylvania

HAMBURG-AMERICAN LINE
Hamburg—New York
(Continued)

N. Y.

Arrival	Steamer
May 18	Amerika
May 22	Sicilia
May 23	Pallanza
May 23	Deutschland
May 24	Batavia
May 27	Otavi
May 31	Pretoria
June 1	Badenia
June 2	Luecher
June 6	Swakopmund
June 7	Patricia
June 8	K. Auguste Victoria
June 13	Lincoln
June 16	Amerika
June 20	Bosnia
June 21	Graf Waldersee
June 21	Deutschland
June 28	Pisa
June 29	Pennsylvania
July 4	Andalusia
July 6	K. Auguste Victoria
July 9	Batavia
July 13	Amerika
July 14	Arcadia
July 19	Deutschland
July 20	Patricia
July 25	President Lincoln
July 31	Badenia
Aug. 2	Graf Waldersee
Aug. 3	K. Auguste Victoria
Aug. 8	Pennsylvania
Aug. 13	Bluecher
Aug. 17	Amerika
Aug. 17	Bosnia
Aug. 22	Pretoria
Aug. 22	Deutschland
Aug. 31	K. Auguste Victoria
Aug. 29	Patricia
Sept. 3	President Lincoln
Sept. 8	Bluecher
Sept. 12	Graf Waldersee
Sept. 13	Oceana
Sept. 14	Amerika
Sept. 18	Pennsylvania
Sept. 19	Deutschland
Sept. 23	Batavia
Sept. 25	President Grant
Sept. 28	K. Auguste Victoria
Oct. 3	Pretoria
Oct. 6	Bluecher
Oct. 11	Patricia
Oct. 12	Amerika
Oct. 16	President Lincoln
Oct. 17	Deutschland
Oct. 26	K. Auguste Victoria
Oct. 25	Graf Waldersee
Nov. 1	Pennsylvania
Nov. 3	Bluecher
Nov. 4	President Grant
Nov. 9	Amerika
Nov. 16	Pretoria
Nov. 23	K. Auguste Victoria
Nov. 23	Patricia
Nov. 27	President Lincoln

HAMBURG-AMERICAN LINE
Hamburg—New York
(Continued)

N. Y.

Arrival	Steamer
Dec. 2	Bluecher
Dec. 6	Graf Waldersee
Dec. 8	Amerika
Dec. 15	Pennsylvania
Dec. 20	President Grant
Dec. 21	K. Auguste Victoria
Dec. 29	Pretoria

HAMBURG-AMERICAN LINE
Mediterranean—New York

N. Y.

Arrival	Steamer
Jan. 18	Moltke
Feb. 17	Hamburg
Mar. 3	Deutschland
Mar. 5	Romanic
Mar. 27	Hamburg
Apr. 20	Moltke
May 1	Bulgaria
May 2	Hamburg
May 4	Oceana
May 24	Moltke
June 7	Hamburg
June 28	Bulgaria
June 30	Moltke
Aug. 5	Hamburg
Aug. 27	Moltke
Sept. 19	Hamburg
Oct. 10	Moltke
Oct. 23	Bulgaria
Nov. 1	Hamburg
Nov. 17	Batavia
Nov. 22	Moltke
Dec. 16	Bulgaria
Dec. 23	Hamburg

HOLLAND-AMERICA LINE
Rotterdam—New York

N. Y.

Arrival	Steamer
Jan. 15	Ryndam
Jan. 29	Potsdam
Feb. 12	Statendam
Feb. 20	Noordam
Feb. 27	Ryndam
Mar. 6	Potsdam
Mar. 13	New Amsterdam
Mar. 19	Statendam
Mar. 27	Noordam
Apr. 1	Ryndam
Apr. 12	Potsdam
Apr. 16	New Amsterdam
Apr. 24	Statendam
Apr. 30	Noordam
May 7	Ryndam
May 14	Potsdam
May 21	New.. Amsterdam
May 28	Statendam
June 4	Noordam
June 11	Ryndam
June 18	Potsdam
June 24	New Amsterdam

Year 1907

HOLLAND-AMERICA LINE
Rotterdam—New York
(Continued)
N. Y.

Arrival	Steamer
July 3	Statendam
July 9	Noordam
July 16	Ryndam
July 30	Potsdam
Aug. 5	New Amsterdam
Aug. 13	Statendam
Aug. 19	Noordam
Aug. 26	Ryndam
Sept. 3	Potsdam
Sept. 9	New Amsterdam
Sept. 16	Statendam
Sept. 23	Noordam
Oct. 1	Ryndam
Oct. 8	Potsdam
Oct. 14	New Amsterdam
Oct. 22	Statendam
Oct. 29	Noordam
Nov. 4	Ryndam
Nov. 12	Potsdam
Nov. 18	New Amsterdam
Nov. 24	Statendam
Dec. 11	Ryndam
Dec. 19	Potsdam

INSULAR NAVIGATION COMPANY
Azores, Lisbon—New York,
New Bedford, Mass.
N. Y.

Arrival	Steamer
Sept. 28	Peninsular
Nov. 15	Peninsular

LA VELOCE LINE
Mediterranean—New York
N. Y.

Arrival	Steamer
Feb. 21	Brasile
Mar. 11	Citta di Milano
Mar. 16	Nord America
Mar. 24	Citta di Torino
Mar. 30	Brasile
Mar. 30	Citta di Napoli
Apr. 27	Citta di Milano
Apr. 28	Nord America
May 4	Brasile
May 5	Citta di Torino
May 16	Citta di Napoli
May 22	Europa
June 9	Nord America
June 12	Washington
June 28	Citta di Torino
June 28	Europa
July 14	Citta di Milano
July 25	Nord America
Aug. 9	Europa
Sept. 4	Nord America
Sept. 17	Europa
Oct. 8	Citta di Torino
Oct. 18	Nord America
Oct. 27	Europa
Nov. 25	Nord America
Dec. 5	Europa

LEYLAND LINE
Liverpool—Boston
Boston

Arrival	Steamer
Jan. 1	Winifredian
Jan. 18	Canadian
Jan. 24	Bohemian
Jan. 28	Devonian
Feb. 6	Winifredian
Feb. 20	Canadian
Feb. 26	Bohemian
Mar. 3	Devonian
Mar. 12	Winifredian
Apr. 3	Bohemian
Apr. 11	Devonian
Apr. 24	Winifredian
May 8	Bohemian
May 14	Devonian
May 22	Canadian
May 28	Winifredian
June 11	Bohemian
June 18	Devonian
June 26	Canadian
July 2	Winifredian
July 17	Cestrian
July 23	Devonian
July 31	Canadian
Aug. 13	Bohemian
Aug. 20	Cestrian
Aug. 26	Devonian
Sept. 3	Canadian
Sept. 10	Winifredian
Sept. 17	Bohemian
Sept. 24	Cestrian
Sept. 30	Devonian
Oct. 8	Canadian
Oct. 14	Winifredian
Oct. 22	Bohemian
Nov. 5	Devonian
Nov. 12	Canadian
Nov. 18	Winifredian
Dec. 4	Bohemian
Dec. 13	Devonian
Dec. 20	Canadian
Dec. 25	Winifredian

LLOYD ITALIANO
Mediterranean—New York
N. Y.

Arrival	Steamer
Feb. 27	Luisiana
Mar. 16	Virginia
Mar. 26	Indiana
Apr. 9	Luisiana
Apr. 24	Virginia
May 2	Florida
May 13	Indiana
May 23	Luisiana
June 4	Virginia
June 15	Florida
June 23	Indiana
July 6	Luisiana
July 21	Virginia
Aug. 9	Florida
Sept. 2	Luisiana
Sept. 27	Florida
Oct. 15	Luisiana
Nov. 11	Florida
Nov. 25	Luisiana
Dec. 24	Florida

LLOYD SABAUDO
Mediterranean—New York
N. Y.

Arrival	Steamer
Apr. 27	Re d'Italia
May 31	Regina d'Italia
June 21	Re d'Italia
July 6	Prin'pe di Piemonte
July 20	Regina d'Italia
Aug. 3	Re d'Italia
Aug. 16	Prin'pe di Piemonte
Sept. 1	Regina d'Italia
Sept. 14	Re d'Italia
Oct. 2	Prin'pe di Piemonte
Oct. 27	Re d'Italia
Nov. 20	Prin'pe di Piemonte
Dec. 7	Re d'Italia
Dec. 22	Regina d'Italia

NAVIGAZIONE GENE-RALE ITALIANA
Mediterranean—New York
N. Y.

Arrival	Steamer
Mar. 3	Lombardia
Mar. 11	Liguria
Mar. 19	Sannio
Mar. 26	Campania
Apr. 1	Lazio
Apr. 10	Lombardia
Apr. 20	Liguria
Apr. 27	Sannio
May 6	Campania
May 11	Lazio
May 20	Liguria
June 10	Sannio
June 23	Campania
June 27	Lazio
July 11	Liguria
Aug. 3	Sannio
Aug. 19	Campania
Sept. 1	Lazio
Sept. 26	Sannio
Oct. 24	Campania
Nov. 2	Liguria
Nov. 22	Sannio
Dec. 6	Campania
Dec. 23	Liguria

NORTH GERMAN LLOYD
Express Service
Bremen—New York
N. Y.

Arrival	Steamer
Jan. 15	Kronprinz Wilhelm
Jan. 23	K. Wm. der Grosse
Feb. 5	Kaiser Wilhelm II
Feb. 20	Kronprinz Wilhelm
Mar. 6	Kaiser Wilhelm II
Mar. 19	Kronprinz Wilhelm
Mar. 27	K. Wm. der Grosse
Apr. 3	Kaiser Wilhelm II
Apr. 16	Kronprinz Wilhelm
May 1	K. Wm. der Grosse
May 7	Kaiser Wilhelm II
May 14	Kronprinz Wilhelm
May 28	K. Wm. der Grosse
June 4	Kaiser Wilhelm II
June 12	Kronprinz Wilhelm

Year 1907

NORTH GERMAN LLOYD
Express Service
Bremen—New York

N. Y.

Arrival	Steamer
June 26	K. Wm. der Grosse
July 3	Kaiser Wilhelm II
July 10	Kronprinz Wilhelm
July 24	K. Wm. der Grosse
Aug. 6	Kronprinz Wilhelm
Aug. 13	Kronprinz'n Cecilie
Aug. 20	K. Wm. der Grosse
Aug. 27	Kaiser Wilhelm II
Sept. 3	Kronprinz Wilhelm
Sept. 10	Kronprinz'n Cecilie
Sept. 17	K. Wm. der Grosse
Sept. 24	Kaiser Wilhelm II
Oct. 1	Kronprinz Wilhelm
Oct. 9	Kronprinz'n Cecilie
Oct. 15	K. Wm. der Grosse
Oct. 23	Kaiser Wilhelm II
Oct. 30	Kronprinz Wilhelm
Nov. 5	Kronprinz'n Cecilie
Nov. 17	Kaiser Wilhelm II
Nov. 26	Kronprinz Wilhelm
Dec. 3	Kronprinz'n Cecilie
Dec. 21	Kronprinz Wilhelm

NORTH GERMAN LLOYD
Regular Service
Bremen—New York

N. Y.

Arrival	Steamer
Jan. 4	Main
Jan. 14	Chemnitz
Jan. 18	Rhein
Jan. 24	York
Jan. 30	Neckar
Feb. 9	Cassel
Feb. 15	Main
Feb. 22	Fried. der Grosse
Mar. 2	Rhein
Mar. 10	Brandenburg
Mar. 11	Trave
Mar. 15	Weimar
Mar. 16	Chemnitz
Mar. 23	Main
Mar. 27	Grosser Kurfuerst
Mar. 29	Wuerzberg
Apr. 1	Frankfurt
Apr. 6	Rhein
Apr. 7	Trave
Apr. 7	Breslau
Apr. 13	Brandenburg
Apr. 20	Chemnitz
Apr. 25	Gera
Apr. 27	Main
May 1	Grosser Kurfuerst
May 8	Trave
May 12	Rhein
May 14	Prinzess Alice
May 20	Brandenberg
May 22	Bremen
May 31	Main
June 5	Grosser Kurfuerst
June 15	Rhein
June 18	Fried. der Grosse
June 20	Prinzess Alice
June 27	Bremen

NORTH GERMAN LLOYD
Regular Service
Bremen—New York
(Continued)

N. Y.

Arrival	Steamer
July 6	Main
July 8	Barbarossa
July 10	Grosser Kurfuerst
July 18	Fried. der Grosse
July 25	Prinzess Alice
Aug. 1	Rhein
Aug. 2	Bremen
Aug. 4	Trave
Aug. 6	Breslau
Aug. 7	Barbarossa
Aug. 14	Grosser Kurfuerst
Aug. 22	Main
Aug. 27	Gneisenau
Sept. 3	Bremen
Sept. 12	Barbarossa
Sept. 15	Trave
Sept. 17	Grosser Kurfuerst
Sept. 25	Fried. der Grosse
Oct. 1	Gneisenau
Oct. 2	Brandenberg
Oct. 6	Cassel
Oct. 12	Main
Oct. 16	Barbarossa
Oct. 22	Grosser Kurfuerst
Oct. 23	Rhein
Oct. 27	Zieten
Oct. 30	Fried. der Grosse
Nov. 6	Trave
Nov. 9	Wittekind
Nov. 14	Main
Nov. 14	Seydlitz
Nov. 21	Oldenburg
Nov. 24	Barbarossa
Nov. 26	Grosser Kurfuerst
Dec. 1	Rhein
Dec. 7	Koeln
Dec. 14	Breslau
Dec. 21	Main
Dec. 26	Barbarossa

NORTH GERMAN LLOYD
Mediterranean—New York

N. Y.

Arrival	Steamer
Jan. 20	Prinzess Irene
Jan. 31	Koenigin Luise
Feb. 15	Koenig Albert
Mar. 2	K. Wm. der Grosse
Mar. 2	Prinzess Irene
Mar. 14	Neckar
Mar. 21	Koenigin Luise
Apr. 1	Koenig Albert
Apr. 3	Fried. der Grosse
Apr. 12	Prinzess Irene
Apr. 24	Neckar
Apr. 27	Barbarossa
May 2	Koenigin Luise
May 8	Koenig Albert
May 16	Fried. der Grosse
May 23	Prinzess Irene
May 31	Neckar
June 7	Barbarossa
June 14	Koenigin Luise
June 20	Koenig Albert

NORTH GERMAN LLOYD
Mediterranean—New York
(Continued)

N. Y.

Arrival	Steamer
July 3	Prinzess Irene
July 10	Neckar
July 18	Koenigin Luise
Aug. 1	Koenig Albert
Aug. 15	Prinzess Irene
Aug. 21	Neckar
Aug. 28	Koenigin Luise
Sept. 5	Koenig Albert
Sept. 18	Prinzess Irene
Oct. 3	Koenigin Luise
Oct. 10	Koenig Albert
Oct. 16	Neckar
Oct. 25	Prinzess Irene
Nov. 9	Koenigin Luise
Nov. 21	Koenig Albert
Nov. 27	Neckar
Dec. 5	Fried. der Grosse
Dec. 21	Koenigin Luise

NORTH GERMAN LLOYD
Bremen—Baltimore

Baltimore

Arrival	Steamer
Jan. 17	Breslau
Jan. 24	Brandenburg
Feb. 3	Hannover
Feb. 6	Oldenburg
Feb. 15	Darmstadt
Feb. 24	Frankfurt
Mar. 1	Breslau
Mar. 8	Koeln
Mar. 14	Oldenburg
Mar. 19	Cassel
Mar. 22	Gera
Mar. 30	Hannover
Apr. 1	Prof. Woermann
Apr. 6	Wittekind
Apr. 13	Stuttgart
Apr. 18	Weimer
Apr. 26	Halle
Apr. 26	Cassel
Apr. 26	Willehad
May 1	Koeln
May 4	Frankfurt
May 8	Karlsruhe
May 11	Hannover
May 17	Wittekind
May 18	Breslau
May 25	Weimer
May 31	Chemnitz
June 4	Gera
June 6	Darmstadt
June 14	Koeln
June 17	Rhein
June 22	Cassel
June 27	Breslau
July 4	Frankfurt
July 9	Main
July 20	Brandenburg
July 26	Hannover
Aug. 3	Rhein
Aug. 8	Breslau
Aug. 15	Chemnitz
Aug. 23	Main
Aug. 28	Cassel

Year 1907

NORTH GERMAN LLOYD
Bremen—Baltimore
(Continued)

Baltimore

Arrival	Steamer
Sept. 4	Rhein
Sept. 11	Breslau
Sept. 26	Koeln
Oct. 4	Brandenburg
Oct. 9	Cassel
Oct. 11	Hannover
Oct. 17	Chemnitz
Oct. 25	Rhein
Oct. 31	Breslau
Nov. 6	Willehad
Nov. 8	Frankfurt
Nov. 14	Brandenburg
Nov. 22	Cassel
Nov. 28	Hannover
Nov. 28	Oldenburg
Dec. 1	Rhein
Dec. 10	Koeln
Dec. 16	Willehad
Dec. 21	Chemnitz
Dec. 27	Brandenburg

PRINCE LINE
Mediterranean—New York

N. Y.

Arrival	Steamer
Jan. 15	Napolitan Prince
Feb. 7	Sicilian Prince
Mar. 29	Napolitan Prince
Apr. 13	Sicilian Prince
May 15	Napolitan Prince
June 3	Sicilian Prince
July 5	Napolitan Prince
July 22	Sicilian Prince
Sept. 15	Napolitan Prince
Oct. 6	Sicilian Prince
Nov. 4	Napolitan Prince
Nov. 28	Sicilian Prince
Dec. 28	Napolitan Prince

RED STAR LINE
Antwerp—New York

N. Y.

Arrival	Steamer
Jan. 7	Samland
Jan. 9	Finland
Jan. 29	Kroonland
Feb. 10	Westernland
Feb. 12	Finland
Feb. 21	Samland
Feb. 26	Zeeland
Mar. 5	Kroonland
Mar. 14	Vaderland
Mar. 19	Finland
Mar. 25	Cambroman
Mar. 26	Zeeland
Apr. 2	Kroonland
Apr. 11	Vaderland
Apr. 16	Finland
Apr. 23	Zeeland
Apr. 30	Kroonland
May 3	Cambroman

RED STAR LINE
Antwerp—New York
(Continued)

N. Y.

Arrival	Steamer
May 7	Vaderland
May 13	Finland
May 13	Samland
May 21	Zeeland
May 28	Kroonland
June 3	Vaderland
June 12	Finland
June 17	Cambroman
June 18	Zeeland
June 27	Samland
July 3	Vaderland
July 9	Kroonland
July 17	Zeeland
July 24	Finland
July 30	Vaderland
Aug. 6	Kroonland
Aug. 13	Zeeland
Aug. 20	Finland
Aug. 26	Vaderland
Sept. 3	Kroonland
Sept. 9	Zeeland
Sept. 16	Finland
Sept. 23	Vaderland
Sept. 30	Kroonland
Oct. 8	Zeeland
Oct. 14	Finland
Oct. 22	Vaderland
Oct. 29	Kroonland
Nov. 6	Samland
Nov. 11	Zeeland
Nov. 23	Cambroman
Nov. 28	Merion
Dec. 3	Vaderland
Dec. 13	Samland
Dec. 24	Zeeland

RED STAR LINE
Antwerp—Phila.—Boston

Boston

Arrival	Steamer
Jan. 4	Menominee
Jan. 23	Marquette
Feb. 6	Manitou
Mar. 5	Marquette
Mar. 20	Manitou
Apr. 16	Marquette
Apr. 29	Manitou
May 14	Menominee
May 27	Marquette
June 12	Manitou
June 25	Menominee
July 9	Marquette
July 22	Manitou
Aug. 12	Menominee
Aug. 26	Marquette
Sept. 12	Manitou
Sept. 24	Menominee
Oct. 8	Marquette
Oct. 22	Manitou
Nov. 5	Menominee
Nov. 19	Marquette
Dec. 4	Manitou
Dec. 19	Menominee

RUSSIAN EAST ASIATIC STEAMSHIP COMPANY
Libau—New York

N. Y.

Arrival	Steamer
Feb. 10	Korea
Mar. 26	Livonia
May 26	Korea
June 10	Arconia
June 20	Livonia
July 5	Estonia
July 19	Lituania
Aug. 2	Arconia
Aug. 17	Korea
Aug. 30	Estonia
Sept. 13	Lituania
Oct. 3	Arconia
Oct. 13	Korea
Oct. 26	Estonia
Nov. 29	Arconia
Dec. 8	Korea
Dec. 22	Lituania

RUSSIAN VOLUNTEER FLEET
Libau—New York

N. Y.

Arrival	Steamer
Jan. 15	Smolensk
Feb. 21	Petersburg
Mar. 12	Smolensk
Apr. 12	Petersburg
May 2	Smolensk
May 30	Moskova
June 13	Petersburg
June 27	Smolensk
July 13	Saratov
July 24	Moskova
Aug. 8	Petersburg
Aug. 23	Smolensk
Sept. 4	Saratov
Sept. 18	Moskova
Oct. 2	Petersburg
Oct. 17	Smolensk
Oct. 31	Saratov
Nov. 13	Petersburg
Nov. 30	Smolensk
Dec. 13	Kherson
Dec. 27	Saratov

SCANDINAVIAN AMERICAN LINE
Scandinavian Ports—New York

N. Y.

Arrival	Steamer
Jan. 24	C. F. Tietgen
Feb. 6	Oscar II
Feb. 20	Hellig Olav
Mar. 6	United States
Mar. 14	C. F. Tietgen
Mar. 21	Oscar II
Apr. 3	Hellig Olav
Apr. 16	United States
Apr. 24	C. F. Tietgen
Apr. 30	Oscar II
May 14	Hellig Olav
May 27	United States

Year 1907

SCANDINAVIAN-AMERICAN LINE
Scandinavian Ports—New York
(Continued)

N. Y.

Arrival	Steamer
June 4	C. F. Tietgen
June 11	Oscar II
June 26	Hellig Olav
July 9	United States
July 16	C. F. Tietgen
July 23	Oscar II
Aug. 6	Hellig Olav
Aug. 19	United States
Aug. 27	C. F. Tietgen
Sept. 3	Oscar II
Sept. 17	Hellig Olav
Oct. 1	United States
Oct. 9	C. F. Tietgen
Oct. 15	Oscar II
Oct. 30	Hellig Olav
Nov. 12	United States
Nov. 21	C. F. Tietgen
Nov. 27	Oscar II
Dec. 11	Hellig Olav
Dec. 26	United States

SICULA-AMERICANA
Mediterranean—New York

N. Y.

Arrival	Steamer
Mar. 26	Italia
May 13	Italia
July 3	Italia
Aug. 8	San Giorgio
Aug. 27	Italia
Sept. 28	San Giorgio
Oct. 18	Italia
Oct. 31	San Giovanni
Nov. 14	San Giorgio
Dec. 7	Italia
Dec. 8	San Giovanni
Dec. 28	San Giorgio

WHITE STAR LINE
Liverpool—New York

N. Y.

Arrival	Steamer
Jan. 3	Teutonic
Jan. 11	Celtic
Jan. 17	Majestic
Jan. 25	Arabic
Jan. 31	Teutonic
Feb. 8	Baltic
Feb. 15	Majestic
Feb. 20	Oceanic
Feb. 28	Teutonic
Mar. 8	Baltic
Mar. 14	Majestic
Mar. 21	Oceanic
Mar. 28	Teutonic
Apr. 5	Baltic
Apr. 11	Majestic
Apr. 15	Cedric
Apr. 17	Oceanic
Apr. 25	Teutonic
May 2	Baltic

WHITE STAR LINE
Liverpool—New York
(Continued)

N. Y.

Arrival	Steamer
May 9	Majestic
May 12	Cedric
May 16	Adriatic
May 23	Teutonic
May 29	Oceanic
June 6	Majestic
June 8	Baltic
June 14	Cedric
June 22	Celtic
June 29	Arabic
July 5	Baltic
July 12	Cedric
July 20	Celtic
July 27	Arabic
Aug. 3	Baltic
Aug. 9	Cedric
Aug. 17	Celtic
Aug. 23	Arabic
Aug. 30	Baltic
Sept. 6	Cedric
Sept. 13	Celtic
Sept. 20	Arabic
Sept. 27	Baltic
Oct. 4	Cedric
Oct. 11	Celtic
Oct. 19	Arabic
Oct. 26	Baltic
Nov. 2	Cedric
Nov. 8	Celtic
Nov. 16	Arabic
Nov. 22	Baltic
Nov. 30	Cedric
Dec. 7	Celtic
Dec. 15	Arabic
Dec. 21	Baltic
Dec. 29	Cedric

WHITE STAR LINE
Southampton—New York

N. Y.

Arrival	Steamer
June 13	Adriatic
June 20	Teutonic
June 26	Oceanic
July 4	Majestic
July 11	Adriatic
July 18	Teutonic
July 24	Oceanic
Aug. 1	Majestic
Aug. 8	Adriatic
Aug. 15	Teutonic
Aug. 21	Oceanic
Aug. 28	Majestic
Sept. 5	Adriatic
Sept. 11	Teutonic
Sept. 18	Oceanic
Sept. 26	Majestic
Oct. 3	Adriatic
Oct. 10	Teutonic
Oct. 16	Oceanic
Oct. 24	Majestic
Oct. 31	Adriatic
Nov. 7	Teutonic
Nov. 13	Oceanic
Nov. 21	Majestic

WHITE STAR LINE
Southampton—New York
(Continued)

N. Y.

Arrival	Steamer
Nov. 28	Adriatic
Dec. 5	Teutonic
Dec. 12	Oceanic
Dec. 19	Majestic
Dec. 27	Adriatic

WHITE STAR LINE
Mediterranean—New York

N. Y.

Arrival	Steamer
Feb. 11	Cedric
Feb. 26	Celtic
Mar. 18	Cedric
Mar. 26	Cretic
Mar. 31	Celtic
Apr. 17	Republic
May 3	Cretic
May 23	Republic
June 15	Cretic
July 27	Cretic
Sept. 21	Cretic
Nov. 1	Cretic
Nov. 24	Republic
Dec. 8	Cretic

WHITE STAR LINE
Liverpool—Boston

Boston

Arrival	Steamer
Jan. 13	Cymric
Feb. 18	Cymric
Mar. 25	Cymric
Apr. 22	Cymric
May 4	Arabic
May 20	Cymric
June 1	Arabic
June 14	Cymric
June 27	Republic
July 12	Cymric
July 25	Republic
Aug. 9	Cymric
Aug. 22	Republic
Sept. 6	Cymric
Sept. 19	Republic
Oct. 4	Cymric
Oct. 17	Republic
Nov. 2	Cymric
Nov. 29	Cymric

WHITE STAR LINE
Mediterranean—Boston

Boston

Arrival	Steamer
Jan. 9	Canopic
Jan. 24	Republic
Feb. 19	Canopic
Mar. 11	Republic
Apr. 7	Canopic
Apr. 22	Romanic
May 13	Canopic
June 3	Romanic

Year 1907

WHITE STAR LINE
Mediterranean—Boston
(Continued)

Boston Arrival	Steamer
June 24	Canopic
July 8	Romanic
Aug. 2	Canopic
Sept. 5	Romanic
Sept. 30	Canopic
Oct. 21	Romanic
Nov. 11	Canopic
Nov. 28	Romanic

ADDITIONAL ARRIVALS
Mediterranean—New York
N. Y.

Arrival	Steamer
Jan. 16	Massilia (Fabre, Marseilles)
Jan. 26	Gallia (Fabre, Marseilles)
Feb. 21	Neustria (Fabre, Marseilles)
Feb. 21	Gregory Morch (R's'n-Odessa Line)
Mar. 12	Massilia (Fabre, Marseilles)
Apr. 20	Neustria (Fabre, Marseilles)

ADDITIONAL ARRIVALS
Mediterranean—New York
(Continued)
N. Y.

Arrival	Steamer
Apr. 27	America (Fabre, Marseilles)
July 9	America (Fabre, Marseilles)
Aug. 21	Gallia (Fabre, Marseilles)
Sept. 2	America (Fabre, Marseilles)
Nov. 1	Gallia (Fabre, Marseilles

Year 1908

ALLAN LINE	
Glasgow—Boston	
Boston	
Arrival	**Steamer**
Jan. 2........	Carthaginian
Jan. 25...........	Corinthian
Feb. 6.........	Laurentian
Feb. 19..........	Mongolian
Mar. 4..........	Corinthian
Mar. 18..........	Laurentian
Apr. 2..........	Pretorian
May 12..........	Laurentian
May 31..........	Numidian
June 16..........	Laurentian
June 30...........	Numidian
July 13..........	Laurentian
July 27..........	Numidian
Aug. 10..........	Laurentian
Aug. 13...........	Grampian
Aug. 24..........	Numidian
Aug. 26..........	Numidian
Sept. 7..........	Laurentian
Sept. 22..........	Numidian
Oct. 5..........	Laurentian
Oct. 20..........	Numidian
Nov. 4..........	Laurentian
Dec. 1..........	Hesperian
Dec. 18..........	Laurentian

AMERICAN LINE	
Southampton—New York	
N.Y.	
Arrival	**Steamer**
Jan. 5........	Philadelphia
Jan. 11............	St. Paul
Jan. 19..........	New York
Jan. 27............	St. Louis
Feb. 2..........	Philadelphia
Feb. 9............	St. Paul
Feb. 16..........	New York
Feb. 23............	St. Louis
Feb. 29..........	Philadelphia
Mar. 8............	St. Paul
Mar. 15..........	New York
Mar. 21............	St. Louis
Mar. 29..........	Philadelphia
Apr. 6............	St. Paul
Apr. 12..........	New York
Apr. 19............	St. Louis
Apr. 25..........	Philadelphia
May 9..........	New York
May 17............	St. Louis
May 23..........	Philadelphia
June 6..........	New York
June 13............	St. Louis
June 20..........	Philadelphia
June 27..........	St. Paul
July 4..........	New York
July 12............	St. Louis
July 25.........	Philadelphia
Aug. 1............	St. Paul
Aug. 8..........	New York
Aug. 15............	St. Louis
Aug. 22.........	Philadelphia
Aug. 29............	St. Paul
Sept. 5..........	New York
Sept. 12............	St. Louis

AMERICAN LINE	
Southampton—New York	
(Continued)	
N.Y.	
Arrival	**Steamer**
Sept. 19........	Philadelphia
Sept. 26............	St. Paul
Oct. 3..........	New York
Oct. 10............	St. Louis
Oct. 17........	Philadelphia
Oct. 24............	St. Paul
Nov. 1............	New York
Nov. 7............	St. Louis
Nov. 14........	Philadelphia
Nov. 22............	St. Paul
Nov. 29..........	New York
Dec. 6............	St. Louis
Dec. 13........	Philadelphia
Dec. 21............	St. Paul
Dec. 27..........	New York

AMERICAN LINE	
Liverpool—Philadelphia	
Phila.	
Arrival	**Steamer**
Jan. 1..........	Friesland
Jan. 13..........	Haverford
Jan. 29...........	Merion
Feb. 17..........	Haverford
Mar. 5............	Merion
Mar. 26..........	Haverford
Apr. 8...........	Merion
Apr. 21..........	Friesland
Apr. 27..........	Haverford
May 11...........	Merion
May 25..........	Friesland
June 1..........	Haverford
June 7........	Westernland
June 14...........	Merion
June 23..........	Noordland
June 28..........	Friesland
July 6..........	Haverford
July 20...........	Merion
Aug. 2...........	Friesland
Aug. 10..........	Haverford
Aug. 23...........	Merion
Aug. 31..........	Noordland
Sept. 6..........	Friesland
Sept. 14..........	Haverford
Sept. 20........	Westernland
Sept. 28...........	Merion
Oct. 11..........	Friesland
Oct. 20..........	Haverford
Nov. 1...........	Merion
Nov. 15..........	Friesland
Nov. 25..........	Haverford
Dec. 8............	Merion
Dec. 31..........	Dominion

ANCHOR LINE	
Glasgow—New York	
N.Y.	
Arrival	**Steamer**
Jan. 7..........	Furnessia
Jan. 25............	Astoria
Jan. 28..........	California
Feb. 4..........	Caledonia

ANCHOR LINE	
Glasgow—New York	
(Continued)	
N.Y.	
Arrival	**Steamer**
Feb. 10..........	Columbia
Feb. 25..........	California
Mar. 2..........	Caledonia
Mar. 9...........	Columbia
Mar. 18..........	Furnessia
Mar. 23..........	California
Mar. 30..........	Caledonia
Apr. 7..........	Columbia
Apr. 15..........	Furnessia
Apr. 20..........	California
Apr. 26..........	Caledonia
May 3..........	Columbia
May 11..........	Furnessia
May 18..........	California
May 24..........	Caledonia
May 31..........	Columbia
June 8..........	Furnessia
June 14..........	California
June 21..........	Caledonia
June 28..........	Columbia
July 12..........	California
July 20..........	Caledonia
July 26..........	Columbia
Aug. 10..........	California
Aug. 16..........	Caledonia
Aug. 23..........	Columbia
Sept. 1...........	Furnessia
Sept. 6..........	California
Sept. 13..........	Caledonia
Sept. 20..........	Columbia
Sept. 29..........	Furnessia
Oct. 5..........	California
Oct. 11..........	Caledonia
Oct. 19..........	Columbia
Oct. 27..........	Furnessia
Nov. 1..........	California
Nov. 8..........	Caledonia
Nov. 15..........	Columbia
Dec. 3..........	California
Dec. 7..........	Caledonia
Dec. 16..........	Columbia
Dec. 29..........	California

ANCHOR LINE	
Mediterranean—New York	
N.Y.	
Arrival	**Steamer**
Jan. 7............	Algeria
Jan. 27............	Calabria
Feb. 20............	Italia
Mar. 17............	Perugia
Mar. 30............	Algeria
Apr. 10............	Calabria
Apr. 30............	Italia
May 22............	Perugia
June 15............	Algeria
July 4............	Calabria
Aug. 14............	Italia
Sept. 29............	Algeria
Oct. 25............	Italia
Dec. 17............	Perugia

Year 1908

ATLANTIC TRANS. LINE
London—New York

N. Y.

Arrival	Steamer
Jan. 4	Minnehaha
Jan. 19	Minnetonka
Feb. 3	Minneapolis
Feb. 23	Minnetonka
Mar. 3	Mesaba
Mar. 8	Minneapolis
Mar. 15	Minnehaha
Apr. 8	Mesaba
Apr. 12	Minnetonka
Apr. 21	Minnehaha
May 5	Minneapolis
May 11	Minnetonka
May 20	Mesaba
May 26	Minnehaha
June 2	Minneapolis
June 8	Minnetonka
June 16	Mesaba
June 22	Minnehaha
June 29	Minneapolis
July 6	Minnetonka
July 14	Mesaba
July 20	Minnehaha
July 27	Minneapolis
Aug. 3	Minnetonka
Aug. 11	Mesaba
Aug. 17	Minnehaha
Aug. 24	Minneapolis
Aug. 31	Minnetonka
Sept. 8	Minnehaha
Sept. 22	Minneapolis
Sept. 28	Minnetonka
Oct. 6	Mesaba
Oct. 12	Minnehaha
Oct. 19	Minneapolis
Oct. 26	Minnetonka
Nov. 4	Mesaba
Nov. 9	Minnehaha
Nov. 16	Minneapolis
Nov. 28	Minnetonka
Dec. 13	Minnehaha
Dec. 20	Minneapolis

AUSTRO-AMERICANA LINE
Mediterranean—New York

N. Y.

Arrival	Steamer
Jan. 14	Gerty
Jan. 26	Laura
Feb. 18	Alice
Mar. 4	Eugenia
Mar. 25	Laura
Apr. 1	Francesca
Apr. 1	Carolina
Apr. 13	Ida
Apr. 14	Alice
May 3	Argentina
May 15	Laura
May 28	Alice
June 7	Martha Washington
June 17	Argentina
July 1	Laura
July 9	Eugenia
July 14	Alice
July 23	Irene

AUSTRO-AMERICANA LINE
Mediterranean—New York
(Continued)

N. Y.

Arrival	Steamer
July 29	Martha Washington
Aug. 7	Argentina
Aug. 27	Alice
Sept. 26	Argentina
Oct. 2	Laura
Oct. 17	Oceania
Oct. 27	Martha Washington
Nov. 5	Alice
Nov. 14	Argentina
Nov. 19	Laura
Dec. 8	Oceania
Dec. 12	Martha Washington
Dec. 25	Alice

CUNARD LINE
Liverpool—New York

N. Y.

Arrival	Steamer
Jan. 3	Lusitania
Jan. 13	Carmania
Jan. 17	Mauretania
Jan. 25	Campania
Feb. 1	Lusitania
Feb. 8	Lucania
Feb. 16	Etruria
Feb. 22	Campania
Feb. 28	Mauretania
Mar. 7	Lucania
Mar. 13	Lusitania
Mar. 22	Etruria
Mar. 26	Carmania
Mar. 27	Mauretania
Apr. 3	Umbria
Apr. 5	Lucania
Apr. 9	Caronia
Apr. 10	Lusitania
Apr. 16	Etruria
Apr. 17	Mauretania
Apr. 23	Carmania
Apr. 25	Lucania
Apr. 29	Campania
May 1	Lusitania
May 7	Caronia
May 8	Mauretania
May 14	Etruria
May 16	Lucania
May 21	Carmania
May 22	Lusitania
May 30	Campania
June 1	Mauretania
June 6	Caronia
June 11	Umbria
June 12	Lusitania
June 18	Carmania
June 19	Mauretania
June 25	Etruria
June 27	Campania
July 1	Caronia
July 4	Lucania
July 9	Umbria
July 10	Lusitania
July 16	Carmania
July 17	Mauretania

CUNARD LINE
Liverpool—New York
(Continued)

N. Y.

Arrival	Steamer
July 22	Campania
July 25	Lucania
July 29	Etruria
July 31	Lusitania
Aug. 6	Umbria
Aug. 7	Mauretania
Aug. 12	Caronia
Aug. 15	Lucania
Aug. 18	Campania
Aug. 20	Lusitania
Aug. 26	Carmania
Aug. 28	Mauretania
Sept. 4	Lucania
Sept. 5	Umbria
Sept. 9	Caronia
Sept. 10	Lusitania
Sept. 16	Etruria
Sept. 18	Mauretania
Sept. 24	Carmania
Sept. 26	Campania
Oct. 1	Umbria
Oct. 3	Lucania
Oct. 7	Caronia
Oct. 9	Lusitania
Oct. 16	Mauretania
Oct. 24	Campania
Oct. 30	Lusitania
Nov. 7	Lucania
Nov. 14	Caronia
Nov. 20	Lusitania
Nov. 28	Campania
Dec. 5	Lucania
Dec. 11	Lusitania
Dec. 20	Campania
Dec. 26	Lucania

CUNARD LINE
Mediterranean—Adriatic—
New York

N. Y.

Arrival	Steamer
Feb. 12	Caronia
Feb. 23	Carmania
Mar. 4	Slavonia
Mar. 19	Pannonia
Mar. 25	Carpathia
Apr. 8	Ultonia
Apr. 23	Slavonia
May 6	Pannonia
May 19	Carpathia
May 26	Ultonia
June 10	Slavonia
June 24	Pannonia
July 7	Carpathia
July 15	Ultonia
July 29	Slavonia
Aug. 12	Pannonia
Aug. 26	Carpathia
Sept. 2	Ultonia
Sept. 17	Slavonia
Oct. 2	Pannonia
Oct. 15	Carpathia
Oct. 23	Ultonia
Nov. 7	Slavonia
Nov. 12	Ultonia

Year 1908

CUNARD LINE
Mediterranean—Adriatic—
New York
(Continued)

N. Y.

Arrival	Steamer
Nov. 21	Pannonia
Dec. 2	Carpathia
Dec. 28	Slavonia

CUNARD LINE
Liverpool—Boston

Boston

Arrival	Steamer
Jan. 16	Ivernia
Jan. 30	Saxonia
Feb. 13	Ivernia
Feb. 27	Saxonia
Mar. 19	Ivernia
Apr. 3	Saxonia
Apr. 16	Ivernia
Apr. 30	Saxonia
May 14	Ivernia
May 29	Saxonia
June 11	Ivernia
June 25	Saxonia
July 9	Ivernia
July 23	Saxonia
Aug. 5	Ivernia
Aug. 20	Saxonia
Sept. 3	Ivernia
Sept. 17	Saxonia
Oct. 1	Ivernia
Oct. 16	Saxonia
Oct. 29	Ivernia
Nov. 12	Saxonia
Nov. 26	Ivernia
Dec. 11	Saxonia
Dec. 24	Ivernia

FABRE LINE
Mediterranean—New York

N. Y.

Arrival	Steamer
Jan. 10	Venezia
Jan. 31	Roma
Feb. 12	Germania
Feb. 25	Venezia
Mar. 8	Madonna
Mar. 24	Roma
Apr. 1	Germania
Apr. 10	Venezia
Apr. 28	Madonna
May 7	Roma
May 19	Germania
May 28	Venezia
June 16	Madonna
July 3	Germania
July 16	Venezia
Aug. 2	Madonna
Aug. 19	Germania
Sept. 1	Venezia
Sept. 16	Madonna
Sept. 29	Roma
Oct. 7	Germania
Oct. 18	Venezia
Nov. 4	Madonna
Dec. 2	Venezia
Dec. 24	Madonna

FRENCH LINE
(Compagnie Generale Transatlantique)
Havre, Bordeaux—New York

N. Y.

Arrival	Steamer
Jan. 6	La Gascogne
Jan. 11	La Lorraine
Jan. 20	La Bretagne
Jan. 26	La Touraine
Feb. 2	La Savoie
Feb. 8	La Lorraine
Feb. 17	La Bretagne
Feb. 23	La Touraine
Feb. 28	La Savoie
Mar. 6	La Provence
Mar. 16	La Bretagne
Mar. 21	La Touraine
Mar. 31	La Gascogne
Apr. 4	La Provence
Apr. 11	La Lorraine
Apr. 18	La Touraine
Apr. 25	La Savoie
Apr. 26	Californie
May 2	La Provence
May 9	La Lorraine
May 16	La Touraine
May 23	La Savoie
May 26	Louisiane
May 30	La Provence
June 7	La Lorraine
June 13	La Savoie
June 10	Chicago
June 18	Californie
June 19	La Provence
June 29	La Lorraine
July 4	La Touraine
July 13	La Bretagne
July 17	La Provence
July 19	Louisiane
July 27	La Touraine
July 31	La Savoie
Aug. 10	La Bretagne
Aug. 14	Californie
Aug. 15	La Lorraine
Aug. 19	Floride
Aug. 22	La Touraine
Aug. 31	La Gascogne
Aug. 31	Chicago
Sept. 4	La Provence
Sept. 12	Louisiane
Sept. 12	La Lorraine
Sept. 19	La Savoie
Sept. 26	La Provence
Sept. 29	Chicago
Oct. 3	La Lorraine
Oct. 9	Californie
Oct. 11	La Touraine
Oct. 17	La Savoie
Oct. 23	Louisiane
Oct. 23	La Provence
Oct. 26	Chicago
Oct. 31	La Lorraine
Nov. 7	La Touraine
Nov. 12	Hudson
Nov. 14	La Savoie
Nov. 21	La Provence
Nov. 28	La Lorraine
Dec. 6	La Touraine
Dec. 7	Chicago
Dec. 7	Louisiane

FRENCH LINE
(Compagnie Generale Transatlantique)
Havre, Bordeaux—New York
(Continued)

N. Y.

Arrival	Steamer
Dec. 8	Californie
Dec. 15	La Bretagne
Dec. 20	La Provence
Dec. 26	La Lorraine

HAMBURG-AMERICAN LINE
Hamburg—New York

N. Y.

Arrival	Steamer
Jan. 4	Patricia
Jan. 7	Bluecher
Jan. 24	Graf Waldersee
Jan. 24	President Lincoln
Jan. 25	Amerika
Feb. 1	Pennsylvania
Feb. 7	K. Aug. Victoria
Feb. 17	Albano
Feb. 21	Pretoria
Feb. 29	Amerika
Mar. 14	Graf Waldersee
Mar. 21	Pennsylvania
Mar. 28	Patricia
Apr. 5	Amerika
Apr. 8	Pretoria
Apr. 17	President Lincoln
Apr. 18	K. Aug. Victoria
Apr. 23	Deutschland
Apr. 25	President Grant
Apr. 30	Pennsylvania
May 2	Amerika
May 10	Bluecher
May 16	K. Aug. Victoria
May 16	Pretoria
May 21	Deutschland
May 22	Graf Waldersee
May 29	Amerika
May 27	President Lincoln
June 3	President Grant
June 7	Bluecher
June 10	Pennsylvania
June 13	K. Aug. Victoria
June 18	Patricia
June 18	Deutschland
June 27	Amerika
June 27	Pretoria
July 8	President Lincoln
July 11	K. Aug. Victoria
July 16	Deutschland
July 23	Pennsylvania
July 30	Patricia
Aug. 1	Amerika
Aug. 6	Pretoria
Aug. 9	Bluecher
Aug. 13	Graf Waldersee
Aug. 15	K. Aug. Victoria
Aug. 18	President Lincoln
Aug. 20	Deutschland
Aug. 25	President Grant
Aug. 29	Amerika
Sept. 4	Pennsylvania
Sept. 6	Bluecher
Sept. 10	Patricia
Sept. 11	Hamburg

Year 1908

HAMBURG-AMERICAN LINE
Hamburg—New York
(Continued)

N. Y.

Arrival	Steamer
Sept. 11	K. Aug. Victoria
Sept. 17	Deutschland
Sept. 18	Pretoria
Sept. 25	Graf Waldersee
Sept. 26	Amerika
Sept. 30	President Lincoln
Oct. 2	Moltke
Oct. 4	Bluecher
Oct. 7	President Grant
Oct. 9	K. Aug. Victoria
Oct. 16	Deutschland
Oct. 16	Pennsylvania
Oct. 22	Patricia
Oct. 25	Amerika
Oct. 30	Pretoria
Nov. 3	Bluecher
Nov. 7	K. Aug. Victoria
Nov. 14	President Lincoln
Nov. 21	Amerika
Dec. 6	Patricia
Dec. 8	K. Aug. Victoria
Dec. 21	Amerika
Dec. 25	Pretoria

HAMBURG-AMERICAN LINE
Mediterranean—New York

N. Y.

Arrival	Steamer
Jan. 23	Moltke
Feb. 11	Hamburg
Mar. 25	Hamburg
Apr. 18	Moltke
May 10	Hamburg
May 26	Moltke
June 23	Hamburg
July 6	Moltke
Oct. 17	Hamburg
Nov. 21	Batavia
Nov. 30	Moltke
Dec. 23	Hamburg

HELLENIC TRANS. LINE
Italy—Greece—New York

N. Y.

Arrival	Steamer
Jan. 27	Moraitis
Apr. 3	Moraitis
May 25	Moraitis
July 29	Moraitis
Sept. 30	Moraitis
Dec. 7	Themistocles

HOLLAND-AMERICA LINE
Rotterdam—New York

N. Y.

Arrival	Steamer
Jan. 1	Statendam
Jan. 14	Ryndam

HOLLAND-AMERICA LINE
Rotterdam—New York
(Continued)

N. Y.

Arrival	Steamer
Jan. 29	Noordam
Feb. 6	Statendam
Feb. 18	Ryndam
Mar. 3	Noordam
Mar. 10	Statendam
Mar. 24	Ryndam
Apr. 1	Potsdam
Apr. 8	Noordam
Apr. 15	Statendam
Apr. 20	New Amsterdam
Apr. 29	Ryndam
May 11	Noordam
May 19	Statendam
May 25	New Amsterdam
June 2	Ryndam
June 9	Potsdam
June 16	Noordam
June 22	Rotterdam
June 29	New Amsterdam
July 7	Ryndam
July 21	Noordam
Aug. 3	Rotterdam
Aug. 10	New Amsterdam
Aug. 17	Ryndam
Aug. 24	Statendam
Sept. 1	Noordam
Sept. 7	Rotterdam
Sept. 14	New Amsterdam
Sept. 22	Ryndam
Sept. 29	Statendam
Oct. 5	Noordam
Oct. 12	Rotterdam
Oct. 19	New Amsterdam
Oct. 27	Ryndam
Nov. 3	Statendam
Nov. 9	Noordam
Nov. 25	New Amsterdam
Dec. 1	Ryndam
Dec. 9	Statendam
Dec. 23	Noordam

INSULAR NAVIGATION COMPANY
Azores—Lisbon—New York

N. Y.

Arrival	Steamer
Jan. 11	Peninsular
June 1	Peninsular
July 15	Peninsular

ITALIA LINE
Mediterranean—New York

N. Y.

Arrival	Steamer
Apr. 10	Ancona
June 1	Ancona
July 17	Ancona
Aug. 25	Verona
Sept. 19	Taormina
Oct. 14	Verona
Nov. 6	Toarmina
Dec. 19	Ancona

LA VELOCE LINE
Mediterranean—New York

N. Y.

Arrival	Steamer
Jan. 14	Nord America
Feb. 11	Europa
Feb. 27	Nord America
Mar. 31	Brasile
Apr. 24	Nord America
May 14	Brasile
June 8	Nord America
June 24	Brasile
July 24	Nord America
Aug. 18	Europa
Sept. 16	Nord America
Oct. 27	Nord America
Dec. 6	Nord America

LEYLAND LINE
Liverpool—Boston

Boston

Arrival	Steamer
Mar. 25	Devonian
Apr. 3	Canadian
Apr. 9	Winifredian
Apr. 22	Bohemian
May 11	Winifredian
June 5	Devonian
June 14	Winifredian
June 24	Canadian
July 7	Devonian
Aug. 5	Cestrian
Aug. 19	Bohemian
Aug. 25	Winifredian
Sept. 1	Devonian
Sept. 9	Cestrian
Sept. 15	Canadian
Sept. 22	Bohemian
Sept. 29	Winifredian
Oct. 5	Devonian
Oct. 26	Bohemian
Nov. 4	Winifredian
Nov. 11	Canadian
Nov. 18	Devonian
Nov. 24	Bohemian

LLOYD ITALIANO
Mediterranean—New York

N. Y.

Arrival	Steamer
Jan. 23	Mendoza
Mar. 4	Florida
Mar. 24	Luisiana
Apr. 20	Florida
May 9	Luisiana
June 6	Florida
June 30	Indiana
July 30	Luisiana
Sept. 11	Luisiana
Oct. 18	Indiana
Nov. 11	Luisiana
Nov. 29	Indiana
Dec. 23	Luisiana

LLOYD SABAUDO
Mediterranean—New York

N. Y.

Arrival	Steamer
Feb. 28	Princ. di Piemonte
Mar. 22	Regina d'Italia

Year 1908

LLOYD SABAUDO
Mediterranean—New York
(Continued)

N.Y. Arrival	Steamer
Apr. 4	Re d'Italia
Apr. 24	Princ. di Piemonte
May 16	Regina d'Italia
June 1	Principe di Udine
July 2	Princ. di Piemonte
Aug. 13	Re d'Italia
Sept. 16	Princ. di Piemonte
Oct. 7	Re d'Italia
Oct. 23	Regina d'Italia
Nov. 24	Re d'Italia
Dec. 4	Regina d'Italia

NAVIGAZIONE GENE-RALE ITALIANA
Mediterranean—New York

N.Y. Arrival	Steamer
Jan. 8	Sannio
Jan. 31	Lazio
Feb. 17	Duca degli Abruzzi
Mar. 20	Sannio
Mar. 31	Duca degli Abruzzi
Apr. 23	Campagnia
May 12	Duca degli Abruzzi
May 29	Liguria
June 17	Duca degli Abruzzi
July 11	Sannio
Aug. 6	Liguria
Sept. 1	Duca degli Abruzzi
Sept. 30	Sannio
Oct. 10	Duca degli Abruzzi
Nov. 2	Duca di Genoa
Nov. 27	Lombardia
Dec. 8	Duca di Genoa
Dec. 24	Liguria

N.Y. AND CONTINENTAL LINE
Rotterdam, Hamburg—New York

N.Y. Arrival	Steamer
Apr. 9	Volturno
Apr. 26	Avoca
May 2	Jelunga
June 13	Jelunga
July 18	Jelunga
Aug. 13	Volturno

NORTH GERMAN LLOYD
Express Service
Bremen—New York

N.Y. Arrival	Steamer
Jan. 14	Kronprinzes. Cecilie
Jan. 31	Kaiser Wilhelm II
Feb. 11	Kronprinzes. Cecilie
Feb. 26	Kaiser Wilhelm II
Mar. 11	Kronprinzes. Cecilie
Mar. 18	Kronprinz Wilhelm
Mar. 25	Kaiser Wilhelm II
Apr. 2	K. Wm. der Grosse
Apr. 8	Kronprinzes. Cecilie

NORTH GERMAN LLOYD
Bremen—New York
(Continued)

N.Y. Arrival	Steamer
Apr. 15	Kronprinz Wilhelm
Apr. 21	Kaiser Wilhelm II
Apr. 29	K. Wm. der Grosse
May 6	Kronprinzes. Cecilie
May 13	Kronprinz Wilhelm
May 20	Kaiser Wilhelm II
May 27	K. Wm. der Grosse
June 2	Kronprinzes. Cecilie
June 10	Kronprinz Wilhelm
June 17	Kaiser Wilhelm II
June 23	K. Wm. der Grosse
June 30	Kronprinzes. Cecilie
July 7	Kronprinz Wilhelm
July 14	Kaiser Wilhelm II
July 21	K. Wm. der Grosse
July 28	Kronprinzes. Cecilie
Aug. 5	Kronprinz Wilhelm
Aug. 11	Kaiser Wilhelm II
Aug. 18	K. Wm. der Grosse
Aug. 25	Kronprinzes. Cecilie
Sept. 1	Kronprinz Wilhelm
Sept. 8	Kaiser Wilhelm II
Sept. 15	K. Wm. der Grosse
Sept. 22	Kronprinzes. Cecilie
Sept. 29	Kronprinz Wilhelm
Oct. 6	Kaiser Wilhelm II
Oct. 14	K. Wm. der Grosse
Oct. 20	Kronprinzes. Cecilie
Oct. 28	Kronprinz Wilhelm
Nov. 4	Kaiser Wilhelm II
Nov. 11	K. Wm. der Grosse
Nov. 18	Kronprinzes. Cecilie
Dec. 2	Kaiser Wilhelm II
Dec. 23	K. Wm. der Grosse

NORTH GERMAN LLOYD
Bremen—New York

N.Y. Arrival	Steamer
Jan. 3	Prinzess Irene
Jan. 9	Seydlitz
Jan. 18	Koeln
Jan. 24	Buelow
Jan. 30	Barbarossa
Feb. 8	Neckar
Feb. 15	Cassel
Feb. 21	Rhein
Feb. 29	Koeln
Mar. 5	Seydlitz
Mar. 14	Breslau
Mar. 21	Main
Mar. 30	Rhein
Apr. 3	Barbarossa
Apr. 12	Chemnitz
Apr. 16	Seydlitz
Apr. 22	Leutzow
Apr. 29	Grosser Kurfuerst
May 8	Main
May 14	Barbarossa
May 22	Derfflinger
May 28	Luetzow
June 3	Grosser Kurfuerst
June 11	Bremen
June 15	Prinz F. Wilhelm
June 25	Barbarossa

NORTH GERMAN LLOYD
Bremen—New York
(Continued)

N.Y. Arrival	Steamer
July 1	Luetzow
July 8	Prinzess Alice
July 15	Bremen
July 21	Prinz F. Wilhelm
July 29	Barbarossa
Aug. 5	Buelow
Aug. 11	Grosser Kurfuerst
Aug. 18	Bremen
Aug. 24	Prinz F. Wilhelm
Aug. 25	Rhein
Sept. 2	Barbarossa
Sept. 8	Main
Sept. 9	Friedrich d. Grosse
Sept. 15	Grosser Kurfuerst
Sept. 21	Neckar
Sept. 25	Buelow
Sept. 28	Prinz F. Wilhelm
Oct. 6	Rhein
Oct. 7	Barbarossa
Oct. 14	Friedrich d. Grosse
Oct. 20	Grosser Kurfuerst
Oct. 29	Main
Nov. 4	Prinz F. Wilhelm
Nov. 12	Barbarossa
Nov. 18	Friedrich d. Grosse
Nov. 27	Grosser Kurfuerst
Dec. 5	Main
Dec. 8	Prinz F. Wilhelm
Dec. 19	Scharnhorst
Dec. 26	Gneisenau

NORTH GERMAN LLOYD
Mediterranean—New York

N.Y. Arrival	Steamer
Jan. 25	Friedrich d. Grosse
Feb. 7	Koenig Albert
Feb. 20	Prinzess Irene
Mar. 5	Friedrich d. Grosse
Mar. 13	Koenigin Luise
Mar. 27	Koenig Albert
Apr. 2	Prinzess Irene
Apr. 9	Friedrich d. Grosse
Apr. 17	Koenigin Luise
Apr. 30	Koenig Albert
May 8	Prinzess Irene
May 14	Friedrich d. Grosse
May 21	Koenigin Luise
June 4	Koenig Albert
June 10	Prinzess Irene
June 18	Friedrich d. Grosse
July 2	Koenigin Luise
July 9	Koenig Albert
July 22	Prinzess Irene
Aug. 6	Koenigin Luise
Aug. 20	Koenig Albert
Sept. 3	Prinzess Irene
Sept. 17	Koenigin Luise
Sept. 25	Koenig Albert
Oct. 9	Prinzess Irene
Oct. 30	Koenigin Luise
Nov. 12	Koenig Albert
Nov. 27	Prinzess Irene
Dec. 10	Koenigin Luise
Dec. 26	Barbarossa

Year 1908

NORTH GERMAN LLOYD
Bremen—Baltimore
Baltimore

Arrival	Steamer
Jan. 5	Cassel
Jan. 11	Frankfurt
Jan. 20	Koeln
Jan. 26	Breslau
Jan. 31	Hannover
Feb. 7	Brandenburg
Feb. 19	Cassel
Feb. 28	Chemnitz
Mar. 18	Breslau
Mar. 21	Frankfurt
Apr. 15	Chemnitz
Apr. 23	Breslau
May 8	Cassel
May 20	Neckar
June 4	Breslau
June 17	Main
June 30	Neckar
July 9	Hannover
July 15	Breslau
July 29	Main
Aug. 7	Koeln
Aug. 10	Neckar
Aug. 25	Rhein
Sept. 3	Chemnitz
Sept. 9	Main
Sept. 22	Neckar
Oct. 1	Hannover
Oct. 8	Rhein
Oct. 15	Koeln
Oct. 22	Brandenburg
Nov. 4	Neckar
Nov. 12	Chemnitz
Nov. 19	Rhein
Dec. 7	Main
Dec. 17	Neckar

PRINCE LINE
Mediterranean—New York
N. Y.

Arrival	Steamer
Jan. 20	Sicilian Prince
Mar. 24	Napolitan Prince
Apr. 20	Sicilian Prince

RED STAR LINE
Antwerp—New York
N. Y.

Arrival	Steamer
Jan. 2	Finland
Jan. 7	Vaderland
Jan. 15	Samland
Jan. 22	Zeeland
Jan. 30	Kroonland
Feb. 6	Finland
Feb. 11	Vaderland
Feb. 19	Zeeland
Feb. 25	Samland
Mar. 3	Kroonland
Mar. 10	Finland
Mar. 18	Vaderland
Mar. 24	Kroonland
Apr. 1	Kroonland
Apr. 8	Finland

RED STAR LINE
Antwerp—New York
(Continued)
N. Y.

Arrival	Steamer
Apr. 15	Vaderland
Apr. 21	Zeeland
Apr. 28	Kroonland
May 5	Finland
May 12	Vaderland
May 19	Zeeland
May 27	Kroonland
June 2	Finland
June 10	Vaderland
June 15	Zeeland
June 29	Finland
July 6	Vaderland
July 13	Zeeland
July 22	Gothland
July 28	Kroonland
Aug. 3	Vaderland
Aug. 10	Finland
Aug. 17	Zeeland
Aug. 25	Kroonland
Aug. 31	Vaderland
Sept. 7	Finland
Sept. 14	Zeeland
Sept. 22	Kroonland
Sept. 28	Vaderland
Oct. 5	Finland
Oct. 13	Zeeland
Oct. 20	Kroonland
Oct. 30	Samland
Nov. 3	Finland
Nov. 9	Vaderland
Nov. 18	Kroonland
Nov. 27	Zeeland
Dec. 3	Samland
Dec. 9	Finland
Dec. 17	Vaderland
Dec. 23	Kroonland
Dec. 29	Zeeland

RED STAR LINE
Antwerp—Philadelphia
Phila.

Arrival	Steamer
Jan. 2	Marquette
Jan. 14	Manitou
Jan. 30	Menominee
Feb. 11	Marquette
Feb. 26	Manitou
Apr. 8	Manitou
May 4	Marquette
May 19	Manitou
June 2	Menominee
June 15	Marquette
June 29	Manitou
July 13	Menominee
Aug. 10	Marquette
Aug. 24	Manitou
Sept. 7	Menominee
Sept. 21	Marquette
Oct. 5	Manitou
Oct. 20	Menominee
Nov. 3	Marquette
Nov. 17	Manitou
Dec. 19	Marquette
Dec. 31	Manitou

RUSSIAN-AMERICAN LINE
Rotterdam—New York
N. Y.

Arrival	Steamer
Jan. 3	Estonia
Feb. 16	Korea
Mar. 5	Lituania
Mar. 26	Estonia
Apr. 25	Korea
May 21	Estonia
June 13	Russia
July 15	Estonia
July 28	Russia
Aug. 10	Korea
Aug. 26	Estonia
Sept. 9	Russia
Sept. 26	Korea
Oct. 5	Estonia
Nov. 12	Korea
Dec. 3	Estonia
Dec. 23	Birma

RUSSIAN VOLUNTEER FLEET
Rotterdam—New York
N. Y.

Arrival	Steamer
Jan. 9	Soskwa
Jan. 25	Petersburg
Feb. 20	Kherson
Mar. 20	Saratov
Apr. 2	Petersburg
Apr. 17	Kherson
May 28	Petersburg
June 11	Kherson

SCANDINAVIAN-AMERICAN LINE
Scandinavian Ports—
New York
N. Y.

Arrival	Steamer
Jan. 30	Oscar II
Feb. 16	Hellig Olav
Feb. 27	United States
Mar. 5	C. F. Tietgen
Mar. 10	Oscar II
Mar. 27	Hellig Olav
Apr. 8	United States
Apr. 22	Oscar II
May 5	Hellig Olav
May 20	C. F. Tietgen
June 3	Oscar II
June 16	Hellig Olav
June 30	United States
July 14	C. F. Tietgen
July 28	Hellig Olav
Aug. 11	United States
Aug. 25	Oscar II
Sept. 1	C. F. Tietgen
Sept. 8	Hellig Olav
Sept. 22	United States
Oct. 6	Oscar II
Oct. 15	C. F. Tietgen
Oct. 21	Hellig Olav
Nov. 4	United States
Nov. 19	Oscar II
Nov. 21	C. F. Tietgen
Dec. 2	Hellig Olav
Dec. 22	United States

Year 1908

SICULA-AMERICAN LINE
Mediterranean—New York
N.Y.

Arrival	Steamer
Jan. 26	San Giovanni
Feb. 20	San Giorgio
Mar. 23	San Giovanni
Apr. 11	San Giovanni
May 11	San Giovanni
May 22	San Giorgio
June 17	San Giovanni
July 1	San Giorgio
July 28	San Giovanni
Aug. 14	San Giorgio
Sept. 6	San Giovanni
Sept. 23	San Giorgio
Oct. 19	San Giovanni
Nov. 2	San Giorgio
Nov. 26	San Giovanni
Dec. 10	San Giorgio

WHITE STAR LINE
Liverpool—New York
N.Y.

Arrival	Steamer
Jan. 3	Celtic
Jan. 18	Baltic
Jan. 26	Arabic
Jan. 31	Celtic
Feb. 15	Baltic
Feb. 29	Celtic
Mar. 14	Baltic
Mar. 29	Celtic
Apr. 11	Baltic
Apr. 18	Cedric
Apr. 25	Arabic
May 1	Celtic
May 9	Baltic
May 16	Cedric
May 24	Arabic
May 30	Celtic
June 5	Baltic
June 12	Cedric
June 20	Arabic
June 26	Celtic
July 3	Baltic
July 10	Cedric
July 17	Arabic
July 25	Celtic
July 31	Baltic
Aug. 7	Cedric
Aug. 15	Arabic
Aug. 21	Celtic
Aug. 28	Baltic
Sept. 4	Cedric
Sept. 11	Arabic
Sept. 18	Celtic
Sept. 25	Baltic
Oct. 2	Cedric
Oct. 10	Arabic
Oct. 17	Celtic
Oct. 23	Baltic
Oct. 30	Cedric
Nov.. 8	Arabic
Nov. 14	Celtic
Nov. 28	Cedric
Nov. 31	Baltic
Dec. 7	Arabic
Dec. 14	Celtic
Dec. 21	Baltic

WHITE STAR LINE
Southampton—New York
N.Y.

Arrival	Steamer
Jan. 8	Oceanic
Jan. 16	Majestic
Jan. 25	Adriatic
Feb. 5	Oceanic
Feb. 20	Adriatic
Feb. 27	Majestic
Mar. 4	Oceanic
Mar. 12	Teutonic
Mar. 19	Adriatic
Mar. 27	Majestic
Apr. 1	Oceanic
Apr. 9	Teutonic
Apr. 16	Adriatic
Apr. 23	Majestic
Apr. 29	Oceanic
May 9	Teutonic
May 14	Adriatic
May 21	Majestic
May 27	Oceanic
June 4	Teutonic
June 11	Adriatic
June 18	Majestic
June 24	Oceanic
July 1	Teutonic
July 9	Adriatic
July 16	Majestic
July 22	Oceanic
July 30	Teutonic
Aug. 6	Adriatic
Aug. 13	Majestic
Aug. 19	Oceanic
Aug. 26	Teutonic
Sept. 3	Adriatic
Sept. 9	Majestic
Sept. 16	Oceanic
Sept. 23	Teutonic
Oct. 1	Adriatic
Oct. 7	Majestic
Oct. 14	Oceanic
Oct. 21	Teutonic
Oct. 29	Adriatic
Nov. 5	Majestic
Nov. 11	Oceanic
Nov. 19	Teutonic
Nov. 26	Adriatic
Dec. 3	Majestic
Dec. 10	Oceanic
Dec. 19	Teutonic
Dec. 24	Adriatic

WHITE STAR LINE
Mediterranean—New York
N.Y.

Arrival	Steamer
Jan. 16	Republic
Feb. 9	Cedric
Mar. 3	Republic
Mar. 18	Cedric
Mar. 24	Cretic
Apr. 15	Republic
May 4	Cretic
May 21	Republic
June 13	Cretic
June 29	Romanic
Sept. 11	Cretic

WHITE STAR LINE
Mediterranean—New York
(Continued)
N.Y.

Arrival	Steamer
Oct. 30	Cretic
Dec. 8	Cretic

WHITE STAR LINE
Liverpool—Boston
Boston

Arrival	Steamer
Jan. 1	Cymric
Feb. 5	Cymric
Mar. 10	Cymric
Apr. 14	Cymric
May 19	Cymric
June 15	Cymric
June 28	Republic
July 13	Cymric
July 26	Republic
Aug. 9	Cymric
Aug. 23	Republic
Sept. 7	Cymric
Sept. 20	Republic
Oct. 5	Cymric
Oct. 19	Republic
Nov. 2	Cymric
Nov. 22	Republic
Dec. 1	Cymric

WHITE STAR LINE
Mediterranean—Boston
Boston

Arrival	Steamer
Jan. 3	Canopic
Jan. 25	Romanic
Feb. 17	Canopic
Mar. 9	Romanic
Mar. 30	Canopic
Apr. 20	Romanic
May 12	Canopic
May 25	Romanic
June 23	Canopic
Aug. 20	Romanic
Sept. 27	Canopic
Oct. 20	Romanic
Nov. 16	Canopic
Nov. 30	Romanic
Dec. 29	Canopic

ADDITIONAL ARRIVALS
Mediterranean—New York
N.Y.

Arrival	Steamer
Jan. 25	Gallia (Fabre Marseilles
Mar. 25	Gallia (Fabre, Marseilles)
June 21	Roma (Fabre, Marseilles)
Aug. 7	Roma (Fabre, Marseilles
Oct. 18	Neustria (Fabre, Marseilles
Nov. 2	Massilia (Fabre, Marseilles)
Dec. 14	Gallia (Fabre, Marseilles)

Year 1909

ALLAN LINE
Glasgow—Boston
Boston

Arrival	Steamer
Jan. 3	Carthaginian
Jan. 13	Sicilian
Jan. 31	Laurentian
Feb. 11	Ionian
Mar. 1	Carthaginian
Mar. 11	Laurentian
Mar. 26	Corinthian
Apr. 7	Grampian
Apr. 21	Hesperian
May 5	Laurentian
May 24	Numidian
June 8	Laurentian
June 21	Numidian
July 5	Laurentian
July 20	Numidian
Aug. 2	Laurentian
Aug. 16	Numidian
Aug. 30	Laurentian
Sept. 13	Numidian
Sept. 27	Parisian
Oct. 11	Numidian
Nov. 8	Numidian
Dec. 1	Pretorian
Dec. 16	Numidian
Dec. 28	Ionian

AMERICAN LINE
Southampton—New York
N.Y.

Arrival	Steamer
Jan. 4	St. Louis
Jan. 9	Philadelphia
Jan. 24	New York
Feb. 2	St. Louis
Feb. 6	Philadelphia
Feb. 14	St. Paul
Feb. 21	New York
Mar. 6	Philadelphia
Mar. 14	St. Paul
Mar. 22	New York
Mar. 28	St. Louis
Apr. 3	Philadelphia
Apr. 10	St. Paul
Apr. 18	New York
Apr. 24	St. Louis
May 1	Philadelphia
May 9	St. Paul
May 16	New York
May 22	St. Louis
May 29	Philadelphia
June 6	St. Paul
June 13	New York
June 19	St. Louis
June 26	Philadelphia
July 3	St. Paul
July 11	New York
July 17	St. Louis
July 31	Philadelphia
Aug. 8	St. Paul
Aug. 14	New York
Aug. 21	St. Louis
Aug. 28	Philadelphia
Sept. 4	St. Paul

AMERICAN LINE
Southampton—New York
(Continued)
N.Y.

Arrival	Steamer
Sept. 11	New York
Sept. 18	St. Louis
Sept. 25	Philadelphia
Oct. 2	St. Paul
Oct. 9	New York
Oct. 17	St. Louis
Oct. 23	Philadelphia
Oct. 31	St. Paul
Nov. 6	New York
Nov. 14	St. Louis
Nov. 20	Philadelphia
Nov. 27	St. Paul
Dec. 5	New York
Dec. 11	St. Louis
Dec. 18	Philadelphia
Dec. 24	St. Paul
Dec. 30	New York

AMERICAN LINE
Liverpool—Philadelphia
Phila.

Arrival	Steamer
Jan. 10	Friesland
Feb. 5	Dominion
Feb. 17	Merion
Mar. 9	Haverford
Mar. 27	Merion
Apr. 5	Friesland
Apr. 13	Haverford
Apr. 28	Merion
May 9	Friesland
May 17	Haverford
May 31	Merion
June 13	Friesland
June 20	Haverford
July 5	Merion
July 18	Friesland
July 26	Haverford
Aug. 8	Merion
Aug. 22	Friesland
Aug. 29	Haverford
Sept. 12	Merion
Sept. 25	Friesland
Oct. 3	Haverford
Oct. 14	Merion
Nov. 1	Friesland
Nov. 8	Haverford
Nov. 22	Merion
Dec. 7	Friesland
Dec. 15	Haverford
Dec. 27	Merion

ANCHOR LINE
Glasgow—New York
N.Y.

Arrival	Steamer
Jan. 4	Caledonia
Jan. 25	Furnessia
Feb. 2	California
Feb. 7	Columbia
Feb. 25	Furnessia

ANCHOR LINE
Glasgow—New York
(Continued)
N.Y.

Arrival	Steamer
Feb. 28	Caledonia
Mar. 8	California
Mar. 15	Columbia
Mar. 28	Caledonia
Apr. 6	California
Apr. 12	Columbia
Apr. 20	Furnessia
Apr. 25	Caledonia
May 3	California
May 9	Columbia
May 17	Furnessia
May 23	Caledonia
May 30	California
June 6	Columbia
June 15	Furnessia
June 20	Caledonia
June 28	California
July 4	Columbia
July 13	Furnessia
July 18	Caledonia
July 26	California
Aug. 1	Columbia
Aug. 10	Furnessia
Aug. 15	Caledonia
Aug. 23	California
Aug. 29	Columbia
Sept. 7	Furnessia
Sept. 12	Caledonia
Sept. 20	California
Sept. 26	Columbia
Oct. 5	Furnessia
Oct. 10	Caledonia
Oct. 18	California
Oct. 24	Columbia
Nov. 7	Caledonia
Nov. 15	California
Nov. 21	Columbia
Nov. 30	Furnessia
Dec. 6	Caledonia
Dec. 13	California
Dec. 29	Furnessia

ANCHOR LINE
Mediterranean—New York
N.Y.

Arrival	Steamer
Jan. 2	Italia
Feb. 1	Calabria
Feb. 21	Perugia
Mar. 13	Italia
Mar. 29	Calabria
Apr. 22	Perugia
Apr. 30	Italia
May 21	Calabria
June 10	Italia
July 10	Calabria
July 30	Perugia
Aug. 13	Italia
Sept. 2	Calabria
Sept. 24	Perugia
Oct. 8	Italia
Oct. 25	Calabria

Year 1909

ANCHOR LINE
Mediterranean—New York
(Continued)

N. Y.

Arrival	Steamer
Nov. 14	Perugia
Nov. 27	Italia
Dec. 17	Calabria

ATLANTIC TRANSPORT LINE
London—New York

N. Y.

Arrival	Steamer
Jan. 2	Minnetonka
Jan. 18	Minnehaha
Jan. 23	Minneapolis
Feb. 8	Minnetonka
Mar. 1	Minnehaha
Mar. 14	Minnetonka
Mar. 22	Minneapolis
Apr. 13	Minnehaha
Apr. 20	Minneapolis
May 4	Minnetonka
May 10	Minnewaska
May 17	Minnehaha
May 25	Minneapolis
May 31	Minnetonka
June 7	Minnewaska
June 14	Minnehaha
June 21	Minneapolis
June 28	Minnetonka
July 5	Minnewaska
July 12	Minnehaha
July 19	Minneapolis
July 26	Minnetonka
Aug. 2	Minnewaska
Aug. 9	Minnehaha
Aug. 16	Minneapolis
Aug. 23	Minnetonka
Aug. 30	Minnewaska
Sept. 6	Minnehaha
Sept. 13	Minneapolis
Sept. 20	Minnetonka
Sept. 27	Minnewaska
Oct. 4	Minnehaha
Oct. 11	Minneapolis
Oct. 19	Minnetonka
Oct. 25	Minnewaska
Nov. 1	Minnehaha
Nov. 13	Minneapolis
Nov. 20	Minnetonka
Nov. 27	Minnewaska
Dec. 5	Minnehaha
Dec. 18	Minneapolis
Dec. 25	Minnetonka

AUSTRO-AMERICANA
Mediterranean—New York

N. Y.

Arrival	Steamer
Jan. 6	Laura
Feb. 2	Martha W.
Feb. 17	Alice
Feb. 25	Laura
Mar. 2	Giulia
Mar. 4	Oceania
Mar. 17	Martha W.
Mar. 25	Atlanta
Mar. 26	Argentina

AUSTRO-AMERICANA
Mediterranean—New York
(Continued)

N. Y.

Arrival	Steamer
Apr. 8	Alice
Apr. 15	Columbia
Apr. 14	Laura
Apr. 21	Oceania
May 3	Martha W.
May 12	Argentina
May 26	Alice
June 2	Laura
June 9	Oceania
June 14	Martha W.
July 1	Argentina
July 9	Atlanta
July 13	Alice
July 20	Laura
July 28	Oceania
Aug. 1	Martha W.
Aug. 24	Argentina
Sept. 7	Laura
Sept. 17	Martha W.
Oct. 1	Alice
Oct. 6	Oceania
Oct. 13	Argentina
Oct. 28	Laura
Nov. 2	Martha W.
Nov. 16	Alice
Nov. 24	Oceania
Dec. 1	Argentina
Dec. 16	Laura
Dec. 20	Martha W.

COMPANIA TRANSATLANTICA LINE
(Spanish Line)
Spanish Ports—New York

N. Y.

Arrival	Steamer
Jan. 11	Buenos Aires
Feb. 11	Manuel Calvo
Mar. 12	Antonio Lopez
Apr. 13	Manuel Calvo
May 11	Montevideo
June 10	Antonio Lopez
July 11	Montserrat
Aug. 16	Buenos Aires
Sept. 10	Antonio Lopez
Oct. 12	Montevideo
Nov. 12	Manuel Calvo
Dec. 11	Montserrat

CUNARD LINE
Liverpool—New York

N. Y.

Arrival	Steamer
Jan. 1	Lusitania
Jan. 9	Campania
Jan. 17	Carmania
Jan. 24	Lucania
Jan. 29	Mauretania
Feb. 6	Campania
Feb. 14	Lusitania
Feb. 18	Mauretania
Feb. 27	Lucania
Mar. 5	Lusitania
Mar. 11	Mauretania
Mar. 20	Campania

CUNARD LINE
Liverpool—New York
(Continued)

N. Y.

Arrival	Steamer
Mar. 26	Lusitania
Apr. 3	Lucania
Apr. 7	Caronia
Apr. 9	Mauretania
Apr. 17	Campania
Apr. 21	Carmania
Apr. 23	Lusitania
Apr. 30	Mauretania
May 5	Caronia
May 8	Campania
May 14	Lusitania
May 19	Carmania
May 20	Mauretania
May 29	Campania
June 2	Caronia
June 4	Lusitania
June 10	Mauretania
June 16	Carmania
June 19	Campania
June 25	Lusitania
June 29	Caronia
July 3	Lucania
July 8	Mauretania
July 14	Carmania
July 16	Campania
July 23	Lusitania
July 27	Caronia
July 29	Mauretania
Aug. 6	Campania
Aug. 10	Carmania
Aug. 12	Lusitania
Aug. 19	Mauretania
Aug. 24	Caronia
Aug. 28	Campania
Sept. 2	Lusitania
Sept. 7	Carmania
Sept. 9	Mauretania
Sept. 17	Campania
Sept. 21	Caronia
Sept. 23	Lusitania
Sept. 30	Mauretania
Oct. 5	Carmania
Oct. 9	Campania
Oct. 16	Caronia
Oct. 21	Lusitania
Oct. 28	Mauretania
Nov. 2	Carmania
Nov. 6	Campania
Nov. 11	Lusitania
Nov. 20	Caronia
Nov. 25	Mauretania
Nov. 25	Carpathia
Dec. 3	Lusitania
Dec. 3	Carmania
Dec. 11	Campania
Dec. 16	Mauretania
Dec. 23	Lusitania

CUNARD LINE
Mediterranean—New York

N. Y.

Arrival	Steamer
Jan. 2	Caronia
Jan. 2	Carmania
Jan. 29	Pannonia

Year 1909

CUNARD LINE
Mediterranean—New York
(Continued)

N. Y. Arrival	Steamer
Feb. 13	Caronia
Mar. 1	Carmania
Mar. 19	Pannonia
Mar. 26	Carpathia
Apr. 9	Slavonia
Apr. 21	Ultonia
May 6	Pannonia
May 11	Carpathia
May 27	Slavonia
June 10	Ultonia
June 25	Pannonia
June 30	Carpathia
July 29	Ultonia
Aug. 13	Pannonia
Aug. 24	Carpathia
Sept. 16	Ultonia
Oct. 2	Pannonia
Oct. 14	Carpathia
Nov. 8	Ultonia
Nov. 8	Carmania
Nov. 21	Pannonia
Nov. 21	Caronia
Dec. 2	Carpathia
Dec. 2	Saxonia
Dec. 9	Carmania

CUNARD LINE
Liverpool—Boston

Boston Arrival	Steamer
Jan. 23	Saxonia
Feb. 4	Ivernia
Feb. 18	Saxonia
Mar. 4	Ivernia
Mar. 18	Saxonia
Apr. 1	Ivernia
Apr. 15	Saxonia
Apr. 29	Ivernia
May 13	Saxonia
May 27	Ivernia
June 10	Saxonia
June 24	Ivernia
July 9	Saxonia
July 22	Ivernia
Aug. 5	Saxonia
Aug. 19	Ivernia
Sept. 1	Saxonia
Sept. 15	Ivernia
Sept. 29	Saxonia
Oct. 14	Ivernia
Oct. 29	Saxonia
Nov. 11	Ivernia
Nov. 25	Saxonia
Nov. 25	Pannonia
Dec. 10	Ivernia

FABRE LINE
Mediterranean—New York

N. Y. Arrival	Steamer
Jan. 7	Germania
Jan. 28	Venezia
Feb. 14	Madonna
Feb. 19	Roma
Feb. 28	Germania

FABRE LINE
Mediterranean—New York
(Continued)

N. Y. Arrival	Steamer
Mar. 18	Venezia
Mar. 29	Gallia
Mar. 29	Maronna
Apr. 8	Massilia
Apr. 9	Roma
Apr. 16	Germania
May 12	Madonna
May 16	Gallia
May 24	Roma
June 4	Germania
June 9	Massilia
June 23	Venezia
June 23	Madonna
July 4	Gallia
July 8	Roma
July 20	Germania
Aug. 2	Venezia
Aug. 9	Madonna
Aug. 19	Roma
Aug. 31	Germania
Sept. 9	Gallia
Sept. 13	Venezia
Sept. 22	Madonna
Oct. 2	Massilia
Oct. 5	Roma
Oct. 16	Germania
Oct. 30	Gallia
Nov. 1	Venezia
Nov. 9	Madonna
Nov. 23	Roma
Dec. 3	Germania
Dec. 21	Venezia
Dec. 28	Madonna

FRENCH LINE
(Compagnie Generale Transatlantique)
Havre, Bordeaux—New York

N. Y. Arrival	Steamer
Jan. 3	La Touraine
Jan. 5	Hudson
Jan. 8	Caroline
Jan. 10	La Bretagne
Jan. 16	La Savoie
Jan. 24	La Lorraine
Jan. 29	Louisiane
Feb. 1	La Gascogne
Feb. 3	Californie
Feb. 8	La Bretagne
Feb. 13	La Provence
Feb. 20	La Savoie
Feb. 20	Caroline
Feb. 23	Chicago
Feb. 28	La Touraine
Mar. 4	Hudson
Mar. 8	La Bretagne
Mar. 9	La Gascogne
Mar. 13	La Provence
Mar. 20	Louisiane
Mar. 21	La Savoie
Mar. 23	Chicago
Mar. 28	La Touraine
Mar. 31	La Bretagne
Apr. 2	Californie
Apr. 3	La Lorraine

FRENCH LINE
(Compagnie Generale Transatlantique)
Havre, Bordeaux—New York
(Continued)

N. Y. Arrival	Steamer
Apr. 6	La Gascogne
Apr. 9	La Provence
Apr. 15	Floride
Apr. 17	La Savoie
Apr. 24	Hudson
Apr. 26	La Bretagne
Apr. 27	Chicago
May 1	La Lorraine
May 4	La Gascogne
May 7	La Provence
May 15	La Savoie
May 16	Caroline
May 23	La Bretagne
May 23	Californie
May 28	Floride
May 29	La Lorraine
May 31	Chicago
June 5	La Provence
June 11	Louisiane
June 14	La Savoie
June 19	La Lorraine
June 20	Mexico
June 26	La Provence
June 26	Caroline
June 28	Chicago
July 3	La Savoie
July 11	La Touraine
July 16	Hudson
July 18	La Bretagne
July 23	Louisiane
July 24	La Lorraine
July 31	La Savoie
Aug. 5	Floride
Aug. 8	La Touraine
Aug. 13	Californie
Aug. 15	La Bretagne
Aug. 20	Mexico
Aug. 21	La Lorraine
Aug. 30	La Touraine
Aug. 30	Chicago
Sept. 3	La Provence
Sept. 9	Louisiane
Sept. 10	Hudson
Sept. 11	La Savoie
Sept. 13	La Gascogne
Sept. 17	La Lorraine
Sept. 22	Floride
Sept. 24	La Provence
Sept. 27	Chicago
Oct. 3	La Touraine
Oct. 6	Caroline
Oct. 8	Californie
Oct. 8	La Savoie
Oct. 11	La Gascogne
Oct. 18	La Bretagne
Oct. 23	La Provence
Oct. 28	Chicago
Oct. 29	Louisiane
Nov. 1	La Touraine
Nov. 6	Floride
Nov. 7	La Savoie
Nov. 18	La Gascogne
Nov. 18	Caroline
Nov. 19	La Provence

Year 1909

FRENCH LINE
(Compagnie Generale Transatlantique)
Havre—Bordeaux—New York
(Continued)

N.Y. Arrival	Steamer
Nov. 21	Hudson
Nov. 28	La Touraine
Dec. 6	La Bretagne
Dec. 7	Chicago
Dec. 12	La Lorraine
Dec. 15	Californie
Dec. 17	La Provence
Dec. 19	Floride
Dec. 26	La Touraine
Dec. 30	Caroline

GREEK LINE
Italy—Greece—New York

N.Y. Arrival	Steamer
Feb. 17	Themistocles
Apr. 19	Themistocles
June 3	Athinai
June 25	Themistocles
July 31	Athinai
Aug. 25	Themistocles
Sept. 27	Athinai
Oct. 25	Themistocles
Nov. 24	Athinai

HAMBURG-AMERICAN LINE
Hamburg—New York

N.Y. Arrival	Steamer
Feb. 3	Deutschland
Apr. 22	Deutschland
May 27	Deutschland
Sept. 9	Deutschland
Oct. 15	Deutschland
Nov. 1	Amerika
Jan. 8	Batavia
Jan. 13	Arcadia
Jan. 25	Pennsylvania
Jan. 25	K. Auguste Victoria
Feb. 5	Graf Waldersee
Feb. 14	Patricia
Feb. 16	Amerika
Feb. 25	Pisa
Feb. 28	Pretoria
Mar. 6	Pennsylvania
Mar. 8	K. Auguste Victoria
Mar. 18	Graf Waldersee
Mar. 27	Patricia
Mar. 31	Amerika
Apr. 2	Badenia
Apr. 7	Cleveland
Apr. 8	Rhaetia
Apr. 15	President Grant
Apr. 17	K. Auguste Victoria
Apr. 24	Pennsylvania
Apr. 29	President Lincoln
May 5	Bluecher
May 8	Amerika
May 16	Cleveland
May 20	President Grant

HAMBURG-AMERICAN LINE
Hamburg—New York
(Continued)

N.Y. Arrival	Steamer
May 22	K. Auguste Victoria
May 29	Pennsylvania
June 3	President Lincoln
June 6	Cincinnati
June 9	Bluecher
June 12	Amerika
June 20	Cleveland
June 24	President Grant
June 26	K. Auguste Victoria
July 2	Pennsylvania
July 8	President Grant
July 11	Cincinnati
July 17	Amerika
July 25	Cleveland
July 29	President Grant
July 31	K. Auguste Victoria
Aug. 5	Pennsylvania
Aug. 11	President Lincoln
Aug. 15	Cincinnati
Aug. 18	Bluecher
Aug. 21	Amerika
Aug. 26	Graf Waldersee
Aug. 29	President Grant
Sept. 1	President Grant
Sept. 3	K. Auguste Victoria
Sept. 9	Pennsylvania
Sept. 15	President Lincoln
Sept. 18	Cincinnati
Sept. 22	Bluecher
Sept. 25	Amerika
Oct. 2	Graf Waldersee
Oct. 3	Cleveland
Oct. 6	President Grant
Oct. 8	K. Auguste Victoria
Oct. 16	Pennsylvania
Oct. 22	President Lincoln
Oct. 24	Cincinnati
Oct. 27	Bluecher
Oct. 30	Amerika
Nov. 11	President Grant
Nov. 13	K. Auguste Victoria
Nov. 21	Pennsylvania
Nov. 25	Graf Waldersee
Dec. 4	Amerika
Dec. 6	Bulgaria
Dec. 16	President Grant
Dec. 20	K. Auguste Victoria
Dec. 23	Prinz Adalbert
Dec. 30	Pennsylvania

HAMBURG-AMERICAN LINE
Mediterranean—New York

N.Y. Arrival	Steamer
Jan. 19	Moltke
Feb. 10	Hamburg
Mar. 5	Deutschland
Mar. 20	Hamburg
Apr. 3	Bulgaria
Apr. 10	Batavia
Apr. 18	Moltke
May 2	Hamburg

HAMBURG-AMERICAN LINE
Mediterranean—New York
(Continued)

N.Y. Arrival	Steamer
May 20	Bulgaria
May 28	Batavia
June 3	Moltke
June 20	Hamburg
July 11	Moltke
Aug. 7	Hamburg
Aug. 26	Moltke
Sept. 20	Hamburg
Oct. 11	Moltke
Nov. 9	Hamburg
Nov. 29	Moltke
Dec. 24	Hamburg

HOLLAND-AMERICA LINE
Rotterdam—New York

N.Y. Arrival	Steamer
Jan. 4	Ryndam
Jan. 13	Statendam
Jan. 26	Noordam
Feb. 9	Rotterdam
Feb. 16	Statendam
Mar. 1	Noordam
Mar. 16	Ryndam
Mar. 23	New Amsterdam
Mar. 30	Potsdam
Apr. 7	Noordam
Apr. 12	Rotterdam
Apr. 20	Ryndam
Apr. 27	New Amsterdam
May 4	Potsdam
May 11	Noordam
May 16	Rotterdam
May 26	Ryndam
May 31	New Amsterdam
June 8	Potsdam
June 15	Noordam
June 20	Rotterdam
June 29	Ryndam
July 5	New Amsterdam
July 13	Potsdam
July 26	Noordam
Aug. 1	Rotterdam
Aug. 10	Ryndam
Aug. 16	New Amsterdam
Aug. 24	Potsdam
Aug. 30	Noordam
Sept. 5	Rotterdam
Sept. 14	Ryndam
Sept. 20	New Amsterdam
Sept. 27	Potsdam
Oct. 4	Noordam
Oct. 11	Rotterdam
Oct. 20	Ryndam
Oct. 25	New Amsterdam
Nov. 2	Potsdam
Nov. 8	Noordam
Nov. 16	Rotterdam
Nov. 23	Ryndam
Dec. 7	Statendam
Dec. 14	Noordam
Dec. 28	Ryndam

Year 1909

ITALIA LINE
Mediterranean—New York
N. Y.

Arrival	Steamer
Feb. 7	Ancona
Feb. 22	Verona
Mar. 7	Taormina
Mar. 23	Ancona
Apr. 1	Verona
Apr. 22	Ancona
Apr. 29	Taormina
May 13	Verona
May 28	Ancona
June 10	Taormina
June 28	Verona
July 29	Taormina
Aug. 26	Verona
Sept. 16	Taormina
Oct. 7	Ancona
Oct. 30	Verona
Dec. 6	Verona
Dec. 24	Taormina

ITALIA LINE
Mediterranean—Philadelphia
Phila.

Arrival	Steamer
Feb. 8	Ancona
Feb. 23	Verona
Mar. 9	Taormina
Mar. 24	Ancona
Apr. 3	Verona
Apr. 24	Ancona
May 1	Taormina
May 15	Verona
May 31	Ancona
June 12	Taormina
June 30	Verona
July 31	Taormina
Aug. 28	Verona
Sept. 17	Taormina
Oct. 8	Ancona
Nov. 1	Verona
Dec. 7	Verona
Dec. 26	Taormina

LA VELOCE LINE
Mediterranean—New York
N. Y.

Arrival	Steamer
Feb. 1	Europa
Feb. 28	Nord America
Mar. 18	Europa
Mar. 26	Liguria
Apr. 2	Lombardia
Apr. 11	Nord America
Apr. 29	Europa
May 7	Liguria
May 16	Lombardia
June 5	America
June 12	Europa
July 12	America
July 28	Europa
Aug. 19	America
Sept. 14	Europa
Oct. 25	Europa
Dec. 2	America
Dec. 17	Oceania

LEYLAND LINE
Liverpool—Boston
Boston

Arrival	Steamer
Apr. 8	Winifredian
Apr. 14	Bohemian
Apr. 22	Crestrian
May 6	Canadian
May 19	Bohemian
June 3	Winifredian
June 16	Devonian
June 30	Canadian
July 13	Winifredian
Aug. 9	Devonian
Aug. 24	Canadian
Aug. 31	Bohemian
Sept. 6	Winifredian
Sept. 20	Devonian
Sept. 28	Cestrian
Oct. 4	Bohemian
Oct. 20	Winifredian
Oct. 27	Devonian
Nov. 3	Cestrian
Nov. 16	Bohemian

LLOYD ITALIANO LINE
Mediterranean—New York
N. Y.

Arrival	Steamer
Feb. 12	Indiana
Feb. 22	Luisiana
Mar. 17	Virginia
Mar. 29	Indiana
Apr. 5	Luisiana
Apr. 21	Virginia
May 6	Indiana
May 14	Luisiana
May 29	Virginia
June 6	Florida
June 14	Indiana
July 11	Luisiana
Aug. 5	Virginia
Sept. 1	Mendoza
Sept. 20	Virginia
Oct. 14	Mendoza
Oct. 31	Virginia
Nov. 30	Luisiana
Dec. 19	Virginia

LLOYD SABAUDO
Mediterranean—New York
N. Y.

Arrival	Steamer
Jan. 13	Re d'Italia
Feb. 26	Re d'Italia
Mar. 12	Prin. di Piemonte
Mar. 27	Regina d'Italia
Apr. 8	Re d'Italia
Apr. 21	Prin. di Piemonte
May 6	Regina d'Italia
May 19	Re d'Italia
June 1	Prin. di Piemonte
June 16	Regina d'Italia
June 21	Tomaso di Savoia
July 22	Prin. di Piemonte
Aug. 19	Regina d'Italia
Sept. 16	Prin. di Piemonte
Oct. 19	Regina d'Italia
Nov. 1	Prin. di Piemonte
Nov. 29	Regina d'Italia
Dec. 21	Prin. di Piemonte

NATIONAL GREEK LINE
Mediterranean—New York
N. Y.

Arrival	Steamer
Apr. 21	Patris
June 2	Patris
July 14	Patris
Aug. 29	Patris
Oct. 10	Patris
Nov. 22	Patris

NAVIGAZIONE GENER-ALE ITALIANA
Mediterranean—New York
N. Y.

Arrival	Steamer
Jan. 19	Duca d. Abruzzi
Feb. 5	Duca di Genoa
Feb. 22	Campania
Mar. 1	Duca d. Abruzzi
Mar. 13	Duca di Genoa
Mar. 18	Lazio
Mar. 25	Sannio
Apr. 6	Duca d. Abruzzi
Apr. 17	Duca di Genoa
Apr. 16	Campania
May 7	Lazio
May 9	Duca d. Abruzzi
May 14	Sannio
May 24	Duca di Genoa
June 5	Campania
June 12	Duca d. Abruzzi
July 1	Duca di Genoa
July 18	Sannio
Aug. 8	Duca d. Abruzzi
Aug. 30	Duca di Abruzzi
Sept. 14	Duca di Abruzzi
Sept. 30	Sannio
Oct. 11	Duca di Genoa
Oct. 25	Duca d. Abruzzi
Nov. 23	Duca D'Aosta
Nov. 22	Sannio
Dec. 6	Duca di Genoa
Dec. 22	Duca d. Abruzzi

NAVIGAZIONE GENER-ALE ITALIANA
Mediterranean—Boston
Boston

Arrival	Steamer
Nov. 12	Lazio
Dec. 24	Duca degli Abruzzi

NORTH GERMAN LLOYD
Express Service
Bremen—New York
N. Y.

Arrival	Steamer
Jan. 26	K. Wm. der Grosse
Feb. 10	Kronprinzes. Cecilie
Feb. 25	Kaiser Wilhelm II
Mar. 17	Kronprinzes. Cecilie
Mar. 24	K. Wm. der Grosse
Mar. 31	Kaiser Wilhelm II
Apr. 7	Kronprinzes Wilhelm
Apr. 13	Kronprinzes. Cecilie
Apr. 21	K. Wm. der Grosse
Apr. 28	Kaiser Wilhelm II
May 5	Kronprinz Wilhelm

Year 1909

NORTH GERMAN LLOYD
Express Service
Bremen—New York
(Continued)
N.Y.

Arrival	Steamer
May 11...Kronprinzes. Cecilie
May 18..K. Wm. der Grosse
May 26...Kaiser Wilhelm II
June 2..Kronprinz Wilhelm
June 8..Kronprinzes. Cecilie
June 16...K. Wm. der Grosse
June 22...Kaiser Wilhelm II
June 30...Kronprinz Wilhelm
July 7..Kronprinzes. Cecilie
July 13...K. Wm. der Grosse
July 20...Kaiser Wilhelm II
July 27...Kronprinz Wilhelm
Aug. 3..Kronprinzes. Cecilie
Aug. 17..K. Wm. der Grosse
Aug. 25...Kaiser Wilhelm II
Aug. 31...Kronprinz Wilhelm
Sept. 7..Kronprinzes. Cecilie
Sept. 14..K. Wm. der Grosse
Sept. 21...Kaiser Wilhelm II
Sept. 28...Kronprinz Wilhelm
Oct. 5..Kronprinzes. Cecilie
Oct. 13..K. Wm. der Grosse
Oct. 20...Kaiser Wilhelm II
Oct. 27...Kronprinz Wilhelm
Nov. 2..Kronprinzes. Cecilie
Nov. 16...Kaiser Wilhelm II
Nov. 30...Kronprinzes. Cecilie
Dec. 21...Kaiser Wilhelm II

NORTH GERMAN LLOYD
Regular Service
Bremen—New York
N.Y.

Arrival	Steamer
Jan. 3............. Rhein
Jan. 9....... Brandenburg
Jan. 12............. Main
Jan. 14..Pr. Fried'h Wilhelm
Jan. 25.......... Chemnitz
Jan. 28......Koenig Albert
Feb. 1............. Neckar
Feb. 3....Grosser Kurfuerst
Feb. 13......... Scharnhorst
Feb. 17........ Brandenburg
Feb. 18..Pr. Fried'h Wilhelm
Feb. 19............. Koeln
Feb. 27............. Main
Mar. 2.......... Chemnitz
Mar. 3.......... Gneisenau
Mar. 15............. Roon
Mar. 17......... Scharnhorst
Mar. 23..Pr. Fried'h Wilhelm
Mar. 25............. Rhein
Mar. 30....... Brandenburg
Apr. 1............. Yorck
Apr. 10.......... Wittekind
Apr. 11............. Main
Apr. 14.......... Gneisenau
Apr. 23............. Breslau
Apr. 27..Pr. Fried'h Wilhelm
May 5....Fried'h der Grosse
May 10............. Berlin
May 18......Prinzess Alice
May 26............. Bremen

NORTH GERMAN LLOYD
Regular Service
Bremen—New York
(Continued)
N.Y.

Arrival	Steamer
June 1..P. Fried'h Wilhelm
June 9....Fried'h der Grosse
June 16....Grosser Kurfuerst
June 21...George Washington
June 30............. Bremen
July 6..Pr. Fried'h Wilhelm
July 14....Fried'h der Grosse
July 20....Grosser Kurfuerst
July 26...George Washington
Aug. 4............. Bremen
Aug. 12..Pr. Fried'h Wilhelm
Aug. 18....Fried'h der Grosse
Aug. 24....Grosser Kurfuerst
Aug. 30...George Washington
Sept. 7............. Bremen
Sept. 13..Pr. Fried'h Wilhelm
Sept. 20............. Main
Sept. 21....Fried'h der Grosse
Sept. 28...Grosser Kurfuerst
Oct. 4...George Washington
Oct. 13............. Bremen
Oct. 19..Pr. Fried'h Wilhelm
Oct. 20............. Neckar
Oct. 29.......... Barbarossa
Nov. 3....Grosser Kurfuerst
Nov. 11..George Washington
Nov. 12............. Cassel
Nov. 17............. Main
Nov. 25............. Hannover
Nov. 26..Pr. Fried'h Wilhelm
Dec. 3............. Rhein
Dec. 10............. Neckar
Dec. 17............. Breslau
Dec. 19............. Zieten
Dec. 22............. Roon
Dec. 28............. Main

NORTH GERMAN LLOYD
Mediterranean—New York
N.Y.

Arrival	Steamer
Feb. 8......... Barbarossa
Feb. 19......Koenigin Luise
Feb. 27......Prinzess Irene
Mar. 4.......Koenig Albert
Mar. 12............. Barbarossa
Mar. 20......... Barbarossa
Apr. 2......Koenigin Luise
Apr. 9......Prinzess Irene
Apr. 15......Koenig Albert
Apr. 21............. Neckar
Apr. 24....Grosser Kurfuerst
Apr. 30......... Barbarossa
May 13......Koenigin Luise
May 27......Prinzess Irene
June 4............. Neckar
June 9......Koenig Albert
June 18......... Barbarossa
June 22............. Berlin
July 1......Koenigin Luise
July 8......Prinzess Irene
Aug. 3............. Berlin
Aug. 18......Prinzess Irene
Sept. 2....Koenig Albert

NORTH GERMAN LLOYD
Mediterranean—New York
(Continued)
N.Y.

Arrival	Steamer
Sept. 14............. Berlin
Sept. 30.......Prinzess Irene
Oct. 14.......Koenig Albert
Oct. 27............. Berlin
Nov. 11.......Prinzess Irene
Nov. 25.......Koenig Albert
Dec. 8............. Berlin
Dec. 24.......Prinzess Irene

NORTH GERMAN LLOYD
Bremen—Baltimore
Baltimore

Arrival	Steamer
Jan. 6............. Rhein
Jan. 15............. Main
Jan. 29............. Breslau
Feb. 5............. Hannover
Feb. 14............. Rhein
Mar. 1............. Main
Mar. 5............. Cassel
Mar. 13............. Breslau
Mar. 27............. Rhein
Apr. 2............. Koeln
Apr. 12............. Hannover
Apr. 22............. Frankfurt
Apr. 25............. Breslau
May 6............. Rhein
May 19............. Main
June 5............. Koeln
June 10............. Rhein
June 17............. Breslau
June 24............. Hannover
June 29............. Main
July 15............. Frankfurt
July 21............. Cassel
Aug. 4............. Breslau
Aug. 10............. Main
Aug. 26............. Chemnitz
Sept. 8............. Cassel
Sept. 15............. Rhein
Sept. 22............. Main
Oct. 6............. Breslau
Oct. 21............. Neckar
Nov. 5............. Chemnitz
Nov. 20............. Main
Nov. 28............. Hannover
Dec. 2............. Brandenburg
Dec. 19............. Breslau
Dec. 30............. Main

NORTH-WEST TRANS-
PORTATION LINE
Halifax—Rotterdam—Ham-
burg—New York
N.Y.

Arrival	Steamer
Feb. 21............. Volturno
Mar. 20.......Raglan Castle
Apr. 4............. Volturno
Apr. 18............. Uranium
May 8.......Raglan Castle
May 16............. Volturno
June 2............. Uranium
June 23.......Raglan Castle
July 4............. Volturno

Year 1909

NORTH-WEST TRANS-PORTATION LINE
Halifax—Rotterdam—Ham-
burg—New York
(Continued)

N. Y.

Arrival	Steamer
July 17	Uranium
Aug. 2	Raglan Castle
Aug. 14	Volturno
Sept. 3	Uranium
Sept. 17	Napolitan Prince
Oct. 3	Volturno
Oct. 18	Uranium
Oct. 30	Napolitan Prince
Nov. 12	Volturno
Nov. 26	Uranium
Dec. 11	Napolitan Prince
Dec. 20	Sicilian Prince
Dec. 28	Volturno

RED STAR LINE
Antwerp—New York

N. Y.

Arrival	Steamer
Jan. 7	Samland
Jan. 13	Finland
Jan. 19	Vaderland
Jan. 27	Kroonland
Feb. 3	Zeeland
Feb. 10	Samland
Feb. 18	Gothland
Feb. 24	Vaderland
Mar. 2	Kroonland
Mar. 8	Zeeland
Mar. 17	Samland
Mar. 24	Gothland
Mar. 30	Vaderland
Apr. 7	Zeeland
Apr. 13	Kroonland
Apr. 19	Lapland
Apr. 27	Vaderland
May 4	Zeeland
May 11	Kroonland
May 16	Lapland
May 24	Vaderland
June 1	Zeeland
June 8	Kroonland
June 13	Lapland
June 20	Vaderland
July 5	Kroonland
July 11	Lapland
July 19	Vaderland
July 26	Zeeland
Aug. 2	Kroonland
Aug. 8	Lapland
Aug. 16	Vaderland
Aug. 23	Zeeland
Aug. 30	Kroonland
Sept. 5	Lapland
Sept. 13	Vaderland
Sept. 20	Zeeland
Sept. 27	Kroonland
Oct. 3	Lapland
Oct. 12	Vaderland
Oct. 19	Zeeland
Oct. 27	Kroonland
Nov. 1	Lapland
Nov. 8	Finland
Nov. 17	Zeeland

RED STAR LINE
Antwerp—New York
(Continued)

N. Y.

Arrival	Steamer
Nov. 23	Vaderland
Nov. 29	Kroonland
Dec. 6	Lapland
Dec. 14	Finland
Dec. 20	Zeeland
Dec. 27	Vaderland

RED STAR LINE
Antwerp—Philadelphia—
Boston

Boston

Arrival	Steamer
Jan. 11	Menominee
Jan. 27	Marquette
Feb. 10	Manitou
Feb. 23	Menominee
Mar. 9	Marquette
Mar. 24	Manitou
Apr. 7	Menominee
Apr. 20	Marquette
May 5	Manitou
May 17	Menominee
June 1	Marquette
June 15	Manitou
June 28	Menominee
July 12	Marquette
Aug. 9	Manitou
Aug. 23	Menominee
Sept. 5	Marquette
Sept. 20	Manitou
Oct. 4	Menominee
Oct. 20	Marquette
Nov. 3	Manitou
Nov. 15	Menominee
Nov. 29	Marquette
Dec. 15	Manitou
Dec. 27	Menominee

RUSSIAN-AMERICAN LINE
Rotterdam, Libau—New York

N. Y.

Arrival	Steamer
Jan. 12	Estonia
Feb. 16	Korea
Feb. 26	Estonia
Mar. 19	Lituania
Apr. 8	Russia
May 5	Lituania
May 21	Estonia
May 30	Russia
June 18	Lituania
July 3	Estonia
July 15	Russia
July 31	Lituania
Aug. 17	Birma
Aug. 30	Russia
Sept. 14	Estonia
Sept. 27	Birma
Nov. 1	Russia
Nov. 16	Estonia
Nov. 29	Lituania
Dec. 15	Birma
Dec. 26	Russia

SCANDINAVIAN-AMERICAN LINE
Scandinavian—New York

N. Y.

Arrival	Steamer
Jan. 29	C. F. Tietgen
Feb. 10	Hellig Olav
Feb. 25	Oscar II
Mar. 9	United States
Mar. 24	Hellig Olav
Apr. 8	Oscar II
Apr. 20	United States
Apr. 28	C. F. Tietgen
May 5	Hellig Olav
May 18	Oscar II
June 1	United States
June 9	C. F. Tietgen
June 15	Hellig Olav
June 28	Oscar II
July 13	United States
July 27	Hellig Olav
Aug. 9	Oscar II
Aug. 24	United States
Aug. 31	C. F. Tietgen
Sept. 7	Hellig Olav
Sept. 21	Oscar II
Oct. 5	United States
Oct. 13	C. F. Tietgen
Oct. 20	Hellig Olav
Nov. 2	Oscar II
Nov. 16	United States
Nov. 24	C. F. Tietgen
Nov. 30	Hellig Olav
Dec. 22	Oscar II

SICULA AMERICANA
Mediterranean—New York

N. Y.

Arrival	Steamer
Jan. 25	San Giovanni
Feb. 7	San Giorgio
Mar. 4	San Giovanni
Mar. 20	San Giorgio
Apr. 14	San Giovanni
Apr. 30	San Giorgio
May 25	San Giovanni
June 9	San Giorgio
July 12	San Giovanni
Aug. 7	San Giorgio
Sept. 10	San Giovanni
Oct. 9	San Giorgio
Oct. 23	San Giovanni
Nov. 20	San Giorgio
Dec. 2	San Giovanni

WHITE STAR LINE
Liverpool—New York

N. Y.

Arrival	Steamer
Jan. 2	Cedric
Jan. 10	Celtic
Jan. 25	Baltic
Feb. 1	Arabic
Feb. 7	Celtic
Feb. 20	Baltic
Mar. 7	Celtic
Mar. 21	Baltic
Apr. 4	Celtic
Apr. 18	Baltic

Year 1909

WHITE STAR LINE
Liverpool—New York
(Continued)

N.Y. Arrival	Steamer
Apr. 25	Arabic
May 2	Celtic
May 9	Cedric
May 16	Baltic
May 23	Arabic
May 30	Celtic
June 6	Cedric
June 12	Baltic
June 20	Arabic
June 27	Celtic
July 3	Cedric
July 10	Baltic
July 19	Arabic
July 25	Celtic
Aug. 1	Cedric
Aug. 8	Baltic
Aug. 16	Arabic
Aug. 22	Celtic
Aug. 29	Cedric
Sept. 5	Baltic
Sept. 12	Arabic
Sept. 19	Celtic
Sept. 26	Cedric
Oct. 3	Baltic
Oct. 11	Arabic
Oct. 18	Celtic
Oct. 25	Cedric
Oct. 31	Baltic
Nov. 8	Arabic
Nov. 14	Celtic
Nov. 21	Cedric
Nov. 28	Baltic
Dec. 6	Arabic
Dec. 12	Celtic
Dec. 26	Laurentic

WHITE STAR LINE
Southampton—New York

N.Y. Arrival	Steamer
Jan. 7	Oceanic
Jan. 14	Teutonic
Jan. 29	Adriatic
Feb. 5	Majestic
Feb. 11	Oceanic
Feb. 18	Teutonic
Feb. 26	Adriatic
Mar. 4	Majestic
Mar. 10	Oceanic

WHITE STAR LINE
Southampton—New York
(Continued)

N.Y. Arrival	Steamer
Mar. 18	Teutonic
Mar. 26	Adriatic
Apr. 1	Majestic
Apr. 7	Oceanic
Apr. 15	Teutonic
Apr. 22	Adriatic
Apr. 29	Majestic
May 5	Oceanic
May 13	Teutonic
May 20	Adriatic
May 27	Majestic
June 2	Oceanic
June 9	Teutonic
June 17	Adriatic
June 23	Majestic
June 30	Oceanic
July 8	Teutonic
July 15	Adriatic
July 21	Majestic
July 28	Oceanic
Aug. 5	Teutonic
Aug. 12	Adriatic
Aug. 18	Majestic
Aug. 25	Oceanic
Sept. 1	Teutonic
Sept. 9	Adriatic
Sept. 15	Majestic
Sept. 22	Oceanic
Sept. 29	Teutonic
Oct. 7	Adriatic
Oct. 14	Majestic
Oct. 20	Oceanic
Oct. 28	Teutonic
Nov. 4	Adriatic
Nov. 10	Majestic
Nov. 17	Oceanic
Nov. 25	Teutonic
Dec. 3	Adriatic
Dec. 9	Majestic
Dec. 15	Oceanic
Dec. 23	Teutonic

WHITE STAR LINE
Mediterranean—New York

N.Y. Arrival	Steamer
Jan. 14	Republic
Jan. 16	Cedric

WHITE STAR LINE
Mediterranean—New York
(Continued)

N.Y. Arrival	Steamer
Mar. 18	Finland
Mar. 26	Cedric
Mar. 29	Cretic
Apr. 23	Finland
May 10	Cretic
June 2	Finland
June 21	Cretic
Sept. 17	Cretic
Nov. 1	Cretic
Dec. 30	Cretic

WHITE STAR LINE
Mediterranean—Boston

Boston Arrival	Steamer
Jan. 22	Romanic
Feb. 9	Canopic
Feb. 24	Cretic
Mar. 8	Romanic
Mar. 23	Canopic
Apr. 12	Romanic
May 4	Canopic
May 17	Romanic
June 7	Canopic
June 28	Romanic
July 31	Cretic
Sept. 9	Romanic
Sept. 27	Canopic
Oct. 19	Romanic
Nov. 8	Canopic
Nov. 26	Romanic

WHITE STAR LINE
Liverpool—Boston

Boston Arrival	Steamer
Jan. 8	Cymric
Feb. 9	Cymric
Mar. 16	Cymric
Apr. 26	Cymric
May 24	Cymric
June 21	Cymric
July 23	Cymric
Aug. 20	Cymric
Sept. 17	Cymric
Oct. 16	Cymric
Nov. 12	Cymric

Year 1910

ALLAN LINE
Glasgow—Boston
Boston

Arrival	Steamer
Jan. 13	Pretorian
Feb. 5	Numidian
Feb. 19	Ionian
Mar. 5	Pretorian
Mar. 18	Numidian
Apr. 1	Ionian
Apr. 13	Hesperian
Apr. 20	Numidian
May 9	Parisian
May 23	Numidian
June 7	Parisian
June 20	Numidian
July 5	Parisian
July 18	Numidian
Aug. 1	Parisian
Aug. 17	Numidian
Aug. 28	Parisian
Sept. 12	Numidian
Sept. 25	Parisian
Oct. 11	Numidian
Oct. 24	Parisian
Nov. 7	Numidian
Nov. 30	Pretorian
Dec. 15	Corinthian
Dec. 27	Lake Erie

AMERICAN LINE
Southampton—New York
N. Y.

Arrival	Steamer
Jan. 15	St. Louis
Jan. 16	Philadelphia
Jan. 27	New York
Feb. 19	St. Louis
Feb. 24	Philadelphia
Mar. 10	St. Louis
Mar. 24	Philadelphia
Apr. 7	St. Louis
Apr. 16	New York
Apr. 24	St. Paul
Apr. 30	Philadelphia
May 7	St. Louis
May 15	New York
May 21	St. Paul
May 28	Philadelphia
June 5	St. Louis
June 12	New York
June 19	St. Paul
June 27	Philadelphia
July 4	St. Louis
July 10	New York
July 16	St. Paul
July 23	Philadelphia
July 31	St. Louis
Aug. 7	New York
Aug. 13	St. Paul
Aug. 20	Philadelphia
Aug. 27	St. Louis
Sept. 3	New York
Sept. 10	St. Paul
Sept. 17	Philadelphia
Sept. 24	St. Louis
Oct. 1	New York

AMERICAN LINE
Southampton—New York
(Continued)
N. Y.

Arrival	Steamer
Oct. 8	St. Paul
Oct. 15	Philadelphia
Oct. 22	St. Louis
Oct. 29	New York
Nov. 5	St. Paul
Nov. 12	Philadelphia
Nov. 20	St. Louis
Nov. 27	New York
Dec. 4	St. Paul
Dec. 11	Philadelphia
Dec. 23	St. Louis

AMERICAN LINE
Liverpool—Philadelphia
Phila.

Arrival	Steamer
Jan. 11	Friesland
Jan. 20	Haverford
Feb. 1	Merion
Feb. 16	Friesland
Mar. 4	Haverford
Mar. 15	Merion
Mar. 20	Friesland
Apr. 6	Haverford
Apr. 17	Merion
Apr. 24	Friesland
May 9	Haverford
May 23	Merion
May 29	Friesland
June 13	Haverford
June 27	Merion
July 3	Friesland
July 18	Haverford
Aug. 1	Merion
Aug. 8	Friesland
Aug. 21	Haverford
Sept. 4	Merion
Sept. 10	Friesland
Sept. 25	Haverford
Oct. 11	Merion
Oct. 16	Friesland
Oct. 31	Haverford
Nov. 14	Merion
Nov. 21	Friesland
Dec. 4	Haverford
Dec. 21	Merion

ANCHOR LINE
Glasgow—New York
N. Y.

Arrival	Steamer
Jan. 4	Caledonia
Jan. 19	California
Jan. 31	Columbia
Feb. 7	Caledonia
Feb. 15	California
Feb. 23	Furnessia
Mar. 1	Columbia
Mar. 7	Caledonia
Mar. 13	California
Mar. 22	Furnessia
Mar. 27	Columbia

ANCHOR LINE
Glasgow—New York
(Continued)
N. Y.

Arrival	Steamer
Apr. 3	Caledonia
Apr. 10	California
Apr. 18	Furnessia
Apr. 24	Columbia
May 1	Caledonia
May 8	California
May 17	Furnessia
May 22	Columbia
May 29	Caledonia
June 6	California
June 13	Furnessia
June 19	Columbia
June 26	Caledonia
July 3	California
July 12	Furnessia
July 17	Columbia
July 24	Caledonia
Aug. 1	California
Aug. 8	Furnessia
Aug. 14	Columbia
Aug. 21	Caledonia
Aug. 28	California
Sept. 5	Furnessia
Sept. 11	Columbia
Sept. 17	Caledonia
Sept. 25	California
Oct. 4	Furnessia
Oct. 9	Columbia
Oct. 16	Caledonia
Oct. 24	California
Nov. 1	Furnessia
Nov. 6	Columbia
Nov. 13	Caledonia
Nov. 21	California
Nov. 29	Furnessia
Dec. 4	Columbia
Dec. 11	Caledonia
Dec. 19	California

ANCHOR LINE
Mediterranean—New York
N. Y.

Arrival	Steamer
Jan. 9	Perugia
Jan. 27	Italia
Feb. 14	Calabria
Mar. 5	Perugia
Mar. 17	Italia
Apr. 7	Calabria
Apr. 23	Perugia
May 4	Italia
May 29	Calabria
June 11	Perugia
June 24	Italia
July 15	Calabria
Aug. 17	Italia
Sept. 16	Calabria
Oct. 1	Perugia
Oct. 14	Italia
Nov. 22	Perugia
Dec. 5	Italia
Dec. 30	Calabria

Year 1910

ATLANTIC TRANSPORT LINE
London—New York
N.Y.

Arrival	Steamer
Jan. 2	Minnewaska
Jan. 9	Minnehaha
Jan. 25	Minneapolis
Feb. 1	Minnetonka
Feb. 7	Minnewaska
Feb. 15	Minnehaha
Mar. 8	Minnetonka
Mar. 14	Minnewaska
Mar. 21	Minneapolis
Apr. 4	Minnehaha
Apr. 11	Minnewaska
Apr. 18	Minneapolis
Apr. 25	Minnetonka
May 9	Minnewaska
May 16	Minneapolis
May 23	Minnetonka
May 31	Mesaba
June 6	Minnewaska
June 13	Minneapolis
June 21	Minnetonka
June 29	Mesaba
July 4	Minnewaska
July 12	Minneapolis
July 18	Minnetonka
Aug. 1	Minnewaska
Aug. 9	Minneapolis
Aug. 15	Minnetonka
Aug. 24	Mesaba
Aug. 29	Minnewaska
Sept. 5	Minneapolis
Sept. 12	Minnetonka
Sept. 20	Mesaba
Sept. 26	Minnewaska
Oct. 3	Minneapolis
Oct. 10	Minnetonka
Oct. 18	Mesaba
Oct. 24	Minnewaska
Oct. 31	Minneapolis
Nov. 5	Minnehaha
Nov. 12	Minnetonka
Nov. 26	Minnewaska
Dec. 3	Minneapolis
Dec. 11	Minnehaha
Dec. 20	Minnetonka

AUSTRO-AMERICANA LINE
Mediterranean—New York
N.Y.

Arrival	Steamer
Jan. 6	Alice
Jan. 19	Oceania
Feb. 3	Argentina
Feb. 12	Martha Washington
Feb. 27	Alice
Mar. 11	Oceania
Mar. 23	Argentina
Mar. 28	Martha Washington
Apr. 9	Eugenia
Apr. 14	Alice
Apr. 20	Laura
Apr. 27	Oceania
May 12	Argentina
May 17	Martha Washington
May 31	Alice

AUSTRO-AMERICANA LINE
Mediterranean—New York
(Continued)
N.Y.

Arrival	Steamer
June 11	Eugenia
June 17	Columbia
June 23	Oceania
June 29	Argentina
July 4	Martha Washington
July 22	Atlanta
Aug. 9	Oceania
Aug. 18	Columbia
Aug. 21	Martha Washington
Sept. 9	Argentina
Sept. 23	Atlanta
Sept. 28	Oceania
Oct. 5	Alice
Oct. 10	Martha Washington
Oct. 21	Columbia
Oct. 29	Eugenia
Nov. 9	Laura
Nov. 16	Oceania
Nov. 23	Alice
Nov. 28	Martha Washington
Dec. 28	Laura

COMPANIA TRANSATLANTICA LINE
(Spanish Line)
Mediterranean—New York
N.Y.

Arrival	Steamer
Jan. 10	Buenos Aires
Feb. 13	Montserrat
Mar. 11	Montevideo
Apr. 12	Manuel Calvo
May 12	Antonio Lopez
June 10	Buenos Aires
July 11	Manuel Calvo
Aug. 10	Montevideo
Sept. 10	Manuel Calvo
Oct. 12	Antonio Lopez
Nov. 11	Buenos Aires
Dec. 14	Montserrat

CUNARD LINE
Liverpool—New York
N.Y.

Arrival	Steamer
Jan. 2	Umbria
Jan. 10	Carmania
Jan. 15	Lusitania
Jan. 23	Campania
Jan. 31	Umbria
Feb. 3	Mauretania
Feb. 13	Campania
Feb. 21	Umbria
Feb. 25	Mauretania
Mar. 4	Lusitania
Mar. 12	Campania
Mar. 17	Mauretania
Mar. 24	Lusitania
Apr. 2	Campania
Apr. 7	Mauretania
Apr. 13	Caronia
Apr. 14	Lusitania
Apr. 23	Campania
May 1	Carmania

CUNARD LINE
Liverpool—New York
(Continued)
N.Y.

Arrival	Steamer
May 5	Mauretania
May 11	Caronia
May 13	Lusitania
May 20	Campania
May 25	Carmania
May 26	Mauretania
June 2	Lusitania
June 7	Caronia
June 11	Campania
June 16	Mauretania
June 22	Carmania
June 24	Lusitania
July 1	Campania
July 5	Caronia
July 7	Mauretania
July 14	Lusitania
July 20	Carmania
July 22	Campania
July 31	Caronia
Aug. 4	Mauretania
Aug. 11	Lusitania
Aug. 17	Carmania
Aug. 20	Campania
Aug. 25	Mauretania
Aug. 30	Caronia
Sept. 1	Lusitania
Sept. 9	Campania
Sept. 13	Carmania
Sept. 15	Mauretania
Sept. 22	Lusitania
Sept. 27	Caronia
Sept. 30	Campania
Oct. 6	Mauretania
Oct. 11	Carmania
Oct. 13	Lusitania
Oct. 22	Campania
Oct. 29	Caronia
Nov. 3	Mauretania
Nov. 10	Lusitania
Nov. 20	Carmania
Nov. 24	Mauretania
Dec. 2	Campania
Dec. 11	Caronia
Dec. 16	Mauretania
Dec. 23	Lusitania
Dec. 30	Campania

CUNARD LINE
Mediterranean—Adriatic— New York
N.Y.

Arrival	Steamer
Jan. 2	Caronia
Jan. 25	Saxonia
Feb. 3	Pannonia
Feb. 14	Caronia
Mar. 1	Carmania
Mar. 18	Saxonia
Mar. 25	Carpathia
Apr. 5	Pannonia
Apr. 21	Ultonia
May 10	Carpathia
May 26	Pannonia
June 8	Ultonia
June 28	Carpathia

Year 1910

CUNARD LINE
Mediterranean—Adriatic—
New York
(Continued)

N. Y.

Arrival	Steamer
July 14	Pannonia
July 29	Ultonia
Aug. 16	Carpathia
Aug. 31	Pannonia
Sept. 14	Ultonia
Oct. 5	Carpathia
Oct. 21	Pannonia
Nov. 3	Ultonia
Nov. 18	Carpathia
Dec. 3	Saxonia
Dec. 10	Pannonia
Dec. 24	Ultonia
Dec. 31	Carmania

CUNARD LINE
Liverpool—Boston

Boston

Arrival	Steamer
Feb. 3	Ivernia
Mar. 11	Ivernia
Apr. 7	Ivernia
May 5	Ivernia
May 19	Saxonia
June 2	Ivernia
June 16	Saxonia
June 30	Ivernia
July 14	Saxonia
July 28	Ivernia
Aug. 11	Saxonia
Aug. 25	Ivernia
Sept. 8	Saxonia
Sept. 22	Ivernia
Oct. 6	Saxonia
Oct. 20	Ivernia
Nov. 17	Ivernia

FABRE LINE
Mediterranean—New York

N. Y.

Arrival	Steamer
Jan. 15	Gallia
Jan. 22	Germania
Jan. 28	Roma
Feb. 7	Venezia
Feb. 28	Madonna
Mar. 15	Roma
Mar. 22	Venezia
Mar. 30	Germania
Apr. 11	Madonna
Apr. 27	Roma
May 2	Massilia
May 9	Venezia
May 18	Germania
May 27	Madonna
June 13	Roma
June 22	Venezia
June 27	Massilia
July 4	Germania
July 12	Madonna
July 26	Roma
Aug. 6	Venezia
Aug. 14	Germania
Aug. 17	Sant' Anna
Aug. 29	Madonna

FABRE LINE
Mediterranean—New York
(Continued)

N. Y.

Arrival	Steamer
Sept. 6	Massilia
Sept. 7	Roma
Sept. 18	Venezia
Sept. 26	Germania
Oct. 3	Sant' Anna
Oct. 9	Madonna
Oct. 21	Roma
Nov. 1	Venezia
Nov. 9	Germania
Nov. 13	Sant' Anna
Nov. 26	Madonna
Dec. 6	Roma
Dec. 22	Venezia
Dec. 28	Germania

FRENCH LINE
(Compagnie Generale Transatlantique)
Havre—Bordeaux—New York

N. Y.

Arrival	Steamer
Jan. 3	La Bretagne
Jan. 9	La Savoie
Jan. 15	Hudson
Jan. 16	La Lorraine
Jan. 19	Mexico
Jan. 23	La Lorraine
Jan. 30	Floride
Jan. 31	La Bretagne
Feb. 5	La Savoie
Feb. 10	St. Laurent
Feb. 12	Caroline
Feb. 13	La Provence
Feb. 16	La Gascogne
Feb. 24	La Bretagne
Feb. 27	La Savoie
Mar. 3	Chicago
Mar. 6	La Lorraine
Mar. 10	Hudson
Mar. 12	La Provence
Mar. 14	Floride
Mar. 15	La Gascogne
Mar. 20	La Touraine
Mar. 25	Caroline
Mar. 26	La Savoie
Mar. 29	Chicago
Apr. 2	La Lorraine
Apr. 5	St. Laurent
Apr. 5	Niagara
Apr. 9	La Provence
Apr. 12	La Gascogne
Apr. 16	La Touraine
Apr. 23	Floride
Apr. 25	La Bretagne
Apr. 25	Chicago
Apr. 30	La Lorraine
May 2	Hudson
May 5	Caroline
May 7	La Savoie
May 10	La Gascogne
May 13	La Provence
May 17	Niagara
May 22	La Touraine
May 23	Chicago
May 28	St. Laurent
May 28	La Lorraine

FRENCH LINE
(Compagnie Generale Transatlantique)
Havre—Bordeaux—New York
(Continued)

N. Y.

Arrival	Steamer
June 2	Floride
June 4	La Savoie
June 7	La Gascogne
June 10	La Provence
June 17	Caroline
June 18	La Lorraine
June 20	Chicago
June 25	La Savoie
June 25	Hudson
July 2	La Provence
July 10	Californie
July 11	La Bretagne
July 15	Floride
July 16	La Lorraine
July 18	Chicago
July 23	La Savoie
July 23	La Laurent
July 29	Caroline
July 31	La Touraine
Aug. 7	La Bretagne
Aug. 12	La Provence
Aug. 19	Californie
Aug. 19	Hudson
Aug. 21	La Touraine
Aug. 27	La Lorraine
Aug. 30	Chicago
Sept. 3	La Provence
Sept. 6	Niagara
Sept. 10	La Savoie
Sept. 12	La Gascogne
Sept. 18	La Lorraine
Sept. 18	Mexico
Sept. 21	Floride
Sept. 25	La Touraine
Sept. 26	Chicago
Sept. 30	La Provence
Oct. 7	Caroline
Oct. 8	La Savoie
Oct. 12	La Gascogne
Oct. 12	St. Laurent
Oct. 15	La Lorraine
Oct. 18	Niagara
Oct. 23	La Touraine
Oct. 26	Chicago
Oct. 29	La Provence
Nov. 2	Floride
Nov. 5	La Savoie
Nov. 8	La Gascogne
Nov. 12	Hudson
Nov. 12	La Lorraine
Nov. 17	Caroline
Nov. 22	Chicago
Nov. 28	La Bretagne
Nov. 29	Niagara
Nov. 30	La Touraine
Dec. 3	La Savoie
Dec. 6	La Gascogne
Dec. 10	La Lorraine
Dec. 19	La Touraine
Dec. 21	Floride
Dec. 21	Chicago
Dec. 26	La Bretagne
Dec. 30	Caroline
Dec. 31	La Lorraine

Year 1910

GREEK LINE
Greece—New York
N.Y.

Arrival	Steamer
Jan. 4	Themistocles
Jan. 23	Athinai
Mar. 12	Themistocles
Mar. 28	Athinai
Apr. 30	Themistocles
May 31	Athinai
June 30	Themistocles
July 26	Athinai
Aug. 25	Themistocles
Sept. 21	Athinai
Oct. 19	Themistocles
Nov. 11	Athinai
Dec. 18	Themistocles

HAMBURG-AMERICAN LINE
Hamburg—New York
N.Y.

Arrival	Steamer
Jan. 8	Graf Waldersee
Jan. 15	Pretoria
Jan. 17	Bluecher
Jan. 21	President Lincoln
Jan. 24	Cincinnati
Jan. 29	President Grant
Feb. 1	Amerika
Feb. 18	Pennsylvania
Feb. 19	Graf Waldersee
Feb. 22	K. Auguste Victoria
Mar. 4	President Lincoln
Mar. 10	President Grant
Mar. 12	Amerika
Mar. 25	Pretoria
Mar. 30	Pisa
Mar. 31	Graf Waldersee
Apr. 4	K. Auguste Victoria
Apr. 13	President Lincoln
Apr. 20	President Grant
Apr. 23	Amerika
May 5	Pennsylvania
May 12	Graf Waldersee
May 14	K. Auguste Victoria
May 18	Bluecher
May 18	Deutschland
May 26	President Lincoln
May 28	Amerika
June 1	President Grant
June 5	Cincinnati
June 10	Pennsylvania
June 12	Cleveland
June 17	Graf Waldersee
June 18	K. Auguste Victoria
June 23	Bluecher
June 23	Deutschland
June 30	President Lincoln
July 2	Amerika
July 7	President Grant
July 10	Cincinnati
July 15	Pennsylvania
July 17	Cleveland
July 23	K. Auguste Victoria
Aug. 4	President Lincoln
Aug. 6	Amerika
Aug. 12	Graf Waldersee
Aug. 14	Cincinnati

HAMBURG-AMERICAN LINE
Hamburg—New York
(Continued)
N.Y.

Arrival	Steamer
Aug. 21	Allemannia
Aug. 25	Pennsylvania
Aug. 27	K. Auguste Victoria
Aug. 31	Bluecher
Sept. 2	Patricia
Sept. 5	Cleveland
Sept. 6	Deutschland
Sept. 8	President Lincoln
Sept. 9	Amerika
Sept. 13	Pisa
Sept. 14	President Grant
Sept. 17	Cincinnati
Sept. 22	Graf Waldersee
Sept. 25	Prinz Oskar
Sept. 25	K. Auguste Victoria
Sept. 29	Pennsylvania
Oct. 1	Deutschland
Oct. 5	Pretoria
Oct. 5	Bluecher
Oct. 9	Cleveland
Oct. 13	Pallanza
Oct. 13	President Lincoln
Oct. 15	Amerika
Oct. 20	President Grant
Oct. 23	Cincinnati
Oct. 30	K. Auguste Victoria
Nov. 3	Pennsylvania
Nov. 7	Patricia
Nov. 12	Bluecher
Nov. 14	Amerika
Nov. 22	Cleveland
Nov. 24	Batavia
Nov. 28	K. Auguste Victoria
Dec. 2	Barcelona
Dec. 7	President Grant
Dec. 12	Pretoria
Dec. 16	Pennsylvania
Dec. 20	Amerika
Dec. 26	Arcadia
Dec. 28	President Lincoln

HAMBURG-AMERICAN LINE
Mediterranean—New York
N.Y.

Arrival	Steamer
Jan. 17	Moltke
Feb. 9	Hamburg
Mar. 19	Batavia
Mar. 26	Hamburg
Apr. 20	Cincinnati
May 2	Batavia
May 2	Hamburg
May 23	Moltke
June 10	Batavia
June 13	Hamburg
July 4	Moltke
Aug. 2	Hamburg
Aug. 22	Moltke
Sept. 13	Hamburg
Oct. 2	Moltke
Nov. 10	Hamburg
Dec. 20	Cincinnati

HAMBURG-AMERICAN LINE
Hamburg—Philadelphia
Phila.

Arrival	Steamer
Nov. 10	Graf Waldersee
Nov. 25	Prinz Oskar
Dec. 26	Graf Waldersee

HOLLAND-AMERICA LINE
Rotterdam—New York
N.Y.

Arrival	Steamer
Jan. 15	Potsdam
Jan. 26	Noordam
Feb. 2	Statendam
Feb. 17	Potsdam
Mar. 3	Noordam
Mar. 15	Ryndam
Mar. 21	Potsdam
Mar. 28	New Amsterdam
Apr. 5	Noordam
Apr. 11	Rotterdam
Apr. 18	Ryndam
Apr. 26	Potsdam
May 2	New Amsterdam
May 9	Noordam
May 16	Rotterdam
May 24	Ryndam
May 30	Potsdam
June 6	New Amsterdam
June 14	Noordam
June 20	Rotterdam
June 27	Ryndam
July 5	Potsdam
July 11	New Amsterdam
July 25	Noordam
Aug. 1	Rotterdam
Aug. 9	Ryndam
Aug. 15	Potsdam
Aug. 21	New Amsterdam
Aug. 28	Noordam
Sept. 4	Rotterdam
Sept. 12	Ryndam
Sept. 19	Potsdam
Sept. 25	New Amsterdam
Oct. 3	Noordam
Oct. 9	Rotterdam
Oct. 18	Ryndam
Oct. 25	Potsdam
Oct. 31	New Amsterdam
Nov. 8	Noordam
Nov. 14	Rotterdam
Nov. 23	Ryndam
Nov. 29	Potsdam
Dec. 5	New Amsterdam
Dec. 13	Noordam
Dec. 28	Ryndam

LLOYD ITALIANO
Mediterranean—New York
N.Y.

Arrival	Steamer
Jan. 30	Luisiana
Feb. 26	Virginia
Mar. 13	Florida
Mar. 21	Luisiana
Apr. 3	Virginia
Apr. 16	Indiana

Year 1910

LLOYD ITALIANO
Mediterranean—New York
(Continued)
N. Y.

Arrival	Steamer
Apr. 24	Florida
May 2	Luisiana
May 13	Virginia
May 26	Mendoza
June 6	Florida
June 18	Luisiana
July 7	Mendoza
Aug. 6	Luisiana
Aug. 31	Mendoza
Sept. 20	Luisiana
Oct. 4	Virginia
Nov. 2	Luisiana
Dec. 7	Indiana
Dec. 28	Mendoza

LLOYD SABAUDO
Mediterranean—New York
N. Y.

Arrival	Steamer
Jan. 24	Re d'Italia
Feb. 11	Regina d'Italia
Feb. 19	Prin. di Piemonte
Mar. 10	Re d'Italia
Mar. 21	Regina d'Italia
Apr. 3	Prin. di Piemonte
Apr. 19	Re d'Italia
Apr. 23	Regina d'Italia
May 16	Prin. di Piemonte
June 3	Re d'Italia
June 24	Tomaso di Savoia
July 18	Re d'Italia
Aug. 18	Regina d'Italia
Sept. 9	Prin. di Piemonte
Sept. 16	Re d'Italia
Oct. 15	Regina d'Italia
Nov. 1	Re d'Italia
Dec. 1	Regina d'Italia
Dec. 21	Re d'Italia

LLOYD SABAUDO
Mediterranean—Boston
Boston

Arrival	Steamer
Jan. 5	Patris
Mar. 17	Patris
Apr. 27	Patris
June 8	Patris
July 19	Patris
Aug. 27	Patris
Oct. 8	Patris
Nov. 21	Patris

NAVIGAZIONE GENE-RALE ITALIANA
Mediterranean—New York
N. Y.

Arrival	Steamer
Jan. 15	Lazio
Jan. 31	Duca di Genoa
Feb. 15	Duca degli Abruzzi
Mar. 2	Duca D'Aosta
Mar. 14	Duca di Genoa
Mar. 28	Duca degli Abruzzi
Apr. 12	Duca D'Aosta
Apr. 26	Duca di Genoa
May 8	Duca degli Abruzzi
May 14	Lombardia

NAVIGAZIONE GENE-RALE ITALIANA
Mediterranean—New York
(Continued)
N. Y.

Arrival	Steamer
May 24	Duca D'Aosta
June 6	Duca di Genoa
June 21	Duca degli Abruzzi
July 4	Duca D'Aosta
July 25	Duca di Genoa
Aug. 16	Duca degli Abruzzi
Aug. 27	Duca D'Aosta
Sept. 14	Duca di Genoa
Sept. 27	Duca degli Abruzzi
Oct. 10	Duca D'Aosta
Nov. 7	Duca degli Abruzzi
Nov. 21	Duca D'Aosta
Dec. 6	Duca di Genoa
Dec. 21	Duca degli Abruzzi

NAVIGAZIONE GENE-RALE ITALIANA
Mediterranean—Boston
Boston

Arrival	Steamer
Feb. 2	Duca di Genoa
Mar. 2	Sannio
Mar. 24	Lombardia
Apr. 19	Lazio
May 6	Sannio
June 14	Lazio
Aug. 14	Sannio
Oct. 9	Sannio
Nov. 21	Lazio

NORTH GERMAN LLOYD
Express Service
Bremen—New York
N. Y.

Arrival	Steamer
Jan. 19	Kronprinz Wilhelm
Feb. 2	K. Wm. der Grosse
Mar. 4	K. Wm. der Grosse
Mar. 16	Kronprinz'n Cecilie
Mar. 30	Kaiser Wilhelm II
Apr. 13	K. Wm. der Grosse
Apr. 19	Kronprinz'n Cecilie
Apr. 27	Kronprinz Wilhelm
May 4	Kaiser Wilhelm II
May 11	K. Wm. der Grosse
May 17	Kronprinz'n Cecilie
May 25	Kronprinz Wilhelm
June 1	Kaiser Wilhelm II
June 8	K. Wm. der Grosse
June 15	Kronprinz'n Cecilie
June 21	Kronprinz Wilhelm
June 28	Kaiser Wilhelm II
July 6	K. Wm. der Grosse
July 12	Kronprinz'n Cecilie
July 20	Kronprinz Wilhelm
July 26	Kaiser Wilhelm II
Aug. 3	K. Wm. der Grosse
Aug. 16	Kronprinz'n Cecilie
Aug. 23	Kronprinz Wilhelm
Aug. 30	Kaiser Wilhelm II
Sept. 6	K. Wm. der Grosse
Sept. 13	Kronprinz'n Cecilie
Sept. 20	Kronprinz Wilhelm
Sept. 27	Kaiser Wilhelm II
Oct. 5	K. Wm. der Grosse

NORTH GERMAN LLOYD
Express Service
Bremen—New York
(Continued)
N. Y.

Arrival	Steamer
Oct. 11	Kronprinz'n Cecilie
Oct. 18	Kronprinz Wilhelm
Oct. 26	Kaiser Wilhelm II
Nov. 1	K. Wm. der Grosse
Nov. 9	Kronprinz'n Cecilie
Nov. 22	Kronprinz Wilhelm
Dec. 7	K. Wm. der Grosse

NORTH GERMAN LLOYD
Bremen—New York
N. Y.

Arrival	Steamer
Jan. 3	Barbarossa
Jan. 13	Rhein
Jan. 16	Prz. Fried. Wilhelm
Jan. 22	Zieten
Jan. 26	Grosser Kurfuerst
Feb. 2	Neckar
Feb. 4	Roon
Feb. 14	Main
Feb. 17	Prinzess Irene
Feb. 18	George Washington
Mar. 2	Rhein
Mar. 5	Zieten
Mar. 8	Prz. Fried. Wilhelm
Mar. 14	Darmstadt
Mar. 17	Fried. der Grosse
Mar. 20	Oldenburg
Mar. 21	George Washington
Mar. 31	Neckar
Apr. 7	Rhein
Apr. 12	Prz. Fried. Wilhelm
Apr. 21	Zieten
Apr. 23	Oldenburg
Apr. 26	George Washington
May 4	Bremen
May 10	Grosser Kurfuerst
May 16	Prz. Fried. Wilhelm
May 25	Prinzess Alice
May 31	George Washington
June 8	Bremen
June 16	Main
June 21	Prz. Fried. Wilhelm
July 1	Koenigin Luise
July 5	George Washington
July 13	Bremen
July 21	Main
July 25	Prz. Fried. Wilhelm
Aug. 3	Rhein
Aug. 4	Barbarossa
Aug. 11	George Washington
Aug. 16	Bremen
Aug. 23	Grosser Kurfuerst
Aug. 29	Prz. Fried. Wilhelm
Sept. 8	Barbarossa
Sept. 12	George Washington
Sept. 19	Neckar
Sept. 21	Fried. der Grosse
Sept. 28	Grosser Kurfuerst
Oct. 3	Prz. Fried. Wilhelm
Oct. 10	George Washington
Oct. 20	Barbarossa
Oct. 25	Rhein
Oct. 26	Fried. der Grosse
Nov. 1	Grosser Kurfuerst

Year 1910

NORTH GERMAN LLOYD
Bremen—New York
(Continued)

N. Y.

Arrival	Steamer
Nov. 6	Neckar
Nov. 6	Prz. Fried. Wilhelm
Nov. 17	George Washington
Nov. 17	Roon
Nov. 25	Breslau
Nov. 30	Fried. der Grosse
Dec. 8	Main
Dec. 16	Rhein
Dec. 23	George Washington
Dec. 27	Brandenburg
Dec. 30	Frankfurt

NORTH GERMAN LLOYD
Mediterranean—New York

N. Y.

Arrival	Steamer
Jan. 18	Berlin
Feb. 3	Koenig Albert
Feb. 19	Barbarossa
Mar. 2	Berlin
Mar. 17	Koenig Albert
Apr. 1	Barbarossa
Apr. 7	Prinzess Irene
Apr. 13	Berlin
Apr. 23	Fried. der Grosse
Apr. 28	Koenig Albert
May 5	Neckar
May 12	Prinzess Irene
May 21	Barbarossa
May 25	Berlin
June 4	Fried. der Grosse
June 10	Neckar
June 17	Koenig Albert
June 24	Prinzess Irene
July 1	Barbarossa
July 16	Berlin
July 15	Fried. der Grosse
July 21	Koenig Albert
Aug. 3	Prinzess Irene
Aug. 11	Koenigin Luise
Aug. 23	Berlin
Sept. 1	Koenig Albert
Sept. 14	Prinzess Irene
Sept. 23	Koenigin Luise
Sept. 28	Berlin
Oct. 14	Koenig Albert
Oct. 29	Prinzess Irene
Nov. 4	Koenigin Luise
Nov. 12	Berlin
Nov. 25	Koenig Albert
Dec. 8	Prinzess Irene
Dec. 21	Berlin
Dec. 21	Koenigin Luise

NORTH GERMAN LLOYD
Bremen—Baltimore

Baltimore

Arrival	Steamer
Jan. 16	Rhein
Jan. 23	Cassel
Jan. 29	Frankfurt
Feb. 4	Neckar
Feb. 16	Main
Feb. 22	Koeln
Feb. 25	Chemnitz
Mar. 7	Cassel

NORTH GERMAN LLOYD
Bremen—Baltimore
(Continued)

Baltimore

Arrival	Steamer
Mar. 13	Hannover
Mar. 17	Brandenburg
Mar. 30	Main
Apr. 13	Cassel
Apr. 30	Brandenburg
May 12	Rhein
May 25	Cassel
June 11	Wittekind
June 23	Rhein
July 7	Cassel
July 23	Main
Aug. 5	Rhein
Aug. 17	Cassel
Sept. 1	Chemnitz
Sept. 7	Main
Sept. 13	Rhein
Sept. 20	Neckar
Sept. 28	Cassel
Oct. 19	Breslau
Oct. 27	Rhein
Nov. 19	Neckar
Nov. 26	Koeln
Dec. 11	Main
Dec. 29	Brandenburg

NORTH GERMAN LLOYD
Bremen—Philadelphia

Phila.

Arrival	Steamer
Mar. 4	Main
May 19	Frankfurt
Mar. 23	Frankfurt
Apr. 7	Breslau
Apr. 20	Hannover
June 1	Breslau
June 15	Hannover
July 1	Koeln
July 14	Frankfurt
July 28	Brandenburg
Aug. 10	Hannover
Aug. 24	Breslau
Sept. 7	Frankfurt
Sept. 19	Koeln
Oct. 5	Hannover
Oct. 18	Main
Nov. 2	Frankfurt
Nov. 17	Brandenburg
Nov. 30	Cassel
Dec. 17	Chemnitz
Dec. 31	Frankfurt

RED STAR LINE
Antwerp—New York

N. Y.

Arrival	Steamer
Jan. 5	Kroonland
Jan. 15	Samland
Jan. 17	Lapland
Jan. 26	Finland
Feb. 2	Vaderland
Feb. 8	Zeeland
Feb. 16	Lapland
Feb. 24	Kroonland
Mar. 3	Finland
Mar. 8	Vaderland

RED STAR LINE
Antwerp—New York
(Continued)

N. Y.

Arrival	Steamer
Mar. 14	Zeeland
Mar. 15	Gothland
Mar. 20	Lapland
Mar. 29	Kroonland
Apr. 5	Finland
Apr. 11	Vaderland
Apr. 17	Lapland
Apr. 26	Kroonland
May 3	Finland
May 10	Vaderland
May 15	Lapland
May 28	Kroonland
May 31	Finland
June 7	Vaderland
June 12	Lapland
June 23	Kroonland
June 28	Finland
July 4	Vaderland
July 10	Lapland
July 20	Kroonland
July 25	Finland
Aug. 2	Vaderland
Aug. 7	Lapland
Aug. 16	Kroonland
Aug. 22	Finland
Aug. 29	Vaderland
Sept. 4	Lapland
Sept. 12	Kroonland
Sept. 19	Finland
Sept. 26	Vaderland
Oct. 3	Lapland
Oct. 11	Kroonland
Oct. 18	Finland
Oct. 24	Vaderland
Oct. 30	Lapland
Nov. 9	Samland
Nov. 15	Finland
Nov. 22	Kroonland
Nov. 30	Gothland
Dec. 4	Lapland
Dec. 15	Samland
Dec. 21	Vaderland
Dec. 27	Kroonland

RED STAR LINE
Antwerp—Philadelphia—
Boston

Boston

Arrival	Steamer
Jan. 16	Marquette
Jan. 26	Manitou
Feb. 9	Menominee
Feb. 28	Marquette
Mar. 21	Menominee
Apr. 8	Marquette
Apr. 18	Manitou
May 2	Menominee
May 17	Marquette
May 30	Manitou
June 13	Menominee
June 28	Marquette
July 12	Manitou
Aug. 8	Menominee
Aug. 22	Manitou
Sept. 5	Marquette
Sept. 19	Menominee

Year 1910

RED STAR LINE
Antwerp—Philadelphia—
Boston
(Continued)

Boston

Arrival	Steamer
Oct. 3	Manitou
Oct. 17	Marquette
Oct. 31	Menominee
Nov. 15	Manitou
Nov. 28	Marquette
Dec. 23	Menominee
Dec. 28	Manitou

RUSSIAN-AMERICAN LINE
Rotterdam—Libau—New
York

N. Y.

Arrival	Steamer
Jan. 18	Estonia
Feb. 4	Lituania
Feb. 16	Russia
Mar. 2	Estonia
Mar. 15	Birma
Mar. 29	Lituania
Apr. 11	Russia
Apr. 26	Estonia
May 24	Birma
June 13	Russia
June 22	Estonia
July 5	Lituania
July 20	Birma
Aug. 1	Russia
Aug. 14	Lituania
Aug. 27	Birma
Sept. 11	Russia
Sept. 25	Lituania
Oct. 13	Estonia
Oct. 30	Birma
Nov. 12	Kursk
Dec. 2	Lituania
Dec. 17	Russia
Dec. 30	Kursh

SCANDINAVIAN-AMER. LINE
Scandinavian Ports—New
York

N. Y.

Arrival	Steamer
Jan. 27	C. F. Tietgen
Feb. 19	United States
Feb. 24	Hellig Olav
Mar. 9	Oscar II
Mar. 16	C. F. Tietgen
Apr. 1	Hellig Olav
Apr. 13	Oscar II
Apr. 24	C. F. Tietgen
May 3	United States
May 17	Hellig Olav
May 31	Oscar II
June 8	C. F. Tietgen
June 28	Hellig Olav
June 4	United States
July 12	Oscar II
July 26	Hellig Olav
Aug. 9	United States
Aug. 22	Oscar II
Aug. 30	C. F. Tietgen

SCANDINAVIAN-AMER. LINE
Scandinavian Ports—New
York
(Continued)

N. Y.

Arrival	Steamer
Sept. 6	Hellig Olav
Sept. 20	United States
Oct. 4	Oscar II
Oct. 12	C. F. Tietgen
Oct. 20	Hellig Olav
Nov. 1	United States
Nov. 15	Oscar II
Nov. 22	C. F. Tietgen
Nov. 29	Hellig Olav
Dec. 22	United States

SICULA AMERICANA LINE
Mediterranean Line—New
York

N. Y.

Arrival	Steamer
Jan. 24	San Giorgio
Feb. 27	San Giovanni
Mar. 19	San Giorgia
Apr. 14	San Giovanni
Apr. 28	San Giorgia
May 23	San Giovanni
June 10	San Giorgio
July 6	San Giovanni
Aug. 2	San Giorgio
Sept. 2	San Giovanni
Sept. 29	San Giorgio
Oct. 26	San Giovanni
Nov. 17	San Giorgio
Dec. 2	San Giovanni

WHITE STAR LINE
Liverpool—New York

N. Y.

Arrival	Steamer
Jan. 10	Arabic
Jan. 17	Baltic
Jan. 24	Celtic
Jan. 31	Laurentic
Feb. 15	Baltic
Feb. 27	Laurentic
Mar. 13	Baltic
Mar. 27	Laurentic
Apr. 10	Baltic
Apr. 25	Cedric
May 2	Arabic
May 8	Baltic
May 16	Celtic
May 22	Cedric
May 30	Arabic
June 6	Baltic
June 12	Celtic
June 19	Cedric
June 27	Arabic
July 4	Baltic
July 10	Celtic
July 17	Cedric
July 25	Arabic
July 31	Baltic
Aug. 7	Celtic
Aug. 14	Cedric
Aug. 21	Arabic
Aug. 28	Baltic

WHITE STAR LINE
Liverpool—New York
(Continued)

N. Y.

Arrival	Steamer
Sept. 4	Celtic
Sept. 11	Cedric
Sept. 18	Arabic
Sept. 25	Baltic
Oct. 2	Celtic
Oct. 9	Cedric
Oct. 17	Arabic
Oct. 23	Baltic
Oct. 30	Celtic
Nov. 6	Cedric
Nov. 14	Arabic
Nov. 20	Baltic
Nov. 27	Celtic
Dec. 4	Cedric
Dec. 12	Arabic
Dec. 19	Baltic

WHITE STAR LINE
Southampton—New York

N. Y.

Arrival	Steamer
Jan. 7	Adriatic
Jan. 20	Oceanic
Feb. 3	Adriatic
Feb. 17	Oceanic
Mar. 4	Adriatic
Mar. 16	Oceanic
Mar. 31	Adriatic
Apr. 13	Oceanic
Apr. 21	Majestic
Apr. 28	Adriatic
May 5	Teutonic
May 11	Oceanic
May 18	Majestic
May 26	Adriatic
June 2	Teutonic
June 8	Oceanic
June 15	Majestic
June 23	Adriatic
June 30	Teutonic
July 6	Oceanic
July 14	Majestic
July 21	Adriatic
July 28	Teutonic
Aug. 3	Oceanic
Aug. 11	Majestic
Aug. 18	Adriatic
Aug. 24	Teutonic
Aug. 31	Oceanic
Sept. 7	Majestic
Sept. 15	Adriatic
Sept. 21	Teutonic
Sept. 28	Oceanic
Oct. 6	Majestic
Oct. 13	Adriatic
Oct. 20	Teutonic
Oct. 26	Oceanic
Nov. 2	Majestic
Nov. 10	Adriatic
Nov. 17	Teutonic
Nov. 23	Oceanic
Dec. 1	Majestic
Dec. 8	Adriatic
Dec. 15	Teutonic
Dec. 28	Oceanic

Year 1911

ALLAN LINE
Glasgow—Halifax—Boston
Boston

Arrival	Steamer
Jan. 11	Pretorian
Feb. 5	Sicilian
Feb. 15	Ionian
Mar. 5	Lake Erie
Mar. 19	Numidian
Mar. 31	Ionian
Apr. 13	Hesperian
Apr. 21	Numidian
May 7	Parisian
May 21	Numidian
June 4	Parisian
June 19	Numidian
July 3	Parisian
July 18	Numidian
July 31	Parisian
Aug. 17	Numidian
Aug. 27	Parisian
Sept. 14	Sardinian
Sept. 25	Parisian
Oct. 10	Numidian
Oct. 23	Parisian
Nov. 9	Numidian
Nov. 29	Scotian
Dec. 16	Numidian

AMERICAN LINE
Southampton—New York
N. Y.

Arrival	Steamer
Jan. 5	St. Paul
Jan. 19	New York
Feb. 3	St. Paul
Feb. 16	St. Louis
Mar. 3	St. Paul
Mar. 16	St. Louis
Mar. 20	St. Paul
Apr. 8	Philadelphia
Apr. 16	St. Louis
Apr. 23	St. Paul
Apr. 30	New York
May 6	Philadelphia
May 13	St. Louis
May 25	St. Paul
May 27	New York
June 3	Philadelphia
June 10	St. Louis
June 29	St. Paul
July 1	Philadelphia
July 9	St. Louis
July 16	New York
July 22	St. Paul
July 29	Philadelphia
Aug. 6	St. Louis
Aug. 24	St. Paul
Aug. 27	Philadelphia
Sept. 2	St. Louis
Sept. 9	New York
Sept. 16	St. Paul
Sept. 23	Philadelphia
Sept. 30	St. Louis
Oct. 7	New York
Oct. 19	St. Paul
Oct. 21	Philadelphia

AMERICAN LINE
Southampton—New York
(Continued)
N. Y.

Arrival	Steamer
Oct. 28	St. Louis
Nov. 9	New York
Nov. 16	St. Paul
Nov. 19	Philadelphia
Nov. 30	St. Louis
Dec. 10	New York
Dec. 21	Philadelphia

AMERICAN LINE
Liverpool—Philadelphia
Phila.

Arrival	Steamer
Jan. 1	Friesland
Jan. 16	Haverford
Feb. 2	Merion
Feb. 22	Haverford
Mar. 9	Merion
Mar. 28	Haverford
Apr. 10	Merion
Apr. 16	Friesland
May 2	Haverford
May 15	Merion
May 22	Friesland
June 5	Haverford
June 19	Merion
July 2	Dominion
July 23	Haverford
Aug. 6	Dominion
Aug. 14	Merion
Sept. 11	Dominion
Sept. 18	Haverford
Oct. 3	Merion
Oct. 15	Dominion
Oct. 23	Haverford
Nov. 7	Merion
Nov. 29	Dominion
Dec. 5	Haverford
Dec. 20	Merion

ANCHOR LINE
Mediterranean—New York
N. Y.

Arrival	Steamer
Feb. 4	Italia
Feb. 26	Calabria
Mar. 26	Italia
Apr. 9	Perugia
Apr. 22	Calabria
May 11	Italia
May 26	Perugia
June 10	Calabria
July 1	Italia
July 15	Perugia
Aug. 14	Calabria
Sept. 6	Italia
Sept. 24	Perugia
Oct. 10	Calabria
Oct. 23	Italia
Nov. 12	Perugia
Nov. 28	Calabria
Dec. 25	Italia

ANCHOR LINE
Glasgow—New York
N. Y.

Arrival	Steamer
Jan. 4	Furnessia
Jan. 15	Columbia
Jan. 30	Caledonia
Feb. 7	Furnessia
Feb. 13	California
Feb. 20	Columbia
Feb. 27	Caledonia
Mar. 8	Furnessia
Mar. 13	California
Mar. 19	Columbia
Mar. 26	Caledonia
Apr. 4	Furnessia
Apr. 10	California
Apr. 16	Columbia
Apr. 23	Caledonia
May 2	Furnessia
May 8	California
May 14	Columbia
May 21	Caledonia
May 29	Furnessia
June 5	California
June 11	Columbia
June 18	Caledonia
June 27	Furnessia
July 2	California
July 9	Columbia
July 16	Caledonia
July 24	Furnessia
July 30	California
Aug. 6	Columbia
Aug. 13	Caledonia
Aug. 24	Furnessia
Aug. 27	California
Sept. 3	Caledonia
Sept. 10	Columbia
Sept. 21	Cameronia
Sept. 25	California
Oct. 2	Caledonia
Oct. 8	Columbia
Oct. 15	Cameronia
Oct. 22	California
Oct. 29	Caledonia
Nov. 6	Columbia
Nov. 14	Cameronia
Nov. 21	California
Nov. 27	Caledonia
Dec. 4	Columbia
Dec. 11	Cameronia
Dec. 19	California

ATLANTIC TRANSPORT LINE
London—New York
N. Y.

Arrival	Steamer
Jan. 3	Minnewaska
Jan. 9	Minneapolis
Jan. 16	Minnehaha
Jan. 23	Minnetonka
Feb. 6	Minnewaska
Feb. 13	Minneapolis
Feb. 20	Minnehaha
Feb. 28	Minnetonka

Year 1911

ATLANTIC TRANSPORT LINE
London—New York
(Continued)

N. Y.

Arrival	Steamer
Mar. 13	Minnewaska
Mar. 20	Minnehaha
Mar. 27	Minneapolis
Apr. 3	Minnetonka
Apr. 23	Minnehaha
Apr. 30	Minnewaska
May 6	Minneapolis
May 13	Minnetonka
May 22	Minnehaha
May 29	Minnewaska
June 5	Minneapolis
June 12	Minnetonka
June 19	Minnehaha
July 7	Minneapolis
July 13	Minnetonka
July 18	Minnehaha
July 24	Minnewaska
Aug. 1	Minneapolis
Aug. 7	Minnetonka
Aug. 24	Minnewaska
Aug. 28	Minneapolis
Sept. 4	Minnetonka
Sept. 11	Minnehaha
Sept. 18	Minnewaska
Sept. 25	Minneapolis
Oct. 2	Minnetonka
Oct. 9	Minnehaha
Oct. 16	Minnewaska
Oct. 23	Minneapolis
Oct. 31	Minnetonka
Nov. 6	Minnehaha
Nov. 14	Minneapolis
Nov. 29	Minneapolis
Dec. 5	Minnetonka
Dec. 10	Minnehaha
Dec. 19	Minnewaska

AUSTRO-AMERICANA LINE
Greece—Italy—Azores—
New York

N. Y.

Arrival	Steamer
Jan. 5	Oceania
Jan. 10	Alice
Jan. 23	Martha W.
Feb. 18	Atlanta
Feb. 25	Oceania
Mar. 2	Alice
Mar. 13	Martha W.
Mar. 25	Argentina
Apr. 12	Oceania
Apr. 13	Eugenia
Apr. 21	Alice
Apr. 26	Martha W.
May 2	Laura
May 12	Argentina
May 31	Oceania
June 6	Alice
June 11	Martha W.
June 21	Laura
June 28	Argentina
July 23	Martha W.
Aug. 16	Argentina

AUSTRO-AMERICANA LINE
Greece—Italy—Azores—
New York
(Continued)

N. Y.

Arrival	Steamer
Aug. 31	Columbia
Sept. 4	Martha W.
Sept. 13	Oceania
Sept. 20	Alice
Oct. 7	Argentina
Oct. 23	Martha W.
Nov. 1	Oceania
Nov. 10	Alice
Nov. 28	Argentina
Dec. 5	Martha W.
Dec. 22	Oceania

AUSTRO-AMERICANA LINE
Adriatic—New York

N. Y.

Arrival	Steamer
Jan. 5	Oceania
Jan. 10	Alice
Jan. 23	Martha Washington
Feb. 18	Atlanta
Feb. 25	Oceania
Mar. 2	Alice
Mar. 13	Martha Washington
Mar. 25	Argentina
Apr. 12	Oceania
Apr. 21	Alice
Apr. 26	Martha Washington
May 2	Laura
May 12	Argentina
May 31	Oceania
June 6	Alice
June 11	Martha Washington
June 21	Laura
June 28	Argentina
July 23	Martha Washington
Aug. 16	Argentina
Aug. 31	Columbia
Sept. 4	Martha Washington
Sept. 13	Oceania
Sept. 20	Alice
Oct. 7	Argentina
Oct. 23	Martha Washington
Nov. 1	Oceania
Nov. 10	Alice
Nov. 28	Argentina
Dec. 5	Martha Washington
Dec. 22	Oceania

COMPANIA TRANSATLANTICA LINE
(Spanish Line)
Spain—New York

N. Y.

Arrival	Steamer
Jan. 10	Montevideo
Feb. 12	Manuel Calvo
Mar. 13	Antonio Lopez
Apr. 12	Buenos Aires
May 13	Antonio Lopez
June 10	Montevideo
July 11	Manuel Calvo
Aug. 10	Buenos Aires
Sept. 10	Montserrat

COMPANIA TRANSATLANTICA LINE
(Spanish Line)
Spain—New York
(Continued)

N. Y.

Arrival	Steamer
Oct. 12	Antonio Lopez
Nov. 10	Montevideo
Dec. 12	Antonio Lopez

CUNARD LINE
Liverpool—New York

N. Y.

Arrival	Steamer
Jan. 7	Caronia
Jan. 12	Lusitania
Jan. 21	Campania
Jan. 26	Mauretania
Feb. 3	Lusitania
Feb. 10	Campania
Feb. 16	Mauretania
Feb. 24	Lusitania
Mar. 6	Franconia
Mar. 10	Mauretania
Mar. 16	Lusitania
Mar. 25	Campania
Mar. 30	Mauretania
Apr. 9	Caronia
Apr. 13	Lusitania
Apr. 19	Carmania
Apr. 22	Campania
Apr. 28	Mauretania
May 3	Caronia
May 4	Lusitania
May 13	Campania
May 16	Carmania
May 19	Mauretania
May 25	Lusitania
May 31	Caronia
June 1	Campania
June 8	Mauretania
June 13	Carmania
June 15	Lusitania
June 24	Campania
June 28	Caronia
June 30	Mauretania
July 10	Carmania
July 13	Lusitania
July 22	Campania
July 25	Caronia
July 27	Mauretania
Aug. 3	Lusitania
Aug. 9	Carmania
Aug. 12	Campania
Aug. 17	Mauretania
Aug. 28	Caronia
Sept. 2	Lusitania
Sept. 7	Mauretania
Sept. 8	Carmania
Sept. 16	Lusitania
Sept. 20	Caronia
Sept. 23	Campania
Sept. 28	Mauretania
Oct. 9	Saxonia
Oct. 12	Lusitania
Oct. 21	Campania
Oct. 26	Mauretania
Nov. 3	Lusitania
Nov. 12	Caronia

Year 1911

CUNARD LINE
Liverpool—New York
(Continued)

N. Y.

Arrival	Steamer
Nov. 16	Mauretania
Nov. 23	Lusitania
Dec. 2	Campania
Dec. 10	Carmania
Dec. 15	Lusitania
Dec. 23	Campania

CUNARD LINE
Italian Ports—New York

N. Y.

Arrival	Steamer
Jan. 25	Carpathia
Feb. 12	Pannonia
Feb. 15	Carmania
Feb. 28	Caronia
Mar. 12	Ultonia
Mar. 26	Saxonia
Apr. 7	Pannonia
Apr. 16	Carpathia
May 3	Ultonia
May 8	Saxonia
May 24	Pannonia
June 6	Carpathia
June 30	Saxonia
July 13	Pannonia
July 26	Carpathia
Aug. 21	Saxonia
Aug. 30	Pannonia
Sept. 11	Carpathia
Oct. 6	Ultonia
Oct. 20	Pannonia
Nov. 3	Carpathia
Nov. 27	Ultonia
Dec. 7	Pannonia
Dec. 22	Carpathia
Dec. 23	Caronia

CUNARD LINE
Adriatic Ports—New York

N. Y.

Arrival	Steamer
July 25	Carpathia
Feb. 12	Pannonia
Feb. 15	Carmania
Feb. 28	Caronia
Mar. 12	Ultonia
Mar. 26	Saxonia
Apr. 7	Pannonia
Apr. 16	Carpathia
May 3	Ultonia
May 8	Saxonia
May 24	Pannonia
June 6	Carpathia
June 30	Saxonia
July 13	Pannonia
July 26	Carpathia
Aug. 21	Saxonia
Aug. 30	Pannonia
Sept. 11	Carpathia
Oct. 6	Ultonia
Oct. 20	Pannonia
Nov. 3	Carpathia
Nov. 27	Ultonia
Dec. 7	Pannonia
Dec. 22	Carpathia
Dec. 23	Caronia

CUNARD LINE
Liverpool—Boston

Boston

Arrival	Steamer
Jan. 12	Ivernia
Feb. 16	Ivernia
Mar. 16	Ivernia
Apr. 13	Ivernia
Apr. 27	Franconia
May 11	Ivernia
May 24	Franconia
June 21	Franconia
July 19	Franconia
Aug. 16	Franconia
Sept. 13	Franconia
Oct. 10	Franconia
Oct. 26	Ivernia
Nov. 9	Franconia
Nov. 24	Ivernia
Dec. 7	Franconia

FABRE LINE
Mediterranean—New York

N. Y.

Arrival	Steamer
Jan. 4	Massilia
Jan. 12	Sant' Anna
Jan. 28	Roma
Feb. 4	Madonna
Feb. 14	Venezia
Feb. 23	Germania
Feb. 28	Sant' Anna
Mar. 14	Roma
Mar. 20	Madonna
Mar. 30	Venezia
Apr. 3	Germania
Apr. 13	Sant' Anna
Apr. 25	Roma
May 6	Madonna
May 12	Venezia
May 19	Germania
May 27	Sant' Anna
June 8	Roma
June 18	Madonna
June 19	Venezia
July 2	Germania
July 14	Sant' Anna
July 22	Roma
Aug. 4	Madonna
Aug. 11	Venezia
Aug. 15	Germania
Sept. 2	Sant' Anna
Sept. 11	Roma
Sept. 21	Madonna
Sept. 28	Venezia
Oct. 6	Germania
Oct. 15	Sant' Anna
Oct. 23	Roma
Nov. 4	Madonna
Nov. 11	Venezia
Nov. 22	Germania
Nov. 28	Sant' Anna
Dec. 4	Roma
Dec. 24	Madonna
Dec. 31	Venezia

FRENCH LINE
(Compagnie Generale Transatlantique)
Havre—Bordeaux—
New York

N. Y.

Arrival	Steamer
Jan. 7	La Savoie
Jan. 8	Hudson
Jan. 10	Niagara
Jan. 14	La Provence
Jan. 23	Virginie
Jan. 24	La Bretagne
Jan. 28	La Savoie
Feb. 2	Chicago
Feb. 3	Floride
Feb. 5	La Touraine
Feb. 9	Caroline
Feb. 10	La Provence
Feb. 14	La Gascogne
Feb. 15	St. Laurent
Feb. 19	Espagne
Feb. 28	La Bretagne
Mar. 2	Chicago
Mar. 5	La Lorraine
Mar. 11	La Provence
Mar. 12	Hudson
Mar. 13	Floride
Mar. 14	La Gascogne
Mar. 19	La Touraine
Mar. 24	Caroline
Mar. 25	La Savoie
Mar. 29	Chicago
Apr. 1	La Lorraine
Apr. 4	Niagara
Apr. 8	La Provence
Apr. 11	La Bretagne
Apr. 15	La Touraine
Apr. 22	La Savoie
Apr. 23	Floride
Apr. 27	Chicago
Apr. 29	La Lorraine
May 6	La Provence
May 6	Caroline
May 9	La Bretagne
May 14	La Touraine
May 16	Niagara
May 17	Hudson
May 20	La Savoie
May 24	Chicago
May 27	La Lorraine
June 3	La Provence
June 3	Floride
June 6	La Bretagne
June 10	La Savoie
June 13	St. Laurent
June 14	Caroline
June 17	La Lorraine
June 20	Chicago
June 24	La Provence
June 27	Niagara
July 2	La Touraine
July 7	Hudson
July 8	La Savoie
July 15	La Lorraine
July 16	Floride
July 24	La Touraine
July 27	Caroline
July 31	La Savoie
Aug. 4	St. Laurent
Aug. 4	La Provence

Year 1911

FRENCH LINE
(Compagnie Generale Transatlantique)
Havre—Bordeaux—
New York
(Continued)

N. Y.

Arrival	Steamer
Aug. 4	Virginie
Aug. 8	Niagara
Aug. 12	La Lorraine
Aug. 20	La Bretagne
Aug. 26	Floride
Aug. 27	Espagne
Aug. 29	Chicago
Sept. 1	La Provence
Sept. 2	Hudson
Sept. 9	La Savoie
Sept. 12	Mexico
Sept. 13	La Bretagne
Sept. 16	La Lorraine
Sept. 19	Niagara
Sept. 23	La Provence
Sept. 25	Rochambeau
Sept. 30	La Savoie
Oct. 6	St. Laurent
Oct. 7	La Lorraine
Oct. 9	Virginie
Oct. 9	Chicago
Oct. 16	La Bretagne
Oct. 17	Niagara
Oct. 20	La Provence
Oct. 22	Rochambeau
Oct. 28	La Savoie
Nov. 3	Caroline
Nov. 4	La Lorraine
Nov. 7	Chicago
Nov. 14	La Bretagne
Nov. 19	La Provence
Nov. 21	Rochambeau
Nov. 23	Mexico
Nov. 26	La Savoie
Dec. 2	La Lorraine
Dec. 5	Chicago
Dec. 5	Hudson
Dec. 11	La Touraine
Dec. 16	La Provence
Dec. 18	Rochambeau
Dec. 19	Caroline
Dec. 23	La Savoie
Dec. 29	St. Laurent

GREEK LINE
Greece—New York

N. Y.

Arrival	Steamer
Feb. 25	Athinai
Apr. 3	Themistocles
Apr. 18	Athinai
May 26	Themistocles
June 11	Athinai
July 13	Themistocles
Aug. 3	Athinai
Aug. 30	Themistocles
Sept. 23	Athinai
Oct. 22	Themistocles
Nov. 9	Athinai
Dec. 13	Themistocles
Dec. 26	Athinia

HAMBURG-AMERICAN LINE
Hamburg—Philadelphia

Phila.

Arrival	Steamer
Jan. 5	Prinz Oskar
Jan. 19	Prinz Adalbert
Feb. 10	Graf Waldersee
Feb. 27	Prinz Oskar
Mar. 13	Prinz Adalbert
Mar. 28	Ypiranga
Apr. 13	Prinz Oskar
May 2	Prinz Adalbert
May 15	Graf Waldersee
May 27	Prinz Oskar
June 13	Prinz Adalbert
June 28	Graf Waldersee
July 11	Prinz Oskar
July 28	Prinz Adalbert
Aug. 12	Graf Waldersee
Aug. 28	Prinz Oskar
Sept. 10	Prinz Adalbert
Sept. 24	Graf Waldersee
Oct. 10	Prinz Oskar
Oct. 24	Prinz Adalbert
Nov. 11	Pretoria
Nov. 25	Prinz Oskar
Dec. 8	Prinz Adalbert
Dec. 22	Graf Waldersee

HAMBURG-AMERICAN LINE
Hamburg—New York

N. Y.

Arrival	Steamer
Jan. 10	Bluecher
Jan. 12	Batavia
Jan. 18	President Grant
Jan. 22	Moltke
Feb. 4	K. Aug. Victoria
Feb. 3	Pennsylvania
Feb. 6	Barcelona
Feb. 17	President Lincoln
Feb. 26	Amerika
Feb. 27	Batavia
Mar. 7	Pisa
Mar. 8	President Grant
Mar. 11	K. Aug. Victoria
Mar. 18	Pennsylvania
Mar. 24	President Lincoln
Mar. 27	Amerika
Apr. 4	Pretoria
Apr. 8	Albano
Apr. 8	K. Aug. Victoria
Apr. 17	President Grant
Apr. 30	Bulgaria
May 1	President Lincoln
May 7	Amerika
May 17	Pennsylvania
May 21	K. Aug. Victoria
May 26	Cleveland
June 1	President Grant
June 3	Amerika
June 11	Cincinnati
June 15	President Lincoln
June 15	Batavia
June 17	K. Aug. Victoria
June 20	Bluecher

HAMBURG-AMERICAN LINE
Hamburg—New York
(Continued)

N. Y.

Arrival	Steamer
June 27	Cleveland
July 2	Pennsylvania
July 8	Amerika
July 15	President Grant
July 22	President Lincoln
July 29	Pisa
July 29	K. Aug. Victoria
Aug. 7	Batavia
Aug. 7	Amerika
Aug. 17	Pennsylvania
Aug. 22	President Grant
Aug. 25	K. Aug. Victoria
Aug. 31	Pallanza
Sept. 1	Patricia
Sept. 3	Cleveland
Sept. 7	Amerika
Sept. 12	Bluecher
Sept. 12	Pretoria
Sept. 17	Cincinnati
Sept. 19	President Lincoln
Sept. 22	K. Aug. Victoria
Oct. 1	Batavia
Oct. 2	President Grant
Oct. 3	Victoria Luise
Oct. 7	Amerika
Oct. 11	Armenia
Oct. 12	Pennsylvania
Oct. 13	Cleveland
Oct. 18	Patricia
Oct. 22	Cincinnati
Oct. 28	K. Aug. Victoria
Nov. 2	President Lincoln
Nov. 3	Pallanza
Nov. 9	President Grant
Nov. 11	Amerika
Nov. 25	Pennsylvania
Nov. 27	Barcelona
Dec. 1	Patricia
Dec. 4	K. Aug. Victoria
Dec. 14	President Lincoln
Dec. 22	Amerika
Dec. 23	President Grant

HAMBURG-AMERICAN LINE
Mediterranean—New York

N. Y.

Arrival	Steamer
Jan. 18	Cleveland
Feb. 7	Cincinnati
Mar. 20	Cincinnati
Apr. 20	Cleveland
May 1	Cincinnati
May 23	Hamburg
May 28	Moltke
June 25	Hamburg
July 5	Moltke
Sept. 19	Hamburg
Oct. 3	Moltke
Nov. 7	Hamburg
Nov. 14	Moltke
Dec. 4	Cincinnati
Dec. 20	Hamburg

Year 1911

HOLLAND-AMERICA LINE
Rotterdam—New York

N. Y.

Arrival	Steamer
Jan. 10	Potsdam
Jan. 23	New Amsterdam
Feb. 3	Ryndam
Feb. 14	Potsdam
Mar. 1	Noordam
Mar. 14	Ryndam
Mar. 21	Potsdam
Mar. 27	New Amsterdam
Apr. 4	Noordam
Apr. 10	Rotterdam
Apr. 18	Ryndam
Apr. 25	Potsdam
May 1	New Amsterdam
May 8	Noordam
May 14	Rotterdam
May 23	Ryndam
May 29	Potsdam
June 5	New Amsterdam
June 12	Noordam
June 18	Rotterdam
June 27	Ryndam
July 5	Potsdam
July 10	New Amsterdam
July 24	Noordam
July 31	Rotterdam
Aug. 7	Ryndam
Aug. 15	Potsdam
Aug. 21	New Amsterdam
Aug. 28	Noordam
Sept. 3	Rotterdam
Sept. 11	Ryndam
Sept. 18	Potsdam
Sept. 25	New Amsterdam
Oct. 3	Noordam
Oct. 10	Rotterdam
Oct. 16	Ryndam
Oct. 24	Potsdam
Oct. 30	New Amsterdam
Nov. 7	Noordam
Nov. 13	Rotterdam
Nov. 23	Ryndam
Dec. 4	New Amsterdam
Dec. 13	Noordam
Dec. 27	Ryndam

ITALIA LINE
Mediterranean—New York

N. Y.

Arrival	Steamer
Jan. 24	Taormina
Mar. 3	Taormina
Mar. 16	Ancona
Mar. 31	Verona
Apr. 12	Taormina
Apr. 20	Ancona
May 8	Verona
May 20	Taormina
May 30	Ancona
June 12	Verona
June 30	Taormina
July 11	Ancona
July 27	Verona
Aug. 22	Taormina
Sept. 6	Verona
Oct. 1	Taormina

ITALIA LINE
Mediterranean—New York
(Continued)

N. Y.

Arrival	Steamer
Oct. 28	Ancona
Dec. 7	Ancona

ITALIA LINE
Mediterranean—Philadelphia

Phila.

Arrival	Steamer
Jan. 25	Taormina
Mar. 5	Taormina
Mar. 17	Ancona
Apr. 2	Verona
Apr. 14	Taormina
Apr. 22	Ancona
May 10	Verona
May 21	Taormina
May 31	Ancona
June 13	Verona
July 1	Taormina
July 13	Ancona
Dec. 9	Ancona

LA VELOCE LINE
Mediterranean—New York

N. Y.

Arrival	Steamer
Jan. 26	Oceania
Feb. 17	America
Mar. 8	Oceania
Mar. 22	Europa
Apr. 2	America
Apr. 18	Oceania
May 4	Europa
May 12	America
May 28	Oceania
June 15	Europa
June 28	America
July 25	Oceania
Aug. 25	Europa
Sept. 6	America
Sept. 16	Oceania
Oct. 24	Oceania
Dec. 4	Oceania

LEYLAND LINE
Liverpool—Boston

Boston

Arrival	Steamer
Jan. 4	Winifredian
Jan. 25	Devonian
Feb. 4	Cestrian
Feb. 8	Winifredian
Feb. 22	Bohemian
Mar. 2	Devonian
Mar. 15	Winifredian
Mar. 28	Bohemian
Apr. 10	Devonian
Apr. 26	Winifredian
May 9	Bohemian
May 15	Devonian
May 23	Armenian
May 29	Winifredian
June 6	Canadian
June 12	Devonian
June 20	Bohemian
June 27	Winifredian

LEYLAND LINE
Liverpool—Boston
(Continued)

Boston

Arrival	Steamer
July 4	Canadian
July 15	Devonian
July 24	Winifredian
Aug. 1	Canadian
Aug. 8	Bohemian
Aug. 15	Devonian
Aug. 21	Winifredian
Sept. 9	Caledonian
Sept. 11	Bohemian
Sept. 14	Devonian
Sept. 19	Winifredian
Sept. 26	Canadian
Oct. 10	Bohemian
Oct. 17	Winifredian
Oct. 23	Devonian
Nov. 15	Bohemian
Nov. 20	Winifredian
Nov. 27	Devonian
Dec. 4	Armenian
Dec. 19	Bohemian
Dec. 26	Winifredian

LEYLAND LINE
Liverpool—New York

N. Y.

Arrival	Steamer
Sept. 8	Mesaba

NAVIGAZIONE GENERALE ITALIANA
Mediterranean—New York

N. Y.

Arrival	Steamer
Jan. 17	Duca D'Aosta
Jan. 31	Duca di Genova
Feb. 15	Duca degli Abruzzi
Feb. 27	Duca D'Aosta
Mar. 15	Duca di Genova
Mar. 27	Duca degli Abruzzi
Apr. 8	Lombardia
Apr. 11	Duca D'Aosta
Apr. 26	Duca di Genova
May 8	Duca degli Abruzzi
May 23	Duca D'Aosta
June 6	Duca di Genova
June 20	Duca degli Abruzzi
July 2	Duca D'Aosta
July 30	Duca D'Aosta
Aug. 14	Duca degli Abruzzi
Aug. 30	Duca D'Aosta
Sept. 10	Duca di Genova
Sept. 25	Duca degli Abruzzi
Oct. 9	Duca degli Abruzzi
Nov. 2	Duca degli Abruzzi
Nov. 20	Duca D'Aosta
Dec. 5	Duca degli Abruzzi
Dec. 24	Duca D'Aosta

NAVIGAZIONE GENERALE ITALIANA
Mediterranean—Boston

Boston

Arrival	Steamer
Feb. 26	Liguria
Apr. 23	Sannio

Year 1911

NORTH GERMAN LLOYD
Express Service
Bremen—New York
N. Y.

Arrival	Steamer
Jan. 13	Kronprinz Wilhelm
Feb. 8	Kronprinz Wilhelm
Mar. 8	Kronprinz Wilhelm
Apr. 5	Kronprinz Wilhelm
Apr. 12	Kaiser Wilhelm II
Apr. 19	K. Wm. der Grosse
Apr. 26	Kronprinzes. Cecilie
May 3	Kronprinz Wilhelm
May 10	Kaiser Wilhelm II
May 17	K. Wm. der Grosse
May 24	Kronprinzes. Cecilie
May 31	Kronprinz Wilhelm
June 2	Kaiser Wilhelm II
June 14	K. Wm. der Grosse
June 20	Kronprinzes. Cecilie
June 28	Kronprinz Wilhelm
July 5	Kaiser Wilhelm II
July 12	K. Wm. der Grosse
July 18	Kronprinzes. Cecilie
July 26	Kronprinz Wilhelm
Aug. 2	Kaiser Wilhelm II
Aug. 15	Kronprinzes. Cecilie
Aug. 22	K. Wm. der Grosse
Aug. 29	Kaiser Wilhelm II
Sept. 6	Kronprinz Wilhelm
Sept. 12	Kronprinzes. Cecilie
Sept. 19	K. Wm. der Grosse
Sept. 27	Kaiser Wilhelm II
Oct. 4	Kronprinz Wilhelm
Oct. 10	Kronprinzes. Cecilie
Oct. 18	K. Wm. der Grosse
Oct. 24	Kaiser Wilhelm II
Nov. 1	Kronprinz Wilhelm
Nov. 7	Kronprinzes. Cecilie
Dec. 6	Kronprinz Wilhelm
Dec. 28	Kronprinzes. Cecilie

NORTH GERMAN LLOYD
Bremen—New York
N. Y.

Arrival	Steamer
Jan. 4	Breslau
Jan. 11	Fried'h der Grosse
Jan. 20	Main
Jan. 27	Pr. Fried'h Wilhelm
Jan. 27	Rhein
Feb. 6	Brandenburg
Feb. 10	Roon
Feb. 15	Bremen
Feb. 18	Fried'h der Grosse
Feb. 20	George Washington
Feb. 28	Pr. Fried'h Wilhelm
Mar. 11	Rhein
Mar. 16	Zieten
Mar. 20	George Washington
Mar. 30	Roon
Apr. 3	Pr. Fried'h Wilhelm
Apr. 12	Bremen
Apr. 21	Rhein
Apr. 24	George Washington
May 6	Breslau
May 8	Pr. Fried'h Wilhelm
May 17	Barbarossa
May 24	Bremen
May 29	George Washington

NORTH GERMAN LLOYD
Bremen—New York
(Continued)
N. Y.

Arrival	Steamer
June 6	Grosser Kurfuerst
June 12	Pr. Fried'h Wilhelm
June 22	Barbarossa
June 28	Bremen
July 3	George Washington
July 13	Rhein
July 17	Pr. Fried'h Wilhelm
July 26	Fried'h der Grosse
Aug. 3	Barbarossa
Aug. 9	Neckar
Aug. 12	Bremen
Aug. 14	George Washington
Aug. 21	Pr. Fried'h Wilhelm
Aug. 31	Rhein
Sept. 5	Berlin
Sept. 11	George Washington
Sept. 12	Main
Sept. 19	Grosser Kurfuerst
Sept. 25	Pr. Fried'h Wilhelm
Sept. 25	Neckar
Oct. 5	Barbarossa
Oct. 9	George Washington
Oct. 10	Rhein
Oct. 18	Fried'h der Grosse
Oct. 23	Main
Oct. 24	Grosser Kurfuerst
Oct. 31	Pr. Fried'h Wilhelm
Nov. 10	Barbarossa
Nov. 13	George Washington
Nov. 23	Fried'h der Grosse
Nov. 23	Fried'd der Grosse
Nov. 30	Koenig Albert
Dec. 4	Pr. Fried'h Wilhelm
Dec. 16	Main
Dec. 22	Neckar

NORTH GERMAN LLOYD
Mediterranean—New York
N. Y.

Arrival	Steamer
Jan. 28	Koenig Albert
Feb. 10	Berlin
Feb. 25	Prinzess Irene
Mar. 10	Koenig Albert
Mar. 17	Koenigin Luise
Mar. 22	Berlin
Mar. 31	Fried'h der Grosse
Apr. 8	Prinzess Irene
Apr. 21	Koenig Albert
Apr. 27	Koenigin Luise
May 3	Berlin
May 11	Fried'h der Grosse
June 1	Koenig Albert
June 8	Koenigin Luise
June 17	Berlin
June 24	Fried'h der Grosse
June 29	Prinzess Irene
Aug. 1	Berlin
Aug. 21	Koenig Albert
Sept. 14	Prinzess Irene
Sept. 30	Koenig Albert
Oct. 13	Berlin
Nov. 4	Prinzess Irene
Nov. 22	Berlin
Dec. 22	Prinzess Irene

NORTH GERMAN LLOYD
Bremen—Baltimore
Baltimore

Arrival	Steamer
Jan. 7	Breslau
Jan. 23	Main
Feb. 6	Brandenburg
Feb. 16	Hannover
Mar. 4	Main
Mar. 17	Brandenburg
Mar. 31	Chemnitz
Apr. 11	Main
Apr. 28	Frankfurt
May 11	Brandenburg
May 25	Chemnitz
June 6	Main
June 15	Cassel
July 15	Rhein
July 18	Rhein
Aug. 11	Neckar
Sept. 3	Rhein
Sept. 7	Koeln
Sept. 13	Main
Sept. 21	Chemnitz
Sept. 26	Neckar
Oct. 12	Rhein
Oct. 25	Main
Nov. 7	Neckar
Nov. 25	Rhein
Dec. 9	Willehad
Dec. 24	Neckar

NORTH GERMAN LLOYD
Bremen—Philadelphia
Phila.

Arrival	Steamer
Jan. 12	Koeln
Jan. 26	Cassel
Feb. 10	Chemnitz
Feb. 24	Frankfurt
Mar. 11	Breslau
Mar. 23	Koeln
Apr. 6	Hannover
Apr. 23	Wittekind
May 4	Cassel
May 17	Hannover
May 30	Rhein
June 14	Koeln
June 29	Brandenburg
July 12	Hannover
July 26	Cassel
Aug. 9	Frankfurt
Aug. 23	Brandenburg
Sept. 6	Hannover
Sept. 19	Breslau
Oct. 4	Frankfurt
Oct. 18	Brandenburg
Nov. 3	Chemnitz
Nov. 17	Breslau
Dec. 1	Brandenburg
Dec. 18	Chemnitz
Dec. 31	Hannover

RED STAR LINE
Antwerp—New York
N. Y.

Arrival	Steamer
Jan. 1	Kroonland
Jan. 11	Lapland
Jan. 19	Gothland

Year 1911

RED STAR LINE
Antwerp—New York
(Continued)

N. Y.

Arrival	Steamer
Jan. 25	Samland
Feb. 3	Vaderland
Feb. 7	Kroonland
Feb. 15	Gothland
Feb. 20	Lapland
Mar. 1	Vaderland
Mar. 8	Finland
Mar. 14	Kroonland
Mar. 19	Lapland
Mar. 28	Vaderland
Apr. 4	Finland
Apr. 11	Kroonland
Apr. 16	Lapland
Apr. 26	Vaderland
May 3	Finland
May 10	Kroonland
May 14	Lapland
May 23	Vaderland
May 29	Finland
June 11	Lapland
June 19	Vaderland
June 30	Finland
July 5	Gothland
July 10	Lapland
July 18	Kroonland
July 26	Finland
Aug. 3	Vaderland
Aug. 7	Lapland
Aug. 15	Kroonland
Aug. 22	Finland
Aug. 29	Vaderland
Sept. 3	Lapland
Sept. 11	Kroonland
Sept. 18	Finland
Sept. 25	Vaderland
Oct. 1	Lapland
Oct. 10	Kroonland
Oct. 17	Finland
Oct. 23	Vaderland
Oct. 31	Zeeland
Nov. 7	Kroonland
Nov. 13	Lapland
Nov. 22	Vaderland
Dec. 1	Finland
Dec. 6	Zeeland
Dec. 11	Lapland
Dec. 20	Kroonland
Dec. 28	Finland

RED STAR LINE
Antwerp—Philadelphia—Boston

Phila.
Boston

Arrival	Steamer
Jan. 9	Marquette
Jan. 24	Menominee
Feb. 14	Manitou
Feb. 21	Marquette
Mar. 9	Menominee
Mar. 23	Manitou
Apr. 3	Marquette
Apr. 17	Menominee
May 2	Manitou
May 15	Marquette

RED STAR LINE
Antwerp—Philadelphia—Boston
(Continued)

Phila.
Boston

Arrival	Steamer
May 28	Menominee
June 12	Manitou
June 27	Marquette
July 12	Menominee
Aug. 8	Manitou
Aug. 22	Marquette
Sept. 8	Menominee
Sept. 18	Manitou
Oct. 3	Marquette
Oct. 16	Menominee
Nov. 1	Manitou
Nov. 16	Marquette
Nov. 29	Menominee
Dec. 15	Manitou
Dec. 27	Marquette

RUSSIAN-AMERICAN LINE
Rotterdam—Libau—New York

N. Y.

Arrival	Steamer
Jan. 17	Birma
Feb. 8	Estonia
Feb. 20	Kursk
Mar. 13	Birma
Mar. 22	Estonia
Apr. 8	Kursk
Apr. 17	Lituania
May 10	Birma
May 22	Kursk
June 5	Lituania
July 19	Birma
July 1	Kursk
July 16	Lituania
Aug. 1	Birma
Aug. 14	Kursk
Aug. 27	Lituania
Sept. 12	Birma
Sept. 22	Kursk
Oct. 17	Birma
Nov. 13	Lituania
Nov. 22	Kursk
Dec. 12	Birma
Dec. 26	Kursk

SCANDINAVIAN-AMERICAN LINE
Scandinavian Ports—New York

N. Y.

Arrival	Steamer
Jan. 27	C. F. Tietgen
Feb. 8	Hellig Olav
Feb. 22	United States
Mar. 10	Oscar II
Mar. 16	C. F. Tietgen
Mar. 21	Hellig Olav
Apr. 4	United States
Apr. 19	Oscar II
Apr. 26	C. F. Tietgen
May 3	Hellig Olav
May 16	United States

SCANDINAVIAN-AMERICAN LINE
Scandinavian Ports—New York

N. Y.

Arrival	Steamer
May 31	Oscar II
June 7	C. F. Tietgen
June 13	Hellig Olav
June 27	United States
July 11	Oscar II
July 24	C. F. Tietgen
Aug. 8	Hellig Olav
Aug. 22	Oscar II
Sept. 5	United States
Sept. 19	Hellig Olav
Oct. 4	Oscar II
Oct. 11	C. F. Tietgen
Oct. 17	United States
Oct. 31	Hellig Olav
Nov. 16	Oscar II
Nov. 22	C. F. Tietgen
Nov. 29	United States
Dec. 19	Hellig Olav

SICULA AMERICANA LINE
Mediterranean—New York

N. Y.

Arrival	Steamer
Jan. 28	San Giorgio
Feb. 26	San Giovanni
Mar. 21	San Giorgio
Apr. 10	San Giovanni
May 4	San Giorgio
May 20	San Giovanni
June 15	San Giorgio
July 7	San Giovanni
Sept. 12	San Giorgio
Sept. 29	San Giovanni
Nov. 12	San Guglielmo
Dec. 25	San Guglielmo

URANIUM STEAMSHIP COMPANY
Rotterdam via Halifax—Rotterdam—New York

N. Y.

Arrival	Steamer
Jan. 12	Uranium
Jan. 28	Volturno
Feb. 10	Campanello
Feb. 24	Uranium
Mar. 13	Volturno
Mar. 24	Campanello
Apr. 8	Uranium
Apr. 20	Volturno
May 5	Campanello
May 16	Uranium
May 31	Volturno
June 14	Campanello
June 28	Uranium
July 15	Volturno
July 26	Campanello
Aug. 10	Uranium
Aug. 23	Volturno
Sept. 8	Campanello
Sept. 20	Uranium
Oct. 7	Volturno
Oct. 18	Campanello

Year 1911

URANIUM STEAMSHIP COMPANY
Rotterdam via Halifax—
Rotterdam—New York
(Continued)

N.Y.

Arrival	Steamer
Nov. 4	Uranium
Nov. 21	Volturno
Dec. 2	Campanello
Dec. 17	Uranium

WHITE STAR LINE
Liverpool—New York

N.Y.

Arrival	Steamer
Jan. 1	Cedric
Jan. 8	Megantic
Jan. 15	Celtic
Jan. 22	Laurentic
Jan. 31	Arabic
Feb. 6	Baltic
Feb. 19	Laurentic
Mar. 6	Baltic
Mar. 19	Laurentic
Apr. 2	Baltic
Apr. 16	Laurentic
May 1	Baltic
May 8	Celtic
May 13	Arabic
May 22	Cedric
May 28	Baltic
June 4	Celtic
June 11	Arabic
June 18	Cedric
June 25	Baltic
July 2	Celtic
July 11	Arabic
July 16	Cedric
July 23	Baltic
July 30	Celtic
Aug. 11	Cedric
Aug. 18	Baltic
Aug. 29	Celtic
Sept. 3	Adriatic
Sept. 9	Cedric
Sept. 15	Baltic
Sept. 22	Celtic
Sept. 29	Adriatic
Oct. 7	Cedric
Oct. 13	Baltic
Oct. 20	Celtic
Oct. 27	Adriatic
Nov. 3	Cedric

WHITE STAR LINE
Liverpool—New York
(Continued)

N.Y.

Arrival	Steamer
Nov. 11	Baltic
Nov. 18	Celtic
Dec. 1	Cedric
Dec. 9	Baltic
Dec. 16	Laurentic
Dec. 22	Celtic
Dec. 30	Arabic

WHITE STAR LINE
Southampton—New York

N.Y.

Arrival	Steamer
Jan. 12	Adriatic
Jan. 25	Oceanic
Feb. 9	Adriatic
Feb. 22	Oceanic
Mar. 9	Adriatic
Mar. 22	Oceanic
Apr. 6	Majestic
Apr. 13	Adriatic
Apr. 19	Oceanic
Apr. 27	Teutonic
May 4	Majestic
May 11	Adriatic
May 17	Oceanic
May 31	Majestic
June 8	Adriatic
June 14	Oceanic
June 21	Olympic
July 6	Adriatic
July 12	Oceanic
July 19	Olympic
July 27	Majestic
Aug. 3	Adriatic
Aug. 9	Oceanic
Aug. 16	Olympic
Aug. 30	Oceanic
Sept. 5	Olympic
Sept. 13	Majestic
Sept. 20	Oceanic
Oct. 5	Majestic
Oct. 11	Oceanic
Oct. 25	Majestic
Nov. 1	Oceanic
Nov. 22	Oceanic
Dec. 7	Olympic
Dec. 13	Oceanic
Dec. 27	Olympic

WHITE STAR LINE
Mediterranean—New York

N.Y.

Arrival	Steamer
Feb. 15	Cedric
Mar. 2	Celtic
Mar. 23	Cretic
Mar. 27	Cedric
Apr. 10	Celtic
May 5	Cretic
June 20	Cretic
Sept. 15	Cretic
Oct. 27	Cretic
Dec. 5	Cretic

WHITE STAR LINE
Mediterranean—Boston

Boston

Arrival	Steamer
Feb. 1	Romanic
Mar. 14	Romanic
Apr. 4	Canopic
Apr. 25	Romanic
May 16	Canopic
June 6	Romanic
June 26	Canopic
Aug. 9	Canopic
Sept. 7	Romanic
Sept. 24	Canopic
Oct. 16	Romanic
Nov. 5	Canopic
Nov. 22	Romanic

WHITE STAR LINE
Liverpool—Boston

Boston

Arrival	Steamer
Feb. 23	Zeeland
Apr. 6	Cymric
Apr. 20	Zeeland
May 5	Cymric
May 18	Zeeland
June 1	Cymric
June 15	Zeeland
June 29	Cymric
July 27	Cymric
Aug. 10	Arabic
Sept. 9	Arabic
Sept. 21	Zeeland
Sept. 29	Cymric
Oct. 5	Arabic
Oct. 26	Cymric
Nov. 2	Arabic
Nov. 30	Arabic

Year 1912

ALLAN LINE
Glasgow—Halifax—Boston
Boston

Arrival	Steamer
Jan. 2	Ionian
Feb. 8	Ionian
Mar. 10	Scotian
Apr. 6	Scandinavian
Apr. 20	Parisian
Apr. 26	Numidian
May 23	Parisian
June 10	Numidian
June 22	Parisian
July 9	Numidian
July 22	Parisian
Aug. 6	Numidian
Aug. 20	Parisian
Sept. 3	Numidian
Sept. 17	Parisian
Sept. 30	Numidian
Oct. 16	Parisian
Oct. 31	Numidian
Nov. 19	Parisian
Dec. 4	Numidian
Dec. 14	Corinthian
Dec. 30	Sicilian

AMERICAN LINE
Southampton—New York
N. Y.

Arrival	Steamer
Jan. 4	New York
Jan. 16	St. Louis
Jan. 25	Philadelphia
Feb. 2	New York
Feb. 11	St. Louis
Feb. 23	St. Paul
Feb. 28	New York
Mar. 11	St. Louis
May 9	Philadelphia
May 19	New York
May 26	St. Paul
June 2	Philadelphia
June 9	St. Louis
June 17	New York
June 30	Philadelphia
July 7	St. Louis
July 14	New York
July 21	St. Paul
July 28	Philadelphia
Aug. 5	St. Louis
Aug. 11	New York
Aug. 18	St. Paul
Aug. 25	Philadelphia
Sept. 1	St. Paul
Sept. 8	New York
Sept. 15	St. Paul
Sept. 21	Philadelphia
Sept. 28	St. Louis
Oct. 6	New York
Oct. 17	St. Paul
Oct. 20	Philadelphia
Oct. 27	St. Louis
Nov. 7	New York
Nov. 9	St. Paul
Nov. 16	Philadelphia
Nov. 28	St. Louis

AMERICAN LINE
Southampton—New York
(Continued)
N. Y.

Arrival	Steamer
Dec. 2	New York
Dec. 8	St. Paul
Dec. 19	Philadelphia
Dec. 30	New York

AMERICAN LINE
Liverpool—Philadelphia
Phila.

Arrival	Steamer
Jan. 10	Haverford
Jan. 25	Merion
Feb. 13	Haverford
Mar. 1	Haverford
Mar. 23	Haverford
May 14	Merion
May 20	Dominion
June 4	Haverford
June 17	Merion
June 25	Dominion
July 9	Haverford
July 22	Merion
July 28	Dominion
Aug. 13	Haverford
Aug. 26	Merion
Sept. 2	Dominion
Sept. 16	Haverford
Sept. 30	Merion
Oct. 7	Dominion
Oct. 21	Haverford
Nov. 4	Merion
Nov. 11	Dominion
Dec. 3	Haverford
Dec. 19	Merion

ANCHOR LINE
Mediterranean—New York
N. Y.

Arrival	Steamer
Jan. 15	Perugia
Feb. 12	Calabria
Feb. 26	Italia
Mar. 17	Perugia
Apr. 8	Calabria
May 11	Italia
June 1	Calabria
June 16	Perugia
July 5	Italia
July 29	Calabria
Aug. 16	Perugia
Sept. 6	Italia
Sept. 28	Calabria
Oct. 21	Perugia
Nov. 2	Italia
Nov. 24	Calabria
Dec. 15	Perugia
Dec. 27	Italia

ANCHOR LINE
Glasgow—New York
N. Y.

Arrival	Steamer
Jan. 1	Caledonia

ANCHOR LINE
Glasgow—New York
(Continued)
N. Y.

Arrival	Steamer
Jan. 17	Columbia
Jan. 23	California
Jan. 29	Caledonia
Feb. 5	Cameronia
Mar. 5	Caledonia
Mar. 12	Columbia
Mar. 18	California
Apr. 1	Caledonia
Apr. 7	Columbia
Apr. 15	California
Apr. 22	Cameronia
May 6	Columbia
May 14	California
May 19	Cameronia
May 27	Caledonia
June 3	Columbia
June 10	California
June 16	Cameronia
June 24	Caledonia
June 30	Columbia
July 8	California
July 14	Cameronia
July 21	Caledonia
July 28	Columbia
Aug. 5	California
Aug. 10	Cameronia
Aug. 18	Caledonia
Aug. 25	Columbia
Sept. 2	California
Sept. 8	Cameronia
Sept. 15	Caledonia
Sept. 22	Columbia
Sept. 29	California
Oct. 6	Cameronia
Oct. 14	Caledonia
Oct. 21	Columbia
Oct. 29	California
Nov. 3	Cameronia
Nov. 10	Caledonia
Nov. 18	Columbia
Nov. 25	California
Dec. 2	Cameronia
Dec. 9	Caledonia
Dec. 18	Columbia
Dec. 30	Cameronia

ATLANTIC TRANSPORT LINE
London—New York
N. Y.

Arrival	Steamer
Jan. 3	Minneapolis
Jan. 8	Minnetonka
Jan. 15	Minnehaha
Jan. 23	Minnewaska
Feb. 7	Minneapolis
Feb. 11	Minnetonka
Feb. 20	Minnehaha
Feb. 27	Minnewaska
Mar. 7	Minneapolis
Mar. 29	Minnetonka
Apr. 1	Minnehaha

Year 1912

ATLANTIC TRANSPORT LINE
London—New York
(Continued)

N. Y.

Arrival	Steamer
Apr. 8	Minnewaska
Apr. 30	Minnetonka
May 6	Minnehaha
May 13	Minnewaska
May 28	Minnetonka
June 4	Minneapolis
July 23	Minnehaha
Aug. 6	Minnewaska
Aug. 12	Minnetonka
Aug. 20	Minneapolis
Aug. 27	Minnehaha
Sept. 2	Minnewaska
Sept. 9	Minnetonka
Sept. 17	Minneapolis
Sept. 23	Minnehaha
Sept. 30	Minnewaska
Oct. 7	Minnetonka
Oct. 15	Minneapolis
Oct. 22	Minnehaha
Oct. 29	Minnewaska
Nov. 5	Minnetonka
Nov. 17	Minneapolis
Nov. 26	Minnehaha
Nov. 30	Minnewaska
Dec. 8	Minnetonka
Dec. 25	Minneapolis
Dec. 30	Minnehaha

AUSTRO-AMERICAN LINE
Greece—Italy—Azores—
New York

N. Y.

Arrival	Steamer
Jan. 19	Argentina
Feb. 8	Oceania
Mar. 4	Argentina
Mar. 14	Alice
Mar. 29	Oceania
Apr. 2	Laura
Apr. 5	Atlanta
Apr. 13	Columbia
May 2	Alice
May 14	Oceania
May 20	Martha W.
May 29	Laura
June 5	Carolina
June 8	Columbia
June 8	K. Fr. Jos. I
July 1	Oceania
July 1	Martha W.
July 10	Argentina
July 20	K. Fr. Jos. I
Aug. 12	Columbia
Aug. 13	Martha W.
Aug. 28	Argentina
Aug. 30	K. Fr. Jos. I
Sept. 10	Alice
Sept. 17	Laura
Sept. 29	Laura
Oct. 17	Eugenia
Oct. 18	Argentina
Oct. 30	Alice
Nov. 7	Laura

AUSTRO-AMERICAN LINE
Greece—Italy—Azores—
New York
(Continued)

N. Y.

Arrival	Steamer
Nov. 12	Martha W.
Nov. 20	Oceania
Dec. 3	K. Fr. Jos. I
Dec. 17	Eugenia
Dec. 20	Alice
Dec. 24	Martha W.

COMPANIA TRANSATLANTICA LINE
(Spanish Line)
Spain—New York

N. Y.

Arrival	Steamer
Jan. 15	Buenos Aires
Feb. 25	Manuel Calvo
Mar. 12	Antonio Lopez
Apr. 10	Montserrat
May 11	Montevideo
June 10	Buenos Aires
July 11	Manuel Calvo
Aug. 10	Antonio Lopez
Sept. 10	Montserrat
Oct. 10	Montevideo
Nov. 11	Buenos Aires
Dec. 12	Montevideo

CUNARD LINE
Liverpool—New York

N. Y.

Arrival	Steamer
Jan. 2	Saxonia
Jan. 4	Lusitania
Jan. 15	Franconia
Jan. 21	Carmania
Jan. 29	Laconia
Feb. 5	Cameronia
Feb. 10	Campania
Feb. 18	Carmania
Feb. 24	Lusitania
Mar. 2	Campania
Mar. 8	Mauretania
Mar. 15	Lusitania
Mar. 24	Campania
Mar. 29	Mauretania
Apr. 7	Caronia
Apr. 14	Carmania
Apr. 18	Carpathia
Apr. 19	Mauretania
Apr. 28	Caronia
May 3	Lusitania
May 12	Carmania
May 17	Mauretania
May 24	Lusitania
May 29	Caronia
June 1	Campania
June 7	Mauretania
June 15	Lusitania
June 23	Campania
June 26	Caronia
June 28	Mauretania
July 12	Lusitania
July 18	Mauretania
July 28	Caronia
Aug. 3	Lusitania

CUNARD LINE
Liverpool—New York
(Continued)

N. Y.

Arrival	Steamer
Aug. 10	Campania
Aug. 16	Mauretania
Aug. 21	Caronia
Aug. 23	Lusitania
Aug. 31	Campania
Sept. 4	Carmania
Sept. 6	Mauretania
Sept. 13	Lusitania
Sept. 17	Caronia
Sept. 21	Campania
Sept. 26	Mauretania
Oct. 2	Carmania
Oct. 4	Lusitania
Oct. 12	Caronia
Oct. 18	Mauretania
Oct. 27	Carmania
Nov. 4	Laconia
Nov. 10	Caronia
Nov. 16	Campania
Nov. 22	Mauretania
Dec. 1	Carmania
Dec. 8	Caronia
Dec. 13	Mauretania
Dec. 21	Lusitania
Dec. 29	Campania

CUNARD LINE
Italian Ports—New York

N. Y.

Arrival	Steamer
Jan. 8	Ivernia
Feb. 9	Pannonia
Feb. 15	Caronia
Mar. 1	Franconia
Mar. 17	Laconia
Mar. 29	Carpathia
Apr. 8	Saxonia
Apr. 26	Pannonia
May 9	Ivernia
May 28	Carpathia
June 4	Saxonia
June 12	Pannonia
June 26	Ivernia
July 12	Carpathia
July 25	Saxonia
Aug. 2	Pannonia
Aug. 15	Ivernia
Aug. 27	Carpathia
Sept. 12	Saxonia
Sept. 19	Pannonia
Oct. 5	Ivernia
Oct. 16	Carpathia
Nov. 2	Saxonia
Nov. 9	Pannonia
Nov. 24	Ivernia
Dec. 5	Carpathia
Dec. 18	Laconia
Dec. 31	Pannonia

CUNARD LINE
Liverpool—Boston

Boston

Arrival	Steamer
Feb. 22	Ivernia
Mar. 25	Ivernia

Year 1912

CUNARD LINE
Liverpool—Boston
(Continued)

Boston Arrival	Steamer
Apr. 10	Franconia
Apr. 25	Laconia
May 9	Franconia
May 23	Laconia
June 5	Franconia
June 19	Laconia
July 3	Franconia
July 17	Laconia
July 31	Franconia
Aug. 14	Laconia
Aug. 28	Franconia
Sept. 11	Laconia
Sept. 25	Franconia
Oct. 9	Laconia
Oct. 23	Franconia
Nov. 20	Franconia
Dec. 9	Saxonia

FABRE LINE
Mediterranean—New York

N. Y. Arrival	Steamer
Jan. 10	Germania
Jan. 24	Sant' Anna
Jan. 29	Roma
Feb. 11	Madonna
Feb. 25	Germania
Feb. 28	Venezia
Mar. 10	Sant' Anna
Mar. 16	Roma
Mar. 23	Madonna
Mar. 29	Canada
Apr. 8	Germania
Apr. 12	Venezia
Apr. 25	Sant' Anna
Apr. 29	Roma
May 9	Madonna
May 14	Canada
May 21	Germania
June 1	Venezia
June 7	Sant' Anna
June 15	Roma
June 25	Canada
July 3	Madonna
July 16	Venezia
July 22	Sant' Anna
July 28	Roma
Aug. 13	Canada
Aug. 18	Madonna
Aug. 31	Venezia
Sept. 7	Sant' Anna
Sept. 13	Roma
Sept. 26	Canada
Oct. 3	Madonna
Oct. 16	Venezia
Oct. 22	Sant' Anna
Oct. 27	Roma
Nov. 9	Canada
Nov. 21	Madonna
Nov. 26	Germania
Nov. 30	Venezie
Dec. 4	Sant' Anna
Dec. 9	Roma
Dec. 28	Canada

FRENCH LINE
(Compagnie Generale Transatlantique)
Havre, Bordeaux—New York

N. Y. Arrival	Steamer
Jan. 2	La Lorraine
Jan. 6	La Bretagne
Jan. 6	Chicago
Jan. 7	La Touraine
Jan. 11	Floride
Jan. 22	La Savoie
Jan. 28	La Lorraine
Jan. 28	Caroline
Jan. 29	Rochambeau
Feb. 3	Hudson
Feb. 4	La Touraine
Feb. 7	Niagara
Feb. 10	La Provence
Feb. 19	Espagne
Feb. 19	Chicago
Feb. 22	St Laurent
Feb. 25	La Touraine
Feb. 26	Rochambeau
Mar. 2	La Savoie
Mar. 10	La Provence
Mar. 13	Caroline
Mar. 14	Niagara
Mar. 18	Espagne
Mar. 20	Chicago
Mar. 26	La Bretagne
Mar. 26	Rochambeau
Mar. 30	La Savoie
Apr. 1	La Touraine
Apr. 5	Hudson
Apr. 6	La Provence
Apr. 16	Chicago
Apr. 16	Niagara
Apr. 17	La Bretagne
Apr. 21	La Savoie
Apr. 22	Rochambeau
Apr. 26	France
Apr. 26	La Touraine
May 4	La Provence
May 10	Caroline
May 12	La Savoie
May 14	La Bretagne
May 20	Rochambeau
May 23	La Touraine
May 24	France
May 29	Hudson
June 1	La Provence
June 3	Chicago
June 4	St. Laurent
June 9	La Savoie
June 17	Floride
June 18	La Bretagne
June 22	La Provence
June 26	California
July 23	Niagara
Aug. 4	La Savoie
Aug. 4	Louisiane
Aug. 5	Rochambeau
Aug. 11	La Lorraine
Aug. 13	Chicago
Aug. 17	France
Aug. 24	La Provence
Aug. 25	Virginie
Aug. 26	Mexico
Aug. 27	La Touraine
Sept. 3	Niagara

FRENCH LINE
(Compagnie Generale Transatlantique)
Havre, Bordeaux—New York
(Continued)

N. Y. Arrival	Steamer
Sept. 6	France
Sept. 9	Rochambeau
Sept. 14	La Provence
Sept. 16	Chicago
Sept. 21	La Savoie
Sept. 24	La Touraine
Sept. 29	La Lorraine
Oct. 1	Niagara
Oct. 4	France
Oct. 7	Rochambeau
Oct. 10	St. Laurent
Oct. 12	La Provence
Oct. 15	Chicago
Oct. 19	La Savoie
Oct. 21	La Touraine
Oct. 25	France
Oct. 30	Niagara
Nov. 2	La Provence
Nov. 4	Rochambeau
Nov. 9	La Lorraine
Nov. 11	Chicago
Nov. 12	Californie
Nov. 15	France
Nov. 23	St. Laurent
Nov. 25	La Touraine
Nov. 28	Niagara
Nov. 28	Louisiane
Dec. 1	La Savoie
Dec. 8	La Lorraine
Dec. 11	Chicago
Dec. 14	France
Dec. 16	Floride
Dec. 22	La Provence
Dec. 28	Niagara
Dec. 31	La Touraine

GREEK LINE
Greece—New York

N. Y. Arrival	Steamer
Mar. 2	Athinai
Mar. 18	Themistoclis
Apr. 18	Athinai
May 12	Themistoclis
June 8	Athinai
July 3	Themistoclis
July 29	Athinai
Aug. 23	Themistoclis
Sept. 21	Athinai
Oct. 12	Themistoclis
Nov. 7	Athinai

HAMBURG-AMERICAN LINE
Hamburg—Philadelphia

Phila. Arrival	Steamer
Jan. 7	Pisa
Jan. 28	Prinz Adalbert
Feb. 10	Prinz Oskar
Mar. 3	Pisa
Mar. 18	Graf Waldersee
Mar. 23	Prinz Oskar
Apr. 11	Pallansa

Year 1912

HAMBURG-AMERICAN LINE
Hamburg—Philadelphia
(Continued)

Phila.

Arrival	Steamer
Apr. 21	Prinz Adalbert
May 11	Barcelona
May 20	Prinz Oskar
June 4	Prinz Adalbert
June 21	Graf Waldersee
July 5	Prinz Oskar
July 19	Prinz Adalbert
July 24	Pretoria
Aug. 6	Graf Waldersee
Aug. 20	Prinz Oskar
Sept. 3	Prinz Adalbert
Sept. 22	Graf Waldersee
Oct. 7	Prinz Oskar
Oct. 21	Prinz Adalbert
Nov. 9	Graf Waldersee
Nov. 22	Prinz Oskar
Dec. 11	Prinz Adalbert

HAMBURG-AMERICAN LINE
Hamburg—New York
N. Y.

Arrival	Steamer
Jan. 5	Pennsylvania
Jan. 9	Pallanza
Jan. 10	Bluecher
Jan. 18	Moltke
Jan. 21	Victoria Luise
Jan. 22	Pretoria
Jan. 25	President Lincoln
Feb. 5	Graf Waldersee
Feb. 5	K. Auguste Victoria
Feb. 15	President Grant
Feb. 27	Pennsylvania
Feb. 27	Amerika
Mar. 7	President Lincoln
Mar. 20	Graf Waldersee
Mar. 22	Barcelona
Mar. 26	Batavia
Mar. 28	President Grant
Apr. 5	Pennsylvania
Apr. 6	Amerika
Apr. 16	President Lincoln
Apr. 26	K. Auguste Victoria
Apr. 28	Pretoria
May 7	Batavia
May 7	President Grant
May 11	Amerika
May 16	Pennsylvania
May 20	Cincinnati
May 25	K. Auguste Victoria
May 30	President Lincoln
June 1	Victoria Luise
June 7	Pretoria
June 8	Amerika
June 11	Cleveland
June 20	President Grant
June 23	K. Auguste Victoria
June 26	Cincinnati
June 30	Pennsylvania
July 6	Amerika
July 10	President Lincoln

HAMBURG-AMERICAN LINE
Hamburg—New York
(Continued)

N. Y.

Arrival	Steamer
July 16	Cleveland
July 22	K. Auguste Victoria
July 24	Hamburg
July 31	President Grant
Aug. 5	Amerika
Aug. 10	Pennsylvania
Aug. 13	Cincinnati
Aug. 21	President Lincoln
Aug. 23	Armenia
Aug. 24	K. Auguste Victoria
Aug. 30	Batavia
Sept. 1	Cleveland
Sept. 3	Patricia
Sept. 9	Kronprinz'n Cecilie
Sept. 11	Pretoria
Sept. 11	President Grant
Sept. 14	Amerika
Sept. 14	Hamburg
Sept. 17	Cincinnati
Sept. 21	K. Auguste Victoria
Sept. 26	Pennsylvania
Sept. 29	President Lincoln
Oct. 2	Cleveland
Oct. 5	Victoria Luise
Oct. 10	Patricia
Oct. 12	Amerika
Oct. 17	President Grant
Oct. 22	K. Auguste Victoria
Oct. 27	Cincinnati
Nov. 1	Corcovado
Nov. 5	Pennsylvania
Nov. 10	Pretoria
Nov. 12	President Lincoln
Nov. 16	Amerika
Nov. 21	Patricia
Nov. 24	Barcelona
Nov. 28	President Grant
Dec. 3	K. Auguste Victoria
Dec. 15	Bulgaria
Dec. 15	Pennsylvania
Dec. 21	President Lincoln
Dec. 24	Amerika

HAMBURG-AMERICAN LINE
Mediterranean—New York
N. Y.

Arrival	Steamer
Jan. 22	Cincinnati
Feb. 17	Hamburg
Mar. 27	K. Auguste Victoria
Mar. 28	Hamburg
Apr. 17	Cincinnati
May 10	Hamburg
May 23	Moltke
June 18	Hamburg
July 1	Moltke
Aug. 12	Moltke
Sept. 23	Moltke
Nov. 6	Moltke
Dec. 3	Cincinnati
Dec. 23	Moltke

HOLLAND-AMERICA LINE
Rotterdam—New York
N. Y.

Arrival	Steamer
Jan. 3	Potsdam
Jan. 17	New Amsterdam
Jan. 24	Noordam
Jan. 30	Ryndam
Feb. 13	Potsdam
Feb. 19	New Amsterdam
Feb. 27	Noordam
Mar. 6	Ryndam
Mar. 12	Rotterdam
Mar. 20	Potsdam
Mar. 27	New Amsterdam
Apr. 3	Noordam
Apr. 9	Ryndam
Apr. 16	Rotterdam
Apr. 23	Potsdam
Apr. 29	New Amsterdam
May 6	Noordam
May 14	Ryndam
May 20	Rotterdam
May 28	Potsdam
June 3	New Amsterdam
June 11	Noordam
June 18	Ryndam
June 24	Rotterdam
July 2	Potsdam
July 8	New Amsterdam
July 16	Noordam
July 23	Ryndam
Aug. 5	Rotterdam
Aug. 13	Potsdam
Aug. 19	New Amsterdam
Aug. 27	Noordam
Sept. 3	Ryndam
Sept. 9	Rotterdam
Sept. 17	Potsdam
Sept. 23	New Amsterdam
Sept. 30	Noordam
Oct. 7	Ryndam
Oct. 14	Rotterdam
Oct. 23	Potsdam
Oct. 28	New Amsterdam
Nov. 5	Noordam
Nov. 12	Ryndam
Nov. 18	Rotterdam
Nov. 26	Potsdam
Dec. 4	New Amsterdam
Dec. 11	Noordam
Dec. 19	Ryndam
Dec. 24	Rotterdam

ITALIA LINE
Mediterranean—New York
N. Y.

Arrival	Steamer
Jan. 1	Taormina
Jan. 24	Ancona
Mar. 13	Ancona
Apr. 24	Ancona
June 4	Ancona
July 13	Ancona
Aug. 26	Ancona
Oct. 8	Ancona
Nov. 19	Ancona
Dec. 27	Ancona

Year 1912

ITALIA LINE
Mediterranean—Philadelphia
Phila.

Arrival	Steamer
Jan. 3	Taormina
Mar. 15	Ancona
Apr. 25	Ancona
June 5	Ancona
July 15	Ancona
Aug. 28	Ancona
Oct. 10	Ancona
Nov. 20	Ancona

LA VELOCE LINE
Mediterranean—New York
N.Y.

Arrival	Steamer
Jan. 13	Oceania
Feb. 28	Oceania
Mar. 27	America
Apr. 9	Oceania
May 12	Oceania
June 18	Oceania
Aug. 12	Stampalia
Sept. 22	Stampalia
Oct. 26	Stampalia
Dec. 1	Stampalia

LA VELOCE LINE
Mediterranean—Philadelphia
Phila.

Arrival	Steamer
Mar. 29	America
Apr. 10	Oceania
Dec. 3	Stampalia

LEYLAND LINE
Liverpool—Boston
Boston

Arrival	Steamer
Jan. 1	Devonian
Jan. 10	Armenian
Jan. 20	Columbian
Jan. 31	Cestrian
Feb. 6	Devonian
Feb. 14	Canadian
Feb. 29	Victorian
Mar. 17	Cestrian
Mar. 20	Devonian
Apr. 11	Armenian
Apr. 26	Cestrian
May 2	Colonian
May 8	Devonian
May 16	Canadian
May 22	Armenian
June 1	Californian
June 5	Bohemian
June 17	Winifredian
June 24	Devonian
July 1	Canadian
July 14	Bohemian
July 27	Devonian
Aug. 5	Canadian
Aug. 18	Bohemian
Aug. 25	Winifredian
Sept. 1	Devonian
Sept. 8	Canadian
Sept. 16	Cestrian
Sept. 21	Bohemian
Sept. 29	Winifredian

LEYLAND LINE
Liverpool—Boston
(Continued)
Boston

Arrival	Steamer
Oct. 6	Devonian
Oct. 14	Canadian
Oct. 28	Bohemian
Nov. 4	Winifredian
Nov. 10	Devonian
Nov. 17	Canadian
Dec. 2	Bohemian
Dec. 9	Winifredian
Dec. 18	Devonian
Dec. 25	Canadian

LEYLAND LINE
Liverpool—New York
N.Y.

Arrival	Steamer
Mar. 5	Bohemian
Mar. 31	Canadian

LLOYD ITALIANO
Mediterranean—New York
N.Y.

Arrival	Steamer
Feb. 8	Taormina
Mar. 1	Luisiana
Mar. 20	Taormina
Apr. 16	Luisiana
May 3	Mendoza
May 10	Taormina
June 1	Luisiana
June 13	Taormina
June 25	Mendoza
July 16	Luisiana
July 23	Taormina
Aug. 14	Mendoza
Sept. 3	Taormina
Sept. 28	Mendoza
Oct. 17	Taormina
Nov. 13	Mendoza
Nov. 28	Taormina
Dec. 22	Mendoza

LLOYD ITALIANO
Mediterranean—Philadelphia
Phila.

Arrival	Steamer
Aug. 16	Mendoza
Dec. 25	Mendoza

LLOYD SABAUDO
Mediterranean—New York
N.Y.

Arrival	Steamer
Mar. 8	Princ. di Piemonte
Apr. 26	Princ. di Piemonte
June 7	Princ. di Piemonte
July 20	Princ. di Piemonte
Sept. 5	Princ. di Piemonte
Oct. 20	Princ. di Piemonte
Nov. 30	Princ. di Piemonte

NATIONAL GREEK LINE
Greece—New York
N.Y.

Arrival	Steamer
Mar. 15	Patris
Apr. 20	Macedonia

NATIONAL GREEK LINE
Greece—New York
(Continued)
N.Y.

Arrival	Steamer
May 7	Patris
May 31	Macedonia
June 17	Patris
July 8	Macedonia
July 27	Patris
Aug. 17	Macedonia
Sept. 9	Patris
Sept. 28	Macedonia
Oct. 22	Patris
Dec. 27	Patris

NAVIGAZIONE GENE-RALE ITALIANA
Mediterranean—New York
N.Y.

Arrival	Steamer
Jan. 16	Duca D'Aosta
Mar. 6	Duca D'Aosta
Apr. 16	Duca D'Aosta
May 7	America
May 20	Duca D'Aosta
June 15	America
June 25	Duca D'Aosta
July 29	America
Aug. 20	Duca D'Aosta
Sept. 11	America
Sept. 20	Duca D'Aosta
Sept. 30	Duca di Genova
Oct. 21	America
Oct. 30	Duca D'Aosta
Nov. 12	Duca di Genova
Nov. 26	America
Dec. 4	Duca D'Aosta

NAVIGAZIONE GENE-RALE ITALIANA
Mediterranean—Philadelphia
Phila.

Arrival	Steamer
May 10	America
June 17	America
July 31	America
Sept. 13	America
Oct. 2	Duca di Genova
Nov. 13	Duca di Genova

NORTH GERMAN LLOYD
Express Service
Bremen—New York
N.Y.

Arrival	Steamer
Feb. 7	Kronprinz Wilhelm
Mar. 6	Kronprinz Wilhelm
Mar. 28	K. Wm. der Grosse
Apr. 10	Kronprinz Wilhelm
Apr. 24	Kaiser Wilhelm II
May 1	K. Wm. der Grosse
May 9	Kronprinz'n Cecilie
May 15	Kronprinz Wilhelm
May 22	Kaiser Wilhelm II
May 29	K. Wm. der Grosse
June 5	Kronprinz'n Cecilie
June 12	Kronprinz Wilhelm
June 19	Kaiser Wilhelm II
June 28	K. Wm. der Grosse
July 3	Kronprinz'n Cecilie

Year 1912

NORTH GERMAN LLOYD
Express Service
Bremen—New York
(Continued)
N. Y.

Arrival	Steamer
July 10	Kronprinz Wilhelm
July 17	Kaiser Wilhelm II
July 24	K. Wm. der Grosse
July 31	Kronprinz'n Cecilie
Aug. 14	Kronprinz Wilhelm
Aug. 21	Kaiser Wilhelm II
Aug. 28	K. Wm. der Grosse
Sept. 4	Kronprinz'n Cecilie
Sept. 11	Kronprinz Wilhelm
Sept. 17	Kaiser Wilhelm II
Sept. 25	K. Wm. der Grosse
Oct. 2	Kronprinz'n Cecilie
Oct. 9	Kronprinz Wilhelm
Oct. 16	Kaiser Wilhelm II
Oct. 23	K. Wm. der Grosse
Oct. 30	Kronprinz'n Cecilie
Nov. 6	Kronprinz Wilhelm
Nov. 20	K. Wm. der Grosse
Dec. 4	Kronprinz'n Cecilie

NORTH GERMAN LLOYD
Bremen—New York
N. Y.

Arrival	Steamer
Jan. 2	Barbarossa
Jan. 5	Breslau
Jan. 14	Rhein
Jan. 17	George Washington
Jan. 27	Chemnitz
Jan. 30	Prz. Fred. Wilhelm
Feb. 8	Prinzess Irene
Feb. 16	Neckar
Feb. 22	George Washington
Feb. 29	Breslau
Mar. 1	Prz. Fred. Wilhelm
Mar. 10	Chemnitz
Mar. 17	Main
Mar. 19	George Washington
Mar. 30	Roon
Mar. 31	Koenigin Luise
Apr. 2	Prz. Fred. Wilhelm
Apr. 7	Neckar
Apr. 10	Barbarossa
Apr. 11	Barbarossa
Apr. 16	George Washington
Apr. 24	Bremen
May 2	Koenigin Luise
May 7	Prz. Fred. Wilhelm
May 13	George Washington
May 20	Barbarossa
May 22	Fried. der Grosse
May 29	Bremen
June 5	Koenigin Luise
June 10	George Washington
June 10	Priz. Fred. Wilhelm
June 27	Grosser Kurfuerst
July 2	Berlin
July 8	George Washington
July 17	Koenigin Luise
July 22	Prz. Fred. Wilhelm
July 30	Main
July 31	Koenig Albert
Aug. 6	George Washington
Aug. 12	Berlin

NORTH GERMAN LLOYD
Bremen—New York
(Continued)
N. Y.

Arrival	Steamer
Aug. 19	Prz. Fred. Wilhelm
Aug. 26	Neckar
Aug. 28	Bremen
Sept. 2	George Washington
Sept. 3	Grosser Kurfuerst
Sept. 5	Rhein
Sept. 10	Main
Sept. 11	Fried. der Grosse
Sept. 16	Barbarossa
Sept. 16	Prz. Fred. Wilhelm
Sept. 22	Koenigin Luise
Sept. 23	Berlin
Sept. 30	George Washington
Oct. 7	Neckar
Oct. 8	Grosser Kurfuerst
Oct. 14	Prz. Fred. Wilhelm
Oct. 23	Main
Oct. 24	Fried. der Grosse
Oct. 28	George Washington
Nov. 7	Bremen
Nov. 13	Grosser Kurfuerst
Nov. 15	Barbarossa
Nov. 18	Prz. Fred. Wilhelm
Nov. 25	George Washington
Dec. 5	Main
Dec. 6	Koenigin Luise
Dec. 12	Fried. der Grosse
Dec. 15	Grosser Kurfuerst
Dec. 21	Buelow
Dec. 26	George Washington

NORTH GERMAN LLOYD
Mediterranean—New York
N. Y.

Arrival	Steamer
Jan. 17	Berlin
Feb. 23	Berlin
Mar. 15	Prinzess Irene
Mar. 22	Koenig Albert
Apr. 3	Berlin
Apr. 26	Prinzess Irene
May 3	Koenig Albert
May 15	Berlin
June 1	Prinzess Irene
June 14	Koenig Albert
June 28	Fried. der Grosse
Aug. 9	Fried. der Grosse
Sept. 5	Prinzess Irene
Sept. 20	Koenig Albert
Oct. 10	Prinzess Irene
Oct. 25	Koenig Albert
Nov. 7	Berlin
Nov. 22	Prinzess Irene
Dec. 6	Koenig Albert
Dec. 18	Berlin

NORTH GERMAN LLOYD
Bremen—Baltimore
Baltimore

Arrival	Steamer
Jan. 8	Breslau
Jan. 17	Rhein
Feb. 2	Main
Feb. 18	Neckar
Mar. 2	Breslau

NORTH GERMAN LLOYD
Bremen—Baltimore
(Continued)
Baltimore

Arrival	Steamer
Mar. 13	Rhein
Mar. 20	Main
Mar. 21	Frankfurt
Mar. 30	Koeln
Apr. 6	Brandenburg
Apr. 8	Neckar
Apr. 12	Breslau
Apr. 25	Rhein
May 10	Chemnitz
May 23	Brandenburg
May 31	Neckar
June 6	Rhein
June 20	Main
July 1	Chemnitz
July 6	Brandenburg
July 16	Neckar
July 26	Rhein
July 31	Main
Aug. 14	Koeln
Aug. 25	Brandenburg
Aug. 27	Neckar
Sept. 6	Rhein
Sept. 12	Main
Sept. 19	Koeln
Sept. 27	Brandenburg
Oct. 8	Neckar
Oct. 18	Rhein
Oct. 25	Main
Nov. 7	Brandenburg
Nov. 15	Breslau
Nov. 25	Neckar
Dec. 7	Main
Dec. 19	Brandenburg
Dec. 22	Barbarossa

NORTH GERMAN LLOYD
Bremen—Philadelphia
Phila.

Arrival	Steamer
Jan. 22	Willehad
Jan. 26	Brandenburg
Feb. 9	Koeln
Feb. 24	Hannover
Mar. 10	Rhein
Apr. 4	Brandenburg
Apr. 17	Hannover
May 1	Main
May 16	Breslau
May 28	Neckar
June 13	Hannover
June 27	Chemnitz
July 10	Breslau
July 24	Rhein
Aug. 7	Hannover
Aug. 21	Brandenburg
Sept. 5	Breslau
Sept. 17	Barbarossa
Oct. 2	Hannover
Oct. 16	Rhein
Oct. 29	Koenigin Luise
Nov. 13	Breslau
Nov. 22	Neckar
Dec. 15	Brandenburg
Dec. 27	Breslau

Year 1912

RED STAR LINE
Antwerp—New York
N.Y.

Arrival	Steamer
Jan. 3	Vaderland
Jan. 9	Zeeland
Jan. 16	Lapland
Jan. 24	Kroonland
Feb. 1	Finland
Feb. 6	Vaderland
Feb. 13	Zeeland
Feb. 19	Lapland
Feb. 28	Kroonland
Mar. 6	Finland
Mar. 14	Vaderland
Mar. 18	Lapland
Mar. 28	Kroonland
Apr. 3	Finland
Apr. 9	Vaderland
Apr. 16	Lapland
Apr. 23	Kroonland
Apr. 30	Finland
May 7	Vaderland
May 13	Lapland
May 21	Kroonland
May 28	Zeeland
June 4	Vaderland
June 8	Finland
June 10	Lapland
June 18	Kroonland
June 25	Zeeland
July 2	Vaderland
July 8	Lapland
July 16	Kroonland
July 23	Zeeland
July 31	Vaderland
Aug. 5	Lapland
Aug. 14	Finland
Aug. 20	Zeeland
Aug. 27	Kroonland
Sept. 2	Lapland
Sept. 10	Finland
Sept. 17	Vaderland
Sept. 24	Kroonland
Sept. 29	Lapland
Oct. 8	Finland
Oct. 15	Vaderland
Oct. 22	Kroonland
Oct. 29	Zeeland
Nov. 5	Finland
Nov. 13	Vaderland
Nov. 18	Lapland
Nov. 26	Kroonland
Dec. 4	Zeeland
Dec. 12	Finland
Dec. 19	Vaderland
Dec. 24	Lapland

RED STAR LINE
Antwerp—Philadelphia—
Boston
Boston

Arrival	Steamer
Jan. 8	Menominee
Jan. 25	Manitou
Feb. 6	Marquette
Feb. 21	Menominee
Mar. 7	Manitou
Mar. 20	Marquette
Apr. 3	Menominee

RED STAR LINE
Antwerp—Philadelphia—
Boston
(Continued)
Boston

Arrival	Steamer
Apr. 16	Manitou
May 1	Marquette
May 14	Menominee
May 28	Manitou
June 12	Marquette
June 26	Menominee
July 9	Mesaba
July 24	Manitou
Aug. 6	Marquette
Aug. 19	Menominee
Sept. 3	Manitou
Sept. 16	Marquette
Oct. 1	Menominee
Oct. 14	Manitou
Oct. 29	Marquette
Nov. 11	Menominee
Nov. 26	Manitou
Dec. 13	Marquette
Dec. 27	Menominee

RUSSIAN-AMERICAN LINE
Libau via Halifax—Rotterdam, Libau—New York
N.Y.

Arrival	Steamer
Jan. 12	Lituania
Feb. 6	Kursk
Feb. 24	Birma
Mar. 5	Lituania
Mar. 19	Kursk
Apr. 6	Estonia
Apr. 7	Birma
Apr. 16	Lituania
Apr. 28	Kursk
May 19	Birma
June 3	Kursk
June 13	Czar
June 26	Russia
July 8	Kursk
July 21	Czar
Aug. 5	Russia
Aug. 16	Kursk
Sept. 2	Birma
Sept. 16	Czar
Sept. 29	Kursk
Oct. 19	Birma
Oct. 28	Czar
Nov. 12	Russia
Nov. 24	Kursk
Dec. 6	Birma
Dec. 9	Czar
Dec. 27	Russia

SICULA AMERICANA LINE
Mediterranean—New York
N.Y.

Arrival	Steamer
Jan. 1	San Giovanni
Feb. 8	San Guglielmo
Mar. 3	San Giovanni
Apr. 12	San Giorgio
May 1	San Guglielmo

SICULA AMERICANA LINE
Mediterranean—New York
(Continued)
N.Y.

Arrival	Steamer
May 25	San Giorgio
June 10	San Guglielmo
June 26	San Giovanni
July 12	San Giorgio
Aug. 2	San Guglielmo
Sept. 3	San Giorgio
Sept. 16	San Guglielmo
Oct. 14	San Giorgio
Oct. 25	San Guglielmo
Nov. 20	San Giorgio
Dec. 7	San Guglielmo
Dec. 14	San Giorgio

SCANDINAVIAN-AMERICAN LINE
Mediterranean Ports—New York
N.Y.

Arrival	Steamer
Jan. 25	Oscar II
Feb. 8	C. F. Tietgen
Feb. 21	United States
Mar. 6	Hellig Olav
Mar. 20	Oscar II
Mar. 28	C. F. Tietgen
Apr. 3	United States
Apr. 17	Hellig Olav
May 3	Oscar II
May 9	C. F. Tietgen
May 15	United States
May 29	Hellig Olav
June 12	Oscar II
June 19	C. F. Tietgen
June 26	United States
July 10	Hellig Olav
July 24	Oscar II
Aug. 6	United States
Aug. 20	Hellig Olav
Aug. 28	C. F. Tietgen
Sept. 3	Oscar II
Sept. 17	United States
Oct. 1	Hellig Olav
Oct. 9	C. F. Tietgen
Oct. 16	Oscar II
Oct. 30	United States
Nov. 12	Hellig Olav
Nov. 20	C. F. Tietgen
Nov. 27	Oscar II
Dec. 7	United States
Dec. 26	Hellig Olav

URANIUM STEAMSHIP COMPANY
Rotterdam via Halifax—
Rotterdam—New York
N.Y.

Arrival	Steamer
Jan. 5	Volturno
Jan. 13	Campanello
Feb. 7	Uranium
Feb. 13	Volturno
Feb. 25	Campenello
Mar. 23	Volturno
Mar. 26	Uranium

Year 1912

URANIUM STEAMSHIP COMPANY
Rotterdam via Halifax—
Rotterdam—New York
(Continued)

N. Y.

Arrival	Steamer
Apr. 8	Campanello
Apr. 27	Volturno
May 6	Uranium
May 17	Campanello
June 2	Volturno
June 14	Uranium
June 27	Campanello
July 11	Volturno
July 24	Uranium
Aug. 7	Campanello
Aug. 22	Volturno
Sept. 5	Uranium
Sept. 22	Campanello
Oct. 2	Volturno
Oct. 19	Uranium
Nov. 2	Campanello
Nov. 14	Volturno
Nov. 30	Uranium
Dec. 10	Campanello
Dec. 27	Volturno

WHITE STAR LINE
Mediterranean—New York

N. Y.

Arrival	Steamer
Jan. 3	Adriatic
Feb. 15	Adriatic
Feb. 29	Cedric
Mar. 29	Adriatic
Apr. 11	Cedric

WHITE STAR LINE
Mediterranean—Boston

Boston

Arrival	Steamer
Jan. 31	Canopic
Mar. 14	Canopic
Apr. 3	Cretic
Apr. 24	Canopic
May 14	Cretic
June 4	Canopic
June 26	Cretic
July 9	Canopic
Aug. 11	Canopic
Sept. 11	Cretic
Sept. 23	Canopic
Oct. 14	Cretic
Nov. 4	Canopic
Nov. 19	Cretic
Dec. 9	Canopic

WHITE STAR LINE
Liverpool—New York

N. Y.

Arrival	Steamer
Jan. 7	Baltic
Jan. 15	Laurentic
Jan. 21	Cedric
Jan. 28	Celtic
Feb. 3	Arabic
Feb. 10	Baltic
Feb. 24	Celtic
Mar. 10	Baltic
Mar. 23	Celtic
Apr. 6	Baltic
Apr. 20	Celtic
Apr. 27	Adriatic
May 4	Baltic
May 11	Cedric
May 18	Celtic
May 25	Adriatic
June 1	Baltic
June 8	Cedric
June 15	Celtic
June 22	Adriatic
June 29	Baltic
July 6	Cedric
July 13	Celtic
July 19	Adriatic
July 27	Baltic
Aug. 3	Cedric
Aug. 10	Celtic
Aug. 16	Adriatic
Aug. 24	Baltic
Aug. 31	Cedric
Sept. 7	Celtic
Sept. 13	Adriatic
Sept. 20	Baltic
Sept. 28	Cedric
Oct. 5	Celtic
Oct. 11	Adriatic
Oct. 19	Baltic
Oct. 26	Cedric
Nov. 2	Celtic
Nov. 10	Cymric
Nov. 16	Baltic
Nov. 22	Adriatic
Nov. 30	Celtic
Dec. 7	Cedric
Dec. 15	Baltic
Dec. 21	Megantic
Dec. 29	Celtic

WHITE STAR LINE
Southampton—New York

N. Y.

Arrival	Steamer
Jan. 10	Oceanic
Jan. 17	Olympic
Feb. 8	Oceanic

WHITE STAR LINE
Southampton—New York
(Continued)

N. Y.

Arrival	Steamer
Feb. 14	Olympic
Mar. 7	Oceanic
Mar. 20	Olympic
Apr. 10	Olympic
May 16	Oceanic
May 22	Olympic
May 30	Majestic
June 5	Oceanic
June 12	Olympic
July 3	Olympic
July 10	Majestic
July 17	Oceanic
July 24	Olympic
Aug. 1	Majestic
Aug. 7	Oceanic
Aug. 15	Olympic
Aug. 22	Majestic
Aug. 28	Oceanic
Sept. 5	Olympic
Sept. 12	Majestic
Sept. 18	Oceanic
Sept. 26	Olympic
Oct. 3	Majestic
Oct. 9	Oceanic
Oct. 24	Majestic
Oct. 29	Oceanic
Nov. 14	Majestic
Nov. 20	Oceanic
Dec. 5	Majestic
Dec. 12	Oceanic
Dec. 27	Majestic

WHITE STAR LINE
Liverpool—Boston

Boston

Arrival	Steamer
Feb. 15	Megantic
Mar. 15	Megantic
May 3	Arabic
May 19	Cymric
May 30	Arabic
June 14	Cymric
June 27	Arabic
July 12	Cymric
July 25	Arabic
Aug. 8	Cymric
Aug. 22	Arabic
Sept. 5	Cymric
Sept. 18	Arabic
Oct. 3	Cymric
Oct. 17	Arabic
Nov. 14	Arabic
Dec. 12	Arabic

Year 1913

ALLAN LINE
Glasgow—Halifax—Boston
Boston

Arrival	Steamer
Jan. 14	Numidian
Jan. 23	Pretorian
Feb. 11	Sicilian
Feb. 22	Numidian
Mar. 4	Scandinavian
Mar. 22	Ionian
Apr. 3	Scotian
Apr. 18	Parisian
Apr. 26	Numidian
May 24	Parisian
June 5	Numidian
June 26	Parisian
July 1	Numidian
July 21	Parisian
Aug. 4	Numidian
Aug. 18	Parisian
Sept. 2	Numidian
Sept. 16	Parisian
Sept. 30	Numidian
Oct. 13	Parisian
Oct. 29	Numidian
Nov. 13	Parisian
Dec. 3	Hesperian
Dec. 17	Scotian
Dec. 31	Sicilian

AMERICAN LINE
Southampton—New York
N.Y.

Arrival	Steamer
Jan. 10	St. Paul
Jan. 17	Philadelphia
Jan. 30	New York
Feb. 14	Philadelphia
Feb. 28	New York
Mar. 13	Philadelphia
Mar. 28	New York
Mar. 30	St. Paul
Apr. 6	Philadelphia
Apr. 21	New York
Apr. 27	St. Paul
May 4	Philadelphia
May 18	New York
May 25	St. Paul
June 8	Philadelphia
June 15	New York
June 22	St. Paul
July 5	Philadelphia
July 13	New York
July 24	St. Paul
Aug. 2	Philadelphia
Aug. 10	New York
Aug. 16	St. Paul
Aug. 24	St. Louis
Aug. 31	Philadelphia
Sept. 7	New York
Sept. 13	St. Paul
Sept. 20	St. Louis
Sept. 27	Philadelphia
Oct. 5	New York
Oct. 12	St. Paul
Oct. 18	St. Louis
Oct. 25	Philadelphia

AMERICAN LINE
Southampton—New York
(Continued)
N.Y.

Arrival	Steamer
Nov. 2	New York
Nov. 15	St. Louis
Nov. 23	Philadelphia
Dec. 4	New York
Dec. 14	St. Paul
Dec. 18	St. Louis
Dec. 27	Philadelphia

AMERICAN LINE
Liverpool—Philadelphia
Phila.

Arrival	Steamer
Jan. 9	Haverford
Feb. 17	Haverford
Mar. 21	Merion
Apr. 1	Haverford
Apr. 23	Merion
May 6	Haverford
May 12	Dominion
May 27	Merion
June 16	Dominion
June 20	Merion
July 21	Dominion
Aug. 4	Merion
Aug. 18	Haverford
Aug. 25	Dominion
Sept. 8	Merion
Sept. 21	Haverford
Sept. 28	Dominion
Oct. 13	Merion
Oct. 27	Haverford
Nov. 4	Dominion
Nov. 17	Merion
Dec. 3	Haverford
Dec. 23	Merion

ANCHOR LINE
Glasgow—New York
N.Y.

Arrival	Steamer
Jan. 8	California
Jan. 21	Caledonia
Feb. 3	Cameronia
Feb. 13	California
Feb. 17	Caledonia
Feb. 23	Columbia
Mar. 4	Cameronia
Mar. 12	California
Mar. 18	Caledonia
Mar. 26	Columbia
Mar. 31	Cameronia
Apr. 8	California
Apr. 13	Caledonia
Apr. 21	Columbia
Apr. 27	Cameronia
May 5	California
May 12	Caledonia
May 19	Columbia
May 25	Cameronia
June 2	California
June 8	Caledonia
June 16	Columbia

ANCHOR LINE
Glasgow—New York
(Continued)
N.Y.

Arrival	Steamer
June 22	Cameronia
June 30	California
July 6	Caledonia
July 13	Columbia
July 19	Cameronia
July 27	California
Aug. 3	Caledonia
Aug. 10	Columbia
Aug. 16	Cameronia
Aug. 24	California
Aug. 31	Caledonia
Sept. 7	Columbia
Sept. 14	Cameronia
Sept. 22	California
Sept. 28	Caledonia
Oct. 5	Columbia
Oct. 12	Cameronia
Oct. 20	California
Oct. 26	Caledonia
Nov. 3	Columbia
Nov. 11	Cameronia
Nov. 17	California
Nov. 25	Caledonia
Dec. 1	Columbia
Dec. 7	Cameronia
Dec. 15	California
Dec. 28	Caledonia

ANCHOR LINE
Mediterranean—New York
N.Y.

Arrival	Steamer
Jan. 20	Calabria
Feb. 11	Perugia
Mar. 1	Italia
Mar. 21	Calabria
Apr. 12	Perugia
Apr. 25	Italia
May 16	Calabria
June 7	Perugia
June 19	Italia
July 12	Calabria
Aug. 1	Perugia
Aug. 22	Italia
Sept. 5	Calabria
Sept. 26	Perugia
Oct. 10	Italia
Nov. 3	Calabria
Nov. 22	Perugia
Dec. 6	Italia
Dec. 27	Calabria

ATLANTIC TRANSPORT LINE
London—New York
N.Y.

Arrival	Steamer
Jan. 8	Minnewaska
Jan. 15	Minnetonka
Jan. 28	Minneapolis
Feb. 4	Minnehaha
Feb. 12	Minnewaska

Year 1913

ATLANTIC TRANSPORT LINE
London—New York
(Continued)

N. Y.

Arrival	Steamer
Feb. 18	Minnetonka
Mar. 5	Minneapolis
Mar. 11	Minnehaha
Mar. 18	Minnewaska
Mar. 26	Minnetonka
Apr. 8	Minnehaha
Apr. 14	Minneapolis
Apr. 22	Minnetonka
Apr. 28	Minnewaska
May 13	Minneapolis
May 19	Minnehaha
May 26	Minnewaska
June 2	Minnetonka
June 10	Minneapolis
June 16	Minnehaha
June 23	Minnewaska
June 30	Minnetonka
July 7	Minneapolis
July 14	Minnehaha
July 21	Minnewaska
July 28	Minnetonka
Aug. 4	Minneapolis
Aug. 11	Minnehaha
Aug. 18	Minnewaska
Aug. 25	Minnetonka
Sept. 1	Minneapolis
Sept. 8	Minnehaha
Sept. 15	Minnewaska
Sept. 22	Minnetonka
Sept. 29	Minneapolis
Oct. 6	Minnehaha
Oct. 13	Minnewaska
Oct. 20	Minnetonka
Oct. 28	Minneapolis
Nov. 4	Minnehaha
Nov. 12	Minnewaska
Nov. 18	Minnetonka
Dec. 2	Minneapolis
Dec. 8	Minnehaha
Dec. 14	Minnewaska
Dec. 22	Minnetonka

AUSTRO-AMERICAN LINE
Greece, Italy, Azores—New York

N. Y.

Arrival	Steamer
Jan. 12	Oceania
Jan. 31	Alice
Feb. 5	Martha Washington
Feb. 15	Argentina
Feb. 27	Oceania
Feb. 28	Eugenia
Mar. 18	Alice
Mar. 19	Martha Washington
Apr. 5	Argentina
Apr. 16	Polonia
Apr. 18	Oceania
Apr. 30	Martha Washington
May 9	Laura
May 10	K. Fr. Jos. I
May 23	Argentina

AUSTRO-AMERICAN LINE
Greece, Italy, Azores—New York
(Continued)

N. Y.

Arrival	Steamer
June 5	Oceania
June 8	Martha Washington
June 18	K. Fr. Jos. I
July 9	Alice
July 11	Argentina
July 22	Martha Washington
July 26	K. Fr. Jos. I
Aug. 10	Eugenia
Aug. 27	Alice
Aug. 30	Argentina
Aug. 30	K. Fr. Jos. I
Sept. 8	Martha Washington
Sept. 18	Belvedere
Sept. 25	Oceania
Oct. 5	K. Fr. Jos. I
Oct. 17	Argentina
Oct. 20	Martha Washington
Nov. 7	Laura
Nov. 15	Belvedere
Dec. 5	Argentina
Dec. 8	Martha Washington
Dec. 18	Dora
Dec. 25	Laura

AUSTRO-AMERICAN LINE
Adriatic—New York

N. Y.

Arrival	Steamer
Jan. 12	Oceania
Jan. 31	Alice
Feb. 5	Martha Washington
Feb. 15	Argentina
Feb. 27	Oceania
Feb. 28	Eugenia
Mar. 18	Alice
Mar. 19	Martha Washington
Apr. 5	Argentina
Apr. 16	Polonia
Apr. 18	Oceania
Apr. 30	Martha Washington
May 9	Laura
May 10	Kr. Fr. Jos. I
May 23	Argentina
June 5	Oceania
June 8	Martha Washington
June 18	Kr. Fr. Jos. I
July 9	Alice
July 11	Argentina
July 22	Martha Washington
July 26	Kr. Fr. Jos. I
Aug. 10	Eugenia
Aug. 27	Alice
Aug. 30	Argentina
Aug. 30	Kr. Fr. Jos. I
Sept. 8	Martha Washington
Sept. 18	Belvedere
Sept. 25	Oceania
Oct. 5	Kr. Fr. Jos. I
Oct. 17	Argentina
Oct. 20	Martha Washington
Nov. 7	Laura

AUSTRO-AMERICAN LINE
Adriatic—New York
(Continued)

N. Y.

Arrival	Steamer
Nov. 15	Belvedere
Dec. 5	Argentina
Dec. 8	Martha Washington
Dec. 25	Laura

COMPANIA TRANSATLANTICA LINE
(Spanish Line)
Spain—New York

N. Y.

Arrival	Steamer
Jan. 10	Montserrat
Feb. 13	Manuel Calvo
Mar. 12	Antonio Lopez
Apr. 11	Buenos Aires
May 12	Antonio Lopez
June 11	Montevideo
July 12	Manuel Calvo
Aug. 10	Montserrat
Sept. 11	Buenos Aires
Oct. 11	Montserrat
Nov. 11	Montevideo
Dec. 13	Manuel Calvo

CUNARD LINE
Italian Ports—New York

N. Y.

Arrival	Steamer
Jan. 1	Franconia
Jan. 27	Ultonia
Feb. 10	Laconia
Feb. 25	Pannonia
Mar. 2	Franconia
Mar. 10	Caronia
Mar. 31	Ultonia
Apr. 15	Pannonia
Apr. 21	Saxonia
May 4	Carpathia
May 16	Ivernia
June 7	Saxonia
June 15	Pannonia
June 23	Carpathia
July 5	Ivernia
July 15	Ultonia
July 25	Saxonia
Aug. 8	Pannonia
Aug. 14	Carpathia
Aug. 26	Ivernia
Sept. 5	Ultonia
Sept. 12	Saxonia
Sept. 26	Pannonia
Oct. 2	Carpathia
Oct. 17	Ivernia
Oct. 27	Ultonia
Nov. 4	Saxonia
Nov. 4	Franconia
Nov. 18	Pannonia
Nov. 18	Laconia
Nov. 24	Carpathia
Dec. 5	Ivernia
Dec. 24	Ultonia
Dec. 26	Franconia

Year 1913

CUNARD LINE
Adriatic Ports—New York
N.Y.

Arrival	Steamer
Jan. 1	Laconia
Jan. 1	Pannonia
Jan. 1	Franconia
Jan. 1	Caronia
Jan. 27	Ultonia
Feb. 10	Laconia
Feb. 25	Pannonia
Mar. 2	Franconia
Mar. 10	Caronia
Mar. 31	Ultonia
Mar. 31	Carpathia
Apr. 15	Pannonia
Apr. 15	Ivernia
Apr. 21	Saxonia
May 4	Carpathia
May 16	Ivernia
June 7	Saxonia
June 15	Pannonia
June 23	Carpathia
July 5	Ivernia
July 15	Ultonia
July 25	Saxonia
Aug. 8	Pannonia
Aug. 14	Carpathia
Aug. 26	Ivernia
Sept. 5	Ultonia
Sept. 12	Saxonia
Sept. 26	Pannonia
Oct. 2	Carpathia
Oct. 17	Ivernia
Oct. 27	Ultonia
Nov. 4	Saxonia
Nov. 4	Franconia
Nov. 18	Pannonia
Nov. 18	Laconia
Nov. 24	Carpathia
Dec. 5	Ivernia
Dec. 24	Ultonia
Dec. 26	Franconia

CUNARD LINE
Liverpool—New York
N.Y.

Arrival	Steamer
Jan. 6	Carmania
Jan. 13	Caronia
Jan. 19	Mauretania
Jan. 25	Campania
Feb. 2	Carmania
Feb. 8	Mauretania
Feb. 16	Campania
Feb. 24	Carmania
Feb. 28	Mauretania
Feb. 28	Franconia
Mar. 16	Campania
Mar. 23	Carmania
Mar. 28	Mauretania
Apr. 6	Franconia
Apr. 12	Campania
Apr. 18	Mauretania
Apr. 27	Carmania
May 4	Caronia
May 10	Campania
May 16	Mauretania
May 25	Carmania
June 1	Caronia

CUNARD LINE
Liverpool—New York
(Continued)
N.Y.

Arrival	Steamer
June 6	Mauretania
June 14	Campania
June 22	Carmania
June 27	Mauretania
July 5	Campania
July 13	Caronia
July 18	Mauretania
July 27	Carmania
Aug. 2	Campania
Aug. 9	Caronia
Aug. 15	Mauretania
Aug. 23	Campania
Aug. 29	Lusitania
Sept. 3	Carmania
Sept. 5	Mauretania
Sept. 13	Campania
Sept. 16	Caronia
Sept. 18	Lusitania
Sept. 26	Mauretania
Oct. 1	Carmania
Oct. 4	Campania
Oct. 10	Lusitania
Oct. 14	Caronia
Oct. 17	Mauretania
Oct. 26	Carmania
Oct. 31	Lusitania
Nov. 10	Caronia
Nov. 14	Mauretania
Nov. 23	Carmania
Nov. 28	Lusitania
Dec. 7	Ansonia
Dec. 7	Ivernia
Dec. 7	Caronia
Dec. 12	Mauretania
Dec. 18	Lusitania
Dec. 27	Campania

CUNARD LINE
Liverpool—Boston
Boston

Arrival	Steamer
Jan. 20	Ivernia
Feb. 1	Saxonia
Feb. 16	Carpathia
Feb. 28	Ivernia
Mar. 17	Carpathia
Mar. 28	Ivernia
Mar. 28	Ultonia
May 7	Franconia
May 22	Laconia
June 5	Franconia
June 19	Laconia
July 2	Franconia
July 16	Laconia
July 30	Franconia
Aug. 13	Laconia
Aug. 27	Franconia
Sept. 10	Laconia
Sept. 24	Franconia
Oct. 9	Laconia
Nov. 6	Franconia
Nov. 6	Saxonia
Nov. 19	Laconia
Dec. 6	Alaunia

FABRE LINE
Mediterranean—New York
N.Y.

Arrival	Steamer
Jan. 6	Madonna
Jan. 11	Germania
Jan. 20	Venezia
Jan. 25	Sant' Anna
Feb. 7	Roma
Feb. 23	Canada
Mar. 1	Germania
Mar. 12	Sant' Anna
Mar. 18	Madonna
Mar. 21	Venezia
Mar. 24	Roma
Apr. 2	Canada
Apr. 20	Germania
Apr. 23	Madonna
Apr. 26	Sant' Anna
May 4	Venezia
May 7	Roma
May 16	Canada
May 31	Madonna
June 2	Germania
June 12	Sant' Anna
June 17	Venezia
June 23	Roma
July 2	Canada
July 13	Madonna
July 25	Sant' Anna
Aug. 2	Venezia
Aug. 7	Roma
Aug. 15	Canada
Aug. 29	Madonna
Sept. 9	Sant' Anna
Sept. 17	Venezia
Sept. 22	Roma
Oct. 1	Canada
Oct. 14	Madonna
Oct. 17	Germania
Oct. 24	Sant' Anna
Nov. 2	Venezia
Nov. 7	Roma
Nov. 17	Canada
Nov. 26	Madonna
Dec. 2	Germania
Dec. 7	Sant' Anna
Dec. 18	Venezia
Dec. 30	Canada

FRENCH LINE
(Compagnie Generale Transatlantique)
Havre, Bordeaux, Vigo—New York
N.Y.

Arrival	Steamer
Jan. 3	Hudson
Jan. 6	La Savoie
Jan. 8	Rochambeau
Jan. 12	La Provence
Jan. 15	Chicago
Jan. 20	La Lorraine
Jan. 26	La Savoie
Jan. 29	St. Laurent
Feb. 3	La Touraine
Feb. 3	Rochambeau
Feb. 8	Floride
Feb. 10	La Lorraine
Feb. 14	Chicago
Feb. 16	La Provence

Year 1913

FRENCH LINE
(Compagnie Generale Transatlantique)
Havre, Bordeaux, Vigo—
New York
(Continued)

N. Y.

Arrival	Steamer
Feb. 19	Niagara
Feb. 21	France
Mar. 2	La Lorraine
Mar. 4	Rochambeau
Mar. 7	Virginia
Mar. 11	La Touraine
Mar. 14	Chicago
Mar. 15	La Provence
Mar. 20	St. Laurent
Mar. 22	France
Mar. 22	Niagara
Mar. 31	Rochambeau
Apr. 2	La Touraine
Apr. 6	La Lorraine
Apr. 10	Chicago
Apr. 11	Floride
Apr. 11	France
Apr. 17	Louisiane
Apr. 19	La Provence
Apr. 21	Niagara
Apr. 28	La Touraine
Apr. 28	Hudson
Apr. 28	Rochambeau
May 3	La Lorraine
May 8	Chicago
May 9	France
May 17	La Provence
May 19	Californie
May 22	Niagara
May 25	La Lorraine
May 26	Rochambeau
May 30	France
June 7	La Provence
June 7	Caroline
June 15	Floride
June 16	La Touraine
June 17	Niagara
June 20	France
June 24	Chicago
June 28	La Savoie
June 30	Rochambeau
July 4	Mexico
July 5	La Provence
July 12	La Lorraine
July 15	Niagara
July 19	La Savoie
July 20	Californie
July 25	Caroline
July 26	La Provence
July 29	Chicago
Aug. 2	La Lorraine
Aug. 9	La Savoie
Aug. 11	Rochambeau
Aug. 15	France
Aug. 21	Louisiane
Aug. 23	La Lorraine
Aug. 23	Virginie
Aug. 25	Chicago
Aug. 30	La Provence
Sept. 4	La Touraine
Sept. 5	France
Sept. 9	Niagara
Sept. 13	La Savoie

FRENCH LINE
(Compagnie Generale Transatlantique)
Havre, Bordeaux, Vigo—
New York
(Continued)

N. Y.

Arrival	Steamer
Sept. 15	Rochambeau
Sept. 19	Mexico
Sept. 20	La Provence
Sept. 23	Chicago
Sept. 26	France
Sept. 29	La Touraine
Oct. 4	La Lorraine
Oct. 7	Niagara
Oct. 11	La Savoie
Oct. 11	Louisiane
Oct. 13	Rochambeau
Oct. 18	La Provence
Oct. 20	Chicago
Oct. 25	France
Oct. 27	La Touraine
Nov. 1	La Lorraine
Nov. 9	La Savoie
Nov. 11	Rochambeau
Nov. 15	La Provence
Nov. 18	Chicago
Nov. 19	Caroline
Nov. 22	France
Nov. 22	La Lorraine
Nov. 25	Californie
Dec. 3	Niagara
Dec. 6	La Savoie
Dec. 8	Rochambeau
Dec. 12	France
Dec. 21	La Lorraine
Dec. 23	Chicago
Dec. 24	Louisiane
Dec. 27	La Savoie

GREEK LINE
Greece—New York

N. Y.

Arrival	Steamer
July 14	Athinai
July 30	Themistocles
Sept. 1	Athinai
Sept. 19	Themistocles
Oct. 19	Athinai
Nov. 11	Themistocles
Dec. 25	Athinai

HAMBURG-AMERICAN LINE
Hamburg—Philadelphia

Phila.

Arrival	Steamer
Jan. 2	Graf Waldersee
Jan. 24	Prinz Oskar
Feb. 1	Prinz Adalbert
Feb. 20	Graf Waldersee
Mar. 15	Pallanza
Mar. 20	Prinz Adalbert
Apr. 9	Prinz Oskar
Apr. 17	Graf Waldersee
May 4	Prinz Adalbert
May 20	Prinz Oskar
June 1	Graf Waldersee
June 17	Prinz Adalbert
July 3	Prinz Oskar

HAMBURG-AMERICAN LINE
Hamburg—Philadelphia
(Continued)

Phila.

Arrival	Steamer
July 15	Graf Waldersee
July 30	Prinz Adalbert
Aug. 18	Prinz Oskar
Sept. 1	Graf Waldersee
Sept. 15	Prinz Adalbert
Sept. 20	Bosnia
Oct. 4	Prinz Oskar
Oct. 23	Barcelona
Nov. 1	Prinz Adalbert
Nov. 20	Prinz Oskar
Dec. 5	Graf Waldersee
Dec. 27	Armenia

HAMBURG-AMERICAN LINE
Mediterranean—New York

N. Y.

Arrival	Steamer
Jan. 24	Cincinnati
Feb. 19	Hamburg
Mar. 30	Hamburg
Apr. 16	Cincinnati
May 12	Hamburg
May 27	Moltke
June 24	Hamburg
July 8	Moltke
Aug. 4	Hamburg
Aug. 18	Moltke
Sept. 11	Hamburg
Sept. 30	Moltke
Oct. 21	Hamburg
Nov. 11	Moltke
Dec. 3	Cincinnati
Dec. 23	Cleveland

HAMBURG-AMERICAN LINE
Hamburg—Boston

Boston

Arrival	Steamer
Jan. 21	Pallanza
May 31	Cincinnati
June 19	Bluecher
July 5	Cincinnati
July 20	Cleveland
Aug. 8	Cincinnati
Sept. 5	Cleveland
Sept. 16	Cincinnati
Oct. 10	Cleveland
Oct. 19	Cincinnati
Nov. 14	Cleveland
Nov. 30	Hamburg
Dec. 20	Pisa

HAMBURG-AMERICAN LINE
Hamburg—Baltimore

Baltimore

Arrival	Steamer
Oct. 2	Arcadia
Nov. 2	Pisa
Nov. 17	Bosnia
Dec. 1	Arcadia
Dec. 28	Bulgaria

Year 1913

HAMBURG-AMERICAN LINE
Hamburg—New York

N.Y. Arrival	Steamer
Jan. 5	Patricia
Jan. 6	Hamburg
Jan. 11	Victoria Luise
Jan. 13	President Grant
Jan. 17	K. Auguste Victoria
Jan. 26	Pennsylvania
Jan 29	Barcelona
Jan. 30	President Lincoln
Feb. 1	Amerika
Feb. 16	Patricia
Feb. 21	President Grant
Feb. 26	K. Auguste Victoria
Feb. 28	Pretoria
Mar. 7	Amerika
Mar. 8	Pennsylvania
Mar. 14	President Lincoln
Mar. 15	K. Auguste Victoria
Mar. 30	Patricia
Apr. 2	President Grant
Apr. 7	Amerika
Apr. 10	Pretoria
Apr. 16	Pennsylvania
Apr. 22	President Lincoln
Apr. 26	K. Auguste Victoria
May 8	Patricia
May 9	Salamanca
May 10	Amerika
May 12	Antonina
May 12	Rugia
May 22	Pretoria
May 24	K. Auguste Victoria
May 29	President Grant
June 4	Cleveland
June 6	President Lincoln
June 12	Pennsylvania
June 14	Amerika
June 19	Imperator
June 21	Patricia
June 25	Kronprinz'n Cecilie
June 27	K. Auguste Victoria
June 30	Salamanca
July 5	Pretoria
July 9	President Grant
July 12	Amerika
July 15	Pallanza
July 16	Imperator
July 16	President Lincoln
July 24	Pennsylvania
July 26	K. Auguste Victoria
Aug. 1	Patricia
Aug. 6	Imperator
Aug. 9	Armenia
Aug. 14	Pretoria
Aug. 16	Amerika
Aug. 20	President Grant
Aug. 25	President Lincoln
Aug. 25	K. Auguste Victoria
Aug. 27	Imperator
Sept. 3	Pennsylvania
Sept. 9	Victoria Luise
Sept. 11	Patricia
Sept. 13	Amerika
Sept. 17	Imperator
Sept. 26	Pretoria
Sept. 27	K. Auguste Victoria

HAMBURG-AMERICAN LINE
Hamburg—New York (Continued)

N.Y. Arrival	Steamer
Oct. 1	President Grant
Oct. 4	Victoria Luise
Oct. 8	Imperator
Oct. 8	President Lincoln
Oct. 16	Graf Waldersee
Oct. 18	Amerika
Oct. 23	Patricia
Oct. 25	K. Auguste Victoria
Oct. 29	Imperator
Nov. 5	Armenia
Nov. 10	Pretoria
Nov. 14	President Grant
Nov. 15	Amerika
Nov. 20	Pallanza
Nov. 21	Pennsylvania
Nov. 27	President Lincoln
Dec. 1	K. Auguste Victoria
Dec. 10	Patricia
Dec. 19	Barcelona
Dec. 20	Pretoria
Dec. 20	Amerika
Dec. 24	President Grant

HOLLAND-AMERICA LINE
Rotterdam—New York

N.Y. Arrival	Steamer
Jan. 3	Potsdam
Jan. 14	New Amsterdam
Jan. 23	Noordam
Jan. 29	Ryndam
Feb. 6	Potsdam
Feb. 18	New Amsterdam
Feb. 25	Noordam
Mar. 4	Ryndam
Mar. 11	Rotterdam
Mar. 20	Potsdam
Mar. 26	New Amsterdam
Apr. 1	Noordam
Apr. 9	Ryndam
Apr. 13	Rotterdam
Apr. 24	Potsdam
Apr. 28	New Amsterdam
May 7	Noordam
May 13	Ryndam
May 19	Rotterdam
May 29	Potsdam
June 2	New Amsterdam
June 10	Noordam
June 18	Ryndam
June 23	Rotterdam
July 2	Potsdam
July 7	New Amsterdam
July 14	Noordam
July 22	Ryndam
Aug. 3	Rotterdam
Aug. 12	Potsdam
Aug. 19	New Amsterdam
Aug. 25	Noordam
Sept. 1	Ryndam
Sept. 8	Rotterdam
Sept. 16	Potsdam
Sept. 22	New Amsterdam

HOLLAND-AMERICA LINE
Rotterdam—New York (Continued)

N.Y. Arrival	Steamer
Sept. 29	Noordam
Oct. 6	Ryndam
Oct. 13	Rotterdam
Oct. 21	Potsdam
Oct. 27	New Amsterdam
Nov. 4	Noordam
Nov. 13	Ryndam
Nov. 17	Rotterdam
Dec. 1	New Amsterdam
Dec. 9	Noordam
Dec. 16	Ryndam
Dec. 22	Rotterdam
Dec. 31	Potsdam

ITALIA LINE
Mediterranean—New York

N.Y. Arrival	Steamer
Feb. 5	Ancona
Mar. 16	Ancona
Apr. 14	Napoli
Apr. 29	Ancona
June 3	Napoli
June 9	Ancona
July 18	Napoli
July 21	Ancona
Sept. 2	Ancona
Oct. 13	Ancona
Nov. 21	Ancona
Dec. 20	Napoli

ITALIA LINE
Mediterranean—Philadelphia

Phila. Arrival	Steamer
Feb. 7	Ancona
Mar. 19	Ancona
Apr. 16	Napoli
May 1	Ancona
June 6	Napoli
June 12	Ancona
July 20	Napoli
Sept. 4	Ancona
Oct. 15	Ancona
Nov. 23	Ancona

ITALIA LINE
Mediterranean—Boston

Boston Arrival	Steamer
Sept. 2	Napoli
Oct. 30	Napoli

LA VELOCE LINE
Mediterranean—New York

N.Y. Arrival	Steamer
Feb. 18	Stampalia
Mar. 11	Europa
Mar. 30	Stampalia
Apr. 23	Europa
May 13	Stampalia
June 4	Europa
June 24	Stampalia

Year 1913

LA VELOCE LINE
Mediterranean—New York
(Continued)

N. Y.

Arrival	Steamer
July 13	Stampalia
Aug. 5	Stampalia
Aug. 25	Europa
Sept. 16	Stampalia
Oct. 6	Europa
Oct. 25	Stampalia
Dec. 7	Stampalia

LA VELOCE LINE
Mediterranean—Philadelphia

Phila.

Arrival	Steamer
Feb. 20	Stampalia
May 15	Stampalia
June 26	Stampalia
Aug. 7	Stampalia
Sept. 17	Stampalia
Oct. 27	Stampalia

LEYLAND LINE
Liverpool—Boston

Boston

Arrival	Steamer
Jan. 10	Bohemian
Jan. 17	Winifredian
Jan. 23	Devonian
Jan. 28	Canadian
Feb. 19	Winifredian
Mar. 5	Devonian
Mar. 11	Canadian
Mar. 29	Bohemian
Apr. 1	Winifredian
Apr. 8	Devonian
Apr. 14	Canadian
May 5	Winifredian
May 11	Devonian
May 26	Canadian
June 2	Bohemian
June 8	Winifredian
June 15	Devonian
June 29	Canadian
July 6	Bohemian
July 12	Winifredian
July 20	Devonian
Aug. 3	Canadian
Aug. 10	Bohemian
Aug. 17	Winifredian
Aug. 23	Devonian
Sept. 7	Canadian
Sept. 14	Bohemian
Sept. 20	Winifredian
Sept. 27	Devonian
Oct. 12	Canadian
Oct. 19	Bohemian
Oct. 26	Winifredian
Nov. 2	Devonian
Nov. 17	Canadian
Nov. 25	Bohemian
Dec. 1	Winifredian
Dec. 10	Devonian
Dec. 24	Californian
Dec. 28	Bohemian

LLOYD ITALIANO
Mediterranean—New York

N. Y.

Arrival	Steamer
Feb. 4	Mendoza
Mar. 18	Mendoza
Apr. 9	Taormina
Apr. 19	Indiana
Apr. 29	Mendoza
May 17	Luisiana
May 20	Taormina
June 3	Indiana
June 13	Mendoza
June 28	Luisiana
July 1	Taormina
July 21	Mendoza
Aug. 11	Taormina
Sept. 2	Mendoza
Sept. 23	Taormina
Oct. 12	Mendoza
Nov. 2	Taormina
Dec. 8	Taormina

LLOYD SABAUDO
Mediterranean—New York

N. Y.

Arrival	Steamer
Jan. 17	Princ. di Piemonte
Feb. 27	Re d'Italia
Mar. 22	Princ. di Piemonte
Apr. 5	Re d'Italia
May 2	Princ. di Piemonte
May 15	Re d'Italia
June 14	Principe
June 25	Re d'Italia
July 24	Princ. di Piemonte
Aug. 8	Re d'Italia
Sept. 25	Re d'Italia
Oct. 30	Princ. di Piemonte
Nov. 14	Re d'Italia
Dec. 12	Princ. di Piemonte

NATIONAL GREEK LINE
Greece—New York

N. Y.

Arrival	Steamer
July 1	Patris
Aug. 15	Patris
Oct. 4	Patris
Nov. 28	Patris
Nov. 26	Ioannina

**NAVIGAZIONE GENE-
RALE ITALIANA**
Mediterranean—New York

N. Y.

Arrival	Steamer
Jan. 13	America
Mar. 5	America
Mar. 25	Verona
Apr. 15	America
May 7	Verona
May 25	America
June 9	Lazio
June 13	Verona
June 29	America
July 29	Verona
Aug. 18	America
Sept. 9	Verona

**NAVIGAZIONE GENE-
RALE ITALIANA**
Mediterranean—New York
(Continued)

N. Y.

Arrival	Steamer
Sept. 27	America
Oct. 22	Verona
Nov. 10	America
Dec. 1	Verona
Dec. 19	America

**NAVIGAZIONE GENE-
RALE ITALIANA**
Mediterranean—Boston

Boston

Arrival	Steamer
July 26	Palermo
Sept. 22	Palermo

NORTH GERMAN LLOYD
Express Service
Bremen—New York

N. Y.

Arrival	Steamer
Jan. 16	Kaiser Wilhelm II
Jan. 29	Kronprinz'n Cecilie
Feb. 13	Kaiser Wilhelm II
Feb. 26	Kronprinz'n Cecilie
Mar. 12	Kaiser Wilhelm II
Mar. 27	Kronprinz'n Cecilie
Apr. 16	K. Wm. der Grosse
Apr. 23	Kaiser Wilhelm II
Apr. 30	Kronprinz Wilhelm
May 7	Kronprinz'n Cecilie
May 13	K. Wm. der Grosse
May 21	Kaiser Wilhelm II
May 28	Kronprinz Wilhelm
June 4	Kronprinz'n Cecilie
June 13	K. Wm. der Grosse
June 18	Kaiser Wilhelm II
June 26	Kronprinz Wilhelm
July 2	Kronprinz'n Cecilie
July 9	K. Wm. der Grosse
July 16	Kaiser Wilhelm II
July 23	Kronprinz Wilhelm
July 30	Kronprinz'n Cecilie
Aug. 6	K. Wm. der Grosse
Aug. 20	Kaiser Wilhelm II
Aug. 27	Kronprinz Wilhelm
Sept. 3	Kronprinz'n Cecilie
Sept. 10	K. Wm. der Grosse
Sept. 17	Kaiser Wilhelm II
Sept. 24	Kronprinz Wilhelm
Oct. 1	Kronprinz'n Cecilie
Oct. 9	K. Wm. der Grosse
Oct. 15	Kaiser Wilhelm II
Oct. 22	Kronprinz Wilhelm
Oct. 28	Kronprinz'n Cecilie
Nov. 6	K. Wm. der Grosse
Nov. 13	Kaiser Wilhelm II
Nov. 26	Kronprinz'n Cecilie
Dec. 11	Kaiser Wilhelm II

NORTH GERMAN LLOYD
Mediterranean—New York

N. Y.

Arrival	Steamer
Feb. 5	Berlin
Feb. 21	Prinzess Irene
Mar. 8	Koenig Albert

Year 1913

NORTH GERMAN LLOYD
Mediterranean—New York
(Continued)

N. Y.

Arrival	Steamer
Mar. 19	Berlin
Apr. 11	Prinzess Irene
Apr. 17	Koenig Albert
May 1	Berlin
May 16	Prinzess Irene
June 1	Koenig Albert
June 13	Berlin
June 27	Prinzess Irene
July 19	Barbarossa
Aug. 8	Prinzess Irene
Aug. 29	Barbarossa
Sept. 25	Prinzess Irene
Oct. 11	Barbarossa
Oct. 23	Berlin
Nov. 7	Prinzess Irene
Nov. 22	Barbarossa
Dec. 1	Berlin
Dec. 19	Prinzess Irene

NORTH GERMAN LLOYD
Bremen—New York

N. Y.

Arrival	Steamer
Jan. 4	Neckar
Jan. 16	Main
Jan. 17	Grosser Kurfuerst
Jan. 22	Prz. Fred. Wilhelm
Jan. 31	Barbarossa
Feb. 7	Buelow
Feb. 16	Neckar
Feb. 18	George Washington
Feb. 25	Prz. Fred. Wilhelm
Mar. 7	Kleist
Mar. 14	Barbarossa
Mar. 17	George Washington
Mar. 18	Rhein
Mar. 28	Brandenburg
Mar. 29	Neckar
Apr. 1	Prz. Fred. Wilhelm
Apr. 11	Main
Apr. 14	George Washington
Apr. 19	Wittekind
Apr. 21	Kleist
Apr. 24	Barbarossa
Apr. 27	Bremen
May 5	Neckar
May 6	Prz. Fred. Wilhelm
May 12	George Washington
May 21	Grosser Kurfuerst
May 22	Giessen
May 28	Fried. der Grosse
May 30	Hanover
June 4	Barbarossa
June 10	George Washington
June 12	Brandenburg
June 16	Bremen
June 17	Erlangen
June 3	Prz. Fred. Wilhelm
June 21	Sierra Nevada
June 21	Roon
June 26	Luetzow
June 27	Main
July 3	Fried. der Grosse
July 7	George Washington
July 12	Rhein

NORTH GERMAN LLOYD
Bremen—New York
(Continued)

N. Y.

Arrival	Steamer
July 17	Roon
July 20	Breslau
July 21	Prz. Fred. Wilhelm
July 23	Koenig Albert
July 28	Berlin
Aug. 5	George Washington
Aug. 7	Koenigin Luise
Aug. 14	Main
Aug. 16	Fried. der Grosse
Aug. 20	Bremen
Aug. 25	Prz. Fred. Wilhelm
Aug. 26	Rhein
Sept. 2	George Washington
Sept. 3	Frankfurt
Sept. 8	Grosser Kurfuerst
Sept 9	Berlin
Sept. 9	Neckar
Sept. 15	Koenigin Luise
Sept. 16	Koenig Albert
Sept. 17	Fried. der Grosse
Sept. 23	Main
Sept. 24	Bremen
Sept. 29	George Washington
Oct. 6	Prz. Fred. Wilhelm
Oct. 8	Rhein
Oct. 13	Frankfurt
Oct. 16	Grosser Kurfuerst
Oct. 22	Fried. der Grosse
Oct. 27	George Washington
Oct. 28	Neckar
Nov. 5	Main
Nov. 6	Bremen
Nov. 12	Prz. Fred. Wilhelm
Nov. 15	Hanover
Nov. 19	Grosser Kurfuerst
Nov. 20	Rhein
Nov. 24	George Washington
Dec. 4	Fried. der Grosse
Dec. 6	Koeln
Dec. 9	Prz. Fred. Wilhelm
Dec. 10	Neckar
Dec. 18	Main
Dec. 18	Bremen
Dec. 22	George Washington
Dec. 26	Cassel
Dec. 31	Rhein

NORTH GERMAN LLOYD
Bremen—Baltimore

Baltimore

Arrival	Steamer
Jan. 6	Neckar
Jan. 19	Main
Jan. 31	Brandenburg
Feb. 6	Rhein
Feb. 13	Chemnitz
Feb. 21	Neckar
Feb. 28	Main
Mar. 12	Hannover
Mar. 20	Rhein
Mar. 31	Neckar
Apr. 8	Chemnitz
Apr. 14	Main
Apr. 28	Rhein
May 5	Brandenburg

NORTH GERMAN LLOYD
Bremen—Baltimore
(Continued)

Baltimore

Arrival	Steamer
May 7	Neckar
May 9	Cassell
May 24	Main
May 31	Hannover
June 6	Rhein
June 9	Eisenach
June 15	Breslau
June 19	Erlangen
June 19	Neckar
June 29	Main
July 8	Hannover
July 13	Rhein
July 14	Koeln
July 24	Koenig Albert
July 26	Breslau
July 30	Chemnitz
Aug. 7	Neckar
Aug. 16	Main
Aug. 28	Rhein
Sept. 5	Frankfurt
Sept. 10	Neckar
Sept. 17	Koenig Albert
Sept. 25	Main
Oct. 10	Rhein
Oct. 16	Frankfurt
Oct. 20	Seydlitz
Oct. 24	Brandenburg
Oct. 31	Neckar
Nov. 7	Main
Nov. 21	Rhein
Dec. 4	Frankfurt
Dec. 10	Wittekind
Dec. 13	Neckar
Dec. 30	Main
Dec. 28	Brandenburg

NORTH GERMAN LLOYD
Bremen—Philadelphia

Phila.

Arrival	Steamer
Jan. 18	Willehad
Feb. 1	Rhein
Feb. 11	Chemnitz
Feb. 20	Breslau
Mar. 8	Hannover
Mar. 20	Cassel
Apr. 5	Chemnitz
Apr. 16	Breslau
May 3	Brandenburg
May 18	Frankfurt
May 30	Chemnitz
June 11	Breslau
July 5	Frankfurt
July 11	Koeln
July 22	Breslau
Aug. 2	Brandenburg
Aug. 4	Neckar
Aug. 20	Cassel
Sept. 2	Breslau
Sept. 17	Wittekind
Oct. 1	Chemnitz
Oct. 16	Seydlitz
Oct. 16	Seydlitz ex Volturno
Oct. 29	Neckar
Nov. 15	Breslau

Year 1913

NORTH GERMAN LLOYD
Bremen—Philadelphia
(Continued)

Phila.

Arrival	Steamer
Nov. 30	Frankfurt
Dec. 11	Neckar
Dec. 25	Brandenburg

NORTH GERMAN LLOYD
Bremen—Boston

Boston

Arrival	Steamer
Sept. 30	Koeln
Oct. 20	Cassel
Nov. 13	Hannover
Dec. 3	Koeln
Dec. 24	Cassel

**NORWAY-MEXICO GULF
LINE, LTD.**
Christiania—Philadelphia

Phila.

Arrival	Steamer
Oct. 24	Noruega

**NORWEGIAN-AMERICA
LINE**
Christiania—New York

N. Y.

Arrival	Steamer
June 17	Kristianiafjord
July 28	Kristianiafjord
Sept. 9	Kristianiafjord
Oct. 7	Bergensfjord
Oct. 20	Kristianiafjord
Nov. 11	Bergensfjord
Dec. 2	Kristianiafjord
Dec. 23	Bergensfjord

RED STAR LINE
Antwerp—Philadelphia—
Boston

Boston

Arrival	Steamer
Jan. 13	Manitou
Jan. 25	Marquette
Feb. 5	Menominee
Feb. 22	Manitou
Mar. 6	Marquette
Mar. 19	Menominee
Apr. 2	Manitou
Apr. 14	Marquette
Apr. 29	Menominee
May 13	Manitou
May 27	Marquette
June 10	Menominee
June 23	Mesaba
July 8	Manitou
July 21	Marquette
Aug. 5	Menominee
Aug. 18	Manitou
Sept. 1	Marquette
Sept. 16	Menominee
Sept. 29	Manitou
Oct. 13	Marquette
Oct. 27	Menominee
Nov. 14	Manitou
Nov. 25	Marquette
Dec. 9	Menominee
Dec. 23	Manitou

RED STAR LINE
Antwerp—New York

N. Y.

Arrival	Steamer
Jan. 1	Kroonland
Jan. 9	Zeeland
Jan. 16	Finland
Jan. 24	Vaderland
Jan. 27	Lapland
Feb. 4	Kroonland
Feb. 13	Zeeland
Feb. 19	Finland
Feb. 25	Vaderland
Mar. 3	Lapland
Mar. 12	Kroonland
Mar. 18	Zeeland
Mar. 27	Finland
Mar. 31	Lapland
Apr. 8	Kroonland
Apr. 15	Zeeland
Apr. 19	Vaderland
Apr. 23	Finland
Apr. 28	Lapland
May 5	Gothland
May 6	Kroonland
May 13	Zeeland
May 20	Finland
May 26	Lapland
May 31	Gothland
June 4	Kroonland
June 10	Zeeland
June 17	Finland
June 22	Lapland
June 24	Vaderland
June 30	Gothland
July 1	Kroonland
July 8	Zeeland
July 15	Finland
July 20	Lapland
July 28	Gothland
July 29	Vaderland
Aug. 5	Zeeland
Aug. 12	Finland
Aug. 19	Kroonland
Aug. 26	Vaderland
Sept. 1	Lapland
Sept. 9	Zeeland
Sept. 15	Kroonland
Sept. 22	Finland
Sept. 28	Lapland
Oct. 6	Vaderland
Oct. 16	Kroonland
Oct. 20	Finland
Oct. 28	Zeeland
Nov. 2	Lapland
Nov. 13	Vaderland
Nov. 18	Kroonland
Nov. 26	Finland
Dec. 2	Zeeland
Dec. 8	Lapland
Dec. 16	Vaderland
Dec. 23	Kroonland
Dec. 30	Finland

**RUSSIAN-AMERICAN
LINE**
Libau via Halifax—Rotter-
dam, Libau—New York

N. Y.

Arrival	Steamer
Jan. 8	Kursk

**RUSSIAN-AMERICAN
LINE**
Libau via Halifax—Rotter-
dam, Libau—New York
(Continued)

N. Y.

Arrival	Steamer
Jan. 21	Czar
Feb. 15	Birma
Feb. 18	Kursk
Mar. 4	Czar
Mar. 29	Kursk
Mar. 30	Birma
Apr. 2	Russia
Apr. 14	Czar
Apr. 22	Kursk
May 15	Russia
May 26	Czar
June 9	Kursk
June 26	Russia
June 23	Birma
July 6	Czar
July 20	Kursk
Aug. 4	Russia
Aug. 17	Czar
Aug. 31	Kursk
Sept. 13	Russia
Sept. 28	Czar
Oct. 9	Birma
Oct. 12	Kursk
Oct. 27	Russia
Nov. 11	Czar
Nov. 25	Kursk
Dec. 6	Birma
Dec. 12	Russia
Dec. 23	Czar

**SCANDINAVIAN-
AMERICAN LINE**
Scandinavian Ports—
New York

N. Y.

Arrival	Steamer
Jan. 16	C. F. Tietgen
Jan. 28	Oscar II
Feb. 21	United States
Mar. 5	Hellig Olav
Mar. 21	Oscar II
Mar. 29	C. F. Tietgen ex. Texas
Apr. 4	United States
Apr. 15	Hellig Olav
Apr. 30	Oscar II
May 7	C. F. Tietgen
May 13	United States
May 27	Hellig Olav
June 10	Oscar II
June 18	C. F. Tietgen
June 24	United States
July 8	Hellig Olav
July 23	Oscar II
Aug. 5	United States
Aug. 19	Hellig Olav
Aug. 26	C. F. Tietgen
Sept. 2	Oscar II
Sept. 16	United States
Sept. 29	Hellig Olav
Oct. 8	C. F. Tietgen
Oct. 14	Oscar II
Oct. 26	United States

Year 1913

SCANDINAVIAN-AMERICAN LINE
Scandinavian Ports—
New York
(Continued)

N.Y.

Arrival	Steamer
Nov. 11	Hellig Olav
Nov. 20	C. F. Tietgen
Nov. 27	Oscar II
Dec. 2	United States
Dec. 24	Hellig Olav

SICULA AMERICANA LINE
Mediterranean—New York

N.Y.

Arrival	Steamer
Feb. 15	San Giorgio
Mar. 18	San Guglielmo
Apr. 8	San Giorgio
Apr. 25	San Guglielmo
May 3	San Giovanni
May 15	San Giorgio
June 8	San Guglielmo
June 13	San Giovanni
July 1	San Giorgio
July 25	San Guglielmo
Aug. 1	San Giovanni
Aug. 27	San Giorgio
Sept. 11	San Guglielmo
Sept. 30	San Giovanni
Oct. 24	San Guglielmo
Dec. 4	San Guglielmo

URANIUM STEAMSHIP COMPANY
Rotterdam via Halifax—
Rotterdam—New York

N.Y.

Arrival	Steamer
Jan. 18	Uranium
Feb. 15	Volturno
Mar. 1	Campanello
Mar. 22	Volturno
Apr. 11	Campanello
Apr. 19	Uranium
May 3	Volturno
May 20	Campanello
May 30	Uranium
June 14	Volturno
June 29	Campanello
July 10	Uranium
July 24	Volturno
Aug. 8	Campanello
Aug. 21	Uranium
Sept. 6	Volturno
Sept. 20	Campanello
Oct. 6	Uranium
Oct. 30	Campanello
Nov. 15	Uranium
Dec. 12	Campanello
Dec. 30	Uranium

WARREN LINE
Liverpool—Boston

Boston

Arrival	Steamer
Feb. 27	Michigan
Apr. 10	Michigan

WARREN LINE
Liverpool—Boston
(Continued)

Boston

Arrival	Steamer
Apr. 25	Sachem
May 7	Sagamore
May 23	Michigan
July 16	Sachem
Aug. 1	Sagamore
Sept. 3	Sachem
Sept. 9	Sagamore
Sept. 24	Michigan
Oct. 9	Sachem
Oct. 21	Sagamore
Nov. 8	Michigan
Nov. 20	Sachem
Dec. 20	Michigan
Dec. 31	Sachem

WHITE STAR LINE
Liverpool—New York

N.Y.

Arrival	Steamer
Jan. 3	Laurentic
Jan. 14	Cedric
Jan. 17	Megantic
Jan. 20	Baltic
Jan. 27	Cymric
Feb. 1	Celtic
Feb. 15	Baltic
Mar. 1	Celtic
Mar. 15	Baltic
Mar. 30	Celtic
Apr. 12	Baltic
Apr. 18	Adriatic
Apr. 26	Celtic
May 3	Cedric
May 10	Baltic
May 16	Adriatic
May 23	Celtic
May 31	Cedric
June 7	Baltic
June 13	Adriatic
June 21	Celtic
June 27	Cedric
July 5	Baltic
July 11	Adriatic
July 18	Celtic
July 25	Cedric
Aug. 2	Baltic
Aug. 8	Adriatic
Aug. 16	Celtic
Aug. 22	Cedric
Aug. 30	Baltic
Sept. 5	Adriatic
Sept. 12	Celtic
Sept. 19	Cedric
Sept. 26	Baltic
Oct. 3	Adriatic
Oct. 11	Celtic
Oct. 17	Cedric
Oct. 25	Baltic
Nov. 2	Cymric
Nov. 8	Celtic
Nov. 14	Cedric
Nov. 22	Adriatic
Nov. 29	Baltic
Dec. 5	Celtic
Dec. 15	Cymric
Dec. 26	Cedric

WHITE STAR LINE
Southampton—New York

N.Y.

Arrival	Steamer
Jan. 3	Oceanic
Jan. 23	Majestic
Feb. 7	Oceanic
Feb. 20	Majestic
Mar. 5	Oceanic
Mar. 20	Majestic
Apr. 2	Oceanic
Apr. 9	Olympic
Apr. 17	Majestic
Apr. 23	Oceanic
Apr. 30	Olympic
May 8	Majestic
May 14	Oceanic
May 21	Olympic
May 29	Majestic
June 5	Oceanic
June 11	Olympic
June 19	Majestic
June 25	Oceanic
July 2	Olympic
July 10	Majestic
July 16	Oceanic
July 30	Olympic
Aug. 7	Majestic
Aug. 13	Oceanic
Aug. 20	Olympic
Aug. 28	Majestic
Sept. 3	Oceanic
Sept. 10	Olympic
Sept. 18	Majestic
Sept. 24	Oceanic
Dec. 1	Olympic
Dec. 9	Majestic
Dec. 10	Olympic
Dec. 15	Oceanic
Dec. 22	Olympic
Dec. 25	Majestic
Dec. 30	Majestic
Nov. 6	Oceanic
Nov. 12	Olympic
Nov. 21	Majestic
Nov. 27	Oceanic

WHITE STAR LINE
Mediterranean—New York

N.Y.

Arrival	Steamer
Jan. 1	Adriatic
Feb. 13	Adriatic
Feb. 27	Cedric
Mar. 26	Adriatic
Apr. 10	Cedric

WHITE STAR LINE
Mediterranean—Boston

Boston

Arrival	Steamer
Jan. 29	Canopic
Mar. 12	Canopic
Apr. 1	Cretic
Apr. 22	Canopic
May 12	Cretic

Year 1913

WHITE STAR LINE Mediterranean—Boston (Continued)		WHITE STAR LINE Liverpool—Boston		WHITE STAR LINE Liverpool—Boston (Continued)	
Boston Arrival	**Steamer**	**Boston Arrival**	**Steamer**	**Boston Arrival**	**Steamer**
June 5	Canopic	Jan. 11	Arabic	July 24	Arabic
June 24	Cretic	Feb. 8	Arabic	Aug. 7	Cymric
July 14	Canopic	Mar. 6	Arabic	Aug. 21	Arabic
Sept. 3	Cretic	Apr. 18	Cymric	Sept. 4	Cymric
Sept. 16	Canopic	May 5	Arabic	Sept. 17	Arabic
Oct. 20	Canopic	May 17	Cymric	Oct. 2	Cymric
Oct. 29	Cretic	May 30	Arabic	Oct. 16	Arabic
Nov. 24	Canopic	June 12	Cymric	Nov. 13	Arabic
Dec. 7	Cretic	June 26	Arabic	Dec. 12	Arabic
		July 10	Cymric		

Year 1914

ALLAN LINE
Glasgow
Glasgow—Halifax—Boston

Boston
Arrival	Steamer
Jan. 16	Numidian
Feb. 10	Sicilian
Mar. 7	Pretorian
Mar. 18	Ionian
Apr. 2	Grampian
Apr. 16	Hesperian
May 5	Numidian
May 28	Pretorian
June 8	Numidian
June 27	Pretorian
July 14	Numidian
July 28	Pretorian
Aug. 11	Numidian
Aug. 24	Pretorian
Sept. 8	Numidian
Sept. 21	Pretorian
Oct. 6	Sardinian
Oct. 22	Pomeranian
Nov. 12	Sardinian
Dec. 22	Sardinian

AMERICAN LINE
Southampton—New York

N. Y.
Arrival	Steamer
Jan. 1	New York
Jan. 8	St. Paul
Jan. 18	St. Louis
Feb. 1	Philadelphia
Feb. 6	St. Paul
Feb. 17	St. Louis
Feb. 20	New York
Mar. 3	Philadelphia
Mar. 5	St. Paul
Mar. 20	New York
Mar. 29	Philadelphia
Apr. 3	St. Louis
Apr. 12	St. Paul
Apr. 19	New York
Apr. 23	Philadelphia
May 2	St. Louis
May 10	St. Paul
May 14	New York
May 23	Philadelphia
May 30	St. Louis
June 4	St. Paul
June 14	New York
June 21	Philadelphia
June 25	St. Louis
July 5	St. Paul
July 12	New York
July 16	Philadelphia
July 23	St. Louis
Aug. 2	St. Paul
Aug. 9	New York

AMERICAN LINE
Liverpool—New York

N. Y.
Arrival	Steamer
Aug. 12	Philadelphia
Aug. 22	St. Louis

AMERICAN LINE
Liverpool—New York
(Continued)

N. Y.
Arrival	Steamer
Aug. 30	St. Paul
Sept. 3	New York
Sept. 5	Philadelphia
Sept. 12	St. Louis
Sept. 21	St. Paul
Sept. 24	New York
Sept. 27	Philadelphia
Oct. 3	St. Louis
Oct. 10	St. Paul
Oct. 18	New York
Oct. 25	Philadelphia
Nov. 2	St. Louis
Nov. 7	St. Paul
Nov. 15	New York
Nov. 22	Philadelphia
Dec. 6	St. Paul
Dec. 14	New York
Dec. 20	St. Louis

AMERICAN LINE
Liverpool—Philadelphia

Phila.
Arrival	Steamer
Jan. 13	Haverford
Jan. 29	Merion
Feb. 21	Haverford
Mar. 10	Merion
Mar. 27	Haverford
Apr. 15	Merion
Apr. 28	Haverford
May 18	Merion
June 1	Haverford
June 15	Dominion
June 22	Merion
July 7	Haverford
July 21	Dominion
July 28	Merion
Aug. 10	Haverford
Aug. 23	Dominion
Sept. 1	Merion
Sept. 14	Haverford
Sept. 28	Dominion
Oct. 5	Merion
Oct. 19	Haverford
Nov. 3	Dominion
Nov. 10	Merion
Nov. 25	Haverford
Dec. 16	Dominion
Dec. 30	Haverford

ANCHOR LINE
Mediterranean—New York

N. Y.
Arrival	Steamer
Jan. 22	Perugia
Feb. 7	Italia
Mar. 3	Calabria
Mar. 21	Perugia
Apr. 11	Italia
Apr. 26	Calabria
May 14	Perugia
May 29	Italia

ANCHOR LINE
Mediterranean—New York
(Continued)

N. Y.
Arrival	Steamer
June 22	Calabria
July 11	Perugia
July 30	Italia
Sept. 2	Calabria
Oct. 14	Italia
Oct. 29	Perugia
Dec. 20	Italia

ANCHOR LINE
Glasgow—New York

N. Y.
Arrival	Steamer
Jan. 8	Cameronia
Jan. 19	Columbia
Jan. 28	California
Feb. 2	Caledonia
Feb. 9	Cameronia
Feb. 18	Columbia
Feb. 25	California
Mar. 3	Caledonia
Mar. 9	Cameronia
Mar. 16	Columbia
Mar. 24	California
Mar. 31	Caledonia
Apr. 7	Cameronia
Apr. 14	Columbia
Apr. 21	California
Apr. 27	Caledonia
May 4	Cameronia
May 11	Columbia
May 18	California
May 25	Caledonia
June 1	Campania
June 8	Columbia
June 15	California
June 22	Caledonia
June 29	Campania
July 6	Columbia
July 20	Caledonia
Aug. 3	Columbia
Aug. 12	Ausonia
Aug. 23	Cameronia
Aug. 31	Columbia
Sept. 11	Ausonia
Sept. 21	Cameronia
Sept. 28	Columbia
Oct. 13	Pannonia
Oct. 19	Cameronia
Oct. 26	Columbia
Nov. 16	Pannonia
Nov. 21	Cameronia
Dec. 11	Ausonia
Dec. 29	Cameronia

ATLANTIC TRANSPORT LINE
London—New York

N. Y.
Arrival	Steamer
Jan. 2	Minneapolis
Jan. 18	Minnewaska
Jan. 27	Minnetonka

Year 1914

ATLANTIC TRANSPORT LINE
London—New York
(Continued)

N. Y.

Arrival	Steamer
Feb. 10	Minneapolis
Feb. 24	Minnewaska
Mar. 1	Minnetonka
Mar. 10	Mesaba
Mar. 16	Minneapolis
Mar. 31	Minnetonka
Apr. 7	Minnewaska
Apr. 27	Minneapolis
May 4	Minnewaska
May 12	Minnehaha
May 18	Minnetonka
May 25	Minneapolis
June 1	Minnewaska
June 8	Minnehaha
June 15	Minnetonka
June 23	Minneapolis
June 29	Minnewaska
July 6	Minnehaha
July 13	Minnetonka
July 20	Minneapolis
July 25	Minnewaska
Aug. 3	Minnehaha
Aug. 10	Minnetonka
Aug. 24	Minnewaska
Aug. 31	Minnehaha
Sept. 7	Minnetonka
Sept. 16	Menominee
Sept. 21	Minnewaska
Sept. 28	Minnehaha
Oct. 5	Minnetonka
Oct. 19	Minnewaska
Oct. 26	Minnehaha
Nov. 4	Minnetonka
Nov. 17	Minnewaska
Nov. 29	Minnehaha
Dec. 6	Minnetonka
Dec. 21	Minnewaska
Dec. 31	Minneapolis

AUSTRO-AMERICANA LINE
Greece, Italy—Azores—
New York

N. Y.

Arrival	Steamer
Jan. 17	Belvedere
Jan. 18	Kr. Fr. Jos. I
Feb. 2	Martha Washington
Feb. 16	Argentina
Mar. 2	K. Fr. Jos. I
Mar. 4	Oceania
Mar. 16	Martha Washington
Mar. 27	Belvedere
Apr. 11	Argentina
Apr. 12	K. Fr. Jos. I
Apr. 22	Oceania
Apr. 26	Martha Washington
May 14	Belvedere
May 16	K. Fr. Jos. I
May 25	Laura
May 27	Argentina
June 9	Martha Washington
June 18	Oceania
June 27	K. Fr. Jos. I

AUSTRO-AMERICANA LINE
Greece, Italy—Azores—
New York
(Continued)

N. Y.

Arrival	Steamer
July 9	Belvedere
July 16	Argentina
Aug. 3	Martha Washington

AUSTRO-AMERICANA LINE
Adriatic—New York

N. Y.

Arrival	Steamer
Jan. 17	Belvedere
Jan. 18	K. Fr. Jos. I
Feb. 2	Martha Washington
Feb. 16	Argentina
Mar. 2	K. Fr. Jos. I
Mar. 4	Oceania
Mar. 16	Martha Washington
Mar. 27	Belvedere
Apr. 11	Argentina
Apr. 12	Kr. Fr. Jos. I
Apr. 22	Oceania
Apr. 26	Martha Washington
May 14	Belvedere
May 16	K. Fr. Jos. I
May 25	Laura
May 27	Argentina
June 9	Martha Washington
June 18	Oceania
June 27	K. Fr. Jos. I
July 9	Belvedere
July 16	Argentina
Aug. 3	Martha Washington

COMPANIA TRANSATLANTICA LINE
(Spanish Line)
Spain—New York

N. Y.

Arrival	Steamer
Jan. 15	Antonio Lopez
Feb. 15	Buenos Aires
Mar. 13	Montserrat
Apr. 12	Montevideo
May 12	Manuel Calvo
June 12	Antonio Lopez
July 12	Buenos Aires
Aug. 11	Montserrat
Sept. 10	Montevideo
Oct. 12	Buenos Aires
Nov. 12	Antonio Lopez
Dec. 12	Manuel Calvo

CUNARD LINE
Liverpool—New York

N. Y.

Arrival	Steamer
Jan. 4	Carmania
Jan. 9	Lusitania
Jan. 18	Caronia
Jan. 25	Campania
Feb. 1	Carmania
Feb. 6	Lusitania
Feb. 17	Campania
Feb. 23	Carmania
Mar. 6	Lusitania

CUNARD LINE
Liverpool—New York
(Continued)

N. Y.

Arrival	Steamer
Mar. 13	Mauretania
Mar. 22	Carmania
Mar. 27	Lusitania
Apr. 3	Mauretania
Apr. 12	Campania
Apr. 17	Lusitania
Apr. 23	Mauretania
May 2	Campania
May 10	Caronia
May 15	Lusitania
May 21	Mauretania
May 31	Carmania
June 5	Aquitania
June 12	Mauretania
June 19	Lusitania
June 26	Aquitania
July 2	Mauretania
July 10	Lusitania
July 17	Aquitania
July 26	Carmania
July 30	Lusitania
Aug. 6	Mauretania
Aug. 17	Laconia
Aug. 22	Campania
Sept. 3	Mauretania
Sept. 8	Saxonia
Sept. 12	Campania
Sept. 17	Lusitania
Sept. 24	Mauretania
Oct. 3	Campania
Oct. 8	Lusitania
Oct. 15	Mauretania
Oct. 30	Franconia
Oct. 31	Lusitania
Nov. 10	Orduna
Nov. 16	Transylvania
Nov. 24	Franconia
Nov. 27	Lusitania
Dec. 9	Orduna
Dec. 15	Transylvania
Dec. 22	Lusitania

CUNARD LINE
Italian, Greek Ports—New York

N. Y.

Arrival	Steamer
Jan. 9	Pannonia
Jan. 10	Laconia
Jan. 22	Carpathia
Feb. 1	Saxonia
Feb. 19	Franconia
Feb. 24	Ultonia
Mar. 4	Pannonia
Mar. 10	Caronia
Mar. 22	Carpathia
Apr. 1	Laconia
Apr. 5	Franconia
Apr. 13	Saxonia
Apr. 24	Pannonia
Apr. 25	Ivernia
May 11	Carpathia
May 17	Laconia
May 25	Ultonia
June 3	Saxonia

Year 1914

CUNARD LINE
Italian, Greek Ports—New York
(Continued)

N.Y.

Arrival	Steamer
June 15	Pannonia
June 22	Ivernia
July 3	Carpathia
July 20	Ultonia
July 27	Saxonia
Aug. 5	Pannonia
Aug. 21	Ivernia
Sept. 2	Carpathia
Oct. 27	Carpathia
Dec. 30	Carpathia

CUNARD LINE
Adriatic Ports—New York

N.Y.

Arrival	Steamer
Jan. 9	Pannonia
Jan. 10	Laconia
Jan. 22	Carpathia
Feb. 1	Saxonia
Feb. 19	Franconia
Feb. 24	Ultonia
Mar. 4	Pannonia
Mar. 10	Caronia
Mar. 22	Carpathia
Apr. 1	Laconia
Apr. 5	Franconia
Apr. 11	Saxonia
Apr. 24	Pannonia
Apr. 25	Ivernia
May 11	Carpathia
May 17	Laconia
May 25	Ultonia
June 3	Saxonia
June 15	Pannonia
June 22	Ivernia
July 3	Carpathia
July 20	Ultonia
July 27	Saxonia
Aug. 5	Pannonia
Aug. 21	Ivernia
Sept. 2	Carpathia
Oct. 27	Carpathia
Dec. 30	Carpathia

CUNARD LINE
Liverpool—Boston

Boston

Arrival	Steamer
Jan. 10	Alaunia
Jan. 23	Andania
Feb. 14	Alaunia
Feb. 27	Andania
Mar. 15	Alaunia
Apr. 6	Andania
Apr. 23	Carmania
May 7	Franconia
June 4	Franconia
June 9	Caronia
June 17	Laconia
June 24	Carmania
July 1	Franconia
July 8	Caronia
July 15	Laconia
July 28	Franconia
Aug. 30	Franconia

CUNARD LINE
Liverpool—Boston
(Continued)

Boston

Arrival	Steamer
Sept. 9	Laconia
Sept. 23	Franconia
Oct. 6	Laconia

FABRE LINE
Mediterranean—New York

N.Y.

Arrival	Steamer
Jan. 8	Roma
Jan. 16	Germania
Jan. 20	Madonna
Jan. 26	Sant Anna
Feb. 15	Venezia
Feb. 21	Canada
Mar. 3	Roma
Mar. 6	Madonna
Mar. 7	Germania
Mar. 14	Sant Anna
Mar. 26	Venezia
Apr. 8	Canada
Apr. 9	Germania
Apr. 18	Madonna
Apr. 25	Roma
Apr. 29	Sant Anna
May 6	Venezia
May 8	Patria
May 18	Germania
May 25	Canada
May 31	Madonna
June 4	Roma
June 12	Sant Anna
June 21	Venezia
June 26	Patria
June 29	Germania
July 6	Canada
July 15	Madonna
July 21	Roma
July 28	Sant Anna
Aug. 5	Venezia
Aug. 11	Patria
Aug. 16	Germania
Sept. 17	Patria
Sept. 29	Sant Anna
Oct. 6	Roma
Oct. 14	Madonna
Oct. 23	Britannia
Oct. 31	Patria
Nov. 6	Venezia
Nov. 16	Sant Anna
Nov. 20	Roma
Dec. 2	Madonna
Dec. 6	Britannia
Dec. 14	Patria

FRENCH LINE
(Compagnie Generale Transatlantique)
Havre, Bordeaux, Vigo—New York

N.Y.

Arrival	Steamer
Jan. 3	France
Jan. 7	Caroline
Jan. 10	La Lorraine
Jan. 18	La Provence
Jan. 21	Niagara
Jan. 21	St. Laurent

FRENCH LINE
(Compagnie Generale Transatlantique)
Havre, Bordeaux, Vigo—New York
(Continued)

N.Y.

Arrival	Steamer
Jan. 25	La Savoie
Jan. 27	Rochambeau
Jan. 31	France
Feb. 1	Hudson
Feb. 8	La Provence
Feb. 14	Chicago
Feb. 16	La Savoie
Feb. 17	Louisiane
Feb. 23	La Lorraine
Feb. 25	Rochambeau
Mar. 1	La Provence
Mar. 5	Floride
Mar. 8	La Savoie
Mar. 11	Caroline
Mar. 13	Chicago
Mar. 15	La Lorraine
Mar. 24	Rochambeau
Mar. 25	Hudson
Mar. 28	La Touraine
Mar. 29	La Provence
Apr. 4	France
Apr. 10	Chicago
Apr. 12	La Lorraine
Apr. 14	Louisiane
Apr. 16	Niagara
Apr. 17	Rochambeau
Apr. 19	La Savoie
Apr. 25	La Provence
May 1	France
May 2	Floride
May 9	Chicago
May 10	La Touraine
May 16	La Provence
May 18	Rochambeau
May 22	France
May 31	La Lorraine
June 1	Louisiane
June 1	Caroline
June 4	Chicago
June 6	La Savoie
June 9	Niagara
June 13	La Provence
June 15	Rochambeau
June 19	France
June 25	Virginie
June 27	La Savoie
June 27	Floride
July 4	La Lorraine
July 6	Mexico
July 6	Niagara
July 10	France
July 20	La Touraine
July 22	Louisiane
July 25	La Savoie
Aug. 1	La Lorraine
Aug. 3	Rochambeau
Aug. 20	France
Aug. 23	Chicago
Aug. 30	Espagne
Sept. 7	Rochambeau
Sept. 11	Flandre
Sept. 12	France
Sept. 13	La Touraine

Year 1914

FRENCH LINE
(Compagnie Generale Transatlantique)
Havre, Bordeaux, Vigo—
New York
(Continued)

N. Y.

Arrival	Steamer
Sept. 24	Virginie
Sept. 28	Chicago
Sept. 28	Espagne
Oct. 3	France
Oct. 12	Rochambeau
Oct. 15	Californie
Oct. 19	La Touraine
Oct. 27	Chicago
Nov. 9	Rochambeau
Nov. 11	La Touraine
Nov. 17	Hudson
Nov. 26	Chicago
Dec. 9	Rochambeau
Dec. 18	La Touraine
Dec. 18	Floride
Dec. 21	Californie
Dec. 27	Chicago

GREEK LINE
Greece—New York

N. Y.

Arrival	Steamer
Jan. 9	Themistocles
Feb. 28	Athinai
Mar. 28	Themistocles
Apr. 18	Athinai
May 20	Themistocles
June 9	Athinai
July 9	Themistocles
July 29	Athinai
Aug. 23	Themistocles
Sept. 17	Athinai
Oct. 17	Themistocles

HAMBURG-AMERICAN LINE
Mediterranean—New York

N. Y.

Arrival	Steamer
Jan. 22	Cincinnati
Mar. 2	Cincinnati
Mar. 25	Hamburg
Apr. 19	Cincinnati
Apr. 19	Cleveland
May 12	Hamburg
May 25	Moltke
June 24	Hamburg
July 6	Moltke
July 31	Hamburg

HAMBURG-AMERICAN LINE
Spain—Levant—New York

N. Y.

Arrival	Steamer
June 19	Corcovado
July 23	Pisa

HAMBURG-AMERICAN LINE
Hamburg—New York

N. Y.

Arrival	Steamer
Jan. 1	Pennsylvania

HAMBURG-AMERICAN LINE
Hamburg—New York
(Continued)

N. Y.

Arrival	Steamer
Jan. 10	President Lincoln
Jan. 23	Graf Waldersee
Feb. 1	Pretoria
Feb. 3	President Grant
Feb. 5	Hamburg
Feb. 7	K. Auguste Victoria
Feb. 16	Amerika
Feb. 16	Pennsylvania
Feb. 24	President Lincoln
Mar. 6	Graf Waldersee
Mar. 7	K. Auguste Victoria
Mar. 14	Amerika
Mar. 15	Pretoria
Mar. 19	Imperator
Mar. 20	President Grant
Mar. 28	Pennsylvania
Apr. 3	President Lincoln
Apr. 5	K. Auguste Victoria
Apr. 5	Moltke
Apr. 9	Imperator
Apr. 18	Amerika
Apr. 18	Graf Waldersee
Apr. 26	Pretoria
Apr. 29	President Grant
May 2	K. Auguste Victoria
May 7	Pennsylvania
May 9	Imperator
May 12	President Lincoln
May 18	Amerika
May 20	Batavia
May 21	Vaterland
May 28	Graf Waldersee
May 30	K. Auguste Victoria
June 3	Imperator
June 5	Pretoria
June 10	President Grant
June 13	Vaterland
June 18	Pennsylvania
June 24	Imperator
June 24	President Lincoln
July 2	K. Auguste Victoria
July 4	Vaterland
July 5	Batavia
July 10	Graf Waldersee
July 15	Imperator
July 15	Kronprinz's Cecilie
July 23	President Grant
July 30	Pennsylvania
July 30	Vaterland
Aug. 4	President Lincoln

HAMBURG-AMERICAN LINE
Hamburg—Boston

Boston

Arrival	Steamer
Jan. 17	Furst Bismarck
Feb. 1	Rhaetia
Feb. 23	Furst Bismarck
Mar. 12	Rhaetia
Apr. 11	Arcadia
Apr. 23	Rhaetia
May 24	Cincinnati
June 7	Cleveland

HAMBURG-AMERICAN LINE
Hamburg—Boston
(Continued)

Boston

Arrival	Steamer
June 19	Amerika
June 29	Cincinnati
July 13	Cleveland
July 24	Amerika
Aug. 10	Cincinnati

HAMBURG-AMERICAN LINE
Hamburg—Philadelphia

Phila.

Arrival	Steamer
Jan. 7	Prinz Adalbert
Jan. 28	Prinz Oskar
Feb. 23	Prinz Adalbert
Feb. 24	Barcelona
Mar. 16	Prinz Adalbert
Mar. 27	Corcovado
Apr. 14	Prinz Adalbert
Apr. 29	Prinz Oskar
May 15	Rugia
May 28	Prinz Adalbert
June 18	Prinz Oskar
June 28	Rugia
July 16	Prinz Adalbert
July 22	Rhaetia
Aug. 5	Prinz Oskar

HAMBURG-AMERICAN LINE
Hamburg—Baltimore

Baltimore

Arrival	Steamer
Jan. 7	Bosnia
Jan. 31	Arcadia
Feb. 26	Barcelona
Feb. 28	Bulgaria
Mar. 7	Bosnia
Apr. 2	Batavia
Apr. 29	Bulgaria
May 6	Bosnia
May 19	Armenia
June 2	Barcelona
June 29	Bosnia
July 14	Armenia
July 27	Bulgaria

HOLLAND-AMERICA LINE
Rotterdam—New York

N. Y.

Arrival	Steamer
Jan. 12	New Amsterdam
Jan. 21	Noordam
Jan. 27	Rotterdam
Feb. 5	Potsdam
Feb. 19	New Amsterdam
Feb. 26	Noordam
Mar. 4	Ryndam
Mar. 18	Potsdam
Mar. 24	New Amsterdam
Apr. 1	Noordam
Apr. 9	Ryndam
Apr. 14	Rotterdam
Apr. 23	Potsdam
Apr. 27	New Amsterdam

Year 1914

HOLLAND-AMERICA LINE
Rotterdam—New York
(Continued)

N. Y.

Arrival	Steamer
May 4	Noordam
May 12	Ryndam
May 18	Rotterdam
May 27	Potsdam
June 2	New Amsterdam
June 9	Noordam
June 16	Ryndam
June 22	Rotterdam
July 1	Potsdam
July 6	New Amsterdam
July 14	Noordam
July 21	Ryndam
Aug. 3	Rotterdam
Aug. 12	Potsdam
Aug. 17	New Amsterdam
Aug. 24	Noordam
Aug. 27	Noorderdijk
Sept. 1	Ryndam
Sept 6	Westerdijk
Sept. 7	Rotterdam
Sept. 15	Potsdam
Sept. 21	New Amsterdam
Sept. 21	Andijk
Oct. 2	Noordam
Oct. 3	Palembang
Oct. 7	Ryndam
Oct. 24	Rotterdam
Oct. 30	New Amsterdam
Nov. 3	Potsdam
Nov. 11	Ryndam
Nov. 24	Rotterdam
Dec. 5	New Amsterdam
Dec. 15	Potsdam
Dec. 24	Ryndam

HOLLAND-AMERICA LINE
Rotterdam—Boston

Boston

Arrival	Steamer
Sept. 3	Soestdijk

ITALIA LINE
Mediterranean—New York

N. Y.

Arrival	Steamer
Jan. 12	Ancona
Jan. 23	Ancona
Apr. 6	Ancona
May 15	Ancona
May 31	Napoli
June 25	Ancona
July 26	Napoli
Aug. 5	Ancona
Sept. 12	Ancona
Oct. 3	Napoli
Oct. 28	Ancona
Nov. 23	Napoli
Dec. 3	Ancona

ITALIA LINE
Mediterranean—Philadelphia

Phila.

Arrival	Steamer
Jan. 14	Ancona

ITALIA LINE
Mediterranean—Philadelphia
(Continued)

Phila.

Arrival	Steamer
Feb. 25	Ancona
Apr. 8	Ancona
May 16	Ancona
June 27	Ancona
Aug. 6	Ancona
Sept. 14	Ancona
Oct. 30	Ancona
Dec. 5	Ancona

LA VELOCE LINE
Mediterranean—New York

N. Y.

Arrival	Steamer
Jan. 24	Stampalia
Feb. 13	*Europa
Mar. 6	Stampalia
Mar. 26	Europa
Apr. 15	Stampalia
May 11	Europa
May 25	Stampalia
July 9	Stampalia
Aug. 3	Europa
Aug. 20	Stampalia
Sept. 11	Europa
Oct. 1	Stampalia
Oct. 11	Duca di Genova
Oct. 22	Europa
Nov. 9	Stampalia
Dec. 4	Europa
Dec. 20	Stampalia

LA VELOCE LINE
Mediterranean—Philadelphia

Phila.

Arrival	Steamer
Mar. 8	Stampalia
Apr. 16	Stampalia
May 26	Stampalia
July 11	Stampalia
Aug. 21	Stampalia
Oct. 2	Stampalia

LEYLAND LINE
Liverpool—Boston

Boston

Arrival	Steamer
Jan. 5	Winifredian
Jan. 21	Victorian
Jan. 28	Canadian
Feb. 2	Devonian
Feb. 11	Bohemian
Feb. 25	Winifredian
Mar. 4	Canadian
Mar. 9	Devonian
Mar. 18	Bohemian
Mar. 29	Caledonian
Mar. 31	Winifredian
Apr. 14	Devonian
Apr. 17	Canadian
Apr. 28	Armenian
May 5	Winifredian
May 17	Devonian
May 28	Caledonian
June 2	Bohemian

LEYLAND LINE
Liverpool—Boston
(Continued)

Boston

Arrival	Steamer
June 15	Winifredian
June 22	Devonian
June 30	Canadian
July 6	Bohemian
July 20	Winifredian
July 27	Devonian
Aug. 3	Canadian
Aug. 10	Bohemian
Sept. 1	Devonian
Sept. 21	Bohemian
Oct. 1	Iberian
Oct. 10	Devonian
Oct. 26	Canadian
Nov. 3	Bohemian
Nov. 24	Devonian
Dec. 8	Bohemian
Dec. 30	Devonian

LLOYD ITALIANO
Mediterranean—New York

N. Y.

Arrival	Steamer
Jan. 28	Taormina
Feb. 21	Caserta
Mar. 16	Taormina
Apr. 5	Caserta
Apr. 22	Taormina
May 15	Caserta
June 2	Taormina
June 24	Caserta
July 14	Taormina
Aug. 9	Caserta
Aug. 26	Taormina
Sept. 1	P. Mafalda
Sept. 18	Caserta
Oct. 4	Taormina
Oct. 27	Caserta
Nov. 19	Taormina
Dec. 5	Caserta

LLOYD ITALIANO
Mediterranean—Philadelphia

Phila.

Arrival	Steamer
Jan. 30	Taormina
June 4	Taormina
July 16	Taormina

LLOYD SABAUDO
Mediterranean—New York

N. Y.

Arrival	Steamer
Feb. 17	Regina d'Italia
Apr. 4	Regina d'Italia
May 16	Regina d'Italia
June 29	Re d'Italia
July 15	Regina d'Italia
Aug. 24	Principe di'Udine
Sept. 15	Re d'Italia
Oct. 1	Tomaso di Savoia
Oct. 7	Regina d'Italia
Oct. 30	Re d'Italia
Dec. 3	Regina d'Italia
Dec. 15	Re d'Italia

Year 1914

NATIONAL GREEK LINE
Italy—Greece—New York
N. Y.

Arrival	Steamer
Feb. 14	Patris
Mar. 13	Thessaloniki
Mar. 19	Ioannina
Apr. 5	Patris
May 1	Ioannina
May 16	Thessaloniki
May 28	Patris
June 25	Ioannina
July 15	Patris
Sept. 3	Ioannina
Sept. 17	Thessaloniki
Oct. 3	Patris
Nov. 6	Ioannina
Nov. 13	Athinai
Nov. 23	Thessaloniki
Nov. 26	Patris
Dec. 19	Themistocles

NAVIGAZIONE GENERALE ITALIANA LINE
Mediterranean—New York
N. Y.

Arrival	Steamer
Jan. 16	Verona
Feb. 4	America
Feb. 26	Verona
Mar. 19	America
Apr. 8	Verona
Apr. 28	America
May 11	Palermo
May 21	Verona
June 9	America
July 2	Verona
July 20	Duca d'Aosta
Aug. 11	America
Sept. 2	Verona
Sept. 22	America
Sept. 26	Duca d'Aosta
Oct. 14	Verona
Oct. 25	D. degli Abruzzi
Nov. 1	America
Nov. 10	Duca d'Aosta
Dec. 1	Verona
Dec. 2	D. degli Abruzzi
Dec. 8	America
Dec. 28	Duca d'Aosta

NAVIGAZIONE GENERALE ITALIANA LINE
Mediterranean—Philadelphia
Phila.

Arrival	Steamer
Mar. 21	America
Apr. 29	America
Sept. 4	Verona

NAVIGAZIONE GENERALE ITALIANA LINE
Mediterranean—Boston
Boston

Arrival	Steamer
Mar. 25	Palermo
May 4	Indiana
July 20	Palermo
Oct. 11	Palermo

NORTH GERMAN LLOYD
Express Service
Bremen—New York
N. Y.

Arrival	Steamer
Jan. 15	Kronprinzes. Cecilie
Feb. 19	Kronprinzes. Cecilie
Mar. 4	Kaiser Wilhelm II
Mar. 18	Kronprinzes. Cecilie
Mar. 26	K. Wm. der Grosse
Apr. 1	Kaiser Wilhelm II
Apr. 8	Kronprinz Wilhelm
Aug. 15	Kronprinzes. Cecilie
Apr. 23	K. Wm. der Grosse
Apr. 29	Kaiser Wilhelm II
May 6	Kronprinz Wilhelm
May 13	Kronprinzes. Cecilie
May 21	K. Wm. der Grosse
May 27	Kaiser Wilhelm II
June 3	Kronprinz Wilhelm
June 10	Kronprinzes. Cecilie
June 18	K. Wm. der Grosse
July 1	Kronprinz Wilhelm
July 2	Kronprinzes. Cecilie
July 16	K. Wm. der Grosse
July 22	Kronprinzes. Cecilie
July 29	Kronprinz Wilhelm
Aug. 5	Kaiser Wilhelm II

NORTH GERMAN LLOYD
Mediterranean—New York
N. Y.

Arrival	Steamer
Jan. 22	Berlin
Feb. 13	Prinzess Irene
Mar. 4	Berlin
Mar. 20	Prinzess Irene
Apr. 3	Koenig Albert
Apr. 16	Berlin
Apr. 30	Prinzess Irene
May 14	Koenig Albert
June 11	Prinzess Irene
June 26	Koenig Albert
July 24	Prinzess Irene

NORTH GERMAN LLOYD
Bremen—New York
N. Y.

Arrival	Steamer
Jan. 2	Barbarossa
Jan. 7	Grosser Kurfuerst
Jan. 17	Hannover
Jan. 17	Scharnhorst
Jan. 23	Neckar
Jan. 28	George Washington
Feb. 5	Grosser Kurfuerst
Feb. 11	Prz. Fred. Wilhelm
Feb. 21	Barbarossa
Feb. 26	Koenig Albert
Mar. 6	Scharnhorst
Mar. 12	Bremen
Mar. 17	Prz. Fred. Wilhelm
Mar. 28	Barbarossa
Apr. 4	Seydlitz
Apr. 7	George Washington
Apr. 12	Koeln
Apr. 17	Bremen
Apr. 21	Prz. Fred. Wilhelm
Apr. 22	Rhein
Apr. 29	Koenigin Luise

NORTH GERMAN LLOYD
Bremen—New York
(Continued)
N. Y.

Arrival	Steamer
Apr. 30	Brandenburg
May 6	Neckar
May 7	Seydlitz
May 12	George Washington
May 20	Bremen
May 25	Prz. Fred. Wilhelm
May 27	Cassel
June 3	Grosser Kurfuerst
June 8	George Washington
June 18	Barbarossa
June 23	Prz. Fred. Wilhelm
June 26	Chemnitz
July 2	Bremen
July 6	George Washington
July 14	Berlin
July 22	Grosser Kurfuerst
July 24	Breslau
July 29	Barbarossa
Aug. 4	George Washington

NORTH GERMAN LLOYD
Bremen—Baltimore
Baltimore

Arrival	Steamer
Jan. 4	Rhein
Jan. 18	Breslau
Jan. 26	Neckar
Feb. 19	Chemnitz
Feb. 25	Main
Feb. 28	Cassel
Mar. 13	Rhein
Mar. 21	Neckar
Mar. 29	Breslau
Apr. 6	Main
Apr. 10	Cassel
Apr. 23	Rhein
May 3	Koenigin Luise
May 8	Neckar
May 15	Barbarossa
May 20	Main
June 2	Koenigin Luise
June 13	Rhein
June 15	Fried. der Grosse
July 1	Main
July 8	Koenigin Luise
July 14	Neckar
July 22	Fried. der Grosse
July 29	Rhein

NORTH GERMAN LLOYD
Bremen—Philadelphia
Phila.

Arrival	Steamer
Jan. 15	Breslau
Jan. 28	Wittekind
Feb. 6	Koeln
Feb. 22	Main
Mar. 6	Brandenburg
Mar. 18	Neckar
Apr. 3	Main
Apr. 20	Wittekind
May 1	Koenigin Luise
May 12	Barbarossa
May 29	Cassel
June 10	Rhein

Year 1914

NORTH GERMAN LLOYD
Bremen—Philadelphia
(Continued)

Phila.

Arrival	Steamer
June 28	Chemnitz
July 6	Koenigin Luise
July 20	Fried. der Grosse
Aug. 5	Brandenburg

NORTH GERMAN LLOYD
Bremen—Boston

Boston

Arrival	Steamer
Jan. 14	Hannover
Feb. 4	Koeln
Mar. 1	Frankfurt
Mar. 17	Hannover
Apr. 9	Koeln
Apr. 28	Brandenburg
May 18	Breslau
June 9	Koeln
June 30	Frankfurt
July 21	Breslau
Aug. 11	Koeln

NORWAY-MEXICO GULF LINE, LTD.
Christiania—Boston

Boston

Arrival	Steamer
Feb. 12	Noreuga
Apr. 15	Noreuga

NORWAY-MEXICO GULF LINE, LTD.
Christiania—Philadelphia

Phila.

Arrival	Steamer
June 3	Mexicano

NORWEGIAN AMERICA LINE
Bergen, Kristiania via Halifax
New York

N. Y.

Arrival	Steamer
Feb. 7	Kristianiafjord
Feb. 27	Bergensfjord
Mar. 17	Kristianiafjord
Apr. 8	Bergensfjord
Apr. 28	Kristianiafjord
May 18	Bergensfjord
June 1	Kristianiafjord
June 22	Bergensfjord
July 20	Kristianiafjord
Aug. 3	Bergensfjord
Aug. 24	Kristianiafjord
Sept. 5	Bergensfjord
Sept. 28	Kristianiafjord
Oct. 12	Bergensfjord
Nov. 3	Kristianiafjord
Nov. 19	Bergensfjord
Dec. 7	Kristianiafjord
Dec. 24	Bergensfjord

RED STAR LINE
Antwerp—Liverpool—
New York

N. Y.

Arrival	Steamer
Jan. 9	Samland
Jan. 13	Lapland
Jan. 21	Vaderland
Jan. 28	Kroonland
Feb. 4	Finland
Feb. 15	Samland
Feb. 18	Lapland
Mar. 3	Gothland
Mar. 4	Kroonland
Mar. 12	Finland
Mar. 17	Zeeland
Mar. 24	Lapland
Apr. 1	Vaderland
Apr. 8	Kroonland
Apr. 15	Finland
Apr. 20	Lapland
Apr. 28	Vaderland
May 5	Kroonland
May 12	Finland
May 17	Lapland
May 26	Vaderland
June 2	Kroonland
June 9	Finland
June 15	Lapland
June 24	Zeeland
June 30	Kroonland
July 7	Vaderland
July 13	Lapland
July 21	Finland
July 27	Zeeland
Aug. 4	Vaderland
Aug. 11	Kroonland
Aug. 19	Finland

RED STAR LINE
Liverpool—New York

N. Y.

Arrival	Steamer
Sept. 6	Kroonland
Sept. 9	Lapland
Sept. 13	Finland
Sept. 22	Zeeland
Oct. 2	Vaderland
Oct. 8	Kroonland
Oct. 14	Finland

RED STAR LINE
Antwerp—Philadelphia—
Boston

Boston

Arrival	Steamer
Jan. 6	Marquette
Jan. 21	Menominee
Feb. 4	Manitou
Feb. 20	Marquette
Mar. 5	Menominee
Mar. 19	Manitou
Apr. 2	Marquette
Apr. 17	Menominee
Apr. 28	Manitou
May 11	Marquette
May 25	Mesaba
June 9	Menominee
June 24	Manitou

RED STAR LINE
Antwerp—Philadelphia—
Boston
(Continued)

Boston

Arrival	Steamer
July 6	Marquette
July 21	Menominee
Aug. 3	Manitou
Aug. 17	Marquette

RED STAR LINE
Mediterranean—New York

N. Y.

Arrival	Steamer
Dec. 6	Kroonland
Dec. 28	Finland

RUSSIAN-AMERICAN LINE
Libau via Halifax—Rotter-
dam—Libau, Archangel—
New York

N. Y.

Arrival	Steamer
Jan. 4	Kursk
Jan. 20	Russia
Feb. 7	Czar
Feb. 21	Birma
Feb. 25	Dwinsk
Mar. 8	Russia
Mar. 16	Kursk
Mar. 27	Czar
Apr. 4	Dwinsk
Apr. 19	Russia
Apr. 27	Kursk
May 7	Czar
May 20	Dwinsk
May 29	Russia
June 8	Kursk
June 17	Czar
June 30	Dwinsk
July 9	Russia
July 20	Kursk
July 29	Czar
Aug. 4	Dwinsk
Dec. 8	Dwinsk

SCANDINAVIAN-AMER-ICAN LINE
Scandinavian Ports—New
York

N. Y.

Arrival	Steamer
Jan. 23	Oscar II
Mar. 1	Frederik VIII
Mar. 4	Hellig Olav
Mar. 27	Oscar II
Apr. 8	Frederik VIII
Apr. 23	Hellig Olav
May 9	Oscar II
May 16	Frederik VIII
May 26	United States
June 2	Hellig Olav
June 16	Oscar II
June 22	Frederik VIII
July 7	United States
July 21	Hellig Olav
Aug. 3	Frederik VIII

Year 1914

SCANDINAVIAN-AMER-ICAN LINE
Scandinavian Ports—New York
(Continued)

N.Y.

Arrival	Steamer
Aug. 18	United States
Aug. 26	Oscar II
Sept. 2	Hellig Olav
Sept. 15	Frederik VIII
Sept. 30	United States
Oct. 7	Oscar II
Oct. 13	Hellig Olav
Oct. 25	Frederik VIII
Nov. 10	United States
Nov. 21	Oscar II
Nov. 24	Hellig Olav
Dec. 2	Frederik VIII
Dec. 26	United States

SICULA AMERICANA LINE
Mediterranean—New York

N.Y.

Arrival	Steamer
Jan. 25	San Guglielmo
Mar. 18	San Guglielmo
Apr. 6	San Giovanni
Apr. 29	San Giovanni
May 14	San Giovanni
May 28	San Giorgio
June 8	San Guglielmo
July 11	San Giorgio
July 29	San Guglielmo
Aug. 31	San Giovanni
Sept. 3	San Guglielmo
Sept. 11	San Giorgio
Oct. 8	San Giovanni
Oct. 15	San Giovanni
Oct. 28	San Giorgio
Nov. 27	San Guglielmo

URANIUM STEAMSHIP COMPANY
Rotterdam via Halifax—New York

N.Y.

Arrival	Steamer
Jan. 25	Campanello
Feb. 13	Uranium
Mar. 8	Principello
Mar. 11	Campanello
Mar. 30	Uranium
Apr. 22	Principello
Apr. 30	Campanello
May 13	Uranium
May 31	Principello
June 12	Campanello
June 24	Uranium
July 10	Principello
July 23	Campanello
Aug. 5	Uranium
Sept. 22	Principello

WARREN LINE
Liverpool—Boston

Boston

Arrival	Steamer
Jan. 15	Sagamore

WARREN LINE
Liverpool—Boston
(Continued)

Boston

Arrival	Steamer
Feb. 27	Sagamore
Apr. 3	Sagamore
Apr. 19	Michigan
May 14	Sagamore
May 28	Michigan
June 10	Sachem
June 24	Sagamore
July 9	Michigan
July 29	Sagamore
Aug. 13	Michigan
Sept. 10	Sachem
Sept. 15	Sagamore
Sept. 30	Michigan
Oct. 19	Sachem
Oct. 28	Sagamore
Nov. 27	Sachem
Dec. 13	Sagamore
Dec. 20	Michigan

WHITE STAR LINE
Liverpool—New York

N.Y.

Arrival	Steamer
Jan. 10	Baltic
Jan. 17	Celtic
Jan. 25	Cedric
Jan. 27	Laurentic
Feb. 2	Cymric
Feb. 8	Megantic
Feb. 22	Cedric
Mar. 7	Baltic
Mar. 22	Cedric
Apr. 5	Baltic
Apr. 18	Cedric
May 2	Baltic
May 8	Adriatic
May 15	Cedric
May 30	Baltic
June 5	Adriatic
June 12	Cedric
June 20	Celtic
June 27	Baltic
July 3	Adriatic
July 11	Cedric
July 18	Celtic
July 25	Baltic
July 31	Adriatic
Aug. 11	Cedric
Aug. 15	Celtic
Aug. 22	Baltic
Aug. 29	Olympic
Aug. 29	Adriatic
Sept. 4	Cedric
Sept. 11	Celtic
Sept. 18	Baltic
Sept. 18	Cretic
Sept. 23	Olympic
Sept. 25	Adriatic
Oct. 2	Cedric
Oct. 8	Celtic
Oct. 16	Baltic
Oct. 22	Adriatic
Oct. 30	Cedric
Nov. 7	Lapland

WHITE STAR LINE
Liverpool—New York
(Continued)

N.Y.

Arrival	Steamer
Nov. 13	Baltic
Nov. 20	Adriatic
Dec. 10	Megantic
Dec. 12	Lapland
Dec. 19	Baltic
Dec. 20	Adriatic

WHITE STAR LINE
Southampton—New York

N.Y.

Arrival	Steamer
June 10	Oceanic
June 17	Olympic
July 2	Oceanic
July 8	Olympic
July 29	Oceanic
Aug. 5	Olympic

WHITE STAR LINE
Glasgow—New York

N.Y.

Arrival	Steamer
Oct. 17	Olympic

WHITE STAR LINE
Mediterranean—New York

N.Y.

Arrival	Steamer
Jan. 3	Adriatic
Feb. 16	Adriatic
Mar. 2	Celtic
Mar. 29	Adriatic
Apr. 13	Celtic
May 23	Celtic

WHITE STAR LINE
Mediterranean—Boston

Boston

Arrival	Steamer
Jan. 27	Canopic
Mar. 9	Canopic
Mar. 26	Cretic
Apr. 20	Canopic
May 11	Cretic
June 1	Canopic
June 22	Cretic
July 7	Canopic
Aug. 16	Canopic

WHITE STAR LINE
Southampton—New York

N.Y.

Arrival	Steamer
Jan. 14	Oceanic
Jan. 23	Majestic
Jan. 28	Olympic
Feb. 14	Oceanic
Feb. 25	Olympic
Mar. 12	Oceanic
Mar. 25	Olympic
Apr. 9	Oceanic
Apr. 15	Olympic

Year 1914

WHITE STAR LINE	
Southampton—New York	
(Continued)	
N. Y.	
Arrival	**Steamer**
Apr. 29	Oceanic
May 6	Olympic
May 20	Oceanic
May 27	Olympic
Sept. 24	Canopic
Nov. 2	Canopic
Nov. 16	Cretic
Dec. 11	Canopic

WHITE STAR LINE	
Liverpool—Boston	
Boston	
Arrival	**Steamer**
Jan. 7	Arabic
Feb. 25	Arabic
Mar. 7	Cymric
Apr. 5	Cymric
Apr. 17	Arabic
May 1	Cymric
May 14	Arabic
May 29	Cymric
June 11	Arabic

WHITE STAR LINE	
Liverpool—Boston	
(Continued)	
Boston	
Arrival	**Steamer**
June 25	Cymric
July 9	Arabic
Aug. 6	Arabic
Sept. 3	Arabic
Sept. 30	Arabic
Oct. 29	Arabic
Nov. 27	Arabic

Year 1915

ALLAN LINE
Glasgow—Boston
Boston

Arrival	Steamer
Feb. 5	Carthaginian
Feb. 10	Pretorian
Mar. 25	Pretorian
Apr. 21	Carthaginian

AMERICAN LINE
Liverpool—Philadelphia
Phila.

Arrival	Steamer
Jan. 26	Dominion
Feb. 9	Haverford
Apr. 26	Dominion
June 2	Dominion

AMERICAN LINE
Liverpool—New York
N. Y.

Arrival	Steamer
Jan. 4	St. Paul
Jan. 11	Philadelphia
Jan. 17	St. Louis
Jan. 31	New York
Feb. 9	Philadelphia
Feb. 14	St. Louis
Feb. 22	St. Paul
Mar. 1	New York
Mar. 16	Philadelphia
Mar. 18	St. Louis
Mar. 22	St. Paul
Mar. 29	New York
Apr. 9	Philadelphia
Apr. 11	St. Louis
Apr. 18	St. Paul
Apr. 25	New York
May 2	Philadelphia
May 9	St. Louis
May 16	St. Paul
May 24	New York
June 3	Philadelphia
June 7	St. Louis
June 13	St. Paul
June 20	New York
June 27	Philadelphia
July 5	St. Louis
July 11	St. Paul
July 18	New York
July 25	Philadelphia
Aug. 1	St. Louis
Aug. 8	St. Paul
Aug. 15	New York
Aug. 22	Philadelphia
Sept. 2	St. Paul
Sept. 9	New York
Sept. 12	St. Louis
Sept. 20	Philadelphia
Oct. 1	St. Paul
Oct. 7	New York
Oct. 14	St. Louis
Oct. 17	Philadelphia
Oct. 24	St. Paul
Oct. 31	New York
Nov. 11	St. Louis
Nov. 22	St. Paul

AMERICAN LINE
Liverpool—New York
(Continued)
N. Y.

Arrival	Steamer
Nov. 28	New York
Dec. 6	St. Louis
Dec. 16	Philadelphia
Dec. 20	St. Paul
Dec. 28	New York

AMERICAN LINE
London—New York
N. Y.

Arrival	Steamer
Nov. 25	Finland

ANCHOR LINE
Glasgow—New York
N. Y.

Arrival	Steamer
Jan. 20	Ausonia
Jan. 25	Cameronia
Feb. 16	Tuscania
Mar. 2	Cameronia
Mar. 22	Tuscania
Mar. 30	Cameronia
Apr. 6	Transylvania
Apr. 20	Tuscania
Apr. 26	Cameronia
May 4	Transylvania
May 18	Tuscania
June 7	Cameronia
June 21	Tuscania
July 19	Tuscania
Aug. 2	Cameronia
Aug. 23	Tuscania
Sept. 5	Cameronia
Sept. 21	Tuscania
Oct. 6	Cameronia
Oct. 13	California
Oct. 26	Tuscania
Nov. 5	Cameronia
Nov. 16	California
Dec. 7	Cameronia
Dec. 21	California

ANCHOR LINE
Mediterranean—New York
N. Y.

Arrival	Steamer
Feb. 19	Italia
Apr. 17	Italia
July 25	Italia
Sept. 27	Italia
Nov. 27	Italia

ATLANTIC TRANSPORT LINE
London—New York
N. Y.

Arrival	Steamer
Jan. 6	Minnehaha
Jan. 12	Minnetonka
Jan. 24	Minnewaska
Feb. 12	Minneapolis
Feb. 17	Minnehaha

ATLANTIC TRANSPORT LINE
London—New York
(Continued)
N. Y.

Arrival	Steamer
Apr. 14	Minnehaha
May 18	Minnehaha
June 29	Minnehaha
Aug. 9	Minnehaha
Sept. 21	Minnehaha
Nov. 1	Minnehaha
Dec. 16	Minnehaha

COMPANIA TRANSATLANTICA LINE
(Spanish Line)
Spain—New York
N. Y.

Arrival	Steamer
Jan. 12	Buenos Aires
Feb. 11	Montevideo
Mar. 13	Manuel Calvo
Apr. 12	Antonio Lopez
June 11	Buenos Aires
July 11	Montevideo
Aug. 12	Manuel Calvo
Sept. 12	Antonio Lopez
Oct. 11	Montevideo
Nov. 12	Buenos Aires
Nov. 14	Montserrat
Dec. 14	Montevideo

CUNARD LINE
Mediterranean—New York
N. Y.

Arrival	Steamer
Jan. 11	Calabria
Mar. 9	Carpathia
May 4	Carpathia

CUNARD LINE
Liverpool—New York
N. Y.

Arrival	Steamer
Jan. 4	Franconia
Jan. 12	Orduna
Jan. 19	Transylvania
Jan. 23	Lusitania
Jan. 30	Alaunia
Feb. 1	Franconia
Feb. 10	Orduna
Feb. 16	Tuscania
Feb. 20	Lusitania
Mar. 1	Cameronia
Mar. 15	Orduna
Mar. 22	Tuscania
Mar. 26	Lusitania
Apr. 5	Transylvania
Apr. 15	Orduna
Apr. 20	Tuscania
Apr. 24	Lusitania
May 3	Transylvania
May 11	Saxonia
May 14	Orduna
May 18	Tuscania
June 7	Cameronia

Year 1915

CUNARD LINE
Liverpool—New York
(Continued)

N.Y.

Arrival	Steamer
June 14	Orduna
June 20	Tuscania
June 28	Saxonia
July 17	Orduna
July 19	Tuscania
July 27	Carpathia
July 31	Saxonia
Aug. 2	Cameronia
Aug. 16	Orduna
Aug. 22	Tuscania
Sept. 3	Saxonia
Sept. 5	Cameronia
Sept. 20	Orduna
Oct. 6	Cameronia
Oct. 13	California
Oct. 21	Orduna
Oct. 26	Tuscania
Nov. 4	Cameronia
Nov. 15	Saxonia
Nov. 28	Orduna
Dec. 6	Cameronia
Dec. 21	California

FABRE LINE
Mediterranean—New York

N.Y.

Arrival	Steamer
Jan. 2	Sant' Anna
Jan. 10	Venezia
Jan. 14	Roma
Jan. 24	Madonna
Feb. 4	Patria
Feb. 26	Sant' Anna
Mar. 5	Roma
Mar. 11	Madonna
Mar. 21	Patria
Apr. 16	Sant' Anna
Apr. 20	Roma
Apr. 29	Madonna
May 3	Patria
June 1	Sant' Anna
June 2	Roma
June 18	Patria
June 19	Venezia
June 21	Madonna
July 17	Sant' Anna
July 19	Roma
Aug. 8	Patria
Sept. 1	Sant' Anna
Sept. 2	Roma
Sept. 23	Patria
Oct. 17	Roma
Nov. 12	Patria
Dec. 1	Roma
Dec. 22	Patria

FRENCH LINE
(Compagnie Generale Transatlantique)
Havre, Bordeaux—New
York

N.Y.

Arrival	Steamer
Jan. 8	Niagara
Jan. 14	Hudson
Jan. 15	Rochambeau

FRENCH LINE
(Compagnie Generale Transatlantique)
Havre, Bordeaux—New
York
(Continued)

N.Y.

Arrival	Steamer
Jan. 19	La Touraine
Jan. 26	Chicago
Feb. 11	Niagara
Feb. 15	Rochambeau
Feb. 23	La Touraine
Mar. 2	Chicago
Mar. 11	Niagara
Mar. 15	Rochambeau
Mar. 18	Hudson
Mar. 22	La Touraine
Apr. 2	Chicago
Apr. 12	Niagara
Apr. 14	Rochambeau
Apr. 23	La Touraine
May 1	Californie
May 2	Hudson
May 4	Espagne
May 12	Rochambeau
May 19	Niagara
May 26	Chicago
May 31	Espagne
June 15	Rochambeau
June 22	Niagara
June 30	Chicago
July 7	Espagne
July 13	Rochambeau
July 20	La Touraine
July 30	Chicago
Aug. 2	Espagne
Aug. 10	Rochambeau
Aug. 17	La Touraine
Aug. 30	Espagne
Sept. 6	Rochambeau
Sept. 16	Chicago
Sept. 21	La Touraine
Sept. 30	Espagne
Oct. 5	Rochambeau
Oct. 14	Chicago
Oct. 23	La Touraine
Nov. 2	Rochambeau
Nov. 9	Lafayette
Nov. 15	Espagne
Nov. 24	La Touraine
Nov. 29	Rochambeau
Dec. 6	Lafayette
Dec. 15	Espagne
Dec. 29	Rochambeau

HOLLAND AMERICA LINE
Rotterdam—New York

N.Y.

Arrival	Steamer
Jan. 11	New Amsterdam
Jan. 19	Potsdam
Jan. 27	Ryndam
Feb. 13	New Amsterdam
Feb. 22	Rotterdam
Mar. 6	Ryndam
Mar. 21	New Amsterdam
Mar. 25	Rotterdam
Apr. 1	Potsdam
Apr. 8	Noordam

HOLLAND AMERICA LINE
Rotterdam—New York
(Continued)

N.Y.

Arrival	Steamer
Apr. 13	Ryndam
Apr. 23	Rotterdam
May 6	Potsdam
May 11	Noordam
May 21	Ryndam
May 28	Rotterdam
June 11	New Amsterdam
June 23	Noordam
July 11	Rotterdam
July 18	New Amsterdam
July 29	Noordam
Aug. 5	Ryndam
Aug. 15	Rotterdam
Aug. 25	New Amsterdam
Sept. 1	Noordam
Sept. 8	Ryndam
Sept. 20	Rotterdam
Sept. 30	New Amsterdam
Oct. 7	Noordam
Oct. 17	Ryndam
Oct. 31	Rotterdam
Nov. 4	New Amsterdam
Nov. 13	Noordam
Nov. 24	Ryndam
Dec. 9	New Amsterdam
Dec. 19	Noordam
Dec. 24	Rotterdam

ITALIA LINE
Mediterranean—New York

N.Y.

Arrival	Steamer
Jan. 18	Ancona
Mar. 11	Ancona
Apr. 26	Ancona
June 7	Ancona
July 18	Ancona
Aug. 30	Ancona
Oct. 11	Ancona

ITALIA LINE
Mediterranean—Philadelphia

Phila.

Arrival	Steamer
Apr. 27	Ancona
June 9	Ancona
July 20	Ancona

LA VELOCE LINE
Mediterranean—New York

N.Y.

Arrival	Steamer
Jan. 29	Europa
Feb. 24	Stampalia
Mar. 13	Europa
Apr. 7	Stampalia
May 3	Europa
May 19	Stampalia
June 17	Europa
July 7	Stampalia
July 30	Europa
Aug. 16	Stampalia
Sept. 10	Europa
Sept. 27	Stampalia

Year 1915

LA VELOCE LINE
Mediterranean—New York
(Continued)
N. Y.

Arrival	Steamer
Oct. 23	Europa
Nov. 2	Duca di Genova
Nov. 10	Stampalia

LEYLAND LINE
Liverpool—Boston
Boston

Arrival	Steamer
Jan. 21	Canadian
Feb. 3	Devonian
Feb. 19	Bohemian
Feb. 24	Canadian
Mar. 14	Devonian
Apr. 4	Canadian
Apr. 20	Devonian
May 3	Bohemian
May 26	Devonian
June 10	Bohemian
July 2	Devonian
July 13	Bohemian
Aug. 5	Devonian
Aug. 16	Bohemian
Sept. 12	Devonian
Sept. 22	Bohemian
Oct. 30	Devonian
Oct. 31	Bohemian
Nov. 24	Devonian

LLOYD ITALIANO
Mediterranean—New York
N. Y.

Arrival	Steamer
Jan. 20	Taormina
Feb. 27	Caserta
Mar. 3	Taormina
Apr. 14	Taormina
May 26	Taormina
June 17	Caserta
July 1	Taormina
Aug. 8	Taormina
Sept. 13	Caserta
Sept. 24	Taormina
Oct. 26	Caserta
Nov. 8	Taormina

LLOYD ITALIANO
Mediterranean—Boston
Boston

Arrival	Steamer
Apr. 22	Caserta
June 15	Caserta
July 31	Caserta

LLOYD SABAUDO
Mediterranean—New York
N. Y.

Arrival	Steamer
Jan. 22	Regina d'Italia
Feb. 10	Re d'Italia
Apr. 7	Re d'Italia
Apr. 27	Regina d'Italia
May 28	Principe di Udine
July 10	Principe di Udine
Sept. 3	Tomaso di Savoia

NATIONAL GREEK LINE
Italy—Greece—New York
N. Y.

Arrival	Steamer
Jan. 5	Ioannia
Jan. 12	Athinai
Jan. 21	Patris
Jan. 29	Thessaloniki
Feb. 19	Themistocles
Mar. 15	Ioannina
Mar. 16	Athinai
Mar. 23	Patris
Apr. 11	Thessaloniki
Apr. 20	Themistocles
May 10	Athinai
May 16	Patris
May 27	Vasilefs C'n'tinos
May 29	Ioannina
June 12	Thessaloniki
June 19	Themistocles
July 7	Athinai
July 13	Vasilefs C'n'tinos
July 26	Patris
Aug. 22	Themistocles
Aug. 29	Thessaloniki
Sept. 7	Athinai
Sept. 12	Patris
Sept. 26	Ioannina
Oct. 4	Vasilefs C'n'tinos
Nov. 27	Vasilefs C'n'tinos
Nov. 26	Themistocles
Dec. 25	Ioannina

NAVIGAZIONE GENER-ALE ITALIANA LINE
Mediterranean—Boston
Boston

Arrival	Steamer
Feb. 21	Verona
July 1	Verona
Aug. 14	Verona

NAVIGAZIONE GENER-ALE ITALIANA LINE
Mediterranean—New York
N. Y.

Arrival	Steamer
Jan. 14	Verona
Jan. 25	D. degli Abruzzi
Feb. 10	America
Feb. 15	Duca d'Aosta
Mar. 8	D. degli Abruzzi
Mar. 25	America
Mar. 31	Duca d'Aosta
Apr. 19	D. degli Abruzzi
May 10	Duca d'Aosta
June 1	D. degli Abruzzi
June 20	America
June 21	Duca d'Aosta
July 12	D. degli Abruzzi
July 26	America
Aug. 9	Duca d'Aosta
Aug. 16	Verona
Aug. 23	D. degli Abruzzi
Sept. 7	America
Oct. 4	D. degli Abruzzi
Oct. 18	America
Nov. 17	D. degli Abruzzi

NORWEGIAN AMERICA LINE
Kristiania, Bergen—New York
N. Y.

Arrival	Steamer
Feb. 20	Kristianiafjord
Mar. 13	Bergensfjord
Apr. 3	Kristianiafjord
Apr. 26	Bergensfjord
May 16	Kristianiafjord
June 4	Bergensfjord
June 28	Kristianiafjord
July 17	Bergensfjord
Aug. 6	Kristianiafjord
Aug. 27	Bergensfjord
Sept. 17	Kristianiafjord
Oct. 8	Bergensfjord
Oct. 29	Kristianiafjord
Nov. 20	Bergensfjord
Dec. 4	Kristianiafjord

RED STAR LINE
Mediterranean—New York
N. Y.

Arrival	Steamer
Feb. 23	Finland
Apr. 11	Finland

RUSSIAN AMERICAN LINE
Archangel—New York
N. Y.

Arrival	Steamer
Jan. 31	Kursk
June 18	Kursk
June 28	Czaritza
July 10	Czar
July 22	Dwinsk
July 30	Kursk
Aug. 10	Czaritza
Aug. 23	Czar
Sept. 9	Dwinsk
Sept. 17	Kursk
Sept. 25	Czaritza
Oct. 8	Czar
Oct. 31	Kursk
Oct. 28	Dwinsk
Nov. 7	Czaritza
Nov. 28	Czar

SCANDINAVIAN-AMER-ICAN LINE
Scandinavian Ports—New York
N. Y.

Arrival	Steamer
Jan. 27	Oscar II
Feb. 20	Frederik VIII
Feb. 29	Hellig Olav
Mar. 3	United States
Mar. 13	Oscar II
Mar. 24	Hellig Olav
Mar. 31	Frederik VIII
Apr. 16	United States
Apr. 20	Oscar II
May 6	Hellig Olav
May 11	Frederik VIII
May 25	United States

Year 1915

SCANDINAVIAN-AMER-
ICAN LINE
Scandinavian Ports—New
York
(Continued)

N. Y.

Arrival	Steamer
June 1	Oscar II
June 18	Hellig Olav
June 24	Frederik VIII
July 7	United States
July 21	Oscar II
Aug. 3	Frederik VIII
Aug. 17	United States
Aug. 24	Hellig Olav
Sept. 2	Oscar II
Sept. 13	Frederik VIII
Sept. 29	United States
Oct. 5	Hellig Olav
Oct. 14	Oscar II
Oct. 27	Frederik VIII
Nov. 9	United States
Nov. 16	Hellig Olav
Nov. 28	Oscar II
Dec. 4	Frederik VIII
Dec. 28	United States

SICULA AMERICANA
LINE
Mediterranean—New York

N. Y.

Arrival	Steamer
Jan. 12	San Guglielmo
Feb. 22	San Guglielmo
Mar. 24	San Giorgio
Apr. 28	San Guglielmo
Aug. 10	San Guglielmo
Sept. 20	San Guglielmo
Nov. 2	San Guglielmo
Dec. 23	San Guglielmo

TRANSATLANTICA
ITALIANA LINE
Mediterranean—New York

N. Y.

Arrival	Steamer
Feb. 26	Dante Alighieri

TRANSATLANTICA
ITALIANA LINE
Mediterranean—New York
(Continued)

N. Y.

Arrival	Steamer
May 1	Dante Alighieri
June 12	Dante Alighieri
July 22	Dante Alighieri
Sept. 6	Dante Alighieri
Oct. 18	Dante Alighieri
Nov. 20	Giuseppe Verdi

WHITE STAR LINE
Mediterranean—Boston

Boston

Arrival	Steamer
Jan. 22	Canopic
Feb. 9	Cretic
Mar. 9	Canopic
Apr. 5	Cretic
Apr. 25	Canopic
May 27	Cretic
June 13	Canopic
July 13	Cretic
Aug. 5	Canopic
Aug. 31	Cretic
Sept. 23	Canopic
Oct. 21	Cretic
Nov. 10	Canopic
Dec. 16	Cretic
Dec. 31	Canopic

WHITE STAR LINE
Liverpool—New York

N. Y.

Arrival	Steamer
Jan. 3	Arabic
Jan. 9	Megantic
Jan. 15	Lapland
Jan. 22	Baltic
Jan. 31	Arabic
Feb. 4	Adriatic
Feb. 13	Megantic
Feb. 21	Cymric

WHITE STAR LINE
Liverpool—New York
(Continued)

N. Y.

Arrival	Steamer
Feb. 26	Baltic
Mar. 13	Arabic
Mar. 15	Adriatic
Mar. 20	Lapland
Mar. 27	Megantic
Apr. 7	Cymric
Apr. 11	Arabic
Apr. 16	Adriatic
Apr. 24	Lapland
Apr. 30	Megantic
May 8	Cymric
May 15	Arabic
May 23	Adriatic
May 31	Lapland
June 13	Cymric
June 18	Arabic
June 24	Adriatic
July 2	Lapland
July 11	Baltic
July 18	Cymric
July 23	Arabic
July 29	Adriatic
Aug. 8	Lapland
Aug. 13	Baltic
Aug. 21	Cymric
Sept. 2	Adriatic
Sept. 10	Lapland
Sept. 17	Baltic
Sept. 26	Cymric
Oct. 15	Lapland
Oct. 22	Baltic
Oct. 28	Adriatic
Nov. 6	Cymric
Nov. 23	Lapland
Nov. 26	Baltic
Dec. 2	Adriatic
Dec. 12	Cymric
Dec. 25	Lapland

Year 1916

AMERICAN LINE
Liverpool—New York
N. Y.

Arrival	Steamer
Jan. 2	St. Louis
Jan. 12	Philadelphia
Jan. 15	St. Paul
Jan. 22	New York
Jan. 31	St. Louis
Feb. 15	St. Paul
Feb. 21	Finland
Feb. 22	New York
Mar. 13	St. Paul
Mar. 19	Philadelphia
Mar. 28	Finland
Apr. 14	St. Paul
Apr. 16	New York
Apr. 20	Philadelphia
Apr. 23	St. Louis
May 6	Finland
May 11	New York
May 14	Philadelphia
May 21	St. Louis
June 4	New York
June 9	Finland
June 11	Philadelphia
June 17	St. Louis
June 24	Kroonland
June 25	St. Paul
July 2	New York
July 9	Philadelphia
July 15	Finland
July 15	St. Louis
July 23	St. Paul
July 30	New York
July 30	Kroonland
Aug. 11	Philadelphia
Aug. 13	St. Louis
Aug. 20	St. Paul
Aug. 19	Finland
Aug. 28	New York
Sept. 5	Philadelphia
Sept. 9	St. Louis
Sept. 14	Kroonland
Sept. 17	St. Paul
Sept. 24	New York
Oct. 1	Finland
Oct. 1	Philadelphia
Oct. 8	St. Louis
Oct. 15	St. Paul
Oct. 22	Kroonland
Oct. 23	New York
Oct. 29	Philadelphia
Nov. 4	Finland
Nov. 5	St. Louis
Nov. 12	St. Paul
Nov. 20	New York
Nov. 26	Kroonland
Nov. 26	Philadelphia
Dec. 3	St. Louis
Dec. 8	Finland
Dec. 10	St. Paul
Dec. 18	New York
Dec. 23	Philadelphia
Dec. 31	St. Louis

ANCHOR LINE
Glasgow—New York
N. Y.

Arrival	Steamer
Jan. 10	Cameronia
Jan. 17	Tuscania
Jan. 28	California
Feb. 10	Cameronia
Feb. 23	Tuscania
Mar. 1	California
Mar. 14	Cameronia
Mar. 28	Tuscania
Apr. 5	California
May 3	Tuscania
May 11	California
May 22	Cameronia
June 5	Tuscania
June 13	California
June 26	Cameronia
July 10	Tuscania
July 17	California
July 31	Cameronia
Aug. 15	Tuscania
Aug. 22	California
Sept. 5	Cameronia
Sept. 18	Tuscania
Sept. 25	California
Oct. 10	Cameronia
Oct. 27	Tuscania
Nov. 6	California
Nov. 29	Tuscania
Dec. 11	California
Dec. 18	Cameronia

ANCHOR LINE
Mediterranean—New York
N. Y.

Arrival	Steamer
Feb. 10	Italia
Apr. 19	Italia
June 23	Italia
Aug. 31	Italia
Nov. 2	Italia

COMPANIA TRANSATLANTICA LINE
(Spanish Line)
Spain—New York
N. Y.

Arrival	Steamer
Jan. 11	Montevideo
Feb. 12	Antonio Lopez
Mar. 14	Manuel Calvo
Apr. 15	Antonio Lopez
Apr. 28	Alfonso XIII
May 12	Montevideo
June 9	Alfonso XIII
June 10	Montserrat
July 12	Buenos Aires
July 23	Alfonso XIII
Aug. 10	Montserrat
Sept. 11	Antonio Lopez
Oct. 13	Montevideo
Nov. 13	Montserrat
Nov. 24	Alfonso XIII
Dec. 17	Buenos Aires

CUNARD LINE
London—New York
N. Y.

Arrival	Steamer
Mar. 12	Pannonia
Mar. 31	Andania
May 2	Pannonia
May 15	Andania
May 22	Alaunia
June 19	Pannonia
June 25	Andania
July 2	Alaunia
July 31	Pannonia
Aug. 5	Andania
Aug. 16	Alaunia
Sept. 21	Andania
Sept. 30	Alaunia
Nov. 16	Andania
Nov. 27	Pannonia
Dec. 24	Ascania

CUNARD LINE
Liverpool—New York
N. Y.

Arrival	Steamer
Jan. 10	Cameronia
Jan. 11	Orduna
Jan. 17	Tuscania
Jan. 28	California
Feb. 10	Cameronia
Feb. 15	Orduna
Feb. 23	Tuscania
Feb. 29	California
Mar. 14	Cameronia
Mar. 20	Orduna
Mar. 28	Tuscania
Apr. 5	California
Apr. 27	Orduna
May 2	Tuscania
May 11	California
May 16	Carpathia
May 22	Cameronia
May 30	Orduna
June 5	Tuscania
June 13	California
June 22	Carpathia
June 26	Cameronia
July 3	Orduna
July 10	Tuscania
July 18	Saxonia
July 28	Carpathia
July 31	Cameronia
Aug. 7	Orduna
Aug. 15	Tuscania
Aug. 22	Saxonia
Sept. 1	Carpathia
Sept. 5	Cameronia
Sept. 11	Orduna
Sept. 18	Tuscania
Sept. 25	Saxonia
Oct. 10	Cameronia
Oct. 16	Orduna
Oct. 27	Tuscania
Nov. 6	Carpathia
Nov. 8	Saxonia
Nov. 28	Laconia
Dec. 11	Orduna
Dec. 21	Carpathia

Year 1916

FABRE LINE
Mediterranean—New York

N. Y.

Arrival	Steamer
Jan. 17	Roma
Feb. 2	Patria
Feb. 26	Roma
Mar. 16	Patria
Apr. 4	Roma
May 2	Patria
June 19	Patria
July 13	Roma
Aug. 3	Patria
Aug. 31	Roma
Sept. 19	Patria
Oct. 24	Roma
Nov. 3	Patria
Dec. 26	Roma
Dec. 26	Patria

FRENCH LINE
(Compagnie Generale Transatlantique)
Havre, Bordeaux—New York

N. Y.

Arrival	Steamer
Jan. 6	La Touraine
Jan. 11	Lafayette
Jan. 19	Espagne
Jan. 29	Rochambeau
Feb. 5	Chicago
Feb. 10	La Touraine
Feb. 17	Lafayette
Feb. 22	Espagne
Feb. 29	Rochambeau
Mar. 10	Chicago
Mar. 15	La Touraine
Mar. 29	Rochambeau
Apr. 5	Espagne
Apr. 20	Chicago
Apr. 24	Rochambeau
May 3	Espagne
May 9	La Touraine
May 22	Lafayette
June 1	Chicago
June 5	Rochambeau
June 13	La Touraine
June 19	Lafayette
June 30	Chicago
July 4	Rochambeau
July 11	La Touraine
July 23	Lafayette
July 31	Rochambeau
Aug. 12	Chicago
Aug. 15	La Touraine
Aug. 21	Lafayette
Aug. 29	Rochambeau
Sept. 9	Chicago
Sept. 13	La Touraine
Sept. 18	Lafayette
Sept. 25	Rochambeau
Oct. 10	Espagne
Oct. 16	Lafayette
Oct. 17	Virginie
Oct. 25	Rochambeau
Nov. 9	Espagne
Nov. 15	Chicago
Nov. 20	La Touraine
Nov. 23	Rochambeau
Dec. 6	Espagne
Dec. 13	Chicago
Dec. 22	La Touraine
Dec. 28	Rochambeau

HOLLAND AMERICA LINE
Rotterdam—New York

N. Y.

Arrival	Steamer
Jan. 1	Ryndam
Jan. 15	New Amsterdam
Jan. 29	Rotterdam
Jan. 29	Noordam
Feb. 24	New Amsterdam
Mar. 5	Rotterdam
Mar. 15	Noordam
Apr. 4	New Amsterdam
Mar. 3	Ryndam
May 4	Noordam
May 24	New Amsterdam
June 13	Ryndam
June 22	Noordam
July 6	New Amsterdam
Aug. 5	Noordam
Aug. 21	New Amsterdam
Aug. 27	Ryndam
Sept. 18	Noordam
Oct. 1	New Amsterdam
Oct. 17	Ryndam
Oct. 31	Noordam
Nov. 17	New Amsterdam
Dec. 4	Ryndam
Dec. 17	Noordam

LA VELOCE LINE
Mediterranean—New York

N. Y.

Arrival	Steamer
Feb. 6	Stampalia
Mar. 24	Stampalia
May 5	Duca di Genoa
July 9	Stampalia
Sept. 28	Duca di Genoa

LLOYD ITALIANO
Mediterranean—New York

N. Y.

Arrival	Steamer
Feb. 1	Caserta
Mar. 19	Caserta
May 2	Caserta
Oct. 6	Caserta
Dec. 18	Caserta

LLOYD SABAUDO
Mediterranean—New York

N. Y.

Arrival	Steamer
Jan. 21	Regina d'Italia
Mar. 16	Regina d'Italia
May 11	Regina d'Italia
June 18	Principe di Udine
July 12	Regina d'Italia
Aug. 6	Re d'Italia
Sept. 18	Regina d'Italia
Oct. 6	Re d'Italia
Nov. 18	Regina d'Italia
Dec. 10	Re d'Italia

NATIONAL GREEK LINE
Greece—New York

N. Y.

Arrival	Steamer
Jan. 6	Patris

NATIONAL GREEK LINE
Greece—New York
(Continued)

N. Y.

Arrival	Steamer
Jan. 18	Vasilefs c'n'tinos
Feb. 5	Themistocles
Mar. 7	Vasilefs c'n'tinos
Mar. 13	Ioannina
Mar. 21	Patris
Apr. 14	Themistocles
Apr. 24	Vasilefs c'n'tinos
May 24	Patris
May 29	Ioannina
June 14	Vasilefs c'n'tinos
July 17	Themistocles
Aug. 4	Ioannina
Aug. 6	Vasilefs c'n'tinos
Aug. 18	Patris
Sept. 24	Vasilefs c'n'tinos
Sept. 30	Themistocles
Oct. 10	Patris
Oct. 23	Ioannina
Dec. 16	Themistocles

NAVIGAZIONE GENERALE ITALIANA LINE
Mediterranean—New York

N. Y.

Arrival	Steamer
Jan. 26	America
Mar. 8	America
Apr. 19	America
May 13	D. degli Abruzzi
June 3	D. degli Abruzzi
June 24	Duca d'Aosta
July 15	D. degli Abruzzi
Aug. 12	Duco d'Aosta
Sept. 5	America
Sept. 23	D. degli Abruzzi
Oct. 14	Duca d'Aosta
Nov. 4	D. degli Abruzzi
Nov. 27	Duca d'Aosta

NORWEGIAN AMERICA LINE
Kristiania, Bergen—New York

N. Y.

Arrival	Steamer
Jan. 1	Bergensfjord
Jan. 24	Kristianiafjord
Feb. 14	Bergensfjord
Mar. 6	Kristianiafjord
Mar. 27	Bergensfjord
Apr. 15	Kristianiafjord
May 5	Bergensfjord
Mar. 29	Kristianiafjord
June 18	Bergensfjord
July 8	Kristianiafjord
July 29	Bergensfjord
Aug. 19	Kristianiafjord
Sept. 9	Bergensfjord
Sept. 30	Kristianiafjord
Oct. 22	Bergensfjord
Nov. 11	Kristianiafjord
Dec. 5	Bergensfjord
Dec. 25	Kristianiafjord

Year 1916

RUSSIAN AMERICAN LINE
Archangel—New York
N. Y.

Arrival	Steamer
Jan. 3	Czaritza
Jan. 4	Kursk
Apr. 1	Kursk
July 7	Czar

SCANDINAVIAN-AMER-ICAN LINE
Scandinavian Ports—New York
N. Y.

Arrival	Steamer
Jan. 31	Hellig Olav
Feb. 11	Oscar II
Feb. 22	Frederik VIII
Mar. 12	Hellig Olav
Mar. 23	United States
Mar. 30	Oscar II
Apr. 13	Frederik VIII
Apr. 20	Hellig Olav
May 2	United States
May 11	Oscar II
May 23	Frederik VIII
May 30	Hellig
June 13	United States
June 21	Oscar II
July 11	Hellig Olav
July 18	Frederik VIII
July 25	United States
Aug. 9	Oscar II
Aug. 22	Hellig Olav
Aug. 29	Frederik VIII
Sept. 5	United States
Sept. 19	Oscar II
Oct. 3	Hellig Olav
Oct. 10	Frederik VIII
Oct. 19	United States
Nov. 1	Oscar II
Nov. 14	Hellig Olav
Nov. 27	Frederik VIII
Nov. 30	United States
Dec. 21	Oscar II

SWEDISH-AMERICAN LINE
Gothenburg—New York
N. Y.

Arrival	Steamer
Mar. 8	Stockholm
Apr. 25	Stockholm
June 9	Stockholm
Aug. 19	Stockholm
Oct. 3	Stockholm
Nov. 22	Stockholm

SICULA AMERICANA LINE
Mediterranean—New York
N. Y.

Arrival	Steamer
Feb. 23	San Guglielmo
Apr. 24	San Guglielmo
July 2	San Guglielmo
Sept. 23	San Guglielmo
Nov. 29	San Guglielmo

TRANSATLANTICA ITALIANA LINE
Mediterranean—New York
N. Y.

Arrival	Steamer
Jan. 6	Giuseppe Verdi
Feb. 24	Giuseppe Verdi
Apr. 9	Giuseppe Verdi
Apr. 26	Dante Alighieri
May 30	Giuseppe Verdi
June 20	Dante Alighieri
July 16	Giuseppe Verdi
Aug. 9	Dante Alighieri
Sept. 5	Giuseppe Verdi
Sept. 28	Dante Alighieri
Oct. 23	Giuseppe Verdi
Nov. 21	Dante Alighieri
Dec. 15	Giuseppe Verdi

WHITE STAR LINE
Mediterranean—Boston
Boston

Arrival	Steamer
Feb. 11	Cretic
Feb. 24	Canopic
Apr. 7	Cretic

WHITE STAR LINE
Mediterranean—Boston
(Continued)
Boston

Arrival	Steamer
Apr. 15	Canopic
May 31	Cretic
June 15	Canopic
July 28	Cretic
Aug. 20	Canopic
Sept. 21	Cretic
Oct. 12	Canopic
Dec. 10	Canopic

WHITE STAR LINE
Liverpool—New York
N. Y.

Arrival	Steamer
Jan. 1	Baltic
Jan. 9	Adriatic
Jan. 23	Cymric
Jan. 29	Lapland
Feb. 5	Baltic
Feb. 12	Adriatic
Mar. 6	Lapland
Mar. 15	Baltic
Mar. 24	Adriatic
Apr. 18	Lapland
May 6	Baltic
May 12	Adriatic
May 26	Lapland
June 16	Baltic
June 23	Adriatic
June 30	Lapland
July 21	Baltic
July 28	Adriatic
July 30	Lapland
Aug. 11	Lapland
Aug. 25	Baltic
Sept. 1	Adriatic
Sept. 14	Lapland
Sept. 29	Baltic
Oct. 5	Adriatic
Oct. 23	Lapland
Nov. 3	Baltic
Nov. 10	Adriatic
Nov. 17	Cedric
Nov. 27	Lapland
Dec. 8	Baltic
Dec. 19	Adriatic
Dec. 29	Lapland

Year 1917

AMERICAN LINE
Southampton—Liverpool—
New York

N. Y.

Arrival	Steamer
Jan. 2	St. Louis
Jan. 2	Kroonland
Jan. 9	St. Paul
Jan. 14	New York
Jan. 16	Finland
Jan. 21	Philadelphia
Jan. 28	St. Louis
Feb. 5	St. Paul
Feb. 11	Kroonland
Feb. 12	New York
Feb. 22	Philadelphia
Feb. 28	Finland
Apr. 8	St. Louis
Apr. 17	St. Paul
May 3	Philadelphia
May 9	St. Louis
May 14	St. Paul
June 3	Philadelphia
June 6	St. Louis
June 11	St. Paul
June 26	New York
July 11	St. Paul
July 18	St. Louis
July 18	Philadelphia
July 23	New York
July 24	Kroonland
Aug. 11	St. Paul
Aug. 19	Philadelphia
Aug. 24	New York
Sept. 8	St. Paul
Sept. 12	St. Louis
Sept. 16	Philadelphia
Sept. 22	New York
Oct. 8	St. Paul
Oct. 12	St. Louis
Oct. 15	Philadelphia
Oct. 22	New York
Nov. 10	St. Louis
Nov. 15	Philadelphia
Nov. 19	New York
Nov. 26	St. Paul
Dec. 10	St. Louis
Dec. 14	Philadelphia
Dec. 20	New York
Dec. 23	St. Paul

ANCHOR LINE
Glasgow—New York

N. Y.

Arrival	Steamer
Jan. 3	Tuscania
Jan. 23	California
Feb. 7	Tuscania
Mar. 21	Tuscania
Apr. 28	Tuscania
June 9	Tuscania
July 24	Tuscania
Nov. 11	Carpathia

ANCHOR LINE
Mediterranean—New York

N. Y.

Arrival	Steamer
Jan. 13	Italia
Mar. 30	Italia
Nov. 28	Italia

COMPANIA TRANSATLANTICA LINE
(Spanish Line)
Spain—New York

N. Y.

Arrival	Steamer
Jan. 2	Montserrat
Jan. 8	Alfonso XII
Feb. 14	Antonio Lopez
Feb. 25	Alfonso XII
Mar. 20	Alicante
Mar. 23	Montserrat
Apr. 4	Alfonso XII
Apr. 13	Montevideo
Apr. 21	C. Lopez y Lopez
May 19	Alicante
May 21	Alfonso XII
May 22	Buenos Aires
June 15	C. Lopez y Lopez
June 15	Montevideo
July 4	Alfonso XII
July 14	Antonio Lopez
Aug. 10	C. Lopez y Lopez
Aug. 15	Manuel Calvo
Aug. 30	Alfonso XII
Sept. 12	Montserrat
Oct. 2	P. De Satrustegui
Oct. 13	Buenos Aires
Oct. 21	Alfonso XII
Nov. 16	Montevideo
Dec. 11	Alfonso XII
Dec. 26	P. De Satrustegui

CUNARD LINE
Liverpool—New York

N. Y.

Arrival	Steamer
Jan. 2	Tuscania
Jan. 19	Orduna
Jan. 23	Saxonia
Jan. 29	Carmania
Feb. 12	Andania
Feb. 13	Laconia
Feb. 20	Orduna
Mar. 6	Carmania
Mar. 25	Andania
Mar. 30	Orduna
Apr. 10	Carmania
May 4	Orduna
May 11	Andania
May 14	Carmania
May 24	Aurania
June 8	Orduna
June 16	Carmania
June 24	Andania
July 5	Aurania
July 18	Orduna
July 22	Carmania

CUNARD LINE
Liverpool—New York
(Continued)

N. Y.

Arrival	Steamer
Aug. 6	Andania
Aug. 14	Aurania
Sept. 1	Orduna
Sept. 11	Carmania
Sept. 15	Saxonia
Sept. 20	Andania
Sept. 26	Aurania
Oct. 8	Pannonia
Oct. 18	Orduna
Nov. 1	Andania
Nov. 8	Aurania
Nov. 25	Pannonia
Dec. 5	Orduna
Dec. 16	Andania
Dec. 22	Carmania
Dec. 24	Aurania

CUNARD LINE
London—New York

N. Y.

Arrival	Steamer
Jan. 5	Andania
Jan. 18	Pannonia
Feb. 12	Ascania
Feb. 21	Ausonia
Mar. 18	Saxonia
Apr. 2	Carpathia
Apr. 10	Ausonia
May 9	Pannonia
May 17	Carpathia
June 18	Saxonia
July 3	Carpathia
Aug. 3	Saxonia
Aug. 19	Pannonia
Sept. 2	Carpathia

FABRE LINE
Mediterranean, Azores—
New York

N. Y.

Arrival	Steamer
Feb. 11	Roma
Feb. 21	Patria
Mar. 25	Roma
May 3	Roma
Aug. 8	Roma
Oct. 9	Roma
Dec. 7	Roma

FRENCH LINE
(Compagnie Generale Transatlantique)
Bordeaux—New York

N. Y.

Arrival	Steamer
Jan. 3	Espagne
Jan. 14	Chicago
Jan. 25	La Touraine
Jan. 30	Rochambeau
Feb. 8	Espagne
Feb. 15	Chicago
Mar. 2	La Touraine

Year 1917

FRENCH LINE
(Compagnie Generale Transatlantique)
Bordeaux—New York

N. Y. Arrival	Steamer
Mar. 8	Rochambeau
Mar. 22	Espagne
Apr. 6	Chicago
Apr. 11	Rochambeau
Apr. 20	La Touraine
Apr. 24	Espagne
May 12	Chicago
May 16	Rochambeau
May 24	La Touraine
May 29	Espagne
June 15	Chicago
June 19	Rochambeau
June 27	La Touraine
July 4	Espagne
July 19	Chicago
July 26	Rochambeau
Aug. 2	La Touraine
Aug. 8	Espagne
Aug. 22	Chicago
Aug. 28	Rochambeau
Sept. 8	La Touraine

FRENCH LINE
(Compagnie Generale Transatlantique)
Bordeaux—New York
(Continued)

N. Y. Arrival	Steamer
Sept. 11	Espagne
Oct. 10	Chicago
Oct. 19	Rochambeau
Oct. 25	La Touraine
Oct. 31	Espagne
Nov. 11	Chicago
Nov. 26	Rochambeau
Nov. 29	Espagne
Dec. 7	Niagara
Dec. 14	La Touraine
Dec. 20	Chicago
Dec. 26	Rochambeau

HOLLAND-AMERICAN LINE
Rotterdam—New York

N. Y. Arrival	Steamer
Jan. 2	New Amsterdam
Jan. 24	Ryndam

HOLLAND-AMERICAN LINE
Rotterdam—New York
(Continued)

N. Y. Arrival	Steamer
Feb. 1	Noordam
Feb. 14	Ryndam
May 30	Noordam
June 20	Ryndam
July 13	New Amsterdam

LLOYD SABAUDO
Mediterranean—New York

N. Y. Arrival	Steamer
Mar. 27	Re d'Italia
May 30	Re d'Italia
Aug. 6	Re d'Italia
Oct. 20	Re d'Italia

NATIONAL GREEK LINE
Greece—New York

N. Y. Arrival	Steamer
Feb. 12	Patris

Year 1918

AMERICAN LINE
Liverpool—New York
N. Y.

Arrival	Steamer
Jan. 15	St. Paul
Jan. 20	St. Louis
Feb. 3	Philadelphia
Feb. 10	New York
Feb. 20	St. Paul
Mar. 1	Philadelphia
Mar. 5	New York
Mar. 16	St. Paul
Mar. 23	St. Louis
Mar. 29	Philadelphia
Apr. 6	New York
Apr. 15	St. Paul
Apr. 21	St. Louis
May 7	New York
May 16	Philadelphia

ANCHOR LINE
Glasgow—New York
N. Y.

Arrival	Steamer
Jan. 17	Tuscania
May 1	Orduna
May 10	Ulna
Dec. 24	Oriana

ANCHOR LINE
Mediterranean—New York
N. Y.

Arrival	Steamer
Mar. 7	Italia
June 6	Italia

COMPANIA TRANSATLANTICA LINE
(Spanish Line)
Spain—New York
N. Y.

Arrival	Steamer
Jan. 13	Antonio Lopez
Jan. 24	Manuel Calvo
Apr. 22	Montevideo
June 7	C. Lopez y Lopez
June 19	Montserrat
July 1	Alicante
July 19	Buenos Aires
Oct. 13	C. Lopez y Lopez
Oct. 23	Manuel Calvo
Nov. 1	Montserrat
Nov. 20	Alicante
Dec. 28	Isla de Panay

CUNARD LINE
United Kingdom—New York
N. Y.

Arrival	Steamer
Jan. 4	Carpathia
Jan. 25	Orduna
Feb. 7	Pannonia
Feb. 9	Saxonia
Feb. 13	Carmania
Mar. 4	Carpathia
Mar. 9	Orduna
Mar. 22	Carmania

CUNARD LINE
United Kingdom—New York
(Continued)
N. Y.

Arrival	Steamer
Mar. 27	Saxonia
Apr. 2	Pannonia
Apr. 21	Carpathia
Apr. 24	Ausonia
Apr. 28	Carmania
May 1	Orduna
May 2	Ascania
May 9	Saxonia
June 2	Carmania
June 4	Carpathia
June 11	Orduna
July 1	Briton
July 3	Caronia
July 3	Saxonia
July 13	Carmania
July 19	Orduna
Aug. 13	Caronia
Aug. 26	Carmania
Sept. 2	Orduna
Sept. 10	Balmoral Castle
Sept. 22	Caronia
Oct. 2	Carmania
Oct. 3	Ortega
Oct. 3	Nevasa
Oct. 9	Walmer Castle
Oct. 9	Orduna
Oct. 28	Aquitania
Oct. 28	Saxon
Oct. 29	Plassy
Nov. 5	Mauretania
Nov. 9	Dunvegan Castle
Nov. 9	Carmania
Nov. 11	Ortega
Nov. 19	Orduna
Nov. 26	Balmoral Castle
Dec. 2	Mauretania
Dec. 5	Orca
Dec. 17	Princess Juliana
Dec. 17	Caronia
Dec. 21	Walmer Castle
Dec. 22	Carmania
Dec. 30	Mauretania

FABRE LINE
Mediterranean—New York
N. Y.

Arrival	Steamer
Apr. 23	Roma
June 11	Patria

Prov.

Arrival	Steamer
Apr. 20	Roma

FRENCH LINE
(Compagnie Generale Transatlantique)
Bordeaux—New York
N. Y.

Arrival	Steamer
Jan. 1	Espagne
Jan. 16	Niagara
Feb. 2	La Touraine
Feb. 13	Espagne
Feb. 16	Rochambeau

FRENCH LINE
(Compagnie Generale Transatlantique)
Bordeaux—New York
(Continued)
N. Y.

Arrival	Steamer
Feb. 25	Niagara
Mar. 3	Chicago
Mar. 9	La Touraine
Mar. 21	Espagne
Mar. 24	Rochambeau
Apr. 10	Chicago
Apr. 23	Niagara
Apr. 29	Rochambeau
May 2	Espagne
May 7	La Lorraine
May 17	Chicago
June 5	Espagne
June 9	La Lorraine
June 13	Niagara
June 23	Chicago
June 27	Rochambeau
June 30	La Lorraine
Aug. 5	Rochambeau
Aug. 2	Niagara
Aug. 15	Chicago
Aug. 17	La Lorraine
Aug. 22	Espagne
Sept. 4	Rochambeau
Sept. 19	La Lorraine
Sept. 23	Niagara
Sept. 26	Espagne
Oct. 17	Rochambeau
Oct. 27	Espagne
Oct. 28	Chicago
Nov. 3	La Lorraine
Nov. 10	Niagara
Nov. 24	Rochambeau
Nov. 27	Espagne
Dec. 9	Chicago
Dec. 16	La Lorraine
Dec. 28	Niagara

HOLLAND-AMERICA LINE
Rotterdam—New York
N. Y.

Arrival	Steamer
Feb. 7	New Amsterdam
June 13	New Amsterdam
Aug. 17	New Amsterdam
Oct. 23	New Amsterdam

LLOYD SABAUDO
Mediterranean—New York
N. Y.

Arrival	Steamer
May 5	Re d'Italia

NORWEGIAN AMERICA LINE
Kristiania, Bergen—New York
N. Y.

Arrival	Steamer
Feb. 18	Bergensfjord
Aug. 28	Bergensfjord

Year 1918

NORWEGIAN AMERICA LINE
Kristiania, Bergen—New York
(Continued)

N. Y.

Arrival	Steamer
June 22	Bergensfjord
Aug. 11	Bergensfjord
Sept. 25	Bergensfjord
Oct. 16	Stavangerfjord
Nov. 10	Bergensfjord
Dec. 3	Stavangerfjord
Dec. 25	Bergensfjord

ROYAL HOLLAND LLOYD
Amsterdam—New York

N. Y.

Arrival	Steamer
July 21	Frisia
Nov. 24	Hollandia

SCANDINAVIAN-AMER-ICAN LINE
Scandinavian Ports—New York

N. Y.

Arrival	Steamer
Mar. 7	Hellig Olav
May 26	Hellig Olav
Nov. 23	Oscar II
Dec. 5	Hellig Olav
Dec. 30	United States

SWEDISH-AMERICAN LINE
Gothenburg—New York

N. Y.

Arrival	Steamer
Oct. 4	Stockholm
Dec. 16	Stockholm

TRANSATLANTICA ITALIANA LINE
Mediterranean—New York

N. Y.

Arrival	Steamer
Jan. 1	Giuseppe Verdi
Feb. 23	Dante Alighieri
Apr. 1	Giuseppe Verdi
Apr. 20	Dante Alighieri
May 31	Giuseppe Verdi
Aug. 4	Giuseppe Verdi
Nov. 6	Giuseppe Verdi

TRANSOCEANICA LINE
Mediterranean—New York

N. Y.

Arrival	Steamer
Dec. 23	San Giorgio

WHITE STAR LINE
United Kingdom Ports—New York

N. Y.

Arrival	Steamer
Jan. 2	Baltic
Jan. 20	Adriatic
Jan. 28	Lapland
Mar. 9	Adriatic
Mar. 9	Baltic
Mar. 21	Lapland
Apr. 15	Adriatic
Apr. 19	Baltic
Apr. 28	Megantic
Apr. 29	Canada
May 13	Lapland
May 25	Baltic
May 25	Adriatic
June 8	Megantic
June 22	Lapland
July 6	Adriatic

WHITE STAR LINE
United Kingdom Ports—New York
(Continued)

N. Y.

Arrival	Steamer
July 6	Baltic
July 23	Megantic
July 29	Lapland
Aug. 16	Adriatic
Aug. 22	Baltic
Sept. 2	Megantic
Sept. 11	Lapland
Sept. 30	Adriatic
Oct. 5	Baltic
Oct. 9	Megantic
Oct. 19	Lapland
Oct. 28	Canopic
Nov. 8	Adriatic
Nov. 9	Baltic
Nov. 12	Olympic
Nov. 17	Megantic
Dec. 4	Lapland
Dec. 11	Adriatic
Dec. 17	Celtic
Dec. 20	Megantic
Dec. 21	Baltic
Dec. 23	Cedric

WHITE STAR LINE
United Kingdom—Boston

Boston

Arrival	Steamer
Dec. 11	Canopic

WHITE STAR LINE
Mediterranean—Boston

Boston

Arrival	Steamer
Jan. 30	Cretic
Mar. 30	Canopic

Year 1919

NAVIGAZIONE GENERALE ITALIANA LINE
Mediterranean—New York
(Continued)

N. Y.

Arrival	Steamer
July 5	Caserta
Aug. 13	Duca d'Aosta
Aug. 26	Duca degli Abruzzi
Sept. 5	Taormina
Sept. 11	Caserta
Sept. 19	America
Oct. 17	Duca d'Aosta
Oct. 26	Taormina
Nov. 2	Duca degli Abruzzi
Nov. 13	Caserta
Dec. 1	America
Dec. 19	Duca d'Aosta
Dec. 25	Taormina

NAVIGAZIONE GENERALE ITALIANA LINE
Mediterranean—Philadelphia

Phila.

Arrival	Steamer
Nov. 17	Caserta

NORWEGIAN-AMERICA LINE
Kristiania—Bergen—New York

N. Y.

Arrival	Steamer
Jan. 22	Stavangerfjord
Feb. 11	Bergensfjord
Mar. 4	Stavangerfjord
Mar. 24	Bergensfjord
Apr. 20	Stavangerfjord
May 12	Bergensfjord
June 3	Stavangerfjord
June 24	Bergensfjord
July 15	Stavangerfjord
Aug. 5	Bergensfjord
Aug. 26	Stavangerfjord
Sept. 16	Bergensfjord
Oct. 7	Stavangerfjord
Oct. 28	Bergensfjord
Dec. 2	Stavangerfjord
Dec. 18	Bergensfjord

ROYAL HOLLAND LLOYD
Rotterdam—New York

N. Y.

Arrival	Steamer
Mar. 15	Hollandia

RUSSIAN-VOLUNTEER FLEET
Novorossia—New York

N. Y.

Arrival	Steamer
June 17	Vladimir

SCANDINAVIAN-AMERICAN LINE
Scandinavian Ports—New York

N. Y.

Arrival	Steamer
Jan. 14	Oscar II
Jan. 29	Hellig Olav
Feb. 19	United States

SCANDINAVIAN-AMERICAN LINE
Scandinavian Ports—New York
(Continued)

N. Y.

Arrival	Steamer
Feb. 27	Oscar II
Mar. 19	Hellig Olav
Mar. 31	Frederik VIII
Apr. 14	United States
Apr. 29	Hellig Olav
May 13	Frederik VIII
June 5	United States
June 9	Oscar II
June 19	Hellig Olav
June 26	Frederik VIII
July 15	United States
July 24	Oscar II
July 30	Hellig Olav
Aug. 11	Frederik VIII
Aug. 25	United States
Sept. 14	Oscar II
Oct. 20	Hellig Olav
Oct. 31	Frederik VIII
Nov. 7	United States
Dec. 23	Frederik VIII

SWEDISH-AMERICAN LINE
Gothenburg—New York

N. Y.

Arrival	Steamer
Feb. 12	Stockholm
Apr. 3	Stockholm
May 24	Stockholm
July 14	Stockholm
Aug. 26	Stockholm
Oct. 11	Stockholm
Nov. 30	Stockholm

TRANSATLANTICA ITALIANA LINE
Mediterranean—New York

N. Y.

Arrival	Steamer
Jan. 20	Giuseppe Verdi
Feb. 17	Dante Alighieri
Mar. 21	Giuseppe Verdi
Apr. 18	Dante Alighieri
May 4	Giuseppe Verdi
June 17	Dante Alighieri
July 8	Giuseppe Verdi
Aug. 9	Dante Alighieri
Sept. 3	Giuseppe Verdi
Oct. 2	Dante Alighieri
Oct. 25	Giuseppe Verdi
Dec. 6	Dante Alighieri
Dec. 24	Giuseppe Verdi

TRANSOCEANICA LINE
Mediterranean—New York

N. Y.

Arrival	Steamer
Feb. 4	San Giovanni
Mar. 27	San Giorgio
May 4	San Giovanni
May 27	San Giorgio
July 13	San Giovanni
Aug. 2	San Giorgio
Oct. 6	San Giovanni
Oct. 20	San Giorgio

WHITE STAR LINE
Liverpool—New York

N. Y.

Arrival	Steamer
Jan. 19	Lapland
Jan. 22	Cretic
Jan. 31	Adriatic
Feb. 1	Celtic
Feb. 6	Baltic
Feb. 11	Canopic
Mar. 3	Lapland
Mar. 11	Adriatic
Mar. 17	Celtic
Mar. 20	Baltic
Mar. 24	Cretic
Apr. 12	Lapland
Apr. 17	Megantic
Apr. 22	Adriatic
May 9	Baltic
May 27	Cedric
June 10	Adriatic
July 6	Baltic
July 13	Celtic
July 18	Cedric
Aug. 7	Adriatic
Aug. 11	Lapland
Aug. 24	Baltic
Sept. 4	Celtic
Sept. 15	Cedric
Sept. 16	Cretic
Sept. 25	Lapland
Sept. 29	Baltic
Oct. 17	Adriatic
Oct. 22	Celtic
Oct. 27	Cedric
Nov. 10	Baltic
Dec. 12	Cedric
Dec. 19	Baltic

WHITE STAR LINE
Southampton—New York

N. Y.

Arrival	Steamer
Feb. 24	Olympic
Sept. 13	Adriatic
Nov. 3	Lapland
Nov. 23	Adriatic
Dec. 4	Lapland
Dec. 28	Adriatic

WHITE STAR LINE
Mediterranean—Boston, New York

N. Y.

Arrival	Steamer
Apr. 15	Canopic
Aug. 16	Canopic
Oct. 12	Canopic
Nov. 11	Cretic
Dec. 24	Canopic

WHITE STAR LINE
Liverpool—Boston

Boston

Arrival	Steamer
Mar. 7	Vedic
July 4	Vedic

Year 1920

AMERICAN LINE
Cherbourg, Southampton—
New York
N. Y.

Arrival	Steamer
Mar. 13	New York
Apr. 9	Philadelphia
Apr. 22	New York
Apr. 29	St. Paul
May 10	Philadelphia
May 21	New York
May 28	St. Paul
June 8	Philadelphia
June 19	New York
June 25	St. Paul
July 5	Philadelphia
July 19	New York
July 22	St. Paul
Aug. 2	Philadelphia
Aug. 18	New York
Aug. 23	St. Paul
Aug. 30	Philadelphia
Sept. 13	New York
Sept. 21	St. Paul
Sept. 27	Philadelphia
Oct. 12	New York
Oct. 18	St. Paul
Oct. 25	Philadelphia
Nov. 15	New York

AMERICAN LINE
Hamburg, Spain, Azores—
New York
N. Y.

Arrival	Steamer
Feb. 2	Manchuria
Feb. 17	Mongolia
Mar. 21	Manchuria
Apr. 1	Mongolia
Apr. 29	Manchuria
May 13	Mongolia
June 11	Manchuria
June 25	Mongolia
July 23	Manchuria
Aug. 5	Mongolia
Sept. 4	Manchuria
Sept. 17	Mongolia
Oct. 16	Manchuria
Oct. 27	Mongolia
Nov. 24	Manchuria
Dec. 10	Mongolia

AMERICAN LINE
Black Sea—New York
N. Y.

Arrival	Steamer
Apr. 2	Black Arrow

AMERICAN LINE
Liverpool—Philadelphia
Phila.

Arrival	Steamer
Feb. 15	Haverford
Apr. 3	Haverford
May 21	Haverford
July 6	Haverford
Aug. 26	Haverford
Oct. 13	Haverford
Dec. 9	Haverford

ANCHOR LINE
Glasgow—New York
N. Y.

Arrival	Steamer
Jan. 6	Columbia
Feb. 4	Columbia
Mar. 7	Columbia
Apr. 9	Columbia
May 12	Toloa
May 15	Columbia
May 27	Ulua
June 26	Columbia
July 28	Columbia
Sept. 6	Columbia
Oct. 5	Columbia
Nov. 9	Columbia
Dec. 9	Columbia
Dec. 20	Sixaola

ANCHOR LINE
Mediterranean—New York
N. Y.

Arrival	Steamer
Jan. 10	Italia
Mar. 19	Italia
May 20	Italia
July 22	Italia
Aug. 18	Calabria
Sept. 11	Italia
Oct. 17	Calabria
Nov. 9	Italia
Dec. 16	Calabria

ATLANTIC TRANSPORT LINE
London—New York
N. Y.

Arrival	Steamer
Oct. 20	Minnekahda

BALTIC S. S. CORP. OF AMERICA
Havre, Danzig—New York
N. Y.

Arrival	Steamer
Sept. 17	New Rochelle
Nov. 15	New Rochelle

COMPANIA TRANS-MEDITERRANEAN LINE
Spain—New York
N. Y.

Arrival	Steamer
Apr. 24	Escolano
Nov. 23	Romeu
Dec. 26	Escolano

COMPANIA TRANSATLANTICA LINE
(Spanish Line)
Spain—New York
N. Y.

Arrival	Steamer
Jan. 17	P. de Satrustegui
Jan. 22	Cataluna

COMPANIA TRANSATLANTICA LINE
(Spanish Line)
Spain—New York
(Continued)
N. Y.

Arrival	Steamer
Feb. 18	C. Lopez y Lopez
Mar. 7	Montserrat
Mar. 19	Isla de Panay
Apr. 10	Cataluna
Apr. 23	P. de Satrustegui
May 15	Buenos Aires
May 21	C. Lopez y Lopez
June 21	Montserrat
July 13	P. de Satrustegui
July 19	Isla de Panay
Aug. 8	Cataluna
Aug. 14	Montevideo
Sept. 12	C. Lopez y Lopez
Sept. 14	Buenos Aires
Oct. 17	P. de Satrustegui
Nov. 13	Montserrat
Nov. 20	Isla de Panay
Dec. 17	Buenos Aires

COSULICH LINE
Italy, Greece, Adriatic—
New York
N. Y.

Arrival	Steamer
Jan. 7	Argentina
Jan. 31	Belvedere
Feb. 26	President Wilson
Mar. 24	Argentina
Apr. 27	Belvedere
May 3	President Wilson
June 12	Argentina
July 4	Belvedere
July 14	President Wilson
Aug. 8	Argentina
Sept. 5	Belvedere
Sept. 6	President Wilson
Sent. 18	Columbia
Oct. 5	Argentina
Oct. 27	President Wilson
Nov. 11	Belvedere
Nov. 27	Argentina
Dec. 12	President Wilson

CUNARD LINE
Liverpool—New York
N. Y.

Arrival	Steamer
Jan. 24	Carmania
Feb. 24	K. Aug. Victoria
Mar. 1	Carmania
Mar. 2	Imperator
Mar. 24	Vestris
Apr. 8	Carmania
Apr. 19	K. Aug. Victoria
Apr. 30	Vasari
May 13	Carmania
May 17	Caronia
June 5	K. Aug. Victoria
June 21	Caronia
July 7	Vauban

Year 1920

CUNARD LINE
Liverpool—New York
(Continued)

N. Y.

Arrival	Steamer
July 12	K. Aug. Victoria
July 19	Caronia
July 27	Vestris
Aug. 9	K. Aug. Victoria
Aug. 15	Caronia
Sept. 2	Vasari
Sept. 9	K. Aug. Victoria
Sept. 12	Caronia
Sept. 14	Port Albany
Sept. 22	Carmania
Oct. 3	K. Aug. Victoria
Oct. 16	Caronia
Oct. 17	Carmania
Oct. 19	Vauban
Nov. 12	K. Aug. Victoria
Nov. 16	Vestris
Nov. 20	Carmania
Dec. 13	K. Aug. Victoria
Dec. 20	Carmania

CUNARD LINE
Southampton—New York

N. Y.

Arrival	Steamer
Jan. 24	Royal George
Jan. 27	Mauretania
Mar. 6	Royal George
Mar. 12	Mauretania
Apr. 10	Royal George
Apr. 22	Mauretania
May 16	Royal George
May 16	Mauretania
June 13	Imperator
June 21	Royal George
June 26	Mauretania
July 12	Imperator
July 24	Aquitania
Aug. 8	Imperator
Aug. 21	Aquitania
Aug. 28	Mauretania
Sept. 5	Imperator
Sept. 17	Aquitania
Sept. 25	Mauretania
Oct. 3	Imperator
Oct. 9	Aquitania
Oct. 23	Mauretania
Oct. 30	Aquitania
Nov. 12	Imperator
Nov. 20	Aquitania
Dec. 11	Aquitania
Dec. 19	Imperator
Dec. 31	Caronia

CUNARD LINE
Cherbourg—Plymouth—London—Hamburg—New York

N. Y.

Arrival	Steamer
Feb. 12	Saxonia
Apr. 1	Saxonia
Oct. 25	Saxonia
Nov. 21	Caronia
Dec. 1	Saxonia

CUNARD LINE
Mediterranean—New York

N. Y.

Arrival	Steamer
Jan. 22	Pannonia
Apr. 2	Pannonia
June 7	Pannonia
Aug. 12	Pannonia
Oct. 26	Pannonia

CUNARD LINE
London—Boston

Boston

Arrival	Steamer
Sept. 23	Valacia

FABRE LINE
Mediterranean—New York

N. Y.

Arrival	Steamer
Jan. 7	Madonna
Feb. 4	Roma
Feb. 15	Patria
Feb. 18	Britannia
Mar. 5	Canada
Mar. 22	Madonna
Mar. 25	Roma
Apr. 12	Britannia
Apr. 14	Patria
May 2	Canada
May 11	Madonna
May 13	Roma
June 9	Britannia
June 12	Patria
June 21	Canada
July 3	Roma
July 8	Madonna
July 28	Britannia
July 31	Patria
Aug. 9	Canada
Aug. 24	Roma
Aug. 24	Providence
Sept. 3	Britannia
Sept. 4	Madonna
Sept. 20	Patria
Oct. 4	Canada
Oct. 8	Asia
Oct. 11	Roma
Oct. 13	Providence
Oct. 28	Madonna
Oct. 29	Britannia
Nov. 12	Patria
Nov. 24	Roma
Dec. 1	Providence
Dec. 10	Asia
Dec. 14	Canada
Dec. 20	Madonna

FRENCH LINE
(Compagnie Generale Transatlantique)
Danzig, Hamburg—New York

N. Y.

Arrival	Steamer
Mar. 14	Santaren

FRENCH LINE
(Compagnie Generale Transatlantique)
Havre, Bordeaux—New York

N. Y.

Arrival	Steamer
Jan. 6	La Touraine
Jan. 19	La Touraine
Jan. 21	Lafayette
Jan. 27	La Savoie
Jan. 29	Niagara
Feb. 7	La Touraine
Feb. 12	Rochambeau
Feb. 21	Lafayette
Feb. 23	La Savoie
Feb. 28	Chicago
Mar. 5	La Touraine
Mar. 14	Niagara
Mar. 14	France
Mar. 15	Rochambeau
Mar. 16	Mexico
Mar. 23	La Savoie
Mar. 30	La Lorraine
Apr. 6	Lafayette
Apr. 10	France
Apr. 17	Rochambeau
Apr. 20	La Touraine
Apr. 26	La Lorraine
May 4	Leopoldina
May 27	France
May 30	La Savoie
May 31	Santarem
May 31	La Lorraine
June 8	Rochambeau
June 8	La Touraine
June 16	Leopoldina
June 20	France
June 27	Niagara
June 28	Lafayette
June 28	La Savoie
July 5	La Lorraine
July 9	La Touraine
July 12	Rochambeau
July 17	France
July 26	Lafayette
July 27	Leopoldina
Aug. 2	La Savoie
Aug. 11	Caroline
Aug. 12	Niagara
Aug. 13	Rochambeau
Aug. 16	La Lorraine
Aug. 23	Lafayette
Aug. 30	La Savoie
Sept. 5	France
Sept. 9	Mexico
Sept. 13	La Lorraine
Sept. 16	Leopoldina
Sept. 17	Rochambeau
Sept. 20	Lafayette
Sept. 20	Niagara
Sept. 23	La Touraine
Sept. 27	La Savoie
Oct. 3	France
Oct. 11	La Lorraine
Oct. 18	Lafayette
Oct. 18	Caroline
Oct. 22	La Touraine
Oct. 23	Rochambeau
Oct. 23	Roussillon
Oct. 25	La Savoie

Year 1920

FRENCH LINE
(Compagnie Generale Transatlantique)
Havre, Bordeaux—New York
(Continued)

N. Y.

Arrival	Steamer
Nov. 1	Niagara
Nov. 2	France
Nov. 5	Leopoldina
Nov. 8	La Lorraine
Nov. 19	La Touraine
Nov. 23	La Savoie
Nov. 27	France
Nov. 27	Rochambeau
Dec. 7	La Lorraine
Dec. 17	Roussillon
Dec. 17	La Touraine
Dec. 19	Leopoldina
Dec. 20	Caroline
Dec. 20	La Savoie
Dec. 23	Niagara
Dec. 29	Rochambeau

FRENCH LINE
(Compagnie Generale Transatlantique)
Spain—New York

N. Y.

Arrival	Steamer
May 4	Niagara

FRENCH LINE
(Compagnie Generale Transatlantique)
Portugal—New York

N. Y.

Arrival	Steamer
June 19	Caroline
July 7	Mexico

FURNESS-WARREN LINE
Liverpool—Boston

Boston

Arrival	Steamer
July 19	Fort Victoria
Aug. 22	Fort Victoria
Sept. 29	Fort Victoria

HOLLAND-AMERICA LINE
Rotterdam—New York

N. Y.

Arrival	Steamer
Jan. 23	Noordam
Jan. 28	Rotterdam
Feb. 11	New Amsterdam
May 16	Noordam
May 23	New Amsterdam
May 30	Rotterdam
June 21	Noordam
June 29	New Amsterdam
July 12	Rotterdam
July 29	Noordam
Aug. 4	New Amsterdam
Aug. 12	Ryndam
Aug. 21	Rotterdam
Aug. 31	Noordam
Sept. 7	New Amsterdam
Sept. 14	Ryndam
Sept. 26	Rotterdam
Oct. 6	Noordam

HOLLAND-AMERICA LINE
Rotterdam—New York
(Continued)

N. Y.

Arrival	Steamer
Oct. 12	New Amsterdam
Oct. 18	Ryndam
Oct. 29	Rotterdam
Nov. 10	Noordam
Nov. 17	New Amsterdam
Nov. 26	Ryndam
Dec. 4	Rotterdam
Dec. 20	New Amsterdam

LA VELOCE LINE
Mediterranean—New York

N. Y.

Arrival	Steamer
Feb. 19	Europa

LA VELOCE LINE
Mediterranean—Philadelphia

Phila.

Arrival	Steamer
Feb. 23	Europa

LEYLAND LINE
Liverpool—Boston

Boston

Arrival	Steamer
Jan. 14	Winifredian
Feb. 15	Bohemian
Mar. 3	Winifredian
Apr. 4	Napierian
Apr. 14	Mercian
May 2	Winifredian
June 9	Oxonian
June 15	Winifredian
July 2	Caledonian
July 26	Winifredian
Sept. 22	Winifredian
Oct. 8	Mercian
Nov. 1	Caledonian
Nov. 7	Winifredian
Nov. 30	Mercian
Dec. 21	Winifredian

LEYLAND LINE
Manchester—Boston

Boston

Arrival	Steamer
Feb. 25	Caledonian
June 23	Mercian

LLOYD SABAUDO
Mediterranean—New York

N. Y.

Arrival	Steamer
Jan. 20	Regina d'Italia
Feb. 4	Re d'Italia
Mar. 23	Pesaro
Apr. 20	Re d'Italia
Apr. 29	Regina d'Italia
May 27	Pesaro
July 7	Regina d'Italia
Aug. 7	Re d'Italia
Aug. 23	Pesaro
Oct. 23	Re d'Italia
Oct. 25	Pesaro
Nov. 1	Regina d'Italia
Dec. 19	Re d'Italia

NATIONAL GREEK LINE
Greece—New York

N. Y.

Arrival	Steamer
Feb. 9	Themistocles
Feb. 22	Megali Hellas
Apr. 10	Themistocles
Apr. 22	Megali Hellas
June 18	Themistocles
June 23	Megali Hellas
July 14	Patris
Aug. 10	Megali Hellas
Aug. 23	Themistocles
Sept. 8	Patris
Oct. 4	Megali Hellas
Oct. 22	Themistocles
Nov. 2	Patris
Nov. 25	Megali Hellas
Dec. 15	Themistocles
Dec. 26	Patris

NAVIGAZIONE GENERALE ITALIANA LINE
Mediterranean—New York

N. Y.

Arrival	Steamer
Jan. 3	Duca degli Abruzzi
Jan. 8	Caserta
Feb. 1	America
Feb. 9	Duca D'Aosta
Feb. 14	Taormina
Feb. 23	Duca degli Abruzzi
Mar. 26	Duca D'Aosta
Mar. 27	America
Apr. 10	Taormina
Apr. 16	Duca degli Abruzzi
May 14	Duca D'Aosta
May 22	America
June 4	Taormina
June 10	Duca degli Abruzzi
July 3	F. Palasciano
July 7	Duca D'Aosta
Aug. 3	Duca degli Abruzzi
Aug. 28	F. Palasciano
Sept. 4	Duca D'Aosta
Sept. 29	Duca degli Abruzzi
Oct. 23	F. Palasciano
Oct. 28	Duca D'Aosta
Nov. 11	America
Dec. 2	Duca degli Abruzzi
Dec. 15	F. Palasciano
Dec. 21	Duca D'Aosta
Dec. 31	America

NAVIGAZIONE GENERALE ITALIANA LINE
Mediterranean—Philadelphia

Phila.

Arrival	Steamer
Jan. 22	Caserta
Mar. 30	Duca D'Aosta
Oct. 4	Duca degli Abruzzi

NEW YORK & CUBA MAIL STEAMSHIP COMPANY
Spain—New York

N. Y.

Arrival	Steamer
Feb. 21	Orizaba
Dec. 15	H. R. Mallory

Year 1920

NORWEGIAN-AMERICA LINE
Kristiania—Bergen—New York

N. Y.

Arrival	Steamer
Jan. 9	Stavangerfjord
Feb. 17	Stavangerfjord
Mar. 24	Stavangerfjord
Apr. 9	Bergensfjord
May 4	Stavangerfjord
May 24	Bergensfjord
June 15	Stavangerfjord
July 6	Bergensfjord
July 27	Stavangerfjord
Aug. 16	Bergensfjord
Sept. 7	Stavangerfjord
Sept. 27	Bergensfjord
Oct. 19	Stavangerfjord
Nov. 8	Bergensfjord
Nov. 30	Stavangerfjord
Dec. 21	Bergensfjord

RED STAR LINE
Antwerp—New York

N. Y.

Arrival	Steamer
Jan. 14	Lapland
Feb. 19	Lapland
Mar. 28	Lapland
Apr. 28	Kroonland
May 3	Lapland
May 9	Finland
May 31	Kroonland
June 5	Lapland
June 13	Finland
July 6	Kroonland
July 14	Lapland
July 19	Finland
Aug. 8	Kroonland
Aug. 14	Lapland
Aug. 21	Finland
Aug. 29	Zeeland
Sept. 11	Kroonland
Sept. 18	Lapland
Sept. 25	Finland
Oct. 2	Zeeland
Oct. 17	Kroonland
Oct. 23	Lapland
Oct. 31	Finland
Nov. 6	Zeeland
Nov. 26	Kroonland
Nov. 29	Lapland
Dec. 7	Finland
Dec. 13	Zeeland
Dec. 30	Kroonland

RED STAR LINE
Danzig—New York

N. Y.

Arrival	Steamer
Aug. 22	Gothland
Oct. 10	Gothland
Nov. 27	Gothland

SCANDINAVIAN-AMERICAN LINE
Scandinavian Ports—New York

N. Y.

Arrival	Steamer
Jan. 2	United States
Feb. 2	Hellig Olav
Feb. 15	Oscar II
Mar. 4	Frederik VIII
Mar. 31	Oscar II
June 22	Frederik VIII
July 6	United States
July 20	Oscar II
Aug. 5	Hellig Olav
Aug. 16	Frederik VIII
Aug. 23	United States
Sept. 7	Oscar II
Sept. 21	Hellig Olav
Oct. 4	Frederik VIII
Oct. 11	United States
Oct. 25	Oscar II
Nov. 9	Hellig Olav
Nov. 24	Frederik VIII
Nov. 29	United States
Dec. 9	Oscar II
Dec. 21	Hellig Olav

SICULA AMERICANA LINE
Mediterranean—New York

N. Y.

Arrival	Steamer
Dec. 26	Guglielmo Peirce

SWEDISH-AMERICAN LINE
Gothenburg—New York

N. Y.

Arrival	Steamer
Jan. 23	Stockholm
Mar. 16	Stockholm
May 30	Stockholm
June 9	Drottningholm
July 14	Drottningholm
July 21	Stockholm
Aug. 20	Drottningholm
Sept. 4	Stockholm
Sept. 26	Drottningholm
Oct. 18	Stockholm
Nov. 7	Drottningholm
Nov. 29	Stockholm
Dec. 20	Drottningholm

TRANSATLANTICA ITALIANA LINE
Mediterranean—New York

N. Y.

Arrival	Steamer
Jan. 29	Dante Alighieri
Feb. 14	Giuseppi Verdi
Mar. 1	H. R. Mallory
Mar. 22	Dante Alighieri
Apr. 3	Giuseppi Verdi
May 9	H. R. Mallory
May 14	Dante Alighieri
May 28	Giuseppi Verdi
July 2	Dante Alighieri
July 13	Giuseppe Verdi
Aug. 22	Dante Alighieri

TRANSATLANTICA ITALIANA LINE
Mediterranean—New York
(Continued)

N. Y.

Arrival	Steamer
Sept. 3	Giuseppi Verdi
Oct. 9	Dante Alighieri
Oct. 27	Giuseppe Verdi
Oct. 2	Dante Alighieri
Dec. 17	Giuseppe Verdi

TRANSOCEANICA LINE
Mediterranean—New York

N. Y.

Arrival	Steamer
Jan. 5	San Giovanni
Feb. 6	San Giorgio
Mar. 14	San Giovanni
May 2	San Giorgio
May 22	San Giovanni

TRANSPORTES MARITIMOS DO ESTADO LINE
Portugal—New York

N. Y.

Arrival	Steamer
Nov. 25	Mormugao

UNITED STATES ARMY TRANSPORTS
Italy—Greece—Adriatic—New York

N. Y.

Arrival	Steamer
Sept. 10	Edellyn
Sept. 12	America
Sept. 23	Thomas
Oct. 21	Logan
Nov. 17	Pres. Grant
Dec. 18	Heffron

U. S. MAIL STEAMSHIP COMPANY
Boulogne—London—New York

N. Y.

Arrival	Steamer
Oct. 18	Panhandle State
Nov. 22	Panhandle State
Dec. 4	Old North State
Dec. 25	Panhandle State

U. S. MAIL STEAMSHIP COMPANY
Hamburg—Danzig—New York

N. Y.

Arrival	Steamer
Sept. 18	Susquehanna
Nov. 4	Susquehanna
Dec. 21	Susquehanna

U. S. SHIPPING BOARD
Italy—Greece—Adriatic—New York

N. Y.

Arrival	Steamer
Mar. 11	Susquehanna
June 2	Susquehanna

Year 1920

WHITE STAR LINE
Liverpool—New York
N. Y.

Arrival	Steamer
Jan. 2	Celtic
Jan. 21	Cedric
Jan. 24	Baltic
Feb. 18	Cedric
Mar. 7	Baltic
Apr. 10	Baltic
May 7	Celtic
May 17	Baltic
June 11	Celtic
June 18	Baltic
June 17	Celtic
July 24	Baltic
Aug. 18	Mobile
Aug. 20	Celtic
Aug. 27	Baltic
Sept. 26	Celtic
Sept. 28	Mobile
Oct. 1	Baltic
Oct. 29	Celtic
Nov. 12	Baltic
Dec. 3	Celtic
Dec. 18	Baltic

WHITE STAR LINE
Southampton—New York
N. Y.

Arrival	Steamer
Feb. 8	Adriatic
Mar. 12	Adriatic
Apr. 16	Adriatic
May 21	Adriatic
June 25	Adriatic
July 2	Olympic
July 28	Olympic
Aug. 6	Adriatic
Aug. 25	Olympic
Sept. 10	Adriatic
Sept. 15	Olympic
Oct. 6	Olympic
Oct. 15	Adriatic
Nov. 3	Olympic
Nov. 12	Adriatic
Nov. 24	Olympic
Dec. 11	Adriatic
Dec. 22	Olympic

WHITE STAR LINE
Mediterranean—Boston—
New York
Boston

Arrival	Steamer
Jan. 6	Cretic

WHITE STAR LINE
Mediterranean—Boston—
New York
(Continued)
Boston

Arrival	Steamer
Mar. 2	Canopic
Mar. 21	Cretic
Apr. 28	Canopic
May 13	Cretic
June 26	Canopic
July 13	Cretic
Aug. 20	Canopic
Sept. 7	Cretic
Oct. 17	Canopic
Oct. 30	Cretic
Dec. 10	Canopic
Dec. 22	Cretic

ADDITIONAL ARRIVALS
N. Y.

Arrival	Steamer
Oct. 31	Gul Djemal (Mount Royal S.S. Co., Spain)
Dec. 17	City of Marseilles (America & India Line, Bombay)
Dec. 19	Leca (Compania Da Guire, Spain)

Year 1921

AMERICAN LINE
Hamburg—Vigo—New York
N.Y.

Arrival	Steamer
Jan. 6	Manchuria
Jan. 20	Mongolia
Feb. 23	Manchuria*
Mar. 5	Mongolia*
Apr. 4	Manchuria
Apr. 16	Mongolia
May 13	Minnekahda
May 22	Manchuria
May 29	Mongolia
June 19	Minnekahda
July 3	Manchuria
July 17	Mongolia
July 31	Minnekahda
Aug. 13	Manchuria
Aug. 30	Mongolia
Sept. 12	Minnekahda
Sept. 25	Manchuria
Oct. 10	Mongolia
Oct. 22	Minnekahda
Nov. 5	Manchuria
Nov. 23	Mongolia
Dec. 4	Minnekahda
Dec. 21	Manchuria

*Westbound passengers landed at Boston.

AMERICAN NEAR EAST AND BLACK SEA LINE
Levant—Black Sea—New York
N.Y.

Arrival	Steamer
June 25	Acropolis
Sept. 1	Acropolis
Nov. 11	Acropolis

ANCHOR LINE
Glasgow—New York
N.Y.

Arrival	Steamer
Jan. 8	Columbia
Feb. 15	Columbia
Feb. 23	Massilia
Mar. 1	Algeria
Mar. 20	Columbia
Apr. 7	Algeria
Apr. 18	Columbia
May 9	Algeria
May 28	Albania
June 13	Columbia
June 18	Assyria
June 20	Algeria
June 30	Cameronia
July 5	Castalia
July 10	Columbia
July 27	Cameronia
Aug. 7	Assyria
Aug. 8	Columbia
Aug. 16	Algeria
Aug. 21	Cameronia
Sept. 4	Columbia
Sept. 13	Assyria
Sept. 18	Cameronia

ANCHOR LINE
Glasgow—New York
(Continued)
N.Y.

Arrival	Steamer
Sept. 28	Algeria
Oct. 3	Columbia
Oct. 16	Cameronia
Oct. 24	Assyria
Oct. 31	Columbia
Nov. 7	Algeria
Nov. 17	Cameronia
Nov. 29	Assyria
Dec. 4	Columbia
Dec. 18	Algeria

ANCHOR LINE
Mediterranean—New York—New Bedford
N.Y.

Arrival	Steamer
Jan. 22	Italia
Mar. 13	Calabria
Apr. 4	Italia*
May 15	Calabria
June 11	Italia
Aug. 1	Calabria
Aug. 18	Italia
Oct. 2	Calabria*
Oct. 22	Italia
Nov. 29	Calabria
Dec. 25	Cameronia
Dec. 27	Italia

*Westbound passengers landed at Boston.

BALTIC-AMERICA LINE
Libau via Halifax—Hamburg—Danzig—Libau—New York
N.Y.

Arrival	Steamer
Feb. 27	Lituania*
Mar. 12	Estonia*
Mar. 29	Polonia*
Apr. 10	Lituania
Apr. 29	Estonia
May 12	Polonia
May 26	Lituania
June 16	Estonia
July 1	Polonia
July 13	Lituania*
Aug. 1	Latvia
Aug. 8	Estonia
Aug. 16	Polonia
Sept. 1	Lituania
Sept. 14	Latvia
Sept. 27	Estonia
Oct. 11	Polonia
Oct. 25	Lituania
Nov. 2	Latvia
Nov. 16	Estonia
Dec. 2	Polonia
Dec. 13	Lituania

*Westbound passengers landed at Boston.

COMPANIA TRANSATLANTICA LINE
(Spanish Line)
Spain—New York
N.Y.

Arrival	Steamer
Jan. 14	Leon XIII
Feb. 17	Antonio Lopez
Mar. 14	Montserrat
Apr. 14	Buenos Aires
Apr. 14	Alfonso XIII
May 15	Antonio Lopez
June 11	Alfonso XIII
June 12	Montserrat
July 14	Leon XIII
Aug. 12	Antonio Lopez
Sept. 13	Montserrat
Oct. 15	Buenos Aires
Nov. 15	Montevideo
Dec. 16	Montserrat

COSULICH LINE
Italy—Greece—Adriatic—New York
N.Y.

Arrival	Steamer
Jan. 17	Belvedere
Jan. 24	Argentina
Feb. 1	Pres. Wilson
Feb. 3	Sofia
Feb. 10	San Giusto
Mar. 12	Columbia
Mar. 17	Argentina
Mar. 27	Pres. Wilson
Mar. 30	Belvedere
May 21	Argentina
May 23	Pres. Wilson
June 10	Belvedere
June 14	Columbia
July 4	Pres. Wilson
July 29	Argentina
Aug. 17	Pres. Wilson
Aug. 27	Belvedere
Sept. 21	Argentina
Oct. 4	Pres. Wilson
Nov. 1	Belvedere
Nov. 12	Argentina
Nov. 26	Pres. Wilson

CUNARD LINE
Liverpool—New York
N.Y.

Arrival	Steamer
Jan. 4	Vasari
Jan. 9	K. A. Victoria
Jan. 24	Carmania
Jan. 31	Albania
Feb. 14	Vauban
Feb. 28	Carmania
Mar. 5	Vestris
Mar. 16	Albania
Apr. 8	Carmania
Apr. 24	Caronia
May 12	Carmania
May 21	Cameronia
May 27	Caronia
June 11	Carmania
June 17	Emperor of India

Year 1921

CUNARD LINE
Liverpool—New York
(Continued)

N.Y. Arrival	Steamer
June 26	Caronia
July 6	Albania
July 10	Carmania
Aug. 8	Carmania
Aug. 13	Albania
Aug. 21	Caronia
Aug. 30	Scythia
Sept. 4	Carmania
Sept. 17	Albania
Sept. 18	Caronia
Sept. 26	Vasari
Sept. 30	Scythia
Oct. 16	Caronia
Oct. 25	Albania
Nov. 9	Scythia
Dec. 5	Albania
Dec. 19	Scythia

CUNARD LINE
Southampton—New York

N.Y. Arrival	Steamer
Jan. 18	Imperator
Jan. 23	Saturnia
Jan. 30	Aquitania
Feb. 23	Aquitania
Mar. 7	Imperator
Mar. 19	Aquitania
Apr. 2	Mauretania
Apr. 9	Aquitania
Apr. 30	Aquitania
May 7	Mauretania
May 20	Aquitania
June 10	Aquitania
June 12	Mauretania
July 1	Berengaria
July 13	Mauretania
July 23	Aquitania
Aug. 14	Berengaria
Aug. 20	Aquitania
Sept. 4	Empress of India
Sept. 9	Aquitania
Sept. 18	Berengaria
Sept. 30	Aquitania
Sept. 30	Empress of India
Oct. 6	Carmania
Oct. 17	Berengaria
Oct. 21	Aquitania
Oct. 31	Carmania
Nov. 11	Aquitania
Nov. 28	Carmania
Dec. 9	Aquitania
Dec. 26	Carmania

CUNARD LINE
Mediterranean, Adriatic—
New York

N.Y. Arrival	Steamer
Jan. 10	Pannonia
Mar. 3	Caronia
Mar. 17	Pannonia
May 21	Pannonia
Aug. 12	Pannonia
Oct. 17	Pannonia
Nov. 29	Caronia

CUNARD LINE
Cherbourg—Plymouth—London—Hamburg—New York

N.Y. Arrival	Steamer
Jan. 21	Saxonia
Mar. 5	Saxonia*
Apr. 20	Saxonia
June 4	Saxonia
July 16	Saxonia
Sept. 11	Saxonia
Oct. 26	Saxonia

*Westbound landed at Boston.

ELLERMAN'S WILSON LINE
Cardiff—New York

N.Y. Arrival	Steamer
Sept. 22	City of Lucknow
Oct. 18	City of Valencia

FABRE LINE
Mediterranean—New York

N.Y. Arrival	Steamer
Jan. 6	Braga
Jan. 22	Patria
Jan. 29	Britannia
Feb. 9	Providence
Feb. 24	Canada*
Mar. 16	Patria
Apr. 16	Providence
Apr. 19	Canada
Apr. 28	Asia
May 7	Patria
May 26	Providence
June 12	Canada
June 25	Patria
July 17	Providence
Aug. 12	Patria
Aug. 22	Madonna
Sept. 4	Patria
Sept. 25	Braga
Sept. 27	Patria
Oct. 9	Canada
Oct. 25	Providence
Oct. 27	Madonna
Nov. 22	Patria
Nov. 30	Canada
Dec. 6	Britannia
Dec. 27	Providence

*Westbound Third Class passengers landed as follows:
New York, 45; Philadelphia, 1,710.

FABRE LINE
Mediterranean—Boston

Boston Arrival	Steamer
Oct. 12	Britannia
Nov. 4	Asia

FRENCH LINE
(Compagnie Generale Transatlantique)
Havre—Bordeaux—New York

N.Y. Arrival	Steamer
Jan. 4	La Lorraine
Jan. 15	La Touraine

FRENCH LINE
(Compagnie Generale Transatlantique)
Havre—Bordeaux—New York
(Continued)

N.Y. Arrival	Steamer
Jan. 16	France
Jan. 24	La Savoie
Jan. 31	La Lorraine
Feb. 1	Roussillon
Feb. 13	France
Feb. 17	Chicago
Feb. 19	Caroline
Feb. 22	La Savoie
Feb. 22	Leopoldina
Mar. 5	Rochambeau
Mar. 7	Niagara
Mar. 13	France
Mar. 14	Roussillon
Mar. 22	La Savoie
Mar. 23	La Touraine
Mar. 28	La Lorraine
Mar. 29	Chicago
Apr. 6	Rochambeau
Apr. 14	La Bourdannais
Apr. 16	France
Apr. 22	Roussillon
Apr. 25	La Lorraine
Apr. 26	Caroline
May 2	Lafayette
May 2	Niagara*
May 3	La Touraine
May 7	France
May 7	Rochambeau
May 16	Chicago
May 16	La Savoie
May 23	La Lorraine
May 26	La Bourdonnais
May 30	Roussillon
May 30	Lafayette
June 4	France
June 4	La Touraine
June 11	Rochambeau
June 13	La Savoie
June 20	Chicago
June 22	Paris
June 23	Leopoldina
June 26	Niagara
June 27	Lafayette
July 2	La Lorraine
July 2	France
July 8	Roussillon
July 11	La Savoie
July 16	Rochambeau
July 18	La Bourdonnais
July 19	La Touraine
July 23	Paris
July 23	Chicago
July 27	Leopoldina
July 30	France
Aug. 8	La Savoie
Aug. 13	Paris
Aug. 14	Niagara
Aug. 20	Rochambeau
Aug. 22	France
Aug. 26	Lafayette
Aug. 29	La Lorraine
Sept. 1	Chicago
Sept. 4	La Savoie
Sept. 10	Paris

Year 1921

FRENCH LINE
(Compagnie Generale Transatlantique)
Havre—Bordeaux—New York
(Continued)

N. Y.

Arrival	Steamer
Sept. 11	La Bourdonnais
Sept. 12	La Touraine
Sept. 12	Leopoldina
Sept. 17	France
Sept. 23	Lafayette
Sept. 24	Rochambeau
Sept. 26	La Lorraine
Oct. 1	Paris
Oct. 3	Roussillon
Oct. 4	Chicago
Oct. 11	France
Oct. 15	Leopoldina
Oct. 16	La Savoie
Oct. 18	La Bourdonnais
Oct. 24	La Lorraine
Oct. 28	Paris
Nov. 1	Rochambeau
Nov. 7	Lafayette
Nov. 14	La Savoie
Nov. 19	Paris
Nov. 21	Chicago
Nov. 29	La Touraine
Dec. 7	Roussillon
Dec. 12	Paris
Dec. 19	La Savoie
Dec. 27	La Lorraine
Dec. 27	La Bourdonnais

*To and from Hamburg.

HAMBURG AMERICAN LINE
Hamburg—New York

N. Y.

Arrival	Steamer
Feb. 14	Mount Clay*
Mar. 25	Mount Clay*
May 3	Mount Clay
May 10	Mount Carroll
June 14	Mount Clay
June 21	Mount Carroll
June 30	Mount Clinton
July 25	Mount Clay
Aug. 2	Mount Carroll
Aug. 9	Mount Clinton
Sept. 4	Mount Clay
Sept. 21	Mount Carroll*
Oct. 1	Bayern
Oct. 4	Mount Clinton
Oct. 18	Mount Clay
Nov. 1	Mount Carroll
Nov. 6	Hansa
Nov. 15	Mount Clinton
Nov. 29	Wuerttemberg
Dec. 1	Mount Clay
Dec. 10	Bayern
Dec. 13	Mount Carroll
Dec. 19	Hansa
Dec. 30	Mount Clinton

*Westbound passengers landed at Boston.

HOLLAND-AMERICA LINE
Rotterdam—New York

N. Y.

Arrival	Steamer
Jan. 3	Ryndam
Jan. 19	Rotterdam
Feb. 6	Ryndam
Feb. 13	New Amsterdam
Feb. 23	Rotterdam
Mar. 15	Ryndam
Mar. 20	New Amsterdam
Mar. 27	Noordam
Apr. 2	Rotterdam
Apr. 17	Ryndam
Apr. 23	New Amsterdam
Apr. 30	Noordam
May 14	Rotterdam
May 21	Ryndam
May 28	New Amsterdam
June 6	Noordam
June 18	Rotterdam
June 26	Ryndam
July 3	New Amsterdam
July 10	Noordam
July 22	Rotterdam
Aug. 1	Ryndam
Aug. 6	New Amsterdam
Aug. 13	Noordam
Aug. 26	Rotterdam
Sept. 3	Ryndam
Sept. 9	New Amsterdam
Sept. 17	Noordam
Sept. 30	Rotterdam
Oct. 7	Ryndam
Oct. 15	New Amsterdam
Oct. 23	Noordam
Nov. 5	Rotterdam
Nov. 12	Ryndam
Nov. 20	New Amsterdam
Nov. 26	Noordam
Dec. 6	Rotterdam
Dec. 22	Ryndam
Dec. 28	New Amsterdam

LA VELOCE LINE
Mediterranean—New York

N. Y.

Arrival	Steamer
Aug. 19	Europa
Oct. 14	Europa

LEYLAND LINE
Liverpool—Manchester—Boston

Boston

Arrival	Steamer
Jan. 29	Mercian
Feb. 11	Winifredian
May 17	Winifredian
June 25	Winifredian
July 30	Oxonian
Aug. 7	Winifredian
Aug. 31	Nortonian
Sept. 17	Winifredian
Oct. 1	Scythian
Oct. 5	Belgian
Oct. 24	Winifredian
Nov. 9	Novian
Dec. 1	Winifredian

LLOYD SABAUDO
Mediterranean—New York

N. Y.

Arrival	Steamer
Jan. 4	Pesaro
Jan. 7	Regina d'Italia
Feb. 17	Re d'Italia
Mar. 11	Regina d'Italia*
Mar. 12	San Rossore*
Apr. 5	Pesaro
Apr. 25	Re d'Italia
May 12	Regina d'Italia
May 25	San Rossore*
May 26	Pesaro
July 20	Pesaro
Sept. 16	Regina d'Italia
Nov. 3	Regina d'Italia
Dec. 19	Regina d'Italia

*Westbound passengers landed at Philadelphia.

NATIONAL GREEK LINE
Mediterranean—New York

N. Y.

Arrival	Steamer
Jan. 5	King Alexander
Jan. 20	Megali Hellas
Feb. 20	Themistocles
Feb. 28	King Alexander
Apr. 1	Megali Hellas
May 2	King Alexander
May 29	Megali Hellas
June 18	Themistocles
July 2	King Alexander
Aug. 1	Megali Hellas
Sept. 1	King Alexander
Sept. 14	Themistocles
Oct. 1	Megali Hellas
Nov. 4	King Alexander
Nov. 24	Themistocles
Dec. 1	Megali Hellas

NAVIGAZIONE GENERALE ITALIANA LINE
Mediterranean—New York

N. Y.

Arrival	Steamer
Jan. 25	Duca degli Abruzzi
Feb. 10	Duca D'Aosta
Feb. 18	F. Palasciano
Mar. 3	America*
Mar. 12	Duca degli Abruzzi
Mar. 31	Duca D'Aosta
Apr. 5	Caserta
Apr. 21	America*
Apr. 30	F. Palasciano
May 6	Taormina
May 12	Duca degli Abruzzi
May 18	Duca D'Aosta
May 29	Caserta
July 5	Duca D'Aosta
July 26	America
Aug. 13	Taormina
Sept. 28	Taormina
Oct. 4	America
Oct. 25	Palermo
Nov. 16	Taormina
Nov. 25	America

Year 1921

NAVIGAZIONE GENER-ALE ITALIANA LINE
Mediterranean—New York
(Continued)
N. Y.

Arrival	Steamer
Dec. 6	Colombo
Dec. 17	Palermo

*Westbound passengers landed at Philadelphia.

NORWEGIAN-AMERICA LINE
Kristiania—Bergen
New York
N. Y.

Arrival	Steamer
Jan. 18	Stavangerfjord
Feb. 7	Bergensfjord
Mar. 1	Stavangerfjord
Mar. 24	Bergensfjord
Apr. 13	Stavangerfjord
May 2	Bergensfjord
May 22	Stavangerfjord
June 6	Bergensfjord
June 28	Stavangerfjord
July 18	Bergensfjord
Aug. 9	Stavangerfjord
Aug. 29	Bergensfjord
Sept. 20	Stavangerfjord
Oct. 10	Bergensfjord
Oct. 31	Stavangerfjord
Nov. 23	Bergensfjord
Dec. 20	Stavangerfjord

OTTOMAN AMERICA LINE
Levant—Black Sea—
New York
N. Y.

Arrival	Steamer
July 18	Gul Djemal
Sept. 10	Gul Djemal
Nov. 18	Gul Djemal

POLISH-AMERICAN NAVIGATION CORP.
Danzig—New York
N. Y.

Arrival	Steamer
Jan. 29	Gdansk
Mar. 17	Gdansk
Apr. 27	Gdansk
June 8	Gdansk
July 14	Gdansk
Aug. 26	Gdansk
Oct. 1	Gdansk
Nov. 4	Gdansk
Dec. 7	Gdansk

RED STAR LINE
New York—Antwerp
N. Y.

Arrival	Steamer
Jan. 3	Lapland
Jan. 11	Finland
Jan. 20	Zeeland

RED STAR LINE
New York—Antwerp
(Continued)
N. Y.

Arrival	Steamer
Feb. 2	Poland
Feb. 7	Lapland
Feb. 16	Finland*
Feb. 24	Zeeland*
Mar. 3	Kroonland
Mar. 23	Finland
Mar. 27	Lapland
Apr. 5	Kroonland
Apr. 17	Zeeland
May 1	Lapland
May 4	Finland
May 9	Kroonland
May 28	Zeeland
June 5	Lapland
June 12	Finland
June 24	Kroonland
June 26	Zeeland
July 9	Lapland
July 18	Finland
Aug. 1	Zeeland
Aug. 9	Kroonland
Aug. 14	Lapland
Aug. 21	Finland
Sept. 4	Zeeland
Sept. 12	Kroonland
Sept. 17	Lapland
Sept. 25	Finland
Oct. 9	Zeeland
Oct. 17	Kroonland
Oct. 22	Lapland
Nov. 5	Gothland
Nov. 7	Finland
Nov. 12	Zeeland
Nov. 27	Lapland
Dec. 12	Kroonland
Dec. 20	Zeeland

*Westbound passengers landed at Boston.

RED STAR LINE
Danzig—New York
N. Y.

Arrival	Steamer
Jan. 16	Gothland
Nov. 25	Samland

RED STAR LINE
Danzig—Philadelphia
Phila.

Arrival	Steamer
Mar. 18	Samland
Mar. 29	Gothland
May 19	Poland
July 2	Samland
Oct. 10	Samland

ROYAL MAIL STEAM PACKET COMPANY
Hamburg—New York
N. Y.

Arrival	Steamer
May 13	Orbita
May 27	Oropesa

ROYAL MAIL STEAM PACKET COMPANY
Hamburg—New York
(Continued)
N. Y.

Arrival	Steamer
June 10	Orduna
June 24	Orbita
July 8	Oropesa
July 22	Orduna
Aug. 5	Orbita
Aug. 19	Oropesa
Sept. 2	Orduna
Sept. 16	Orbita
Sept. 30	Oropesa
Oct. 14	Orduna
Nov. 4	Orbita
Nov. 19	Oropesa
Dec. 2	Orduna
Dec. 16	Orbita

ROYAL MAIL STEAM PACKET COMPANY
Scandinavian Ports—
New York
N. Y.

Arrival	Steamer
Jan. 19	Frederik VIII
Feb. 16	United States
Mar. 10	Hellig Olav
Mar. 26	Oscar II
Mar. 31	United States
Apr. 13	Frederik VIII
Apr. 20	Hellig Olav
May 4	Oscar II
May 11	United States
May 24	Frederik VIII
June 1	Hellig Olav
June 15	Oscar II
June 21	United States
July 5	Frederik VIII
July 13	Hellig Olav
July 26	Oscar II
Aug. 3	United States
Aug. 16	Frederik VIII
Aug. 23	Hellig Olav
Sept. 6	Oscar II
Sept. 13	United States
Sept. 27	Frederik VIII
Oct. 4	Hellig Olav
Oct. 17	Oscar II
Oct. 24	United States
Nov. 8	Frederik VIII
Nov. 19	Hellig Olav
Nov. 28	Oscar II
Dec. 4	United States
Dec. 24	Frederik VIII

SICULA AMERICANA LINE
Mediterranean—New York
N. Y.

Arrival	Steamer
Feb. 17	Guglielmo Peirce
Apr. 15	Guglielmo Peirce
June 3	Guglielmo Peirce
Aug. 10	Guglielmo Peirce
Sept. 25	Guglielmo Peirce
Nov. 14	Guglielmo Peirce

Year 1921

SWEDISH-AMERICAN LINE
Gothenburg—New York
N. Y.

Arrival	Steamer
Jan. 12	Stockholm
Feb. 3	Drottningholm
Mar. 1	Stockholm
Mar. 15	Drottningholm
Apr. 14	Stockholm
Apr. 25	Drottningholm
May 24	Stockholm
June 1	Drottningholm
June 30	Stockholm
July 15	Drottningholm
Aug. 11	Stockholm
Aug. 24	Drottningholm
Sept. 21	Stockholm
Oct. 4	Drottningholm
Nov. 2	Stockholm
Nov. 22	Drottningholm
Dec. 14	Stockholm

TRANSATLANTICA ITALIANA LINE
Mediterranean—New York
N. Y.

Arrival	Steamer
Jan. 20	Dante Alighieri
Feb. 3	Giuseppe Verdi
Feb. 17	Henry R. Mallory
Feb. 25	Orizaba
Mar. 9	Dante Alighieri
Mar. 22	Giuseppe Verdi
Apr. 23	Dante Alighieri
May 19	Giuseppe Verdi
June 15	Dante Alighieri
July 12	Giuseppe Verdi
Aug. 3	Dante Alighieri
Sept. 1	Giuseppe Verdi
Sept. 23	Dante Alighieri
Oct. 18	Giuseppe Verdi
Nov. 9	Dante Alighieri
Dec. 5	Giuseppe Verdi
Dec. 31	Dante Alighieri

TRANSMEDITERRANEA LINE
Spain—New York
N. Y.

Arrival	Steamer
Feb. 18	Escolano

TRANSOCEANICA LINE
Mediterranean—New York
N. Y.

Arrival	Steamer
Feb. 2	San Giovanni
Mar. 19	San Giovanni
May 18	San Giovanni
June 3	San Giorgio
July 23	San Giorgio
Aug. 26	San Giovanni
Sept. 21	San Giorgio

TRANSPORTES MARITIMOS ESTADO
(Portuguese Line)
Portugal—New York
N. Y.

Arrival	Steamer
May 3	Mormugao
June 10	Sao Vicente

UNITED AMERICAN LINES, INC.
Joint Service with Hamburg-American Lines, Inc.
See page 205

UNITED STATES LINES
Boulogne—London—
New York
N. Y.

Arrival	Steamer
Sept. 11	Old North State
Oct. 2	Centennial State
Oct. 17	Old North State
Nov. 6	Centennial State
Nov. 21	Panhandle State
Dec. 11	Centennial State
Dec. 21	Panhandle State

UNITED STATES LINES
Bremen—Danzig—
New York
N. Y.

Arrival	Steamer
Aug. 27	George Washington
Sept. 3	Princess Matoika
Sept. 15	Potomac
Sept. 22	America
Sept. 27	George Washington
Oct. 5	Hudson
Oct. 17	Princess Matoika
Oct. 24	America
Oct. 28	George Washington
Nov. 2	Potomac
Nov. 19	Hudson
Nov. 26	America
Dec. 2	Princess Matoika
Dec. 3	George Washington
Dec. 18	Potomac
Dec. 24	America

UNITED STATES MAIL STEAMSHIP CO., INC.
Boulogne—London
New York
N. Y.

Arrival	Steamer
Jan. 15	Old North State
Jan. 30	Panhandle State
Feb. 14	Old North State
Mar. 6	Panhandle State
Mar. 21	Old North State
Apr. 10	Panhandle State
Apr. 24	Old North State
May 16	Panhandle State
June 2	Old North State
June 24	Panhandle State
July 4	Old North State
July 24	Centennial State
Aug. 8	Old North State
Aug. 25	Centennial State

UNITED STATES MAIL STEAMSHIP CO., INC.
Bremen—Danzig—New York
N. Y.

Arrival	Steamer
Feb. 10	Susquehanna
Mar. 28	New Rochelle
Apr. 3	Susquehanna
Apr. 26	Potomac
May 19	Hudson
June 12	Potomac
July 5	Hudson
July 19	America
July 25	Potomac
Aug. 15	Hudson
Aug. 20	America

UNITED STATES MAIL STEAMSHIP CO., INC.
Mediterranean—New York
N. Y.

Arrival	Steamer
Mar. 3	Princess Matoika
Apr. 20	Princess Matoika
May 19	Pocahontas
June 4	Princess Matoika

UNITED STATES MAIL STEAMSHIP CO., INC.
Mediterranean—Boston
Boston

Arrival	Steamer
Apr. 2	Pocahontas

WHITE STAR LINE
Liverpool—New York
N. Y.

Arrival	Steamer
Jan. 8	Celtic
Jan. 19	Megantic
Jan. 20	Vedic
Jan. 29	Cedric
Feb. 18	Celtic
Mar. 2	Vedic
Mar. 4	Cedric
Mar. 26	Celtic
Apr. 8	Cedric
Apr. 25	Celtic
May 9	Cedric
May 27	Celtic
June 6	Cedric
June 20	Celtic
July 3	Cedric
July 18	Celtic
July 25	Baltic
Aug. 1	Cedric
Aug. 15	Celtic
Aug. 22	Baltic
Aug. 28	Cedric
Sept. 12	Celtic
Sept. 19	Baltic
Sept. 25	Cedric
Oct. 10	Celtic
Oct. 17	Baltic
Oct. 24	Cedric
Nov. 2	Vedic
Nov. 14	Baltic
Nov. 22	Cedric
Nov. 28	Celtic
Dec. 11	Baltic
Dec. 19	Cedric
Dec. 26	Celtic

Year 1921

WHITE STAR LINE
Southampton—New York
N. Y.

Arrival	Steamer
Jan. 15	Adriatic
Feb. 12	Adriatic
Mar. 17	Olympic
Apr. 1	Adriatic
Apr. 13	Olympic
Apr. 29	Adriatic
May 11	Olympic
May 27	Adriatic
June 1	Olympic
June 22	Olympic
July 1	Adriatic
July 13	Olympic
July 29	Adriatic
Aug. 10	Olympic
Aug. 25	Adriatic
Aug. 30	Olympic
Sept. 16	Arabic
Sept. 20	Olympic
Sept. 30	Adriatic
Oct. 11	Olympic
Oct. 28	Adriatic

WHITE STAR LINE
Southampton—New York
(Continued)
N. Y.

Arrival	Steamer
Nov. 1	Olympic
Nov. 24	Adriatic
Dec. 6	Olympic
Dec. 23	Adriatic
Dec. 28	Olympic

WHITE STAR LINE
Liverpool—Philadelphia
Phila.

Arrival	Steamer
Jan. 23	Haverford
Mar. 3	Haverford
Apr. 13	Haverford
May 29	Haverford
July 4	Haverford
Aug. 8	Haverford
Sept. 12	Haverford
Oct. 16	Haverford
Nov. 30	Haverford

WHITE STAR LINE
Halifax—Mediterranean—
Boston—New York
Boston

Arrival	Steamer
Feb. 15	Canopic
Mar. 1	Cretic
Apr. 9	Canopic
Apr. 27	Cretic
June 6	Canopic
Aug. 1	Canopic
Aug. 25	Cretic
Sept. 22	Canopic
Oct. 15	Cretic
Nov. 11	Canopic
Nov. 29	Cretic

N. Y.

Arrival	Steamer
June 1	Gothland
Oct. 25	Arabic
Dec. 2	Arabic

Year 1922

AMERICAN LINE
Hamburg—New York
N.Y.

Arrival	Steamer
Jan. 3	Mongolia
Jan. 14	Minnekahda
Feb. 1	Haverford
Feb. 17	Mongolia
Mar. 1	Minnekahda
Mar. 20	Haverford
Apr. 9	Minnekahda
Apr. 28	Haverford
May 17	Minnekahda
May 24	Manchuria
May 30	St. Paul
June 21	Minnekahda
June 27	Manchuria
July 7	St. Paul
July 18	Mongolia
July 26	Minnekahda
Aug. 1	Manchuria
Aug. 10	St. Paul
Aug. 22	Mongolia
Aug. 29	Minnekahda
Sept. 5	Manchuria
Sept. 12	St. Paul
Sept. 27	Mongolia
Oct. 4	Minnekahda
Oct. 10	Manchuria
Oct. 31	Mongolia
Nov. 7	Minnekahda
Nov. 21	Manchuria
Dec. 6	Mongolia
Dec. 15	Minnekahda
Dec. 29	Manchuria

AMERICAN NEAR EAST & BLACK SEA LINE
Levant—Black Sea—
New York
N.Y.

Arrival	Steamer
Jan. 24	Acropolis
Apr. 10	Acropolis
July 7	Acropolis
Sept. 1	Acropolis

ANCHOR LINE
Liverpool—Glasgow—
Boston
Boston

Arrival	Steamer
Aug. 20	Algeria

ANCHOR LINE
Mediterranean—Adriatic
New Bedford—New York
N.Y.

Arrival	Steamer
Mar. 10	Italia
May 30	Italia
Aug. 1	Italia
Sept. 6	Cameronia

ANCHOR LINE
Glasgow—New York
N.Y.

Arrival	Steamer
Jan. 21	Algeria
Jan. 24	Assyria
Mar. 7	Algeria
Mar. 16	Assyria
Apr. 11	Algeria
May 17	Assyria
May 21	Columbia
May 28	Cameronia
June 7	Algeria
June 18	Columbia
June 25	Cameronia
July 3	Assyria
July 10	Algeria
July 16	Columbia
July 29	Elysia
Aug. 6	Assyria
Aug. 13	Columbia
Aug. 21	Algeria
Aug. 28	City of London
Sept. 10	Columbia
Sept. 19	Algeria
Sept. 25	Tuscania
Oct. 1	Cameronia
Oct. 8	Columbia
Oct. 17	Assyria
Oct. 23	Tuscania
Oct. 29	Cameronia
Nov. 5	Columbia
Nov. 15	Algeria
Nov. 22	Assyria
Dec. 4	Columbia
Dec. 22	Saturnia

ANCHOR LINE
Liverpool—New York
N.Y.

Arrival	Steamer
Mar. 8	Cameronia
Apr. 3	Cameronia

ANCHOR LINE
Liverpool—Glasgow—
Boston
Boston

Arrival	Steamer
Aug. 20	Algeria

ANCHOR LINE
Mediterranean & Adriatic—
New Bedford—New York
N.Y.

Arrival	Steamer
May 10	Italia
May 30	Italia
Aug. 1	Italia
Sept. 6	Cameronia

BALTIC-AMERICA LINE
Hamburg—Danzig—Libau
New York
N.Y.

Arrival	Steamer
Jan. 7	Estonia
Jan. 27	Lituania

BALTIC-AMERICA LINE
Hamburg—Danzig—Libau
New York
(Continued)
N.Y.

Arrival	Steamer
Feb. 17	Polonia
Mar. 8	Estonia
Mar. 18	Latvia
Mar. 31	Polonia
Apr. 12	Estonia
Apr. 29	Lituania
May 5	Latvia
May 12	Polonia
May 25	Estonia
June 9	Lituania
June 23	Polonia
July 1	Latvia
July 6	Estonia
July 21	Lituania
Aug. 3	Polonia
Aug. 17	Latvia
Aug. 31	Lituania
Sept. 13	Polonia
Sept. 27	Estonia
Oct. 12	Lituania
Oct. 26	Polonia
Nov. 8	Estonia
Nov. 30	Lituania
Dec. 21	Estonia

COMPANIA TRANSATLANTICA LINE
(Spanish Line)
Spain—New York
N.Y.

Arrival	Steamer
Jan. 15	Manuel Calvo
Feb. 15	Leon XIII
Mar. 16	Montserrat
Apr. 16	Manuel Calvo
May 17	Reina Ma. Cristina
May 28	Antonio Lopez
June 13	P. de Satrustegui
July 13	Manuel Calvo
Aug. 13	Montserrat
Sept. 14	P. de Satrustegui
Oct. 13	Manuel Calvo
Nov. 7	Reina Ma. Cristina
Nov. 13	Montserrat
Dec. 15	P. de Satrustegui

COSULICH LINE
Mediterranean—New York
N.Y.

Arrival	Steamer
Jan. 18	Pres. Wilson
May 15	Pres. Wilson
May 31	Belvedere
July 1	Pres. Wilson
July 1	Argentina
Aug. 3	Belvedere
Aug. 17	Pres. Wilson
Sept. 1	Argentina
Oct. 8	Belvedere
Oct. 16	Pres. Wilson
Nov. 2	Argentina
Nov. 30	Pres. Wilson

Year 1922

CUNARD LINE
Mediterranean—Adriatic New York
N. Y.

Arrival	Steamer
Jan. 15	Caronia
Mar. 30	Caronia
Apr. 15	Carmania

CUNARD LINE
Liverpool—Boston
Boston

Arrival	Steamer
Apr. 28	Samaria
May 25	Samaria
July 1	Laconia
Sept. 15	Tyrrhenia
Oct. 14	Ausonia
Oct. 28	Tyrrhenia
Nov. 12	Samaria
Nov. 26	Albania
Dec. 20	Ausonia

CUNARD LINE
Liverpool—New York
N. Y.

Arrival	Steamer
Jan. 20	Scythia
Jan. 31	Vandyk
Feb. 12	Albania
Feb. 24	Scythia
Mar. 26	Albania
Apr. 18	Scythia
May 12	Carmania
May 20	Scythia
June 4	Laconia
June 10	Carmania
June 17	Scythia
July 3	Laconia
July 8	Carmania
July 15	Scythia
July 29	Laconia
Aug. 12	Carmania
Aug. 26	Scythia
Sept. 3	Laconia
Sept. 8	Carmania
Sept. 22	Scythia
Sept. 30	Laconia
Oct. 6	Carmania
Oct. 15	Ausonia
Oct. 21	Scythia
Oct. 29	Tyrrhenia
Nov. 3	Carmania
Nov. 13	Samaria
Nov. 15	Laconia
Nov. 20	Scythia
Nov. 26	Caronia
Dec. 4	Andania
Dec. 5	Tyrrhenia
Dec. 11	Carmania
Dec. 22	Ausonia
Dec. 27	Caronia

CUNARD LINE
Southampton—New York
N. Y.

Arrival	Steamer
Jan. 17	Saxonia
Jan. 30	Carmania
Feb. 3	Aquitania

CUNARD LINE
Southampton—New York
(Continued)
N. Y.

Arrival	Steamer
Feb. 25	Aquitania
Mar. 17	Aquitania
Mar. 31	Mauretania
Apr. 7	Aquitania
Apr. 21	Mauretania
Apr. 28	Aquitania
May 12	Mauretania
May 19	Aquitania
May 27	Berengaria
June 2	Mauretania
June 9	Aquitania
June 17	Berengaria
June 23	Mauretania
July 1	Aquitania
July 7	Berengaria
July 14	Mauretania
July 28	Aquitania
Aug. 4	Berengaria
Aug. 11	Mauretania
Aug. 18	Aquitania
Sept. 1	Berengaria
Sept. 2	Mauretania
Sept. 8	Aquitania
Sept. 20	Berengaria
Sept. 23	Mauretania
Sept. 30	Aquitania
Oct. 11	Berengaria
Oct. 20	Aquitania
Nov. 3	Mauretania
Nov. 10	Aquitania
Nov. 17	Berengaria
Nov. 24	Mauretania
Dec. 1	Aquitania
Dec. 8	Berengaria
Dec. 18	Antonia
Dec. 31	Berengaria

CUNARD LINE
Cherbourg—Plymouth—London—Hamburg—New York
N. Y.

Arrival	Steamer
Mar. 9	Saxonia
May 9	Caronia
May 17	Saxonia
June 10	Caronia
June 26	Saxonia
July 23	Caronia
July 31	Saxonia
Aug. 26	Caronia
Sept. 2	Saxonia
Sept. 26	Caronia
Oct. 9	Saxonia
Oct. 29	Caronia
Nov. 21	Saxonia

FABRE LINE
Mediterranean—New York
N. Y.

Arrival	Steamer
Jan. 27	Canada
Feb. 17	Providence
Mar. 7	Braga
Mar. 15	Patria
Mar. 26	Canada

FABRE LINE
Mediterranean—New York
(Continued)
N. Y.

Arrival	Steamer
Apr. 4	Britannia
Apr. 14	Providence
Apr. 26	Asia
May 18	Patria
May 22	Canada
June 8	Providence
June 20	Braga
July 8	Patria
July 14	Asia
July 28	Providence
Aug. 10	Britannia
Aug. 26	Patria
Sept. 1	Madonna
Sept. 3	Braga
Sept. 18	Providence
Sept. 23	Roma
Oct. 3	Britannia
Oct. 10	Asia
Nov. 1	Patria
Nov. 2	Madonna
Nov. 3	Canada
Nov. 12	Providence
Dec. 3	Braga
Dec. 4	Roma
Dec. 8	Patria
Dec. 11	Britannia

FRENCH LINE
(Compagnie Generale Transatlantique)
Havre—Bordeaux—New York
N. Y.

Arrival	Steamer
Jan. 3	La Touraine
Jan. 10	Rochambeau
Jan. 16	Paris
Jan. 21	Chicago
Jan. 24	La Lorraine
Jan. 31	La Touraine
Feb. 5	Rousillon
Feb. 6	La Savoie
Feb. 15	Rochambeau
Feb. 18	Paris
Feb. 28	La Lorraine
Mar. 6	Bourdonnais
Mar. 7	La Savoie
Mar. 11	Paris
Mar. 22	Rochambeau
Mar. 27	La Lorraine
Apr. 1	Paris
Apr. 1	Chicago
Apr. 8	France
Apr. 8	La Bourdonnais
Apr. 17	La Touraine
Apr. 21	Rochambeau
Apr. 22	Paris
May 1	La Savoie
May 6	France
May 6	Chicago
May 13	La Bourdonnais
May 15	Lafayette
May 17	Niagara
May 20	Paris
May 18	La Touraine
May 26	Rochambeau

Year 1922

FRENCH LINE
(Compagnie Generale Transatlantique)
Havre—Bordeaux—New York
(Continued)
N. Y.

Arrival	Steamer
May 27	France
May 27	La Lorraine
June 5	La Savoie
June 9	Chicago
June 10	Paris
June 19	Lafayette
June 21	Niagara
June 22	La Touraine
June 24	France
June 24	Roussillon
June 26	La Lorraine
June 30	Rochambeau
July 1	Paris
July 8	La Bourdonnais
July 11	La Savoie
July 14	Chicago
July 22	France
July 29	Paris
July 30	Niagara
Aug. 6	La Savoie
Aug. 11	Roussillon
Aug. 14	Lafayette
Aug. 19	Paris
Aug. 25	Chicago
Aug. 26	France
Sept. 1	La Touraine
Sept. 6	La Savoie
Sept. 6	Niagara
Sept. 8	Rochambeau
Sept. 9	Paris
Sept. 11	La Lorraine
Sept. 15	Roussillon
Sept. 22	France
Sept. 22	La Bourdonnais
Sept. 27	Lafayette
Sept. 29	Chicago
Oct. 1	Paris
Oct. 5	La Touraine
Oct. 11	La Lorraine
Oct. 12	Rochambeau
Oct. 13	France
Oct. 16	La Savoie
Oct. 21	Roussillon
Oct. 22	Lafayette
Oct. 28	Paris
Nov. 7	Chicago
Nov. 12	France
Nov. 17	Rochambeau
Nov. 17	Paris
Nov. 21	Niagara
Nov. 27	La Savoie
Dec. 7	Roussillon
Dec. 9	Paris
Dec. 21	La Bourdonnais
Dec. 27	La Savoie
Dec. 28	Niagara

HAMBURG-AMERICAN LINE
Hamburg—New York
N. Y.

Arrival	Steamer
Jan. 8	Wuerttemberg
Jan. 20	Bayern

HAMBURG-AMERICAN LINE
Hamburg—New York
(Continued)
N. Y.

Arrival	Steamer
Jan. 31	Hansa
Feb. 19	Wuerttemberg
Mar. 30	Wuerttemberg
Apr. 7	Bayern
Apr. 25	Hansa
May 13	Wuerttemberg
May 25	Bayern
June 4	Hansa
June 22	Wuerttemberg
June 26	Bayern
Aug. 16	Wuerttemberg
Aug. 22	Hansa
Sept. 2	Rugia
Sept. 14	Bayern
Sept. 27	Wuerttemberg
Oct. 8	Hansa
Oct. 25	Bayern
Nov. 9	Wuerttemberg
Nov. 19	Hansa

HOLLAND-AMERICA LINE
Rotterdam—New York
N. Y.

Arrival	Steamer
Jan. 16	Noordam
Jan. 30	Ryndam
Feb. 13	New Amsterdam
Feb. 19	Noordam
Mar. 7	Ryndam
Mar. 19	New Amsterdam
Mar. 26	Noordam
Apr. 2	Rotterdam
Apr. 9	Ryndam
Apr. 23	New Amsterdam
May 1	Noordam
May 5	Rotterdam
May 13	Ryndam
May 27	New Amsterdam
June 3	Noordam
June 9	Rotterdam
June 18	Ryndam
July 1	New Amsterdam
July 9	Noordam
July 14	Rotterdam
July 22	Ryndam
Aug. 6	New Amsterdam
Aug. 12	Noordam
Aug. 18	Rotterdam
Aug. 26	Ryndam
Sept. 9	New Amsterdam
Sept. 16	Noordam
Sept. 22	Rotterdam
Sept. 30	Ryndam
Oct. 14	New Amsterdam
Oct. 22	Noordam
Oct. 27	Rotterdam
Nov. 4	Ryndam
Nov. 15	Volendam
Nov. 26	Noordam
Dec. 1	Rotterdam
Dec. 17	Ryndam

LA VELOCE LINE
Mediterranean—New York
N. Y.

Arrival	Steamer
July 8	Europa
Aug. 29	Europa

LEYLAND LINE
Liverpool—Boston
Boston

Arrival	Steamer
Jan. 10	Winifredian
Feb. 3	Caledonian
Mar. 3	Winifredian
Apr. 11	Winifredian
May 26	Winifredian
June 23	Median
July 12	Winifredian
Aug. 23	Winifredian
Sept. 1	Caledonian
Oct. 1	Winifredian
Nov. 11	Winifredian
Dec. 8	Bayern
Dec. 21	Winifredian
Dec. 23	Wuerttemberg

LLOYD SABAUDO
Mediterranean—New York
N. Y.

Arrival	Steamer
Apr. 3	Regina d'Italia
May 26	Conte Rosso
July 1	Conte Rosso
Aug. 5	Conte Rosso
Sept. 9	Conte Rosso
Oct. 21	Conte Rosso
Dec. 1	Conte Rosso

NATIONAL GREEK LINE
Mediterranean—New York
N. Y.

Arrival	Steamer
Jan. 2	Constantinople
Jan. 20	King Alexander
Feb. 7	Megali Hellas
Feb. 18	Themistocles
Mar. 15	Constantinople
Apr. 13	Megali Hellas
May 7	Themistocles
May 21	Constantinople
June 16	Megali Hellas
July 1	King Alexander
July 14	Themistocles
Aug. 1	Constantinople
Aug. 16	Megali Hellas
Sept. 1	King Alexander
Sept. 27	Themistocles
Oct. 2	Constantinople
Nov. 1	King Alexander
Dec. 8	Constantinople

NAVIGAZIONE GENERALE ITALIANA LINE
Mediterranean—New York
N. Y.

Arrival	Steamer
Jan. 12	Taormina
Jan. 28	America
Feb. 8	Colombo
Mar. 2	Taormina

Year 1922

NAVIGAZIONE GENER-ALE ITALIANA LINE
Mediterranean—New York
(Continued)

N. Y.

Arrival	Steamer
Mar. 23	Colombo
Apr. 14	Taormina
Apr. 28	America
May 9	Colombo
May 28	Taormina
June 7	Duca Degli Abruzzi
June 14	America
July 4	Colombo
July 19	Taormina
July 26	America
Aug. 9	Colombo
Aug. 22	Guilio Cesare
Sept. 1	Taormina
Sept. 8	America
Sept. 20	Colombo
Oct. 1	Guilio Cesare
Oct. 12	Taormina
Nov. 1	America
Nov. 8	Colombo
Nov. 25	Taormina
Dec. 5	America
Dec. 20	Colombo

NORTH GERMAN LLOYD
Bremen—New York

N. Y.

Arrival	Steamer
Feb. 26	Seydlitz
Mar. 13	Hannover
Mar. 23	Yorck
Apr. 6	Seydlitz
Apr. 21	Hannover
May 5	Yorck
May 18	Seydlitz
June 1	Hannover
June 15	Yorck
July 1	Seydlitz
July 13	Hannover
Aug. 14	Yorck
Aug. 17	Seydlitz
Aug. 25	Hannover
Sept. 11	Yorck
Sept. 21	Seydlitz
Sept. 28	Sierra Nevada
Oct. 6	Hannover
Oct. 18	Yorck
Oct. 30	Seydlitz
Nov. 2	Sierra Nevada
Nov. 19	Hannover
Nov. 29	Yorck
Dec. 14	Seydlitz

NORWEGIAN-AMERICA LINE
Kristiania—Bergen—New York

N. Y.

Arrival	Steamer
Jan. 25	Bergensfjord
Feb. 14	Stavangerfjord
Mar. 9	Bergensfjord
Mar. 28	Stavangerfjord
Apr. 17	Bergensfjord
May 9	Stavangerfjord

NORWEGIAN-AMERICA LINE
Kristiania—Bergen—New York
(Continued)

N. Y.

Arrival	Steamer
May 29	Bergensfjord
June 20	Stavangerfjord
July 10	Bergensfjord
July 31	Stavangerfjord
Aug. 21	Bergensfjord
Sept. 11	Stavangerfjord
Oct. 2	Bergensfjord
Oct. 24	Stavangerfjord
Nov. 14	Bergensfjord
Dec. 4	Stavangerfjord
Dec. 12	Bergensfjord

RED STAR LINE
Antwerp—New York

N. Y.

Arrival	Steamer
Jan. 4	Finland
Jan. 16	Kroonland
Jan. 27	Zeeland
Jan. 31	Lapland
Feb. 6	Finland
Feb. 17	Gothland
Feb. 21	Kroonland
Mar. 3	Zeeland
Mar. 14	Finland
Mar. 22	Gothland
Mar. 26	Kroonland
Apr. 2	Lapland
Apr. 16	Finland
Apr. 24	Zeeland
May 1	Kroonland
May 7	Lapland
May 16	Gothland
May 22	Finland
May 28	Zeeland
June 4	Kroonland
June 11	Lapland
June 19	Gothland
June 25	Finland
July 2	Zeeland
July 10	Kroonland
July 16	Lapland
July 30	Finland
Aug. 6	Zeeland
Aug. 13	Kroonland
Aug. 19	Lapland
Aug. 28	Gothland
Sept. 3	Finland
Sept. 10	Zeeland
Sept. 17	Kroonland
Sept. 23	Lapland
Oct. 4	Gothland
Oct. 8	Finland
Oct. 15	Zeeland
Oct. 22	Kroonland
Oct. 28	Lapland
Nov. 6	Gothland
Nov. 13	Finland
Nov. 20	Zeeland
Nov. 27	Kroonland
Dec. 3	Lapland
Dec. 25	Zeeland
Dec. 31	Finland

RED STAR LINE
Danzig—New York

N. Y.

Arrival	Steamer
Jan. 11	Samland
Mar. 23	Samland
May 6	Samland
June 17	Samland
July 28	Samland
Sept. 8	Samland
Nov. 1	Samland

ROYAL MAIL STEAM PACKET CO.
Hamburg—New York

N. Y.

Arrival	Steamer
Jan. 1	Araguaya
Jan. 13	Orduna
Feb. 11	Orbita
Feb. 24	Orduna
Mar. 12	Oropesa
Mar. 24	Orbita
Apr. 7	Orduna
Apr. 24	Oropesa
May 8	Orbita
May 22	Orduna
June 5	Oropesa
June 19	Orbita
July 1	Vestris
July 3	Orduna
July 18	Oropesa
July 21	Vandyck
July 31	Orbita
Aug. 7	Orduna
Aug. 18	Vauban
Aug. 22	Oropesa
Sept. 1	Vandyck
Sept. 4	Orbita
Sept. 11	Orduna
Sept. 25	Oropesa
Oct. 9	Orbita
Oct. 16	Orduna
Oct. 31	Oropesa
Nov. 20	Orduna
Dec. 11	Orbita
Dec. 18	Araguaya

SCANDINAVIAN-AMER-ICAN LINE
Scandinavian Ports—New York

N. Y.

Arrival	Steamer
Jan. 31	Hellig Olav
Feb. 25	United States
Mar. 14	Oscar II
Apr. 20	Hellig Olav
May 2	Frederik VIII
May 9	Oscar II
May 22	United States
May 29	Hellig Olav
June 12	Frederik VIII
June 20	Oscar II
July 4	United States
July 10	Hellig Olav
July 24	Frederik VIII
Aug. 1	Oscar II
Aug. 14	United States
Aug. 21	Hellig Olav

Year 1922

SCANDINAVIAN-AMERICAN LINE
Scandinavian Ports—New York
(Continued)

N. Y.

Arrival	Steamer
Sept. 4	Frederik VIII
Sept. 11	Oscar II
Sept. 26	United States
Oct. 3	Hellig Olav
Oct. 16	Frederik VIII
Oct. 24	Oscar II
Nov. 6	United States
Nov. 21	Hellig Olav
Nov. 27	Frederik VIII
Dec. 25	United States

SICULA AMERICANA LINE
Mediterranean—New York

N. Y.

Arrival	Steamer
July 3	Guglielmo Peirce
Aug. 31	Guglielmo Peirce
Oct. 14	Guglielmo Peirce
Nov. 30	Guglielmo Peirce

SWEDISH-AMERICAN LINE
Gothenburg—New York

N. Y.

Arrival	Steamer
Jan. 26	Stockholm
Mar. 6	Stockholm
Apr. 12	Stockholm
May 20	Stockholm
May 30	Drottningholm
July 9	Drottningholm
July 19	Stockholm
Aug. 12	Drottningholm
Aug. 28	Stockholm
Sept. 16	Drottningholm
Oct. 7	Stockholm
Oct. 21	Drottningholm
Nov. 15	Stockholm
Nov. 28	Drottningholm

TRANSATLANTICA ITALIANA LINE
Mediterranean—New York

N. Y.

Arrival	Steamer
Feb. 11	Giuseppe Verdi
Apr. 8	Giuseppe Verdi
May 13	Dante Alighieri
June 6	Giuseppe Verdi
July 1	Dante Alighieri
July 23	Giuseppe Verdi
Aug. 18	Dante Alighieri
Sept. 8	Giuseppe Verdi
Oct. 2	Dante Alighieri
Oct. 20	Giuseppe Verdi
Dec. 1	Giuseppe Verdi

UNITED AMERICAN LINES, INC.
Hamburg—New York

N. Y.

Arrival	Steamer
Jan. 9	Mount Clay

UNITED AMERICAN LINES, INC.
Hamburg—New York
(Continued)

N. Y.

Arrival	Steamer
Jan. 25	Mount Carroll
Feb. 7	Mount Clinton
Mar. 9	Mount Carroll
Mar. 21	Mount Clinton
Apr. 10	Mount Clay
Apr. 23	Resolute
May 3	Mount Clinton
May 13	Reliance
May 17	Mount Clay
May 27	Resolute
May 31	Mount Carroll
June 9	Reliance
June 13	Mount Clinton
June 23	Resolute
June 23	Mount Clay
July 7	Reliance
July 11	Mount Carroll
July 21	Resolute
July 25	Mount Clinton
Aug. 4	Reliance
Aug. 7	Mount Clay
Aug. 18	Resolute
Aug. 23	Mount Carroll
Sept. 1	Reliance
Sept. 5	Mount Clinton
Sept. 14	Resolute
Sept. 17	Mount Clay
Sept. 29	Reliance
Oct. 4	Mount Carroll
Oct. 12	Resolute
Oct. 17	Mount Clinton
Oct. 26	Reliance
Oct. 30	Mount Clay
Nov. 10	Resolute
Nov. 14	Mount Carroll
Nov. 24	Reliance
Nov. 28	Mount Clinton
Dec. 12	Mount Clay
Dec. 26	Mount Carroll

UNITED STATES LINES
Queenstown, Plymouth, Cherbourg, London—New York

N. Y.

Arrival	Steamer
Jan. 10	Centennial State
Jan. 25	Panhandle State
Feb. 14	Centennial State
Mar. 2	Panhandle State
Mar. 20	Centennial State
Apr. 8	Old North State
Apr. 24	Pres. Adams
Apr. 30	Pres. Monroe
May 10	Pres. Van Buren
May 27	Pres. Adams
June 2	Pres. Garfield
June 13	Pres. Van Buren
June 27	Pres. Garfield
July 5	Pres. Monroe
July 12	Pres. Adams
July 18	Pres. Van Buren
July 25	Pres. Polk
Aug. 1	Pres. Garfield
Aug. 12	Pres. Monroe

UNITED STATES LINES
Queenstown, Plymouth, Cherbourg, London—New York
(Continued)

N. Y.

Arrival	Steamer
Aug. 15	Pres. Adams
Aug. 22	Pres. Van Buren
Aug. 29	Pres. Polk
Sept. 5	Pres. Garfield
Sept. 12	Pres. Monroe
Sept. 19	Pres. Adams
Sept. 26	Pres. Van Buren
Oct. 4	Pres. Polk
Oct. 11	Pres. Garfield
Oct. 17	Pres. Monroe
Oct. 24	Pres. Adams
Oct. 31	Pres. Van Buren
Nov. 8	Pres. Polk
Nov. 15	Pres. Garfield
Nov. 21	Pres. Monroe
Nov. 28	Pres. Adams
Dec. 6	Pres. Van Buren
Dec. 13	Pres. Polk
Dec. 21	Pres. Garfield
Dec. 29	Pres. Monroe

UNITED STATES LINES
Plymouth, Cherbourg, Bremen, Danzig—New York

N. Y.

Arrival	Steamer
Jan. 5	Hudson
Jan. 14	George Washington
Jan. 23	Princess Matoika
Jan. 30	America
Feb. 8	Potomac
Feb. 12	George Washington
Feb. 20	Hudson
Mar. 6	America
Mar. 19	Peninsula State
Mar. 18	Potomac
Mar. 26	Hudson
Apr. 5	Susquehanna
Apr. 8	America
Apr. 18	Pres. Arthur
Apr. 21	Pres. Taft
Apr. 29	George Washington
May 2	Pres. Fillmore
May 7	Granite State
May 13	America
May 19	Peninsula State
May 25	Pres. Taft
June 2	Susquehanna
June 2	George Washington
June 11	Pres. Fillmore
June 17	America
June 22	Pres. Roosevelt
June 24	Pres. Arthur
June 30	Pres. Harding
July 8	George Washington
July 14	Susquehanna
July 16	Pres. Fillmore
July 22	America
July 28	Pres. Roosevelt
July 31	Pres. Arthur
Aug. 3	Pres. Harding
Aug. 11	George Washington
Aug. 19	Pres. Fillmore
Aug. 25	Susquehanna

Year 1922

UNITED STATES LINES
Plymouth, Cherbourg, Bremen,
Danzig—New York
(Continued)

N. Y.

Arrival	Steamer
Aug. 26	America
Sept. 1	Pres. Roosevelt
Sept. 5	Pres. Arthur
Sept. 8	Pres. Harding
Sept. 15	George Washington
Sept. 23	Pres. Fillmore
Sept. 30	America
Oct. 6	Susquehanna
Oct. 6	Pres. Roosevelt
Oct. 8	Pres. Arthur
Oct. 13	Pres. Harding
Oct. 20	George Washington
Oct. 29	Pres. Fillmore
Nov. 3	America
Nov. 10	Pres. Roosevelt
Nov. 17	Pres. Arthur
Nov. 17	Pres. Harding
Nov. 24	George Washington
Dec. 3	Pres. Fillmore
Dec. 9	America
Dec. 12	Pres. Roosevelt
Dec. 23	George Washington

WHITE STAR LINE
Liverpool—New York

N. Y.

Arrival	Steamer
Jan. 8	Baltic
Jan. 13	Megantic
Jan. 20	Cedric
Feb. 11	Baltic
Feb. 20	Cedric
Feb. 28	Celtic
Mar. 13	Baltic
Mar. 20	Cedric
Mar. 26	Celtic
Apr. 9	Baltic
Apr. 16	Cedric
Apr. 24	Celtic
May 8	Baltic
May 14	Cedric
May 22	Adriatic
May 29	Celtic
June 5	Baltic
June 11	Cedric
June 19	Adriatic
June 26	Celtic
July 3	Baltic
July 10	Cedric
July 16	Adriatic
July 23	Celtic
July 31	Baltic
Aug. 6	Cedric
Aug. 13	Adriatic
Aug. 20	Celtic
Aug. 28	Baltic
Sept. 3	Cedric

WHITE STAR LINE
Liverpool—New York
(Continued)

N. Y.

Arrival	Steamer
Sept. 10	Adriatic
Sept. 17	Celtic
Sept. 24	Baltic
Oct. 2	Cedric
Oct. 8	Adriatic
Oct. 15	Celtic
Oct. 22	Baltic
Oct. 29	Cedric
Nov. 4	Adriatic
Nov. 12	Celtic
Nov. 19	Baltic
Nov. 26	Cedric
Dec. 3	Adriatic
Dec. 10	Celtic
Dec. 18	Baltic
Dec. 25	Cedric

WHITE STAR LINE
Liverpool—Boston

Boston

Arrival	Steamer
Apr. 24	Canopic
June 2	Haverford
June 15	Pittsburgh
July 20	Pittsburgh
Aug. 24	Pittsburgh
Sept. 1	Haverford
Sept. 27	Pittsburgh
Nov. 2	Pittsburgh

WHITE STAR LINE
Liverpool—Philadelphia

Phila.

Arrival	Steamer
June 4	Haverford
June 17	Pittsburgh
July 15	Haverford
July 22	Pittsburgh
Aug. 26	Pittsburgh
Sept. 3	Haverford
Sept. 29	Pittsburgh
Nov. 4	Pittsburgh

WHITE STAR LINE
Southampton—New York

N. Y.

Arrival	Steamer
Feb. 15	Olympic
Feb. 24	Homeric
Mar. 8	Olympic
Mar. 22	Homeric
Mar. 29	Olympic
Apr. 13	Homeric
Apr. 19	Olympic
May 4	Homeric
May 9	Olympic
May 16	Majestic
May 31	Olympic

WHITE STAR LINE
Southampton—New York
(Continued)

N. Y.

Arrival	Steamer
June 7	Homeric
June 13	Majestic
June 21	Olympic
June 28	Homeric
July 4	Majestic
July 12	Olympic
July 19	Homeric
July 25	Majestic
Aug. 17	Homeric
Aug. 23	Majestic
Aug. 29	Olympic
Sept. 7	Homeric
Sept. 12	Majestic
Sept. 20	Olympic
Sept. 27	Homeric
Oct. 3	Majestic
Oct. 10	Olympic
Oct. 19	Homeric
Oct. 24	Majestic
Oct. 31	Olympic
Nov. 8	Homeric
Nov. 14	Majestic
Nov. 28	Olympic
Dec. 7	Homeric
Dec. 12	Majestic
Dec. 20	Olympic

WHITE STAR LINE
Cherbourg, Southampton,
Bremen—New York

N. Y.

Arrival	Steamer
Nov. 22	Canopic
Dec. 12	Pittsburgh

WHITE STAR LINE
Mediterranean—Boston

Boston

Arrival	Steamer
Jan. 14	Arabic
Aug. 22	Arabic
Sept. 18	Cretic
Oct. 9	Arabic
Nov. 5	Cretic
Nov. 25	Arabic

WHITE STAR LINE
Mediterranean—New York

N. Y.

Arrival	Steamer
Jan. 15	Arabic
Feb. 14	Adriatic
Mar. 6	Arabic
Mar. 29	Adriatic
Apr. 23	Arabic

Year 1923

AMERICAN LINE
Hamburg—New York
N. Y.

Arrival	Steamer
Jan. 10	Mongolia
Jan. 18	Minnekahda
Feb. 2	Manchuria
Feb. 16	Mongolia
Feb. 25	Minnekahda
Mar. 11	Manchuria
Mar. 21	Mongolia
Mar. 30	Minnekahda
Apr. 13	Manchuria
Apr. 25	Mongolia
May 1	Minnekahda
May 15	Manchuria
May 29	Mongolia
June 5	Minnekahda
June 19	Manchuria
June 27	Finland
July 6	Mongolia
July 11	Minnekahda
July 18	Kroonland
July 24	Manchuria
Aug. 1	Finland
Aug. 8	Mongolia
Aug. 15	Minnekahda
Aug. 22	Kroonland
Aug. 29	Manchuria
Sept. 6	Finland
Sept. 11	Mongolia
Sept. 18	Minnekahda
Sept. 26	Kroonland
Oct. 2	Manchuria
Oct. 10	Finland
Oct. 16	Mongolia
Oct. 25	Minnekahda
Nov. 11	Manchuria
Nov. 23	Mongolia
Dec. 1	Minnekahda

ANCHOR LINE
Mediterranean—New York
N. Y.

Arrival	Steamer
Sept. 8	Tuscania

ANCHOR LINE
Glasgow—New York
N. Y.

Arrival	Steamer
Jan. 8	Columbia
Jan. 24	Assyria
Feb. 5	Columbia
Feb. 16	Saturnia
Mar. 4	Assyria
Mar. 13	Columbia
Mar. 27	Cameronia
Apr. 6	Tuscania
Apr. 10	Columbia
Apr. 17	Assyria
Apr. 23	Cameronia
May 1	Tuscania
May 7	Columbia
May 21	Cameronia
June 3	Columbia
June 13	Assyria

ANCHOR LINE
Glasgow—New York
(Continued)
N. Y.

Arrival	Steamer
June 18	Cameronia
June 25	Tuscania
July 3	Columbia
July 11	Assyria
July 14	Cameronia
Aug. 1	Columbia
Aug. 7	Assyria
Aug. 13	Cameronia
Sept. 2	Columbia
Sept. 10	Cameronia
Sept. 18	Assyria
Oct. 1	Columbia
Oct. 2	Tuscania
Oct. 4	Cameronia
Oct. 5	California
Nov. 1	Columbia
Nov. 4	Tuscania
Nov. 17	Assyria
Dec. 3	California
Dec. 18	Columbia

ANCHOR LINE
Glasgow—Liverpool—Boston
Boston

Arrival	Steamer
Mar. 26	Cameronia
Apr. 9	Columbia
Apr. 22	Cameronia
May 6	Columbia
Sept. 1	Columbia
Sept. 8	Cameronia
Oct. 4	Cameronia

ATLANTIC TRANSPORT LINE
London—New York
N. Y.

Arrival	Steamer
Sept. 9	Minnewaska
Oct. 8	Minnewaska
Nov. 6	Minnewaska
Dec. 3	Minnewaska

BOORAS LINE
Mediterranean—New York
Boston
N. Y.

Arrival	Steamer
July 1	Washington

COMPANIA TRANSATLANTICA LINE
(Spanish Line)
Spain—New York
N. Y.

Arrival	Steamer
Jan. 3	Reina M. Cristina
Jan. 15	Manuel Calvo
Feb. 15	Montserrat
Mar. 15	Montevideo
Apr. 13	Antonio Lopez
May 1	Reina M. Cristina
May 14	Montserrat

COMPANIA TRANSATLANTICA LINE
(Spanish Line)
Spain—New York
(Continued)
N. Y.

Arrival	Steamer
July 18	Reina M. Cristina
Sept. 7	Reina M. Cristina
Nov. 13	Reina M. Cristina

COSULICH LINE
Mediterranean—New York,
Boston
N. Y.

Arrival	Steamer
Jan. 19	Pres. Wilson
Mar. 14	Pres. Wilson
May 1	Pres. Wilson
June 7	Argentina
July 1	Pres. Wilson
July 14	Martha Washington
Aug. 1	Argentina
Aug. 16	Pres. Wilson
Sept. 1	Martha Washington
Oct. 1	Pres. Wilson
Nov. 1	Martha Washington
Nov. 21	Pres. Wilson
Dec. 22	Martha Washington

CUNARD LINE
Liverpool—New York
N. Y.

Arrival	Steamer
Jan. 14	Samaria
Jan. 21	Scythia
Jan. 30	Tyrrhenia
Feb. 5	Caronia
Feb. 13	Carmania
Mar. 19	Carmania
Apr. 11	Andania
Apr. 16	Carmania
Apr. 29	Caronia
May 13	Carmania
May 27	Caronia
June 6	Laconia
June 10	Carmania
June 24	Caronia
July 3	Franconia
July 9	Carmania
July 24	Caronia
Aug. 1	Franconia
Aug. 4	Samaria
Aug. 6	Carmania
Aug. 20	Caronia
Aug. 26	Franconia
Sept. 3	Carmania
Sept. 16	Caronia
Sept. 24	Franconia
Oct. 1	Carmania
Oct. 14	Caronia
Nov. 3	Carmania
Nov. 9	Franconia
Nov. 12	Scythia
Nov. 26	Samaria
Dec. 9	Laconia
Dec. 26	Scythia

Year 1923

CUNARD LINE
Mediterranean—New York
N. Y.

Arrival	Steamer
Apr. 4	Scythia

CUNARD LINE
Southampton—New York
N. Y.

Arrival	Steamer
Jan. 27	Berengaria
Feb. 2	Mauretania
Feb. 18	Berengaria
Mar. 17	Aquitania
Apr. 6	Aquitania
Apr. 13	Mauretania
Apr. 16	Antonia
Apr. 21	Berengaria
Apr. 28	Aquitania
May 4	Mauretania
May 11	Berengaria
May 18	Aquitania
May 21	Mauretania
May 28	Albania
June 1	Berengaria
June 8	Aquitania
June 15	Mauretania
June 22	Berengaria
June 27	Saxonia
July 1	Aquitania
July 2	Albania
July 6	Mauretania
July 13	Berengaria
July 20	Aquitania
Aug. 3	Mauretania
Aug. 10	Berengaria
Aug. 17	Aquitania
Aug. 24	Mauretania
Sept. 1	Berengaria
Sept. 6	Aquitania
Sept. 14	Mauretania
Sept. 21	Berengaria
Sept. 26	Albania
Sept. 28	Aquitania
Oct. 5	Mauretania
Oct. 7	Saxonia
Oct. 12	Berengaria
Oct. 19	Aquitania
Oct. 26	Mauretania
Nov. 2	Berengaria
Nov. 9	Aquitania
Nov. 23	Berengaria
Nov. 25	Aquitania
Dec. 1	Ansonia
Dec. 18	Berengaria
Dec. 24	Aquitania

CUNARD LINE
Hamburg—New York
N. Y.

Arrival	Steamer
Jan. 6	Albania
Jan. 24	Antonia
Feb. 18	Saxonia
Mar. 1	Antonia
Mar. 8	Tyrrhenia
Mar. 15	Albania
Mar. 28	Saxonia
Apr. 9	Tyrrhenia
Apr. 23	Albania

CUNARD LINE
Hamburg—New York
(Continued)
N. Y.

Arrival	Steamer
May 7	Saxonia
May 16	Tyrrhenia
June 19	Tyrrhenia
July 6	Laconia
Aug. 2	Tyrrhenia
Aug. 15	Laconia
Sept. 6	Tyrrhenia
Sept. 6	Saxonia
Sept. 19	Laconia
Oct. 24	Laconia
Nov. 1	Albania
Nov. 19	Tyrrhenia
Dec. 15	Andania

CUNARD LINE
Liverpool—Boston
Boston

Arrival	Steamer
Jan. 9	Andania
Jan. 22	Ausonia
Feb. 6	Andania
Feb. 21	Ausonia
Mar. 14	Andania
Mar. 27	Ausonia
Apr. 15	Carmania
May 6	Laconia
May 21	Scythia
June 18	Scythia
July 6	Samaria
July 8	Carmania
July 20	Scythia
Aug. 5	Carmania
Aug. 18	Scythia
Sept. 1	Samaria
Sept. 14	Scythia
Oct. 1	Samaria
Nov. 1	Carmania
Nov. 1	Samaria

FABRE LINE
Mediterranean—New York
N. Y.

Arrival	Steamer
Jan. 3	Canada
Jan. 3	Providence
Jan. 3	Asia
Feb. 1	Madonna
Feb. 9	Patria
Mar. 5	Braga
Mar. 14	Providence
Apr. 3	Asia
Apr. 11	Patria
Apr. 24	Canada
May 2	Britannia
May 30	Patria
June 2	Asia
June 24	Providence
July 1	Canada
July 18	Patria
Aug. 1	Madonna
Aug. 13	Providence
Sept. 1	Braga
Sept. 10	Patria
Oct. 6	Providence
Oct. 20	Britannia

FABRE LINE
Mediterranean—New York
(Continued)
N. Y.

Arrival	Steamer
Nov. 1	Patria
Nov. 30	Providence
Dec. 4	Britannia
Dec. 4	Braga

FRENCH LINE
(Compagnie Generale Transatlantique)
Halifax, Plymouth, Havre, Vigo, Bordeaux—New York
N. Y.

Arrival	Steamer
Jan. 3	Rochambeau
Jan. 11	Roussillon
Jan. 13	Paris
Jan. 24	Chicago
Jan. 30	La Bourdonnais
Feb. 7	Rochambeau
Feb. 18	France
Feb. 18	Roussillon
Mar. 2	Chicago
Mar. 3	Paris
Mar. 11	France
Mar. 15	La Bourdonnais
Mar. 21	Rochambeau
Mar. 24	Paris
Apr. 4	La Savoie
Apr. 12	Roussillon
Apr. 17	France
Apr. 21	Paris
Apr. 21	Chicago
Apr. 26	La Bourdonnais
Apr. 30	La Savoie
May 7	Lafayette
May 12	Paris
May 19	France
May 19	Suffren
May 25	Rochambeau
May 29	Chicago
June 2	Paris
June 3	La Bourdonnais
June 9	France
June 14	Roussillon
June 18	Lafayette
June 23	Paris
June 25	Suffren
June 27	Chicago
June 28	Rochambeau
July 1	France
July 8	La Bourdonnais
July 8	La Savoie
July 14	Paris
July 21	France
July 27	Suffren
July 30	Lafayette
Aug. 1	Rochambeau
Aug. 6	La Savoie
Aug. 11	Paris
Aug. 18	France
Aug. 25	Roussillon
Aug. 27	Lafayette
Sept. 1	Chicago
Sept. 3	La Savoie
Sept. 7	Paris
Sept. 6	Rochambeau
Sept. 9	Suffren

Year 1923

FRENCH LINE
(Compagnie Generale Transatlantique)
Halifax, Plymouth, Havre,
Vigo, Bordeaux—New York
(Continued)
N. Y.

Arrival	Steamer
Sept. 10	La Bourdonnais
Sept. 15	France
Sept. 24	Lafayette
Sept. 29	Roussillon
Oct. 1	Paris
Oct. 6	France
Oct. 6	Chicago
Oct. 11	Rochambeau
Oct. 14	La Savoie
Oct. 20	Paris
Oct. 22	La Bourdonnais
Nov. 1	Suffren
Nov. 7	Chicago
Nov. 9	Paris
Nov. 12	Roussillon
Nov. 20	Rochambeau
Nov. 26	La Savoie
Dec. 4	La Bourdonnais
Dec. 4	Suffren
Dec. 8	Paris
Dec. 19	Chicago
Dec. 23	La Savoie
Dec. 25	Roussillon

HAMBURG-AMERICAN LINE
Hamburg—New York
N. Y.

Arrival	Steamer
Jan. 1	Hansa
Jan. 20	Bayern
Feb. 5	Thuringia
Feb. 13	Hansa
Mar. 7	Bayern
Mar. 15	Thuringia
Mar. 25	Hansa
Apr. 7	Munsterland
Apr. 18	Bayern
Apr. 26	Thuringia
May 6	Hansa
May 27	Bayern
June 6	Thuringia
June 17	Hansa
July 4	Westphalia
July 15	Albert Ballin
July 25	Thuringia
July 29	Hansa
Aug. 14	Westphalia
Aug. 26	Albert Ballin
Sept. 4	Thuringia
Sept. 9	Hansa
Sept. 26	Westphalia
Oct. 6	Albert Ballin
Oct. 16	Thuringia
Oct. 21	Hansa
Oct. 26	Bayern
Nov. 8	Westphalia
Nov. 18	Albert Ballin
Nov. 27	Thuringia
Dec. 1	Hansa
Dec. 19	Westphalia
Dec. 22	Bayern

HOLLAND-AMERICA LINE
Rotterdam—New York
N. Y.

Arrival	Steamer
Jan. 2	Noordam
Jan. 15	Volendam
Jan. 26	Rotterdam
Feb. 4	Noordam
Feb. 19	Volendam
Mar. 5	Ryndam
Mar. 18	New Amsterdam
Apr. 7	Volendam
Apr. 22	New Amsterdam
Apr. 28	Veendam
May 4	Rotterdam
May 12	Volendam
May 26	New Amsterdam
June 2	Veendam
June 9	Rotterdam
June 16	Volendam
June 23	Ryndam
July 1	New Amsterdam
July 7	Veendam
July 14	Rotterdam
July 21	Volendam
Aug. 4	New Amsterdam
Aug. 12	Veendam
Aug. 17	Rotterdam
Aug. 24	Volendam
Sept. 2	Ryndam
Sept. 7	New Amsterdam
Sept. 15	Veendam
Sept. 21	Rotterdam
Sept. 29	Volendam
Oct. 6	Ryndam
Oct. 13	New Amsterdam
Oct. 20	Veendam
Oct. 26	Rotterdam
Nov. 1	Volendam
Nov. 11	Ryndam
Nov. 17	New Amsterdam
Dec. 1	Rotterdam
Dec. 22	New Amsterdam

LEYLAND LINE
Liverpool—Boston
Boston

Arrival	Steamer
Feb. 15	Winifredian
Apr. 6	Winifredian
June 6	Winifredian
June 24	Devonian
July 22	Winifredian
Aug. 13	Devonian
Sept. 2	Winifredian
Sept. 26	Devonian
Oct. 6	Winifredian
Nov. 2	Devonian
Dec. 4	Winifredian
Dec. 25	Devonian

LLOYD SABAUDO
Mediterranean—New York
N. Y.

Arrival	Steamer
Jan. 15	Conte Rosso
Apr. 1	Conte Rosso
May 7	Conte Rosso

LLOYD SABAUDO
Mediterranean—New York
(Continued)
N. Y.

Arrival	Steamer
June 14	Conte Rosso
June 24	Conte Verde
July 19	Conte Rosso
Aug. 1	Conte Verde
Aug. 23	Conte Rosso
Sept. 9	Conte Verde
Sept. 27	Conte Rosso
Oct. 14	Conte Verde
Nov. 1	Conte Rosso
Nov. 10	Conte Re. d'Italia
Dec. 6	Conte Rosso

NATIONAL GREEK LINE
Mediterranean—New York
Boston
N. Y.

Arrival	Steamer
Jan. 8	King Alexander
Feb. 6	Megali Hellas
Mar. 14	Themistocles
May 17	Themistocles
July 1	King Alexander
Aug. 1	Constantinople
Sept. 1	Byron
Oct. 1	Constantinople
Nov. 1	Byron
Nov. 12	Themistocles

NAVIGAZIONE GENER-ALE ITALIANA LINE
Mediterranean—New York
N. Y.

Arrival	Steamer
Jan. 13	Taormina
Jan. 21	America
Feb. 10	Giulio Cesare
Mar. 2	Taormina
Mar. 15	America
Apr. 13	Taormina
May 2	America
June 7	Colombo
June 21	America
July 1	Giulio Cesare
July 10	Taormina
July 17	Colombo
Aug. 1	America
Aug. 11	Giulio Cesare
Aug. 20	Taormina
Sept. 6	Colombo
Sept. 14	America
Sept. 19	Giulio Cesare
Oct. 21	Colombo
Oct. 27	America
Nov. 9	Duilio
Dec. 3	Colombo
Dec. 3	America
Dec. 19	Duilio

NAVIGAZIONE GENER-ALE ITALIANA LINE
Mediterranean—Philadelphia
Phila.

Arrival	Steamer
Dec. 1	Colombo

Year 1923

NORTH GERMAN LLOYD
Bremen—New York
N. Y.

Arrival	Steamer
Jan. 1	Hannover
Jan. 25	Yorck
Feb. 11	Hannover
Feb. 24	Seydlitz
Mar. 11	Yorck
Mar. 21	Hannover
Mar. 29	Seydlitz
Apr. 12	Yorck
Apr. 18	Bremen
Apr. 27	Hannover
May 10	Seydlitz
May 17	Yorck
May 23	Bremen
June 6	Hannover
June 14	Seydlitz
June 21	Yorck
June 26	Bremen
July 2	Muenchen
July 13	Hannover
July 14	Seydlitz
July 25	Yorck
Aug. 1	Bremen
Aug. 7	Muenchen
Aug. 17	Hannover
Aug. 22	Seydlitz
Aug. 30	Yorck
Sept. 10	Muenchen
Sept. 15	Bremen
Sept. 20	Sierra Ventana
Sept. 24	Hannover
Sept. 26	Seydlitz
Oct. 3	Derfflinger
Oct. 5	Yorck
Oct. 9	Muenchen
Oct. 19	Bremen
Oct. 22	Sierra Ventana
Nov. 3	Seydlitz
Nov. 6	Derfflinger
Nov. 9	Yorck
Nov. 14	Muenchen
Nov. 18	Canopic
Nov. 26	Sierra Ventana
Nov. 27	Bremen
Dec. 9	Derfflinger
Dec. 10	Muenchen
Dec. 17	Seydlitz
Dec. 19	Yorck
Dec. 22	Canopic
Dec. 26	Sierra Ventana

NORTH GERMAN LLOYD
Bremen—Galveston
Galveston

Arrival	Steamer
Oct. 17	Werra
Dec. 15	Hannover

NORTH GERMAN LLOYD
Bremen—Baltimore
Baltimore

Arrival	Steamer
May 6	Porta
May 24	Eisenach
July 2	Porta
July 21	Eisenach
Aug. 24	Porta

NORTH GERMAN LLOYD
Bremen—Baltimore
(Continued)
Baltimore

Arrival	Steamer
Sept. 13	Eisenach
Oct. 18	Porta
Nov. 7	Eisenach
Dec. 31	Eisenach

NORTH GERMAN LLOYD
Bremen—Philadelphia
Phila.

Arrival	Steamer
May 3	Porta
May 21	Eisenach
June 28	Porta
July 16	Eisenach
Aug. 21	Porta
Sept. 9	Eisenach
Oct. 14	Porta
Nov. 3	Eisenach
Dec. 28	Eisenach

NORWEGIAN-AMERICA LINE
Bergen—New York
N. Y.

Arrival	Steamer
Jan. 9	Skiensfjord
Feb. 14	Stavangerfjord
Mar. 6	Bergensfjord
Mar. 24	Stavangerfjord
Apr. 4	Tyrifjord
Apr. 15	Bergensfjord
May 1	Stavangerfjord
May 18	Bergensfjord
June 3	Tyrifjord
June 5	Stavangerfjord
July 1	Bergensfjord
July 10	Stavangerfjord
Aug. 1	Bergensfjord
Aug. 21	Randsfjord
Aug. 21	Stavangerfjord
Sept. 6	Bergensfjord
Sept. 9	Topdalsfjord
Sept. 25	Stavangerfjord
Oct. 15	Bergensfjord
Oct. 31	Randsfjord
Nov. 2	Stavangerfjord
Nov. 19	Bergensfjord
Dec. 3	Stavangerfjord
Dec. 25	Bergensfjord

RED STAR LINE
Antwerp—New York
N. Y.

Arrival	Steamer
Jan. 8	Lapland
Jan. 27	Kroonland
Feb. 18	Lapland
Mar. 17	Zeeland
Mar. 24	Lapland
Apr. 3	Finland
Apr. 14	Belgenland
Apr. 22	Zeeland
Apr. 27	Lapland
May 11	Belgenland
May 25	Lapland
June 8	Belgenland

RED STAR LINE
Antwerp—New York
(Continued)
N. Y.

Arrival	Steamer
June 16	Zeeland
June 22	Lapland
July 6	Belgenland
July 14	Zeeland
July 20	Lapland
Aug. 1	Gothland
Aug. 4	Belgenland
Aug. 10	Zeeland
Aug. 17	Lapland
Sept. 2	Belgenland
Sept. 8	Zeeland
Sept. 14	Lapland
Sept. 29	Belgenland
Oct. 6	Zeeland
Oct. 13	Lapland
Nov. 3	Belgenland
Nov. 10	Zeeland
Dec. 19	Zeeland

RED STAR LINE
Danzig—New York
N. Y.

Arrival	Steamer
Jan. 3	Samland
Sept. 22	Gothland

RED STAR LINE
Scandinavian Ports—Boston
Boston

Arrival	Steamer
May 21	Oscar II
Sept. 3	Hellig Olav
Nov. 6	Oscar II

ROYAL MAIL STEAM PACKET CO.
Hamburg—New York
N. Y.

Arrival	Steamer
Jan. 1	Orduna
Jan. 16	Orca
Jan. 22	Orbita
Feb. 13	Orduna
Mar. 6	Orbita
Apr. 10	Orduna
Apr. 16	Ohio
Apr. 30	Orbita
May 8	Orca
May 14	Orduna
May 28	Ohio
June 5	Orbita
June 11	Orca
June 18	Orduna
July 3	Ohio
July 9	Orbita
July 16	Orca
July 23	Orduna
Aug. 5	Ohio
Aug. 13	Orbita
Aug. 20	Orca
Sept. 3	Orduna
Sept. 9	Ohio
Sept. 17	Orbita
Oct. 1	Orca
Oct. 8	Orduna

Year 1923

ROYAL MAIL STEAM PACKET CO.
Hamburg—New York
(Continued)
N. Y.

Arrival	Steamer
Oct. 14	Ohio
Oct. 22	Orbita
Oct. 29	Arcadian
Nov. 1	Orca
Nov. 12	Orduna
Nov. 18	Ohio
Dec. 1	Orbita

SCANDINAVIAN-AMERICAN LINE
Scandinavian Ports—New York
N. Y.

Arrival	Steamer
Jan. 22	Oscar II
Feb. 6	Hellig Olav
Feb. 20	Frederik VIII
Mar. 1	Oscar II
Mar. 14	United States
Mar. 21	Hellig Olav
Apr. 4	Frederik VIII
Apr. 10	Oscar II
Apr. 24	United States
May 1	Hellig Olav
May 14	Frederik VIII
May 22	Oscar II
June 4	United States
June 12	Hellig Olav
June 25	Frederik VIII
July 3	Oscar II
July 17	United States
July 24	Hellig Olav
Aug. 6	Frederik VIII
Aug. 14	Oscar II
Aug. 27	United States
Sept. 5	Hellig Olav
Sept. 17	Frederik VIII
Sept. 25	Oscar II
Oct. 9	United States
Oct. 16	Hellig Olav
Oct. 24	Frederik VIII
Nov. 7	Oscar II
Nov. 19	United States
Nov. 24	Hellig Olav
Dec. 1	Frederik VIII
Dec. 27	Oscar II

SICULA AMERICANA LINE
Mediterranean—New York
N. Y.

Arrival	Steamer
July 8	Guglielmo Peirce
Oct. 5	Guglielmo Peirce
Nov. 22	Guglielmo Peirce

SWEDISH-AMERICAN LINE
Gothenburg—New York
N. Y.

Arrival	Steamer
Jan. 8	Drottningholm
Feb. 6	Drottningholm
Mar. 6	Drottningholm
Mar. 28	Kungsholm

SWEDISH-AMERICAN LINE
Gothenburg—New York
(Continued)
N. Y.

Arrival	Steamer
Apr. 7	Drottningholm
Apr. 17	Stockholm
May 1	Kungsholm
May 7	Drottningholm
May 22	Stockholm
June 4	Drottningholm
June 12	Kungsholm
July 1	Stockholm
July 2	Drottningholm
July 18	Kungsholm
Aug. 1	Drottningholm
Aug. 7	Stockholm
Aug. 22	Kungsholm
Sept. 1	Drottningholm
Sept. 11	Stockholm
Sept. 24	Drottningholm
Oct. 3	Kungsholm
Oct. 16	Stockholm
Oct. 22	Drottningholm
Nov. 7	Kungsholm
Nov. 23	Stockholm
Dec. 1	Drottningholm
Dec. 20	Kungsholm

TRANSATLANTICA ITALIANA LINE
Mediterranean—New York
N. Y.

Arrival	Steamer
Jan. 19	Giuseppe Verdi
Mar. 7	Giuseppe Verdi
Mar. 25	Dante Alighieri
Apr. 21	Giuseppe Verdi
May 8	Dante Alighieri
June 3	Giuseppe Verdi
July 1	Dante Alighieri
July 25	Giuseppe Verdi
Aug. 18	Dante Alighieri
Sept. 7	Giuseppe Verdi
Oct. 6	Dante Alighieri
Oct. 25	Giuseppe Verdi
Dec. 1	Dante Alighieri

UNITED AMERICAN LINES, INC.
Hamburg—New York
N. Y.

Arrival	Steamer
Jan. 12	Mount Clinton
Jan. 23	Mount Clay
Feb. 15	Mount Carroll
Feb. 23	Mount Clinton
Mar. 7	Mount Clay
Apr. 11	Mount Clay
Apr. 23	Reliance
Apr. 30	Mount Carroll
May 15	Mount Clinton
May 25	Reliance
May 28	Mount Clay
June 8	Resolute
June 11	Mount Carroll
June 22	Reliance
July 2	Mount Clinton
July 6	Resolute

UNITED AMERICAN LINES, INC.
Hamburg—New York
(Continued)
N. Y.

Arrival	Steamer
July 8	Mount Clay
July 20	Reliance
Aug. 2	Mount Carroll
Aug. 3	Resolute
Aug. 7	Mount Clinton
Aug. 17	Reliance
Aug. 20	Mount Clay
Aug. 31	Resolute
Sept. 13	Reliance
Sept. 17	Mount Clinton
Sept. 28	Resolute
Oct. 1	Mount Clay
Oct. 12	Reliance
Oct. 26	Resolute
Nov. 1	Cleveland
Nov. 9	Reliance
Nov. 12	Mount Clay
Nov. 27	Resolute
Dec. 10	Cleveland
Dec. 11	Reliance

UNITED STATES LINES
Southampton—New York
N. Y.

Arrival	Steamer
July 23	Leviathan
Aug. 13	Leviathan
Sept. 3	Leviathan
Sept. 25	Leviathan
Oct. 15	Leviathan
Nov. 3	Leviathan
Nov. 26	Leviathan
Dec. 21	Leviathan

UNITED STATES LINES
London—New York
N. Y.

Arrival	Steamer
Jan. 3	Pres. Adams
Jan. 10	Pres. Van Buren
Jan. 18	Pres. Polk
Jan. 24	Pres. Garfield
Feb. 8	Pres. Adams
Feb. 17	Pres. Monroe
Feb. 21	Pres. Van Buren
Mar. 1	Pres. Polk
Mar. 10	Pres. Garfield
Mar. 15	Pres. Adams
Mar. 22	Pres. Monroe
Mar. 28	Pres. Van Buren
Apr. 5	Pres. Polk
Apr. 11	Pres. Garfield
Apr. 26	Pres. Monroe
May 1	Pres. Van Buren
May 8	Pres. Polk
May 15	Pres. Garfield
May 22	Pres. Adams
May 29	Pres. Monroe
June 5	Pres. Van Buren
June 13	Pres. Polk
June 19	Pres. Garfield
July 1	Pres. Adams
July 3	Pres. Monroe
July 10	Pres. Van Buren

Year 1923

UNITED STATES LINES London—New York (Continued)	
N. Y.	
Arrival	**Steamer**
July 15	Pres. Polk
July 31	Pres. Garfield
Aug. 1	Pres. Adams
Aug. 8	Pres. Monroe
Aug. 14	Pres. Van Buren
Aug. 21	Pres. Polk
Sept. 5	Pres. Garfield
Sept. 5	Pres. Adams
Sept. 11	Pres. Monroe
Sept. 18	Pres. Van Buren
Oct. 1	Pres. Polk
Oct. 3	Pres. Garfield
Oct. 7	Pres. Adams
Oct. 16	Pres. Monroe
Oct. 23	Pres. Van Buren
Nov. 1	Pres. Polk
Nov. 11	Pres. Adams
Nov. 21	Pres. Monroe
Nov. 27	Pres. Garfield
Dec. 5	Pres. Van Buren
Dec. 12	Pres. Polk
Dec. 19	Pres. Adams
Dec. 26	Pres. Monroe

UNITED STATES LINES Bremen—New York	
N. Y.	
Arrival	**Steamer**
Jan. 10	Pres. Fillmore
Jan. 14	America
Jan. 17	Pres. Harding
Jan. 26	Pres. Roosevelt
Feb. 19	America
Feb. 25	Pres. Harding
Mar. 3	George Washington
Mar. 11	Pres. Roosevelt
Mar. 19	Pres. Arthur
Mar. 27	Pres. Fillmore
Mar. 31	Pres. Harding
Apr. 7	George Washington
Apr. 13	Pres. Roosevelt
Apr. 29	Pres. Fillmore
May 4	Pres. Harding
May 11	George Washington
May 18	Pres. Roosevelt
May 27	Pres. Arthur
June 1	Pres. Fillmore
June 4	Pres. Harding
June 15	George Washington
June 22	Pres. Roosevelt
June 26	America
July 1	Pres. Fillmore
July 6	Pres. Harding
July 15	Pres. Harding
July 20	George Washington
Aug. 1	America
Aug. 3	Pres. Roosevelt
Aug. 6	Pres. Fillmore
Aug. 10	Pres. Harding
Aug. 17	Pres. Arthur
Aug. 24	George Washington
Sept. 1	America
Sept. 7	Pres. Roosevelt
Sept. 10	Pres. Fillmore
Sept. 14	Pres. Harding

UNITED STATES LINES Bremen—New York (Continued)	
N. Y.	
Arrival	**Steamer**
Sept. 22	Pres. Arthur
Oct. 1	George Washington
Oct. 6	America
Oct. 11	Pres. Roosevelt
Oct. 15	Pres. Fillmore
Oct. 19	Pres. Harding
Nov. 1	Pres. Arthur
Nov. 2	George Washington
Nov. 11	America
Nov. 16	Pres. Roosevelt
Nov. 23	Pres. Harding
Dec. 1	Pres. Fillmore
Dec. 6	George Washington
Dec. 15	America
Dec. 21	Pres. Roosevelt

WHITE STAR LINE Liverpool—New York	
N. Y.	
Arrival	**Steamer**
Jan. 1	Adriatic
Jan. 9	Megantic
Jan. 16	Baltic
Jan. 22	Celtic
Jan. 29	Regina
Feb. 5	Cedric
Feb. 13	Baltic
Feb. 19	Celtic
Mar. 1	Regina
Mar. 5	Cedric
Mar. 13	Baltic
Mar. 19	Celtic
Mar. 27	Regina
Apr. 3	Cedric
Apr. 16	Celtic
Apr. 23	Baltic
Apr. 29	Cedric
May 6	Adriatic
May 13	Celtic
May 20	Baltic
May 27	Cedric
June 3	Adriatic
June 10	Celtic
June 22	Baltic
June 24	Cedric
July 2	Adriatic
July 8	Celtic
July 16	Baltic
July 23	Cedric
Aug. 1	Adriatic
Aug. 6	Celtic
Aug. 12	Baltic
Aug. 20	Cedric
Aug. 26	Adriatic
Sept. 4	Celtic
Sept. 9	Baltic
Sept. 16	Cedric
Sept. 23	Adriatic
Oct. 2	Celtic
Oct. 9	Baltic
Oct. 21	Adriatic
Nov. 1	Celtic
Nov. 4	Baltic
Nov. 11	Cedric
Nov. 19	Adriatic

WHITE STAR LINE Liverpool—New York (Continued)	
N. Y.	
Arrival	**Steamer**
Nov. 26	Celtic
Dec. 3	Baltic
Dec. 17	Cedric
Dec. 24	Celtic
Dec. 31	Adriatic

WHITE STAR LINE Hamburg—New York	
N. Y.	
Arrival	**Steamer**
Jan. 16	Pittsburgh
Feb. 26	Pittsburgh
Mar. 19	Canopic
Apr. 4	Pittsburgh
May 8	Pittsburgh
May 23	Canopic
June 12	Pittsburgh
June 28	Canopic
July 18	Pittsburgh
Aug. 21	Pittsburgh
Sept. 5	Canopic
Sept. 25	Pittsburgh
Oct. 10	Canopic
Oct. 27	Pittsburgh
Dec. 10	Pittsburgh

WHITE STAR LINE Liverpool—Boston	
Boston	
Arrival	**Steamer**
Apr. 16	Megantic
Apr. 21	Haverford
July 2	Haverford
Aug. 4	Haverford
Sept. 5	Haverford
Oct. 1	Megantic
Nov. 1	Megantic

WHITE STAR LINE Southampton—New York	
N. Y.	
Arrival	**Steamer**
Jan. 3	Majestic
Jan. 11	Homeric
Jan. 17	Olympic
Feb. 7	Olympic
Mar. 7	Majestic
Mar. 27	Majestic
Apr. 4	Olympic
Apr. 12	Homeric
Apr. 17	Majestic
Apr. 25	Olympic
May 3	Homeric
May 8	Majestic
May 16	Olympic
May 23	Homeric
May 29	Majestic
June 6	Olympic
June 13	Homeric
June 19	Majestic
June 27	Olympic
July 4	Homeric
July 10	Majestic
July 18	Olympic
July 25	Homeric

Year 1923

WHITE STAR LINE
Southampton—New York
(Continued)

N. Y.

Arrival	Steamer
Aug. 1	Majestic
Aug. 15	Olympic
Aug. 22	Homeric
Aug. 28	Majestic
Sept. 5	Olympic
Sept. 12	Homeric
Sept. 18	Majestic
Sept. 25	Olympic
Oct. 4	Homeric
Oct. 10	Majestic
Oct. 16	Olympic
Nov. 1	Majestic
Nov. 6	Olympic

WHITE STAR LINE
Southampton—New York
(Continued)

N. Y.

Arrival	Steamer
Nov. 21	Majestic
Nov. 27	Olympic
Dec. 11	Majestic

WHITE STAR LINE
Halifax—Philadelphia

Phila.

Arrival	Steamer
Apr. 23	Haverford
July 4	Haverford
Aug. 6	Haverford
Sept. 7	Haverford

WHITE STAR LINE
Halifax—Philadelphia
(Continued)

Phila.

Arrival	Steamer
Oct. 12	Haverford

WHITE STAR LINE
Mediterranean—Boston—
New York

Boston

Arrival	Steamer
Nov. 12	Arabic

N. Y.

Arrival	Steamer
Feb. 20	Adriatic
Apr. 9	Adriatic

Year 1924

AMERICAN LINE
Hamburg—New York
N.Y.

Arrival	Steamer
Jan. 1	Mongolia
Jan. 3	Minnekahda
Feb. 6	Minnekahda
Mar. 15	Minnekahda
Apr. 15	Minnekahda
Apr. 23	Mongolia
July 1	Mongolia
July 29	Minnekahda
Aug. 5	Mongolia
Sept. 3	Minnekahda
Sept. 10	Mongolia
Oct. 7	Minnekahda
Oct. 14	Mongolia
Nov. 11	Minnekahda
Nov. 19	Mongolia
Dec. 24	Minnekahda

AMERICAN LINE
Antwerp—New York
N.Y.

Arrival	Steamer
Feb. 18	Mongolia
Mar. 23	Mongolia

ANCHOR LINE
Liverpool—New York
N.Y.

Arrival	Steamer
Mar. 12	Cameronia
Apr. 18	Cameronia

ANCHOR LINE
Glasgow—New York
N.Y.

Arrival	Steamer
Jan. 16	Columbia
Jan. 30	Cameronia
Feb. 7	Assyria
Feb. 12	Tuscania
Feb. 26	Columbia
Mar. 12	Assyria
Mar. 24	Columbia
Apr. 13	Assyria
Apr. 17	Columbia
May 6	Cameronia
May 19	California
May 26	Tuscania
June 2	Cameronia
June 10	Columbia
June 17	Assyria
June 26	California
June 30	Cameronia
July 7	Columbia
July 16	Assyria
July 21	California
July 29	Cameronia
Aug. 3	Columbia
Aug. 17	California
Aug. 26	Assyria
Aug. 31	Cameronia
Sept. 12	California
Sept. 24	Assyria
Sept. 28	Cameronia
Oct. 6	Tuscania

ANCHOR LINE
Glasgow—New York
(Continued)
N.Y.

Arrival	Steamer
Oct. 10	Columbia
Oct. 23	Assyria
Oct. 26	Cameronia
Nov. 5	Tuscania
Nov. 10	Columbia
Nov. 20	Assyria
Nov. 27	Cameronia
Dec. 9	Columbia
Dec. 23	Cameronia

ANCHOR LINE
Mediterranean—New York
N.Y.

Arrival	Steamer
Sept. 2	Tuscania

ATLANTIC TRANSPORT LINE
London—New York
N.Y.

Arrival	Steamer
Apr. 28	Minnewaska
May 12	Minnetonka
May 26	Minnewaska
June 9	Minnetonka
June 22	Minnewaska
July 6	Minnetonka
July 20	Minnewaska
July 20	Menominee
Aug. 3	Minnetonka
Aug. 18	Minnewaska
Sept. 1	Minnetonka
Sept. 14	Minnewaska
Sept. 29	Minnetonka
Oct. 13	Minnewaska
Oct. 27	Minnetonka
Nov. 10	Minnewaska
Nov. 24	Minnetonka
Dec. 9	Minnewaska
Dec. 23	Minnetonka

BALTIC-AMERICAN LINE
Libau via Halifax—Hamburg
—Danzig—Libau—New York
N.Y.

Arrival	Steamer
Jan. 11	Estonia
Feb. 21	Estonia
Mar. 18	Lituania
Apr. 3	Estonia
Apr. 26	Lituania
May 16	Polonia
June 7	Estonia
June 30	Polonia
July 23	Estonia
Aug. 13	Lituania
Sept. 3	Estonia
Sept. 25	Lituania
Oct. 15	Estonia
Nov. 3	Lituania
Nov. 25	Estonia
Dec. 18	Lituania

COMPANIA TRANSATLANTICA LINE
(Spanish Line)
Spain—New York
N.Y.

Arrival	Steamer
Jan. 14	Reina Ma. Cristina
Apr. 8	Reina Ma. Cristina
May 22	Reina Ma. Cristina
July 30	Reina Ma. Cristina
Oct. 25	Reina Ma. Cristina

COSULICH LINE
Mediterranean—New York
N.Y.

Arrival	Steamer
Jan. 7	Pres. Wilson
Mar. 2	Pres. Wilson
Apr. 29	Pres. Wilson
May 5	M. Washington
June 16	Pres. Wilson
June 30	M. Washington
July 31	Pres. Wilson
Aug. 31	M. Washington
Oct. 1	Pres. Wilson
Oct. 16	M. Washington
Nov. 22	Pres. Wilson
Dec. 3	M. Washington

CUNARD LINE
Cherbourg—Plymouth—London—Hamburg—New York
N.Y.

Arrival	Steamer
Jan. 2	Tyrrhenia
Feb. 10	Andania
Feb. 25	Antonia
Mar. 12	Saxonia
Mar. 23	Andania
Apr. 7	Antonia
Apr. 30	Saxonia
June 14	Saxonia
June 30	Lancastria
July 2	Albania
Sept. 6	Lancastria
Sept. 27	Albania
Oct. 15	Lancastria
Nov. 5	Saxonia
Nov. 28	Andania

CUNARD LINE
Cherbourg—Southampton—New York
N.Y.

Arrival	Steamer
Jan. 15	Antonia
Jan. 23	Aquitania
Feb. 13	Berengaria
Mar. 6	Berengaria
Mar. 11	Aquitania
Mar. 28	Berengaria
Apr. 11	Aquitania
Apr. 18	Berengaria
Apr. 22	Albania
Apr. 28	Franconia
May 2	Aquitania
May 10	Berengaria

Year 1924

CUNARD LINE
Cherbourg—Southampton—
New York
(Continued)

N. Y. Arrival	Steamer
May 19	Scythia
May 23	Aquitania
May 26	Albania
May 31	Berengaria
June 6	Mauretania
June 13	Aquitania
June 21	Berengaria
June 27	Mauretania
July 4	Aquitania
July 11	Berengaria
July 28	Lancastria
Aug. 1	Aquitania
Aug. 8	Berengaria
Aug. 12	Albania
Aug. 14	Aquitania
Aug. 22	Mauretania
Aug. 29	Berengaria
Sept. 5	Mauretania
Sept. 12	Aquitania
Sept. 16	Saxonia
Sept. 19	Berengaria
Sept. 25	Mauretania
Oct. 3	Aquitania
Oct. 10	Berengaria
Oct. 16	Mauretania
Oct. 24	Aquitania
Nov. 1	Berengaria
Nov. 7	Mauretania
Nov. 14	Aquitania
Nov. 22	Berengaria
Nov. 28	Mauretania
Dec. 9	Aquitania
Dec. 31	Aquitania

CUNARD LINE
Liverpool—New York

N. Y. Arrival	Steamer
Jan. 9	Laconia
Jan. 17	Ausonia
Jan. 22	Samaria
Jan. 29	Scythia
Feb. 5	Tyrrhenia
Feb. 19	Ausonia
Feb. 26	Athenia
Mar. 18	Ausonia
Mar. 25	Athenia
Apr. 1	Lancastria
Apr. 15	Ausonia
Apr. 22	Scythia
May 12	Lancastria
May 27	Franconia
June 3	Laconia
June 16	Scythia
June 22	Franconia
June 30	Carmania
July 7	Laconia
July 15	Scythia
July 29	Samaria
Aug. 4	Laconia
Aug. 19	Scythia
Sept. 1	Laconia
Sept. 8	Franconia
Sept. 16	Scythia

CUNARD LINE
Liverpool—New York
(Continued)

N. Y. Arrival	Steamer
Sept. 24	Aurania
Sept. 29	Laconia
Oct. 5	Franconia
Oct. 14	Scythia
Oct. 21	Aurania
Oct. 27	Laconia
Nov. 4	Samaria
Nov. 11	Scythia
Nov. 19	Aurania
Nov. 24	Laconia
Nov. 30	Caronia

CUNARD LINE
Liverpool—Boston

Boston Arrival	Steamer
Jan. 16	Ausonia
June 1	Laconia
June 28	Carmania
July 3	Samaria
July 14	Scythia
July 27	Samaria
Aug. 18	Scythia
Aug. 30	Samaria
Sept. 15	Scythia
Oct. 1	Samaria
Oct. 13	Scythia
Nov. 3	Samaria
Nov. 23	Laconia
Dec. 7	Carmania
Dec. 29	Caronia

FABRE LINE
Mediterranean—New York

N. Y. Arrival	Steamer
Jan. 5	Canada
Feb. 7	Providence
Mar. 12	Patria
Apr. 12	Providence
May 13	Patria
June 4	Providence
July 4	Patria
July 14	Britannia
July 22	Providence
Aug. 19	Canada
Aug. 25	Patria
Sept. 1	Madonna
Sept. 12	Providence
Oct. 14	Patria
Oct. 31	Providence
Dec. 4	Asia
Dec. 5	Patria

FRENCH LINE
(Compagnie Generale Transatlantique)
Plymouth—Havre—Vigo—
Bordeaux—New York

N. Y. Arrival	Steamer
Jan. 2	Rochambeau
Jan. 10	Suffren
Jan. 13	Paris
Jan. 21	La Bourdonnais
Jan. 23	Chicago

FRENCH LINE
(Compagnie Generale Transatlantique)
Plymouth—Havre—Vigo—
Bordeaux—New York
(Continued)

N. Y. Arrival	Steamer
Jan. 29	La Savoie
Feb. 3	Paris
Feb. 12	Rochambeau
Feb. 19	Suffren
Feb. 25	La Savoie
Feb. 26	La Bourdonnais
Mar. 4	Chicago
Mar. 8	Paris
Mar. 18	Rochambeau
Mar. 19	Roussillon
Mar. 24	La Savoie
Mar. 29	Paris
Apr. 8	Chicago
Apr. 11	La Bourdonnais
Apr. 14	Rochambeau
Apr. 19	Paris
Apr. 28	La Savoie
May 8	Roussillon
May 8	Suffren
May 10	Paris
May 16	France
May 21	La Bourdonnais
May 26	Rochambeau
June 1	La Savoie
June 7	Paris
June 13	Roussillon
June 13	France
June 14	Chicago
June 20	Suffren
June 23	Lafayette
June 28	Paris
July 1	Rochambeau
July 1	La Bourdonnais
July 5	France
July 14	La Savoie
July 19	Paris
July 23	Roussillon
July 25	France
July 29	Rochambeau
Aug. 5	Suffren
Aug. 13	Lafayette
Aug. 16	Paris
Aug. 23	France
Sept. 1	Roussillon
Sept. 2	La Savoie
Sept. 5	De Grasse
Sept. 5	Rochambeau
Sept. 5	Suffren
Sept. 6	Paris
Sept. 12	France
Sept. 16	Chicago
Sept. 22	Lafayette
Sept. 23	La Bourdonnais
Sept. 26	Paris
Sept. 29	Rochambeau
Oct. 1	De Grasse
Oct. 3	France
Oct. 10	Suffren
Oct. 12	Roussillon
Oct. 12	La Savoie
Oct. 18	Paris
Oct. 24	France
Oct. 30	Chicago

Year 1924

FRENCH LINE
(Compagnie Generale Transatlantique)
Plymouth—Havre—Vigo—
Bordeaux—New York
(Continued)

N. Y.

Arrival	Steamer
Oct. 31	Rochambeau
Nov. 4	De Grasse
Nov. 12	Suffren
Nov. 12	La Bourdonnais
Nov. 15	Paris
Nov. 23	La Savoie
Nov. 24	Roussillon
Dec. 3	Rochambeau
Dec. 6	Paris
Dec. 12	Chicago
Dec. 13	France
Dec. 22	La Savoie
Dec. 26	La Bourdonnais

HAMBURG-AMERICAN LINE
Hamburg—New York

N. Y.

Arrival	Steamer
Jan. 1	Albert Ballin
Jan. 12	Thuringia
Feb. 11	Albert Ballin
Feb. 26	Westphalia
Feb. 22	Albert Ballin
Apr. 5	Deutschland
Apr. 29	Thuringia
May 4	Albert Ballin
May 9	Hansa
May 18	Deutschland
June 2	Westphalia
June 15	Albert Ballin
June 21	Hansa
July 1	Deutschland
July 8	Westphalia
July 20	Albert Ballin
July 27	Njassa
Aug. 3	Deutschland
Aug. 24	Albert Ballin
Aug. 28	Westphalia
Aug. 29	Hansa
Sept. 6	Deutschland
Sept. 25	Thuringia
Sept. 28	Albert Ballin
Oct. 5	Hansa
Oct. 11	Deutschland
Nov. 3	Albert Ballin
Nov. 11	Thuringia
Nov. 16	Deutschland
Dec. 11	Westphalia
Dec. 16	Albert Ballin
Dec. 26	Thuringia
Dec. 29	Deutschland

HOLLAND-AMERICA LINE
Rotterdam—New York

N. Y.

Arrival	Steamer
Jan. 21	Veendam
Jan. 27	Rotterdam
Feb. 4	New Amsterdam
Feb. 26	Veendam
Mar. 12	New Amsterdam
Apr. 6	Veendam

HOLLAND-AMERICA LINE
Rotterdam—New York
(Continued)

N. Y.

Arrival	Steamer
Apr. 13	New Amsterdam
Apr. 25	Rotterdam
May 10	Veendam
May 17	New Amsterdam
May 31	Rotterdam
June 7	Volendam
June 14	Veendam
June 21	New Amsterdam
July 4	Rotterdam
July 13	Volendam
July 19	Veendam
July 26	New Amsterdam
Aug. 8	Rotterdam
Aug. 17	Volendam
Aug. 23	Veendam
Aug. 31	New Amsterdam
Sept. 6	Ryndam
Sept. 12	Rotterdam
Sept. 20	Volendam
Sept. 27	Veendam
Oct. 4	New Amsterdam
Oct. 17	Rotterdam
Oct. 25	Volendam
Nov. 1	Veendam
Nov. 8	New Amsterdam
Nov. 22	Rotterdam
Dec. 7	Veendam
Dec. 30	Ryndam

LEYLAND LINE
Liverpool—Boston

Boston

Arrival	Steamer
Jan. 17	Winifredian
Feb. 14	Devonian
Mar. 10	Winifredian
Apr. 23	Winifredian
May 14	Devonian
June 11	Winifredian
Aug. 11	Nessian
Aug. 16	Belgian
Aug. 27	Devonian
Sept. 16	Winifredian
Oct. 14	Devonian
Nov. 5	Winifredian
Nov. 25	Devonian
Dec. 25	Winifredian

LLOYD SABAUDO
Mediterranean—New York

N. Y.

Arrival	Steamer
Jan. 11	Conte Verde
Feb. 16	Conte Rosso
Feb. 26	Conte Verde
Mar. 29	Conte Rosso
Apr. 19	Conte Rosso
May 24	Conte Verde
June 9	Regina d'Italia
June 21	Conte Rosso
July 5	Conte Verde
July 26	Conte Rosso
Aug. 11	Conte Verde
Sept. 1	Conte Rosso
Sept. 20	Conte Verde

LLOYD SABAUDO
Mediterranean—New York
(Continued)

N. Y.

Arrival	Steamer
Oct. 11	Conte Rosso
Oct. 25	Conte Verde
Nov. 29	Conte Verde

NATIONAL GREEK LINE
Mediterranean—New York

N. Y.

Arrival	Steamer
Jan. 1	Byron
Feb. 2	Themistocles
Mar. 16	Byron
Apr. 12	Themistocles
May 8	Byron
July 17	King Alexander
June 28	Byron
July 21	Themistocles
Aug. 11	King Alexander
Aug. 25	Byron
Sept. 24	Themistocles
Oct. 11	Byron
Oct. 23	King Alexander
Nov. 8	Edison
Nov. 25	Byron
Dec. 18	King Alexander

NAVIGAZIONE GENER- ALE ITALIANA LINE
Mediterranean—New York

N. Y.

Arrival	Steamer
Jan. 23	Colombo
Feb. 11	Duilio
Mar. 2	Colombo
Mar. 22	Duilio
Apr. 10	Colombo
Apr. 25	Duilio
May 22	Colombo
June 8	Duilio
June 26	Colombo
June 27	Guilio Cesare
July 14	Duilio
Aug. 9	Guilio Cesare
Aug. 17	Duilio
Sept. 13	Guilio Cesare
Sept. 19	Duilio
Oct. 21	Duilio
Oct. 30	Colombo
Nov. 25	Duilio
Dec. 6	Colombo
Dec. 26	Duilio

NAVIGAZIONE GENER- ALE ITALIANA LINE
Mediterranean—Boston

Boston

Arrival	Steamer
Mar. 22	America
May 15	America

NORTH GERMAN LLOYD
Bremen—New York

N. Y.

Arrival	Steamer
Jan. 1	Bremen
Jan. 11	Muenchen
Jan. 23	Colombo

Year 1924

NORTH GERMAN LLOYD
Bremen—New York
(Continued)

N.Y. Arrival	Steamer
Jan. 28	Stuttgart
Feb. 14	Bremen
Feb. 26	Stuttgart
Mar. 20	Bremen
Apr. 10	Stuttgart
Apr. 21	Bremen
Apr. 30	Columbus
May 1	York
May 11	Stuttgart
May 19	Bremen
May 26	Muenchen
May 29	Seydlitz
June 5	York
June 6	Columbus
June 15	Stuttgart
June 18	Bremen
June 26	Luetzow
July 1	Muenchen
July 4	Columbus
July 12	Sierra Ventana
July 17	York
July 27	Luetzow
Aug. 1	Columbus
Aug. 14	Sierra Ventana
Aug. 24	Columbus
Aug. 29	Bremen
Sept. 4	Luetzow
Sept. 6	Stuttgart
Sept. 10	Sierra Ventana
Sept. 17	Columbus
Sept. 19	Derfflinger
Sept. 23	Muenchen
Sept. 30	Bremen
Oct. 5	Stuttgart
Oct. 10	Columbus
Oct. 21	Muenchen
Nov. 1	Bremen
Nov. 9	Columbus
Nov. 24	Muenchen
Dec. 6	Stuttgart
Dec. 15	Bremen
Dec. 25	Duilio

NORWEGIAN-AMERICA LINE
Bergen—Stavanger—Kristiansand—Oslo—New York

N.Y. Arrival	Steamer
Feb. 13	Bergensfjord
Mar. 23	Bergensfjord
Apr. 9	Stavangerfjord
Apr. 25	Bergensfjord
May 13	Stavangerfjord
May 30	Bergensfjord
June 16	Stavangerfjord
July 2	Bergensfjord
July 21	Stavangerfjord
Aug. 25	Stavangerfjord
Sept. 29	Stavangerfjord
Oct. 7	Bergensfjord
Oct. 29	Stavangerfjord
Nov. 11	Bergensfjord
Dec. 1	Stavangerfjord
Dec. 23	Bergensfjord

RED STAR LINE
Antwerp—New York

N.Y. Arrival	Steamer
Jan. 9	Lapland
Jan. 15	Belgenland
Feb. 9	Zeeland
May 24	Zeeland
June 20	Zeeland
July 25	Zeeland
Aug. 23	Zeeland
Aug. 31	Belgenland
Sept. 6	Lapland
Sept. 20	Zeeland
Oct. 2	Belgenland
Oct. 11	Lapland
Oct. 18	Zeeland
Nov. 23	Zeeland
Nov. 30	Belgenland
Dec. 29	Zeeland

RED STAR LINE
Mediterranean—New York

N.Y. Arrival	Steamer
Feb. 29	Lapland
Apr. 19	Lapland

RED STAR LINE
Southampton—New York

N.Y. Arrival	Steamer
Mar. 28	Belgenland
May 5	Belgenland

RED STAR LINE
Hamburg—New York

N.Y. Arrival	Steamer
May 19	Lapland

RED STAR LINE
London—New York

N.Y. Arrival	Steamer
June 2	Belgenland
June 17	Lapland
July 1	Belgenland
July 14	Lapland
July 28	Belgenland

ROYAL MAIL STEAM PACKET CO.
Lisbon—Hamburg—New York

N.Y. Arrival	Steamer
Jan. 1	Orca
Jan. 15	Orduna
Mar. 10	Orduna
Apr. 21	Orduna
Apr. 28	Orbita
May 12	Orca
May 19	Araguaya
May 26	Orduna
June 2	Orbita
June 16	Orca
July 1	Ohio
July 2	Orduna
July 7	Orbita

ROYAL MAIL STEAM PACKET CO.
Lisbon—Hamburg—New York
(Continued)

N.Y. Arrival	Steamer
July 22	Orca
Aug. 1	Ohio
Aug. 11	Orbita
Aug. 25	Orca
Aug. 31	Ohio
Sept. 1	Orduna
Sept. 15	Orbita
Sept. 30	Orca
Oct. 6	Ohio
Oct. 13	Orduna
Oct. 20	Orbita
Nov. 19	Orca
Nov. 24	Araguaya
Dec. 1	Orduna
Dec. 24	Ohio

SCANDINAVIAN-AMERICAN LINE
Scandinavian Ports—New York

N.Y. Arrival	Steamer
Jan. 23	Hellig Olav
Feb. 6	Oscar II
Feb. 18	Frederik VIII
Feb. 29	United States
Mar. 19	Oscar II
Apr. 1	Frederik VIII
Apr. 15	United States
Apr. 29	Hellig Olav
May 12	Frederik VIII
May 27	United States
June 10	Hellig Olav
July 1	Frederik VIII
July 20	United States
Aug. 1	Hellig Olav
Aug. 19	Oscar II
Aug. 31	United States
Sept. 9	Hellig Olav
Sept. 20	Frederik VIII
Sept. 30	Oscar II
Oct. 14	United States
Oct. 30	Hellig Olav
Nov. 11	Oscar II
Nov. 25	United States
Dec. 1	Frederik VIII
Dec. 24	Oscar II

SWEDISH-AMERICAN LINE
Gothenburg—New York

N.Y. Arrival	Steamer
Jan. 8	Drottningholm
Jan. 17	Stockholm
Feb. 1	Kungsholm
Feb. 12	Drottningholm
Feb. 24	Stockholm
Mar. 12	Drottningholm
Mar. 24	Kungsholm
Apr. 7	Stockholm
Apr. 22	Kungsholm
May 4	Drittningholm

Year 1924

SWEDISH-AMERICAN LINE
Gothenburg—New York
(Continued)

N.Y. Arrival	Steamer
May 18	Stockholm
May 28	Kungsholm
June 4	Drottningholm
June 29	Stockholm
July 7	Drottningholm
July 21	Kungsholm
Aug. 4	Drottningholm
Aug. 12	Stockholm
Aug. 25	Kungsholm
Sept. 6	Drottningholm
Sept. 16	Stockholm
Sept. 29	Kungsholm
Oct. 6	Drottningholm
Oct. 22	Stockholm
Nov. 3	Drottningholm
Nov. 19	Kungsholm
Nov. 26	Stockholm
Dec. 4	Drottningholm

TRANSATLANTICA ITALIANA LINE
Mediterranean—New York—Boston

N.Y. Arrival	Steamer
Feb. 8	Giuseppe Verdi
Feb. 28	Dante Alighieri
Apr. 16	Dante Alighieri
May 9	Giuseppe Verdi
June 1	Dante Alighieri
June 19	Giuseppe Verdi
Aug. 3	Dante Alighieri
Aug. 27	Giuseppe Verdi
Sept. 21	Dante Alighieri
Oct. 12	Giuseppe Verdi
Nov. 28	Giuseppe Verdi

UNITED AMERICAN LINES, INC.
Hamburg—New York

N.Y. Arrival	Steamer
Jan. 1	Mount Clay
Jan. 27	Cleveland
Mar. 10	Cleveland
Apr. 20	Cleveland
Apr. 25	Reliance
May 23	Reliance
May 26	Cleveland
June 7	Mount Clay
June 20	Reliance
July 1	Cleveland
July 4	Resolute
July 15	Mount Clay
July 18	Reliance
Aug. 1	Resolute
Aug. 11	Cleveland
Aug. 15	Reliance
Aug. 29	Resolute
Sept. 12	Reliance
Sept. 14	Cleveland
Sept. 22	Mount Clay
Sept. 25	Resolute
Oct. 9	Reliance

UNITED AMERICAN LINES, INC.
Hamburg—New York
(Continued)

N.Y. Arrival	Steamer
Oct. 19	Cleveland
Oct. 26	Resolute
Oct. 27	Mount Clay
Nov. 11	Reliance
Nov. 23	Cleveland
Dec. 2	Mount Clay

UNITED STATES LINES
Queenstown—Cherbourg—London—New York

N.Y. Arrival	Steamer
Jan. 2	Pres. Garfield
Jan. 10	Pres. Van Buren
Jan. 16	Pres. Polk
Jan. 23	Pres. Adams
Jan. 31	Pres. Monroe
Feb. 6	Pres. Garfield
Feb. 13	Pres. Van Buren
Feb. 20	Pres. Polk
Mar. 12	Pres. Monroe
Mar. 19	Pres. Van Buren

UNITED STATES LINES
Plymouth—Cherbourg—Bremen—New York

N.Y. Arrival	Steamer
Jan. 7	George Washington
Jan. 16	Pres. Harding
Jan. 27	America
Feb. 5	George Washington
Feb. 14	Pres. Roosevelt
Feb. 21	Pres. Harding
Mar. 3	America
Mar. 17	Pres. Roosevelt
Mar. 24	Pres. Harding
Apr. 3	George Washington
Apr. 7	America
Apr. 13	Pres. Roosevelt
Apr. 20	Pres. Harding
Apr. 29	George Washington
May 4	America
May 11	Pres. Roosevelt
May 21	Pres. Harding
May 27	Republic
May 29	George Washington
June 7	America
June 8	Pres. Roosevelt
June 19	Pres. Harding
June 30	George Washington
July 1	Republic
July 3	Pres. Roosevelt
July 9	America
July 16	Pres. Harding
July 29	Republic
July 31	George Washington
Aug. 3	Pres. Roosevelt
Aug. 6	America
Aug. 14	Pres. Harding
Aug. 31	George Washington
Sept. 1	Republic
Sept. 3	Pres. Roosevelt
Sept. 7	America

UNITED STATES LINES
Plymouth—Cherbourg—Bremen—New York
(Continued)

N.Y. Arrival	Steamer
Sept. 14	Pres. Harding
Sept. 28	George Washington
Oct. 3	Republic
Oct. 3	Pres. Roosevelt
Oct. 9	America
Oct. 16	Pres. Harding
Oct. 26	George Washington
Nov. 9	Republic
Nov. 18	America
Nov. 21	Pres. Harding
Nov. 24	George Washington
Dec. 8	Pres. Roosevelt
Dec. 23	Republic
Dec. 22	America

UNITED STATES LINES
Cherbourg—Southampton—New York

N.Y. Arrival	Steamer
Apr. 28	Leviathan
May 19	Leviathan
June 9	Leviathan
June 30	Leviathan
July 21	Leviathan
Aug. 12	Leviathan
Sept. 1	Leviathan
Sept. 22	Leviathan
Oct. 22	Leviathan
Nov. 10	Leviathan
Dec. 2	Leviathan
Dec. 21	Leviathan

WHITE STAR LINE
Hamburg—New York

N.Y. Arrival	Steamer
Jan. 21	Pittsburgh
Feb. 24	Pittsburgh
Apr. 11	Canopic
Apr. 26	Pittsburgh
May 18	Canopic
June 2	Pittsburgh
June 19	Canopic
July 7	Pittsburgh
Aug. 11	Pittsburgh
Aug. 27	Arabic
Sept. 16	Pittsburgh
Sept. 29	Arabic
Nov. 4	Pittsburgh

WHITE STAR LINE
Liverpool—New York

N.Y. Arrival	Steamer
Jan. 15	Cedric
Jan. 21	Megantic
Jan. 29	Baltic
Feb. 5	Doric
Feb. 11	Cedric
Mar. 11	Cedric
Apr. 1	Celtic
Apr. 14	Cedric
Apr. 21	Baltic

Year 1924

WHITE STAR LINE		WHITE STAR LINE		WHITE STAR LINE	
Liverpool—New York		Liverpool—New York		Southampton—New York	
	(Continued)		(Continued)		(Continued)
N. Y.		**N. Y.**		**N. Y.**	
Arrival	**Steamer**	**Arrival**	**Steamer**	**Arrival**	**Steamer**
Apr. 28	Celtic	Dec. 9	Celtic	July 2	Olympic
May 5	Adriatic	Dec. 16	Doric	July 7	Homeric
May 11	Cedric	Dec. 23	Cedric	July 15	Majestic
May 19	Baltic	Dec. 30	Regina	July 29	Olympic
May 26	Celtic			Aug. 6	Homeric
June 2	Adriatic			Aug. 12	Majestic
June 9	Cedric	**WHITE STAR LINE**		Aug. 19	Olympic
June 16	Baltic	Liverpool—Philadelphia		Aug. 27	Homeric
June 23	Celtic	**Phila.**		Sept. 2	Majestic
July 1	Adriatic	**Arrival**	**Steamer**	Sept. 9	Olympic
July 7	Cedric	Sept. 10	Haverford	Sept. 17	Homeric
July 14	Baltic	Sept. 29	Canopic	Sept. 23	Majestic
July 21	Celtic			Sept. 30	Olympic
July 27	Adriatic			Oct. 8	Homeric
Aug. 4	Cedric	**WHITE STAR LINE**		Oct. 14	Majestic
Aug. 11	Baltic	Southampton—New York		Oct. 21	Olympic
Aug. 18	Celtic	**N. Y.**		Oct. 30	Homeric
Aug. 24	Adriatic	**Arrival**	**Steamer**	Nov. 4	Majestic
Sept. 1	Cedric	Jan. 10	Majestic	Nov. 11	Olympic
Sept. 8	Baltic	Jan. 30	Majestic	Nov. 20	Homeric
Sept. 15	Celtic	Feb. 27	Olympic	Nov. 25	Majestic
Sept. 22	Adriatic	Mar. 18	Olympic	Dec. 3	Olympic
Sept. 29	Cedric	Apr. 8	Olympic	Dec. 15	Majestic
Oct. 6	Baltic	Apr. 15	Majestic	Dec. 24	Olympic
Oct. 13	Celtic	Apr. 29	Olympic		
Oct. 19	Adriatic	May 7	Homeric		
Oct. 28	Cedric	May 13	Majestic	**WHITE STAR LINE**	
Nov. 4	Baltic	May 20	Olympic	Mediterranean—New York	
Nov. 10	Celtic	May 28	Homeric	**N. Y.**	
Nov. 17	Adriatic	June 3	Majestic	**Arrival**	**Steamer**
Nov. 24	Cedric	June 11	Olympic	Feb. 19	Adriatic
Dec. 1	Baltic	June 18	Homeric	Apr. 8	Adriatic
		June 24	Majestic		

Year 1925

AMERICAN LINE
Hamburg—New York
N. Y.

Arrival	Steamer
Jan. 12	Mongolia
Jan. 21	Minnekahda

AMERICAN PALESTINE LINE
Levant—New York
N. Y.

Arrival	Steamer
May 8	President Arthur
July 14	President Arthur

ANCHOR LINE
Glasgow—Boston
Boston

Arrival	Steamer
July 19	California
Sept. 20	Transylvania

ANCHOR LINE
Mediterranean—New York
N. Y.

Arrival	Steamer
Sept. 3	Tuscania

ANCHOR LINE
Glasgow—New York
N. Y.

Arrival	Steamer
Jan. 4	Assyria
Jan. 7	Columbia
Jan. 15	California
Jan. 19	Tuscania
Jan. 27	Cameronia
Feb. 5	Assyria
Feb. 17	Columbia
Feb. 23	Cameronia
Mar. 5	Athenia
Mar. 17	Columbia
Mar. 23	Cameronia
Apr. 6	Athenia
Apr. 14	Columbia
Apr. 20	Cameronia
Apr. 28	Tuscania
May 5	Assyria
May 11	Columbia
May 17	Cameronia
May 25	Tuscania
June 3	Assyria
June 8	Columbia
June 15	Cameronia
June 22	California
June 30	Assyria
July 1	Tuscania
July 6	Columbia
July 12	Cameronia
July 20	California
Aug. 2	Columbia
Aug. 9	Cameronia
Aug. 16	California
Aug. 25	Assyria
Aug. 30	Columbia
Sept. 6	Cameronia
Sept. 13	California

ANCHOR LINE
Glasgow—New York
(Continued)
N. Y.

Arrival	Steamer
Sept. 21	Transylvania
Sept. 28	Tuscania
Oct. 4	Cameronia
Oct. 12	Caledonia
Oct. 18	Transylvania
Oct. 27	Tuscania
Nov. 3	Cameronia
Nov. 9	Caledonia
Nov. 16	Transylvania
Dec. 1	Cameronia
Dec. 16	Athenia
Dec. 29	Caledonia

ATLANTIC TRANSPORT LINE
London—New York—Boston
N. Y.

Arrival	Steamer
Jan. 13	Minnewaska
Jan. 26	Minnetonka
Feb. 9	Minnewaska
Feb. 23	Minnetonka
Mar. 9	Minnewaska
Mar. 23	Minnetonka
Apr. 2	Minnekahda
Apr. 20	Minnewaska
May 4	Minnetonka
May 18	Minnewaska
May 25	Minnekahda
June 1	Minnetonka
June 15	Minnewaska
June 22	Minnekahda
June 29	Minnetonka
July 14	Minnewaska
July 20	Minnekahda
July 27	Minnetonka
Aug. 10	Minnewaska
Aug. 17	Minnekahda
Aug. 23	Minnetonka
Sept. 7	Minnewaska
Sept. 14	Minnekahda
Sept. 21	Minnetonka
Oct. 5	Minnewaska
Oct. 13	Minnekahda
Oct. 19	Minnetonka
Nov. 3	Minnewaska
Nov. 9	Minnekahda
Nov. 16	Minnetonka
Nov. 30	Minnewaska
Dec. 8	Minnekahda
Dec. 14	Minnetonka

BALTIC-AMERICA LINE
Halifax—New York
N. Y.

Arrival	Steamer
Jan. 8	Estonia
Jan. 28	Lituania
Feb. 18	Estonia
Mar. 9	Lituania
Apr. 2	Estonia
Apr. 22	Lituania

BALTIC-AMERICA LINE
Halifax—New York
(Continued)
N. Y.

Arrival	Steamer
May 9	Estonia
May 21	Lituania
June 20	Estonia
July 12	Lituania
Aug. 1	Estonia
Aug. 23	Lituania
Sept. 11	Estonia
Oct. 4	Lituania
Oct. 26	Estonia
Dec. 2	Estonia

COMPANIA TRANSATLANTICA LINE
(Spanish Line)
Spain— New York
N. Y.

Arrival	Steamer
May 16	Reina Ma. Cristina
Oct. 5	Reina Ma. Cristina
Nov. 24	Reina Ma. Cristina

COSULICH LINE
Italy, Greece, Adriatic— New York
N. Y.

Arrival	Steamer
Jan. 26	President Wilson
Feb. 16	Martha Washington
Mar. 15	President Wilson
Apr. 6	Martha Washington
May 3	President Wilson
May 27	Martha Washington
June 22	President Wilson
July 14	Martha Washington
Aug. 9	President Wilson
Sept. 1	Martha Washington
Sept. 27	President Wilson
Oct. 21	Martha Washington
Nov. 18	President Wilson
Dec. 1	Martha Washington

CUNARD LINE
Cherbourg—Southampton— New York
N. Y.

Arrival	Steamer
May 1	Berengaria
May 8	Mauretania
May 15	Aquitania
May 23	Berengaria
May 29	Mauretania
June 5	Aquitania
June 10	Albania
June 12	Berengaria
June 19	Mauretania
June 26	Aquitania
July 3	Berengaria
July 10	Mauretania
July 24	Aquitania
July 31	Berengaria
Aug. 7	Mauretania
Aug. 14	Aquitania
Aug. 21	Berengaria

Year 1925

CUNARD LINE
Cherbourg—Southampton—
New York
(Continued)

N. Y. Arrival	Steamer
Aug. 28	Mauretania
Aug. 30	Caronia
Sept. 4	Aquitania
Sept. 9	Albania
Sept. 11	Berengaria
Sept. 18	Mauretania
Sept. 21	Lancastria
Sept. 25	Aquitania
Sept. 28	Caronia
Oct. 2	Berengaria
Oct. 9	Mauretania
Oct. 16	Aquitania
Oct. 19	Lancastria
Oct. 24	Berengaria
Oct. 30	Mauretania
Nov. 3	Caronia
Nov. 6	Aquitania
Nov. 13	Berengaria
Nov. 20	Mauretania
Nov. 23	Antonia
Nov. 27	Aquitania
Dec. 4	Berengaria
Dec. 14	Mauretania
Dec. 20	Ausonia

CUNARD LINE
Liverpool—New York

N. Y. Arrival	Steamer
Jan. 12	Caronia
Jan. 20	Scythia
Jan. 27	Laconia
Feb. 3	Samaria
Feb. 10	Caronia
Feb. 18	Lancastria
Feb. 23	Carmania
Mar. 5	Aurania
Mar. 9	Caronia
Mar. 17	Lancastria
Mar. 23	Carmania
Mar. 31	Aurania
Apr. 6	Caronia
Apr. 14	Scythia
Apr. 20	Laconia
Apr. 27	Carmania
May 4	Samaria
May 11	Caronia
May 19	Scythia
May 24	Carmania
June 2	Samaria
June 8	Caronia
June 15	Laconia
June 21	Carmania
June 29	Franconia
July 5	Caronia
July 13	Laconia
July 19	Carmania
July 28	Samaria
Aug. 2	Caronia
Aug. 10	Laconia
Aug. 16	Carmania
Aug. 24	Franconia
Aug. 31	Carinthia
Sept. 7	Laconia
Sept. 13	Carmania

CUNARD LINE
Liverpool—New York
(Continued)

N. Y. Arrival	Steamer
Sept. 20	Franconia
Sept. 30	Scythia
Oct. 5	Carinthia
Oct. 12	Carmania
Oct. 19	Franconia
Oct. 29	Scythia
Nov. 10	Samaria
Nov. 16	Franconia
Nov. 23	Alaunia
Nov. 30	Laconia
Dec. 7	Samaria
Dec. 15	Aurania
Dec. 30	Alaunia

CUNARD LINE
Liverpool—Boston

Boston Arrival	Steamer
Jan. 26	Aurania
Feb. 8	Caronia
Feb. 21	Carmania
Mar. 7	Caronia
Mar. 21	Carmania
Apr. 4	Caronia
Apr. 26	Carmania
May 3	Samaria
May 9	Caronia
May 18	Scythia
May 31	Samaria
June 7	Caronia
June 14	Scythia
June 22	Lancastria
June 27	Samaria
July 12	Laconia
July 26	Samaria
Aug. 7	Scythia
Aug. 21	Samaria
Sept. 5	Scythia
Sept. 16	Samaria
Sept. 28	Scythia
Oct. 11	Carmania
Oct. 18	Franconia
Oct. 28	Scythia
Nov. 9	Samaria
Nov. 15	Franconia
Nov. 29	Laconia

CUNARD LINE
Cherbourg—Southampton—
New York

N. Y. Arrival	Steamer
Jan. 12	Aquitania
Jan. 14	Antonia
Jan. 19	Mauretania
Jan. 26	Ausonia
Feb. 4	Berengaria
Feb. 13	Mauretania
Feb. 17	Antonia
Feb. 18	Aquitania
Feb. 25	Berengaria
Mar. 3	Ausonia
Mar. 10	Aquitania
Mar. 20	Berengaria
Mar. 23	Antonia
Mar. 27	Mauretania

CUNARD LINE
Cherbourg—Southampton—
New York
(Continued)

N. Y. Arrival	Steamer
Apr. 3	Aquitania
Apr. 6	Ausonia
Apr. 10	Berengaria
Apr. 18	Mauretania
Apr. 24	Aquitania

CUNARD LINE
Cherbourg—New York

N. Y. Arrival	Steamer
Feb. 3	Andania
Mar. 9	Andania
Apr. 14	Andania
May 18	Andania
June 22	Andania
July 27	Andania
Aug. 22	Lancastria
Aug. 31	Andania
Oct. 5	Andania
Nov. 9	Andania
Dec. 6	Ascania
Dec. 14	Andania

FABRE LINE
Mediterranean—New York

N. Y. Arrival	Steamer
Jan. 3	Providence
Feb. 10	Patria
Mar. 6	Asia
Mar. 13	Providence
Apr. 21	Patria
May 29	Providence
June 5	Asia
June 26	Patria
Aug. 6	Braga
Aug. 7	Providence
Aug. 21	Canada
Sept. 3	Asia
Sept. 4	Patria
Oct. 6	Providence
Nov. 21	Patria
Nov. 28	Providence
Dec. 3	Canada

FRENCH LINE
(Compagnie Generale Transatlantique)
Halifax—New York

N. Y. Arrival	Steamer
Jan. 1	Suffren
Jan. 4	Paris
Jan. 10	France
Jan. 19	La Savoie
Jan. 24	Paris
Feb. 1	France
Feb. 4	La Bourdonnais
Feb. 14	De Grasse
Feb. 21	Rochambeau
Feb. 24	Roussillon
Feb. 25	France
Mar. 8	Suffren
Mar. 12	De Grasse
Mar. 17	La Bourdonnais
Mar. 18	France
Mar. 24	Paris

Year 1925

FRENCH LINE
(Compagnie Generale Transatlantique)
Halifax—New York
(Continued)
N. Y.

Arrival	Steamer
Apr. 3	Rochambeau
Apr. 5	Roussillon
Apr. 10	De Grasse
Apr. 14	Suffren
Apr. 16	France
Apr. 21	Paris
Apr. 29	La Bourdonnais
May 1	La Savoie
May 6	France
May 12	De Grasse
May 13	Paris
May 18	Roussillon
May 22	Suffren
May 27	France
June 1	La Savoie
June 3	Paris
June 8	De Grasse
June 8	La Bourdonnais
June 13	Rochambeau
June 17	France
June 22	Suffren
June 24	Paris
June 29	La Savoie
June 29	Roussillon
July 2	De Grasse
July 9	France
July 13	Rochambeau
July 14	Paris
July 24	La Savoie
July 30	De Grasse
Aug. 8	Suffren
Aug. 12	Paris
Aug. 13	Roussillon
Aug. 21	Rochambeau
Aug. 24	Chicago
Aug. 28	De Grasse
Aug. 30	La Savoie
Sept. 1	Paris
Sept. 9	France
Sept. 10	La Bourdonnais
Sept. 14	Suffren
Sept. 18	Rochambeau
Sept. 23	Paris
Sept. 24	Roussillon
Sept. 28	De Grasse
Sept. 30	France
Oct. 8	Chicago
Oct. 9	La Savoie
Oct. 13	Suffren
Oct. 14	Paris
Oct. 19	Rochambeau
Oct. 22	La Bourdonnais
Oct. 31	De Grasse
Nov. 4	Paris
Nov. 8	Roussillon
Nov. 12	La Savoie
Nov. 20	Chicago
Nov. 21	Rochambeau
Nov. 27	De Grasse
Dec. 2	Paris
Dec. 4	Le Bourdonnais
Dec. 11	La Savoie
Dec. 19	Rochambeau
Dec. 23	Paris

HAMBURG-AMERICAN LINE
Halifax—New York—Boston
N. Y.

Arrival	Steamer
Jan. 21	Westphalia
Jan. 27	Albert Ballin
Feb. 5	Thuringia
Feb. 10	Deutschland
Mar. 6	Westphalia
Mar. 9	Albert Ballin
Mar. 18	Thuringia
Mar. 24	Deutschland
Apr. 17	Westphalia
Apr. 21	Albert Ballin
Apr. 29	Thuringia
May 4	Deutschland
May 27	Westphalia
June 1	Albert Ballin
June 11	Thuringia
June 15	Deutschland
July 13	Albert Ballin
July 22	Thuringia
July 27	Deutschland
Aug. 19	Westphalia
Aug. 24	Albert Ballin
Sept. 2	Thuringia
Sept. 7	Deutschland
Sept. 30	Westphalia
Oct. 5	Albert Ballin
Oct. 14	Thuringia
Oct. 19	Deutschland
Nov. 11	Westphalia
Nov. 16	Albert Ballin
Nov. 25	Thuringia
Nov. 30	Deutschland
Dec. 22	Westphalia
Dec. 29	Albert Ballin

HOLLAND-AMERICA LINE
Halifax— New York
N. Y.

Arrival	Steamer
Jan. 12	Veendam
Jan. 24	Rotterdam
Jan. 31	New Amsterdam
Feb. 14	Veendam
Mar. 8	New Amsterdam
Mar. 22	Veendam
Apr. 4	Volendam
Apr. 13	New Amsterdam
Apr. 25	Rotterdam
May 2	Veendam
May 10	Volendam
May 15	New Amsterdam
May 24	Ryndam
May 29	Rotterdam
June 7	Veendam
June 13	Volendam
June 20	New Amsterdam
June 28	Ryndam
July 3	Rotterdam
July 10	Veendam
July 18	Volendam
July 25	New Amsterdam
Aug. 7	Rotterdam
Aug. 14	Veendam
Aug. 24	Volendam
Aug. 29	New Amsterdam

HOLLAND-AMERICA LINE
Halifax—New York
(Continued)
N. Y.

Arrival	Steamer
Sept. 5	Ryndam
Sept. 10	Rotterdam
Sept. 19	Veendam
Sept. 25	Volendam
Oct. 3	New Amsterdam
Oct. 10	Ryndam
Oct. 16	Rotterdam
Oct. 24	Veendam
Nov. 3	Volendam
Nov. 8	New Amsterdam
Nov. 20	Rotterdam
Dec. 6	Volendam
Dec. 21	New Amsterdam

LEYLAND LINE
Liverpool—Boston
Boston

Arrival	Steamer
Jan. 8	Devonian
Feb. 11	Winifredian
Feb. 24	Devonian
June 8	Winifredian
June 16	Devonian
July 19	Winifredian
Aug. 8	Devonian
Sept. 6	Winifredian
Sept. 19	Devonian
Oct. 20	Winifredian
Nov. 5	Devonian
Dec. 23	Winifredian

LLOYD SABAUDO
Mediterranean—New York
N. Y.

Arrival	Steamer
Jan. 18	Conte Verde
Jan. 31	Conte Rosso
Feb. 28	Conte Verde
Mar. 15	Conte Rosso
Apr. 6	Conte Verde
May 11	Conte Verde
June 6	Conte Rosso
June 20	Conte Verde
July 13	Conte Rosso
July 27	Conte Verde
Aug. 16	Conte Rosso
Aug. 31	Conte Verde
Sept. 21	Conte Rosso
Oct. 3	Conte Verde
Oct. 25	Conte Rosso
Nov. 30	Conte Viancamano
Dec. 21	Conte Rosso

NATIONAL GREEK LINE
Mediterranean—New York—
Boston
N. Y.

Arrival	Steamer
Jan. 3	Edison
Jan. 31	Byron
Feb. 26	King Alexander
Mar. 23	Byron
Apr. 24	King Alexander
May 18	Byron

Year 1925

NATIONAL GREEK LINE
Mediterranean—New York—
Boston
(Continued)

N. Y.

Arrival	Steamer
June 21	Edison
July 14	Byron
Aug. 15	Edison
Sept. 10	Byron
Oct. 7	Edison
Nov. 3	Byron
Nov. 25	Edison
Dec. 31	Byron

NAVIGAZIONE GENE-RALE ITALIANA LINE
Mediterranean—New York—
Philadelphia

N. Y.

Arrival	Steamer
Feb. 8	Duilio
Mar. 2	Duilio
Apr. 9	Colombo
May 2	Duilio
May 21	Colombo
June 13	Duilio
June 26	Colombo
June 30	Guilio Cesare
July 25	Duilio
Aug. 2	Colombo
Aug. 25	Duilio
Sept. 9	Colombo
Sept. 18	Guilio Cesare
Sept. 27	Duilio
Oct. 21	Colombo
Nov. 1	Duilio
Nov. 25	Colombo
Dec. 6	Duilio

NAVIGAZIONE GENE-RALE ITALIANA LINE
Mediterranean—Philadelphia

Phila.

Arrival	Steamer
May 19	Colombo
June 25	Colombo

NORTH GERMAN LLOYD
Halifax—Bremen—New York

N. Y.

Arrival	Steamer
Jan. 14	Stuttgart
Jan. 28	Muenchen
Feb. 18	Stuttgart
Mar. 6	Bremen
Mar. 16	Luetzow
Mar. 23	Stuttgart
Apr. 7	Bremen
Apr. 10	Columbus
Apr. 21	Luetzow
Apr. 28	Stuttgart
May 9	Columbus
May 14	Bremen
May 19	Muenchen
May 28	Luetzow
June 4	Sierra Ventana
June 5	Columbus
June 10	Stuttgart

NORTH GERMAN LLOYD
Halifax—Bremen—New York
(Continued)

N. Y.

Arrival	Steamer
June 17	Bremen
June 23	Muenchen
July 2	Columbus
July 11	Sierra Ventana
July 14	Stuttgart
July 22	Bremen
Aug. 7	Columbus
Aug. 17	Stuttgart
Aug. 19	Sierra Ventana
Aug. 25	Bremen
Aug. 30	Columbus
Sept. 8	Muenchen
Sept. 16	Luetzow
Sept. 18	Stuttgart
Sept. 24	Sierra Ventana
Sept. 25	Columbus
Sept. 29	Bremen
Oct. 7	Berlin
Oct. 13	Muenchen
Oct. 21	Luetzow
Oct. 25	Columbus
Nov. 3	Stuttgart
Nov. 12	Bremen
Nov. 18	Berlin
Nov. 25	Muenchen
Dec. 2	Luetzow
Dec. 7	Columbus
Dec. 21	Berlin

NORWEGIAN-AMERICA LINE
Bergen—New York

N. Y.

Arrival	Steamer
Feb. 3	Bergensfjord
Feb. 20	Stavangerfjord
Mar. 17	Stavangerfjord
Mar. 31	Bergensfjord
Apr. 28	Stavangerfjord
May 16	Bergensfjord
June 2	Stavangerfjord
June 20	Bergensfjord
July 6	Stavangerfjord
July 24	Bergensfjord
Aug. 18	Norefjord
Aug. 21	Stavangerfjord
Sept. 5	Bergensfjord
Sept. 7	Topdalsfjord
Sept. 14	Idefjord
Sept. 25	Stavangerfjord
Oct. 16	Bergensfjord
Oct. 23	Tyrifjord
Nov. 3	Stavangerfjord
Nov. 13	Idefjord
Nov. 24	Bergensfjord
Dec. 15	Stavangerfjord

RED STAR LINE
Mediterranean—New York

N. Y.

Arrival	Steamer
Mar. 4	Lapland
Apr. 23	Lapland

RED STAR LINE
Halifax—New York

N. Y.

Arrival	Steamer
Jan. 10	Lapland
Feb. 1	Pittsburgh
Feb. 22	Zeeland
Mar. 8	Pittsburgh
Apr. 4	Zeeland
Apr. 12	Pittsburgh
May 2	Zeeland
May 17	Pittsburgh
May 23	Belgenland
May 30	Zeeland
June 5	Lapland
June 13	Pittsburgh
June 20	Belgenland
June 27	Zeeland
July 2	Lapland
July 11	Pittsburgh
July 18	Belgenland
July 25	Zeeland
Aug. 8	Pittsburgh
Aug. 22	Zeeland
Aug. 29	Lapland
Sept. 5	Pittsburgh
Sept. 12	Belgenland
Sept. 19	Zeeland
Sept. 26	Lapland
Oct. 3	Pittsburgh
Oct. 10	Belgenland
Oct. 17	Zeeland
Oct. 26	Lapland
Nov. 1	Pittsburgh
Nov. 14	Zeeland
Nov. 19	Belgenland
Dec. 7	Pittsburgh
Dec. 21	Zeeland

ROYAL MAIL STEAM PACKET CO.
Halifax—Southampton—
New York—Boston

N. Y.

Arrival	Steamer
Jan. 13	Orca
Jan. 19	Orduna
Feb. 7	Ohio
Mar. 9	Orduna
Apr. 14	Orbita
Apr. 21	Orduna
Apr. 23	Ohio
May 12	Orbita
May 19	Orca
May 26	Orduna
June 9	Orbita
June 16	Orca
June 23	Orduna
June 29	Ohio
July 7	Orbita
July 14	Orca
July 21	Orduna
July 27	Ohio
Aug. 4	Orbita
Aug. 11	Orca
Aug. 18	Orduna
Aug. 24	Ohio
Sept. 1	Orbita
Sept. 8	Orca
Sept. 15	Orduna

Year 1925

ROYAL MAIL STEAM PACKET CO.
Halifax—Southampton—
New York—Boston
(Continued)

N. Y.

Arrival	Steamer
Sept. 20	Ohio
Sept. 29	Orbita
Oct. 6	Orca
Oct. 13	Orduna
Oct. 19	Ohio
Oct. 29	Orbita
Nov. 4	Orca
Nov. 30	Araguaya
Dec. 22	Orduna

SCANDINAVIAN-AMER-ICAN LINE
Halifax—Boston—New York

N. Y.

Arrival	Steamer
Jan. 22	Oscar II
Feb. 12	Hellig Olav
Feb. 25	Frederik VIII
Mar. 11	Oscar II
Mar. 18	Hellig Olav
Mar. 23	Frederik VIII
Apr. 8	United States
Apr. 23	Oscar II
May 5	Hellig Olav
May 11	Frederik VIII
May 20	United States
June 3	Oscar II
June 21	Hellig Olav
June 24	Frederik VIII
July 1	United States
Aug. 1	Frederik VIII
Aug. 11	United States
Aug. 27	Oscar II
Sept. 8	Frederik VIII
Sept. 23	United States
Oct. 7	Hellig Olav
Oct. 18	Frederik VIII
Nov. 4	United States
Nov. 18	Hellig Olav
Nov. 30	Frederik VIII
Dec. 31	Oscar II

SWEDISH-AMERICAN LINE
Halifax—New York

N. Y.

Arrival	Steamer
Jan. 2	Stockholm
Jan. 19	Drottningholm
Feb. 14	Stockholm
Feb. 24	Drottningholm
Mar. 16	Stockholm
Mar. 30	Drottningholm
Apr. 20	Stockholm
May 4	Drottningholm
May 23	Stockholm
June 2	Drottningholm
June 24	Stockholm
July 6	Drottningholm
July 27	Stockholm
Aug. 15	Drottningholm
Sept. 5	Stockholm
Sept. 14	Drottningholm

SWEDISH-AMERICAN LINE
Halifax—New York
(Continued)

N. Y.

Arrival	Steamer
Oct. 7	Stockholm
Oct. 17	Drottningholm
Nov. 10	Stockholm
Nov. 24	Drottningholm
Nov. 30	Gripsholm
Dec. 29	Stockholm

TRANSATLANTICA ITALIANA LINE
Mediterranean—New York—Boston

N. Y.

Arrival	Steamer
Jan. 13	Dante Alighieri
Feb. 1	Giuseppe Verdi
Feb. 25	Dante Alighieri
Mar. 27	Giuseppe Verdi
Apr. 23	Dante Alighieri
May 9	Giuseppe Verdi
June 20	Dante Alighieri
July 7	Giuseppe Verdi
Aug. 6	Dante Alighieri
Aug. 21	Giuseppe Verdi
Sept. 22	Dante Alighieri
Oct. 11	Giuseppe Verdi
Nov. 8	Dante Alighieri
Nov. 28	Giuseppe Verdi
Dec. 23	Dante Alighieri

TRANSATLANTICA ITALIANA LINE
Mediterranean—Boston

Boston

Arrival	Steamer
June 8	Leonardo Da Vinci
Oct. 27	Leonardo Da Vinci

UNITED AMERICAN LINES, Inc.
Hamburg—Halifax—New York

N. Y.

Arrival	Steamer
Jan. 3	Mount Clay
Jan. 11	Cleveland
Feb. 18	Mount Clay
Feb. 24	Cleveland
Mar. 30	Mount Clay
Apr. 6	Cleveland
Apr. 19	Reliance
Apr. 30	Resolute
May 11	Mount Clay
May 15	Reliance
May 18	Cleveland
May 29	Resolute
June 12	Reliance
June 22	Mount Clay
June 26	Resolute
June 29	Cleveland
July 9	Reliance
July 23	Resolute
Aug. 3	Mount Clay
Aug. 6	Reliance
Aug. 10	Cleveland

UNITED AMERICAN LINES, Inc.
Hamburg—Halifax—New York
(Continued)

N. Y.

Arrival	Steamer
Aug. 20	Resolute
Sept. 3	Reliance
Sept. 14	Mount Clay
Sept. 17	Resolute
Sept. 21	Cleveland
Oct. 1	Reliance
Oct. 15	Resolute
Oct. 28	Mount Clay
Oct. 31	Reliance
Nov. 2	Cleveland
Dec. 13	Cleveland

UNITED STATES LINES
Bremen—New York

N. Y.

Arrival	Steamer
Jan. 8	President Roosevelt
Jan. 27	Republic
Feb. 2	America
Feb. 6	George Washington
Feb. 13	President Roosevelt
Feb. 20	President Harding
Mar. 5	Republic
Mar. 6	George Washington
Mar. 19	President Roosevelt
Mar. 27	President Harding
Apr. 4	America
Apr. 9	George Washington
Apr. 18	President Roosevelt
Apr. 30	President Harding
May 5	Republic
May 8	George Washington
May 15	America
May 21	President Roosevelt
May 28	President Harding
June 7	George Washington
June 9	Republic
June 13	America
June 21	President Roosevelt
June 26	President Harding
July 3	George Washington
July 11	Republic
July 17	America
July 22	President Roosevelt
July 25	President Harding
July 31	George Washington
Aug. 9	Republic
Aug. 15	America
Aug. 20	President Roosevelt
Aug. 27	President Harding
Sept. 3	George Washington
Sept. 7	Republic
Sept. 11	America
Sept. 15	President Harding
Sept. 17	President Roosevelt
Oct. 2	George Washington
Oct. 12	Republic
Oct. 16	America
Oct. 18	President Roosevelt
Oct. 27	President Harding
Nov. 6	George Washington
Nov. 14	Republic
Nov. 17	America

Year 1925

UNITED STATES LINES
Bremen—New York
(Continued)

N.Y.

Arrival	Steamer
Nov. 20..	President Roosevelt
Nov. 27...	President Harding
Dec. 3..	George Washington
Dec. 19	Republic
Dec. 23	America

UNITED STATES LINES
Southampton—New York

N.Y.

Arrival	Steamer
Mar. 16	Leviathan
Apr. 6	Leviathan
Apr. 27	Leviathan
May 18	Leviathan
June 8	Leviathan
June 29	Leviathan
July 20	Leviathan
Aug. 10	Leviathan
Aug. 31	Leviathan
Sept. 21	Leviathan
Oct. 19	Leviathan
Nov. 10	Leviathan
Nov. 30	Leviathan
Dec. 21	Leviathan

WHITE STAR LINE
Liverpool—Boston

Boston

Arrival	Steamer
Mar. 17	Canada
Mar. 30	Baltic
Apr. 27	Baltic
May 4	Canopic
May 10	Celtic
May 24	Cedric
May 31	Baltic
June 8	Celtic
June 21	Cedric
July 5	Celtic
July 19	Cedric
Aug. 2	Celtic
Aug. 16	Cedric
Aug. 30	Celtic
Sept. 7	Canopic
Sept. 13	Cedric
Sept. 28	Celtic
Oct. 11	Cedric
Oct. 27	Celtic
Nov. 9	Cedric
Nov. 29	Doric
Dec. 8	Celtic
Dec. 29	Doric

WHITE STAR LINE
Liverpool—New York

N.Y.

Arrival	Steamer
Jan. 6	Adriatic
Jan. 13	Doric

WHITE STAR LINE
Liverpool—New York
(Continued)

N.Y.

Arrival	Steamer
Jan. 20	Megantic
Jan. 26	Cedric
Feb. 3	Baltic
Feb. 9	Celtic
Feb. 17	Doric
Feb. 23	Cedric
Mar. 3	Baltic
Mar. 9	Celtic
Mar. 23	Cedric
Mar. 31	Baltic
Apr. 6	Celtic
Apr. 21	Doric
Apr. 28	Baltic
May 5	Canopic
May 11	Celtic
May 18	Adriatic
May 25	Cedric
June 2	Baltic
June 9	Celtic
June 15	Adriatic
June 22	Cedric
June 29	Baltic
July 7	Celtic
July 12	Adriatic
July 20	Cedric
July 27	Baltic
Aug. 4	Celtic
Aug. 9	Adriatic
Aug. 17	Cedric
Aug. 24	Baltic
Aug. 31	Celtic
Sept. 7	Adriatic
Sept. 14	Cedric
Sept. 21	Baltic
Sept. 29	Celtic
Oct. 5	Adriatic
Oct. 13	Cedric
Oct. 19	Baltic
Nov. 2	Adriatic
Nov. 10	Cedric
Nov. 16	Baltic
Dec. 1	Doric
Dec. 9	Celtic
Dec. 14	Baltic
Dec. 21	Regina
Dec. 30	Doric

WHITE STAR LINE
Southampton—New York

N.Y.

Arrival	Steamer
Jan. 17	Olympic
Jan. 22	Homeric
Feb. 11	Olympic
Mar. 4	Olympic
Mar. 24	Olympic
Apr. 1	Homeric
Apr. 15	Olympic
Apr. 22	Homeric
Apr. 28	Majestic

WHITE STAR LINE
Southampton—New York
(Continued)

N.Y.

Arrival	Steamer
May 6	Olympic
May 13	Homeric
May 19	Majestic
May 26	Olympic
June 3	Homeric
June 9	Majestic
June 16	Olympic
June 24	Homeric
June 30	Majestic
July 7	Olympic
July 15	Homeric
July 21	Majestic
Aug. 5	Olympic
Aug. 12	Homeric
Aug. 18	Majestic
Aug. 26	Olympic
Sept. 2	Homeric
Sept. 8	Majestic
Sept. 15	Olympic
Sept. 23	Homeric
Sept. 29	Majestic
Oct. 6	Olympic
Oct. 14	Homeric
Oct. 20	Majestic
Nov. 5	Homeric
Nov. 11	Majestic
Dec. 1	Majestic
Dec. 9	Homeric
Dec. 22	Majestic
Dec. 30	Homeric

WHITE STAR LINE
Hamburg—New York

N.Y.

Arrival	Steamer
Feb. 20	Arabic
Mar. 27	Arabic
Apr. 30	Arabic
June 5	Arabic
July 12	Arabic
Aug. 12	Arabic
Sept. 16	Arabic
Oct. 21	Arabic
Nov. 27	Arabic

WHITE STAR LINE
Mediterranean—New York

N.Y.

Arrival	Steamer
Feb. 22	Adriatic
Apr. 13	Adriatic

ADDITIONAL ARRIVALS
Around-the-World Cruises

N.Y.

Arrival	Steamer
Apr. 15	Belgenland
May 30	Ohio

Year 1926

AMERICAN MERCHANT LINES
London—New York

N. Y.

Arrival	Steamer
Jan. 14	American Banker
Jan. 19	American Merchant
Jan. 28	American Shipper
Feb. 5	American Farmer
Feb. 10	American Trader
Feb. 25	American Banker
Feb. 25	American Merchant
Mar. 15	American Farmer
Mar. 16	American Trader
Mar. 23	American Banker
Mar. 30	American Merchant
Apr. 6	American Shipper
Apr. 21	American Trader
May 3	American Merchant
May 10	American Shipper
May 30	American Trader
June 1	American Merchant
June 7	American Shipper
June 14	American Banker
June 21	American Farmer
June 28	American Merchant
July 5	American Shipper
July 12	American Banker
July 19	American Farmer
July 26	American Trader
Aug. 2	American Shipper
Aug. 9	American Banker
Aug. 16	American Farmer
Auc. 23	American Trader
Aug. 30	American Merchant
Sept. 6	American Banker
Sept. 13	American Farmer
Sept. 20	American Trader
Sept. 27	American Merchant
Oct. 4	American Banker
Oct. 10	American Shipper
Oct. 18	American Trader
Oct. 25	American Merchant
Nov. 1	American Banker
Nov. 8	American Shipper
Nov. 15	American Trader
Nov. 26	American Merchant
Nov. 29	American Farmer
Dec. 6	American Banker
Dec. 14	American Shipper
Dec. 21	American Trader
Dec. 28	American Merchant

ANCHOR LINE
Liverpool, Londonderry, Glasgow—New York, Boston

N. Y.

Arrival	Steamer
Jan. 19	California
Jan. 26	Transylvania
Jan. 31	Caledonia
Feb. 8	Cameronia
Feb. 23	Tuscania
Mar. 9	Cameronia
Mar. 23	Caledonia
Apr. 6	Cameronia
Apr. 13	Athenia

ANCHOR LINE
Liverpool, Londonderry, Glasgow—New York, Boston
(Continued)

N. Y.

Arrival	Steamer
Apr. 20	Transylvania
May 3	California
May 10	Tuscania
May 17	Cameronia
May 24	Transylvania
May 31	California
June 7	Caledonia
June 13	Cameronia
June 20	Transylvania
June 27	California
July 1	Caledonia
July 11	Cameronia
July 19	Transylvania
July 26	Caledonia
Aug. 8	Cameronia
Aug. 16	Transylvania
Aug. 26	Caledonia
Sept. 5	Cameronia
Sept. 12	Transylvania
Sept. 20	Caledonia
Sept. 27	California
Oct. 3	Cameronia
Oct. 12	Transylvania
Oct. 18	Caledonia
Oct. 31	Cameronia
Nov. 8	Transylvania
Nov. 15	Caledonia
Nov. 29	Cameronia
Dec. 6	Transylvania
Dec. 19	Caledonia
Dec. 27	Athenia

ANCHOR LINE
Liverpool—New York

N. Y.

Arrival	Steamer
Oct. 12	Transylvania
Nov. 8	Transylvania

ANCHOR LINE
Londonderry, Glasgow—Boston

Boston

Arrival	Steamer
Apr. 19	Transylvania
May 30	California
July 25	Caledonia
Sept. 19	Caledonia
Oct. 11	Transylvania
Nov. 7	Transylvania
Dec. 18	Caledonia

ANCHOR LINE
Plymouth, Havre, London—New York

N. Y.

Arrival	Steamer
June 14	Tuscania
July 12	Tuscania
Aug. 9	Tuscania
Sept. 6	Tuscania
Oct. 3	Tuscania
Nov. 1	Tuscania

ATLANTIC TRANSPORT LINE
London—New York

N. Y.

Arrival	Steamer
Jan. 8	Minnekahda
Jan. 13	Minnetonka
Feb. 9	Minnetonka
Feb. 23	Minnewaska
Mar. 22	Minnetonka
Mar. 29	Minnekahda
Apr. 5	Minnewaska
Apr. 20	Minnetonka
Apr. 27	Minnekahda
May 3	Minnewaska
May 28	Minnekahda
May 31	Minnetonka
June 14	Minnewaska
June 21	Minnekahda
June 28	Minnetonka
July 12	Minnewaska
July 19	Minnekahda
July 26	Minnetonka
Aug. 9	Minnewaska
Aug. 16	Minnekahda
Aug. 23	Minnetonka
Sept. 8	Minnewaska
Sept. 13	Minnekahda
Sept. 20	Minnetonka
Oct. 4	Minnewaska
Oct. 11	Minnekahda
Oct. 18	Minnetonka
Nov. 1	Minnewaska
Nov. 9	Minnekahda
Nov. 15	Minnetonka
Nov. 29	Minnewaska
Dec. 7	Minnekahda
Dec. 13	Minnetonka
Dec. 27	Minnewaska

BALTIC-AMERICA LINE
Halifax—Copenhagen, Danzig, Libau—New York

N. Y.

Arrival	Steamer
Jan. 28	Lituania
Mar. 11	Lituania
Mar. 31	Estonia
Apr. 21	Lituania
May 10	Estonia
June 1	Lituania
June 18	Estonia
July 9	Lituania
Aug. 2	Estonia
Aug. 24	Lituania
Sept. 9	Estonia
Oct. 5	Lituania
Oct. 26	Estonia
Dec. 4	Estonia
Dec. 20	Lituania

CANADIAN PACIFIC STEAMSHIP COMPANY
Southampton—New York

N. Y.

Arrival	Steamer
Feb. 5	Empress of France

Year 1926

COMPANIA TRANS-ATLANTICA
(Spanish Line)
Spain—New York

N. Y.

Arrival	Steamer
Mar. 10	Reina M. Cristina
June 5	Manuel Arnus
July 15	Manuel Arnus
Aug. 22	Manuel Arnus
Sept. 28	Manuel Arnus
Nov. 12	Manuel Arnus
Dec. 21	Manuel Arnus

COSULICH LINE
Mediterranean—New York, Boston

N. Y.

Arrival	Steamer
Jan. 23	Martha Washington
Mar. 15	Martha Washington
May 3	Martha Washington
May 17	President Wilson
June 16	Martha Washington
June 30	President Wilson
Aug. 2	Martha Washington
Aug. 22	President Wilson
Sept. 20	Martha Washington
Oct. 10	President Wilson
Nov. 9	Martha Washington
Nov. 29	President Wilson
Dec. 31	Martha Washington

CUNARD LINE
Cherbourg, Southampton—New York

N. Y.

Arrival	Steamer
Jan. 7	Berengaria
Jan. 28	Aquitania
Feb. 9	Mauretania
Feb. 15	Antonia
Feb. 17	Aquitania
Mar. 2	Berengaria
Mar. 18	Aquitania
Mar. 27	Berengaria
Mar. 30	Antonia
Apr. 2	Mauretania
Apr. 10	Aquitania
Apr. 17	Berengaria
Apr. 20	Aquitania
Apr. 23	Mauretania
Apr. 27	Lancastria
May 7	Berengaria
May 14	Mauretania
May 21	Aquitania
May 28	Berengaria
June 4	Mauretania
June 11	Aquitania
June 18	Berengaria
June 25	Mauretania
July 2	Aquitania
July 9	Berengaria
July 16	Mauretania
July 30	Aquitania
Aug. 6	Berengaria
Aug. 17	Mauretania
Aug. 20	Aquitania
Aug. 27	Berengaria
Sept. 3	Mauretania

CUNARD LINE
Cherbourg, Southampton—New York
(Continued)

N. Y.

Arrival	Steamer
Sept. 10	Aquitania
Sept. 17	Berengaria
Sept. 24	Mauretania
Oct. 1	Aquitania
Oct. 8	Berengaria
Oct. 15	Mauretania
Oct. 22	Aquitania
Oct. 29	Berengaria
Nov. 5	Mauretania
Nov. 7	Caronia
Nov. 15	Franconia
Nov. 20	Berengaria
Nov. 26	Mauretania
Dec. 9	Antonia
Dec. 14	Berengaria
Dec. 19	Ascania

CUNARD LINE
Liverpool—New York

N. Y.

Arrival	Steamer
Jan. 11	Franconia
Jan. 13	Aurania
Jan. 16	Laconia
Jan. 20	Scythia
Jan. 25	Samaria
Feb. 3	Alaunia
Feb. 9	Carmania
Feb. 16	Aurania
Feb. 23	Caronia
Mar. 3	Alaunia
Mar. 9	Carmania
Mar. 16	Aurania
Mar. 22	Caronia
Mar. 30	Carinthia
Mar. 30	Antonia
Apr. 5	Alaunia
Apr. 13	Samaria
Apr. 20	Scythia
Apr. 26	Caronia
May 2	Carmania
May 10	Samaria
May 17	Scythia
May 24	Caronia
May 31	Carinthia
June 8	Samaria
June 14	Scythia
June 22	Laconia
June 26	Carinthia
June 28	Franconia
July 6	Samaria
July 12	Scythia
July 20	Laconia
July 26	Franconia
Aug. 3	Samaria
Aug. 9	Scythia
Aug. 17	Laconia
Aug. 23	Franconia
Aug. 30	Samaria
Sept. 6	Carinthia
Sept. 14	Laconia
Sept. 20	Franconia
Sept. 27	Samaria
Oct. 3	Carinthia

CUNARD LINE
Liverpool—New York
(Continued)

N. Y.

Arrival	Steamer
Oct. 19	Franconia
Oct. 26	Samaria
Nov. 1	Scythia
Nov. 7	Caronia
Nov. 15	Lancastria
Nov. 23	Samaria
Nov. 29	Scythia
Dec. 6	Alaunia
Dec. 14	Aurania
Dec. 20	Franconia
Dec. 29	Samaria

CUNARD LINE
Plymouth, Havre, London—New York

N. Y.

Arrival	Steamer
May 31	Lancastria
June 6	Carmania
June 20	Caronia
June 28	Lancastria
July 4	Carmania
July 18	Caronia
Aug. 1	Carmania
Aug. 15	Caronia
Aug. 21	Lancastria
Aug. 29	Carmania
Sept. 11	Caronia
Sept. 20	Lancastria
Sept. 26	Carmania
Oct. 9	Caronia
Oct. 18	Lancastria
Oct. 24	Carmania
Nov. 7	Caronia
Nov. 30	Ausonia
Dec. 6	Carmania
Dec. 14	Andania

CUNARD LINE
Cherbourg, Plymouth, London, Hamburg—New York

N. Y.

Arrival	Steamer
Jan. 19	Andania
Jan. 19	Ascania
Feb. 3	Ausonia
Mar. 2	Ascania
Mar. 10	Andania
Mar. 16	Ausonia
Apr. 5	Ascania
Apr. 13	Andania
May 17	Andania
June 24	Andania
July 26	Andania
Aug. 29	Andania
Oct. 3	Andania
Nov. 8	Andania

CUNARD LINE
Liverpool—Boston

Boston

Arrival	Steamer
Jan. 10	Franconia
Jan. 19	Scythia
Feb. 8	Carmania

Year 1926

CUNARD LINE
Liverpool—Boston
(Continued)

Boston Arrival	Steamer
Feb. 23	Caronia
Mar. 7	Carmania
Mar. 21	Caronia
Apr. 12	Samaria
Apr. 25	Caronia
Apr. 25	Lancastria
May 9	Samaria
May 23	Caronia
June 7	Samaria
June 28	Laconia
July 5	Samaria
July 19	Laconia
Aug. 2	Samaria
Aug. 16	Laconia
Sept. 3	Scythia
Sept. 12	Laconia
Sept. 29	Scythia
Oct. 24	Samaria
Nov. 22	Samaria
Dec. 27	Samaria

FABRE LINE
Mediterranean—New York

N.Y. Arrival	Steamer
Jan. 7	Patria
Feb. 14	Britannia
Feb. 14	Providence
Mar. 23	Patria
Apr. 27	Providence
June 12	Patria
July 6	Providence
Aug. 2	Asia
Aug. 2	Patria
Aug. 9	Roma
Sept. 3	Providence
Sept. 20	Patria
Nov. 11	Asia
Nov. 13	Providence
Dec. 4	Patria

FRENCH LINE
(Compagnie Generale Transatlantique)
Havre—New York

N.Y. Arrival	Steamer
Jan. 1	De Grasse
Jan. 9	La Savoie
Jan. 23	Suffren
Feb. 5	La Savoie
Feb. 19	De Grasse
Feb. 28	Suffren
Mar. 12	La Savoie
Mar. 20	De Grasse
Mar. 27	Suffren
Apr. 12	De Grasse
Apr. 16	La Savoie
Apr. 23	Chicago
May 7	De Grasse
May 18	Suffren
May 28	La Savoie
May 31	Chicago
June 7	De Grasse
June 20	Suffren
June 28	La Savoie

FRENCH LINE
(Compagnie Generale Transatlantique)
Havre—New York
(Continued)

N.Y. Arrival	Steamer
June 29	Chicago
July 5	De Grasse
July 30	La Savoie
Aug. 7	Suffren
Aug. 17	Rochambeau
Aug. 23	La Savoie
Aug. 27	De Grasse
Sept. 7	Suffren
Sept. 17	Rochambeau
Sept. 20	La Savoie
Sept. 27	De Grasse
Oct. 9	Suffren
Oct. 18	Rochambeau
Oct. 24	De Grasse
Oct. 29	La Savoie
Nov. 20	Rochambeau
Nov. 26	De Grasse
Dec. 12	Suffren
Dec. 17	Rochambeau

FRENCH LINE
(Compagnie Generale Transatlantique)
Plymouth, Havre—New York

N.Y. Arrival	Steamer
Jan. 13	Paris
Jan. 28	France
Feb. 10	Paris
Mar. 3	France
Mar. 31	France
Apr. 7	Paris
Apr. 21	France
Apr. 27	Paris
May 12	France
May 19	Paris
June 2	France
June 9	Paris
June 23	France
June 30	Paris
July 14	France
July 20	Paris
Aug. 11	France
Sept. 1	France
Sept. 7	Paris
Sept. 22	France
Sept. 29	Paris
Oct. 13	France
Oct. 20	Paris
Nov. 3	France
Nov. 10	Paris
Dec. 1	Paris
Dec. 22	Paris

FRENCH LINE
(Compagnie Generale Transatlantique)
Halifax, Vigo, Bordeaux—
New York

N.Y. Arrival	Steamer
Jan. 17	La Bourdonnais
Mar. 6	La Bourdonnais
Mar. 27	Roussillon
Apr. 16	La Bourdonnais
May 6	Roussillon
May 20	La Bourdonnais

FRENCH LINE
(Compagnie Generale Transatlantique)
Halifax, Vigo, Bordeaux—
New York
(Continued)

N.Y. Arrival	Steamer
June 10	Roussillon
July 8	La Bourdonnais
July 22	Roussillon
Aug. 19	La Bourdonnais
Sept. 2	Chicago
Sept. 16	Roussillon
Oct. 16	Chicago
Oct. 28	Roussillon
Nov. 12	La Bourdonnais
Nov. 27	Chicago
Dec. 6	Roussillon

HAMBURG-AMERICAN LINE
Hamburg, Cobh, Southampton,
Cherbourg, Boulogne S/M
—New York

N.Y. Arrival	Steamer
Jan. 8	Thuringia
Jan. 15	Deutschland
Feb. 6	Westphalia
Feb. 7	Albert Ballin
Feb. 17	Thuringia
Feb. 23	Deutschland
Mar. 17	Westphalia
Mar. 22	Albert Ballin
Mar. 31	Thuringia
Apr. 5	Deutschland
Apr. 20	Hamburg
Apr. 27	Westphalia
May 3	Albert Ballin
May 11	Thuringia
May 17	Deutschland
May 31	Hamburg
June 8	Westphalia
June 14	Albert Ballin
June 23	Thuringia
June 28	Deutschland
July 12	Hamburg
July 20	Westphalia
July 26	Albert Ballin
Aug. 9	Deutschland
Aug. 16	Cleveland
Aug. 20	Resolute
Aug. 23	Hamburg
Aug. 31	Westphalia
Sept. 3	Reliance
Sept. 6	Albert Ballin
Sept. 14	Thuringia
Sept. 17	Resolute
Sept. 20	Deutschland
Sept. 25	Cleveland
Sept. 30	Reliance
Oct. 4	Hamburg
Oct. 11	Westphalia
Oct. 15	Resolute
Oct. 18	Albert Ballin
Oct. 25	Thuringia
Oct. 28	Reliance
Nov. 1	Deutschland
Nov. 9	Cleveland
Nov. 15	Hamburg

Year 1926

HAMBURG-AMERICAN LINE
Hamburg, Cobh, Southampton, Cherbourg, Boulogne S/M —New York
(Continued)

N. Y.

Arrival	Steamer
Nov. 25	Westphalia
Nov. 29	Albert Ballin
Dec. 7	Thuringia
Dec. 10	Reliance
Dec. 14	Deutschland
Dec. 20	Cleveland
Dec. 27	Hamburg
Dec. 31	Resolute

HAMBURG-AMERICAN LINE
Cobh, Hamburg—Boston

Boston

Arrival	Steamer
Feb. 16	Westphalia
Mar. 30	Thuringia
Apr. 26	Westphalia
May 10	Thuringia
June 7	Westphalia
June 22	Thuringia
July 19	Westphalia
Aug. 30	Westphalia
Sept. 13	Thuringia
Oct. 10	Westphalia
Oct. 24	Thuringia
Nov. 24	Westphalia
Dec. 6	Thuringia

HOLLAND-AMERICA LINE
Rotterdam, Boulogne-Sur-Mer, Southampton—Halifax— New York

N. Y.

Arrival	Steamer
Jan. 12	Volendam
Jan. 22	Rotterdam
Feb. 10	Veendam
Feb. 21	Volendam
Mar. 6	New Amsterdam
Mar. 28	Volendam
Apr. 12	New Amsterdam
Apr. 24	Rotterdam
May 1	Veendam
May 8	Volendam
May 15	New Amsterdam
May 22	Ryndam
May 28	Rotterdam
June 5	Veendam
June 13	Volendam
June 18	New Amsterdam
June 28	Rotterdam
July 3	Ryndam
July 10	Veendam
July 18	Volendam
July 24	New Amsterdam
July 31	Rotterdam
Aug. 14	Veendam
Aug. 21	Volendam
Aug. 28	New Amsterdam
Sept. 3	Rotterdam
Sept. 12	Ryndam

HOLLAND-AMERICA LINE
Rotterdam, Boulogne-Sur-Mer, Southampton—Halifax— New York
(Continued)

N. Y.

Arrival	Steamer
Sept. 17	Veendam
Sept. 25	Volendam
Oct. 1	New Amsterdam
Oct. 8	Rotterdam
Oct. 23	Veendam
Oct. 29	Volendam
Nov. 7	New Amsterdam
Nov. 13	Rotterdam
Dec. 4	Volendam
Dec. 11	New Amsterdam
Dec. 20	Veendam
Dec. 26	Noordam

LEYLAND LINE
Liverpool—Boston

Boston

Arrival	Steamer
Jan. 12	Devonian
May 8	Devonian
June 1	Winifredian
June 19	Devonian
July 11	Winifredian
July 31	Devonian
Aug. 23	Winifredian
Sept. 11	Devonian
Oct. 3	Winifredian
Oct. 26	Devonian
Nov. 19	Winifredian
Dec. 8	Devonian
Dec. 30	Winifredian

LLOYD SABAUDO
Mediterranean—New York

N. Y.

Arrival	Steamer
Jan. 16	Conte Biancamano
Feb. 6	Conte Rosso
Feb. 21	Conte Biancamano
Mar. 13	Conte Rosso
Mar. 27	Conte Biancamano
Apr. 17	Conte Rosso
May 3	Conte Biancamano
May 29	Conte Rosso
June 7	Conte Biancamano
July 3	Conte Rosso
July 16	Conte Biancamano
Aug. 10	Conte Rosso
Aug. 28	Conte Biancamano
Sept. 14	Conte Rosso
Oct. 4	Conte Biancamano
Oct. 23	Conte Rosso
Nov. 8	Conte Biancamano
Nov. 30	Conte Rosso
Dec. 20	Conte Biancamano

NATIONAL GREEK LINE
Mediterranean—New York— Boston

N. Y.

Arrival	Steamer
Jan. 28	Edison
Feb. 24	Byron

NATIONAL GREEK LINE
Mediterranean—New York— Boston
(Continued)

N. Y.

Arrival	Steamer
Mar. 23	Edison
Apr. 20	Byron
May 15	Edison
June 12	Byron
July 10	Edison
Aug. 7	Byron
Aug. 31	Edison
Sept. 21	Moreas
Oct. 5	Byron
Oct. 25	Edison
Nov. 9	Moreas
Nov. 24	Byron
Dec. 26	Edison

NAVIGAZIONE GENE-RALE ITALIANA LINE
Mediterranean—New York

N. Y.

Arrival	Steamer
Jan. 11	Colombo
Jan. 26	Duilio
Feb. 19	Colombo
Mar. 6	Duilio
Apr. 2	Colombo
Apr. 19	Duilio
May 12	Colombo
May 23	Duilio
June 19	Colombo
June 28	Duilio
July 31	Duilio
Aug. 19	Colombo
Sept. 6	Duilio
Sept. 29	Colombo
Oct. 1	Roma
Oct. 15	Duilio
Nov. 1	Roma
Nov. 13	Colombo
Nov. 23	Duilio
Dec. 4	Roma
Dec. 28	Duilio

NORTH GERMAN LLOYD
Bremen—New York

N. Y.

Arrival	Steamer
Jan. 15	Bremen
Jan. 25	Stuttgart
Jan. 27	Columbus
Feb. 11	Berlin
Feb. 22	Muenchen
Mar. 2	York
Mar. 11	Bremen
Mar. 15	Berlin
Mar. 27	Muenchen
Apr. 5	York
Apr. 17	Columbus
Apr. 19	Bremen
Apr. 24	Berlin
May 1	Muenchen
May 9	Sierra Ventana
May 13	Columbus
May 14	York
May 20	Bremen
May 22	Stuttgart

Year 1926

NORTH GERMAN LLOYD
Bremen—New York
(Continued)
N. Y.

Arrival	Steamer
May 26	Berlin
June 2	Muenchen
June 7	Columbus
June 15	Sierra Ventana
June 16	Luetzow
June 21	Stuttgart
June 24	Bremen
June 26	Berlin
July 1	Columbus
July 11	York
July 18	Muenchen
July 25	Bremen
Aug. 1	Sierra Ventana
Aug. 4	Seydlitz
Aug. 5	Columbus
Aug. 13	Berlin
Aug. 19	York
Aug. 21	Muenchen
Aug. 26	Derfflinger
Aug. 29	Bremen
Aug. 30	Columbus
Sept. 4	Stuttgart
Sept. 4	Sierra Ventana
Sept. 11	Berlin
Sept. 15	Luetzow
Sept. 16	Seydlitz
Sept. 22	Muenchen
Sept. 25	Columbus
Sept. 29	Derfflinger
Oct. 1	Bremen
Oct. 8	Stuttgart
Oct. 17	Berlin
Oct. 22	Columbus
Oct. 22	Seydlitz
Oct. 23	Luetzow
Oct. 31	Muenchen
Nov. 3	Derfflinger
Nov. 8	Bremen
Nov. 15	Stuttgart
Nov. 21	Berlin
Dec. 3	Muenchen
Dec. 9	Columbus
Dec. 21	Berlin
Dec. 30	Bremen

NORTH GERMAN LLOYD
Bremen—Philadelphia
Phila.

Arrival	Steamer
May 15	York
June 17	Derfflinger

NORWEGIAN-AMERICA LINE
Bergen, Stavanger, Kristian-
sand, Oslo—New York
N. Y.

Arrival	Steamer
Feb. 3	Bergensfjord
Feb. 16	Stavangerfjord
Mar. 10	Bergensfjord
Mar. 26	Stavangerfjord
Apr. 23	Bergensfjord
Apr. 30	Stavangerfjord
May 22	Bergensfjord

NORWEGIAN-AMERICA LINE
Bergen, Stavanger, Kristian-
sand, Oslo—New York
(Continued)
N. Y.

Arrival	Steamer
June 8	Stavangerfjord
June 26	Bergensfjord
Aug. 2	Stavangerfjord
Aug. 20	Bergensfjord
Sept. 6	Stavangerfjord
Sept. 24	Bergensfjord
Oct. 15	Stavangerfjord
Oct. 20	Norefjord
Nov. 5	Bergensfjord
Nov. 26	Stavangerfjord
Dec. 18	Bergensfjord

RED STAR LINE
Mediterranean—New York
N. Y.

Arrival	Steamer
Mar. 3	Lapland
Apr. 23	Lapland

RED STAR LINE
Antwerp—New York
N. Y.

Arrival	Steamer
Jan. 13	Lapland
Jan. 27	Zeeland
Feb. 9	Pittsburgh
Mar. 2	Zeeland
Mar. 16	Pittsburgh
Apr. 13	Pennland
May 3	Zeeland
May 17	Pennland
May 23	Belgenland
May 31	Zeeland
June 7	Lapland
June 15	Pennland
June 20	Belgenland
June 29	Zeeland
July 4	Lapland
July 12	Pennland
Aug. 9	Pennland
Aug. 15	Belgenland
Aug. 23	Zeeland
Aug. 30	Lapland
Sept. 6	Pennland
Sept. 12	Belgenland
Sept. 20	Zeeland
Sept. 27	Lapland
Oct. 4	Pennland
Oct. 11	Belgenland
Oct. 18	Zeeland
Nov. 1	Pennland
Nov. 15	Lapland
Nov. 30	Pennland
Dec. 6	Belgenland
Dec. 25	Arabic
Dec. 31	Lapland

ROYAL MAIL STEAM PACKET COMPANY
Cherbourg, Southampton—
New York, Boston
N. Y.

Arrival	Steamer
Jan. 14	Orca

ROYAL MAIL STEAM PACKET COMPANY
Cherbourg, Southampton—
New York, Boston
(Continued)
N. Y.

Arrival	Steamer
Jan. 16	Ohio
Feb. 4	Orduna
Mar. 3	Orduna
Mar. 29	Orduna
May 10	Ohio
May 24	Orduna
May 31	Orbita
June 5	Ohio
June 14	Orca
June 21	Orduna
June 28	Orbita
July 3	Ohio
July 12	Orca
July 19	Orduna
July 26	Orbita
July 31	Ohio
Aug. 9	Orca
Aug. 16	Orduna
Aug. 23	Orbita
Aug. 29	Ohio
Sept. 6	Orca
Sept. 13	Orduna
Sept. 20	Orbita
Sept. 26	Ohio
Oct. 11	Orca
Oct. 24	Ohio

SCANDINAVIAN-AMERICAN LINE
Scandinavian Ports—New
York
N. Y.

Arrival	Steamer
Jan. 20	Hellig Olav
Feb. 9	United States
Mar. 5	Oscar II
Mar. 24	United States
Apr. 7	Hellig Olav
Apr. 28	Oscar II
May 3	Frederik VIII
May 10	United States
May 19	Hellig Olav
June 2	Oscar II
June 14	Frederik VIII
June 23	United States
July 14	Hellig Olav
July 26	Frederik VIII
Aug. 4	United States
Aug. 18	Oscar II
Aug. 24	Hellig Olav
Sept. 5	Frederik VIII
Sept. 15	United States
Sept. 28	Oscar II
Oct. 5	Hellig Olav
Oct. 17	Frederik VIII
Oct. 26	United States
Nov. 10	Oscar II
Nov. 24	Hellig Olav
Nov. 30	Frederik VIII
Dec. 22	Oscar II

Year 1926

SWEDISH-AMERICAN LINE
Gothenburg—New York

N. Y.

Arrival	Steamer
Jan. 14	Gripsholm
Feb. 3	Drottningholm
Feb. 23	Gripsholm
Mar. 4	Stockholm
Mar. 22	Drottningholm
Apr. 7	Stockholm
Apr. 24	Gripsholm
May 3	Drottningholm
May 12	Stockholm
May 27	Gripsholm
June 6	Drottningholm
June 16	Stockholm
June 29	Gripsholm
July 11	Drottningholm
July 17	Stockholm
Aug. 7	Gripsholm
Aug. 17	Stockholm
Aug. 23	Drottningholm
Sept. 6	Gripsholm
Sept. 20	Drottningholm
Sept. 28	Stockholm
Oct. 4	Gripsholm
Oct. 19	Drottningholm
Oct. 26	Stockholm
Nov. 4	Gripsholm
Nov. 17	Drottningholm
Nov. 29	Stockholm
Dec. 3	Gripsholm
Dec. 21	Drottningholm

TRANSATLANTICA ITALIANA LINE
Mediterranean—New York

N. Y.

Arrival	Steamer
Jan. 26	Giuseppe Verdi
Feb. 20	Dante Alighieri
Mar. 7	Giuseppe Verdi
Apr. 28	Giuseppe Verdi
May 25	Dante Alighieri
June 17	Giuseppe Verdi
July 11	Dante Alighieri
Aug. 1	Giuseppe Verdi
Aug. 24	Dante Alighieri
Sept. 26	Giuseppe Verdi
Oct. 12	Dante Alighieri
Nov. 12	Giuseppe Verdi
Nov. 28	Dante Alighieri

UNITED AMERICAN LINES, INC.
Hamburg—Southampton— Cherbourg—Boulogne S/M—New York

N. Y.

Arrival	Steamer
Jan. 19	Cleveland
Mar. 2	Cleveland
Apr. 13	Cleveland
May 13	Reliance
May 24	Cleveland
June 10	Reliance
June 24	Resolute
July 2	Cleveland
July 9	Reliance
July 22	Resolute

UNITED STATES LINES
Cherbourg—Southampton— New York

N. Y.

Arrival	Steamer
Jan. 27	Leviathan
Apr. 5	Leviathan
Apr. 26	Leviathan
May 17	Leviathan
June 7	Leviathan
June 28	Leviathan
July 19	Leviathan
Aug. 16	Leviathan
Sept. 6	Leviathan
Sept. 27	Leviathan
Oct. 18	Leviathan
Nov. 8	Leviathan
Nov. 29	Leviathan
Dec. 20	Leviathan

UNITED STATES LINES
Cobh, Plymouth—Cherbourg —Bremen—New York

N. Y.

Arrival	Steamer
Jan. 8	George Washington
Jan. 14	Pres. Roosevelt
Feb. 15	Pres. Roosevelt
Mar. 15	Pres. Roosevelt
Apr. 2	George Washington
Apr. 19	Republic
Apr. 30	Pres. Harding
May 7	George Washington
May 23	Republic
May 28	Pres. Harding
June 4	George Washington
June 11	Pres. Roosevelt
June 25	Pres. Harding
June 30	Republic
July 2	George Washington
July 9	Pres. Roosevelt
July 23	Pres. Harding
July 30	George Washington
July 31	Republic
Aug. 5	Pres. Roosevelt
Aug. 20	Pres. Harding
Aug. 27	George Washington
Sept. 2	Pres. Roosevelt
Sept. 4	Republic
Sept. 17	Pres. Harding
Sept. 24	George Washington
Sept. 30	Pres. Roosevelt
Oct. 5	Republic
Oct. 15	Pres. Harding
Oct. 22	George Washington
Oct. 29	Pres. Roosevelt
Nov. 5	Republic
Nov. 13	Pres. Harding
Nov. 20	George Washington
Nov. 26	Pres. Roosevelt
Dec. 7	Republic
Dec. 11	Pres. Harding
Dec. 18	George Washington
Dec. 23	Pres. Roosevelt

WHITE STAR LINE
Southampton—New York

N. Y.

Arrival	Steamer
Jan. 13	Majestic

WHITE STAR LINE
Southampton—New York (Continued)

N. Y.

Arrival	Steamer
Jan. 20	Homeric
Feb. 3	Olympic
Feb. 24	Olympic
Mar. 9	Majestic
Mar. 24	Olympic
Mar. 30	Majestic
Apr. 13	Olympic
Apr. 20	Majestic
Apr. 28	Homeric
May 5	Olympic
May 11	Majestic
May 19	Homeric
May 25	Olympic
June 1	Majestic
June 9	Homeric
June 15	Olympic
June 22	Majestic
June 30	Homeric
July 6	Olympic
July 14	Majestic
July 22	Homeric
July 28	Olympic
Aug. 3	Majestic
Aug. 11	Homeric
Aug. 17	Olympic
Aug. 25	Majestic
Sept. 1	Homeric
Sept. 7	Olympic
Sept. 14	Majestic
Sept. 22	Homeric
Sept. 28	Olympic
Oct. 5	Majestic
Oct. 13	Homeric
Oct. 19	Olympic
Oct. 26	Majestic
Nov. 3	Homeric
Nov. 9	Olympic
Nov. 17	Majestic
Nov. 25	Homeric
Nov. 30	Olympic
Dec. 7	Majestic
Dec. 21	Olympic
Dec. 28	Majestic

WHITE STAR LINE
Liverpool—New York

N. Y.

Arrival	Steamer
Jan. 3	Adriatic
Jan. 13	Celtic
Jan. 19	Megantic
Jan. 27	Regina
Feb. 2	Baltic
Feb. 9	Celtic
Feb. 16	Doric
Feb. 23	Cedric
Mar. 2	Baltic
Mar. 8	Celtic
Mar. 17	Regina
Mar. 22	Cedric
Mar. 29	Baltic
Apr. 6	Celtic
Apr. 20	Cedric
Apr. 26	Baltic
May 3	Celtic

Year 1926

WHITE STAR LINE Liverpool—New York	
N. Y. Arrival	Steamer
May 9	Adriatic
May 26	Baltic
June 1	Celtic
June 6	Adriatic
June 14	Cedric
June 21	Baltic
June 29	Celtic
July 4	Adriatic
July 12	Cedric
July 19	Baltic
July 27	Celtic
Aug. 1	Adriatic
Aug. 9	Cedric
Aug. 16	Baltic
Aug. 23	Celtic
Aug. 29	Adriatic
Sept. 6	Cedric
Sept. 13	Baltic
Sept. 20	Celtic
Sept. 26	Adriatic

WHITE STAR LINE Liverpool—New York (Continued)	
N. Y. Arrival	Steamer
Oct. 4	Cedric
Oct. 11	Baltic
Oct. 19	Celtic
Oct. 24	Adriatic
Nov. 1	Cedric
Nov. 8	Baltic
Nov. 16	Celtic
Nov. 22	Adriatic
Nov. 30	Cedric
Dec. 6	Baltic
Dec. 14	Megantic
Dec. 21	Doric
Dec. 28	Celtic

WHITE STAR LINE Mediterranean—New York	
N. Y. Arrival	Steamer
Feb. 22	Adriatic
Apr. 12	Adriatic

WHITE STAR LINE Liverpool—Boston	
Boston Arrival	Steamer
Jan. 26	Regina
Mar. 1	Baltic
Apr. 5	Celtic
Apr. 19	Cedric
May 12	Celtic
May 31	Celtic
June 13	Cedric
June 28	Celtic
July 11	Cedric
July 26	Celtic
Aug. 8	Cedric
Aug. 22	Celtic
Sept. 5	Cedric
Sept. 19	Celtic
Oct. 3	Cedric
Oct. 17	Celtic
Oct. 31	Cedric
Nov. 15	Celtic
Nov. 29	Cedric
Dec. 26	Celtic

Year 1927

AMERICAN MERCHANT LINE
London—New York

N. Y.

Arrival	Steamer
Jan. 3	American Farmer
Jan. 11	American Banker
Jan. 19	American Shipper
Jan. 25	American Trader
Feb. 3	American Merchant
Feb. 10	American Farmer
Feb. 15	American Banker
Feb. 23	American Shipper
Mar. 2	American Trader
Mar. 10	American Merchant
Mar. 15	American Farmer
Mar. 23	American Banker
Mar. 31	American Shipper
Apr. 5	American Trader
Apr. 12	American Merchant
Apr. 18	American Farmer
Apr. 25	American Banker
May 2	American Trader
May 10	American Merchant
May 16	American Farmer
May 23	American Banker
May 31	American Trader
June 6	American Shipper
June 13	American Farmer
June 21	American Banker
June 27	American Trader
July 5	American Shipper
July 11	American Farmer
July 18	American Merchant
July 25	American Trader
Aug. 1	American Shipper
Aug. 8	American Farmer
Aug. 9	American Banker
Aug. 15	American Merchant
Aug. 22	American Trader
Aug. 29	American Shipper
Sept. 6	American Banker
Sept. 12	American Merchant
Sept. 19	American Trader
Sept. 26	American Shipper
Oct. 3	American Banker
Oct. 10	American Merchant
Oct. 17	American Farmer
Oct. 25	American Shipper
Nov. 1	American Banker
Nov. 9	American Merchant
Nov. 14	American Farmer
Nov. 21	American Trader
Nov. 29	American Shipper
Dec. 7	American Banker
Dec. 15	American Merchant
Dec. 20	American Farmer
Dec. 27	American Trader

ATLANTIC TRANSPORT LINE
London, Boulogne—New York

N. Y.

Arrival	Steamer
Jan. 10	Minnetonka
Jan. 18	Minnekahda
Jan. 24	Minnewaska

ATLANTIC TRANSPORT LINE
London, Boulogne—New York
(Continued)

N. Y.

Arrival	Steamer
Feb. 9	Minnetonka
Feb. 15	Minnekahda
Feb. 25	Minnewaska
Mar. 8	Minnetonka
Mar. 15	Minnekahda
Apr. 5	Minnewaska
Apr. 12	Minnekahda
Apr. 21	Minnetonka
May 2	Minnewaska
May 10	Minnesota
May 16	Minnetonka
May 23	Minnekahda
May 31	Minnewaska
June 6	Minnesota
June 14	Minnetonka
June 20	Minnekahda
June 27	Minnewaska
July 5	Minnesota
July 11	Minnetonka
July 18	Minnekahda
July 25	Minnewaska
Aug. 2	Minnesota
Aug. 8	Minnetonka
Aug. 16	Minnekahda
Aug. 22	Minnewaska
Aug. 30	Minnesota
Sept. 6	Minnetonka
Sept. 13	Minnekahda
Sept. 19	Minnewaska
Sept. 26	Minnesota
Oct. 3	Minnetonka
Oct. 17	Minnewaska
Oct. 25	Minnesota
Oct. 31	Minnetonka
Nov. 9	Minnekahda
Nov. 14	Minnewaska
Nov. 22	Minnesota
Nov. 28	Minnetonka
Dec. 6	Minnekahda
Dec. 12	Minnewaska
Dec. 20	Minnesota
Dec. 27	Minnetonka

BALTIC AMERICAN LINE
Danzig, Copenhagen—New York

N. Y.

Arrival	Steamer
Jan. 10	Estonia
Feb. 4	Lituania
Feb. 23	Estonia
Mar. 21	Lituania
Apr. 4	Estonia
Apr. 25	Lituania
May 16	Estonia
June 7	Lituania
June 27	Estonia
July 15	Lituania
Aug. 6	Estonia

BALTIC AMERICAN LINE
Danzig, Copenhagen—New York
(Continued)

N. Y.

Arrival	Steamer
Aug. 29	Lituania
Sept. 9	Estonia
Oct. 4	Lituania
Oct. 25	Polonia
Nov. 15	Lituania
Dec. 6	Polonia
Dec. 19	Estonia

CANADIAN PACIFIC LINE
Southampton, Cherbourg—New York

N. Y.

Arrival	Steamer
Feb. 8	Empress of France
Nov. 28	Empress of Australia

COMPANIA TRANSATLANTICA LINE
(Spanish Line)
Cadiz, Barcelona, Vigo—New York

N. Y.

Arrival	Steamer
Jan. 6	Alicante
Feb. 4	Manuel Arnus
Feb. 13	Alfonso 13
Mar. 4	Cristobal Colon
Mar. 16	Manuel Arnus
Mar. 27	Alfonso 13
Apr. 13	Alicante
Apr. 17	Cristobal Colon
May 7	Manuel Arnus
May 8	Alfonso 13
May 30	Cristobal Colon
June 16	Manuel Arnus
June 21	Alfonso 13
June 27	Alicante
July 13	Cristobal Colon
July 29	Manuel Arnus
Aug. 5	Manuel Calvo
Aug. 10	Alfonso 13
Aug. 29	Alicante
Aug. 29	Antonio Lopez
Sept. 1	Cristobal Colon
Sept. 6	Manuel Arnus
Sept. 19	Montevideo
Sept. 23	Alfonso 13
Oct. 9	Manuel Arnus
Oct. 10	Manuel Calvo
Oct. 15	Cristobal Colon
Nov. 4	Antonio Lopez
Nov. 6	Alfonso 13
Nov. 9	Alicante
Nov. 25	Montevideo
Nov. 28	Cristobal Colon
Nov. 30	Manuel Arnus
Dec. 1	Manuel Arnus
Dec. 15	Manuel Calvo
Dec. 20	Alfonso 13

Year 1927

CUNARD-ANCHOR LINE
Glasgow, Belfast—New York
N.Y.

Arrival	Steamer
Jan. 11	Cameronia
Jan. 17	California
Jan. 25	Transylvania
Feb. 9	Aurania
Feb. 10	Cameronia
Feb. 24	Letitia
Mar. 8	Aurania
Mar. 9	Cameronia
Mar. 23	Letitia
Apr. 5	Aurania
Apr. 5	Cameronia
Apr. 20	Transylvania
May 3	Cameronia
May 16	Caledonia
May 21	Aurania
May 23	Transylvania
May 31	California
June 6	Cameronia
June 13	Caledonia
June 20	Transylvania
June 28	California
July 1	Cameronia
July 11	Caledonia
July 18	Transylvania
July 25	Cameronia
Aug. 9	Caledonia
Aug. 15	Transylvania
Aug. 26	Cameronia
Sept. 4	Caledonia
Sept. 12	Transylvania
Sept. 19	Cameronia
Sept. 27	California
Oct. 3	Caledonia
Oct. 10	Transylvania
Oct. 17	Cameronia
Oct. 30	Caledonia
Nov. 7	Transylvania
Nov. 14	Cameronia
Nov. 21	Aurania
Nov. 28	Caledonia
Dec. 5	Transylvania
Dec. 20	Letitia

CUNARD-ANCHOR LINE
Mediterranean Ports—
New York
N.Y.

Arrival	Steamer
Sept. 3	California

CUNARD LINE
Southampton, Cherbourg,
Halifax, Havre—New York
N.Y.

Arrival	Steamer
Jan. 5	Berengaria
Jan. 11	Ausonia
Jan. 12	Aquitania
Jan. 18	Andania
Jan. 24	Antonia
Feb. 1	Ascania
Feb. 3	Aquitania
Feb. 8	Tuscania
Feb. 14	Ausonia
Feb. 16	Mauretania
Feb. 23	Aquitania

CUNARD LINE
Southampton, Cherbourg,
Halifax, Havre—New York
(Continued)
N.Y.

Arrival	Steamer
Mar. 1	Antonia
Mar. 8	Ascania
Mar. 9	Berengaria
Mar. 15	Tuscania
Mar. 16	Aquitania
Mar. 23	Ausonia
Apr. 2	Berengaria
Apr. 7	Ascania
Apr. 8	Mauretania
Apr. 12	Lancastria
Apr. 16	Aquitania
Apr. 23	Berengaria
Apr. 26	Carmania
Apr. 29	Mauretania
May 2	Tuscania
May 7	Aquitania
May 14	Berengaria
May 16	Lancastria
May 20	Mauretania
May 23	Carmania
May 28	Aquitania
June 3	Berengaria
June 6	Tuscania
June 10	Mauretania
June 18	Aquitania
June 20	Carmania
June 25	Berengaria
June 27	Lancastria
July 1	Mauretania
July 5	Tuscania
July 8	Aquitania
July 15	Berengaria
July 18	Carmania
July 22	Mauretania
July 25	Aurania
July 30	Aquitania
Aug. 1	Tuscania
Aug. 6	Berengaria
Aug. 12	Mauretania
Aug. 15	Carmania
Aug. 19	Aquitania
Aug. 23	Lancastria
Aug. 27	Berengaria
Aug. 30	Tuscania
Sept. 2	California
Sept. 2	Mauretania
Sept. 7	Antonia
Sept. 9	Aquitania
Sept. 12	Carmania
Sept. 16	Berengaria
Sept. 19	Lancastria
Sept. 23	Mauretania
Sept. 30	Aquitania
Oct. 1	Tuscania
Oct. 8	Berengaria
Oct. 11	Carmania
Oct. 14	Mauretania
Oct. 19	Lancastria
Oct. 21	Aquitania
Oct. 29	Berengaria
Nov. 1	Tuscania
Nov. 4	Mauretania
Nov. 7	Carmania
Nov. 11	Aquitania

CUNARD LINE
Southampton, Cherbourg,
Halifax, Havre—New York
(Continued)
N.Y.

Arrival	Steamer
Nov. 14	Lancastria
Nov. 18	Berengaria
Nov. 25	Mauretania
Nov. 28	Antonia
Dec. 3	Aquitania
Dec. 6	Ascania
Dec. 14	Berengaria
Dec. 21	Ausonia
Dec. 24	Lancastria
Dec. 27	Mauretania

CUNARD LINE
Liverpool, Queenstown—
New York
N.Y.

Arrival	Steamer
Jan. 3	Tuscania
Jan. 11	Aurania
Jan. 17	Scythia
Jan. 24	Laconia
Jan. 26	Alaunia
Feb. 3	Samaria
Feb. 7	Tuscania
Feb. 9	Aurania
Feb. 14	Caronia
Feb. 26	Alaunia
Feb. 28	Carmania
Mar. 1	Carmania
Mar. 8	Aurania
Mar. 15	Caronia
Mar. 23	Alaunia
Mar. 28	Carinthia
Apr. 5	Aurania
Apr. 13	Scythia
Apr. 18	Caronia
Apr. 26	Samaria
May 2	Laconia
May 10	Scythia
May 16	Caronia
May 21	Aurania
May 23	Carinthia
May 24	Samaria
June 6	Laconia
June 13	Scythia
June 16	Caronia
June 22	Samaria
June 27	Carinthia
June 30	Franconia
July 5	Laconia
July 11	Caronia
July 12	Scythia
July 19	Samaria
July 25	Aurania
July 25	Franconia
Aug. 2	Laconia
Aug. 5	Caronia
Aug. 8	Scythia
Aug. 16	Samaria
Aug. 22	Franconia
Aug. 29	Laconia
Sept. 4	Caronia
Sept. 6	Carinthia
Sept. 13	Samaria
Sept. 15	Aurania

Year 1927

CUNARD LINE
Liverpool, Queenstown—
New York
(Continued)

N.Y. Arrival	Steamer
Sept. 19	Franconia
Sept. 27	Laconia
Sept. 29	Caronia
Oct. 3	Carinthia
Oct. 4	Scythia
Oct. 11	Samaria
Oct. 13	Carmania
Oct. 17	Aurania
Oct. 24	Caronia
Oct. 25	Laconia
Nov. 1	Andania
Nov. 7	Carmania
Nov. 9	Samaria
Nov. 14	Scythia
Nov. 21	Laconia
Nov. 22	Aurania
Nov. 28	Carinthia
Dec. 7	Andania
Dec. 14	Alaunia
Dec. 14	Scythia
Dec. 19	Franconia
Dec. 27	Aurania

CUNARD LINE
World Ports—New York

N.Y. Arrival	Steamer
June 2	Franconia

DOLLAR STEAMSHIP LINE
World Ports—New York

N.Y. Arrival	Steamer
Jan. 15	President Van Buren
Jan. 27	President Hayes
Feb. 14	President Polk
Feb. 26	President Adams
Mar. 12	President Garfield
Mar. 26	President Harrison
Apr. 7	President Monroe
Apr. 21	President Wilson
May 5	President Van Buren
May 19	President Hayes
June 2	President Polk
June 16	President Adams
June 30	President Garfield
July 15	President Harrison
July 28	President Monroe
Aug. 11	President Wilson
Aug. 26	President Van Buren
Sept. 8	President Hayes
Sept. 22	President Polk
Oct. 6	President Adams
Oct. 20	President Garfield
Nov. 4	President Harrison
Nov. 18	President Monroe
Nov. 30	President Wilson
Dec. 14	President Van Buren
Dec. 29	President Hayes

FABRE LINE
Piraeus, Lisbon, Marseilles,
Palermo, Constantinople—
New York

N.Y. Arrival	Steamer
Jan. 3	Sinaia
Jan. 4	Providence
Feb. 28	Providence
Mar. 1	Asia
Apr. 1	Patria
Apr. 4	Roma
Apr. 29	Sinaia
May 11	Providence
May 31	Asia
June 13	Patria
July 5	Roma
July 11	Providence
Aug. 1	Sinaia
Aug. 10	Patria
Aug. 23	Canada
Sept. 2	Providence
Sept. 6	Asia
Oct. 4	Patria
Oct. 7	Roma
Nov. 4	Sinaia
Nov. 14	Providence
Dec. 7	Asia
Dec. 12	Patria

FRENCH LINE
(Compagnie Generale Transatlantique)
Havre, Plymouth—New York

N.Y. Arrival	Steamer
Jan. 6	France
Jan. 12	Paris
Jan. 24	Rochambeau
Jan. 27	France
Feb. 3	Paris
Feb. 11	De Grasse
Feb. 16	France
Feb. 23	Paris
Mar. 5	Rochambeau
Mar. 6	La Fayette
Mar. 10	France
Mar. 19	La Savoie
Mar. 29	Suffren
Mar. 31	France
Apr. 9	De Grasse
Apr. 15	Rochambeau
Apr. 20	Paris
Apr. 26	Suffren
Apr. 27	France
May 6	De Grasse
May 11	Paris
May 16	Rochambeau
May 18	France
May 27	La Savoie
June 1	Paris
June 6	De Grasse
June 8	France
June 14	Rochambeau
June 18	Suffren
June 22	France
June 27	La Savoie
June 29	Ile de France
July 5	De Grasse

FRENCH LINE
(Compagnie Generale Transatlantique)
Havre, Plymouth—New York
(Continued)

N.Y. Arrival	Steamer
July 6	France
July 11	Rochambeau
July 13	Paris
July 25	Suffren
July 27	France
Aug. 1	De Grasse
Aug. 3	Paris
Aug. 12	Rochambeau
Aug. 17	Ile de France
Aug. 24	Suffren
Aug. 24	France
Aug. 31	Paris
Aug. 31	De Grasse
Sept. 6	La Savoie
Sept. 7	Ile de France
Sept. 12	Rochambeau
Sept. 14	France
Sept. 21	Paris
Sept. 21	Suffren
Sept. 28	Ile de France
Oct. 4	La Savoie
Oct. 5	De Grasse
Oct. 6	France
Oct. 10	Rochambeau
Oct. 13	Paris
Oct. 19	Ile de France
Oct. 26	Suffren
Oct. 26	France
Nov. 4	De Grasse
Nov. 11	Rochambeau
Nov. 16	Ile de France
Nov. 23	Paris
Dec. 5	Suffren
Dec. 11	De Grasse
Dec. 15	Paris
Dec. 23	Rochambeau

FRENCH LINE
(Compagnie Generale Transatlantique)
Bordeaux, Vigo, Halifax—
New York

N.Y. Arrival	Steamer
Jan. 4	La Bourdonnais
Jan. 31	Lafayette
Mar. 16	La Bourdonnais
Apr. 7	Chicago
Apr. 14	Roussillon
Apr. 26	La Bourdonnais
May 16	Chicago
May 24	Roussillon
June 8	La Bourdonnais
June 22	Chicago
July 5	Roussillon
Aug. 1	La Bourdonnais
Aug. 29	Roussillon
Sept. 27	La Bourdonnais
Oct. 18	Roussillon
Nov. 10	La Bourdonnais
Nov. 26	Chicago
Dec. 12	Roussillon
Dec. 27	La Bourdonnais

Year 1927

HAMBURG-AMERICAN LINE
Hamburg, Southampton, Cherbourg—New York

N. Y.

Arrival	Steamer
Jan. 11	Albert Ballin
Jan. 19	Thuringia
Jan. 24	Deutschland
Feb. 9	Hamburg
Feb. 16	Westphalia
Feb. 23	Albert Ballin
Mar. 2	Thuringia
Mar. 8	Deutschland
Mar. 16	Cleveland
Mar. 23	Hamburg
Mar. 31	Westphalia
Apr. 5	Albert Ballin
Apr. 12	New York
Apr. 13	Thuringia
Apr. 18	Deutschland
Apr. 26	Cleveland
May 2	Hamburg
May 11	Westphalia
May 17	Albert Ballin
May 20	Reliance
May 23	New York
May 24	Thuringia
May 31	Deutschland
June 7	Cleveland
June 13	Hamburg
June 17	Reliance
June 21	Westphalia
June 28	Albert Ballin
July 5	Thuringia
July 5	New York
July 11	Deutschland
July 21	Cleveland
July 25	Hamburg
Aug. 3	Westphalia
Aug. 8	Albert Ballin
Aug. 9	Reliance
Aug. 15	New York
Aug. 16	Thuringia
Aug. 22	Deutschland
Aug. 26	Resolute
Aug. 31	Cleveland
Sept. 6	Hamburg
Sept. 9	Reliance
Sept. 13	Westphalia
Sept. 19	Albert Ballin
Sept. 23	Resolute
Sept. 26	New York
Sept. 27	Thuringia
Oct. 3	Deutschland
Oct. 7	Reliance
Oct. 11	Cleveland
Oct. 17	Hamburg
Oct. 21	Resolute
Oct. 25	Westphalia
Oct. 31	Albert Ballin
Nov. 9	Thuringia
Nov. 9	New York
Nov. 14	Deutschland
Nov. 21	Cleveland
Nov. 28	Hamburg
Dec. 7	Westphalia
Dec. 13	Albert Ballin
Dec. 14	Reliance
Dec. 19	New York

HAMBURG-AMERICAN LINE
Hamburg, Southampton, Cherbourg—New York
(Continued)

N. Y.

Arrival	Steamer
Dec. 21	Thuringia
Dec. 27	Deutschland

HAMBURG-AMERICAN LINE
World Ports—New York

N. Y.

Arrival	Steamer
May 26	Resolute

HOLLAND-AMERICA LINE
Rotterdam, Southampton, Cherbourg—New York

N. Y.

Arrival	Steamer
Jan. 17	Volendam
Jan. 25	Veendam
Jan. 31	Rotterdam
Feb. 14	Noordam
Feb. 21	New Amsterdam
Mar. 13	Volendam
Mar. 14	Veendam
Mar. 22	Noordam
Apr. 11	New Amsterdam
Apr. 18	Volendam
Apr. 22	Rotterdam
Apr. 29	Noordam
May 3	Ryndam
May 7	Veendam
May 16	New Amsterdam
May 27	Rotterdam
June 6	Volendam
June 11	Veendam
June 18	New Amsterdam
June 22	Ryndam
June 28	Rotterdam
July 11	Volendam
July 18	Veendam
July 25	New Amsterdam
July 29	Rotterdam
Aug. 15	Volendam
Aug. 22	Veendam
Aug. 29	New Amsterdam
Sept. 2	Rotterdam
Sept. 12	Ryndam
Sept. 16	Volendam
Sept. 24	Veendam
Oct. 3	New Amsterdam
Oct. 7	Rotterdam
Oct. 17	Ryndam
Oct. 21	Volendam
Oct. 29	Veendam
Nov. 11	Rotterdam
Nov. 21	Ryndam
Nov. 30	Volendam
Dec. 8	Veendam
Dec. 27	Ryndam
Dec. 30	Volendam

ITALIA AMERICA LINE
(Formerly Navigazione Generale Italiana)
Genoa, Naples, Palermo—New York

N. Y.

Arrival	Steamer
Jan. 14	Colombo
Jan. 22	Roma
Feb. 14	Duilio
Feb. 21	Colombo
Mar. 4	Roma
Mar. 23	Duilio
Mar. 30	Colombo
Apr. 8	Roma
May 2	Duilio
May 13	Roma
May 21	Taormina
May 31	Duilio
June 14	Colombo
June 18	Roma
July 2	Duilio
July 22	Roma
Aug. 9	Duilio
Aug. 22	Roma
Sept. 13	Duilio
Sept. 21	Colombo
Oct. 1	Roma
Oct. 18	Duilio
Oct. 26	Colombo
Nov. 4	Roma
Dec. 5	Colombo
Dec. 7	Roma

LLOYD SABAUDO
Genoa, Naples—New York

N. Y.

Arrival	Steamer
Feb. 7	Conte-Biancamano
Feb. 23	Conte-Rosso
Mar. 12	Conte-Biancamano
Mar. 30	Conte-Rosso
Apr. 16	Conte-Biancamano
May 4	Conte-Rosso
May 21	Conte-Biancamano
June 8	Conte-Rosso
June 25	Conte-Biancamano
July 12	Conte-Rosso
July 30	Conte-Biancamano
Aug. 17	Conte-Rosso
Sept. 3	Conte-Biancamano
Sept. 20	Conte-Rosso
Oct. 8	Conte-Biancamano
Oct. 25	Conte-Rosso
Nov. 14	Conte-Biancamano
Dec. 3	Conte-Rosso
Dec. 22	Conte-Biancamano

McDONNELL & TRUDA LINE
Genoa, Naples, Palermo, Lisbon—New York

N. Y.

Arrival	Steamer
Mar. 15	Giuseppi Verdi
May 5	Giuseppi Verdi
June 20	Giuseppi Verdi
Aug. 10	Giuseppi Verdi
Sept. 30	Giuseppi Verdi
Nov. 5	Dante Alighieri
Nov. 25	Giuseppi Verdi

Year 1927

NATIONAL STEAM NAVIGATION OF GREECE
Piraeus, Patras—New York

N. Y.

Arrival	Steamer
Feb. 2	Moreas
Mar. 3	Edison
Mar. 28	Byron
Apr. 23	Edison
May 31	Byron
June 27	Edison
July 26	Byron
Aug. 30	Edison
Sept. 28	Byron
Oct. 4	Themistocles
Oct. 26	Edison
Nov. 23	Byron
Dec. 30	Edison

NORTH GERMAN LLOYD LINE
Bremen, Southampton, Cherbourg—New York

N. Y.

Arrival	Steamer
Jan. 15	Stuttgart
Jan. 24	Muenchen
Jan. 24	Columbus
Jan. 31	Seydlitz
Feb. 9	Bremen
Feb. 15	Berlin
Feb. 26	Muenchen
Mar. 7	Stuttgart
Mar. 15	Bremen
Mar. 23	Berlin
Mar. 24	Seydlitz
Apr. 4	Muenchen
Apr. 11	Stuttgart
Apr. 18	Yorck
Apr. 18	Columbus
Apr. 25	Bremen
May 2	Berlin
May 7	Muenchen
May 14	Columbus
May 16	Derflinger
May 23	Stuttgart
May 31	Bremen
June 3	Berlin
June 6	Columbus
June 11	Muenchen
June 16	Yorck
June 20	Sierre Ventana
June 27	Stuttgart
June 29	Bremen
July 1	Columbus
July 6	Berlin
July 9	Luetzow
July 16	Muenchen
July 25	Sierre Ventana
Aug. 1	Bremen
Aug. 6	Columbus
Aug. 9	Berlin
Aug. 15	Seydlitz
Aug. 16	Dresden
Aug. 19	Muenchen
Aug. 29	Sierre Ventana
Sept. 1	Bremen
Sept. 6	Sierra Cordoba

NORTH GERMAN LLOYD LINE
Bremen, Southampton, Cherbourg—New York
(Continued)

N. Y.

Arrival	Steamer
Sept. 6	Stuttgart
Sept. 7	Yorck
Sept. 12	Berlin
Sept. 15	Derflinger
Sept. 17	Luetzow
Sept. 19	Seydlitz
Sept. 20	Dresden
Sept. 23	Muenchen
Sept. 29	Sierre Ventana
Oct. 4	Stuttgart
Oct. 10	Bremen
Oct. 11	Berlin
Oct. 17	Yorck
Oct. 22	Columbus
Oct. 22	Dresden
Oct. 31	Muenchen
Nov. 7	Luetzow
Nov. 9	Berlin
Nov. 12	Stuttgart
Nov. 18	Columbus
Nov. 28	Dresden
Dec. 5	Muenchen
Dec. 6	Berlin
Dec. 15	Stuttgart
Dec. 19	Columbus
Dec. 28	Dresden

NORWEGIAN AMERICAN LINE
Oslo, Bergen—New York

N. Y.

Arrival	Steamer
Jan. 29	Stavangerfjord
Feb. 19	Bergensfjord
Mar. 7	Stavangerfjord
Mar. 28	Bergensfjord
Apr. 13	Stavangerfjord
May 2	Bergensfjord
May 16	Stavangerfjord
May 31	Bergensfjord
June 20	Stavangerfjord
July 5	Bergensfjord
Aug. 1	Bergensfjord
Aug. 19	Stavangerfjord
Sept. 6	Bergensfjord
Sept. 23	Stavangerfjord
Oct. 10	Bergensfjord
Oct. 28	Stavangerfjord
Nov. 25	Bergensfjord
Dec. 16	Stavangerfjord

PHELPS BROTHERS LINE
Trieste, Patras, Naples—New York

N. Y.

Arrival	Steamer
Jan. 19	President Wilson
Feb. 24	Martha Washington
Mar. 17	President Wilson
Apr. 7	Martha Washington
May 5	President Wilson

PHELPS BROTHERS LINE
Trieste, Patras, Naples—New York
(Continued)

N. Y.

Arrival	Steamer
May 20	Martha Washington
June 15	President Wilson
July 1	Martha Washington
Aug. 1	President Wilson
Aug. 26	Martha Washington
Sept. 14	President Wilson
Oct. 8	Martha Washington
Oct. 26	President Wilson
Dec. 5	President Wilson

RED STAR LINE
Antwerp—New York

N. Y.

Arrival	Steamer
Jan. 3	Pennland
Jan. 10	Lapland
Jan. 27	Samland
Mar. 2	Pennland
Mar. 2	Lapland
Mar. 25	Samland
Mar. 29	Pennland
Apr. 9	Winifredian
Apr. 19	Lapland
Apr. 24	Belgenland
May 2	Pennland
May 16	Lapland
May 23	Belgenland
May 31	Pennland
June 7	Samland
June 20	Belgenland
June 28	Pennland
July 5	Lapland
July 21	Samland
July 24	Lapland
July 25	Belgenland
Aug. 1	Pennland
Aug. 15	Lapland
Aug. 23	Belgenland
Sept. 6	Pennland
Sept. 12	Lapland
Sept. 19	Belgenland
Oct. 3	Pennland
Oct. 11	Lapland
Oct. 17	Belgenland
Oct. 31	Pennland
Nov. 7	Lapland
Nov. 30	Pennland
Dec. 12	Belgenland
Dec. 13	Samland
Dec. 22	Winifredian
Dec. 27	Pennland

ROYAL MAIL STEAM PACKET COMPANY
Southampton, Cherbourg—New York

N. Y.

Arrival	Steamer
Jan. 4	Orca
Jan. 13	Asturias
Jan. 24	Avon
Apr. 26	Asturias

Year 1927

SCANDINAVIAN LINE
Copenhagen, Oslo, Halifax—
New York

N. Y.

Arrival	Steamer
Jan. 22	Hellig Olav
Feb. 10	United States
Mar. 2	Hellig Olav
Mar. 10	Oscar II
Mar. 23	United States
Apr. 13	Hellig Olav
Apr. 21	Oscar II
May 4	Frederik VIII
May 12	United States
May 25	Hellig Olav
June 2	Oscar II
June 14	Frederik VIII
June 22	United States
July 16	Hellig Olav
July 25	Frederik VIII
Aug. 3	United States
Aug. 16	Oscar II
Aug. 24	Hellig Olav
Sept. 6	Frederik VIII
Sept. 14	United States
Sept. 28	Oscar II
Oct. 5	Hellig Olav
Oct. 17	Frederik VIII
Oct. 26	United States
Nov. 9	Oscar II
Nov. 23	Hellig Olav
Nov. 29	Frederik VIII
Dec. 27	Oscar II

SWEDISH-AMERICAN LINE
Gothenburg—New York

N. Y.

Arrival	Steamer
Jan. 17	Stockholm
Feb. 2	Drottningholm
Feb. 23	Stockholm
Mar. 15	Drottningholm
Mar. 29	Stockholm
Apr. 12	Gripsholm
Apr. 19	Drottningholm
May 2	Stockholm
May 10	Gripsholm
May 23	Drottningholm
May 31	Stockholm
June 6	Gripsholm
June 21	Drottningholm
June 29	Stockholm
July 8	Gripsholm
July 25	Stockholm
Aug. 8	Gripsholm
Aug. 15	Drottningholm
Aug. 27	Stockholm
Sept. 6	Gripsholm
Sept. 20	Drottningholm
Sept. 27	Stockholm
Oct. 4	Gripsholm
Oct. 18	Drottningholm
Oct. 28	Stockholm
Nov. 4	Gripsholm
Nov. 21	Drottningholm
Nov. 30	Stockholm
Dec. 9	Gripsholm
Dec. 27	Drottningholm

UNITED STATES LINE
Bremen, Southampton, Cherbourg—New York

N. Y.

Arrival	Steamer
Jan. 7	President Harding
Jan. 7	Republic
Jan. 24	President Roosevelt
Feb. 10	President Harding
Feb. 19	Republic
Mar. 7	President Roosevelt
Mar. 18	George Washington
Mar. 23	Republic
Mar. 28	President Harding
Apr. 4	President Roosevelt
Apr. 15	George Washington
Apr. 21	Republic
Apr. 22	President Harding
Apr. 29	President Roosevelt
May 13	George Washington
May 20	President Harding
May 25	Republic
May 27	President Roosevelt
June 10	George Washington
June 17	President Harding
June 24	President Roosevelt
June 24	Republic
July 8	George Washington
July 13	President Harding
July 22	President Roosevelt
July 29	Republic
Aug. 5	George Washington
Aug. 6	President Harding
Aug. 19	President Roosevelt
Sept. 2	President Harding
Sept. 6	Republic
Sept. 9	George Washington
Sept. 17	President Roosevelt
Oct. 3	President Harding
Oct. 7	George Washington
Oct. 11	Republic
Oct. 14	President Roosevelt
Oct. 28	President Harding
Nov 5	George Washington
Nov. 11	President Roosevelt
Nov. 12	Republic
Nov. 26	President Harding
Dec. 14	President Roosevelt
Dec. 23	President Harding

UNITED STATES LINE
Southampton, Cherbourg—
New York

N. Y.

Arrival	Steamer
Mar. 15	Leviathan
Apr. 4	Leviathan
Apr. 25	Leviathan
May 16	Leviathan
June 7	Leviathan
June 28	Leviathan
July 18	Leviathan
Aug. 15	Leviathan
Sept. 6	Leviathan
Sept. 26	Leviathan
Oct. 18	Leviathan
Nov. 9	Leviathan
Nov. 29	Leviathan
Dec. 21	Leviathan

WHITE STAR LINE
Southampton, Cherbourg &
Antwerp—New York

N. Y.

Arrival	Steamer
Jan. 21	Homeric
Jan. 25	Majestic
Feb. 3	Arabic
Feb. 9	Olympic
Mar. 2	Olympic
Mar. 16	Arabic
Mar. 23	Olympic
Mar. 30	Majestic
Apr. 7	Homeric
Apr. 12	Arabic
Apr. 13	Olympic
Apr. 20	Majestic
Apr. 27	Homeric
May 4	Olympic
May 9	Arabic
May 11	Majestic
May 19	Homeric
May 25	Olympic
June 1	Majestic
June 9	Homeric
June 14	Arabic
June 15	Olympic
June 21	Majestic
June 30	Homeric
July 6	Olympic
July 12	Arabic
July 13	Majestic
July 21	Homeric
July 27	Olympic
Aug. 2	Majestic
Aug. 18	Homeric
Aug. 24	Olympic
Aug. 30	Arabic
Aug. 31	Majestic
Sept. 7	Homeric
Sept. 14	Olympic
Sept. 21	Majestic
Sept. 26	Arabic
Sept. 28	Homeric
Oct. 5	Olympic
Oct. 11	Majestic
Oct. 19	Homeric
Oct. 24	Arabic
Oct. 26	Olympic
Nov. 2	Majestic
Nov. 9	Homeric
Nov. 16	Olympic
Nov. 22	Arabic
Nov. 23	Majestic
Dec. 7	Olympic
Dec. 21	Majestic

WHITE STAR LINE
Liverpool, Queenstown—
New York

N. Y.

Arrival	Steamer
Jan. 3	Adriatic
Jan. 25	Celtic
Feb. 2	Baltic
Feb. 9	Cedric
Feb. 15	Regina
Feb. 21	Adriatic
Mar. 1	Baltic
Mar. 8	Cedric

Year 1927

WHITE STAR LINE	
Liverpool, Queenstown—	
New York	
(Continued)	

N. Y. Arrival	Steamer
Mar. 16	Regina
Mar. 23	Celtic
Mar. 29	Baltic
Apr. 6	Cedric
Apr. 11	Adriatic
Apr. 20	Celtic
Apr. 25	Baltic
May 3	Cedric
May 9	Adriatic
May 17	Celtic
May 23	Baltic
May 31	Cedric
June 6	Adriatic
June 14	Celtic

WHITE STAR LINE	
Liverpool, Queenstown—	
New York	
(Continued)	

N. Y. Arrival	Steamer
June 20	Baltic
June 28	Cedric
July 5	Adriatic
July 12	Celtic
July 18	Baltic
July 26	Cedric
Aug. 1	Adriatic
Aug. 9	Celtic
Aug. 15	Baltic
Aug. 23	Cedric
Aug. 29	Adriatic
Sept. 6	Celtic
Sept. 12	Baltic
Sept. 20	Cedric

WHITE STAR LINE	
Liverpool, Queenstown—	
New York	
(Continued)	

N. Y. Arrival	Steamer
Sept. 26	Adriatic
Oct. 4	Celtic
Oct. 10	Baltic
Oct. 18	Cedric
Oct. 25	Adriatic
Nov. 1	Celtic
Nov. 9	Baltic
Nov. 15	Cedric
Nov. 21	Laurentic
Nov. 29	Celtic
Dec. 6	Baltic
Dec. 14	Cedric
Dec. 21	Calgaric
Dec. 27	Albertic

Year 1928

AMERICAN MERCHANT LINE
London—New York

N. Y.

Arrival	Steamer
Jan. 3	American Shipper
Jan. 9	American Banker
Jan. 18	American Merchant
Jan. 26	American Farmer
Feb. 2	American Trader
Feb. 9	American Shipper
Feb. 15	American Banker
Feb. 23	American Merchant
Mar. 2	American Farmer
Mar. 6	American Trader
Mar. 13	American Shipper
Mar. 22	American Banker
Mar. 27	American Merchant
Apr. 3	American Farmer
Apr. 9	American Trader
Apr. 16	American Shipper
Apr. 23	American Banker
May 1	American Merchant
May 7	American Trader
May 14	American Shipper
May 21	American Banker
May 28	American Merchant
June 4	American Trader
June 11	American Shipper
June 18	American Farmer
June 25	American Merchant
July 2	American Trader
July 9	American Shipper
July 16	American Farmer
July 23	American Merchant
July 30	American Banker
Aug. 6	American Shipper
Aug. 13	American Farmer
Aug. 21	American Merchant
Aug. 27	American Banker
Sept. 4	American Trader
Sept. 10	American Farmer
Sept. 17	American Merchant
Sept. 24	American Banker
Oct. 1	American Trader
Oct. 9	American Farmer
Oct. 16	American Shipper
Oct. 23	American Banker
Oct. 31	American Trader
Nov. 7	American Farmer
Nov. 14	American Shipper
Nov. 21	American Banker
Nov. 28	American Merchant
Dec. 4	American Trader
Dec. 10	American Farmer
Dec. 18	American Shipper
Dec. 24	American Banker

ATLANTIC TRANSPORT LINE
London, Boulogne—New York

N. Y.

Arrival	Steamer
Jan. 4	Minnekahda
Jan. 9	Minnewaska
Jan. 25	Minnetonka
Feb. 1	Minnekahda

ATLANTIC TRANSPORT LINE
London, Boulogne—New York
(Continued)

N. Y.

Arrival	Steamer
Feb. 7	Minnewaska
Feb. 23	Minnetonka
Mar. 5	Minnekahda
Mar. 5	Minnewaska
Mar. 6	Mississippi
Mar. 19	Minnetonka
Mar. 28	Minnesota
Apr. 10	Minnekahda
Apr. 18	Minnewaska
Apr. 24	Minnesota
May 2	Minnetonka
May 8	Minnekahda
May 14	Minnewaska
May 21	Minnesota
May 28	Minnetonka
June 5	Minnekahda
June 11	Minnewaska
June 18	Minnesota
June 25	Minnetonka
July 3	Minnekahda
July 9	Minnewaska
July 17	Minnesota
July 22	Mississippi
July 23	Minnetonka
July 31	Minnekahda
Aug. 7	Minnewaska
Aug. 14	Minnesota
Aug. 20	Minnetonka
Aug. 28	Minnekahda
Sept. 4	Minnewaska
Sept. 10	Minnesota
Sept. 17	Minnetonka
Sept. 25	Minnekahda
Oct. 1	Mississippi
Oct. 1	Minnewaska
Oct. 10	Minnesota
Oct. 16	Minnetonka
Oct. 23	Minnekahda
Oct. 30	Minnewaska
Nov. 7	Minnesota
Nov. 13	Minnetonka
Nov. 20	Minnekahda
Nov. 27	Minnewaska
Nov. 27	Mississippi
Dec. 6	Minnesota
Dec. 10	Minnetonka
Dec. 18	Minnekahda
Dec. 24	Minnewaska

BALTIC AMERICAN LINE
Danzig, Copenhagen—New York

N. Y.

Arrival	Steamer
Jan. 26	Lituania
Feb. 17	Estonia
Mar. 7	Lituania
Mar. 27	Estonia
Apr. 16	Lituania
Apr. 30	Estonia

BALTIC AMERICAN LINE
Danzig, Copenhagen—New York
(Continued)

N. Y.

Arrival	Steamer
May 21	Lituania
June 8	Estonia
June 18	Polonia
June 28	Lituania
July 17	Estonia
Aug. 2	Lituania
Aug. 28	Estonia
Sept. 1	Polonia
Sept. 6	Lituania
Oct. 1	Estonia
Oct. 22	Polonia
Nov. 8	Estonia
Nov. 27	Polonia
Dec. 17	Lituania

CANADIAN PACIFIC LINE
Southampton, Cherbourg—New York

N. Y.

Arrival	Steamer
Jan. 23	Empress of France
Nov. 27	Empress of Australia
Dec. 20	Duchess of Bedford

COMPANIA TRANSATLANTICA LINE
(Spanish Line)
Cadiz, Barcelona, Vigo—New York

N. Y.

Arrival	Steamer
Jan. 9	Antonio Lopez
Jan. 11	Cristobal Colon
Jan. 11	Manuel Arnus
Feb. 3	Montevideo
Feb. 9	Alfonso XIII
Feb. 27	Manuel Calvo
Mar. 3	Cristobal Colon
Mar. 12	Manuel Arnus
Mar. 20	Antonio Lopez
Mar. 25	Alfonso XIII
Apr. 13	Montevideo
Apr. 16	Cristobal Colon
Apr. 23	Manuel Arnus
May 3	Manuel Calvo
May 8	Alfonso XIII
May 24	Antonio Lopez
May 30	Cristobal Colon
June 5	Manuel Arnus
June 21	Alfonso XIII
July 7	Manuel Calvo
July 13	Cristobal Colon
July 20	Manuel Arnus
Aug. 6	Juan Sebastin Elcano
Aug. 10	Alfonso XIII
Aug. 28	Antonio Lopez
Sept. 1	Cristobal Colon
Sept. 7	Manuel Arnus
Sept. 23	Alfonso XIII

Year 1928

COMPANIA TRANSATLANTICA LINE
(Spanish Line)
Cadiz, Barcelona, Vigo— New York
(Continued)

N. Y.

Arrival	Steamer
Sept. 24	Manuel Calvo
Oct. 10	Juan Sebastin Elcano
Oct. 15	Cristobol Colon
Oct. 23	Manuel Arnus
Nov. 6	Alfonso XIII
Nov. 22	Marques de Cornillas
Nov. 28	Cristobol Colon
Dec. 4	Manuel Arnus
Dec. 15	Juan Sebastin Elcano
Dec. 20	Alfonso XIII

COSULICH LINE
Trieste, Patras, Palermo, Naples—New York

N. Y.

Arrival	Steamer
Feb. 16	Saturnia
Mar. 29	Saturnia
May 1	Saturnia
June 5	Saturnia
July 11	Saturnia
Aug. 14	Saturnia
Sept. 18	Saturnia
Nov. 2	Saturnia
Dec. 8	Saturnia
Dec. 31	Vulcania

CUNARD-ANCHOR LINE
Glasgow, Belfast—New York

N. Y.

Arrival	Steamer
Jan. 2	Cameronia
Jan. 4	Athenia
Jan. 9	Caledonia
Jan. 18	California
Jan. 23	Transylvania
Feb. 2	Cameronia
Feb. 16	Athenia
Mar. 2	Cameronia
Mar. 14	Athenia
Apr. 4	Cameronia
Apr. 12	Athenia
Apr. 18	Transylvania
May 1	California
May 7	Cameronia
May 21	Transylvania
May 29	California
June 5	Cameronia
June 11	Caledonia
June 18	Transylvania
June 24	California
June 28	Cameronia
July 9	Caledonia
July 15	Transylvania
July 23	Cameronia
Aug. 6	Transylvania
Aug. 13	Caledonia
Aug. 24	Cameronia
Sept. 2	Transylvania
Sept. 10	Caledonia
Sept. 18	Cameronia
Sept. 24	California

CUNARD-ANCHOR LINE
Glasgow, Belfast—New York
(Continued)

N. Y.

Arrival	Steamer
Oct. 8	Caledonia
Oct. 16	Cameronia
Oct. 29	Transylvania
Nov. 8	Caledonia
Nov. 12	Cameronia
Nov. 30	Transylvania
Dec. 10	Caledonia
Dec. 26	Transylvania

CUNARD LINE
Southampton, Cherbourg, Halifax, Havre—New York

N. Y.

Arrival	Steamer
Jan. 3	Antonia
Jan. 4	Aquitania
Jan. 9	Ascania
Jan. 17	Alaunia
Jan. 26	Aquitania
Feb. 2	Ausonia
Feb. 7	Berengaria
Feb. 8	Ascania
Feb. 14	Antonia
Feb. 14	Mauretania
Feb. 28	Alaunia
Feb. 28	Berengaria
Mar. 7	Ausonia
Mar. 13	Tuscania
Mar. 21	Antonia
Mar. 21	Aquitania
Mar. 26	Ascania
Mar. 31	Berengaria
Apr. 2	Alaunia
Apr. 6	Mauretania
Apr. 9	Ausonia
Apr. 14	Aquitania
Apr. 17	Tuscania
Apr. 21	Berengaria
Apr. 27	Mauretania
May 1	Lancastria
May 4	Aquitania
May 11	Berengaria
May 14	Tuscania
May 18	Mauretania
May 21	Carmania
May 25	Aquitania
May 28	Lancastria
May 31	Franconia
June 1	Berengaria
June 4	Caronia
June 8	Mauretania
June 11	Tuscania
June 16	Aquitania
June 18	Carmania
June 22	Berengaria
June 24	Franconia
June 28	Lancastria
June 29	Mauretania
July 2	Caronia
July 7	Aquitania
July 9	Tuscania
July 14	Berengaria
July 16	Carmania
July 20	Mauretania

CUNARD LINE
Southampton, Cherbourg, Halifax, Havre—New York
(Continued)

N. Y.

Arrival	Steamer
July 27	Aquitania
July 30	Caronia
Aug. 3	Berengaria
Aug. 7	Tuscania
Aug. 10	Mauretania
Aug. 13	Carmania
Aug. 18	Aquitania
Aug. 21	Lancastria
Aug. 25	Berengaria
Aug. 27	Caronia
Aug. 31	Mauretania
Aug. 31	California
Sept. 4	Tuscania
Sept. 8	Aquitania
Sept. 10	Carmania
Sept. 15	Berengaria
Sept. 17	Lancastria
Sept. 21	Mauretania
Sept. 24	Caronia
Sept. 28	Aquitania
Oct. 2	Tuscania
Oct. 5	Berengaria
Oct. 8	Carmania
Oct. 13	Mauretania
Oct. 17	Lancastria
Oct. 20	Aquitania
Oct. 22	Caronia
Oct. 27	Berengaria
Oct. 31	Tuscania
Nov. 2	Mauretania
Nov. 5	Carmania
Nov. 10	Aquitania
Nov. 13	Lancastria
Nov. 17	Berengaria
Nov. 27	Franconia
Nov. 28	Alaunia
Dec. 1	Aquitania
Dec. 5	Tuscania
Dec. 11	Berengaria
Dec. 18	Aurania
Dec. 24	Caronia
Dec. 31	Ausonia

CUNARD LINE
Liverpool, Queenstown— New York

N. Y.

Arrival	Steamer
Jan. 3	Andania
Jan. 10	Laconia
Jan. 14	Carinthia
Jan. 17	Scythia
Jan. 26	Samaria
Feb. 2	Andania
Feb. 9	Ascania
Feb. 14	Caronia
Feb. 23	Aurania
Feb. 29	Carmania
Mar. 6	Andania
Mar. 13	Caronia
Mar. 19	Aurania
Mar. 28	Carmania
Mar. 29	Samaria
Apr. 2	Carinthia

Year 1928

CUNARD LINE Liverpool, Queenstown— New York (Continued)		DOLLAR STEAMSHIP LINE World Ports—New York (Continued)		FRENCH LINE (Compagnie Generale Transatlantique) Havre, Plymouth—New York (Continued)	
N. Y. Arrival	**Steamer**	**N. Y. Arrival**	**Steamer**	**N. Y. Arrival**	**Steamer**
Apr. 4	Andania	July 10	President Wilson	Apr. 12	France
Apr. 9	Caronia	July 24	President Van Buren	Apr. 18	Paris
Apr. 17	Scythia	Aug. 7	President Hayes	Apr. 25	Ile de France
Apr. 24	Carmania	Aug. 21	President Polk	May 1	Rochambeau
Apr. 30	Laconia	Sept. 4	President Adams	May 2	France
May 7	Caronia	Sept. 17	President Garfield	May 7	De Grasse
May 14	Samaria	Oct. 2	President Harrison	May 9	Paris
May 22	Scythia	Oct. 17	President Monroe	May 15	Ile de France
May 28	Carinthia	Oct. 30	President Wilson	May 22	Suffern
June 5	Laconia	Nov. 15	President Van Buren	May 23	France
June 11	Samaria	Nov. 28	President Hayes	May 31	Paris
June 19	Scythia	Dec. 11	President Polk	June 4	De Grasse
June 25	Carinthia	Dec. 27	President Adams	June 6	Ile de France
June 25	Franconia			June 13	France
July 3	Laconia			June 15	Rochambeau
July 9	Samaria	**FABRE LINE**		June 20	Paris
July 18	Scythia	Piraeus, Lisbon, Marseilles,		June 26	Ile de France
July 23	Franconia	Palermo, Constantinople—		June 27	Suffern
July 31	Laconia	New York		July 2	De Grasse
Aug. 6	Samaria	**N. Y.**		July 5	France
Aug. 14	Scythia	**Arrival**	**Steamer**	July 10	Rochambeau
Aug. 20	Franconia	Jan. 3	Canada	July 11	Paris
Aug. 28	Laconia	Jan. 30	Providence	July 18	Ile de France
Sept. 4	Carinthia	Mar. 5	Patria	July 27	De Grasse
Sept. 10	Samaria	Mar. 15	Sinaia	Aug. 1	France
Sept. 10	Scythia	Apr. 6	Asia	Aug. 6	Suffern
Sept. 17	Franconia	Apr. 9	Providence	Aug. 7	Rochambeau
Sept. 25	Laconia	May 14	Roma	Aug. 8	Paris
Oct. 1	Carinthia	May 17	Patria	Aug. 14	Ile de France
Oct. 9	Scythia	June 8	Sinaia	Aug. 22	France
Oct. 16	Franconia	June 12	Asia	Aug. 27	De Grasse
Oct. 24	Laconia	June 25	Providence	Aug. 29	Paris
Oct. 30	Samaria	July 18	Patria	Sept. 4	Suffern
Nov. 7	Scythia	Aug. 20	Canada	Sept. 5	Ile de France
Nov. 12	Carinthia	Aug. 29	Providence	Sept. 10	Rochambeau
Nov. 21	Laconia	Sept. 13	Sinaia	Sept. 12	France
Nov. 27	Samaria	Sept. 18	Patria	Sept. 19	Paris
Dec. 6	Antonia	Oct. 17	Asia	Sept. 24	De Grasse
Dec. 10	Carinthia	Nov. 15	Providence	Sept. 26	Ile de France
Dec. 18	Aurania	Nov. 27	Patria	Oct. 2	Suffern
Dec. 19	Laconia	Dec. 17	Sinaia	Oct. 3	France
Dec. 26	Andania			Oct. 9	Rochambeau
Dec. 31	Scythia			Oct. 10	Paris
		FRENCH LINE (Compagnie Generale Transatlantique) Havre, Plymouth—New York		Oct. 17	Ile de France
		N. Y.		Oct. 23	De Grasse
DOLLAR STEAMSHIP LINE World Ports—New York		**Arrival**	**Steamer**	Oct. 24	France
N. Y.		Jan. 4	Suffern	Oct. 31	France
Arrival	**Steamer**	Jan. 5	France	Nov. 10	Rochambeau
Jan. 4	President Hayes	Jan. 11	Paris	Nov. 14	Ile de France
Jan. 11	President Polk	Jan. 21	De Grasse	Nov. 24	De Grasse
Jan. 27	President Adams	Jan. 30	Rochambeau	Nov. 28	Paris
Feb. 9	President Garfield	Feb. 2	Paris	Dec. 5	Ile de France
Feb. 23	President Harrison	Feb. 6	France	Dec. 15	Rochambeau
Mar. 6	President Monroe	Feb. 14	Suffern	Dec. 17	Paris
Mar. 21	President Wilson	Feb. 18	De Grasse	Dec. 28	De Grasse
Apr. 4	President Van Buren	Feb. 23	Paris		
Apr. 17	President Hayes	Mar. 3	Rochambeau		
May 1	President Polk	Mar. 14	Suffern	**FRENCH LINE** (Compagnie Generale Transatlantique) Marseilles, Naples, Etc.— New York	
May 15	President Adams	Mar. 14	Ile de France	**N. Y.**	
May 29	President Garfield	Mar. 21	Paris	**Arrival**	**Steamer**
June 13	President Harrison	Mar. 31	Rochambeau	Mar. 10	France
June 26	President Monroe	Apr. 4	Ile de France		
		Apr. 7	De Grasse		

Year 1928

FRENCH LINE
(Compagnie Generale Transatlantique)
Bordeaux, Vigo, Halifax—
New York
N. Y.

Arrival	Steamer
Jan. 23	Chicago
Feb. 27	La Bourdonnais
Mar. 16	Roussillon
Apr. 2	Chicago
Apr. 13	La Bourdonnais
Apr. 28	Roussillon
May 24	La Bourdonnais
June 11	Roussillon
June 22	Chicago
July 5	La Bourdonnais
July 19	Roussillon
Aug. 30	La Bourdonnais
Sept. 28	Roussillon
Oct. 19	La Bourdonnais
Dec. 9	Roussillon

HAMBURG-AMERICAN LINE
Hamburg, Southampton, Cher-
bourg—New York
N. Y.

Arrival	Steamer
Jan. 3	Resolute
Jan. 4	Cleveland
Jan. 10	Hamburg
Jan. 20	Westphalia
Jan. 22	Reliance
Jan. 25	Albert Ballin
Feb. 1	New York
Feb. 4	Thuringia
Feb. 7	Deutschland
Feb. 14	Cleveland
Feb. 16	Cap Polonia
Feb. 21	Hamburg
Mar. 2	Westphalia
Mar. 5	Albert Ballin
Mar. 13	New York
Mar. 15	Thuringia
Mar. 19	Deutschland
Mar. 26	Cleveland
Apr. 2	Hamburg
Apr. 12	Westphalia
Apr. 13	Reliance
Apr. 16	Albert Ballin
Apr. 23	New York
Apr. 25	Thuringia
Apr. 30	Deutschland
May 7	Cleveland
May 14	Hamburg
May 18	Westphalia
May 21	Albert Ballin
May 24	Reliance
May 26	Resolute
May 28	New York
June 4	Deutschland
June 6	Thuringia
June 11	Cleveland
June 18	Hamburg
June 22	Reliance
June 25	Albert Ballin
June 26	Westphalia
July 3	New York
July 9	Deutschland
July 16	Cleveland

HAMBURG-AMERICAN LINE
Hamburg, Southampton, Cher-
bourg—New York
(Continued)
N. Y.

Arrival	Steamer
July 18	Thuringia
July 23	Hamburg
July 30	Albert Ballin
Aug. 6	New York
Aug. 8	Westphalia
Aug. 13	Deutschland
Aug. 20	Cleveland
Aug. 24	Reliance
Aug. 27	Hamburg
Aug. 29	Thuringia
Aug. 31	Resolute
Sept. 4	Albert Ballin
Sept. 10	New York
Sept. 17	Deutschland
Sept. 18	Westphalia
Sept. 21	Reliance
Sept. 24	Cleveland
Sept. 27	Resolute
Oct. 1	Hamburg
Oct. 9	Albert Ballin
Oct. 9	Thuringia
Oct. 15	New York
Oct. 19	Reliance
Oct. 23	Deutschland
Oct. 30	Cleveland
Oct. 31	Westphalia
Nov. 5	Hamburg
Nov. 12	Albert Ballin
Nov. 20	New York
Nov. 21	Thuringia
Nov. 27	Deutschland
Dec. 4	Cleveland
Dec. 10	Hamburg
Dec. 12	Reliance
Dec. 18	Albert Ballin
Dec. 24	New York
Dec. 31	Resolute

HOLLAND-AMERICA LINE
Rotterdam, Southampton,
Cherbourg—New York
N. Y.

Arrival	Steamer
Jan. 3	Volendam
Jan. 25	Veendam
Jan. 25	Rotterdam
Jan. 31	Ryndam
Feb. 6	Volendam
Mar. 5	Ryndam
Mar. 12	New Amsterdam
Mar. 26	Volendam
Apr. 9	Ryndam
Apr. 16	New Amsterdam
Apr. 21	Rotterdam
Apr. 30	Volendam
May 14	Veendam
May 21	New Amsterdam
May 25	Rotterdam
June 4	Volendam
June 19	New Amsterdam
June 25	Rotterdam
July 2	Ryndam

HOLLAND-AMERICA LINE
Rotterdam, Southampton,
Cherbourg—New York
(Continued)
N. Y.

Arrival	Steamer
July 9	Volendam
July 14	Veendam
July 23	New Amsterdam
July 27	Rotterdam
Aug. 13	Volendam
Aug. 20	Veendam
Aug. 27	New Amsterdam
Sept. 1	Rotterdam
Sept. 10	Ryndam
Sept. 17	Volendam
Sept. 22	Veendam
Sept. 28	New Amsterdam
Oct. 5	Rotterdam
Oct. 17	New Amsterdam
Oct. 22	Volendam
Oct. 29	Veendam
Nov. 5	Ryndam
Nov. 12	Rotterdam
Nov. 19	New Amsterdam
Dec. 3	Volendam
Dec. 10	Ryndam
Dec. 24	New Amsterdam

ITALIA AMERICA LINE
Genoa, Naples, Palermo—
New York
N. Y.

Arrival	Steamer
Jan. 12	Colombo
Jan. 21	Roma
Feb. 24	Colombo
Mar. 3	Roma
Mar. 19	Duilio
Apr. 3	Colombo
Apr. 6	Roma
Apr. 23	Duilio
May 14	Roma
May 26	Duilio
June 18	Roma
June 26	Colombo
July 3	Duilio
July 20	Roma
Aug. 4	Duilio
Aug. 11	Colombo
Aug. 24	Roma
Sept. 8	Augustus
Sept. 17	Colombo
Sept. 28	Roma
Oct. 15	Augustus
Nov. 2	Roma
Nov. 19	Augustus
Dec. 7	Roma
Dec. 24	Augustus

LLOYD SABAUDO
Genoa, Naples—New York
N. Y.

Arrival	Steamer
Feb. 4	Conte Biancamano
Mar. 10	Conte Rosso
Apr. 14	Conte Grande
May 5	Conte Biancamano

Year 1928

LLOYD SABAUDO
Genoa, Naples—New York
(Continued)
N. Y.

Arrival	Steamer
May 19	Conte Grande
June 8	Conte Biancamano
June 23	Conte Grande
July 13	Conte Biancamano
July 28	Conte Grande
Aug. 17	Conte Biancamano
Sept. 1	Conte Grande
Sept. 21	Conte Biancamano
Oct. 6	Conte Grande
Oct. 27	Conte Biancamano
Nov. 10	Conte Grande
Nov. 30	Conte Biancamano
Dec. 15	Conte Grande

NATIONAL STEAM NAVIGATION OF GREECE
Piraeus, Patras—New York
N. Y.

Arrival	Steamer
Jan. 3	Edison
Feb. 20	Edison
Apr. 6	Edison
Apr. 24	Byron
May 31	Edison
June 19	Byron
July 23	Edison
Aug. 10	Byron
Sept. 10	Edison
Oct. 4	Byron
Nov. 3	Edison
Nov. 30	Byron

NORTH GERMAN LLOYD
Bremen, Southampton, Cherbourg—New York
N. Y.

Arrival	Steamer
Jan. 16	Berlin
Jan. 23	Muenchen
Feb. 2	Dresden
Feb. 6	Columbus
Feb. 11	Karlsruhe
Feb. 20	Muenchen
Feb. 27	Berlin
Mar. 5	Dresden
Mar. 8	Karlsruhe
Mar. 17	Muenchen
Mar. 26	Berlin
Apr. 2	Dresden
Apr. 9	Karlsruhe
Apr. 9	Columbus
Apr. 16	Muenchen
Apr. 23	Berlin
Apr. 30	Dresden
May 7	Columbus
May 7	Karlsruhe
May 14	Muenchen
May 21	Yorck
May 22	Berlin
May 28	Dresden
June 4	Columbus
June 5	Karlsruhe
June 11	Muenchen

NORTH GERMAN LLOYD
Bremen, Southampton, Cherbourg—New York
(Continued)
N. Y.

Arrival	Steamer
June 18	Stuttgart
June 19	Berlin
June 21	Yorck
June 25	Dresden
June 28	Sierra Cordoba
July 2	Columbus
July 3	Karlsruhe
July 9	Muenchen
July 16	Stuttgart
July 23	Yorck
July 30	Dresden
Aug. 6	Columbus
Aug. 6	Karlsruhe
Aug. 13	Muenchen
Aug. 16	Seydlitz
Aug. 20	Stuttgart
Aug. 21	Berlin
Aug. 27	Dresden
Sept. 4	Columbus
Sept. 4	Karlsruhe
Sept. 4	Luetzow
Sept. 6	Sierra Cordoba
Sept. 10	Muenchen
Sept. 12	Yorck
Sept. 17	Stuttgart
Sept. 18	Berlin
Sept. 24	Dresden
Oct. 1	Columbus
Oct. 1	Karlsruhe
Oct. 8	Muenchen
Oct. 13	Luetzow
Oct. 15	Stuttgart
Oct. 17	Berlin
Oct. 22	Dresden
Oct. 30	Columbus
Oct. 30	Karlsruhe
Nov. 5	Muenchen
Nov. 12	Stuttgart
Nov. 14	Berlin
Nov. 20	Dresden
Nov. 26	Columbus
Dec. 3	Karlsruhe
Dec. 3	Muenchen
Dec. 10	Berlin
Dec. 17	Stuttgart
Dec. 21	Columbus
Dec. 31	Dresden

NORWEGIAN AMERICAN LINE
Oslo, Bergen—New York
N. Y.

Arrival	Steamer
Feb. 1	Bergensfjord
Feb. 14	Stavangerfjord
Mar. 5	Bergensfjord
Mar. 19	Stavangerfjord
Apr. 9	Bergensfjord
Apr. 23	Stavangerfjord
May 14	Bergensfjord
May 31	Stavangerfjord
June 18	Bergensfjord
July 2	Stavangerfjord

NORWEGIAN AMERICAN LINE
Oslo, Bergen—New York
(Continued)
N. Y.

Arrival	Steamer
July 24	Bergensfjord
Aug. 7	Stavangerfjord
Aug. 27	Bergensfjord
Sept. 10	Stavangerfjord
Oct. 1	Bergensfjord
Oct. 15	Stavangerfjord
Nov. 7	Bergensfjord
Nov. 27	Stavangerfjord
Dec. 17	Bergensfjord

PHELPS BROTHERS LINE
Trieste, Patras, Naples—New York
N. Y.

Arrival	Steamer
Feb. 1	President Wilson
Mar. 15	President Wilson
Apr. 25	President Wilson
June 20	President Wilson
Aug. 3	President Wilson
Sept. 26	President Wilson
Nov. 7	President Wilson
Dec. 20	President Wilson

RED STAR LINE
Antwerp—New York
N. Y.

Arrival	Steamer
Jan. 3	Lapland
Jan. 10	Devonian
Jan. 30	Winifredian
Jan. 31	Lapland
Feb. 15	Devonian
Mar. 5	Lapland
Mar. 21	Devonian
Apr. 11	Pennland
Apr. 16	Lapland
May 15	Pennland
May 21	Lapland
June 4	Belgenland
June 18	Lapland
July 2	Belgenland
July 9	Pennland
July 18	Lapland
July 30	Belgenland
Aug. 7	Pennland
Aug. 14	Lapland
Aug. 27	Belgenland
Sept. 4	Pennland
Sept. 10	Lapland
Sept. 24	Belgenland
Oct. 1	Pennland
Oct. 8	Lapland
Oct. 22	Belgenland
Oct. 30	Pennland
Nov. 5	Lapland
Nov. 27	Pennland
Dec. 3	Lapland
Dec. 14	Belgenland
Dec. 24	Pennland
Dec. 26	Winifredian

Year 1928

RED STAR LINE
World Ports—New York
N. Y.

Arrival	Steamer
Apr. 27	Belgenland

SCANDINAVIAN LINE
Copenhagen, Oslo, Halifax—
New York
N. Y.

Arrival	Steamer
Jan. 24	United States
Feb. 2	Hellig Olav
Feb. 15	Frederik VIII
Feb. 29	United States
Mar. 5	Hellig Olav
Mar. 12	Oscar II
Mar. 19	Frederik VIII
Apr. 2	United States
Apr. 10	Hellig Olav
Apr. 16	Oscar II
Apr. 24	Frederik VIII
May 7	United States
May 15	Hellig Olav
May 22	Oscar II
May 28	Frederik VIII
June 11	United States
June 18	Hellig Olav
June 25	Oscar II
July 2	Frederik VIII
July 17	United States
July 24	Hellig Olav
July 30	Oscar II
Aug. 6	Frederik VIII
Aug. 20	United States
Aug. 27	Hellig Olav
Sept. 4	Oscar II
Sept. 10	Frederik VIII
Sept. 24	United States
Oct. 1	Hellig Olav
Oct. 8	Oscar II
Oct. 15	Frederik VIII
Oct. 29	United States
Nov. 5	Hellig Olav
Nov. 19	Oscar II
Dec. 3	Frederik VIII
Dec. 27	Oscar II

SWEDISH-AMERICAN LINE
Gothenburg—New York
N. Y.

Arrival	Steamer
Jan. 18	Stockholm
Feb. 2	Drottningholm
Feb. 23	Stockholm
Mar. 5	Drottningholm
Mar. 29	Stockholm
Apr. 10	Gripsholm
Apr. 16	Drottningholm
May 2	Stockholm
May 8	Gripsholm
May 15	Drottningholm
May 31	Stockholm
June 5	Gripsholm
June 19	Drottningholm
June 27	Stockholm
July 2	Gripsholm
July 17	Drottningholm
Aug. 7	Gripsholm

SWEDISH-AMERICAN LINE
Gothenburg—New York
(Continued)
N. Y.

Arrival	Steamer
Aug. 15	Stockholm
Aug. 20	Drottningholm
Sept. 4	Gripsholm
Sept. 12	Stockholm
Sept. 17	Drottningholm
Oct. 1	Gripsholm
Oct. 9	Stockholm
Oct. 16	Drottningholm
Oct. 30	Gripsholm
Nov. 13	Drottningholm
Nov. 26	Gripsholm
Dec. 3	Kungsholm
Dec. 24	Drottningholm

UNITED STATES LINE
Bremen, Southampton, Cherbourg—New York
N. Y.

Arrival	Steamer
Jan. 8	Republic
Jan. 13	President Roosevelt
Jan. 20	George Washington
Feb. 14	Republic
Feb. 25	George Washington
Mar. 19	Republic
Mar. 23	George Washington
Apr. 16	America
Apr. 20	George Washington
Apr. 30	Republic
May 4	President Harding
May 11	President Roosevelt
May 15	George Washington
May 26	America
June 1	President Harding
June 4	Republic
June 8	President Roosevelt
June 15	George Washington
June 26	America
June 29	President Harding
July 4	Republic
July 6	President Roosevelt
July 10	George Washington
July 24	America
July 27	President Harding
Aug. 7	Republic
Aug. 17	George Washington
Aug. 22	President Roosevelt
Aug. 25	America
Aug. 31	President Harding
Sept. 10	Republic
Sept. 14	George Washington
Sept. 24	America
Sept. 28	President Harding
Oct. 5	President Roosevelt
Oct. 13	George Washington
Oct. 17	Republic
Oct. 26	America
Oct. 27	President Harding
Nov. 2	President Roosevelt
Nov. 10	George Washington
Nov. 20	Republic
Nov. 24	President Harding
Dec. 1	President Roosevelt
Dec. 8	George Washington

UNITED STATES LINE
Bremen, Southampton, Cherbourg—New York
(Continued)
N. Y.

Arrival	Steamer
Dec. 17	America
Dec. 21	President Harding

UNITED STATES LINE
Algiers, Genoa, Naples—
New York
N. Y.

Arrival	Steamer
Feb. 14	President Roosevelt
Feb. 29	President Harding
Mar. 15	President Roosevelt
Apr. 3	President Harding

UNITED STATES LINE
Southampton, Cherbourg—
New York
N. Y.

Arrival	Steamer
Feb. 27	Leviathan
Mar. 19	Leviathan
Apr. 9	Leviathan
Apr. 30	Leviathan
May 21	Leviathan
June 11	Leviathan
June 30	Leviathan
July 19	Leviathan
Aug. 20	Leviathan
Sept. 10	Leviathan
Oct. 1	Leviathan
Oct. 22	Leviathan
Nov. 9	Leviathan
Nov. 30	Leviathan
Dec. 20	Leviathan

WHITE STAR LINE
Southampton, Cherbourg,
Antwerp—New York
N. Y.

Arrival	Steamer
Jan. 11	Majestic
Jan. 18	Arabic
Jan. 20	Homeric
Jan. 26	Montroyal
Feb. 1	Olympic
Feb. 21	Arabic
Feb. 23	Olympic
Mar. 7	Majestic
Mar. 14	Olympic
Mar. 27	Arabic
Mar. 28	Majestic
Apr. 4	Olympic
Apr. 12	Homeric
Apr. 17	Majestic
Apr. 23	Arabic
Apr. 25	Olympic
Mar. 3	Homeric
May 8	Majestic
May 16	Olympic
May 24	Homeric
May 28	Arabic
May 31	Majestic
June 6	Olympic
June 14	Homeric
June 20	Majestic

Year 1928

WHITE STAR LINE		WHITE STAR LINE		WHITE STAR LINE	
Southampton, Cherbourg, Antwerp—New York (Continued)		Liverpool, Queenstown— New York		Liverpool, Queenstown— New York (Continued)	
N.Y. Arrival	**Steamer**	**N.Y. Arrival**	**Steamer**	**N.Y. Arrival**	**Steamer**
June 25	Arabic	Jan. 3	Adriatic	June 18	Baltic
June 27	Olympic	Jan. 10	Laurentic	June 26	Cedric
July 5	Homeric	Jan. 13	Megantic	July 2	Adriatic
July 10	Majestic	Jan. 18	Celtic	July 10	Celtic
July 19	Olympic	Jan. 26	Albertic	July 16	Baltic
July 27	Homeric	Feb. 2	Calgaric	July 24	Cedric
Aug. 1	Majestic	Feb. 6	Doric	July 30	Adriatic
Aug. 8	Olympic	Feb. 15	Regina	Aug. 7	Celtic
Aug. 16	Homeric	Feb. 23	Adriatic	Aug. 13	Baltic
Aug. 21	Arabic	Feb. 24	Celtic	Aug. 21	Cedric
Aug. 22	Majestic	Feb. 29	Albertic	Aug. 27	Adriatic
Aug. 29	Olympic	Mar. 5	Laurentic	Aug. 30	Caledonian
Sept. 6	Homeric	Mar. 7	Cedric	Sept. 4	Celtic
Sept. 12	Majestic	Mar. 13	Baltic	Sept. 10	Baltic
Sept. 17	Arabic	Mar. 16	Caledonian	Sept. 17	Cedric
Sept. 19	Olympic	Mar. 21	Celtic	Sept. 24	Adriatic
Sept. 27	Homeric	Apr. 3	Cedric	Oct. 1	Celtic
Oct. 2	Majestic	Apr. 3	Megantic	Oct. 9	Baltic
Oct. 10	Olympic	Apr. 9	Albertic	Oct. 16	Cedric
Oct. 16	Arabic	Apr. 11	Adriatic	Oct. 22	Adriatic
Oct. 17	Homeric	Apr. 17	Celtic	Oct. 31	Celtic
Oct. 23	Majestic	Apr. 24	Baltic	Nov. 5	Baltic
Oct. 31	Olympic	May 1	Cedric	Nov. 13	Cedric
Nov. 9	Homeric	May 7	Adriatic	Nov. 19	Adriatic
Nov. 14	Majestic	May 15	Celtic	Nov. 28	Celtic
Nov. 21	Olympic	May 21	Baltic	Dec. 6	Baltic
Nov. 30	Homeric	May 29	Cedric	Dec. 10	Regina
Dec. 5	Majestic	June 4	Adriatic	Dec. 19	Calgaric
Dec. 19	Olympic	June 7	Caledonian		
Dec. 26	Majestic	June 12	Celtic		

Year 1929

AMERICAN MERCHANT LINE
London—New York
N. Y.

Arrival	Steamer
Jan. 2	American Merchant
Jan. 10	American Trader
Jan. 14	American Farmer
Jan. 23	American Shipper
Jan. 30	American Banker
Feb. 4	American Merchant
Feb. 11	American Trader
Feb. 23	American Shipper
Mar. 6	American Banker
Mar. 11	American Merchant
Mar. 12	American Farmer
Mar. 19	American Trader
Mar. 26	American Shipper
Apr. 2	American Banker
Apr. 8	American Merchant
Apr. 15	American Trader
Apr. 23	American Shipper
Apr. 29	American Banker
May 6	American Merchant
May 13	American Trader
May 22	American Farmer
May 27	American Shipper
June 3	American Banker
June 10	American Merchant
June 17	American Farmer
June 24	American Shipper
July 2	American Banker
July 8	American Trader
July 15	American Farmer
July 22	American Shipper
July 29	American Merchant
Aug. 5	American Trader
Aug. 13	American Farmer
Aug. 19	American Banker
Aug. 26	American Merchant
Sept. 3	American Trader
Sept. 10	American Shipper
Sept. 16	American Banker
Sept. 23	American Merchant
Sept. 30	American Trader
Oct. 8	American Shipper
Oct. 15	American Banker
Oct. 21	American Merchant
Oct. 29	American Trader
Nov. 5	American Shipper
Nov. 12	American Banker
Nov. 22	American Merchant
Nov. 27	American Trader
Dec. 3	American Farmer
Dec. 11	American Banker
Dec. 20	American Shipper
Dec. 23	American Trader
Dec. 31	American Merchant

ATLANTIC TRANSPORT LINE
London, Boulogne—New York
N. Y.

Arrival	Steamer
Jan. 15	Minnekahda
Jan. 21	Minnewaska
Jan. 29	Minnetonka

ATLANTIC TRANSPORT LINE
London, Boulogne—New York
(Continued)
N. Y.

Arrival	Steamer
Feb. 26	Minnetonka
Mar. 6	Minnekahda
Mar. 11	Minnewaska
Mar. 26	Minnetonka
Apr. 2	Minnekahda
Apr. 8	Minnewaska
Apr. 23	Minnetonka
Apr. 30	Minnekahda
May 6	Minnewaska
May 14	Minnesota
May 21	Minnetonka
May 28	Minnekahda
June 3	Minnewaska
June 11	Minnesota
June 18	Minnetonka
June 25	Minnekahda
July 1	Minnewaska
July 9	Minnesota
July 15	Minnetonka
July 23	Minnekahda
July 29	Minnewaska
Aug. 6	Minnesota
Aug. 12	Minnetonka
Aug. 20	Minnekahda
Aug. 26	Minnewaska
Sept. 2	Minnesota
Sept. 9	Minnetonka
Sept. 17	Minnekahda
Sept. 23	Minnewaska
Oct. 1	Minnesota
Oct. 7	Minnetonka
Oct. 15	Minnekahda
Oct. 21	Minnewaska
Nov. 4	Minnetonka
Nov. 12	Minnekahda
Nov. 19	Minnewaska
Dec. 3	Minnetonka
Dec. 11	Minnekahda
Dec. 20	Minnewaska
Dec. 31	Minnetonka

BALTIC AMERICAN LINE
Danzig, Copenhagen—New York
N. Y.

Arrival	Steamer
Jan. 23	Lituania
Feb. 4	Polonia
Mar. 22	Lituania
Mar. 27	Estonia
Apr. 27	Estonia
May 7	Polonia
May 14	Lituania
May 27	Estonia
June 11	Polonia
June 17	Lituania
July 1	Estonia
July 23	Lituania
Aug. 6	Estonia
Aug. 27	Lituania

BALTIC AMERICAN LINE
Danzig, Copenhagen—New York
(Continued)
N. Y.

Arrival	Steamer
Sept. 4	Polonia
Sept. 10	Estonia
Oct. 1	Lituania
Oct. 9	Polonia
Oct. 21	Estonia
Nov. 14	Polonia
Dec. 3	Estonia
Dec. 20	Lituania

CANADIAN PACIFIC LINE
Southampton, Cherbourg, Liverpool, Quebec—New York
N. Y.

Arrival	Steamer
Jan. 7	Duchess Bedford
Jan. 21	Duchess Athol
Jan. 28	Empress of Scotland
Apr. 15	Empress of Australia
Sept. 25	Empress of Canada
Nov. 27	Empress of Australia
Dec. 20	Duchess Bedford

COMPANIA TRANSATLANTICA LINE
(Spanish Line)
Cadiz, Barcelona, Vigo, Havana—New York
N. Y.

Arrival	Steamer
Jan. 7	Manuel Calvo
Jan. 11	Cristobal Colon
Jan. 14	Manuel Arnus
Jan. 28	Marques Comillas
Feb. 7	Marques Comillas
Feb. 12	Alfonso XIII
Mar. 4	Magallanes
Mar. 11	Cristobal Colon
Mar. 12	Antonio Lopez
Mar. 22	Leon XIII
Apr. 4	Alfonso XIII
Apr. 5	Leon XIII
Apr. 16	Manuel Calvo
Apr. 26	Juan Sebastin Elcano
May 1	Cristobal Colon
May 10	Manuel Arnus
May 21	Manuel Arnus
May 26	Alfonso XIII
June 7	Antonio Lopez
June 17	Marques Comillas
June 21	Cristobal Colon
June 29	Magallanes
July 11	Magallanes
July 17	Alfonso XIII
July 29	Manuel Calvo
Aug. 7	Buenos Ayres
Aug. 13	Cristobal Colon
Aug. 21	Juan Sebastin Elcano
Sept. 3	Juan Sebastin Elcano
Sept. 7	Alfonso XIII

Year 1929

COMPANIA TRANSATLANTICA LINE
(Spanish Line)

Cadiz, Barcelona, Vigo, Havana—New York
(Continued)

N. Y.

Arrival	Steamer
Sept. 20	Antonio Lopez
Oct. 4	Cristobal Colon
Oct. 4	Manuel Arnus
Oct. 14	Marques Comillas
Oct. 29	Alfonso XIII
Nov. 11	Manuel Calvo
Nov. 19	Leon XIII
Nov. 25	Cristobal Colon
Dec. 20	Alfonso XIII
Dec. 31	Antonio Lopez

COSULICH LINE
Trieste, Patras, Palermo, Naples—New York

N. Y.

Arrival	Steamer
Jan. 2	Vulcania
Feb. 20	Vulcania
Mar. 26	Vulcania
May 1	Vulcania
June 4	Vulcania
June 20	Saturnia
July 9	Vulcania
July 30	Saturnia
Aug. 20	Vulcania
Sept. 9	Saturnia
Sept. 24	Vulcania
Oct. 14	Saturnia
Oct. 29	Vulcania
Nov. 18	Saturnia
Dec. 4	Vulcania

CUNARD-ANCHOR LINE
Glasgow, Belfast—New York

N. Y.

Arrival	Steamer
Jan. 2	Athenia
Jan. 8	Caledonia
Jan. 14	California
Jan. 22	Letitia
Jan. 28	Transylvania
Feb. 5	Athenia
Feb. 5	Cameronia
Feb. 20	Caledonia
Mar. 6	Cameronia
Mar. 22	Caledonia
Apr. 4	Athenia
Apr. 4	Cameronia
Apr. 16	Caledonia
Apr. 23	California
May 7	Cameronia
May 21	California
May 27	Caledonia
June 3	Cameronia
June 17	Transylvania
June 23	Caledonia
June 28	California
July 1	Cameronia
July 15	Transylvania

CUNARD-ANCHOR LINE
Glasgow, Belfast—New York
(Continued)

N. Y.

Arrival	Steamer
July 22	Caledonia
July 29	Cameronia
Aug. 12	Transylvania
Aug. 22	Caledonia
Sept. 3	Cameronia
Sept. 9	Transylvania
Sept. 16	Caledonia
Sept. 23	California
Sept. 30	Cameronia
Oct. 7	Transylvania
Oct. 14	Caledonia
Oct. 29	Cameronia
Nov. 4	Transylvania
Nov. 11	Caledonia
Nov. 25	Cameronia
Dec. 2	Transylvania
Dec. 11	Caledonia
Dec. 18	Letitia
Dec. 23	Cameronia
Dec. 30	Transylvania

CUNARD LINE
Southampton, Cherbourg, Halifax, Havre—New York

N. Y.

Arrival	Steamer
Jan. 2	Ausonia
Jan. 3	Berengaria
Jan. 9	Mauretania
Jan. 14	Ascania
Jan. 21	Alaunia
Jan. 28	Aurania
Jan. 30	Aquitania
Feb. 4	Ausonia
Feb. 13	Mauretania
Feb. 18	Ascania
Feb. 25	Alaunia
Feb. 27	Aquitania
Mar. 5	Aurania
Mar. 6	Berengaria
Mar. 12	Ausonia
Mar. 20	Aquitania
Mar. 26	Ascania
Mar. 27	Berengaria
Apr. 2	Alaunia
Apr. 5	Mauretania
Apr. 8	Aurania
Apr. 8	Carinthia
Apr. 12	Aquitania
Apr. 15	Ausonia
Apr. 20	Berengaria
Apr. 24	Caronia
Apr. 26	Mauretania
Apr. 29	Laconia
May 4	Aquitania
May 10	Berengaria
May 13	Tuscania
May 17	Mauretania
May 21	Caronia
May 24	Aquitania
May 27	Lancastria
May 28	Carinthia
May 31	Berengaria
June 3	Carmania

CUNARD LINE
Southampton, Cherbourg, Halifax, Havre—New York
(Continued)

N. Y.

Arrival	Steamer
June 7	Mauretania
June 10	Tuscania
June 16	Aquitania
June 17	Caronia
June 22	Berengaria
June 25	Carinthia
June 27	Lancastria
June 28	Mauretania
July 1	Carmania
July 5	Aquitania
July 8	Tuscania
July 13	Berengaria
July 15	Caronia
July 19	Mauretania
July 26	Aquitania
July 29	Carmania
Aug. 2	Berengaria
Aug. 5	Tuscania
Aug. 9	Mauretania
Aug. 12	Caronia
Aug. 17	Aquitania
Aug. 19	Lancastria
Aug. 23	Berengaria
Aug. 26	Carmania
Aug. 30	California
Aug. 30	Mauretania
Sept. 3	Tuscania
Sept. 7	Aquitania
Sept. 9	Caronia
Sept. 13	Berengaria
Sept. 16	Lancastria
Sept. 20	Mauretania
Sept. 23	Carmania
Sept. 27	Aquitania
Sept. 30	Tuscania
Oct. 4	Berengaria
Oct. 11	Mauretania
Oct. 14	Lancastria
Oct. 18	Aquitania
Oct. 21	Carmania
Oct. 25	Berengaria
Oct. 28	Tuscania
Nov. 1	Mauretania
Nov. 8	Aquitania
Nov. 11	Carmania
Nov. 11	Lancastria
Nov. 16	Berengaria
Nov. 23	Mauretania
Nov. 26	Alaunia
Dec. 3	Franconia
Dec. 3	Tuscania
Dec. 13	Berengaria
Dec. 14	Ausonia
Dec. 20	Lancastria
Dec. 23	Carmania
Dec. 23	Mauretania
Dec. 31	Berengaria

CUNARD LINE
World Ports—New York

N. Y.

Arrival	Steamer
May 31	Franconia

Year 1929

CUNARD LINE
Liverpool, Queenstown, Alexandria—New York

N. Y.

Arrival	Steamer
Jan. 2	Scythia
Jan. 15	Antonia
Jan. 17	Samaria
Jan. 23	Lancastria
Jan. 29	Andania
Feb. 6	Athenia
Feb. 13	Antonia
Feb. 20	Lancastria
Feb. 28	Andania
Mar. 7	Athenia
Mar. 12	Antonia
Mar. 19	Lancastria
Mar. 27	Andania
Apr. 4	Athenia
Apr. 9	Antonia
Apr. 17	Scythia
Apr. 22	Samaria
Apr. 30	Lancastria
May 6	Carmania
May 14	Scythia
May 21	Samaria
May 28	Carinthia
June 3	Laconia
June 11	Scythia
June 17	Samaria
June 25	Franconia
July 1	Laconia
July 9	Scythia
July 15	Samaria
July 23	Laconia
July 28	Carmania
Aug. 6	Scythia
Aug. 12	Samaria
Aug. 20	Laconia
Aug. 25	Franconia
Sept. 3	Scythia
Sept. 9	Carinthia
Sept. 13	Samaria
Sept. 17	Laconia
Sept. 23	Franconia
Oct. 2	Scythia
Oct. 7	Samaria
Oct. 7	Carinthia
Oct. 15	Laconia
Oct. 21	Andania
Oct. 29	Scythia
Nov. 12	Laconia
Nov. 19	Samaria
Nov. 26	Scythia
Dec. 3	Franconia
Dec. 4	Antonia
Dec. 11	Laconia
Dec. 18	Carinthia
Dec. 19	Lancastria
Dec. 23	Caronia

DOLLAR STEAMSHIP LINE
World Ports—New York

N. Y.

Arrival	Steamer
Jan. 2	President Adams
Jan. 10	President Garfield
Jan. 28	President Harrison

DOLLAR STEAMSHIP LINE
World Ports—New York
(Continued)

N. Y.

Arrival	Steamer
Jan. 28	President Johnson
Feb. 6	President Monroe
Feb. 20	President Wilson
Mar. 6	President Van Buren
Mar. 21	President Hayes
Apr. 3	President Polk
Apr. 18	Ruth Alexander
Apr. 30	President Garfield
May 7	President Harrison
May 13	President Johnson
May 28	President Monroe
June 6	President Adams
June 10	President Wilson
June 25	President Van Buren
July 9	President Hayes
July 23	President Polk
Aug. 6	President Adams
Aug. 24	President Harrison
Sept. 3	President Johnson
Sept. 17	President Monroe
Oct. 1	President Wilson
Oct. 15	President Van Buren
Oct. 30	President Garfield
Nov. 13	President Polk
Nov. 27	President Adams
Dec. 14	President Harrison
Dec. 24	President Johnson

FABRE LINE
Piraeus, Lisbon, Marseilles, Palermo, Constantinople—New York

N. Y.

Arrival	Steamer
Jan. 24	Providence
Feb. 11	Asia
Feb. 13	Patria
Mar. 12	Alesia
Apr. 8	Sinaia
Apr. 9	Providence
May 6	Patria
May 15	Asia
June 11	Alesia
June 25	Providence
July 9	Sinaia
July 25	Patria
Aug. 12	Asia
Aug. 22	Providence
Sept. 13	Alesia
Sept. 16	Patria
Oct. 14	Sinaia
Nov. 13	Asia
Nov. 15	Providence
Nov. 27	Patria
Dec. 16	Alesia

FRENCH LINE
(Compagnie Generale Transatlantique)
Havre, Plymouth—New York

N. Y.

Arrival	Steamer
Jan. 2	France

FRENCH LINE
(Compagnie Generale Transatlantique)
Havre, Plymouth—New York
(Continued)

N. Y.

Arrival	Steamer
Jan. 10	Ile de France
Jan. 19	Rochambeau
Jan. 24	Paris
Jan. 30	Ile de France
Feb. 8	De Grasse
Feb. 13	Paris
Feb. 23	Rochambeau
Feb. 27	Ile de France
Mar. 9	De Grasse
Mar. 13	Paris
Mar. 25	Rochambeau
Mar. 27	Ile de France
Apr. 3	Paris
Apr. 12	De Grasse
Apr. 17	Ile de France
Apr. 29	France
May 8	Ile de France
May 8	De Grasse
May 15	Paris
May 21	Rochambeau
May 22	France
May 29	Ile de France
June 3	De Grasse
June 5	Paris
June 17	Rochambeau
June 19	Ile de France
June 25	Paris
June 29	France
July 1	De Grasse
July 5	Ile de France
July 11	Paris
July 13	Rochambeau
July 17	France
July 24	Ile de France
July 29	De Grasse
July 31	Paris
Aug. 9	Rochambeau
Aug. 14	France
Aug. 20	Ile de France
Aug. 26	De Grasse
Aug. 30	France
Sept. 3	Cuba
Sept. 4	Ile de France
Sept. 10	Rochambeau
Sept. 12	Mexique
Sept. 17	France
Sept. 23	De Grasse
Sept. 25	Ile de France
Oct. 5	Mexique
Oct. 8	Rochambeau
Oct. 9	France
Oct. 15	Ile de France
Oct. 25	De Grasse
Nov. 8	Ile de France
Nov. 15	Rochambeau
Nov. 20	France
Nov. 30	De Grasse
Dec. 4	Ile de France
Dec. 13	France
Dec. 21	Rochambeau
Dec. 28	De Grasse

Year 1929

FRENCH LINE
(Compagnie Generale Transatlantique)
Mediterranean Ports—New York

N. Y.

Arrival	Steamer
Feb. 4	France
Mar. 12	France

FRENCH LINE
(Compagnie Generale Transatlantique)
Bordeaux, Vigo, Halifax— New York

N. Y.

Arrival	Steamer
Feb. 1	Roussillon
Mar. 22	De La Salle
Apr. 11	La Bourdonnais
Apr. 25	Niagara
June 3	De La Salle
June 3	La Bourdonnais
June 14	Roussillon
June 22	Niagara
July 11	La Bourdonnais
July 26	Roussillon
Aug. 15	La Bourdonnais
Sept. 11	Roussillon
Sept. 26	La Bourdonnais
Oct. 19	Roussillon
Nov. 4	La Bourdonnais
Dec. 3	Roussillon
Dec. 14	La Bourdonnais

HAMBURG-AMERICAN LINE
Hamburg, Southampton, Cherbourg—New York

N. Y.

Arrival	Steamer
Jan. 2	Thuringia
Jan. 8	Deutschland
Jan. 14	Hamburg
Jan. 21	Cleveland
Jan. 22	Albert Ballin
Jan. 28	New York
Feb. 4	Westphalia
Feb. 11	Deutschland
Feb. 19	Hamburg
Feb. 26	Albert Ballin
Mar. 5	Cleveland
Mar. 18	Deutschland
Mar. 18	Westphalia
Mar. 26	Hamburg
Apr. 3	Albert Ballin
Apr. 9	St. Louis
Apr. 11	Reliance
Apr. 16	Thuringia
Apr. 16	New York
Apr. 23	Deutschland
Apr. 24	Westphalia
Apr. 29	Hamburg
May 6	Albert Ballin
May 10	Reliance
May 14	St. Louis
May 21	New York
May 22	Cleveland
May 27	Deutschland

HAMBURG-AMERICAN LINE
Hamburg, Southampton, Cherbourg—New York
(Continued)

N. Y.

Arrival	Steamer
June 3	Hamburg
June 5	Westphalia
June 10	Albert Ballin
June 18	St. Louis
June 20	Thuringia
June 22	Reliance
June 25	New York
June 29	Milwaukee
July 1	Deutschland
July 6	Cleveland
July 8	Hamburg
July 13	Albert Ballin
July 20	Westphalia
July 22	St. Louis
July 29	New York
Aug. 2	Thuringia
Aug. 3	Milwaukee
Aug. 5	Deutschland
Aug. 11	Cleveland
Aug. 13	Hamburg
Aug. 20	Albert Ballin
Aug. 23	Resolute
Aug. 27	St. Louis
Aug. 27	Westphalia
Aug. 30	Reliance
Sept. 3	New York
Sept. 9	Deutschland
Sept. 11	Thuringia
Sept. 16	Milwaukee
Sept. 20	Resolute
Sept. 23	Albert Ballin
Sept. 23	Cleveland
Sept. 27	Reliance
Sept. 30	St. Louis
Oct. 8	New York
Oct. 8	Westphalia
Oct. 14	Deutschland
Oct. 21	Milwaukee
Oct. 21	Resolute
Oct. 26	Thuringia
Oct. 28	Cleveland
Oct. 28	Reliance
Nov. 4	St. Louis
Nov. 12	New York
Nov. 19	Deutschland
Nov. 26	Milwaukee
Nov. 26	Westphalia
Dec. 5	Cleveland
Dec. 9	St. Louis
Dec. 11	Reliance
Dec. 17	Resolute
Dec. 21	Thuringia
Dec. 23	Deutschland

HAMBURG-AMERICAN LINE
World Ports—New York

N. Y.

Arrival	Steamer
May 28	Resolute

HOLLAND-AMERICA LINE
Rotterdam, Southampton, Cherbourg—New York

N. Y.

Arrival	Steamer
Jan. 14	Ryndam
Jan. 21	Volendam
Jan. 28	New Amsterdam
Feb. 1	Rotterdam
Feb. 5	Veendam
Feb. 18	Ryndam
Mar. 4	New Amsterdam
Mar. 27	Ryndam
Apr. 8	New Amsterdam
Apr. 15	Veendam
Apr. 20	Statendam
Apr. 29	Ryndam
May 4	Rotterdam
May 11	New Amsterdam
May 20	Veendam
May 27	Statendam
June 3	Volendam
June 10	Rotterdam
June 15	New Amsterdam
June 24	Statendam
June 29	Veendam
July 8	Volendam
July 11	Rotterdam
July 22	New Amsterdam
July 29	Statendam
Aug. 5	Veendam
Aug. 12	Volendam
Aug. 17	Rotterdam
Aug. 23	New Amsterdam
Sept. 3	Statendam
Sept. 9	Veendam
Sept. 14	Volendam
Sept. 21	Rotterdam
Sept. 30	New Amsterdam
Oct. 7	Statendam
Oct. 14	Veendam
Oct. 21	Volendam
Oct. 29	New Amsterdam
Nov. 15	Statendam
Nov. 27	New Amsterdam
Dec. 4	Veendam
Dec. 8	Volendam
Dec. 18	Statendam
Dec. 30	New Amsterdam

ITALIA AMERICA LINE
Genoa, Naples, Palermo— New York

N. Y.

Arrival	Steamer
Jan. 29	Roma
Feb. 13	Augustus
Mar. 5	Roma
Mar. 20	Augustus
Apr. 5	Roma
Apr. 24	Augustus
May 13	Roma
May 29	Augustus
June 17	Roma
July 2	Augustus
July 22	Roma
Aug. 14	Augustus

Year 1929

ITALIA-AMERICA LINE
Genoa, Naples, Palermo—
New York
(Continued)

N. Y.

Arrival	Steamer
Sept. 3	Roma
Sept. 17	Augustus
Oct. 7	Roma
Oct. 22	Augustus
Nov. 8	Roma
Nov. 26	Augustus
Dec. 10	Roma

LLOYD SABAUDO
Genoa, Naples—New York

N. Y.

Arrival	Steamer
Jan. 22	Conte Biancamano
Feb. 4	Conte Grande
Feb. 26	Conte Biancamano
Mar. 11	Conte Grande
Apr. 1	Conte Biancamano
Apr. 15	Conte Grande
May 6	Conte Biancamano
May 20	Conte Grande
June 10	Conte Biancamano
June 24	Conte Grande
July 15	Conte Biancamano
Aug. 5	Conte Grande
Aug. 26	Conte Biancamano
Sept. 10	Conte Grande
Oct. 2	Conte Biancamano
Oct. 14	Conte Grande
Nov. 6	Conte Biancamano
Nov. 18	Conte Grande
Dec. 7	Conte Biancamano
Dec. 20	Conte Grande

NATIONAL STEAM NAVIGATION OF GREECE
Piraeus, Patras—New York

N. Y.

Arrival	Steamer
Jan. 5	Edison
Jan. 31	Byron
Mar. 11	Edison
Mar. 26	Byron
June 3	Byron
June 26	Edison
July 24	Byron
Aug. 21	Edison
Sept. 20	Byron
Oct. 21	Edison
Nov. 13	Byron
Dec. 4	Edison

NORTH GERMAN LLOYD
Bremen, Southampton, Cherbourg—New York

N. Y.

Arrival	Steamer
Jan. 2	Dresden
Jan. 14	Muenchen
Jan. 21	Berlin
Jan. 26	Columbus
Jan. 28	Stuttgart
Feb. 4	Dresden

NORTH GERMAN LLOYD
Bremen, Southampton, Cherbourg—New York
(Continued)

N. Y.

Arrival	Steamer
Feb. 11	Muenchen
Feb. 18	Berlin
Feb. 26	Stuttgart
Mar. 5	Dresden
Mar. 13	Muenchen
Mar. 17	Yorck
Mar. 18	Berlin
Mar. 26	Stuttgart
Apr. 3	Dresden
Apr. 8	Muenchen
Apr. 12	Karlsruhe
Apr. 15	Berlin
Apr. 22	Stuttgart
Apr. 23	Columbus
Apr. 30	Dresden
May 6	Muenchen
May 8	Berlin
May 14	Karlsruhe
May 17	Columbus
May 21	Stuttgart
May 27	Dresden
June 1	Berlin
June 3	Muenchen
June 10	Columbus
June 10	Leutzow
June 13	Karlsruhe
June 17	Stuttgart
June 25	Dresden
June 26	Berlin
July 1	Muenchen
July 2	Columbus
July 15	Karlsruhe
July 15	Stuttgart
July 22	Berlin
July 23	Bremen
July 29	Dresden
Aug. 5	Muenchen
Aug. 16	Karlsruhe
Aug. 19	Stuttgart
Aug. 21	Bremen
Aug. 26	Dresden
Aug. 27	Berlin
Sept. 1	Yorck
Sept. 3	Muenchen
Sept. 6	Leutzow
Sept. 11	Bremen
Sept. 12	Karlsruhe
Sept. 16	Stuttgart
Sept. 23	Berlin
Sept. 23	Dresden
Sept. 30	Muenchen
Oct. 1	Bremen
Oct. 9	Leutzow
Oct. 10	Karlsruhe
Oct. 14	Stuttgart
Oct. 21	Dresden
Oct. 22	Berlin
Oct. 23	Bremen
Oct. 28	Muenchen
Nov. 7	Karlsruhe
Nov. 11	Stuttgart
Nov. 13	Bremen
Nov. 20	Dresden
Nov. 26	Muenchen

NORTH GERMAN LLOYD
Bremen, Southampton, Cherbourg—New York
(Continued)

N. Y.

Arrival	Steamer
Dec. 3	Berlin
Dec. 10	Stuttgart
Dec. 13	Bremen
Dec. 21	Dresden
Dec. 23	Columbus
Dec. 31	Berlin

NORWEGIAN AMERICAN LINE
Oslo, Bergen—New York

N. Y.

Arrival	Steamer
Jan. 14	Stavangerfjord
Feb. 28	Bergensfjord
Mar. 18	Stavangerfjord
Apr. 2	Bergensfjord
Apr. 22	Stavangerfjord
May 6	Bergensfjord
May 27	Stavangerfjord
June 11	Bergensfjord
July 2	Stavangerfjord
July 15	Bergensfjord
Aug. 5	Stavangerfjord
Aug. 19	Bergensfjord
Sept. 9	Stavangerfjord
Sept. 24	Bergensfjord
Oct. 14	Stavangerfjord
Oct. 29	Bergensfjord
Nov. 19	Stavangerfjord
Dec. 3	Bergensfjord
Dec. 21	Stavangerfjord

PHELPS BROTHERS LINE
Trieste, Patras, Naples—
New York

N. Y.

Arrival	Steamer
Feb. 2	President Wilson
Mar. 18	President Wilson
Apr. 15	President Wilson
May 20	President Wilson
June 24	President Wilson
Dec. 7	President Wilson

RED STAR LINE
Antwerp—New York

N. Y.

Arrival	Steamer
Jan. 28	Lapland
Feb. 28	Pennland
Mar. 13	Lapland
Mar. 26	Pennland
Apr. 23	Pennland
May 1	Belgenland
May 13	Lapland
May 21	Pennland
May 25	Belgenland
June 10	Lapland
June 17	Pennland
June 24	Belgenland
July 8	Lapland
July 15	Pennland
July 22	Belgenland

Year 1929

RED STAR LINE
Antwerp—New York
(Continued)
N. Y.

Arrival	Steamer
Aug. 5	Lapland
Aug. 12	Pennland
Aug. 19	Belgenland
Sept. 3	Lapland
Sept. 9	Pennland
Sept. 16	Belgenland
Sept. 30	Lapland
Oct. 8	Pennland
Oct. 14	Belgenland
Oct. 28	Lapland
Nov. 6	Pennland
Dec. 3	Pennland
Dec. 16	Belgenland
Dec. 23	Lapland

SCANDINAVIAN LINE
Copenhagen, Oslo, Halifax—
New York

Jan. 21	United States
Jan. 28	Hellig Olav
Feb. 11	Frederik VIII
Feb. 25	United States
Mar. 4	Hellig Olav
Mar. 12	Oscar II
Mar. 19	Frederik VIII
Apr. 3	United States
Apr. 8	Hellig Olav
Apr. 15	Oscar II
Apr. 23	Frederik VIII
May 7	United States
May 14	Hellig Olav
May 21	Oscar II
May 27	Frederik VIII
June 8	United States
June 18	Hellig Olav
June 25	Oscar II
July 2	Frederik VIII
July 15	United States
July 23	Hellig Olav
July 30	Oscar II
Aug. 5	Frederik VIII
Aug. 19	United States
Aug. 28	Hellig Olav
Sept. 3	Oscar II
Sept. 10	Frederik VIII
Sept. 23	United States
Sept. 30	Hellig Olav
Oct. 8	Oscar II
Oct. 14	Frederik VIII
Oct. 28	United States
Nov. 6	Hellig Olav
Nov. 19	Oscar II
Dec. 2	Frederik VIII
Dec. 16	Hellig Olav
Dec. 30	Oscar II

SWEDISH-AMERICAN LINE
Gothenburg—New York
N. Y.

Arrival	Steamer
Jan. 9	Gripsholm
Jan. 14	Kungsholm
Jan. 22	Drottningholm
Feb. 5	Gripsholm

SWEDISH-AMERICAN LINE
Gothenburg—New York
(Continued)
N. Y.

Arrival	Steamer
Feb. 20	Drottningholm
Mar. 5	Gripsholm
Mar. 19	Drottningholm
Apr. 8	Kungsholm
Apr. 16	Gripsholm
Apr. 23	Drottningholm
May 6	Kungsholm
May 14	Gripsholm
May 21	Drottningholm
June 1	Kungsholm
June 17	Gripsholm
June 22	Drottningholm
July 1	Kungsholm
July 15	Gripsholm
July 29	Drottningholm
Aug. 6	Kungsholm
Aug. 20	Gripsholm
Aug. 26	Drottningholm
Sept. 1	Kungsholm
Sept. 17	Gripsholm
Sept. 23	Drottningholm
Sept. 30	Kungsholm
Oct. 15	Gripsholm
Nov. 4	Kungsholm
Dec. 3	Gripsholm
Dec. 16	Kungsholm

UNITED STATES LINE
Southampton, Cherbourg—
New York
N. Y.

Arrival	Steamer
Feb. 21	Leviathan
Mar. 15	Leviathan
Apr. 5	Leviathan
Apr. 26	Leviathan
May 21	Leviathan
June 8	Leviathan
June 26	Leviathan
July 15	Leviathan
Aug. 13	Leviathan
Sept. 3	Leviathan
Sept. 23	Leviathan
Oct. 11	Leviathan
Oct. 29	Leviathan
Nov. 18	Leviathan
Dec. 6	Leviathan
Dec. 26	Leviathan

UNITED STATES LINE
Bremen, Southampton, Cher-
bourg—New York
N. Y.

Arrival	Steamer
Jan. 2	President Roosevelt
Jan. 8	George Washington
Jan. 15	Republic
Jan. 28	America
Feb. 5	George Washington
Feb. 8	President Harding
Feb. 19	Republic
Feb. 23	America
Mar. 8	President Harding
Mar. 12	George Washington

UNITED STATES LINE
Bremen, Southampton, Cher-
bourg—New York
(Continued)
N. Y.

Arrival	Steamer
Mar. 25	Republic
Mar. 28	America
Apr. 6	President Harding
Apr. 24	Republic
Apr. 29	America
May 4	President Harding
May 13	President Roosevelt
May 18	George Washington
May 27	America
May 31	President Harding
June 6	Republic
June 7	President Roosevelt
June 15	George Washington
June 24	America
June 27	President Harding
July 2	Republic
July 8	President Roosevelt
July 11	George Washington
July 22	America
July 23	President Harding
July 29	Republic
Aug. 9	President Roosevelt
Aug. 16	George Washington
Aug. 24	America
Aug. 31	President Harding
Sept. 3	President Roosevelt
Sept. 3	Republic
Sept. 13	George Washington
Sept. 21	America
Sept. 27	President Harding
Oct. 2	Republic
Oct. 4	President Roosevelt
Oct. 9	George Washington
Oct. 21	America
Oct. 23	President Harding
Nov. 1	Republic
Nov. 4	President Roosevelt
Nov. 9	George Washington
Nov. 20	America
Nov. 25	President Harding
Nov. 29	President Roosevelt
Dec. 10	Republic
Dec. 26	President Roosevelt

WHITE STAR LINE
Liverpool, Queenstown,
Glasgow—New York
N. Y.

Arrival	Steamer
Jan. 2	Baltic
Jan. 8	Adriatic
Jan. 16	Laurentic
Jan. 30	Cedric
Feb. 5	Doric
Feb. 13	Albertic
Feb. 13	Megantic
Feb. 20	Regina
Feb. 26	Cedric
Mar. 8	Doric
Mar. 13	Albertic
Mar. 19	Megantic
Mar. 20	Regina
Mar. 27	Cedric
Apr. 2	Baltic

Year 1929

WHITE STAR LINE Liverpool, Queenstown, Glasgow—New York (Continued) **N. Y.**		WHITE STAR LINE Liverpool, Queenstown, Glasgow—New York (Continued) **N. Y.**		WHITE STAR LINE Southampton, Cherbourg, Antwerp—New York (Continued) **N. Y.**	
Arrival	**Steamer**	**Arrival**	**Steamer**	**Arrival**	**Steamer**
Apr. 11	Albertic	Dec. 20	Albertic	May 23	Homeric
Apr. 24	Cedric	Dec. 26	Doric	May 28	Majestic
Apr. 27	Baltic	Dec. 31	Megantic	June 3	Arabic
May 9	Albertic			June 4	Olympic
May 13	Adriatic	**WHITE STAR LINE** Mediterranean Ports—New York		June 13	Homeric
May 21	Cedric			June 19	Majestic
May 27	Baltic	**N. Y.**		June 26	Olympic
June 5	Albertic	**Arrival**	**Steamer**	July 2	Arabic
June 10	Adriatic	Feb. 26	Adriatic	July 3	Homeric
June 18	Cedric	Mar. 7	Laurentic	July 10	Majestic
June 25	Baltic	Apr. 15	Adriatic	July 18	Olympic
July 3	Albertic			July 25	Homeric
July 8	Adriatic			July 29	Arabic
July 16	Cedric	**WHITE STAR LINE** Southampton, Cherbourg, Antwerp—New York		July 31	Majestic
July 22	Baltic			Aug. 7	Olympic
July 31	Albertic	**N. Y.**		Aug. 15	Homeric
Aug. 5	Adriatic	**Arrival**	**Steamer**	Aug. 20	Majestic
Aug. 13	Cedric	Jan. 9	Arabic	Aug. 26	Arabic
Aug. 19	Baltic	Jan. 16	Majestic	Aug. 28	Olympic
Aug. 27	Albertic	Jan. 25	Homeric	Sept. 5	Homeric
Sept. 3	Adriatic	Feb. 7	Majestic	Sept. 10	Majestic
Sept. 10	Cedric	Feb. 20	Olympic	Sept. 18	Olympic
Sept. 16	Baltic	Mar. 11	Doric	Sept. 24	Arabic
Sept. 25	Albertic	Mar. 13	Olympic	Sept. 26	Homeric
Sept. 30	Adriatic	Apr. 4	Olympic	Oct. 1	Majestic
Oct. 8	Cedric	Apr. 9	Arabic	Oct. 9	Olympic
Oct. 14	Baltic	Apr. 10	Homeric	Oct. 17	Homeric
Oct. 23	Albertic	Apr. 17	Majestic	Oct. 22	Majestic
Oct. 28	Adriatic	Apr. 24	Olympic	Oct. 30	Olympic
Nov. 6	Cedric	May 2	Homeric	Nov. 7	Homeric
Nov. 11	Baltic	May 6	Arabic	Nov. 13	Majestic
Nov. 20	Albertic	May 9	Majestic	Nov. 20	Olympic
Nov. 26	Doric	May 15	Olympic	Nov. 29	Homeric
Dec. 3	Cedric			Dec. 4	Majestic
Dec. 11	Baltic			Dec. 19	Olympic

Year 1930

AMERICAN MERCHANT LINE
London, Hamburg, Cherbourg —New York

N. Y.

Arrival	Steamer
Jan. 9	American Banker
Jan. 14	American Farmer
Jan. 14	American Shipper
Jan. 21	American Trader
Jan. 27	American Merchant
Feb. 5	American Banker
Feb. 11	American Farmer
Feb. 17	American Shipper
Feb. 24	American Trader
Mar. 3	American Merchant
Mar. 10	American Banker
Mar. 18	American Shipper
Mar. 24	American Farmer
Mar. 25	American Trader
Mar. 31	American Merchant
Apr. 9	American Banker
Apr. 14	American Shipper
Apr. 18	American Farmer
Apr. 21	American Trader
Apr. 28	American Merchant
May 6	American Banker
May 13	American Shipper
May 19	American Farmer
May 26	American Trader
June 2	American Banker
June 9	American Shipper
June 16	American Farmer
June 23	American Merchant
June 30	American Trader
July 7	American Banker
July 14	American Shipper
July 21	American Farmer
July 28	American Trader
Aug. 4	American Banker
Aug. 12	American Shipper
Aug. 13	American Merchant
Aug. 25	American Trader
Sept. 2	American Farmer
Sept. 8	American Banker
Sept. 15	American Shipper
Sept. 16	American Merchant
Sept. 22	American Trader
Sept. 29	American Farmer
Oct. 4	American Banker
Oct. 15	American Merchant
Oct. 20	American Trader
Oct. 27	American Farmer
Nov. 5	American Shipper
Nov. 12	American Banker
Nov. 17	American Trader
Nov. 24	American Farmer
Dec. 2	American Shipper
Dec. 8	American Banker
Dec. 17	American Merchant
Dec. 22	American Farmer
Dec. 29	American Shipper

ATLANTIC TRANSPORT LINE
London, Boulogne—New York

N. Y.

Arrival	Steamer
Jan. 2	Minnetonka
Jan. 28	Minnetonka
Feb. 5	Minnekahda
Feb. 11	Minnewaska
Mar. 4	Minnekahda
Mar. 5	Minnesota
Mar. 10	Minnewaska
Mar. 25	Minnetonka
Apr. 1	Minnekahda
Apr. 8	Minnewaska
Apr. 15	Missouri
Apr. 21	Minnetonka
Apr. 29	Minnekahda
May 5	Minnewaska
May 16	Minnesota
May 19	Minnetonka
May 27	Minnekahda
June 2	Minnewaska
June 7	Minnesota
June 11	Missouri
June 16	Minnetonka
June 24	Minnekahda
June 30	Minnewaska
July 14	Minnetonka
July 22	Minnekahda
July 28	Minnewaska
Aug. 11	Missouri
Aug. 11	Minnetonka
Aug. 19	Minnekahda
Aug. 25	Minnewaska
Sept. 8	Minnetonka
Sept. 16	Minnekahda
Sept. 22	Minnewaska
Oct. 6	Minnetonka
Oct. 6	Missouri
Oct. 14	Minnekahda
Oct. 20	Minnewaska
Nov. 3	Minnetonka
Nov. 17	Minnewaska
Dec. 1	Missouri
Dec. 2	Minnetonka
Dec. 16	Minnewaska

BALTIC AMERICAN LINE
Danzig, Copenhagen—New York

N. Y.

Arrival	Steamer
Jan. 24	Lituania
Feb. 15	Estonia
Mar. 5	Lituania
Mar. 26	Estonia
Apr. 10	Lituania
Apr. 23	Polonia
May 8	Pulaski
May 21	Kosciusko
June 11	Polonia
June 19	Pulaski
June 30	Kosciusko
July 23	Pulaski
Aug. 4	Kosciusko

BALTIC AMERICAN LINE
Danzig, Copenhagen—New York

(Continued)

N. Y.

Arrival	Steamer
Aug. 27	Polonia
Sept. 2	Pulaski
Sept. 8	Kosciusko
Sept. 30	Polonia
Oct. 20	Kosciusko
Nov. 5	Polonia
Nov. 5	Pulaski
Nov. 28	Kosciusko
Dec. 17	Pulaski

CANADIAN PACIFIC
Southampton, Cherbourg, Liverpool, Quebec—New York

N. Y.

Arrival	Steamer
Jan. 28	Empress of Scotland
Feb. 6	Empress of France
Nov. 28	Empress of Australia

CANADIAN PACIFIC
World Cruise

N. Y.

Arrival	Steamer
Apr. 17	Empress of Australia

COMPANIA TRANSATLANTICA
(Spanish Line)
Cadiz, Barcelona, Vigo, Havana, Vera Cruz— New York

N. Y.

Arrival	Steamer
Jan. 10	Juan Sebastin Elcano
Jan. 17	Cristobol Colon
Jan. 31	Manuel Arnus
Feb. 13	Manuel Arnus
Feb. 14	Alfonso XIII
Feb. 26	Manuel Calvo
Mar. 5	Marques de Comillas
Mar. 11	Cristobol Colon
Mar. 18	Magallanes
Mar. 31	Magallanes
Apr. 7	Alfonso XIII
Apr. 16	Antonio Lopez
Apr. 26	Buenos Ayres
May 2	Cristobol Colon
May 23	Manuel Calvo
May 28	Alfonso XIII
June 4	Manuel Calvo
June 18	Manuel Arnus
June 23	Cristobol Colon
June 30	Antonio Lopez
June 30	Marques de Comillas
July 14	Marques de Comillas
July 19	Alfonso XIII
Aug. 7	Magallanes
Aug. 15	Cristobol Colon
Aug. 21	Buenos Ayres
Aug. 25	Manuel Calvo

Year 1930

COMPANIA TRANSAT-LANTICA
(Spanish Line)
Cadiz, Barcelona, Vigo
Havana, Vera Cruz—
New York
(Continued)

N.Y.

Arrival	Steamer
Sept. 2	Buenos Ayres
Sept. 10	Alfonso XIII
Sept. 18	Antonio Lopez
Sept. 29	Juan Sebastin Elcano
Oct. 6	Cristobol Colon
Oct. 14	Manuel Arnus
Oct. 27	Manuel Arnus
Oct. 31	Alfonso XIII
Nov. 12	Manuel Calvo
Nov. 19	Marques de Comillas
Nov. 28	Cristobol Colon
Dec. 5	Magallanes
Dec. 14	Magallanes
Dec. 23	Alfonso XIII
Dec. 31	Antonio Lopez

COSULICH LINE
Trieste, Patras, Palermo,
Naples—New York

N.Y.

Arrival	Steamer
Jan. 2	Saturnia
Jan. 22	Vulcania
Feb. 11	Saturnia
Mar. 18	Saturnia
Apr. 8	Vulcania
Apr. 22	Saturnia
May 12	Vulcania
May 27	Saturnia
June 16	Vulcania
July 1	Saturnia
July 29	Vulcania
Aug. 12	Saturnia
Aug. 30	Vulcania
Sept. 16	Saturnia
Oct. 6	Vulcania
Oct. 21	Saturnia
Nov. 10	Vulcania
Nov. 25	Saturnia
Dec. 8	Vulcania
Dec. 30	Saturnia

CUNARD-ANCHOR LINE
Glasgow, Belfast, London-derry—New York

N.Y.

Arrival	Steamer
Jan. 14	Caledonia
Jan. 20	California
Jan. 26	Pennsylvania
Feb. 5	Cameronia
Feb. 17	California
Mar. 5	Cameronia
Mar. 18	California
Apr. 1	Cameronia
Apr. 7	Pennsylvania
Apr. 16	Tuscania

CUNARD-ANCHOR LINE
Glasgow, Belfast, London-derry—New York
(Continued)

N.Y.

Arrival	Steamer
Apr. 17	California
Apr. 28	Caledonia
May 5	Cameronia
May 11	Pennsylvania
May 19	California
May 26	Caledonia
June 2	Cameronia
June 15	Pennsylvania
June 23	Caledonia
June 30	California
July 8	Cameronia
July 13	Pennsylvania
July 21	Caledonia
July 25	California
Aug. 4	Cameronia
Aug. 11	Caledonia
Aug. 16	Pennsylvania
Aug. 29	California
Sept. 2	Cameronia
Sept. 8	Caledonia
Sept. 14	Pennsylvania
Sept. 22	California
Sept. 28	Cameronia
Oct. 6	Caledonia
Oct. 12	Pennsylvania
Oct. 28	Cameronia
Nov. 3	Caledonia
Nov. 9	Pennsylvania
Nov. 24	Cameronia
Dec. 1	Caledonia
Dec. 9	Pennsylvania
Dec. 23	California

CUNARD LINE
Southampton, Cherbourg,
Havre—New York

N.Y.

Arrival	Steamer
Jan. 2	Aurania
Jan. 15	Aquitania
Jan. 15	Ascania
Jan. 21	Alaunia
Jan. 28	Ausonia
Feb. 5	Aquitania
Feb. 6	Aurania
Feb. 11	Mauretania
Feb. 18	Ascania
Feb. 25	Aquitania
Feb. 25	Alaunia
Mar. 4	Ausonia
Mar. 5	Berengaria
Mar. 12	Aurania
Mar. 18	Aquitania
Mar. 25	Ascania
Mar. 29	Berengaria
Apr. 1	Alaunia
Apr. 5	Mauretania
Apr. 7	Carinthia
Apr. 10	Ausonia
Apr. 11	Aquitania
Apr. 16	Aurania
Apr. 21	Berengaria

CUNARD LINE
Southampton, Cherbourg,
Havre—New York
(Continued)

N.Y.

Arrival	Steamer
Apr. 25	Mauretania
Apr. 28	Lancastria
May 2	Aquitania
May 10	Berengaria
May 16	Mauretania
May 23	Aquitania
May 26	Lancastria
May 31	Berengaria
June 2	Caronia
June 5	Mauretania
June 10	Tuscania
June 13	Aquitania
June 16	Carmania
June 22	Berengaria
June 23	Carinthia
June 26	Lancastria
June 27	Mauretania
June 30	Caronia
July 4	Aquitania
July 7	Tuscania
July 11	Berengaria
July 14	Carmania
July 18	Mauretania
July 25	Aquitania
July 28	Caronia
Aug. 2	Berengaria
Aug. 4	Tuscania
Aug. 8	Mauretania
Aug. 11	Carmania
Aug. 15	Aquitania
Aug. 19	Lancastria
Aug. 23	Berengaria
Aug. 25	Caronia
Aug. 29	Mauretania
Sept. 5	Aquitania
Sept. 8	Carmania
Sept. 13	Berengaria
Sept. 15	Lancastria
Sept. 19	Mauretania
Sept. 22	Caronia
Sept. 26	Aquitania
Oct. 1	Tuscania
Oct. 4	Berengaria
Oct. 6	Carmania
Oct. 10	Mauretania
Oct. 14	Lancastria
Oct. 17	Aquitania
Oct. 20	Caronia
Oct. 25	Berengaria
Oct. 30	Tuscania
Oct. 31	Mauretania
Nov. 3	Carmania
Nov. 8	Aquitania
Nov. 12	Aurania
Nov. 17	Franconia
Nov. 21	Mauretania
Nov. 24	Ausonia
Dec. 3	Lancastria
Dec. 15	Mauretania
Dec. 19	Aurania
Dec. 23	Antonia
Dec. 28	Aquitania
Dec. 30	Ausonia

Year 1930

CUNARD LINE
Liverpool, Queenstown—
New York

N.Y.

Arrival	Steamer
Jan. 2	Antonia
Jan. 8	Andania
Jan. 14	Scythia
Jan. 21	Lancastria
Jan. 28	Samaria
Feb. 6	Antonia
Feb. 11	Scythia
Feb. 18	Lancastria
Feb. 25	Andania
Mar. 4	Antonia
Mar. 12	Scythia
Mar. 17	Lancastria
Mar. 26	Andania
Apr. 3	Antonia
Apr. 11	Caronia
Apr. 15	Scythia
Apr. 21	Carmania
Apr. 29	Laconia
May 5	Caronia
May 13	Scythia
May 18	Carmania
May 19	Samaria
May 27	Carinthia
June 1	Caronia
June 1	Laconia
June 10	Scythia
June 16	Samaria
June 24	Franconia
June 29	Laconia
July 7	Scythia
July 13	Samaria
July 22	Laconia
July 28	Franconia
Aug. 5	Scythia
Aug. 11	Samaria
Aug. 18	Laconia
Aug. 25	Franconia
Sept. 2	Scythia
Sept. 7	Carinthia
Sept. 11	Samaria
Sept. 15	Laconia
Sept. 20	Antonia
Sept. 21	Franconia
Oct. 6	Samaria
Oct. 14	Laconia
Oct. 28	Scythia
Nov. 12	Samaria
Nov. 24	Scythia
Dec. 9	Samaria
Dec. 23	Carinthia

DOLLAR STEAMSHIP LINE
World Ports—New York

N.Y.

Arrival	Steamer
Jan. 7	President Monroe
Jan. 22	President Wilson
Feb. 7	President Van Buren
Feb. 19	President Garfield
Mar. 4	President Polk
Mar. 18	President Adams
Apr. 3	President Harrison

DOLLAR STEAMSHIP LINE
World Ports—New York
(Continued)

N.Y.

Arrival	Steamer
Apr. 15	President Johnson
Apr. 30	President Fillmore
May 13	President Wilson
May 27	President Van Buren
June 10	President Garfield
June 24	President Polk
July 8	President Adams
July 21	President Harrison
Aug. 4	President Johnson
Aug. 19	President Fillmore
Sept. 2	President Wilson
Sept. 16	President Van Buren
Sept. 30	President Garfield
Oct. 15	President Polk
Oct. 28	President Adams
Nov. 11	President Harrison
Nov. 25	President Johnson
Dec. 9	President Fillmore
Dec. 22	President Wilson

FABRE LINE
Piraeus, Lisbon, Marseilles,
Palermo, Constantinople
—New York

N.Y.

Arrival	Steamer
Jan. 23	Providence
Feb. 15	Patria
Mar. 15	Alesia
Apr. 7	Providence
Apr. 28	Sinaia
Apr. 30	Patria
June 12	Alesia
June 21	Providence
July 21	Patria
July 21	Sinaia
Aug. 25	Providence
Sept. 5	Alesia
Sept. 13	Patria
Oct. 16	Sinaia
Nov. 15	Providence
Dec. 1	Patria
Dec. 5	Alesia

FRENCH LINE
(Compagnie Generale Transatlantique)
Havre, Plymouth—New York

N.Y.

Arrival	Steamer
Jan. 8	Roussillon
Jan. 10	France
Jan. 15	Ile de France
Jan. 22	Paris
Jan. 31	De Grasse
Feb. 7	Ile de France
Feb. 10	France
Feb. 15	Rochambeau
Feb. 19	Paris
Feb. 28	De Grasse
Mar. 5	Ile de France
Mar. 15	Rochambeau
Mar. 18	France

FRENCH LINE
(Compagnie Generale Transatlantique)
Havre, Plymouth—New York
(Continued)

N.Y.

Arrival	Steamer
Mar. 26	Ile de France
Apr. 9	Paris
Apr. 11	Roussillon
Apr. 16	Ile de France
Apr. 18	Rochambeau
Apr. 21	De Grasse
Apr. 22	France
Apr. 30	Paris
May 12	Roussillon
May 14	Ile de France
May 19	De Grasse
May 21	Paris
May 26	Lafayette
May 28	France
June 3	Rochambeau
June 4	Ile de France
June 10	Paris
June 16	De Grasse
June 17	France
June 19	Roussillon
June 23	Lafayette
June 24	Ile de France
June 28	Paris
July 1	Rochambeau
July 3	France
July 7	De Grasse
July 9	Ile de France
July 17	Paris
July 21	Lafayette
July 22	France
July 29	Roussillon
July 30	Ile de France
Aug. 4	Rochambeau
Aug. 8	De Grasse
Aug. 13	Paris
Aug. 18	Lafayette
Aug. 19	France
Aug. 26	Ile de France
Aug. 30	Paris
Sept. 4	France
Sept. 4	De Grasse
Sept. 6	Roussillon
Sept. 8	Rochambeau
Sept. 11	Ile de France
Sept. 15	Lafayette
Sept. 18	Paris
Sept. 24	France
Sept. 29	De Grasse
Sept. 30	Ile de France
Oct. 6	Rochambeau
Oct. 8	Paris
Oct. 14	Lafayette
Oct. 15	France
Oct. 23	Ile de France
Oct. 31	De Grasse
Nov. 5	Rochambeau
Nov. 6	Lafayette
Nov. 12	France
Nov. 19	Ile de France
Nov. 28	De Grasse
Dec. 2	Paris
Dec. 10	Ile de France
Dec. 20	Lafayette
Dec. 23	Paris

Year 1930

FRENCH LINE
(Compagnie Generale Transatlantique)
Bordeaux, Vigo, Halifax—
New York
N. Y.

Arrival	Steamer
Jan. 7	Roussillon
Jan. 27	La Bourdonnais
Mar. 24	De La Salle
Apr. 11	Roussillon
May 26	La Bourdonnais
June 19	Roussillon
July 15	La Bourdonnais
July 29	Roussillon
Aug. 20	La Bourdonnais
Sept. 6	Roussillon
Sept. 29	La Bourdonnais
Dec. 8	La Bourdonnais

HAMBURG-AMERICAN LINE
Hamburg, Southampton, Cher-
bourg—New York
N. Y.

Arrival	Steamer
Jan. 2	Milwaukee
Jan. 11	Westphalia
Jan. 14	Cleveland
Jan. 24	Thuringia
Jan. 28	St. Louis
Feb. 7	Milwaukee
Feb. 14	Westphalia
Feb. 18	Cleveland
Feb. 24	Hamburg
Mar. 4	St. Louis
Mar. 11	Milwaukee
Mar. 20	Westphalia
Mar. 22	Hamburg
Mar. 25	Cleveland
Mar. 31	Albert Ballin
Apr. 8	St. Louis
Apr. 15	Milwaukee
Apr. 21	Hamburg
Apr. 28	Albert Ballin
Apr. 28	Cleveland
May 5	New York
May 10	St. Louis
May 12	Reliance
May 19	Hamburg
May 26	Albert Ballin
May 26	Resolute
May 26	Milwaukee
May 31	New York
June 3	Cleveland
June 7	Deutschland
June 16	Hamburg
June 16	St. Louis
June 23	Albert Ballin
June 24	Reliance
June 30	Milwaukee
June 30	New York
July 7	Deutschland
July 8	Cleveland
July 12	Hamburg
July 21	Albert Ballin
July 21	St. Louis
July 28	New York
Aug. 4	Deutschland
Aug. 4	Milwaukee
Aug. 11	Hamburg

HAMBURG-AMERICAN LINE
Hamburg, Southampton, Cher-
bourg—New York
(Continued)
N. Y.

Arrival	Steamer
Aug. 12	Cleveland
Aug. 18	Albert Ballin
Aug. 22	Reliance
Aug. 25	New York
Aug. 28	St. Louis
Sept. 2	Deutschland
Sept. 5	Resolute
Sept. 6	Hamburg
Sept. 8	Milwaukee
Sept. 15	Albert Ballin
Sept. 16	Cleveland
Sept. 19	Reliance
Sept. 22	New York
Sept. 29	Deutschland
Sept. 29	St. Louis
Oct. 3	Resolute
Oct. 4	Hamburg
Oct. 11	Albert Ballin
Oct. 11	Milwaukee
Oct. 20	Cleveland
Oct. 20	New York
Oct. 25	Deutschland
Nov. 3	St. Louis
Nov. 3	Hamburg
Nov. 10	Albert Ballin
Nov. 17	New York
Nov. 24	Cleveland
Nov. 29	Hamburg
Dec. 4	St. Louis
Dec. 6	Deutschland
Dec. 15	New York
Dec. 18	Reliance
Dec. 22	Albert Ballin
Dec. 29	Cleveland

HOLLAND-AMERICA LINE
Rotterdam, Southampton,
Cherbourg—New York
N. Y.

Arrival	Steamer
Jan. 22	Volendam
Jan. 31	Rotterdam
Feb. 8	Veendam
Feb. 24	New Amsterdam
Mar. 29	New Amsterdam
Apr. 21	Statendam
Apr. 28	Rotterdam
May 6	Volendam
May 12	New Amsterdam
May 19	Statendam
May 26	Rotterdam
June 3	Volendam
June 10	New Amsterdam
June 16	Statendam
June 21	Rotterdam
June 30	Veendam
July 1	Volendam
July 7	New Amsterdam
July 14	Statendam
July 20	Rotterdam
July 28	Volendam
Aug. 5	New Amsterdam

HOLLAND-AMERICA LINE
Rotterdam, Southampton,
Cherbourg—New York
(Continued)
N. Y.

Arrival	Steamer
Aug. 11	Statendam
Aug. 18	Rotterdam
Aug. 26	Volendam
Sept. 2	New Amsterdam
Sept. 8	Statendam
Sept. 15	Rotterdam
Sept. 22	Volendam
Sept. 30	New Amsterdam
Oct. 6	Statendam
Oct. 14	Rotterdam
Oct. 21	Volendam
Oct. 29	New Amsterdam
Nov. 3	Statendam
Nov. 11	Rotterdam
Nov. 28	New Amsterdam
Dec. 8	Rotterdam
Dec. 8	Volendam
Dec. 15	Statendam
Dec. 31	New Amsterdam

ITALIA AMERICA LINE
Genoa, Naples, Palermo—
New York
N. Y.

Arrival	Steamer
Jan. 7	Roma
Jan. 10	Augustus
Feb. 19	Augustus
Mar. 1	Roma
Mar. 26	Augustus
Apr. 7	Roma
Apr. 28	Augustus
May 12	Roma
June 3	Augustus
June 16	Roma
July 7	Augustus
July 22	Roma
Aug. 19	Augustus
Sept. 2	Roma
Sept. 23	Augustus
Oct. 7	Roma
Oct. 28	Augustus
Nov. 10	Roma
Dec. 1	Augustus
Dec. 9	Roma

LLOYD SABAUDO
Genoa, Naples—New York
N. Y.

Arrival	Steamer
Jan. 18	Conte Biancamano
Feb. 4	Conte Grande
Feb. 25	Conte Biancamano
Mar. 10	Conte Grande
Apr. 1	Conte Biancamano
Apr. 15	Conte Grande
May 6	Conte Biancamano
May 19	Conte Grande
June 10	Conte Biancamano
June 23	Conte Grande
July 15	Conte Biancamano
Aug. 4	Conte Grande
Aug. 26	Conte Biancamano

Year 1930

LLOYD SABAUDO
Genoa, Naples—New York
(Continued)
N.Y.

Arrival	Steamer
Sept. 8	Conte Grande
Sept. 30	Conte Biancamano
Oct. 14	Conte Grande
Nov. 5	Conte Biancamano
Nov. 18	Conte Grande
Dec. 6	Conte Biancamano
Dec. 20	Conte Grande

NATIONAL STEAM NAVIGATION CO. OF GREECE
Piraeus, Patras—New York
N.Y.

Arrival	Steamer
Feb. 24	Byron
Apr. 16	Edison
May 20	Byron
June 17	Edison
July 18	Byron
Aug. 15	Edison
Sept. 8	Byron
Oct. 10	Edison
Nov. 6	Byron

NORTH GERMAN LLOYD
Bremen, Southampton, Cherbourg—New York
N.Y.

Arrival	Steamer
Jan. 2	Berlin
Jan. 10	Bremen
Jan. 14	Muenchen
Jan. 20	Columbus
Jan. 20	Stuttgart
Jan. 27	Berlin
Jan. 29	Bremen
Feb. 5	Dresden
Feb. 13	Muenchen
Feb. 17	Stuttgart
Feb. 19	Bremen
Feb. 24	Berlin
Mar. 5	Dresden
Mar. 11	Yorck
Mar. 12	Bremen
Mar. 17	Stuttgart
Mar. 24	Berlin
Mar. 25	Europa
Mar. 29	Karlsruhe
Apr. 1	Dresden
Apr. 9	Bremen
Apr. 14	Seydlitz
Apr. 14	Stuttgart
Apr. 21	Berlin
Apr. 22	Europa
Apr. 28	Dresden
Apr. 30	Bremen
May 7	Karlsruhe
May 9	Columbus
May 13	Stuttgart
May 13	Europa
May 19	Berlin
May 20	Bremen
May 26	Dresden

NORTH GERMAN LLOYD
Bremen, Southampton, Cherbourg—New York
(Continued)
N.Y.

Arrival	Steamer
May 28	Europa
May 31	Columbus
June 6	Bremen
June 7	Stuttgart
June 12	Karlsruhe
June 14	Europa
June 14	St. Louis
June 16	Berlin
June 21	Columbus
June 23	Dresden
June 26	Bremen
June 30	Yorck
July 3	Europa
July 7	Stuttgart
July 12	Columbus
July 14	Karlsruhe
July 14	Berlin
July 15	Bremen
July 22	Europa
July 28	Dresden
July 28	Chemnitz
Aug. 1	Bremen
Aug. 4	Yorck
Aug. 6	Columbus
Aug. 11	Stuttgart
Aug. 12	Europa
Aug. 18	Berlin
Aug. 18	Karlsruhe
Aug. 20	Bremen
Aug. 25	Dresden
Aug. 26	Columbus
Aug. 28	Europa
Sept. 3	Yorck
Sept. 5	Bremen
Sept. 8	Stuttgart
Sept. 13	Seydlitz
Sept. 13	Leutzow
Sept. 15	Berlin
Sept. 15	Columbus
Sept. 16	Europa
Sept. 22	Dresden
Sept. 22	Karlsruhe
Sept. 23	Bremen
Oct. 1	Europa
Oct. 2	Yorck
Oct. 6	Stuttgart
Oct. 7	Columbus
Oct. 9	Bremen
Oct. 14	Berlin
Oct. 20	Dresden
Oct. 23	Europa
Oct. 27	Karlsruhe
Nov. 3	Columbus
Nov. 3	Stuttgart
Nov. 10	Berlin
Nov. 11	Bremen
Nov. 17	Dresden
Nov. 24	Columbus
Dec. 2	Stuttgart
Dec. 3	Bremen
Dec. 8	Berlin
Dec. 15	Europa
Dec. 18	Dresden
Dec. 23	Bremen

NORWEGIAN AMERICAN LINE
Oslo, Bergen—New York
N.Y.

Arrival	Steamer
Jan. 28	Bergensfjord
Feb. 17	Stavangerfjord
Mar. 4	Bergensfjord
Mar. 24	Stavangerfjord
Apr. 7	Bergensfjord
Apr. 26	Stavangerfjord
May 10	Bergensfjord
May 24	Larviksfjord
May 26	Stavangerfjord
June 11	Bergensfjord
June 24	Stavangerfjord
July 8	Bergensfjord
July 9	Larviksfjord
July 28	Stavangerfjord
Aug. 11	Bergensfjord
Aug. 18	Larviksfjord
Aug. 26	Stavangerfjord
Sept. 15	Bergensfjord
Sept. 29	Stavangerfjord
Sept. 30	Larviksfjord
Oct. 17	Bergensfjord
Oct. 31	Stavangerfjord
Nov. 19	Bergensfjord
Nov. 24	Larviksfjord
Dec. 2	Stavangerfjord
Dec. 23	Bergensfjord

RED STAR LINE
Antwerp—New York
N.Y.

Arrival	Steamer
Jan. 2	Pennland
Jan. 22	Westernland
Feb. 18	Westernland
Mar. 5	Pennland
Mar. 25	Westernland
Apr. 9	Pennland
Apr. 15	Lapland
Apr. 22	Westernland
May 5	Pennland
May 12	Lapland
May 20	Westernland
May 26	Belgenland
June 2	Pennland
June 9	Lapland
June 16	Westernland
June 23	Belgenland
June 30	Pennland
July 7	Lapland
July 16	Westernland
July 21	Belgenland
July 28	Pennland
Aug. 4	Lapland
Aug. 11	Westernland
Aug. 18	Belgenland
Aug. 25	Pennland
Sept. 2	Lapland
Sept. 8	Westernland
Sept. 15	Belgenland
Sept. 23	Pennland
Sept. 29	Lapland
Oct. 6	Westernland
Oct. 14	Belgenland
Oct. 21	Pennland
Nov. 5	Westernland

Year 1930

RED STAR LINE
Antwerp—New York
(Continued)

N.Y.

Arrival	Steamer
Nov. 19	Pennland
Dec. 2	Westernland
Dec. 11	Belgenland
Dec. 23	Pennland

SCANDINAVIAN AMERICAN LINE
Copenhagen, Oslo, Halifax—New York

N.Y.

Arrival	Steamer
Jan. 20	United States
Jan. 28	Hellig Olav
Feb. 11	Frederik VIII
Feb. 24	United States
Mar. 4	Hellig Olav
Mar. 11	Oscar II
Mar. 18	Frederik VIII
Mar. 31	United States
Apr. 8	Hellig Olav
Apr. 14	Oscar II
Apr. 22	Frederik VIII
May 5	United States
May 12	Hellig Olav
May 19	Oscar II
May 26	Frederik VIII
June 9	United States
June 23	Oscar II
June 30	Frederik VIII
July 14	United States
July 28	Oscar II
Aug. 4	Frederik VIII
Aug. 18	United States
Aug. 25	Hellig Olav
Sept. 2	Oscar II
Sept. 8	Frederik VIII
Sept. 22	United States
Sept. 26	Hellig Olav
Oct. 6	Oscar II
Oct. 14	Frederik VIII
Oct. 27	United States
Nov. 3	Hellig Olav
Nov. 18	Oscar II
Dec. 8	Hellig Olav
Dec. 15	United States
Dec. 30	Oscar II

SWEDISH-AMERICAN LINE
Gothenburg—New York

N.Y.

Arrival	Steamer
Jan. 2	Gripsholm
Jan. 21	Drottningholm
Jan. 29	Gripsholm
Feb. 5	Gripsholm
Feb. 18	Drottningholm
Mar. 5	Gripsholm
Mar. 18	Drottningholm
Apr. 2	Gripsholm
Apr. 8	Kungsholm
Apr. 22	Drottningholm
Apr. 28	Gripsholm
May 6	Kungsholm
May 20	Drottningholm

SWEDISH-AMERICAN LINE
Gothenburg—New York
(Continued)

N.Y.

Arrival	Steamer
May 26	Gripsholm
June 2	Kungsholm
June 17	Drottningholm
June 24	Gripsholm
June 30	Kungsholm
July 14	Drottningholm
Aug. 5	Gripsholm
Aug. 11	Kungsholm
Aug. 18	Drottningholm
Sept. 2	Gripsholm
Sept. 8	Kungsholm
Sept. 15	Drottningholm
Sept. 29	Gripsholm
Oct. 6	Kungsholm
Oct. 14	Drottningholm
Oct. 28	Gripsholm
Nov. 3	Kungsholm
Nov. 24	Drottningholm
Dec. 1	Gripsholm
Dec. 16	Kungsholm
Dec. 23	Drottningholm

UNITED STATES LINE
Southampton, Cherbourg—New York

N.Y.

Arrival	Steamer
Apr. 29	Leviathan
May 19	Leviathan
June 9	Leviathan
June 25	Leviathan
July 12	Leviathan
July 30	Leviathan
Aug. 18	Leviathan
Sept. 3	Leviathan
Sept. 22	Leviathan
Oct. 14	Leviathan
Nov. 3	Leviathan
Nov. 24	Leviathan
Dec. 22	Leviathan

UNITED STATES LINE
Bremen, Southampton, Cherbourg—New York

N.Y.

Arrival	Steamer
Jan. 6	George Washington
Jan. 18	President Harding
Jan. 27	President Roosevelt
Feb. 4	George Washington
Feb. 10	America
Feb. 14	President Harding
Feb. 24	President Roosevelt
Mar. 1	George Washington
Mar. 10	America
Mar. 14	President Harding
Mar. 28	George Washington
Apr. 7	America
Apr. 11	President Harding
Apr. 21	George Washington
Apr. 26	President Roosevelt
May 5	America
May 19	George Washington
May 24	President Roosevelt

UNITED STATES LINE
Bremen, Southampton, Cherbourg—New York
(Continued)

N.Y.

Arrival	Steamer
June 2	America
June 6	President Harding
June 13	Republic
June 16	George Washington
June 18	President Roosevelt
June 30	America
July 5	President Harding
July 10	George Washington
July 14	President Roosevelt
July 21	Republic
July 26	America
Aug. 1	President Harding
Aug. 6	President Roosevelt
Aug. 15	George Washington
Aug. 22	Republic
Aug. 23	America
Aug. 27	President Harding
Sept. 2	President Roosevelt
Sept. 10	George Washington
Sept. 19	America
Sept. 26	President Harding
Oct. 2	Republic
Oct. 3	President Roosevelt
Oct. 6	George Washington
Oct. 18	America
Oct. 24	President Harding
Nov. 3	Republic
Nov. 7	George Washington
Nov. 14	President Roosevelt
Nov. 22	America
Dec. 1	President Harding
Dec. 6	George Washington
Dec. 13	President Roosevelt
Dec. 24	America
Dec. 27	President Harding

WHITE STAR LINE
Southampton, Cherbourg, Antwerp—New York

N.Y.

Arrival	Steamer
Jan. 8	Arabic
Jan. 9	Olympic
Jan. 15	Colgaric
Jan. 23	Homeric
Jan. 29	Olympic
Feb. 19	Majestic
Mar. 12	Majestic
Mar. 26	Olympic
Apr. 2	Majestic
Apr. 10	Homeric
Apr. 16	Olympic
Apr. 22	Majestic
May 1	Homeric
May 7	Olympic
May 14	Majestic
May 22	Homeric
May 29	Olympic
June 4	Majestic
June 12	Homeric
June 18	Olympic
June 25	Majestic
June 25	Colgaric
July 3	Homeric

Year 1930

WHITE STAR LINE Southampton, Cherbourg, Antwerp—New York (Continued)		WHITE STAR LINE Liverpool, Queenstown— New York		WHITE STAR LINE Liverpool, Queenstown— New York (Continued)	
N.Y. Arrival	**Steamer**	**N.Y. Arrival**	**Steamer**	**N.Y. Arrival**	**Steamer**
July 8	Olympic	Jan. 7	Laurentic	June 23	Baltic
July 15	Majestic	Jan. 14	Adriatic	July 1	Cedric
July 25	Homeric	Jan. 21	Albertic	July 7	Britannic
July 30	Olympic	Jan. 30	Baltic	July 14	Adriatic
Aug. 6	Majestic	Feb. 7	Doric	July 21	Baltic
Aug. 14	Homeric	Feb. 13	Cedric	July 29	Cedric
Aug. 20	Olympic	Feb. 19	Albertic	Aug. 5	Arabic
Aug. 27	Majestic	Mar. 5	Baltic	Aug. 12	Britannic
Sept. 3	Homeric	Mar. 5	Adriatic	Aug. 18	Baltic
Sept. 10	Olympic	Mar. 12	Cedric	Aug. 26	Cedric
Sept. 17	Majestic	Mar. 20	Albertic	Sept. 2	Adriatic
Sept. 25	Homeric	Mar. 24	Arabic	Sept. 8	Britannic
Oct. 1	Olympic	Mar. 25	Laurentic	Sept. 15	Baltic
Oct. 8	Majestic	Apr. 2	Baltic	Sept. 23	Cedric
Oct. 16	Homeric	Apr. 9	Cedric	Sept. 29	Adriatic
Oct. 23	Olympic	Apr. 16	Albertic	Oct. 6	Britannic
Oct. 29	Majestic	Apr. 22	Arabic	Oct. 14	Baltic
Nov. 6	Homeric	Apr. 28	Baltic	Oct. 21	Cedric
Nov. 12	Olympic	May 6	Cedric	Oct. 27	Adriatic
Nov. 19	Majestic	May 12	Adriatic	Nov. 3	Britannic
Nov. 28	Homeric	May 20	Arabic	Nov. 19	Baltic
Dec. 3	Olympic	May 26	Baltic	Dec. 1	Adriatic
Dec. 9	Majestic	June 3	Cedric	Dec. 17	Baltic
Dec. 23	Olympic	June 6	Baltic	Dec. 22	Britannic
		June 10	Adriatic	Dec. 31	Cedric
		June 17	Arabic		

CPSIA information can be obtained
at www.ICGtesting.com
Printed in the USA
LVHW01s0046230518
578141LV00014B/178/P